Global Politics

Emerging Networks, Trends, and Challenges

W. Andy Knight and Tom Keating

OXFORD
UNIVERSITY PRESS

OXFORD
UNIVERSITY PRESS

8 Sampson Mews, Suite 204, Don Mills, Ontario M3C 0H5
www.oupcanada.com

Oxford University Press is a department of the University of Oxford.
It furthers the University's objective of excellence in research, scholarship,
and education by publishing worldwide in

Oxford   New York
Auckland   Cape Town   Dar es Salaam   Hong Kong   Karachi
Kuala Lumpur   Madrid   Melbourne   Mexico City   Nairobi
New Delhi   Shanghai   Taipei   Toronto

With offices in
Argentina   Austria   Brazil   Chile   Czech Republic   France   Greece
Guatemala   Hungary   Italy   Japan   Poland   Portugal   Singapore
South Korea   Switzerland   Thailand   Turkey   Ukraine   Vietnam

Oxford is a trade mark of Oxford University Press
in the UK and in certain other countries

Published in Canada
by Oxford University Press

Library and Archives Canada Cataloguing in Publication

Knight, W. Andy
Global politics : emerging networks, trends and challenges / W. Andy Knight & Tom Keating.

Includes bibliographical references and index.
ISBN 978-0-19-541717-3

1. International relations–Textbooks. I. Keating, Thomas F
II. Title.

JZ1242.K64 2010   327   C2009-906153-8

Cover image: Stephanie Cabrera/Getty Images

This book is printed on permanent acid-free paper ∞.

Printed and bound in Canada.

1 2 3 4 — 13 12 11 10

Contents

Figures, Tables, and Boxes   vi
Publisher's Preface   viii
Acknowledgements   ix

Introduction: Context and Changing Perceptions of a Globe in Flux   1

Re-imaging Global Politics   1
Understanding Globalization   5
The Context of Global Politics: Multi-Level
    Governance   7
Outline of the Book   12
Key Terms   14
Suggested Readings   15
Global Links   15

Part I ●●●●●○

International and Global Politics

1 Making Sense of International and Global Politics: Contesting Concepts, Theories, Approaches   18

Introduction   18
Early Approaches to Understanding
    Inter-State Relations   19
Idealism/Utopianism   20
Realism   24
International Society   32
Liberalism   33
Traditional Methods and Scientific
    Behaviouralism   39
Conclusion   41
Key Terms   42
Discussion Questions   42
Suggested Readings   43
Global Links   43

2 Alternative Conceptions of Global Politics   44

Introduction   44

Marxism   45
Critical Theories   56
Conclusion   71
Key Terms   71
Discussion Questions   71
Suggested Readings   71
Global Links   72

3 World Civilizations and the Origins of the International System   73

Introduction   73
A Brief History: Tribes, Clans, City-States,
    and Empires   73
Other World Civilizations   82
The Renaissance, Westphalia, and the
    Evolution of the European States
    System   88
Conclusion   90
Key Terms   91
Discussion Questions   91
Suggested Readings   92
Global Links   92

Part II ●●●●●○

Turbulence and Change in World Order

4 Conceptualizing Global Change and Continuity   96

Introduction   96
Towards a Theory of Global Change and
    Continuity   98
Conceptualizing Discontinuity in Global
    Politics   98
Problematizing Global Change and the
    Persistence of Continuities   104
Conclusion   105
Key Terms   106
Discussion Questions   106
Suggested Readings   107
Global Links   107

Contents

5 Conflict, Violence, and War in Global Politics 108

Introduction 108
War and Global Politics 109
The Changing Practice of War 121
Alternatives to War 126
From State to Human Security 131
Conclusion 134
Key Terms 135
Discussion Questions 136
Suggested Readings 136
Global Links 136

6 Global Structures: Historical and Contemporary Experiences 138

Introduction 138
Global Order, Globalization, and Globalism 141
Empires Past and Present 152
Conclusion 156
Key Terms 156
Discussion Questions 156
Suggested Readings 157
Global Links 157

7 Changes to the Institutions of Global Order since 1945: The UN System 158

Introduction 158
Brief History of the Founding of the United Nations 158
The Multi-Faceted Goals of the UN 171
The UN Approach to Managing and Suppressing Conflicts 173
Building Sustainable Peace 183
Conclusion 185
Appendix 1: UN Member States and Dates of Membership 188
Appendix 2: Specialized Agencies and Related Organizations Maintaining Liaison Offices at United Nations Headquarters 192
Key Terms 193
Discussion Questions 194
Suggested Readings 194
Global Links 194

Part III ●●●●●
Globalization

8 Globalization's Impact on the State and the Inter-State System 198

Introduction 198
Characteristics and Drivers of Globalization 200
The Political and Policy Context 206
Globalization and the Theory of the State in Global Politics 211
Conclusion 216
Key Terms 217
Discussion Questions 217
Suggested Readings 218
Global Links 218

9 The Globalization of Business and Business in Global Governance 219

Introduction 219
Multinational Corporations Defined 221
Emerging Markets 226
The Growth of Private Power 229
Corporate Social Responsibility 231
Conclusion and Future Directions 234
Key Terms 235
Discussion Questions 235
Suggested Readings 236
Global Links 236

10 Anti-Globalization Transnational Movements 237

Introduction 237
Precursors of Counter-Globalization Movements 240
Counter-Movements 241
Conclusion 251
Key Terms 252
Discussion Questions 252
Suggested Readings 252
Global Links 253

11 Resistance Movements in the Global South   254

Introduction   254
The Ogoni Resistance Movement   254
The Chipko and Green Belt
    Movements   257
Zapatista Uprising in Chiapas   260
Movimento Trabalhadores Rurais
    Sêm Terra   263
The Porto Alegre World Social
    Forum   265
Conclusion   270
Key Terms   272
Discussion Questions   272
Suggested Readings   273
Global Links   273

12 Transnational Organized Crime   274

Introduction   274
Who Are Transnational Organized
    Criminals?   277
Criminal Gangs and Covert Groups   287
Conclusion   298
Key Terms   299
Discussion Questions   299
Suggested Readings   299
Global Links   300

13 Terrorism: Understanding the Causes of Radicalism and Extremism   301

Introduction   301
Terrorism as Radical Extremism   305
Drawing on History to Understand
    Extremism   307
Explaining Multiple Causes of Extremism
    Using 'Levels of Analysis'   309
The Response of the United Nations
    to Terrorism   320
Conclusion   324
Key Terms   324
Discussion Questions   324
Suggested Readings   325
Global Links   325

Part IV ●●○○○
Multi-Level Governance

14 Governing the Global Environment   328

Introduction   328
Environmental Issues   329
A Precursor to Global Governance of the
    Environment   331
The Launch of Global Negotiations   333
Climate Change, Kyoto, and an Uncertain
    Future   337
Environmental Governance   343
Conclusion   347
Key Terms   348
Discussion Questions   348
Suggested Readings   348
Global Links   349

15 Governing Global Politics in an Era of Globalization   350

Introduction   350
The Evolution of Global Governance   351
The Expanding Agenda of Global
    Governance   362
Assessing Global Governance   367
Conclusion   370
Key Terms   371
Discussion Questions   372
Suggested Readings   372
Global Links   372

Conclusion   374

Introduction   374
Identifying the Terrain of Global Politics   379
Using Theory as a Guide   381
Key Terms   385
Discussion Questions   385
Suggested Readings   385
Global Links   386

Glossary   387
Notes   397
References   422
Index   438

● FIGURES ●●●●

I.1 The World Trade Center attacks of 9/11: victims by country   4
3.1 Nubia   86
3.2 Early Mesoamerica   89
5.1 World military expenditures, 1988–2007   130
5.2 Global distribution of military expenditures, 2007   131
5.3 Increase in military expenditures, 1998–2007   131
6.1 The US coalition against Al-Qaeda   154
7.1 The United Nations system   160
8.1 Interregional Internet bandwidth, 2005   209
12.1 United Nations Office on Drugs and Crime   276
12.2 Colombia, the cocaine gateway to the world   293
13.1 Deaths from International Terrorism, 1990–2005   302
C.1 The Crash of 1929   377

● TABLES ●●●●

2.1 Women Presidents and Prime Ministers, 1950–present   62
7.1 Millennium Development Goals of 2000, To Be Achieved by 2015   162
7.2 Non-Permanent Members of the UN Security Council, and Date When Term Expires   164
7.3 Membership in the Economic and Social Council for 2010 and the Expiration Date of Membership   167
7.4 UN Secretaries-General: Nationality and Term of Office   171
7.5 UN Peacekeeping Operations, 1947–2007   177
7.6 Membership of the UN Peacebuilding Commission, 2009   185
8.1 Global Growth in Communications and Finance   202
11.1 WSF Expansion since 2001: Thematic and Regional Forums   270
13.1 International Conventions to Address the Problem of Terrorism   321

● BOXES ●●●●

1.1 Woodrow Wilson's Fourteen Points   35
1.2 Keohane and Nye on Complex Interdependence   39
Debate 1: Be it resolved that Utopianism provides an important normative starting point for thinking about global politics.   43
2.1 Karl Marx: The Eulogy of Friedrich Engels   48
2.2 The Bombing of the *Rainbow Warrior*   68
Debate 2: Be it resolved that theory should provide an emancipatory project for reforming global politics.   72
3.1 King Nebuchadnezzar   75
3.2 A Lost Tribe of Israel in Africa?   87
3.3 Decolonization   90
Debate 3: Be it resolved that religion has played a significant role in shaping the evolution of global politics.   92
4.1 The Berlin Wall   103
Debate 4: Be it resolved that the Cold War is not over; it has merely been transformed with different antagonists and different issues.   107
5.1 The Vietnam War   116
5.2 The Cuban Missile Crisis   118
5.3 Nuclear Proliferation   120
5.4 The 'Two Darfurs'   122
5.5 Military and UN System Spending   129
Debate 5: Be it resolved that preparing for war makes war more likely.   137
6.1 Gramsci and Hegemony   141

6.2 The Bretton Woods System   149

Debate 6: Be it resolved that military power is of declining importance in the contemporary global order.   157

7.1 The League of Nations Mandate System   170

7.2 The End of Apartheid   180

Debate 7: Be it resolved that the UN should be dissolved.   195

8.1 Containerization and Controversy   204

8.2 The International Slow Food Movement   210

Debate 8: Be it resolved that globalization is responsible for global economic downturns.   218

9.1 The Global Compact   233

Debate 9: Be it resolved that the UN's Global Compact cannot provide a proper check to unfettered capitalism.   236

10.1 50 Years Is Enough   241

Debate 10: Be it resolved that globalization is not new and there is no alternative to it.   253

11.1 World Social Forum Charter of Principles   267

Debate 11: Be it resolved that the World Economic Forum is an anachronism and needs to be replaced.   273

12.1 Offshore Bank Accounts   281

12.2 The End of Slavery   284

12.3 From Romania to the UK   285

Debate 12: Be it resolved that no areas of international affairs have been left untouched by transnational crime.   300

13.1 The Murder of Theo van Gogh   304

13.2 The Unabomber   311

13.3 How to Keep Your Children from Becoming Terrorists and Extremists   313

13.4 Wahabbism   315

13.5 Palestinian Jihad   318

Debate 13: Be it resolved that Hamas extremists are not terrorists but freedom fighters.   325

14.1 What Is Global Warming?   338

14.2 Definitions of Climate Change   342

Debate 14: Be it resolved that the 'tragedy of the commons' is nothing more than a myth.   349

15.1 The Trans-Pacific Partnership   357

15.2 Multilateralism   360

15.3 The 2005 World Summit   364

Debate 15: Be it resolved that the UN has lost its relevance and should be replaced by a world government.   373

C.1 Fragmegration   380

Debate Conclusion: Be it resolved that we are living in a new world disorder that cannot be explained using traditional theories of IR.   386

Publisher's Preface

I am not Athenian or Greek but a citizen of the world.
—Socrates

The planet Earth as seen from space reveals no signs of international borders and divisions. Yet those borders exist and persist: we may live in a world that has become increasingly globalized, both economically and culturally, but the questions of politics remain. Today, as humanity faces environmental and economic crises of astonishing complexity, issues of global politics may hold the key to our very survival.

W. Andy Knight and Tom Keating are two of Canada's pre-eminent scholars in the field of international relations. *Global Politics* grows out of their decades of experience as researchers, teachers, and scholars, and is perhaps the first international relations text to be fully grounded in the realities of the twenty-first century. Addressing issues of conflict and conflict resolution, war and peace, environmental crisis and economic challenge, *Global Politics* encourages students to become informed global citizens.

A variety of learning tools make key concepts clear and illuminate the dark corners of difficult subjects. These include:

- **Special-topic boxes** that provide additional details about topics of interest and importance, as well as excerpts from primary sources;
- **Debate boxes**, which pose high-interest questions designed to stimulate class discussion;
- **End-of-chapter discussion questions, lists of key terms, suggested readings, and links to web resources** that provide the basis for further study; and
- **A lively design** that incorporates striking, contemporary photographs and a variety of charts and tables.

Tying everything together is a clear, concise narrative that draws on perspectives from a variety of fields—history, economics, sociology, and geography, as well as politics—to help readers understand how the many different aspects of global politics are interrelated.

Global Politics is accompanied by robust ancillary packages for both instructors and students.

- **The Online Student Study Guide** includes self-grading interactive quizzes, study tips, RSS feeds, and annotated lists of additional print and web resources.
- **The Instructor's Site** provides access to a host of resources, including PowerPoint slides and a test generator.

The result is the most comprehensive suite of supplements available to accompany any international relations text.

Twenty-four hundred years later, Socrates' ideal of the 'citizen of the world' often seems as distant as ever. Oxford is proud to publish *Global Politics* in the hope of advancing in some small measure progress toward that ancient goal.

Acknowledgements

Writing this book about global politics allowed both of us to reflect on how we have been teaching international relations over many years. We realized a few years ago that we were increasingly shifting the paradigm from international relations (IR) to global politics and that our students at the University of Alberta were benefitting from this broadening of the conceptual terrain. Oxford University Press provided us with the opportunity of bringing this expanded view of IR to a wider audience beyond our classes. For this we are truly grateful.

We would therefore like to thank editorial, production, and marketing staff at Oxford University Press Canada for their support and guidance in helping us bring this book project to a successful conclusion. In particular we are grateful to Richard Tallman for copy-editing and proofreading each chapter and for his detailed queries on the entire manuscript. The book is much better because of his meticulous attention to detail and his thoughtful suggestions. Also, we very much appreciate the diligence, constant communication, and encouragement that came from key OUP staff, David Stover (president), Sophia Fortier (vice-president and director, Higher Education Division), Phyllis Wilson (managing editor), Katherine Skene (acquisition editor), and Jennifer Charlton (developmental editor). At times when we thought that, due to personal setback, the project might not come to fruition, both Katherine and Jennifer demonstrated their confidence in us and took the time to lift our spirits and assist us to the finish line.

Our sincere thanks go to the students who worked conscientiously and unfailingly on segments of the research for this book as our research assistants. Some of them have now graduated from the University of Alberta, but we want to thank them for their remarkable assistance. These individuals are: Edward Akuffo, Greg Bereza, Vandana Bhatia, John McCoy, Dan Preece, Laura Samaroo, Saarah Shivji, and Dan Webb. But we also want to take this opportunity to thank all of the international relations students who have passed through our classes at both the undergraduate and graduate levels. They have inspired us with their inquisitiveness and challenged us through their thoughtful questions to rethink our understanding of what ought to constitute the study of international relations. In many respects, our wonderful students have served as 'guinea pigs' for our experimental lectures. We thank them for their patience and good humour, which allowed us to work through some of the more difficult material during a time of great flux and uncertainty.

We are truly indebted to the reviewers commissioned by Oxford University Press, who provided us with critical and exceedingly useful feedback. We want them to know that we took their suggestions and criticisms seriously and, in many cases, we were able to reorganize sections of the book, add new cases, and eliminate irrelevant material based largely on their insightful comments. We think that the volume holds together much better because of their input.

The Department of Political Science and Faculty of Arts at the University of Alberta provided us with the intellectual environment within which we were able to hone our thinking about the changes taking place in politics at the global level. We also benefitted from the support of our Dean in the Faculty of Arts and from the offices of the University's Vice President Academic and Vice President Research. Colleagues in the department who provided us with timely and critical feedback on drafts include Rob Aitken, Greg Anderson, and Mojtaba Mahdavi. Outside our department, colleagues who were very helpful during discussions about various aspects of the book include David Charters (University of New Brunswick), Hans Machel (Earth and Atmospheric Studies), and Ingrid Johnston (Education). We also received valuable input on certain chapters from Robert Cox (York University), Michael Schechter (Michigan State University), Charles Jones (University of Western Ontario), Mel Capp (Institute for Research on Public Policy), and Wesley Wark (University of Ottawa). We thank each and every one of these individuals.

Lastly, but most importantly, we want to give our heartfelt appreciation to our families. A special word of thanks goes to our loving spouses and life partners, Mitra and Sandra, who put up with us and with the long hours we spent researching and writing this book. Our children, Bayan, Nauzanin, Amy, and Nic, share a lot in common. They have been exposed to a university environment all their lives and while we hope that this has been a positive experience for them, we want them to know that we appreciate their willingness to forgive us when our research preoccupations result in too little time for them and their pursuits.

While we are deeply grateful for the many suggestions and inputs we received from those mentioned above, in the end we take full responsibility for the content of this work. Any errors and mistakes are ours and ours alone.

W. Andy Knight and Tom Keating
Department of Political Science
University of Alberta

Introduction

Context and Changing Perceptions of a Globe in Flux

The twenty-first century will prove to be as challenging as the past one for students and practitioners of global politics. Issues of conflict and conflict resolution, war and peace, will continue to be central to the study of relations between the actors that operate on the global stage, but so, too, will issues of the global political economy, the environment, poverty, health, and human rights. In some sense, therefore, the continuities of what has been labelled 'politics' require that, as students of global politics, we try to understand both past and current history. However, as has been demonstrated in the immediate post-Cold War era, the nature of politics may indeed be undergoing some transformation as the world moves from a world order that had its origins in the Westphalian Treaty (1648) to a 'new' world order (NWO) or new world disorder (NWD).

We also must be attentive to the changes that are taking place in our world. Most importantly, we need to separate significant and pertinent changes from inconsequential ones and to recognize those patterns that have persisted from those that have atrophied. This is not always an easy task, but it requires both a close reading of the past and a willingness to 'think outside the box'.

Re-imaging Global Politics

This textbook is about global politics, globalization, and multi-level governance. As such, it marks a departure from most traditional textbooks dealing with international relations (IR). When Jeremy Bentham coined the term 'international' back in the late 1700s, he conceptualized a phenomenon that was becoming pervasive in his day, namely the emergence of a states system and a noticeable amount of cross-border transactions between the independent states making up that system. Traditional IR texts usually begin with the premise that states are the main actors in world politics and that, therefore, the central focus of any study of such politics ought to revolve around the interactions among these states. This premise stands on the assumption that the human community is divided up, politically, into states operating in accordance with principles of sovereignty, territoriality, and sovereign equality.

The first principle assumes that the governments of states possess both autonomy from external influences and authority over the people who live within their borders, and are thus free to make decisions affecting their domestic and foreign relations. The second principle assumes that states have a demarcated territorial boundary that contains a population (citizens) and material resources. State leaders and governments, rather than, say, a Sovereign God, are entrusted with protecting their sovereign space and the people they govern.[1] The governors of particular state spaces thus assume responsibility for what takes place within those jurisdictions. The authority of these individuals is shored up with the centralization of power and control over institutions such as the military. The inter-state system, on the other hand, is considered to be anarchic, i.e., lacking a centralized authority. Therefore, states, according to this position, have no sovereign body above them that can dictate to them. As a result, all states are in a **self-help** mode at all times, which means simply that they must look out for themselves, finding the means (usually military, economic, and diplomatic-legal) to protect their sovereignty from intruders. This 'container' principle has been both reinforced by, and partly responsible for, the development of national military establishments and the appearance of formal governments/bureaucratic administrations with mandates to conduct the foreign and defence policies of these states.

The third principle implies that all states are more or less legally equal to each other, despite the fact that some have larger territories, bigger populations, more resources, greater military power, and heavier responsibilities than others do. Thus, at the United Nations, for example, independent states assert their right to be recognized as such. In turn, they extend recognition to other states that can lay claim to independence and control over their domestic space. And they are all granted an equal vote in the General Assembly of the UN. This reciprocal

The United Nations building, New York City.

© iStockphoto.com/zinchik

recognition, supported by embryonic positive international law, advanced the concept of the legal equality of sovereigns.

International relations, in this view, have always been about 'the relations undertaken between separate national states pursuing separate national interests: a diplomatic dialogue between diverse power-centres. It is those power-centres which remain the essential political entities.'[2] This concept of the international arena, as being in a state of anarchy in which the foreign policies of individual states collide, has dominated the literature on international relations and is a view held by scholars spanning the ideological spectrum, including political realists, Marxists, and even some liberal internationalists.

The atomistic conceptualization of traditional IR scholars is being questioned today. While we do not dismiss the assertion that states are the key—and perhaps the most vital—players on the world stage, we also notice multiple players besides states vying for position under the spotlight on the world stage. This observation has an impact on the way we study politics. Given the prominence and influence of non-state actors—individuals, non-governmental organizations, transnational and **multinational corporations**, regional bodies, and international and global institutions—it would be irresponsible for us to maintain a rigid conception of world politics that is entirely **state-centric**. States matter, but other actors now seem to matter as well.

The first thing a contemporary student of politics will notice about politics at the world level is the extent to which the interactions that matter globally are between a multitude of actors (including states) operating within a shrunken globe. While the welfare of citizens still very much depends on actions taken by their government, actions and decisions reached by groups, institutions, and bodies beneath the state, across the state, and far beyond the frontiers of the state also can play a pivotal role with respect to the welfare of individuals. Thus, while the term 'international relations' will still carry some resonance for the subject matter in question, the term we have chosen for this book, 'global politics', appears much more inclusive and better reflects our subject matter. Similar to Steve Smith and John Baylis, we are interested in 'political patterns in the world, and not only those between nation-states'.[3]

The events of 11 September 2001 clearly demonstrate the rationale for viewing politics at the world level as 'global politics' rather than simply as 'international relations' or 'international politics'. The terrorist attacks on the citizens of a sovereign state were carried out by a **non-state actor**. Evidence points to the fact that the deaths of nearly 3,000 individuals, the demolition of the World Trade Center towers in New York City, and the destruction of a portion of the Pentagon building outside Washington, DC, by commercial aircraft loaded with fuel were actions masterminded by individuals within the Al-Qaeda terrorist organization. That organization, although harboured and financially supported by some states, is a non-state actor. Its actions had implications for about 60 states within the international system, affected the stock markets around the globe, and were met by military actions of the United States and its coalition partners. In addition, the United Nations and other intergovernmental bodies passed resolutions outlawing the activities of this terrorist organization and are trying to find ways to ensure that such organizations are not supplied with resources in the future nor given safe haven within states.

The attack itself represented both the national and the global dimensions of politics in the contemporary era. The targeting of the Pentagon demonstrated a

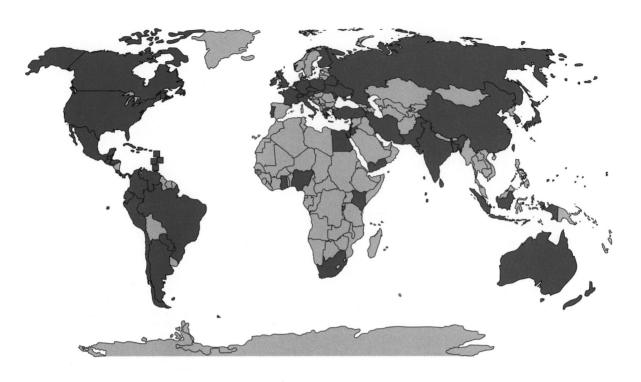

Figure I.1 The World Trade Center attacks of 9/11: victims by country.
Although the 9/11 terrorist attacks struck the United States and the large majority of victims were Americans, the impact truly was global.
Source: <www.cnn.com/SPECIALS/2001/trade.center/interactives.html>.

direct challenge to the United States and its national power. At the same time, in response to these attacks, many states, including the United States, sought to reassert their authority over both their own populations and, more specifically, against foreigners. Border patrols and border security measures were reinforced. Individual liberties were circumscribed and freedom of movement across national borders was significantly curtailed. Passports and points of entry took on greater significance as states, and especially the United States, sought to assert their ability to secure their territorial borders against similar attacks in the future. Their ability to do so, however, is increasingly challenged by the sheer volume of activity that passes across national boundaries.

The attack on the World Trade Center reflects a different set of images, one that identifies a more global (non-national) character. The towers were named for 'world' trade not national trade, and the occupants came from many different countries. Their occupations—mainly international finance—were distinctively and explicitly non-territorial. Thus, apart from states, a variety of sub-national and transnational organizations, both governmental and non-governmental, must be part of any study of global politics. This is particularly important when we examine the relationship between politics and economics. If, according to Harold Lasswell, **politics** is about who gets what, when, and how,[4] then certainly economics matters, and so does the global pattern of resource distribution. Not only have states been forced to yield to other actors in the realm of politics, security, and governance issues, they have also very much been pushed aside by a wide range of economic actors and practices. The prevalence of economic activity that shows no respect for borders—trade, production, investment, military adventurism, etc.—has led some to argue that the territorial **state** is a thing of the past. However, while this level of integrated economic activity has become a prominent feature of late twentieth- and early twenty-first-century global politics, some analysts have noted previous occurrences of international economic integration and have called attention to the striking similarity between late nineteenth-century practices in Europe and contemporary trends. Nevertheless, while such comparisons are important and worthy of attention here, they should not obscure the fact that for many students of politics these economic, social, and political transactions have become the defining feature of the contemporary period, and are captured by the term **globalization**.

Understanding Globalization

When we speak of globalization, what comes to mind are instantaneous communication and rapid transportation, which essentially collapse time and space and dissolve the physical barriers separating states. We also envision rapid and voluminous exchanges of goods and services across national borders and multiple interactions between actors across state boundaries. Certainly, we think of global media outlets like CNN and BBC that can expose people everywhere, and at the same time, to events occurring in all corners of the globe. We also conjure up images of the chain of McDonald's joints that expose people all across the globe to the same brand of fast food, or of sportswear and sports equipment endorsed by Yao Ming, Tiger Woods, and Usain Bolt being worn and used by individuals of diverse cultures, races, and predilections, or of *Harry Potter* filling bookstores and movie theatres around the planet. Clearly, all of these images speak to one truth: that state borders are becoming less relevant in distinguishing communities and can no longer adequately define global politics in an era of globalization.

James Mittleman explains that globalization is causing an integration of economic activities across state boundaries. Advancements in technology have accelerated the movement of capital across the globe and, consequently, for Mittleman the world is no longer 'organized into a set of discrete sovereign states exercising a large (though never complete) degree of control over their domestic economies. Globalizing patterns add new complexity to what is quaintly called international relations; they transcend, blur, and even redefine territorial boundaries.'[5] In addition, globalization has accelerated migratory movements of populations as it disrupts the modes and means of production. In this sense, globalization can be considered a social force that, through its principal agents—multinational corporations, banks, the stock market,

© Paul Colangelo/Corbis

Onlookers view the collapse of the twin towers of the World Trade Center, New York City, 11 September 2001.

and **bond rating agencies**—is aiding and abetting the withering of the sovereign state and forcing us to 'think globally'.

But globalization is also an ideology. It is based on the ideas of **hyper-liberal capitalism** that posit its inevitability. So, while globalization is causing major dislocations between economies and advancing some over others, hyper-liberal capitalist ideology emphasizes this trend as a positive aspect and turns a blind eye to the negative consequences. For example, the collapse of financial markets in 2008 sent governments, banks, and private investors reeling. In addition, recent reports on economic trends conclude that globalization has provided for a net increase in global wealth—despite the fact that this increase has come at the expense of a growing gap between rich and poor.[6] Policy-makers have used reports like these to implement policies and programs such as the Heavily Indebted Poor Country (HIPC) Initiative of the International Monetary Fund, in order to further propel the project of globalization. The HIPC Initiative, launched in 1996 by the World Bank and the IMF, is a comprehensive agreement made by official bilateral and multilateral creditors to assist the poorest, most heavily indebted countries in getting out from under the burden of unsustainable debt. Its intent is to help poor countries focus their policy-making on developing the institutional foundations that will help them sustain development and reduce poverty. This Initiative represents the first effort to co-ordinate all creditors. Consequently, for the first time, creditors are reducing, and not just refinancing, debt and impoverished countries are being forced to include poverty reduction as one of the measurements used to indicate their governments' commitment to reform. But critics of the Initiative, or the 'enhanced' version introduced in 1999, argue that it has not succeeded in resolving the debt crisis in Africa and, furthermore, that its economic policy conditions simply mirror the structural adjustment policies imposed by the international financial institutions on poor countries for two decades with disastrous social results.

Thus, many who are disadvantaged by globalization increasingly feel that this ideology is being forced on them. Faced with such multi-faceted pressure, opponents of globalization have found themselves forced outside of the traditional avenues of state-centric democratic resistance, so that opposition to the project has primarily been manifested within the many anti-globalization protests, from Seattle to Genoa.[7] In this sense, globalization has given rise to a counter-project—one ostensibly driven by a global civil society that has little respect for the buffers of state boundaries. These global protestors are collectively a social force that is chipping away at the **legitimacy** of states and their leaders. James Rosenau refers to their actions as **explosive sub-groupism**,[8] actions that are, in effect, fragmenting power and pointing to the need for alternatives to hyper-liberal globalization.

Whether or not one is pro- or anti-globalization, one thing is certain. Along with the traditional world of states, there is also a rather 'complex **multi-centric world** of diverse actors replete with structures, processes, and decision rules of their own'.[9] Indeed, the so-called 'international' stage has truly become a 'global' stage on which a dialectical clash between these two worlds is occurring. The large number and vast range of collectivities that clamber onto this global stage are exhibiting both organized and disorganized complexity. Besides states, we can also identify literally thousands of factions, associations, organizations, movements, and interest groups in this complicated network that reminds one of John Burton's 'cobweb' metaphor.[10] The whirl of interlocking, and at times conflicting, activities of these various actors places global politics in a state of turbulence and flux. Territorially based state governance no longer seems adequate for effectively handling this new political environment. The intersection of both **sovereignty-bound** and **sovereignty-free** actors opens up an opportunity for us to rethink global political activity. It also provides conditions that may be propitious for entertaining the idea of **multi-level governance**.

The Context of Global Politics: Multi-Level Governance

For many, the changing patterns of activities that have marked global politics in recent decades represent what Rosenau has referred to as 'turbulence'. In his words, this turbulence represents a 'historical breakthrough . . . the likes of which (global life) has not known for three hundred years and the outcomes of which are still far from clear.'[11] This turbulence has been brought on by the convergence of different factors, including: the dynamics of technology; the emergence of transnational issues; the reduced capacity of national governments to address these issues; the growth of regional and local responses (and, hence, decentralizing tendencies); and the growth and enhanced capacity of civil society actors. These developments, in the view of some, have upset the tradition of global politics and left in its place a less stable and predictable future. The apparently settled patterns of inter-state politics that dominated the Cold War between the late 1940s and 1989 had left the impression that global politics followed a rather predictable course. Yet the shape and pattern of global politics have never been as fully settled as the Cold War years, or the portraits presented in some texts, might suggest. At any given time, numerous forces—social, economic, political, ideological, and personal—are shaping the interests and behaviours of states and other actors and defining the context in which these actors relate with one another. The result, however, for students of global politics is the need to recognize and respond to the contingent and multi-faceted nature of global politics. Such views are somewhat easier to accept during periods of more transparent (or apparently transparent) change. The end of the Cold War era may have altered the primary venue for conducting global politics, but the demise of a **bipolar world** with two superpowers left no clear alternative in its wake. The result has been a degree of uncertainty surrounding the state of international order and the sources of support for this order.

This is not the first time that such transformations have been both the overriding characteristic and underlying fissure of global politics. Indeed, flux is more a natural feature of global politics than it is a periodic occurrence in an otherwise unchanging sea of stability. Even the origins of what is commonly labelled 'the modern states system' is likely best viewed as an ongoing process rather than a single event. For example, while many see the European states system originating at the time of the **Peace of Westphalia** in 1648, others place its origins anywhere from 100 years earlier or to a century later. This debate is not irrelevant to us, as it demonstrates two very important characteristics of global politics. One is that global politics is best understood as an ongoing process involving social, political, and economic forces rather than a set of discrete events preceded or followed by periods of stability. The second is that what we have traditionally understood as international relations, i.e., inter-state politics, accounts for only a brief period of human history and therefore should not be assumed to be a permanent feature of our collective history. Moreover, throughout much of the period that is generally considered to constitute the historical record of inter-state relations, state members have repeatedly been subjected to challenges from above and, perhaps more importantly, from below. Thus, the analysis of this historical period provides an insight into the continued significance of looking at global politics by examining its principal characteristics—politics, the state, power, and security.

On Politics

Politics is the means by which various global orders are defined, contested, and resolved—Lasswell's classic definition from 1936 of who gets what, when, how. Similarly, when we study global politics we are concerned with which individuals and groups get power, wealth, health, and status, and how they do it. Our study of global politics requires us to take a rather broad view of each of Lasswell's characteristics. The 'who' of global politics includes the state, but also includes a variety of other actors—corporations such as IBM and Shell, **transnational movements** such as Greenpeace and Oxfam, **sub-national actors** such as provinces and cities, international actors such as the European Union and the International Monetary Fund, and individuals such as Osama bin Laden and Bill Gates. Many actors, or agents as they are sometimes called, have played a role in shaping global politics and use a variety of means to exercise this influence. The 'how' of Lasswell's definition, when applied to the global arena, needs to include military force, but also capital, trade, knowledge, technology, ideas, and norms, for each of these has played some part in defining the issues and parameters within which global politics has been pursued. Finally, a student of contemporary global politics must recognize that the objectives actors pursue are multi-faceted, and that they change across time and space. As a result, traditional realist assertions that global politics is concerned with the pursuit of power, or defending the **national interest**, obscure the multi-dimensional and variable content of terms such as the 'national interest'.

CEM ERSAVCI/Reuters/Landov

Greenpeace activists in one of their less confrontational protests, calling for real action at the 2009 UN Climate Change Conference in Copenhagen.

On the State

The state is the common starting point for most traditional accounts of global politics. By and large, this identification is correct, as the state retains a degree of legitimacy and capacity (both actual and potential) that other actors in global politics do not possess. Moreover, as history ably demonstrates, the state, as a form of political organization, has received a great deal of support, such that at the present juncture units patterned on this organizational form now encompass the entire planet. The persistence and prevalence of the state should not, however, lead us to ignore the very politics that created and sustains states. More importantly, it should not obscure the numerous and influential activities that take place behind, under, around, and above the state by actors that are in no way affiliated with the state. No study of global politics would be complete without giving extensive attention to the state. Yet, a full understanding of the state's place in global politics should not look upon the state as an autonomous actor that was, is, and always will be. Sometimes states may act autonomously, but they are best understood as products of particular histories, societies, cultures, economies, and politics. Studying global politics also requires a study of the state, and requires one to be as attentive to the differences among states as to their similarities.

On Power

Power has often been referred to as the currency of global politics and the instrument that global actors use to get what they want. While it can be a confusing concept, power is central to understanding global politics. Within realist approaches to global politics, the concept of power is treated as the pre-eminent explanatory variable for state action, receiving primary attention in Thucydides's account of the Peloponnesian Wars and providing the centrepiece for a number of realist texts on global politics. For example, John Mearsheimer's text is devoted to a discussion of power, its sources, its applications, and its persistence across time and space.[12]

Traditionally, power has been measured in terms of the capacity of a state to wage war. Materials that could be used to wage war—people, natural resources, industrial capacity, and weapons—were considered to be the most important elements of power. However, recognizing that wars are not the only means to achieve state objectives, a number of scholars have begun to accept the premise that power is a more complex collection of elements. Following the work of Susan Strange, this broad conception of power argues that its critical elements are knowledge, capital, technology, and military capacity, leading one to consider further the very real potentiality that power in global politics does not reside entirely at the state level. Strange and others also have noted the different ways in which power is used in global politics. For example, it is worth distinguishing between structural power and relational power. Another important aspect of the changing contexts of global politics has been in the shifts that have occurred in the distribution of power. Global politics, in the view of Adam Watson, has reflected conflicting pressures towards hegemony (concentrations of power) and independence (diffusion of power among states).[13]

On Security

Long before 9/11, security has been a central concern of global politics and most traditional analyses of global politics have paid particular attention to the security of independent states. At its most exaggerated form, this attention led to the conception of '*raison d'état*', or reason of state, which claimed that 'the well-being of the State and its population is . . . the ultimate value and the goal; and power, maintenance of power, extension of power, is the indispensable means which must—without qualification—be procured.'[14] The security of states took precedence over the security of peoples or individual citizens, in part because it was given a higher value, but in part because it was seen as the necessary shell in which people could exist and prosper. However, this view of security has been subjected to numerous challenges. Critical theorists, and especially feminists, have questioned the credibility and validity of a secure state in which women and others are threatened by current economic and social practices and thus are robbed of their personal security. Other critics, including both philosophers and practitioners, have challenged the concept of state security because it has often been pursued at the expense of personal or **human security**. Yet others have sought to expand our conceptualization of security to address such concerns as environmental sustainability and economic well-being. The United Nations Development Programme, for example, identified human security as a matter of priority and defined the concept primarily in economic and social terms. These more critical views suggest the importance of adopting a more comprehensive view of security that acknowledges both state and personal security and accepts the multi-dimensional character of security, encompassing physical, social, economic, and environmental concerns.

For many, the history of global politics has been a history of war. As survivors of the twentieth century, we should hardly be surprised by the prevalence of war. While wars have occurred with considerable frequency in the history of the modern states system, the twentieth century will stand as one of the bloodiest periods of human existence. Perhaps more importantly, war over the past century has taken on different characteristics, the most notable being the increased threat that war now presents to non-combatants. Often warfare, as it has been conducted in recent years, poses a greater risk to civilians than it does to professional soldiers, those employed to conduct war on behalf of the state, and civilians increasingly have become the primary victims. A second feature of war has been the influence of technology. It has both created a tremendous disparity or asymmetry in the ability to use force and has become a great leveller, allowing even relatively inconsequential groups to gain access to both the means and the material to bring death and destruction to the very centre of the most powerful state in the world. Changing technology, especially the increased use of air power and 'smart' weapons launched great distances from the 'battlefield', has also created a psychological gap between those who use force and their victims on the ground, a condition that Michael Ignatieff has referred to as 'virtual war'.[15]

On Multi-level Governance Networks

As one considers the central features of global politics—the state, power, and security—it becomes evident that global politics is conducted on multiple levels. International orders, both contemporary and historical, have been based on structures and processes operating at various levels—local, national, regional, and global. Such orders have also relied on both procedural and substantive norms that have shaped the beliefs and practices of actors at each of these levels. Thus, as we examine the practice of global politics we should be sensitive to the fact that governance is an integral part of these politics and that governance is carried out at different levels, many of which are reinforcing but some of which may be in conflict and thus challenge the dominant norms and practices.

To best explain the dynamic context of contemporary global politics, the ideological position of critical realism has been adopted in this text, if only because it seeks to capture the different perspectives that we as co-authors of this text are comfortable using. As readers will see, a multiplicity of perspectives has been proffered in the study of global politics and many different viewpoints can be found in the literature. Some of these differences are reflected in the different theoretical orientations of this book's two authors.

Critical Realist Theory

Critical realist theory grounds its analysis on an assessment of the realities of all forms of power in global life, enveloping both a broader concept of the nature of power and a more inclusive understanding of which actors may be able to exert that power. Thus, this approach recognizes that, along with states, a variety of sub-national and transnational organizations, both governmental and non-governmental, must be part of any study of global politics. Moreover, critical realist theory echoes Susan Strange's conception of power, expanding it to include knowledge, capital, technology, and military capacity.

At the same time, it is both historically contingent and philosophically attuned. Emphasizing contextual factors in analysis, critical realist theory accords priority to the dynamic diversity of political arrangements both spatially and temporally, offering a panoramic view or broad interpretive analysis of a given **world order**. Furthermore, the critical realist approach highlights future possibilities with respect to the character of world order in terms of alternatives to the status quo, while recognizing that, because humans have limited understandings, there is no sure way of knowing precisely where the trajectory of world order will lead.

What makes critical realist theory 'realist' is its rejection of the fanciful teleological interpretations of the future that are projected by so-called visionaries and Utopian writers. All of the interpretations of critical realists are rooted in the realities of the current period. Yet, this realism is 'new' in the sense that it departs from the cynical, hopeless position of those realists who see no possible way of transcending the constraints of man's evil nature. Critical realist theorists, while grounding their analysis on the existing system of political actors, offer alternative visions of the future and proffer strategies that can get us to a particular destination (one that is derived from a normative position). They see the character of the existing system as evolving through the pressure of political, social, cultural, economic, ideological, and civilizational forces, as well as changing due to the impact of conjunctural or defining political moments, such as wars, cold wars, catastrophic events, and economic downturns.

VIVEK PRAKASH/Reuters/Landov

Oxfam, a British-based NGO with a broad mandate that includes aid to poor peoples, climate change, and health care, regularly stages street theatre protests with their 'Big Head' leaders at summits of world leaders. Here, at a G8 meeting, the 'Big Heads' protest the power of oil interests in the global economy.

Critical realism is an alternative lens through which we can observe the changing global political environment. This lens provides a better focus and allows us more accurately to describe what we are seeing, that is, the trends that are shifting traditional conceptualizations of 'international' politics towards those of a complex and evolving 'global' politics. Within this lens the authors part company with each other as to the likely direction of future developments and the agents most likely to drive that change. One of us is more firmly rooted in a realist framework that sees the power and capacity of states as essential to the broader transformations of global governance that are both necessary and likely. Such a view does not reject the need and opportunity for change—or its normative content—but acknowledges the necessity of recognizing the role of power and states in shaping that change. In contrast to this view, the other author sees the greater likelihood of positive change and empowerment arising from a more grassroots, bottom-up set of processes where the principal agents lie outside of the states system and where states are forced to yield control to these other agents of change. This position also gives primacy to a set of normative and emancipatory objectives that will both rally support and inform a more radical and substantial reform of global governance. Thus, we both see the occurrence and ongoing likelihood of change and transformation while differing on its source, scope, and longer-term implications. These differences will sometimes show through at various points in the text. As such, they represent the diversity that exists in the field and the value of considering and evaluating alternative approaches as we seek to understand the complex arena of global politics.

Outline of the Book

The first section of the present work deals with the concepts and theories used to describe, understand, and explain both 'international' and 'global' politics. In Chapter 1 the emphasis is on theoretical concepts that proffer a statist conception of 'international' politics. The role and significance of theoretical formulations such as idealism, realism, liberalism, neo-liberalism, and scientific behaviouralism are discussed. Chapter 2 outlines alternative conceptions of international politics found in the theoretical formulations of Marxism, dependency theory, world systems analysis, post-dependency positions, neo-structural realism, and postmodernism (including feminism and environmentalism). The chapter concludes with an examination of a few new paradigms that have been used to indicate the shift from 'international' to 'global' politics. These are the post-internationalist paradigm, constructivism, and historical structuralism. Chapter 3 explores the historical terrain of global politics as an intrinsically interesting prehistory to the modern state system and as an illustrative guide to some continuing patterns of political order and change.

Part II shifts from conceptualization and theory to an empirical analysis of the turbulence and change to the historical structure of world order. Chapter 4 argues that the examination of global dynamics and change should take precedence at this time over preoccupations with stability and the static elements of the Westphalian era that is drawing to a close. Anomalous events in the immediate post-Cold War period seem to be at least jockeying for position, if not replacing recurrent patterns, as the defining element of global politics. Here, we advocate the need to study global politics with the recognition that certain dynamic dialectical forces foster intensive, swift, and decisive changes globally, and that these dynamic forces stem from the proliferation of actors on the global stage, the advancements in technology, changing sources and expressions of power, globalization of national economies, the interdependent and interlocking nature of issues, and the weakening of certain forms of state and state/society complexes.

Chapter 5 looks at one of the enduring features of politics at the global level, i.e., conflict. Even though there may be a shift from 'international' to 'global' politics, war and conflict remain with us. This chapter identifies both the changing nature of war and the reconceptualization of security that has taken place over the past decade or so. Conflict itself is one of the major signs of potential change in politics at the global level. Major conflicts, in the past, have been the vehicle through which the political system is reformed or transformed, and inherent to all global orders are dialectical and conflictual forces with disruptive potential. This chapter focuses on the changes in the sources and character of conflict that are critical indicators of flux in the existing global order.

Chapter 6 continues the theme of 'turbulence and flux' by showing how this has had an impact on the existing global historical structure. As ideas change, so do institutions within which those ideas are embedded. And when the material capabilities that support those institutions change in configuration, then institutional crisis becomes a real possibility. Chapter 7 provides a more in-depth examination of change in the institutions of global order. In particular, the chapter considers the United Nations and how it has evolved and responded to changing practices and ideas.

Part III assesses the contemporary global order and the manner in which practices of globalization are shaping states, the private sector, and a variety of civil society actors. Chapter 8, on the globalization phenomenon, evaluates the impact of globalization on international politics and the inter-state system. Beginning with the premise that globalization is not a new phenomenon, this chapter traces its political and ideological elements and evaluates its differential impact on various forms of state/society complexes. Chapter 9 further elaborates on this impact, focusing on the activities of corporations in the postwar global political economy. It explains how corporations have shaped social and economic relations since the emergence of a truly global economy. It also raises the notion that the differential impact of globalization—the negative as well as the positive aspects—is causing further integration in the global political economy for some states, while marginalizing others from that political economy.

Chapter 10 examines the emergence of anti-globalization movements. Globalization has required that we rethink how politics are conducted and policies are generated at various levels. This rethinking can begin with the realization that civil society has become a much more significant source of dynamic tension within the global political economy. Chapter 11 continues this theme but directs our attention to resistance movements in the global South. Civil society actors in the South have a much more precarious relationship with the global economy and local points of resistance frequently take on much wider significance. Chapter 12 uncovers some of the less attractive aspects of globalization by discussing the prominence and range of transnational crime. Often supported by the same processes of globalization that fuel the legal economy, trans-border criminal activity has flourished under conditions of globalization and now accounts for nearly one-fifth of global economic activity. Finally in this section, Chapter 13 reviews the sources of extremism, using a levels-of-analysis framework, and examines how at times such extremism is manifest in acts of terrorism.

Part IV explores the nature of multi-level governance to show that it is more than an 'idea'. Governance networks are considered in Chapter 14 through an examination of institutions and practices of governance that have sought to address a range of environmental problems confronting the planet. Environmental issues stand on their own as intrinsically important for any student of global politics. They are, however, particularly illustrative of the different forms of governance employed in a search for settling global problems. Chapter 15 looks at the range of actors, interests, and processes involved in global governance. With some reference to historical practices, the chapter outlines the main features of contemporary global governance. Such governance practices and institutions may counter the trend towards global disorder by offering a means of relocating authority in such a way that the conflicts between sovereignty-bound and sovereignty-free actors can be dissipated. Of course, there is no guarantee that the embrace of these practices will ultimately lead to a more orderly, conflict-free world. In fact, they could usher in a messier and more uncertain world unless they are properly thought through.

The Conclusion brings us full circle to an examination of the preferred conceptual lens—critical realism. It is seen as a framework that allows us to envision a multi-level model of governance capable of addressing issues associated with the contemporary turbulence, flux, and disorder while accommodating divergent views—such as those held by the authors. One of the important features of this conceptual framework is its optimism while being grounded in reality. As such, it is compatible with *idealpolitik*. It is certainly not encumbered by the pessimism of neo-realism. Yet, at the same time, it does not allow the student of politics to become carried away with unrealistic visions of how the world ought to be. We find it to be a useful tool for examining conditions of change, turbulence, and flux in global politics, and we hope you do too.

⦿ Key Terms

bipolar world	non-state actor
bond rating agencies	Peace of Westphalia
explosive sub-groupism	politics
globalization	power
human security	self-help
hyper-liberal capitalism	sovereignty-bound
international relations	sovereignty-free
legitimacy	state
multi-centric world	state-centric
multi-level governance	sub-national actors
multinational corporations	transnational movements
national interest	world order

 Suggested Readings

Bache, Ian, and Matthew Flinders, eds. *Multi-Level Governance*. Oxford: Oxford University Press, 2004. *Multi-Level Governance* analyzes the ways in which the concept has been applied across different academic and policy territories. The future of nation-states vis-à-vis sub-national and supra-national organizations and the increasing fluidity of political power is an important subject in the twenty-first century.

Booth, Ken, ed. *Critical Security Studies and World Politics*. Boulder, Colo.: Lynne Rienner, 2005. The book is structured around three concepts—security, community, and emancipation—that are central to the future shape of world politics. The authors argue that critical security is about the problems of real people in real places, and about linking theory and practice.

Mansbach, Richard W., and Edward Rhodes, eds. *Global Politics in a Changing World: A Reader*. Boston: Houghton Mifflin Harcourt, 2009. This collection blends conceptual writings on IR with current events coverage from journalistic sources. Each chapter begins from a scholarly/theoretical view, then follows with readings presenting a news/current events context. The readings encourage students to view daily events within the context of a larger process of change within the international system.

Global Links

The WWW Virtual Library: International Affairs Resources
www2.etown.edu/vl/
    This general site provides links to numerous other sites on a wide variety of selected topics relevant to the study of international affairs; also contains some useful general information on using the web for research.
Global Issues
www.globalissues.org/
    This site deals with many issues and provides links for news stories on a wide variety of global issues.

International and Global Politics

Chapter One

Making Sense of International and Global Politics: Contesting Concepts, Theories, Approaches

> Because all theorizing is rooted in time and space, when circumstances change so too will thinking about world politics.[1]

Introduction

To paraphrase from a statement made by a leading IR scholar, the study of global politics is as much about the contest over the **politics of meaning** as it is about the actual contest over policy and political activity.[2] The 'politics of meaning' in this case refers to the clash of different conceptions and theories about the nature and objective of politics at the global level and over methods of studying, observing, understanding, and explaining global politics. This chapter outlines, describes, and analyzes the origins and principles of the central conceptualizations, or theories, as well as methodologies used to make sense of 'international' and global politics.

Conceptual and theoretical frameworks help us make sense of our world. We can use such frameworks to order and systematize the multiple facts and news items thrown at us daily as we watch television, read the newspaper, or examine scholarly journals and books. Without the use of concepts and theories to guide our thinking process, we would become overwhelmed by the abundance and proliferation of facts and data stemming from the very complex world in which we live. As Stephen Walt put it: 'We need theories to make sense of the blizzard of information that bombards us daily.'[3]

In the study of IR, several conceptual/theoretical approaches or frameworks have been employed to capture the complexities of the interaction between states and transnational actors. Historically, some concepts and theories have exhibited dominance at specific junctures only to be challenged by others later on. The resilience of dominant concepts and theories is usually attributed to their ability to make sense of contemporary issues. This chapter examines what can be referred to as the mainstream or traditional conceptual/theoretical approaches used to explain international/global politics: idealism/Utopianism, realism, and liberalism. We later compare two contrasting methods that can be used to understand and explain global politics: traditionalism and scientific behaviouralism. In the next chapter we will explore challengers to these dominant conceptual, theoretical, and methodological constructs. But first, let's put the process of theorizing about global politics in historical context.

Early Approaches to Understanding Inter-State Relations

E.H Carr, the noted international relations scholar, once said that at the initial stage of a field of study there is a tendency for the normative (an element of wish or purpose) to become overwhelmingly strong, whereas the inclination at that stage to analyze facts is either 'weak or non-existent'.[4] Whether or not this holds true for all fields of study, we can certainly agree with Carr that this is the case for the initial stage of the study of IR, particularly if we date that stage at around the early twentieth century. Dougherty and Pfaltzgraff confirm this when they write: 'The history of international relations theory contains ample evidence of normative theory based on "wish or purpose"'.[5]

However, if one digs deeper, it quickly becomes evident that theorizing about inter-state relations, or about the relationship between entities or actors that make up the human collectivity, began much earlier than the early twentieth century. One only has to peruse the ancient writings of authors like Thucydides, Mo-Ti, Mencius, Confucius, and Kautilya to see rudimentary and abstract ways of trying to conceptualize, describe, and understand interactions that accrue from warfare, diplomacy, and the balance of power between princely state entities. These various early writings on 'inter-state' relations illustrate the extent to which theory can be viewed as basically following reality while at the same time it can be seen as preceding and shaping reality. To provide an example, the failure of the Greek city-state system to develop an effective governance structure led some observers of the time to propose the idealist/Utopianism concept of **cosmopolitanism**, i.e., citizenship in a world state. In that particular case, 'wish' followed analyses of 'facts on the ground'. Out of those 'facts' came the normative drive to create a different kind of polity that would bring better governance to the city-state system. Quite evidently, then, Carr's observation at least needs to be qualified.

Robert Cox, the highly regarded Canadian scholar of international political economy (IPE), offers a more nuanced, and perhaps more satisfactory, explanation of how theory develops:

> there is a real historical world in which things happen; and theory is made through reflection upon what has happened. The separation of theory from historical happenings is, however, only a way of thinking because theory feeds back into the making of history by virtue of the way those who make history (and I am thinking about human collectivities, not just about prominent individuals) think about what they are doing.[6]

But what Cox goes on to say is even more significant in terms of how we understand and make sense of the historical world. He says of the makers of history: 'Their understanding of what the historical context allows them to do, prohibits them from doing, or requires them to do, and the way they formulate their purposes in acting, is a product of theory.'[7]

So, in essence, as students of global politics we reflect on the events that occur and from that reflection we can devise a theoretical framework for understanding those events and for examining future events. But once we have constructed a specific theoretical lens for viewing the world, that construct can influence how we respond to future events and, as Cox puts it, how we think about what we are doing. Thus, theory can be both a constraining and facilitating device. It can be used to limit agency or it can cause agents to act by providing reasons for them to do so. Furthermore, if we really want to make sense of the world around us, we need to be clear about our conceptual, theoretical, and methodological tools and how those tools were developed in the first place. We shall begin by examining three traditional conceptual/theoretical approaches to the study of international relations/global politics, realizing, of course, that none of these theories are monolithic and that there are a variety of strains within each.

Idealism/Utopianism

Sir Thomas More first introduced the term 'Utopia' into modern political discourse through his 1516 work of that name, which describes the ideal city-state. More alerts his readers to the Greek origin of the word and to its double meaning (*eutopia*: 'the good place', and *outopia*: 'no place').[8] Maurice Meisner suggests that the haziness of the concept of Utopia:

> reflects the ambiguity inherent in utopian modes of thought and their ambiguous relationship to history. For utopians are the products of trans-historical moral ideals, and the relationship between moral demands and historical realities is a most tenuous and uncertain one. Utopia, the perfect future that men wish for, and history, the imperfect future that men are in the process of creating, do not correspond. And, it is the consciousness of that lack of correspondence which gives utopian thought its sense of moral pathos and its historical ambiguity. Morally, utopia may be the 'good place,' but historically it may be 'no place'.[9]

Such ambiguity can *generally* be considered a virtue rather than a vice—generally, because many Western scholars, unaware of the genealogy of **Utopianism**, assume, unreflectively, that Utopia is something unrealizable. In their view, those who trumpet Utopias are hopeless daydreamers in search of 'no place', or dangerous illusory fanatics driven by irrational actions in pursuit of unreachable, 'lofty' goals. As Meisner further explains, this position is generally held by Western thinkers who, by and large, have given the Utopian mode of thinking a bad rap sheet by pronouncing it 'irrational', 'unrealistic', and/or 'unpragmatic'.

Indeed, we are constantly being warned by those individuals that we should 'beware of the danger of utopian visions and messianic prophecies intruding into the practical and secular realm of politics', and we are further encouraged 'to applaud the demise of utopian aspirations and ideologies, and to deplore their survivals and revivals'. The general sense we get from those who are critical of Utopianism is that subscribers to this concept of the world are 'politically dangerous and historically pernicious'.[10]

Is this really so? It is true that a Utopian vision of the world would likely clash with conceptions of the world as it is at the moment. But this could create what Max Weber describes as a healthy tension between the existent and the ideal.

Out of this tension can derive a sense of hope for the future, which in turn produces essential pre-conditions for agency that aims to improve and transform the world along the lines of the Utopian vision of 'what ought to be'. This striving for a better world—not its actual accomplishment—produces the dynamic force in history. As Weber put it, the only reason why people are able to attain the possible is because they tend to reach out, time and again, for the impossible.[11] Karl Mannhein, in agreement with Weber, noted: 'With the relinquishment of utopias, man would lose his will to shape history and therewith his ability to understand it.'[12]

From the early body of Utopian writings came such ideas as the development of a law to govern the activities of nations (*jus gentium*), just war principles (a set of laws that would govern how states behaved during wartime). This tendency to envision how the world ought to be governed led writers like Dante Alighieri (1265–1321) to posit a theoretical construct for world government[13]—an idea still found today in embryonic form in such institutions as the United Nations (UN). His idea, however, went much further than the conceptions of the founders of the UN. Dante imagined an international organization under the tutelage of a world ruler who would be in a position to monopolize and harness military power in order to enforce peace among the princes without infringing too much on 'the internal authority of political communities'.[14]

Sr. THOMAS MORE.

Sir Thomas More.

© Corbis

Variations on this Utopian theoretical construct appeared in a number of so-called 'peace plans'. Pierre Dubois (1250–1322), for instance, proposed a regional union of Christian princes that would bring peace to Europe and organize as a collectivity to take back the Holy Land from the Turks. Within Dubois's plan was the notion of an arbitration court for the peaceful settlement of disputes.[15] This idea is more or less captured today in the idea and actuality of the International Court of Justice (ICJ) located in The Hague. Along a similar line of thought is the work of Emeric Crucé (1590–1648), who developed further this Utopian construct by advocating co-operative ventures in the marketplace as a recipe for ending wars and bringing about peace—the kernel of which is found in various free trade arrangements. He also called for an end to colonialism and imperialism, the development of a neutral city that would act as the centre for peacemaking activity, and the eventual termination of war as an instrument for dealing with conflicts.

International Court of Justice, The Hague.

Other early Utopian thinkers include: Duc de Sully (1560–1641), who worked for Henry IV of France as chief minister and who proposed a balance-of-power system for Christian Western European principalities of the day as well as a confederal system that would regulate their interactions; Abbé de Saint Pierre (1659–1743), who had a similar idea for a federal union among European states; William Penn (1644–1718), who called for a system of international law and order; and Immanuel Kant (1724–1804), who, among other things, proposed the creation of republican states as a means of expanding zones of peace and advocated a perpetual peace plan that included the renunciation of war and the elimination of arms races. These are just a few examples, but they serve to underscore the normative quest of Utopian thinkers.

Underlying their thinking are some basic assumptions about human nature that have not always been eagerly embraced, as we shall see later. In fact, some of these assumptions are highly controversial and widely disputed:

1. Human nature is, in essence, good, malleable, and peaceful.
2. Human beings have the dialectical ability to be rational as well as passionate, and education can be the instrument used to ensure that reason prevails over passion.
3. Humans become warlike only when they enter 'society'.
4. Governments, and the media, tend to manipulate public opinion in support of war even when the majority of people (citizens) are opposed to it.
5. War is a product of clashing societies/civilizations that, through ignorance, prejudice, and selfishness, resort to violence; it is not necessarily inherent in individual humans.
6. State leaders in their quest for power are more prone to war than their subjects.
7. Democracies, especially republican states, tend to be peaceful and do not go to war with one another.
8. Arms races are a major cause of warfare between states.
9. Collective security, through centrally organized forces, can be used to deter deviant states.
10. The global rule of law, coupled with the practice of diplomacy and the establishment of effective international organizations, can act as a rational constraint on state actors and lead to global and sustainable peace.

From the above one can quickly recognize views expressed, even today, by some politicians, activists, and scholars. You may have heard them being labelled as 'idealists'. This is not uncommon, because the terms 'idealist' and 'Utopian' are frequently used interchangeably to signify those who hold some or all of the above-stated positions.

'Idealism' is a label generally reserved for that first wave in the development of modern international relations as a systematic study. This occurred immediately after World War I as the carnage of that war gave rise to a sense of revulsion among those who observed international relations at the time. Ultimately, this revulsion led to the growth in the number of idealists who, like earlier Utopians, wanted to prevent such wars from recurring. Hedley Bull acknowledges that these idealists strongly believed that the international system could be:

> transformed into a fundamentally more peaceful and just world order; that under the impact of the awakening of democracy, the growth of 'the international mind', the development of the League of Nations, the good works of men of peace or the enlightenment spread by their own teachings, it was in fact being transformed; and that their responsibility as students of international relations was to assist this march of progress to overcome the ignorance, the prejudices, the ill-will, and the sinister interests that stood in its way.[16]

It is no wonder then that the interwar years were dominated by Utopian thinkers focused on ways of managing international relations in a more peaceful manner than had been the case during the nineteenth century. These individuals directed their attention towards reforming the international system and its institutions so as to ensure peaceful change within the international system. This focus put international lawyers, historians, and students of international organization at the centre of the study of IR.[17]

During the interwar years, IR became 'firmly located within an essentially historical epistemology, in which the major focus for explanations of war was the decision-makers involved.' For this reason, the modern study of IR was quite different from other branches of social sciences. It was 'prescriptive, normative and based on a conception of scholarship activity that stressed the immediate policy-relevance of work'[18] for the simple reason that many thinkers of the time were preoccupied with trying to develop procedures and techniques that would help state decision-makers avoid a carnage similar to that of World War I.

Idealists of the early twentieth century, like Utopians of an earlier time, emphasized the reformation of the international system in the normative hope of establishing global peace. Many of them did so by drawing up blueprints for a better world. They assumed, like the earlier Utopians, that humankind could be enlightened enough to agitate for a world community in which those values common to all people would be stressed and the differences minimized or eliminated. Idealism in the study of IR during that period was defined as an approach that stressed 'the importance of moral and legal norms and internationalism', and called for the establishment of 'effective international organizations' to govern what was considered an anarchic environment dominated by state actors. The term 'idealism', then, became widely associated with the Wilsonian doctrine of US President Woodrow Wilson, the establishment of the League of Nations, and the Kellogg-Briand Pact (1928) renouncing war that was signed by a number of states. These idealist initiatives were expected to usher in and guarantee peace throughout the

© Bettmann/Corbis

US President Woodrow Wilson promoting the formation of the League of Nations. Wilson was awarded the Nobel Peace Prize in 1919 for his efforts.

world or, at the very least, act as a buffer against violent tendencies.[19] As Steve Smith puts it: 'with Idealism intimately connected with the interests of those who had defined the terms of the peace settlements, the tendency was to assume that the benefits of peaceful change channeled through international law and organizations applied universally.'[20]

If there was a difference between the idealist view and the real world, according to those who promoted Utopianism, it was simply because individuals lacked proper education, or because there are evil forces in operation in the world that violate the peace and law of the community, or because governments were simply following their ambitions and not the interests of their own people. In the latter case, it was felt that this could only happen in the case of autocratic or dictatorial governments, the implication being that democracy ought to be the chosen form of government for all states, and that government in a representative democracy necessarily reflected the will of the people.

Most IR scholars today tend to give short shrift to Utopian/idealist ideas because they view Utopianism as having lost 'its credibility and significance with the rise of Nazi Germany, the onset of the Second World War and the post-1945 hostility between the US and the Soviet Union'.[21] But Utopianism/idealism shares with realism a foundational place in the IR discipline. Indeed, Utopianism/idealism is one branch of the root of modern IR scholarship, the other being **realism**. Carr put it best when he stated that Utopianism was an ever-present element of political reality along with realism, and at certain times one would prevail over the other. In that sense, history has been 'a product of the perennial tension between them'.[22]

Realism

E.H. Carr documented well the major problems with idealist/Utopian views of international relations in his book on the *Twenty Years' Crisis*. Those problems became most evident during the 1930s when events revealed certain flaws in the basic assumptions of Utopian thought. The mechanisms imagined by idealists as the best hope for preventing war simply failed to accomplish what they were expected to do. The failure of Utopianism and idealism to explain the events of the 1930s, coupled with the demise of the League of Nations, provided impetus for the emergence of an alternative **paradigm**—realism.

Hans Morgenthau believed, like Carr, that the history of modern political thought is a story about the contest between idealism and realism. In his words, the idealist paradigm asserts:

that a rational and moral political order, derived from universally valid abstract principles, can be achieved here and now. It assumes the essential goodness and infinite malleability of human nature, and blames the failure of the social order to measure up to the rational standards on lack of knowledge and understanding, obsolescent social institutions, or the depravity of certain isolated individuals or groups. It trusts in education, reform, and the sporadic use of force to remedy these defects.[23]

The differences between idealism and realism are cogently elaborated by John H. Herz, who argues that the distinction is really one of emphasis:

> Realist thought is determined by an insight into the overpowering impact of the security factor and the ensuing power-political, oligarchic, authoritarian, and similar trends and tendencies in society and politics, whatever its ultimate conclusion and advocacy. Idealist thought, on the other, tends to concentrate on conditions and solutions which are supposed to overcome the egoistic instincts and attitudes of individuals and groups in favor of considerations beyond mere security and self-interest. It therefore usually appears in one or another form of individualism, humanism, liberalism, pacifism, anarchism, internationalism—in short, as one of the ideologies in favor of limiting (or, more radically, eliminating) the power and authority which organized groups claim over men.[24]

Realism became the dominant theoretical paradigm after World War II and during the height of the Cold War period (1945 until roughly the late 1970s). Initially, it owed its rise primarily to a group of European scholars who migrated to the United States during the 1930s and 1940s in order to flee the war that began in Europe. This group was concerned with 'large-scale questions' and wanted to 'find out the meaning and causes of the catastrophe that had uprooted them'.[25] But there was another reason why this paradigm rose to prominence. As Robert Rothchild notes, realism became popular because it 'encapsulated what they [the politicians] took for granted, especially after the failures of the 1930s and during the height of the Cold War.'[26] Events in the *real* world called into question the idealist approach to reality. British Prime Minister Neville Chamberlain's attempts to appease Hitler's Germany and the failure of the League of Nations to stop the onset of World War II provided skeptics of idealism with the ammunition to shatter the idealist world view. Add this to the competitive and conflictual Cold War environment that followed the end of World War II and one can understand why scholars and practitioners would want to search out an alternative to the Utopian/idealist theory of international politics. Hans Morgenthau, one of the European émigrés, provided such an alternative paradigm to challenge that of the idealists.

Morgenthau called his paradigm 'political realism' and in many respects it was more a counter to the assumptions of idealism than a distinct theory of its own. Morgenthau laid out six basic principles that guided his way of looking at the world of politics. He asserted that, first, politics, like society in general, is governed by a set of objective laws rooted in human nature. By searching empirically throughout history, Morgenthau saw a dominant pattern of opposing interests, competition, conflict, and war throughout generations. Evil, rather than good, appeared to be the central feature in human relations and political reality. If there was any hope for society to improve, state leaders would have to first understand the laws by which society was ruled. In Morgenthau's opinion, the operation

© Bettmann/Corbis

The liberal historian Arthur Schlesinger Jr (at podium) debating President Johnson's Vietnam policy with Hans Morgenthau (seated far right) and the Marxist writer Isaac Deutscher (centre), May 1965, Washington, DC.

of these laws is impervious to our preferences and we 'challenge them only at risk of failure.'[27] If there can be objective laws of politics, then, logically, there ought to be a rational theory that reflects those objective laws. Morgenthau sought to develop such a theory in his work and assumed that one should be able to distinguish between objective truth, supported by empirical evidence and the logic of reason, and subjective judgement, which in his opinion was in the main 'informed by prejudice and wishful thinking.'[28]

The second principle—that international politics is at base about the concept of interest defined in terms of power—is clearly identifiable with Morgenthau's writing:

the struggle for power is universal in time and space and is an undeniable fact of experience. It cannot be denied that throughout historic time, regardless of social, economic, and political considerations, states have met each other in contests for power. Even though anthropologists have shown that certain primitive peoples seem to be free from the desire for power, nobody has yet shown how their state of mind and the conditions under which they live can be recreated on a world-wide scale so as to eliminate the struggle for power from the international scene. It would be useless and even self-destructive to free one or the other of the peoples of the earth from the desire for power while leaving it extant in others. If the desire for power cannot be abolished everywhere in the world, those who might be cured would simply fall victims to the power of others.[29]

This concept of interest defined in terms of power is what, for Morgenthau, demarcates politics as an autonomous sphere of action from such realms as ethics, religion, or even economics (i.e., the study of how resources can best be distributed to meet the needs of the greatest number of people). According to Morgenthau, this interest–power dynamic distinguishes the political from the non-political. So, for political realists, concerns with motives, morality, ideological preferences, or philosophical and political sympathies are not significant areas of investigation when it comes to an examination of international politics or foreign policies of states. While there is no doubt that desirable policies may occupy the thoughts of leaders, political realism is much more concerned with the art of the possible, and thereby stresses the 'rational elements of political reality' in decision-making.[30]

Third, this version of realism does not give the concept of 'interest defined as power' a fixed meaning for all time. While acknowledging that, throughout time, even going back to the days of Thucydides, the clash of interests and the struggle for power among political entities has been an enduring essence of politics, Morgenthau contextualizes these two concepts by saying that the actual meanings of 'interest' and 'power' are determined by historical and social contexts.

The fourth principle of Morgenthau's political realism holds that morality must of necessity give way to prudent political action when it comes to decision-making by states. In other words, states' leaders need to weigh carefully the consequences of alternative political actions and make sound judgements based on the principle of national survival, rather than on any abstract moral sentiment.

On a related point, the fifth principle of political realism is based on the notion of **moral relativism**. As Morgenthau puts it: 'To know that nations are subject to the moral law is one thing, while to pretend to know with certainty what is good and evil in the relations among nations is quite another.' Political realists therefore refuse to identify moral aspirations of any particular state with so-called universal moral laws. If the rulers of a state are convinced that they are on the side of the righteous, this, according to Morgenthau, is 'liable to engender the distortion in judgment which, in the blindness of crusading frenzy, destroys nations and civilizations—in the name of moral principle, ideal, or God himself.'[31] This is why political realism appears 'amoral'—emphasizing prudence over abstract moralizing when it comes to political decision-making.

The sixth principle really underlies the essence of any theory of political realism. Accepting that humans are 'plural' in nature, political realists deliberately subordinate the many facets of the human being (religious, moral, economic, social) to focus specifically on the 'political' as it is—warts and all—rather than as it ought to be. In essence, this constitutes the real difference between realist thought and Utopian/idealist views. Unlike Utopian/idealist analyses, political realists like Morgenthau aim to lessen evil rather than attempt to realize the absolute good.[32] They also see these other facets of human activity as essentially serving political interests. Thus, while Morgenthau and many other realists tend to ignore economic activities, they also tend to interpret such activity as primarily serving political objectives.

As mentioned earlier, there are different strains of realism. It is not a monolithic theory of international relations. However, an examination of the different realist positions reveals some unifying themes with respect to the underlying assumptions of this paradigm. The following are major suppositions usually ascribed to realism.

1. Nation-states are the most important actors in world politics.
2. Operating as a group of sovereign entities, states constitute a multi-state system.
3. All units of the system behave essentially the same.
4. Each state is constantly seeking to enhance and maximize its own power.
5. A clear distinction can be made between domestic and international politics.
6. World politics is a struggle for power that pervades all foreign policy issues.
7. States are completely separate from each other and have no affinities or bonds of community that can interfere with their egotistical pursuit of power.
8. States compete for power and engage in a continuous struggle for survival.

9. This competition makes all states potential, if not actual, enemies.
10. States align with each other out of convenience or only if they are being confronted by a common foe.
11. The primary instrument for bringing about a temporary peace between states is through the mechanism of 'balance of power'.

The last assumption has been used by Kenneth Waltz as a point of departure. Waltz, who developed a structuralist strain of realism, built on Morgenthau's political realist principles but also departed from them. Specifically, Waltz reformulated the realist notion of balance of power into what Karen Mingst and Jack Snyder have called 'an elegant logical theory' that tries to make sense of international politics.[33] Waltz is really a direct descendant of Morgenthau's realist school of thought. But he differs from the more traditional or classical school of realism in at least two significant ways.

First, Waltz dismisses outright the notion that conflict among states is mainly due to the character of human nature. Instead, he posits that the character of the international system itself is to blame for this perennial struggle. That character, he explains, is one of anarchy, since there is no higher power in the international system, other than states, to act as a referee between them, to force them to follow rules, or to get them to keep their promises. For Waltz, anarchy is the permanent condition of the international system, a condition that explains the seemingly endless cycle of violent conflict between states within that system. Second, Waltz is more explicitly theoretical than Morgenthau. He proposes a social scientific theory of international politics based on adherence to rigorous logical deductions derived from specific assumptions about international relations. He develops explicit hypotheses about those relations in such a manner that they can be tested for verifiability or falsification. In that sense, Waltz consciously began to push the study of IR closer to becoming a 'scientistic' discipline.

Waltz compares the search for theory in IR to that of the search for economic theory by the French physiocrats of the eighteenth century. The first major theoretical leap forward by these economists came with the invention of the concept of an economy that was distinct from the actual society and polity in which it was embedded. 'An invention was needed that would permit economic phenomena to be seen as distinct processes, that would permit an economy to be viewed as a realm of affairs marked off from social and political life.'[34] In other words, pre-theoretical economists conceived of the economy as an abstraction of the reality. The theory that emerged was therefore an intellectual construction by which economists were able to select among a myriad of facts and then interpret the selected facts. In essence, what the physiocrats did was to simplify radically the workings of the economy in order to develop general assumptions that could then be tested against and applied to the workings of the real economy. In the process, these economists developed concepts such as 'distribution', 'circulation', and 'the social product' to help them gain a handle on economic causality.

Waltz then compares what the physiocrats did in economics to what Raymond Aron and Hans Morgenthau, two of the most theoretically self-conscious traditional realists, accomplished in the study of IR. Aron, in particular, suggested reasons why international politics as a field of study was much different from economics and concluded that the development of an international politics theory, in a scientistic sense, was nigh impossible. He gave six reasons:

- It is inherently difficult to separate the internal from the external when it comes to factors that affect the international system.
- States cannot be endowed with a single aim.
- In international relations no distinction can be drawn between dependent and independent variables.
- No mechanism exists for restoring a disrupted equilibrium within the international system.
- In the study of international politics there is no way to predict with accuracy in a way that would lead to the development of specified policy goals.
- The complexity of international relations makes it virtually impossible to develop a theory in this subject.

Waltz disagreed with Aron on every one of those points. Morgenthau was closer to Waltz in the sense that, like the physiocrats in economics, he did try to develop abstract concepts—'the national interest' and 'power', for example—to help make sense of international politics. But as Waltz is careful to point out, 'Morgenthau and other realists failed to take the fateful step beyond developing concepts to the fashioning of recognizable theory.'[35] Like Aron, Morgenthau, in fact, also believed that it was difficult to develop a grand theory of international politics simply because of his appreciation of the role of accident and the occurrence of unexpected events and behaviour in politics.

So this is what separates traditional realism from Waltzian neo-realism. Neo-realists consciously seek to develop a grand theory of international politics along the lines of the physiocratic economists, who determined that agriculture was the basis for all subsequent wealth production.

It is instructive here to examine the Waltzian view of 'theory'. For him, theory is a depiction of the organization of a domain and of the connections that exist among its parts. Theory allows one to make a decision about which factors are more important than others and to specify the relations among the selected factors. Theory is an abstraction that allows the scholar to isolate one realm from all others in order to deal with that realm intellectually. In disagreement with Aron, Waltz argues that complexity does not necessarily work against the development of theory. In fact, theory is about the simplification of that complexity, the pushing aside of subtleties, and the distortion of reality. But Waltz also admits that 'since theory abstracts from much of the complication of the world in an effort to explain it, the application of theory in any realm is a perplexing and uncertain matter.' Here, he makes a distinction between theory construction, theory application and, later, theory testing.[36] One should note, also, that Waltz preferred a deductive approach over the primarily inductive approach of traditional realists.

Close scrutiny of Waltz's writing reveals the extent to which he draws on traditional or classical realism in many respects. But it also uncovers several ways in which his structural realism differs. First, it makes an effort to separate internal from external factors in international politics. Second, it views the international system as a whole with structural and unit levels that are at the same time distinct and connected. Third, it demonstrates that structure can influence outcomes of the interacting units and can act as a constraining device on those units, and, thus, the structure of the international system becomes an 'object of inquiry'. Fourth, it asserts that the structure of the international system is defined by a certain ordering principle—'anarchy'—and by the distribution of capabilities across units. Finally, and related to the previous point, since any structure is itself defined by its major units, for neo-realists the nature and character of the international structure will vary depending on the number of great powers within it. In Waltz's words, 'Great powers are marked off from others by the combined capabilities (or power) they command. When their number changes consequentially, the calculations and behavior of states, and the outcomes their interactions produce, vary.'[37]

Thus, the primary departure of neo-realism from traditional realism is the notion that international politics can be viewed as operating within a system with a precisely defined structure—one that has an inordinate (deterministic) influence on the outcome of international relations, i.e., the relations between the units of the system (states).

Unlike traditional realists, Waltz shifted focus from human nature to the structural qualities of the international system. He observed that the international system consisted of both strong and weak powers. In his opinion, the great powers within the system are the entities that really matter when it comes to the functioning of the system. These great powers are bent on survival and aggrandizement. This causes them, more often than not, to engage in war and conflict. Since the international system does not have an overarching sovereign body capable of constraining the activity of these great powers, the entire international system is described as anarchic, with each state adopting self-help as the *raison d'état.*

Both traditional realists and neo-realists generally share a rather pessimistic view of international politics in which war and conflict are predominant, with anarchy and unbridled competition the main descriptors of the environment within which state entities operate. However, during the latter part of the Cold War, some realists adopted a more optimistic view. This branch of realism can be labelled 'defensive realism'. Defensive realists argue that states merely seek to survive and

NIKOLA SOLIC/Reuters/Landov

NATO paratrooper in Croatia.

that great powers are, in fact, capable of guaranteeing their survival by forming alliances that create a balance of power and an equilibrium within the normally anarchic international system.[38] The balance-of-power system created by NATO and the Warsaw Pact, for instance, established stability, albeit precarious, between the great powers—the US and the USSR. Each was able to deter the other from engaging in direct violent confrontation.

Defensive realism builds on Waltz's structural realism and incorporates elements of *realpolitik.* Those elements are: (1) the state's interest provides the basis for its foreign policy, or international action; (2) the need for this policy stems from the unregulated competition of states (anarchy); (3) rational calculations based on *raison d'état* (the necessities of the state) will ultimately result in policies that best serve the state's interests; (4) success is the ultimate test of a state's policy and that success is defined in terms of the preservation and strengthening of the state. Out of this combination of structural realism and *realpolitik,* Waltz constructs a balance-of-power theory as one means of securing order in the anarchic world of inter-state politics. In some ways this is a response to Aron, in that it is a specific policy option designed to restore the equilibrium of the international system and ameliorate the mortal dangers that stem from the normally anarchic system.[39] The balance-of-power theory itself begins with the following assumptions about states: (1) they are unitary actors that pursue self-preservation, at minimum, and universal domination, at maximum; (2) they use whatever means are available to them to achieve their ends; (3) those means include—internally—economic capability and military strength, and—externally—the strengthening and enlargement of alliances; and (4) such alignments can facilitate the manufacture of a balance-of-power mechanism that could bring temporary stability to the international system.[40]

A less optimistic reading of the contemporary international system

Warsaw Pact conference, Sofia, Bulgaria, 1968.

© Bettmann/Corbis

is provided by John Mearsheimer, who in contrast to Waltz, adopts the perspective of 'offensive realism' in his *The Tragedy of Great Power Politics*.[41] Mearsheimer accepts the structuralist arguments of the neo-realists and the pervasive influence of anarchy on the behaviour of great powers. Rather than accepting the likelihood that these states will accept a balance of power, however, Mearsheimer argues that states will instead be driven to expand their power capabilities to gain a position of hegemony over potential rivals. Given this inclination, Mearsheimer argues that great powers will pursue a more offensive strategy in their response to the anarchic structure of the international system. The perpetual competition for hegemony among great powers will render the potential for great power conflict a permanent feature of global politics.

Neo-realism has left an indelible mark on the study of world politics. It sparked a major debate within the IR field that no student of global politics can ignore. While many scholars are critical of Kenneth Waltz's structural approach to realism, it cannot be denied that neo-realism forced international relations scholars to develop a more precise language and method for explaining and understanding world politics. It certainly tried to weed out the eschatological ideas implicit in traditional realism and replace them with 'the secularized idea of science' and instrumental rationality.[42] In many respects, though, neo-realism helped to systematize the field of study in a way that was not done in the past. Furthermore, the Cold War period seemed conducive to both realist and neo-realist theories, or put another way, there seemed to be a fit between those theories and Cold War political practice, resulting in what some have called a 'common-sense' ideology.[43] This gave neo-realism its clout and explains its dominance.

Steve Smith argues that the intellectual predisposition of the period helped to make realism dominant. First, there was the belief in the role of value-free science in resolving problems with which the US, as the emerging hegemonic power, was occupied. Second, scholars who had moved to the US from Europe in the 1930s and 1940s had a significant impact on the study of IR. As mentioned earlier, most of them were concerned with 'large-scale questions' related to the root causes of the catastrophes that had uprooted them. Third, the Cold War environment seemed to confirm and consolidate the theory of realism. Indeed, realism became 'a rationalization for Cold War policies'.[44] Fourth, realism proved to be a good fit for US foreign policy and vice versa. Several major grant-awarding and philanthropic foundations, as well as major universities in the US, were willing to spur research that adopted the realist paradigm. In fact, one would be hard-pressed to find any other country in the Western world with 'this combination of an intellectual community receptive to social science theory and a foreign policy agenda that so closely mirrored the theoretical agenda of Realism'.[45]

International Society

In contrast to the normative aspirations of Utopian writers and the more pessimistic view adopted by realists, a group of writers that coalesced in and around the British Committee on the Theory of International Relations spawned an approach that focused on international society as the central feature of international relations. The position took its lead from the work of Martin Wight, who in a series of lectures in the 1950s outlined what he saw as three traditions in the study of international relations.[46] These traditions Wight labelled as realist, rationalist, and radical, corresponding respectively to realist, international society, and more Utopian and radical theories. In calling attention to the existence of an alternative between realist and more idealist approaches, Wight was arguing for an approach to international relations that both accepted the central significance of states while acknowledging a degree of common purpose among them. This common purpose did not rely on notions of a collection of like-minded democratic states or some universal cosmopolitan civil society, but rested instead on the actions and behaviour of sovereign states.

One of the leading proponents of this international society approach was the Australian scholar Hedley Bull. Bull outlined his argument in *The Anarchical Society*.[47] He begins with a definition of international society:

> A **society of states** (or international society) exists when a group of states, conscious of certain common interests and common values, form a society in the sense that they conceive themselves to be bound by a common set of rules in their relations with one another, and share in the working of common institutions . . . such as the forms of procedures of international law, the machinery of diplomacy and general international organization, and the customs and conventions of war.[48]

Bull goes on to discuss the goals of this international society, highlighting its preservation and the preservation of the sovereignty and independence of the individual states as among the foremost goals. Bull also notes that peace would be another goal of the international society, but that this would be subordinate to the foremost goals of preserving state sovereignty and the society of states itself. Thus, the goal would not be to eliminate war, but to regulate it and minimize its effects on the international society and on the individuals who live within states through such means as international law, international institutions, and the balance of power.

Much of Bull's work focuses on the idea of order. For Bull, it is worth distinguishing between world order, which refers to humanity as a whole, and international order, that is, order among sovereign states. 'Order among mankind as a whole is something wider than order among states; something more fundamental and primordial than it; and also, I should argue, something morally prior to it.'[49] Andrew Hurrell calls attention to the importance of distinguishing between examining order as a fact and order as a value.[50] Bull, while not ignoring the potential value that may be found in international order, is quite clear as to where primary value lies: 'If any value attaches to order in world politics, it is order among all mankind which we must treat as being of primary value, not order within the society of states. If international order does have value, this can only be because it is instrumental to the goal of order in human society as a whole.'[51] Bull would later confront the issue of order as a value in competition with other values such as justice, noting the tensions and potential incompatibility between them.

Unlike the more scientific versions of realism, the international society approach remained firmly rooted within a more interpretivist methodology. There has been a considerable interest in history as well, as writers within this tradition have explored both the occurrence of historical societies of states and the evolution and expansion of international society.[52] As Bull and Adam Watson write: 'We certainly hold that our subject can be understood only in historical perspective, and that without an awareness of the past that generated it, the universal international society of the present can have no meaning.'[53]

The international society approach stands as perhaps the most eclectic of the approaches considered in this text. There is a good deal of debate and discussion among those who situate themselves within the school as to where international society came from and how it might evolve in the future. There is, for example, a debate among those of a more pluralist view who see 'an international order among states sharing different conceptions of justice', where 'states and not individuals are the principal bearers of rights and duties in international law', and solidarists whose 'conception of international society recognizes that individuals have rights and duties in international law.'[54] There is also a commitment to methodological pluralism. 'Because international society is composed of a large number of different material and ideational structures, agents, cultures, beliefs, and perspectives, we need to use a variety of methodologies to understand and explain the phenomena.'[55]

Liberalism

Mark Zacher and Richard Matthew remind us that theories of **liberalism** can be traced in a body of literature that spans three centuries. However, the resurgence of liberalism can be linked to the waning of the Cold War and the noticeable dissatisfaction with realism (and Marxism, which we will discuss in the next chapter). This resurgent liberalism, which some have labelled 'neo-liberalism', is rooted in liberal political theories of the seventeenth century.[56] Those theories helped to propel modernity and the Enlightenment period. At essence, early liberal theory, like Utopianism/idealism, was optimistic about the rationality and malleability of human beings and their capacity to improve the moral and material conditions of their lives. This belief was combined with the notion and commitment to human freedoms.[57] Such freedoms were expected to come from the expansion of democratization, the freeing of the market, and the advance of technologies.

It is important to recognize here that liberalism, like the other theoretical frameworks discussed above, is not a monolithic school of thought. Michael Doyle, who is one of the best-known scholars and advocates of liberalism, identifies at least three distinct schools of liberal thought, each rooted in slightly different conceptions of the citizen and the state. These branches are: liberal pacifism (espoused by Schumpeter), liberal imperialism (associated with Machiavelli), and liberal internationalism (whose best known advocate is Kant).[58]

In trumpeting liberal pacifism, Joseph Schumpeter made the case that the combination of capitalism and democracy provides the foundation for peace. He was confident that imperialism would disappear over time as economic rationalism and democratic governance became more widespread.[59] Later, Michael Haas conducted empirical research that seemed to support Schumpeter's assumptions. Haas, in the course of his research, discovered a cluster of variables that associated democracy, development, and sustained modernization with the development of peaceful conditions.[60]

Niccolò Machiavelli, on the other hand, disagrees with the premise that all free republics are pacifistic. He pointed out that from recorded history free citizens have tended to equip large armies and provide soldiers who fight for public glory and the so-called 'common good'. In many cases, liberal states find it best to export their values via imperialism. In his opinion, 'necessity', or political survival of the state, usually calls for expansion. And, as Doyle points out, there is considerable evidence for liberal imperialism when one examines the annals of history.[61] It should be noted here that although Machiavelli is placed within the liberal camp by Doyle, he is more often claimed as a realist by those who focus on his cynical views of the motives of human beings.[62] We consider Machiavelli as someone who was able to straddle the fence of both theories.

Liberal internationalism has commonly taken the form of a general idealism centred on pacifism. This view of international relations is based on the assumption that mankind will ultimately choose socio-political and economic integration, which over time will progress into a single community. As Herz puts it, this was expected to become a 'progress toward internally ever more democratic, internationally ever more comprehensive societies, which will eventually constitute one great community'.[63] This line of thinking was later embraced by neo-functionalist and integration theorists.

Another approach to liberal internationalism is connected to laissez-faire economics. It assumes that once the '"irrational' monopolistic, militaristic, and nationalist obstacles to free exchange of goods among nations were eliminated, all nations would readily realize their common interest in peace.'[64] This thinking, promoted by such nineteenth-century theorists as August Comte, Herbert Spencer, and Richard Cobden, stressed the importance of free enterprise and free trade as a principle that would draw people together and push aside the antagonisms usually associated with race, language, and creed and unite the world under a banner of peace.

Getty Images

Niccolò Machiavelli.

Liberal theorists generally dispute realist and neo-realist assumptions that deficiency in human nature writ large, or the structure of the international system, leads to aggression and war. Instead, liberal theorists begin with the assumption that aggressive instincts of authoritarian leaders and totalitarian rulers lead to war, and that liberal states, which usually have democratic or republican governments (and are founded on such principles as freedom, equality, civil liberties, respect for private property, and elected representation), are fundamentally opposed to war. As such, liberalism presents a strong challenge to the various strains of realism and, at the same time, has much in common with Utopianism/idealism.

One can see traces of liberalism in the works of Angell, Bentham, Cobden, Hobson, Kant, Locke, Mill, Rousseau, Smith, Spencer, and Wilhem, among others. But Immanuel Kant provides us with the most comprehensive theory of liberalism. Kant argued that the best hope for global peace was through the gradual emergence of republican states whose democratic constitutionalism would allow their citizens the freedom to oppose wars and support free commerce. Such states, in Kant's opinion, would adhere to cosmopolitan law, which would further strengthen the norms that lead to global peace and prosperity. He posited that human beings had a moral responsibility to look after their fellow creatures. But he also maintained that international organizations would be needed to implement and support perpetual peace.

Earlier, we classified Woodrow Wilson as an interwar idealist. But he is also known as a liberal internationalist. Like Kant, Wilson, in his famous 'Fourteen Points' address to the US Congress in 1918, for instance, advocated among other things the establishment of the League of Nations, the removal of barriers to free trade, the promotion of national self-determination, and the establishment of

BOX 1.1

Woodrow Wilson's Fourteen Points

President Wilson's program for world peace was to be built on the following 'Fourteen Points', which were part of his 8 January 1918 address to the US Congress.

   I. Open covenants of peace, openly arrived at, after which there shall be no private international understanding of any kind but diplomacy shall proceed always frankly and in the public view.

   II. Absolute freedom of navigation upon the seas, outside territorial waters, alike in peace and in war, except as the seas may be closed in whole or in part by international action for the enforcement of international covenants.

   III. The removal, so far as possible, of all economic barriers and the establishment of an equality of trade conditions among all the nations consenting to the peace and associating themselves for its maintenance.

   IV. Adequate guarantees given and taken that national armaments will be reduced to the lowest point consistent with domestic safety.

   V. A free, open-minded, and absolutely impartial adjustment of all colonial claims, based upon a strict observance of the principle that in determining all such questions of sovereignty the interests of the populations concerned must have equal weight with the equitable claims of the government whose title is to be determined.

VI. The evacuation of all Russian territory and such a settlement of all questions affecting Russia as will secure the best and freest cooperation of the other nations of the world in obtaining for her an unhampered and unembarrassed opportunity for the independent determination of her own political development and national policy and assure her of a sincere welcome into the society of free nations under institutions of her own choosing; and, more than a welcome, assistance also of every kind that she may need and may herself desire. The treatment accorded Russia by her sister nations in the months to come will be the acid test of their good will, of their comprehension of her needs as distinguished from their own interests, and of their intelligent and unselfish sympathy.

VII. Belgium, the whole world will agree, must be evacuated and restored, without any attempt to limit the sovereignty which she enjoys in common with all other free nations. No other single act will serve as this will serve to restore confidence among the nations in the laws which they have themselves set and determined for the government of their relations with one another. Without this healing act the whole structure and validity of international law is forever impaired.

VIII. All French territory should be freed and the invading portions restored, and the wrong done to France by Prussia in 1871 in the matter of Alsace-Lorraine, which has unsettled the peace of the world for nearly fifty years, should be righted, in order that peace may once more be made secure in the interest of all.

IX. A readjustment of the frontiers of Italy should be effected along clearly recognizable lines of nationality.

X. The peoples of Austria-Hungary, whose place among the nations we wish to see safeguarded and assured, should be accorded the freest opportunity of autonomous development.

XI. Rumania, Serbia, and Montenegro should be evacuated; occupied territories restored; Serbia accorded free and secure access to the sea; and the relations of the several Balkan states to one another determined by friendly counsel along historically established lines of allegiance and nationality; and international guarantees of the political and economic independence and territorial integrity of the several Balkan states should be entered into.

XII. The Turkish portion of the present Ottoman Empire should be assured a secure sovereignty, but the other nationalities which are now under Turkish rule should be assured an undoubted security of life and an absolutely unmolested opportunity of autonomous development, and the Dardanelles should be permanently opened as a free passage to the ships and commerce of all nations under international guarantees.

XIII. An independent Polish state should be erected which should include the territories inhabited by indisputably Polish populations, which should be assured a free and secure access to the sea, and whose political and economic independence and territorial integrity should be guaranteed by international covenant.

XIV. A general association of nations must be formed under specific covenants for the purpose of affording mutual guarantees of political independence and territorial integrity of great and small states alike.

collective security mechanisms. He believed that these steps would ultimately lead to a peaceful, prosperous, and just global order (see Box 1.1). The internationalization of liberal theories is evident in the writings of many of the above-named proponents of liberalism. This explains why the label 'liberal internationalism' is used to describe a variant of the liberalism paradigm.

The following are 10 central assumptions of liberal internationalism:

1. Individual human beings are the most important actors in global politics. They are rational and moral and as such can act, if they so wish, to change the world and themselves so that their full potential can be realized.
2. Social and political institutions can be reformed and improved towards the above end.
3. International relations are being slowly transformed in a manner that promotes progressively greater human freedom, peace, equality, prosperity, and justice.
4. The growth of international co-operation will help to spur human freedom, equality, prosperity, justice, and global peace.
5. International co-operation is being driven by expanding processes of modernization and democratization.
6. Governments, or states, are a necessary evil—they were needed to provide security, education, welfare, and mediation for their citizens, but ought to be constrained to allow for individual freedom and the flourishing of the private sector.
7. Democratic (or republican) governments are less likely to engage in war with one another.
8. Free trade and commerce will bind states together through interdependence and lead to global integration, eventually bringing prosperity and peace to the majority of humankind.
9. Robust international institutions and enforceable international/cosmopolitan law are vehicles for widening the circle of co-operation envisaged by liberalism and for the provision of global security and peace.
10. Education will be the key to the transformation of the human mind so that global sustainable peace will result.

While one can see that liberals obviously share a great deal with idealists, most of them actually draw an important distinction between themselves and Utopian thinkers. Unlike Utopians/idealists, most liberals do not believe that an 'ideal' or perfect harmony of interests is waiting to be discovered.[65] In fact, they accept the realist position that discord and coercion have always been a part of international life. But they are more optimistic than realists—over time, they believe, mutuality of interest, non-coercive bargaining, and collaboration and co-operation will gradually become prominent features among the collectivities that make up the global political system.

When we examine the key assumptions in liberal thought, we can immediately see similarities with idealism and, by extension, differences with realism. But as Ole Holsti reminds us, 'Liberalism shares with realism the stress on explaining the behavior of separate and typically self-interested units of action.'[66] But the differences between liberalism and realism are clear: liberalism does not limit its focus of inquiry to states. Rather, it is particularly concerned with the individual human being and with privately organized social groups and firms; both transnational and domestic activities of these actors—individuals, states, social groups and firms—are fair game in liberalism's analysis, and liberalism does not limit its conception of the international system to one that is anarchical: 'liberalism does not emphasize the significance of military force, but rather seeks to discover ways in which separate actors, with distinct interests, can organize themselves to promote economic efficiency and avoid destructive physical conflict, without renouncing either the economic or political freedoms that liberals hold dear.' Liberalism, like Utopianism/idealism, believes in the possibility of cumulative progress even though it does not constrain itself by forcing this progress towards a predetermined end (teleology) and sees progress as uneven and gradual. Also, and importantly, liberalism forces us to contemplate a much broader range of issues, other than security, in analyses of global politics.[67]

Liberal assumptions are found in several theories—functionalism, neofunctionalism, and global governance and integration theories—that seek to explain the behaviour of hegemons,[68] complex interdependence,[69] and patterns of co-operation among state and non-state actors in the global community.[70] Functionalism appeared in response to the development of co-operation among Western European states after World War II. In an effort to account for the extensive range of co-operative endeavours adopted by previously hostile and competing states, functionalist theories identified the manner in which interactions in non-sensitive areas could develop patterns of co-operation among states. These co-operative experiences, in the view of functionalists, would spill over into other areas, thereby leading to a more inclusive set of co-operative measures and a wider collection of like-minded states. David Mitrany outlined the functionalist perspective in *A Working Peace System* as a method for circumventing the state that would 'overlay political divisions with a spreading web of international activities and agencies, in which and through . . . all nations would be gradually integrated.'[71] This gradual but inevitable integration would see the replacement of states by rendering 'frontier lines meaningless by overlaying them with a natural growth of common activities and common administrative agencies'.[72] Functionalism gained popularity after 1945, particularly in response to postwar developments in Europe that eventually led to the formation of the European Union. Theoretical work by Karl Deutsch and Ernst Haas, among others, refined the functionalism of Mitrany and began to emphasize such factors as patterns of communications and the role of elites.[73] Subsequent attempts to extend the theory to other regions of the world were less successful and suggested that the factors that had facilitated economic and subsequent political co-operation in Europe were not yet developed in other regions of the world. These theories borrowed extensively from liberal assumptions about the nature of the state and its non-security interests, as well as the significant role that societal forces and economic interests played in modifying the security concerns of states.

While some have criticized liberalism as being too general, complex, and wide-ranging in scope to be a useful theoretical guide in explaining global politics, it has become evident, particularly since the end of the Cold War, that this paradigm may provide a better and more accurate reflection of the complex, plural, and messy world in which we live. Indeed, Michael Mandelbaum has argued that the development and expansion of liberal principles and practice define much of global politics over the past century.[74] As Zacher and Matthew correctly note, while the complexity of liberalism may 'undermine theoretical parsimony', the reality is that 'if the world is not simple, thinking it is simple does not enhance intellectual understanding.'[75]

BOX 1.2

Keohane and Nye on Complex Interdependence

At the heart of the argument of Robert O. Keohane and Joseph S. Nye, in *Power and Interdependence* (1977), is the notion that multiple channels now connect societies in contemporary international politics. In essence, these authors express the view that the activity of the conventional Westphalian system of states is no longer the only activity of importance in our political world. We can see their point when we witness the cobweb of interactions between multiple actors on the international stage, including those stemming from informal governmental contacts to the economic activity of multinational corporations (MNCs) and the societal relations between non-governmental organizations (NGOs) and intergovernmental organizations (IGOs).

Keohane and Nye provide us with clear definitions of these various types of interactions. For instance, *inter-state relations* are those channels assumed by realists that connect states to each other; *transgovernmental relations* occur when one relaxes the realist assumption that states act coherently as units; *transnational* applies when one removes the assumption that states act coherently. According to Keohane and Nye, political exchange at the global level occurs through these multiple channels, not simply through the limited Westphalian state channels.

Keohane and Nye also argue that there is not really a hierarchy among issues that places military-security (hard power) issues at the top of the agenda while demoting all other (soft power) issues to the bottom of that agenda. In fact, in our contemporary world, a multitude of different issues compete for position on the agendas of states and other actors. As a result, the line between domestic and foreign policy generally becomes blurred.

Finally, Keohane and Nye suggest that military force will most likely not be exercised in a situation when complex interdependence prevails. In fact, in such cases, the role of the military in resolving disputes may be negated.

To truly make sense of our complex and diverse world it is important to develop a conceptual and theoretical lens that can accommodate and project the images of that complexity, heterogeneity, and diversity. Thus, flexibility and contextualization are important features that any student of global politics should look for in a theory that purports to describe, understand, and explain global politics. The various strains of liberalism contain these features, and this probably explains the renaissance of liberalism in the post-Cold War period (see Box 1.2).[76]

Traditional Methods and Scientific Behaviouralism

Whatever lens one uses to view the world, the issue of what method should be used to make sense of the information and data collected from that observation still needs to be addressed. Historically, there have been two broad methodological approaches used in theorizing about world politics. The first is a deductive method that can be traced back to Plato. 'Deduction is a *formal* process of deriving hypotheses from axioms, assumptions, and concepts logically integrated.' The hypotheses are then tested against observable data in order to be falsified or confirmed.[77] The difference between the deductive approach and the inductive approach has to do with how 'historical factual evidence is collected, converted into useable data, analyzed, and interpreted for the purpose of theory.'[78] The deductive scholar tends to arrive at a particular concept, model, or paradigm in an impressionistic, intuitive manner.

Those who use the inductive approach, on the other hand, are following a method traceable to Aristotle. These individuals are careful about observing, categorizing, and analyzing facts and data that surround them. They tend to describe in detail what they have observed as well as the research procedures followed. The purpose for doing so is to allow other scholars to try and duplicate the same work to see if they will arrive at similar conclusions. This latter approach is one that has been perfected by natural scientists and is generally preferred by social scientists.

As Steve Smith reminds us, there has been a major debate about the way international relations ought to be studied. This debate, initially termed 'the Great Debate' by Hedley Bull, divided American and British IR scholars for many years. The British school of international relations scholarship questioned whether their field of study could ever be considered a branch of social sciences. Indeed, the study of inter-state relations in the UK grew out of such disciplines as history, diplomatic studies, philosophy, and law. Smith elaborates on this point:

> Not only is there a strong body of opinion [in the UK] that concentrates on analyzing current events solely from a policy dimension, but there is also a distinctive 'English School' of studying international relations, usually identified with the work of Martin Wight and Hedley Bull. Even more importantly there is a very vocal body of opinion, centered on the work of Charles Reynolds, which fundamentally takes issue with the notion that International Relations can ever be a social science.[79]

Reynolds believes that IR could never be studied using the canons of inquiry of the natural sciences and adopted by the social sciences. For him, IR is essentially a branch of history, since it seeks to understand the thought of political decision-makers.[80]

Unlike their US counterparts, UK specialists of international relations were not interested in searching for general laws that would describe the generic behaviour of states or explain their actions. 'In line with the diplomatic historian it was assumed that the future course of events was neither predetermined nor beyond the control of decision-makers; instead it was accepted that the course of history would unfold on the basis of deliberate actions taken by the key decision-makers.'[81] In the US, international relations as a study found its home in the social sciences, where emphasis was placed on quantification in the hope of building cumulative theory into a grand theory of IR.

The debate about methodology between the British school of IR (traditionalists) and the US school (behaviouralists) intensified during the 1960s. In essence, this was a disagreement over how knowledge about inter-state relations was acquired. The disagreement was chiefly epistemological. Whereas the British school of IR chose to glean knowledge of the field through introspection, intuition, reasoning, and reflection (the deductive approach), the US school opted for an inductive approach that can be called a positivist epistemology—the gathering of knowledge through the use of our sensory experience and the accumulation of observable data through empirical methods (surveys, content analysis, simulations, gaming, statistical correlations, regression analysis, multivariate analysis, model-building, and computer-driven analysis, to name a few). The latter became known as **scientific**

behaviouralism because it tried to imitate the scientific method of the natural sciences to understand the behaviour of international actors and to look for recurring trends and patterns from which predictions could be made.

The intellectual predisposition of the period when IR became a major study in the US was a belief in the role of a value-free science in resolving problems that the hegemonic power was trying to resolve. This was an imitation of the methodologies of the natural sciences and reflected an almost blind faith in the 'science' of economics.[82] When one combines this with the rise of the US as a superpower and the political environment of the Cold War, one can see why the intellectual and political climate was ripe not only for realism but also for behaviouralism.

The traditionalists were highly skeptical of the adoption of the scientific method in IR study. In their opinion, it is virtually impossible to use quantitative data to predict international events or human affairs. Unlike the natural sciences, in which scientific experiments can be conducted in controlled environments (as in a laboratory, or in a test tube), in the human sciences it is difficult to set up a controlled environment. Traditionalists became indignant about the so-called scientific claims of behaviouralists. They were especially 'critical of the proclivity of some contemporary analysts to quantify in order to demonstrate by tortuous statistical analysis a proposition that ought to be obvious to a person of common sense.'[83] Most traditionalists remain convinced that the essence of global politics lies in the qualitative difference—i.e., subtle shades of meaning that are difficult to quantify. In addition, they argue that the methodology of the hard sciences may not be appropriate for use in the social and human sciences.

Nevertheless, this note of caution has not stopped IR scholars from imitating inductive and positivistic methodologies in an attempt to be more rigorous and to develop an 'objective' theory of IR. The reality, though, is that deductive and inductive methods are not necessarily to be regarded as competing or mutually exclusive approaches. The epistemological approach you use in your attempt to better understand the world around you is best determined by what is being studied, what information is being sought, and at what level of analysis you choose to tackle the subject. Theory-building requires both approaches, sometimes in tandem, and the student of global politics should be equally adept at using both tools.

Conclusion

Purpose precedes and conditions thought. So it should not be surprising that 'when the human mind begins to exercise itself in some fresh field, an initial stage occurs in which the element of wish or purpose is overwhelmingly strong, and the inclination to analyse facts and means weak or nonexistent.'[84]

This, to some extent, explains the chronological sequence of the emergence of Utopian/idealist thought coming before realist thinking as IR developed into a serious field of study. The initial stage of aspiration leading towards an end state is an essential foundational element of human thinking. The teleological aspect of international relations was present from the beginning. It started as a response to World War I as Utopians expressed the desire to prevent such wars. They concentrated on the end-game and did not spend too much time thinking about the obstacles in their path on the way to achieving their 'ideal'. But when the immediate post-1930 events 'revealed the inadequacy of pure aspiration as the basis for a science of international politics', this opened the door for the emergence (or some would say, the re-emergence) of realism—what was considered 'a hard, ruthless, and sometimes cynical' analysis of how the world actually was, an analysis founded to a considerable extent by refugee scholars who had seen and experienced the beginnings of a European world gone mad. 'In the field of action, realism tends to emphasise the irresistible strength of existing forces and the inevitable character of existing tendencies, and to insist that the highest wisdom lies in accepting and adapting oneself to these forces and these tendencies.'[85]

While realism can be a necessary corrective to the exuberance of Utopianism/idealism, as Andrew Linklater warns, it can quickly become 'the sterilization of thought and the negation of action'. When that happens, there is a need for Utopianism/idealism 'to counteract the barrenness of realism'. If immature thought is equated with Utopian thinking, then it can also be associated with certain aspects of realist thinking. 'Mature thought combines purpose with observation and analysis. . . . Sound political thought and sound political life will be found only where both have their place.'[86]

Herz notes that despite the competition between Utopian/idealist and realist thought over the years, 'there have also been possibilities and actualities of synthesis, of a combination of Political Realism and Political Idealism in the sense that the given facts and phenomena were recognized which Realism has stressed, coupled with an attempt to counteract such forces within the realm of the possible on the basis of the ideals of Political Idealism.' Herz calls this synthesis 'Realist Liberalism'. He states that 'Realist Liberalism is the theory and practice of the *realizable* ideal.' He continues:

> if successful, Realist Liberalism will prove to be more lastingly rewarding than utopian idealism or crude power-realism. While less glamorous than Political Idealism, it is also less utopian; while less emotional, it is more sober; while less likely ever to become the battleground of great political movements which stir the imagination of the masses, it has more of a chance to contribute to lasting achievements for human freedom.[87]

It would appear that liberalism offers a plausible way out for both Utopians/idealists and realists. It certainly seems to straddle the fence between these positions while capturing the reality of the world around us. It is in the spirit of paradigmatic pluralism that we now turn to an examination of alternatives to the mainstream approaches used in IR study.

Key Terms

cosmopolitanism
jus gentium
liberalism
moral relativism
paradigm
politics of meaning

raison d'état
realism
scientific behaviouralism
society of states
Utopianism

Discussion Questions

1. What role does theory play in the study of global politics?
2. What are the principal criticisms of Utopianism?
3. What are the principal tenets of realism?
4. What is the difference between classical and structural realism?

5. Why did liberals react against realism?
6. What are some of the distinguishing features of liberalism?

Suggested Readings

Franceschet, Antonio. 'Sovereignty and Freedom: Immanuel Kant's Liberal Internationalist "Legacy"', *Review of International Studies* 27 (2001): 209–28. This article exposes the ambiguity of Kant's political philosophical theorizing on sovereignty and demonstrates that the legacy of liberal internationalist theory is not all that straightforward due to Kant's dualistic understanding of state sovereignty.

Pestritto, Ronald J. *Woodrow Wilson and the Roots of Modern Liberalism*. Lanham, Md: Rowman & Littlefield, 2005. This work illuminates the political thought of US President Woodrow Wilson and thus provides insight into his clear and consistent liberal ideology that laid the foundation for his later actions as a public leader.

Weber, Cynthia. *International Relations Theory: A Critical Introduction*, 3rd edn. Oxford: Taylor & Francis, 2009. This innovative textbook introduces students to the main theories in international relations. It explains and analyzes each theory and exposes the myths and assumptions behind them. Each theory is illustrated using the example of a popular film, which allows students to get a clearer idea of how the theories work.

Global Links

Utopian Thinking
www.enlightennext.org/magazine/j36/utopian-propensity.asp?page = 4
Enlighten Next magazine provides an interesting interview with historian Fritzie P. Manuel on the human impulse to create new and better worlds.

International Political Theory
international-political-theory.net/
This site compiles journal articles and other resources that address themes related to international political theory.

English School of International Relations Theory
www.polis.leeds.ac.uk/research/international-relations-security/english-school/
Dedicated to advancing and reporting research on the English School or international society approach to the study of international relations.

Debate 1

Be it resolved that Utopianism provides an important normative starting point for thinking about global politics.

Chapter Two

Alternative Conceptions of Global Politics

No theory has exclusive claims to the truth.[1]

Introduction

As we have seen in the previous chapter, there are several traditional theoretical approaches to understanding international relations. None of these theories can claim to provide a comprehensive view of how politics work at the global level. At best, each theory offers only an impartial picture of global politics. To illustrate this, John Godfrey Saxe (1816–87) has provided us with a poetic version of a famous Indian legend about the encounter of six blind men with an elephant:

> It was six men of Indostan
> To learning much inclined,
> Who went to see the Elephant
> (Though all of them were blind),
> That each by observation
> Might satisfy his mind.
>
> The First approached the Elephant,
> And happening to fall
> Against his broad and sturdy side,
> At once began to bawl:
> 'God bless me! but the Elephant
> Is very like a wall!'
>
> The Second, feeling of the tusk
> Cried, 'Ho! what have we here,
> So very round and smooth and sharp?
> To me 'tis mighty clear
> This wonder of an Elephant
> Is very like a spear!'

The Third approached the animal,
And happening to take
The squirming trunk within his hands,
Thus boldly up he spake:
'I see,' quoth he, 'the Elephant
Is very like a snake!'

The Fourth reached out an eager hand,
And felt about the knee:
'What most this wondrous beast is like
Is mighty plain,' quoth he;
''Tis clear enough the Elephant
Is very like a tree!'

The Fifth, who chanced to touch the ear,
Said: 'E'en the blindest man
Can tell what this resembles most;
Deny the fact who can,
This marvel of an Elephant
Is very like a fan!'

The Sixth no sooner had begun
About the beast to grope,
Than, seizing on the swinging tail
That fell within his scope.
'I see,' quoth he, 'the Elephant
Is very like a rope!'

And so these men of Indostan
Disputed loud and long,
Each in his own opinion
Exceeding stiff and strong,
Though each was partly in the right,
And all were in the wrong![2]

The moral of this legend, as it applies to global politics theories, can be summed up as follows: each individual theory cannot hope to offer anything more than a glimpse of perceived realities of what goes on in politics at the global level. In this chapter, we review alternative ways of viewing global politics with the hope that they can provide a sufficiently broad arsenal of theoretical and conceptual tools to draw on as we study the behaviour, interaction, and activity of actors on the global stage.

Here we are especially interested in the theoretical formulations of Marxism, modernization theory, dependency theory, post-dependency theory, world systems analyses, and the critical theories of postmodernism (including **feminism** and **environmentalism**). Each of these theoretical constructs offers a stiff challenge to the traditional theories and concepts discussed in the previous chapter. We begin with Marxism.

Marxism

In most global politics classes Marxist thought may not be as prevalent as realist, idealist, or liberal thinking. Certainly, traditional IR theorists seldom engage

Karl Marx.

in serious discussions of **Marxism**. Likewise, mainstream and popular newspapers and television channels usually do not devote much time to analyses of Marxism, let alone employ it to analyze world events. Perhaps this has to do with the fact that Marxist conceptions of the world and of global politics require the kind of serious analyses that cannot be reduced to sound bites. According to Hobden and Jones, Marxist theories 'aim to expose a deeper, underlying—indeed hidden—truth'. In other words, the familiar events of world politics, such as wars, treaties, international aid operations, and summit meetings of world leaders, all occur within structures that have a tremendous influence on those events. Those structures are the structures of the global capitalist system.

Karl Marx and His Critique of Capitalism

The best-known critic of the global capitalist system is Karl Heinrich Marx (1818–83), one of the most important political philosophers of all time. Marx began his analysis of **capitalism** with the assumption that history is progressively unfolding towards the establishment of **communism** (an ideology based on the notion that society can be organized without class distinctions) and that capitalism would be the last stage to be reached before the unfolding of a communist system. By capitalism, Marx was referring to an exploitative system of private ownership of capital that depended heavily on market forces to regulate the distribution of goods and that exploited workers in the process. His revolutionary economic theory posited that the history of societal relationships was one dominated by class struggle; something that was evident not only at the domestic level but also at the international or global level.

Marx did not write much on the subject of international relations per se, since the discipline of IR really did not exist when he was writing and he envisioned a revolution of the proletariat (the working class) at the national level. However, some of his journalistic articles touched on elements of what we would call today global politics. In fact, the entire body of Marx's work has had an incredible influence over the past century and a half on the thinking of many scholars whose research focuses on the workings of the international/global system. Marx's ideas are complex and multi-faceted, but it is important for us to understand some of the key concepts that emerged from his

The opening of the New York Stock Exchange, 1914.

work precisely because of the resonance they have had in terms of influencing alternative approaches to studying global politics.

Marx's greatest contribution to global politics was perhaps the posing and answering of a simple question: How does capitalism work? In answering his own question he began with the common assumption of nineteenth-century German philosophy that history is progressive, or teleological (i.e., that history can be understood as rationally moving towards a certain end state that is better than the current state).[3] Georg Wilhelm Friedrich Hegel (1770–1831), one of Marx's primary intellectual influences, had earlier made the assertion that history unfolds via a series of contradictions as society becomes ever-more rational and self-aware. In its most basic form, we can understand this unfolding process this way: a thesis is presented (e.g., a claim that is understood to be true about the world), but this is soon followed by an antithesis that challenges the validity of the original thesis. The dialectical outcome of this confrontation results in a new synthesis that advances understanding. History, for Hegel, comes to an end when there are no more contradictions and the real and the rational become identical.

Marx expands on this dialectical method but, unlike Hegel, suggests that it is not really in the realm of ideas that this process works itself out; rather, this is done in the actual social world of human interaction, and more specifically in the realm of labour. To support this claim, Marx developed a conceptual model of history characterized by a series of modes of production—the way in which labour and the owners of production are structurally organized to produce wealth. A mode of production is constituted by two key features: (1) the economic base (system of wealth creation); and (2) the political superstructure (the formal, legal-political system that best allows the economic base to function optimally). Although this may be considered a contentious point in some circles, it is commonly understood that the economic base always determines the political superstructure; that is, economic needs will always produce the most appropriate political-legal system in which to operate. In terms of history, then, Marx demonstrates that while many modes of production have existed (e.g., slavery, feudalism, capitalism), they all collapse as the nature of their economic base begins to change. Eventually, the political system that governs those relations is no longer able to facilitate increased production of wealth. When something like this occurs, the contradictions between the economic and political spheres create a revolution and a new mode of production is established.

For Marx, capitalism is the penultimate mode of production in history. As he most famously suggested, by virtue of its internal contradictions, capitalism would be overthrown by a new (and final) historical mode of production—communism—which, in his opinion, does not possess the type of contradictions that previous modes of production did. This is all well and good, but to understand the relevance of this process to global politics we need first to consider the nature of the contradictions that are expected to lead to capitalism's downfall. In other words, we need to return to the earlier question posed: How does capitalism work?

As we all know, capitalism is a profit-driven system of wealth creation. However, for Marx, it is not enough to posit that profit is simply created from the exploitation of labour; instead, he suggests that capitalism requires continued *growth* in profit margins. There are three primary ways in which capitalists can increase their returns on investment: (1) find new markets; (2) decrease labour costs; and (3) raise prices. With respect to the first option, it seems logical that markets will eventually become saturated, thus forcing the capitalists to focus on the second strategy. When this happens, firms will lower wages, lay off workers, or replace human labour with mechanized labour. As a result, unemployment rises and purchasing power plummets. Ironically, the capitalist's last option is to raise prices—a strategy that only intensifies the crisis. This, Marx refers to as a 'crisis of overproduction' (or underconsumption) because more goods are being produced than can be purchased and, as a result, profit margins plunge. Under this scenario, with an increasing consciousness of themselves as a collective revolu-

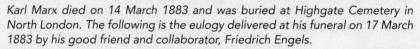

BOX 2.1

Karl Marx: The Eulogy of Friedrich Engels

Karl Marx died on 14 March 1883 and was buried at Highgate Cemetery in North London. The following is the eulogy delivered at his funeral on 17 March 1883 by his good friend and collaborator, Friedrich Engels.

On the 14th of March, at a quarter to three in the afternoon, the greatest living thinker ceased to think. He had been left alone for scarcely two minutes, and when we came back we found him in his armchair, peacefully gone to sleep—but for ever.

An immeasurable loss has been sustained both by the militant proletariat of Europe and America, and by historical science, in the death of this man. The gap that has been left by the departure of this mighty spirit will soon enough make itself felt.

Just as Darwin discovered the law of development or organic nature, so Marx discovered the law of development of human history: the simple fact, hitherto concealed by an overgrowth of ideology, that mankind must first of all eat, drink, have shelter and clothing, before it can pursue politics, science, art, religion, etc.; that therefore the production of the immediate material means, and consequently the degree of economic development attained by a given people or during a given epoch, form the foundation upon which the state institutions, the legal conceptions, art, and even the ideas on religion, of the people concerned have been evolved, and in the light of which they must, therefore, be explained, instead of vice versa, as had hitherto been the case.

But that is not all. Marx also discovered the special law of motion governing the present-day capitalist mode of production, and the bourgeois society that this mode of production has created. The discovery of **surplus value** suddenly threw light on the problem, in trying to solve which all previous investigations, of both bourgeois economists and socialist critics, had been groping in the dark.

For Marx was before all else a revolutionist. His real mission in life was to contribute, in one way or another, to the overthrow of capitalist society and of the state institutions which it had brought into being, to contribute to the liberation of the modern proletariat, which he was the first to make conscious of its own position and its needs, conscious of the conditions of its emancipation. Fighting was his element. And he fought with a passion, a tenacity and a success such as few could rival. His work on the first *Rheinische Zeitung* (1842), the Paris *Vorwarts* (1844), the *Deutsche Brusseler Zeitung* (1847), the *Neue Rheinische Zeitung* (1848–49), the *New York Tribune* (1852–61), and, in addition to these, a host of militant pamphlets, work in organisations in Paris, Brussels and London, and finally, crowning all, the formation of the great International

Working Men's Association—this was indeed an achievement of which its founder might well have been proud even if he had done nothing else.

And, consequently, Marx was the best hated and most calumniated man of his time. Governments, both absolutist and republican, deported him from their territories. Bourgeois, whether conservative or ultra-democratic, vied with one another in heaping slanders upon him. All this he brushed aside as though it were a cobweb, ignoring it, answering only when extreme necessity compelled him. And he died beloved, revered and mourned by millions of revolutionary fellow workers—from the mines of Siberia to California, in all parts of Europe and America—and I make bold to say that, though he may have had many opponents, he had hardly one personal enemy.

His name will endure through the ages, and so also will his work.

Source: The History Guide: Lectures on Modern European Intellectual History, 'Karl Marx, 1818–1883', at: <www.historyguide.org/intellect/marx.html>. (26 July 2005)

tionary agent, the proletariat will likely overthrow bourgeois bosses, thus paving the way for communism to be established.

Lenin and Imperialism

As noted above, Marx conceived of the proletariat revolution as primarily a domestic process (confined within individual nation-states). However, his theory of overproduction became very important for later Marxist theorists and for the study of global politics. In particular, V.I. Lenin (1870–1924), in *Imperialism, The Highest Stage of Capitalism* (1917), sought to explain global politics using Marx's position as a point of departure.[4] As we saw earlier, to ensure continued profit, capitalists are structurally compelled to make use of three strategies that will ultimately lead to capitalism's eventual downfall. However, another option could be considered—amalgamation of firms via mergers. To ensure increased production at relatively lower costs, capitalist companies can purchase competing companies, thereby creating 'economies of scale'. Lenin observed that this process had reached its peak in the late nineteenth and early twentieth centuries and that it represented a new stage in capitalism, which he labelled **monopoly capitalism**. This transformation in the nature of capitalism allowed the bourgeoisie to expand their operations beyond the borders of capitalist countries into poorer countries. He called this capitalist expansion **imperialism**.

Through the colonization of other countries, capitalists avoided the internal contradictions they faced in their own nations. Put another way, they found new markets.

© Bettmann/Corbis

Vladimir Ilyich Ulyanov, who first used Lenin, the name he is best known by, at the turn of the century as a radical writer and editor of a revolutionary expatriate periodical that was smuggled into Russia.

More importantly, they found vast sources of cheap labour. Through the hyper-exploitation of this labour, the bourgeoisie were able to offer low-cost products in their own countries and to provide decent wages for their national proletariat, who otherwise would have chosen a revolutionary path. This had major consequences for the international socialist movement because it created a situation where the world became roughly split between a *core* of rich capitalist countries and a *periphery* of poor countries used by the core as a source of affordable labour and cheap resource extraction. The international working class itself became split between highly exploited labourers in the countries of the periphery and a 'privileged' working class in the core, whose immediate interests lay in sustaining this structural situation that put the working classes in the periphery at a distinct disadvantage.

Lenin's analysis ignited a revolution of sorts in terms of Marxian approaches to international and global politics. For one thing, Lenin advanced the idea that the very character of capitalism was changing. His conceptualization of the world as divided between a dominant core and an exploited periphery complicated Marx's more simplistic view of the class conflict between the proletariat and bourgeoisie. The automatic convergence of interests that was expected to occur between working classes globally, according to Marx's theory, no longer held since capitalists in core countries could use profits derived from exploitation of the proletariat in the periphery to improve the conditions of the working class located in the core. The result, at least in the short term, was to intensify the rivalry between states in the imperial system and reinforce nationalist identities among working classes throughout the capitalist core. Lenin argued that over the long term this rivalry would eventually lead to inter-state conflict among the core capitalist states that would weaken these states, thus reviving inter-class conflict in these core states.

Out of Lenin's analysis emerged a new paradigm within international politics that considered the unit of analysis to be the world of states understood as operating within a single capitalist system. When studying the relationship of states through this lens, one must consider their structural positions within the capitalist world economy. Central to the paradigm is the world systems approach to understanding world politics. This approach begins with the premise that all politics, whether domestic or international, occur within the framework of a capitalist world economy. It also assumes that the position of states and classes within the structure of the world capitalist economy determines to a large degree the behaviour of those states and classes and the nature of the interactions between them. Lenin's theory of imperialism was pushed even further by Latin American scholars of the 'dependency school'.

International Political Economy: From Modernization to Dependency Theory

The early twentieth century saw the emergence of *development theory* within the field of international relations. Essentially, development theorists sought to explain how countries 'develop' towards modernity or how poor 'undeveloped' nations could become rich 'industrialized' societies with all the trappings of what Europeans would consider 'modern' (i.e., the existence of a middle class, modern infrastructure, and the production of manufactured goods rather than relying on the export of primary resources). By far the most influential school of thought among developmentalists is **modernization theory**. This theory basically suggests that all states can potentially move towards modernity and that they can achieve this most efficiently by developing policies that include democratization, industrialization, and privatization.

Emerging in the early post-World War II period, modernization theories offered hope that underdeveloped countries would be able to 'catch up' with developed ones. There was a sense within the writings of most adherents to this position that underdeveloped countries would have to overcome certain barriers that were keeping them poor. To overcome those hurdles, it was suggested that the wealthy countries of the core should provide underdeveloped countries of the periphery with the missing ingredients to 'development' (e.g., investment capital, free enterprise, free trade, etc.). Walt W. Rostow was one of the early proponents of this position. In his influential book, *The Stages of Economic Growth* (1960), Rostow argues that for underdeveloped countries to reach the same level of mass consumption and development as European developed countries they would have to go through a series of stages of economic growth.

Rostow begins by identifying five stages through which all developed countries have passed. He assumes that it is possible to identify all societies as lying within one of these five stages of economic development: (1) traditional society; (2) the preconditions for takeoff; (3) takeoff; (4) the drive to maturity; and (5) the age of mass consumption.[5] According to Rostow, the traditional society experiences limited development because of an inability to take advantage of the potentialities that flow from the application of modern science and technology. Countries at this stage of development are 'pre-Newtonian'.[6] Due to their limited productivity, such societies must devote a high proportion of their resources to agriculture. Agricultural economies tend to have a hierarchical social structure in which individuals have few prospects for upward social mobility. Family and clan connections play an important part in the social structure, and the political system tends to be highly decentralized and influenced by regional landowners.

The second stage of growth can be found in societies in the process of transition, or in which the preconditions for industrial takeoff are present. Those preconditions include the ability to take advantage of the fruits of modern science and technology, the ability to fend off diminishing returns on investments, and the possibility of enjoying the benefits of accrued compound interest. Countries in Western Europe during the late seventeenth and eighteenth centuries are classified by Rostow as passing through this second stage. At that time, Western Europe was just beginning to benefit from the insights of modern science, which helped in the creation of new production functions in agriculture and industry. Britain was the first to reach the preconditions

Agriculture in India.

© Lindsay Hebberd/Corbis

for 'takeoff' stage. But there are cases, for example, India and China since the 1950s,[7] in which a traditional society may have experienced an external intrusion by a more advanced society that set in motion the catalytic conditions needed to move it from the traditional stage to precondition to takeoff. Some of the indications of this transitional stage of development include advancements in education, an increasing number of entrepreneurs, the mobilization of savings, increases in investment, the widening of commerce, and the centralization of political organization/authority. However, the old traditional society continues to exist alongside the newer elements helping to transform that society.

During the third stage—takeoff—the resistances of the traditional society to steady economic growth are finally overcome. The forces of economic progress are allowed to expand at this stage so that economic growth becomes the 'normal' condition. Due to surges in technological advancement as well as the emergence of a centralized political power prepared to place modernization of the economy as the highest order of its political business, new industries are created that yield large profits, which are then plowed back into expansion. This is accompanied by urban growth, the emergence of a new class of entrepreneurs, major increases in the flow of investment in the private sector, the spread of new production techniques in the agricultural and industrial sectors, and the commercialization of agriculture. The social and political structure of the society is so transformed that a steady rate of economic growth is regularly sustained.

The fourth stage is characterized by a relatively long interval of sustained growth and progress as the economy extends the modern technology over the whole gamut of economic activity. This is considered the stage of maturity as the economy finds its place in the international economy. Goods formerly imported are now produced domestically. The economy extends its range into more refined and technologically sophisticated processes (e.g., a shift in focus from coal, iron, and heavy engineering industries to machine tools, chemicals, and electrical equipment). At this stage the society has the technological and entrepreneurial ability to make any product it chooses to produce.

The final stage is one of high mass-consumption during which the leading sectors of the society shift towards durable consumer goods and services. This is a phase in which real incomes of individuals rise to the point where large numbers of people have a demand for consumer goods beyond the basics of food, shelter, and clothing. During this phase the structure of the workforce changes distinctly, with a larger proportion of workers found in urban settings. There may also be a preoccupation with allocating increased resources to social welfare and security, to the production of consumer durables, and to the diffusion of services on a mass basis.

By the 1950s, a group of scholars influenced primarily by Marx and Lenin rejected the modernization thesis because, as far as they were concerned, it ignored the structural realities of global capitalism. Known as the *Dependency School*, this paradigm presented an alternative perspective that suggested that the capitalist world economy ensures the 'underdevelopment' of peripheral countries and, indeed, *requires* that those countries remain in such a state. One of the earliest dependency theorists was Paul Baran (1910–64), who argued that due to existing class structures in both rich and poor countries, it was simply not in the interest of the dominant classes to promote industrialization in the underdeveloped Third World (the global South). Because industrialization did not yet exist to any significant degree in those countries, it was the local feudal aristocracy, merchants, money-lenders, and a small number of local manufacturers who benefited greatly from abetting core-based capitalists in exploiting poor countries. Furthermore, it made no economic sense for the bourgeoisie in rich countries to encourage international competition by helping the Third World to develop.[8]

Raúl Prebisch made a significant contribution to this school of thought. He argued that countries in the periphery are at a distinct disadvantage in regard to trade. Those countries in the global South suffer, in his estimation, from 'declining terms of trade'. So, for example, most of those countries produce and sell raw materials that are much less expensive than manufactured or secondary/tertiary products they import from the industrial countries of the core. Thus, over the course of time, the gap between rich countries of the core and poor countries in the periphery becomes increasingly wider.[9]

Another important contributor to *dependencia* is André Gunder Frank (1929–2005), generally regarded as the 'father' of **dependency theory**. While Baran focused primarily on the internal class relations of the core and periphery, Frank emphasized the structural relation between what he called the 'metropoles' and 'satellites' of the international capitalist system. Using Marx's theory of *surplus value* (i.e., that wealth is produced by underpaying workers for their production), Frank suggested that metropoles (or the core) continuously extract surplus value from satellite (or peripheral) areas. However, he also noted that this exploitive relationship does not exist solely between rich and poor countries, but also exists *within* both poor and rich countries. So, for instance, a metropole (urban centre) in a Third World country exploits local satellites (rural areas) and, in turn, metropoles in industrialized countries extract surplus value from those metropoles in the global South until the process ends in the ultimate centre of the capitalist system—the United States.[10]

Thus, to ensure the greatest payoff in the end, capitalists in the industrialized world are able to enjoy the most surplus value by ensuring that their satellites remain underdeveloped. If satellites were to industrialize on their own, they would become competition for core countries and not the equivalent of feudal landholdings. For both Baran and Frank, the only strategy poor countries can use to break out of their dependency is threefold: to end all ties with the international economy; to institute socialism; and to undertake intense programs of state-run industrialization.

Apart from Baran and Frank, a number of Latin American scholars took up the task of explaining why there is a lack of capital accumulation in the global South. Among these scholars are Fernando Henrique Cardoso and Enzo Faletto.[11]

Post-Dependency Scholarship

Dependency theorists were heavily influenced in their thinking by the works of Marx and Lenin. In essence, they were generally concerned with how capitalism created an asymmetric, and rather unfair, global system based on the

© Carlos Cazalis/Corbis

Fernando Henrique Cardoso, Brazilian post-dependency theorist who served as President of Brazil, 1995–2003.

exploitation of the global South. **Post-dependency theory** shared this concern, but scholars of this school pushed the concept of *dependencia* even further.

Brazilian political economist Fernando Henrique Cardoso (who became President of Brazil, 1995–2003) is often included under the umbrella of dependency theorists. However, his work helps us to understand how Marxist theories of international political economy (IPE) began to diverge from dependency orthodoxy. Writing in the 1970s, Cardoso criticizes dependency theorists for their tendency to treat the Third World as a homogenized space. He stresses that every individual country should be examined in terms of its specific socio-historic context, including its particular class makeup, level of industrialization, and geographical factors. In short, according to Cardoso, the extent of the dependency of periphery countries on the core varies from country to country. Furthermore, empirical evidence shows that, since the 1950s, some countries (e.g., Taiwan and South Korea) have achieved significant industrial growth. This fact has caused scholars to question some of the underlying assumptions of traditional dependency theory and forced them to revisit and rework the theory.

Cardoso, for example, suggests that, depending on internal conditions, the bourgeoisies of some Third World countries have much more power and potential than they were given credit for by dependency theorists such as Frank. Prospects for capital accumulation are evident where manufacturing is focused away from luxury goods and onto capital goods and machinery for production. A developing state can then organize and encourage production to those ends and achieve 'development in dependency'.[12] Finally, some post-dependency theorists have argued that instead of moving to socialism and cutting all ties with core countries, Third World countries can embrace liberal democracy and try to integrate into the global economy as a strategy for moving out of underdevelopment. Indeed, Cardoso pursued this strategy when he became the President of Brazil in 1995.

World Systems Theory

Another important departure from dependency theory can be found in the work of Immanuel Wallerstein, who developed an influential IPE paradigm called **world systems theory**.[13] World systems theory does have some things in common with dependency theory. According to both positions, all politics—international and domestic—take place within the framework of a global capitalist economy. Also, states are not the only actors of importance on the global stage. Social classes are important and so are regional groupings of states.

What distinguishes world systems theorists from dependency theorists is that the latter begin their analysis with individual countries and move up to the international system (therefore, the unit of analysis for dependency theorists remains the individual nation-state and the class structure within it), whereas for the former the unit of analysis is the world capitalist system (and one moves down from this level to study individual countries).[14] This has important implications for the way one studies global politics because everything that occurs in and between states is understood as having an effect on the system as a whole. This is one of the greatest strengths and weaknesses of world systems theory: it at once allows for a comprehensive explanatory lens but at the same time provides little room for political (individual or collective) agency.

Second, Wallerstein's approach is decidedly historical, locating the emergence of the world system in Europe around the sixteenth century with the rise of capitalism.[15] This world system expanded to the entire globe as a result of colonization, with capitalism being the driving force behind this expansionary process.[16] But given the dynamics of history, the social institutions that emerge from this world system do not remain static. They are constantly changing as they adapt to new conditions. Consequently, Wallerstein, taking into account the changes he saw in the world system, advanced the notion of another world economic category, the 'semi-periphery', which operates alongside the core and the periphery.

The semi-periphery is key to explaining the reproduction and continued stability of a system defined by exploitation and increasing disparities in wealth. While the core is still understood as the zone that accumulates wealth at the expense of the periphery, the semi-periphery is considered at a mid-level of development in terms of economic and agricultural production, infrastructure, and state apparatuses. The semi-periphery thus acts as a middle man between the core and periphery. Countries located in the semi-periphery benefit from trade with the core, thereby exhibiting some of the characteristics of the core. But they are also exploited in many ways, similar to countries on the periphery. Furthermore, contrary to dependency theory, some world systems theorists, like certain post-dependency theorists, suggest that all states have the potential of moving upward in relation to their structural hierarchical position in the global economy (and, of course, to move downward as well). In other words, theoretically, semi-peripheral states can become core states and can slip to the periphery, and peripheral countries can move into the semi-periphery. This potentiality creates a situation where states (in particular those in the semi-periphery) are in constant competition with each other, and may have an interest in supporting the existing dominant system because of the potential to benefit, i.e., to move up in the international economic pecking order.

The semi-peripheral states help to reproduce the extant system while acting as a buffer against the anger and revolutionary sentiment that might emanate from the periphery. Some Marxian theorists would say that the semi-periphery acts similarly to the domestic middle classes within Western industrialized societies: because they have so much to lose if the status quo is seriously challenged (and the working class has very little or nothing to lose), the middle class will try to prevent any possibility of a genuinely popular revolution.

Christopher Chase-Dunn, Director of the Institute for Research on World Systems, builds on Wallerstein but goes even further to suggest that 'all the human interaction networks small and large, from the household to global trade, constitute the world-system.'[17] Note, here, the use of the hyphen between 'world' and 'system'. Chase-Dunn claims that the hyphen emphasizes the notion of the 'whole system' and that its use connotes a degree of loyalty to Wallerstein. Chase-Dunn's basic argument is that humans have been interacting with one another across political and geographical boundaries for centuries, especially since the fifteenth century. Even before that time there were many local and regional 'world systems' or intersocietal networks. Most of these systems were forced into the European world system as a result of military conquests and colonial expansionism. The populations of these subjugated peoples were more often than not used as 'cheap labour' for the benefit of Europeans and, later, North Americans. As a result, according to Chase-Dunn, the world-system developed a stratified structure consisting of an economically and politically dominant core and dependent periphery and semi-peripheral regions, some of which successfully improve their positions in the larger core/periphery hierarchy, while most tend to maintain their relative positions.

This structural perspective on global history is very much in keeping with Wallerstein's position. Chase-Dunn also notes that the development of the world-system has been driven by capitalist accumulation as well as geopolitics. It is this emphasis on geopolitics that advances Chase-Dunn's work beyond Wallerstein's. Geopolitics explains the environment of competition over power and wealth by states and multinational corporations (MNCs). However, that competition is conditioned, according to Chase-Dunn, by the dynamics of class struggle at both domestic and global levels. Just as the lower classes within a domestic society will tend to resist the dominant classes, so, too, will people of the periphery and semi-periphery try to resist domination by those of the core. Chase-Dunn, perhaps more so than other world systems theorists, uses empiricism (trade statistics, for example) to identify specific countries located in the core, periphery, and semi-periphery. Chase-Dunn argues that the semi-periphery consists of such countries as Mexico, India, Brazil, and China. But he also adds to this mix the newly industrialized countries, the so-called East Asian Tigers of the 1990s (Hong Kong, South Korea, Singapore, and Taiwan). One can add to this list Turkey, Thailand, Malaysia, and South Africa.

All of the above theories are influenced in one way or another by Marxism— either using Marx as a point of departure or disagreeing with a specific point Marx had posited. These alternative schools of thought give primacy to economic relations within and between states and are, for the most part, critical of several of the mainstream theories discussed in the previous chapter. But other theorists of global politics have built their perspectives on an explicitly critical foundation.

Critical Theories

Canadian political economist Robert Cox made the conceptual distinction between 'problem-solving' and 'critical' theories. As shall be further discussed in Chapter 4, Cox sees problem-solving theory as an approach that takes the present world as a given whereas critical theory questions the very framework that problem-solving theory takes for granted and asks how that world came to be.[18]

Cox's conceptualization of critical theory is largely informed by the work of Antonio Gramsci. But he has also drawn on the Frankfurt School of critical theory developed by such scholars as Theodor Adorno, Jürgen Habermas, and Max Horkheimer. There are essentially two branches of critical theories. The first are those postmodern approaches that essentially deconstruct the taken-for-granted assumptions of all social phenomena, particularly those associated with traditional global politics, but do not promote 'reconstruction' or strategies for improving the situation. The second are those critical approaches, such a feminist theory and environmentalism, that not only deconstruct but also have the normative goal of emancipation and of the radical transformation of existing conditions.

Postmodernism

In political philosophy, modernism is associated with a group of theorists from the seventeenth to nineteenth centuries—such as Locke, Rousseau, Kant, Hegel, Marx, and J.S. Mill. These Enlightenment[19] scholars believed that human reason could be used to combat any form of ignorance, superstition, and tyranny and that it would be a vehicle for building a better world. Generally, the Enlightenment has been characterized by the unflinching belief that through our own capacity to reason we can arrive at the 'truth' and thereby rid the world of all irrational ideas. However, these theorists accepted certain ideas as 'givens':

- History is progressive and moving towards an end or *telos*. This position is known as a metanarrative because it posits an overarching and unifying connection between historical developments.
- The state is the most reasonable form of political association and is in the best position to ensure the polity's security and socio-cultural growth.
- Nature is understood to exist for humans to own, use, and exploit.
- Development is conceived as increased wealth and the well-being of society.

Enlightenment thinking is essentially Eurocentric in that it emerged out of a specific socio-historical context centred in Western Europe. These ideas were then universalized through colonialism and military conquest.

Much of traditional IR theory, as discussed in Chapter 1, can be considered 'modern' as per the Enlightenment. The advent of the Westphalian state system is considered by both liberal and realist schools of thought as marking a higher level of human evolution, and, in the case of liberalism, it marks a move, potentially, towards a more peaceful and co-operative epoch. States are generally understood to be the most important actors, and they are assumed to be rational in their relations with one another (even going to war can be considered rational in some situations). Development is generally understood as being synonymous with industrialization—a mode of production based on the exploitation of nature. Note that most of the foundational assumptions of traditional IR thinking emerge out of Western (European) political philosophy (in particular, Kant, Hobbes, Rousseau, Machiavelli, and Thucydides), which has tended to promote a specific understanding of human nature.

Postmodernists deconstruct much of what we have come to accept as 'givens'. While only since the mid-1980s have postmodern approaches been used within international relations,[20] **postmodernism** has been an influential school of thought for a longer period within the social sciences.[21] This approach to understanding society was developed by postwar French theorists who essentially rejected the philosophy of existentialism and were critical of any scholarship that claimed to have direct access to the 'truth' in human affairs. While there are different strands of postmodern thought, Jean-François Lyotard's definition is probably accepted by adherents to all of the various strands. To be postmodern, in his words, is to exhibit 'incredulity towards metanarratives'.[22] Richard Ashley, one of the leading proponents of postmodernism, is especially critical of the metanarratives of modernity and the Enlightenment and disputes their underlying premises.[23] Thus, to be incredulous of metanarratives is to be totally skeptical of any knowledge claim that involves a grand, all-encompassing theory about the historical record. Such theories, after all, are usually transcendent in nature and posit so-called 'universal truths'. This would mean, therefore, that postmodernists are quite keen on rejecting Marxist theories as well.

Steve Smith and Patricia Owens identify three central themes found in the work of postmodernists. These are: (1) the relationship between power and knowledge; (2) the contextual and performative nature of identity; and (3) the ability of people to construct their social world through the use of textual strategies.[24]

The first theme is mostly associated with Michel Foucault, who opposed the idea that knowledge is somehow immune from the influence of power. Foucault instead argues that power produces knowledge and requires knowledge, and that knowledge relies on, as well as reinforces, power.[25] Postmodern theorists in the international relations field have used the insights of Foucault and others to demonstrate that the knowledge claims generally accepted as 'givens' in IR are in fact 'highly contingent on specific power relations'.[26]

To uncover the workings of power in such cases, one can use a method Foucault referred to as 'genealogy'. This methodology involves a number of important steps:

- shifting one's analytical focus away from simply observing and describing the structures of history towards digging deeper into the movements and clashes of historical movements by asking how those structures were created and reproduced;
- rejecting any notion of universal truth and instead trying to understand historical events by examining conjunctural moments and specific contexts;
- always treating the historical emergence of particular institutions and ideas as contested products of multiple practices;
- treating subjects also as by-products of those practices rather than as having an existence prior to practice;
- treating all ideologies as modes of imposed order and domination.[27]

The second theme that is evident in the work of postmodernists relates to the treatment of identity. Unlike many traditional theories of IR, postmodernism sees identity not as a fixed trait but rather as a 'performative site'. Thus, identities are not seen by postmodernists as intrinsic. According to one postmodern theorist, identity ought to have 'no ontological status apart from the various acts which constitute its reality'.[28] Put another way, postmodernism is 'an approach that denies the existence of a single fixed reality, and pays special attention to texts and to discourses—that is, to how people write and talk about a subject.'[29]

This leads to the third theme found in postmodern work: the use of textual strategies as a means of constructing the social world. One of the leading proponents of such strategies is Jacques Derrida.[30] In fact, the notion of deconstruction became popularized through Derrida's work. For him, we construct our social world as we do texts. To interpret our world is to undertake textual analysis of concepts and the structure of language. Derrida used deconstruction to get to the underlying and hidden meanings of concepts that we generally take for granted and to reveal what lies beneath particular artificial constructs in the language that privilege certain actors, practices, and ideas over others. This process of deconstruction 'is a way of showing how all theories and discourses rely on artificial stabilities produced by the use of seemingly objective and natural oppositions (such as public/private, good/bad, male/female, civilized/barbaric, right/wrong).'[31]

Derrida also used a method that has been labelled 'double reading' to demonstrate that any theory, concept, idea, or practice can have more than one interpretation. Drawing on Derrida, Richard Ashley has undertaken a 'double reading' of the concept of anarchy. He does so by providing the traditional interpretation of what this concept has come to mean and then, in a 'second' reading, demonstrating that what we have come to accept as the natural binary opposition between anarchy and sovereignty is in fact a false opposition. This revelation allows Ashley to argue that we ought to be careful not to accept the 'truth' claims of neo-realists who maintain that anarchy within the sovereign state system is more or less a natural 'law'.[32]

Postmodernists also reject the methodology of positivism and empiricism[33] used in mainstream IR, and suggest that the split between subject and object is nothing more than an illusory social construct. For postmodernists, the so-called 'knowledge' of the world of objects is in fact to be treated only as an interpretation of reality and, therefore, not the actual 'truth'. Further, the subject of modern philosophy is not unified by its capacity to reason but is always changing and being produced by social discourses that, in turn, produce 'reality'. Consequently, for postmodern scholars the idea of reason is always historically situated, and it changes over time and space. This fundamental challenge to the philosophical underpinnings of IR theory results in strong critiques of the 'naturalness' of key categories such as sovereignty, the state, security, anarchy, and citizenship, among others.

To sum up, postmodern theorists are critical and suspicious of any universalizing theories that claim to uncover the causes and consequences of human problems and that offer up solutions for improving the world.[34] For them, any attempt to reduce the source of what ails humankind to a single cause masks the complexity of the problems and downplays the variety of ways in which power is used throughout society to maintain inequalities, injustices, and discrimination. Postmodernists are also wary of these universalizing solutions because they tend to legitimate forms of rule that suppress opposition, usually in the name of enlightenment, rationality, progress, and emancipation.[35] The advantage of taking a postmodern approach to the study of global politics is not that it increases our knowledge and takes us closer to the 'truth' but that it opens our eyes to the fact that there are multiple perspectives on global politics and thus allows us to view the world through different lenses, to open up our ears to hear diverse, sometimes suppressed and silenced, voices that articulate a variety of particular issues and problems. And postmodernism forces us to be more critical of views, theories, and practices that have become dominant, hegemonic, and orthodox (or taken-for-granted).[36]

According to some IR scholars, however, there can be a downside to the wholesale adoption of postmodernism. Pauline Rosenau identifies seven major contradictions in postmodernism:

1. Its anti-theoretical position is in fact a theoretical stand.
2. While postmodernism stresses the irrational, instruments of reason are freely employed to advance its perspective.
3. The postmodern prescription to focus on the marginal is itself an evaluative emphasis of precisely the sort that it otherwise attacks.
4. Postmodernism stresses intertextuality but often treats texts in isolation.
5. By adamantly rejecting modern criteria for assessing theory, postmodernists cannot argue that there are no valid criteria for judgement.

6. Postmodernism criticizes the inconsistency of modernism, but refuses to be held to norms of consistency itself.
7. Postmodernists contradict themselves by relinquishing truth claims in their own writings.[37]

We can add the following criticisms of this school of thought:

8. If all theories are biased, then postmodernism also can be considered biased. Thus its critique can be turned on itself.
9. Some have argued that postmodernism degenerates into nihilism, i.e., negativity for its own sake.
10. Narratives and metanarratives are deconstructed by postmodernists but nothing is constructed in their places.
11. Postmodernism makes no contribution to policy. Postmodernists, generally, according to Robert Jackson and Georg Sorensen, have 'become...estranged from the social and political world that they seek to understand.'[38]

Clearly, not all of these criticisms can be applied to all postmodernist thinkers, since various nuanced positions are found within this particular school of thought. But having briefly outlined what some scholars understand postmodernism to mean and having listed some of its strengths and weaknesses, we can now move on to discuss alternative approaches to IR and global politics that, while not always 'postmodern' in the strictest sense, share many similarities with its deconstructivist approach.

Gender and Feminist Theories

Postmodernists have focused attention on the long-silenced voices of the female half of the world's population. Most traditional IR texts do not devote many pages to the points of view of women. The primary reason can be attributed to the penchant for IR to deal only with relations between states and to separate 'public' from 'private' issues. Men have tended to dominate inter-state relations. Men also are traditionally considered to be masters of the public domain, while women have been relegated traditionally to the private realm. Since traditional IR was seen to address issues of the public realm, women and gender issues were considered by IR scholars to be outside of the sphere of 'international relations'. In fact, it is accurate to say that traditional IR discriminated against women or shunted their voices to the margins.

This situation is being slowly corrected by feminist scholars.[39] The majority of these scholars are activists in their demand for equality between the sexes or for equal rights for women. Clearly, their activism is warranted because, despite gender myopia, overwhelming evidence indicates that women across the globe continue to be disadvantaged relative to men across a range of statistics.[40] Realist thinking in IR continues to be influential, however, and some feminists have argued that the very core assumptions of realism reflect a masculine world view. It is generally assumed by realists that men are natural leaders and that they are better able to make the tough decisions required for the protection of sovereignty, the running of the economy, and the use of military force. The impression one gets from most realist IR literature is that women are either incapable of leading and making those 'tough' decisions, or that they are uninterested in such topics. Such stereotypes are no longer valid, if ever they were.

Women Leaders

Feminist scholars are quick to point out that there have been quite a few women in positions of political leadership. For instance, in 1953–4, Suhbaataryn Yanjmaa served as acting head of state in Mongolia. Sirimavo Bandaranaike became the first female Prime Minister in modern times (in 1960) in Ceylon (now Sri Lanka) after her husband, who was Prime Minister at the time, was assassinated by a Buddhist monk. She held the post for three periods: 1960–5, 1970–7, and 1994–2000. Her daughter, Chandrika Bandaranaike Kumaratunga, was elected President of Sri Lanka in 1994 after serving a short period as Prime Minister. Kumaratunga handed over the post of Prime Minister to her mother, who continued in that position until 2000. Golda Meir became the first female Prime Minister of Israel in 1969 after serving as that country's Minister of Labour and Foreign Minister. She was also one of the founders of the state of Israel and was known as the 'Iron Lady' before that label was applied to Margaret Thatcher, the first female Prime Minister of the United Kingdom (1979–90). Soong Ching-Ling acted as the head of state in China from 1968 to 1972 and again for a brief period in 1981. Isabel Martinez de Perón became the first woman President of Argentina in 1974 (and was the first woman to hold that position in South America). She took over when her husband, Juan Perón, died in office, and she served in that capacity for two years. Thirty years later, the Argentinian people elected another woman as their President. Cristina Elisabet Fernández de Kirchner, wife of the former President of Argentina, was elected to this post in 2007 and became the first woman in history to succeed her husband via an election.

Isabel Martinez de Perón, President of Argentina (1974–6).

Current Argentina President, Cristina Elisabet Fernández de Kirchner, elected in 2007.

Indira Gandhi was Prime Minister of India for three consecutive terms, from 1966 to 1977, becoming the first female leader in the most populous democracy in the world. She was elected again in 1980 and served until 1984 before being assassinated by a bodyguard. María Corazón Sumulong Cojuangco Aquino was installed as President of the Philippines in 1986 after President Ferdinand Marcos was ousted in a peaceful people's power revolution. Aquino served as President of the country until 1992. In 1990, pro-democracy activist Aung San Suu Kyi was elected Prime Minister of Burma (Myanmar), but the military junta in Rangoon did not allow her to serve in that capacity and instead placed her under house arrest.

© Burhan Ali/EPA/Corbis

Benazir Bhutto at one of her final campaign rallies before she was assassinated.

The list of women (Table 2.1) who have achieved the pinnacle of political power in their countries over the last half-century is extensive, and includes two women—Mary Robinson and Mary McAleese—who have served as President of Ireland, consecutively, for the past 20 years; former Norwegian Prime Minister Gro Harlem Brundtland, who also chaired the World Commission on Environment and Development, which introduced to the world community the concept of 'sustainable development'; and Angela Merkel, the first female chancellor of Germany, a nation with the largest European economy and a substantial military force. In 2005, Ellen Johnson-Sirleaf became the first woman president of an African country. This Harvard University graduate and former World Bank economist now heads Liberia and is bringing stability to a country that recently experienced many years of civil war. Also educated at Harvard, as well as at Oxford University, Benazir Bhutto, the daughter of a well-known and beloved Prime Minister of Pakistan, Zulfikar Ali Bhutto, served as Prime Minister of her country, 1988–90 and 1993–6. She was the first female

Table 2.1 Women Presidents and Prime Ministers, 1950–present

Suhbaataryn Yanjmaa, President, Mongolia, 1953–4

Sirimavo Bandaranaike, Prime Minister, Sri Lanka, 1960–5, 1970–7, 1994–2000

Indira Gandhi, Prime Minister, India, 1966–77, 1980–4

Soong Ching-Ling, Chair, China, 1968–72; Honorary President, 1981

Golda Meir, Prime Minister, Israel, 1969–74

Elisabeth Domitien, Prime Minister, Central African Republic, 1974–6

Isabel Perón, President, Argentina, 1974–6

Lucinda da Costa Gomez-Matheeuws, Prime Minister, Netherlands Antilles, 1977

Lidia Gueiler Tejada, President, Bolivia, 1979–80

Maria de Lourdes Pintasilgo, Prime Minister, Portugal, 1979–80

Margaret Thatcher, Prime Minister, United Kingdom, 1979–90

Dame Mary Eugenia Charles, Prime Minister, Dominica, 1980–95

Vigdís Finnbogadóttir, President, Iceland, 1980–96

Gro Harlem Brundtland, Prime Minister, Norway, 1981, 1986–9, 1990–6

Milka Planinc, Prime Minister, Yugolavia, 1982–6

Agatha Barbara, President, Malta, 1982–7

(continued)

Maria Liberia-Peters, Prime Minister, Netherlands Antilles, 1984–6, 1988–94

Corazon Aquino, President, The Philippines, 1986–92

Benazir Bhutto, Prime Minister, Pakistan, 1988–90, 1993–6

*Aung San Suu Kyi, Prime Minister, Burma (Myanmar), 1990

Sabine Bergmann-Pohl, President, German Democratic Republic, 1990

Kazimira Prunskien, Prime Minister, Lithuania, 1990–1

Ertha Pascal-Trouillot, President, Haiti, 1990–1

Violeta Barrios de Chamorro, President, Nicaragua, 1990–6

Mary Robinson, President, Ireland, 1990–7

Edith Cresson, Prime Minister, France, 1991–2

Begum Khaleda Zia, Prime Minister, Bangladesh, 1991–6, 2001–6

Hanna Suchocka, Prime Minister, Poland, 1992–3

Agathe Uwilingiyimana, Prime Minister, Rwanda, 1993–4

Marita Petersen, Prime Minister, Faeroe Islands, 1993

Kim Campbell, Prime Minister, Canada, 1993

Sylvie Kinigi, Prime Minister, Burundi, 1993–4

Tansu Çiller, Prime Minister, Turkey, 1993–6

Susanne Camelia-Romer, Prime Minister, Netherlands Antilles, 1993, 1998–9

Reneta Indzhova, Prime Minister (Interim), Bulgaria, 1994–5

Chandrika Kumaratunga, President, Sri Lanka, 1994–2005

Claudette Werleigh, Prime Minister, Haiti, 1995–6

Sheikh Hasina, Prime Minister, Bangladesh, 1996–2001, 2009–present

Rosalia Arteaga Serrano, President (Interim), Ecuador, 1997

Pamela Gordon, Premier, Bermuda, 1997–8

Janet Jagan, President, Guyana, 1997–9

Jenny Shipley, Prime Minister, New Zealand, 1997–9

Mary McAleese, President, Ireland, 1997–present

Ruth Dreifuss, President, Switzerland, 1998–9

Jennifer Meredith Smith, Premier, Bermuda, 1998–2003

Mireya Elisa Moscoso de Arias, President, Panama, 1999–2004

Vaira Vike-Freiberga, President, Latvia, 1999–2007

Helen Clark, Prime Minister, New Zealand, 1999–present

Tarja Kaarina Halonen, President, Finland, 2000–present

Mame Madior Boye, Prime Minister, Senegal, 2001–2

Megawati Sukarnoputri, President, Indonesia, 2001–4

Gloria Macapagal-Arroyo, President, The Philippines, 2001–present

Nataša Mićić, President (Acting), Serbia, 2002–4

Beatriz Merino Lucero, Prime Minister, Peru, 2003

Nino Burjanadze, President (Acting), Georgia, 2003–4, 2007–8

(continued)

Table 2.1 (Continued)

Micheline Calmy-Rey, President, Switzerland, 2003–present

Luísa Dias Diogo, Prime Minister, Mozambique, 2004–present

Yulia Tymoshenko, Prime Minister, Ukraine, 2005, 2007–present

Ellen Johnson-Sirleaf, President, Liberia, 2005–present

Angela Merkel, Chancellor, Germany, 2005–present

Han Myeong-Sook, Prime Minister, South Korea, 2006–7

Portia Simpson-Miller, Prime Minister, Jamaica, 2006–7

Michelle Bachelet, President, Chile, 2006–present

Micheline Calmy-Rey, President, Switzerland, 2007

Emily de Jongh-Elhage, Prime Minister, Netherlands Antilles, 2006–present

Dalia Itzi, President (Acting), Israel, 2007

Pratibha Patil, President, India, 2007–present

Cristina Fernández de Kirchner, President, Argentina, 2007–present

Michèle Pierre-Louis, Prime Minister, Haiti, 2008–present

Dalia Grybauskaite, President, Lithuania, 2009–present

Jóhanna Sigurdardóttir, Prime Minister, Iceland, 2009–present

---

*Aung San Suu Kyi, the 1991 Nobel Peace Prize laureate, won election in 1990 with her party gaining 80 per cent of the vote. The military government refused to accept the results and soon placed her under house arrest, where she has been for most of the last 20 years.

Note: Acting, interim, and caretaker leaders who held office for only a very short time (i.e., days or weeks) are not included in this list.

Sources: Various websites, including especially Judith Hicks Stiehm, 'Women Presidents, Prime Ministers, Chancellors, and Premiers Since 1950', at: <www.fiu.edu/~stiehmj/documents.wom-enppm.html>; Jone Johnson Lewis, 'Women Presidents and Prime Ministers: 20th Century', at: <womenshistory.about.com/od/rulers20th/a/women_heads.htm>; 'Female Heads of State', at <www.wikigender.org/index.php/Female_Heads_of_State>.

leader of a Muslim country in the modern world. During an attempt at a political comeback, Benazir Bhutto was assassinated in a suicide attack at an election rally in Rawalpindi, Pakistan, on 27 December 2007. Besides Gandhi and Bhutto, at least one other woman political leader was assassinated in modern times: Rwandan Prime Minister Agathe Uwilingiyimana, elected in 1993, was killed at the outset of the Rwandan massacre in 1994.

Multiple Approaches in Feminist Analysis

While feminist writings in the international relations field have increased in recent years, there is no singular feminist theory of global politics. In fact, the work of many of these scholars can rightly be labelled under 'gender studies' because they are concerned not solely with women but with the constructions of 'masculinity' and 'femininity' as well as 'the material and ideological relations that exist between the two sexes'.[41] Steve Smith and Patricia Owens identify at least five strands of gender and feminist thinking: (1) liberal; (2) socialist/Marxist; (3) standpoint; (4) postmodern; (5) post-colonial.[42]

Liberal feminists are primarily concerned with the structural position in which women find themselves in the international system. They ask questions such as the following: Why are a vastly disproportionate number of political leaders and policy-makers men? Why are women excluded from the highest levels of political office? Why are women largely paid less than men for the same work? Why do women suffer disproportionately more than men in violent conflicts and from the burdens of poverty? Why is it that in some countries women have limited rights relative to men and are considered chattel?[43] Thus, liberal feminists are normatively driven by the goal of bringing about a world in which there is equality between the sexes. This means demanding that women are better represented in all aspect of politics (local and global) and that they have influence in how the global political system operates. Often, the liberal feminist perspective has been criticized for its 'add women and stir' approach.

But authors such as Cynthia Enloe, who initially began from the premise of liberal feminism, have demonstrated that by simply adding women to the discussion of global politics we will clearly see that they are playing important 'political' roles in the world, albeit overlooked by the 'gender-blind' traditional IR literature. The important contribution Enloe makes to the study of global politics is to deconstruct traditional IR thinking and writing and show that the activities of women are crucial to the functioning of the global economic and political systems.[44] Furthermore, Enloe forces us to consider as part of the analysis of global politics certain women's activities that many IR scholars would prefer to ignore. In her book *Maneuvers* (2000), for example, Enloe explains why female prostitution ought to be a subject for IR analysis:

> Exploring militarized prostitution [i.e., the availability of female prostitutes within or near theatres of war] is important first because the lives of so many women in so many countries have been directly and indirectly affected by this institution. Second, the subject should attract our attention because so many men have had their expectations of, and fantasies about, women shaped by their own participation in militarized prostitution. Third, military policy makers' attempts to construct a type (or a particular array of types) of masculinity that best suits their military's mission are exposed by taking seriously their military prostitution policies. Fourth, we need to think carefully about militarized prostitution because calculations about it have shaped foreign policies and international alliances. Fifth, understanding any military's policies on prostitution will throw light on the thinking that lies behind its policies on rape, recruitment, sexual harassment, morale, homosexuality, pornography, and marriage. Finally, devoting analytical energy to unraveling the politics of military prostitution may help us explain why prostitution policies of a foreign military can often capture the attention of local male nationalists while those same protest leaders not only continue to ignore the prostitution policies of their own country's military but also stubbornly resist local feminists' efforts to make sexuality an explicit issue in the wider nationalist movement.[45]

In many respects, Marxist and socialist feminists ask similar questions to those of Enloe and other liberal feminists. However, their critique of IR is, as would be expected, situated within the broader context of capitalist social relations. Their primary argument is that the global system of production is founded on the backs of women, i.e., that women are materially exploited to a much greater extent than men and that this is a requirement for the reproduction of international capitalism. Thus, we can understand Marxist feminism as a school of thought that analyzes how class exploitation and patriarchy intersect to produce women's inequality in global politics. Similar to the normative claims of Marxist IPE, then, to realize gender equality requires the overthrow of capitalism.[46] Socialist feminists, to a greater extent than their Marxist counterparts, emphasize the effects of patriarchy and male dominance in producing women's inequality and subservience. Both Marxist and socialist feminists, however, demonstrate that systematic disadvantaging of women is due to a combination of the patriarchal system of power and the capitalist system.

Drawing on the position taken by socialist feminists, standpoint feminists have pointed out that the structural subordination of women, viewed as a specific class based on their 'sex', places women theorists in a unique position from which to view global politics—to draw from a traditional IR slogan, 'where you stand depends on where you sit.' Standpoint feminists seek to eliminate the distortions in IR research brought about by 'entrenched misogyny and androcentrism (male centeredness)'.[47] They claim that knowledge is a social construct 'formed by the prevailing ideological, social, and political setting'.[48] Since traditional IR knowledge has been generated primarily by men, standpoint feminists argue that this knowledge will be partial, distorted, and biased, reflecting the interests of men. Thus, when women generate knowledge, they do so from a completely different perspective (or standpoint) and that knowledge will tend to challenge the dominant positions in IR. The greatest contribution of this particular feminist school of thought has been to show the extent of the male domination of most of the IR theories.[49]

Postmodern feminists, on the other hand, have criticized standpoint and other feminists for their retention of the binary opposites of male–female and the sex–gender distinction. These postmodernists argue that 'sex' is as much a social construction as 'gender' and, as a result, the power relations that produce such concepts tend to be obscured from view.[50] For these critical feminists, the differences between women and men are always discursively constructed, or made to seem natural through discourses of power. Thus, they are interested in how we have come to understand 'gendered' differences that often manifest themselves as dichotomies that generally privilege masculine attributes. As V. Spike Peterson writes: 'As a social construct, gender is not "given" but learned (and therefore mutable).'[51] So, for example, whereas the masculine is often associated with aggression, strength, power-over, rationality, and certainty, the feminine is contrasted as passive, weak, power-to, emotional, and indecisive. When we recognize that these masculine attributes are more often associated with the fundamental tenets that inform traditional IR theory, we can begin to see the extent to which the international system is, itself, a 'gendered' construction. Therefore, postmodern feminists argue that we need to rethink IR in light of the category of gender, but more importantly, within the context of the actual values that should be considered important in guiding our global interactions.

While they deny the naturalized distinctions between men and women, some postmodern feminists seek a revaluation of traits often associated with women, e.g., redefining so-called feminine values, such as peace, nurturance, and collectivism or co-operation, so that they are perceived as just as important and credible, if not more so, than their masculine counterparts. Other postmodern feminists point out, however, that it is possible for so-called masculine traits to be held by women. Margaret Thatcher, the former British Prime Minister, was as much a warmonger as US President Ronald Reagan: while he pursued military adventures in such unlikely places as Grenada and Panama in the 1980s, Thatcher went to war with Argentina over the Falkland Islands. Similarly, they argue that feminist perspectives can be held by men. Mahatma Gandhi, for instance, is often cited as an example of a nurturing male. Judith Butler makes the argument (drawing on the mid-twentieth-century French theorist Simone de Beauvoir) that no necessary relationship exists between material/biological sex and discursively produced gender. Someone can have a male body and not display behaviour generally associated with what is regarded as 'masculine'.[52]

Finally, a group of feminist writers can be classified as post-colonial feminists, whose work cuts across gender, race, and class. These scholars are critical of liberal feminism for failing to recognize that poor women of colour in the South are not only unequal to men but are also stuck in a post-colonial structure that further subordinates them within the global political economy. For them, the concerns of women in the North (or the West) are quite different from those of women in the global South. In fact, most post-colonial feminists are extremely critical of their northern counterparts and see them as privileged, patronizing intellectuals who claim to speak for the 'oppressed' but really have little knowledge of how truly oppressed women are in the global South.[53]

Environmentalism: The Green Perspective

Like gender and feminist approaches, the green perspective is generally given short shrift in IR textbooks. Yet, over the past few decades we have become very aware of how important environmental issues are for many people around the globe. This is most evident in the increased media coverage of issues like global warming, climate change, endangered species, ozone depletion, acid rain, and resource scarcity, the growing number of major international conferences and commissions devoted to the environment (e.g., the Rio de Janeiro Summit in 1992 and subsequent global environmental summits; the Brundtland Commission of 1987), and the importance attached to multilateral agreements dealing specifically with the environment (e.g., the Kyoto Accord). There is now a global consciousness about the importance and immediacy of environmental problems. While the scope and legitimacy of these issues continue, in some circles, to be hotly contested, the important question for us is how the green perspective affects traditional approaches to studying IR.

Thinking green offers a significant challenge to the largely problem-solving approach of traditional IR theory. Like gender and feminist approaches, it is not sufficient to 'add and stir' when it comes to environmental issues. That has happened, through industrial development, resource exploitation, and consumerism, and has created the problems the world now faces. From the perspective of 'green thought', or ecologism, the contemporary state system, the major structures of the global economy, and many of the global institutions are part and parcel of the environmental problem facing our globe. As mentioned in the previous chapter, the state as a sovereign entity, with no greater authority above it, remains at the cornerstone of much of IR theory—in particular, realist theory. This means, in essence, that the state has complete authority over its domestic concerns and is assured against external interference in internal matters. However, as we all know, environmental issues are never simply 'domestic'; pollution knows no political or physical borders: an oil spill off the west coast of the United States can have major effects beyond that area; a dust storm resulting from desertification in Africa will impact areas in South America; industrial and medical waste from the North that has been dumped in the global South will have long-term negative impacts.

The Chernobyl accident in April 1986 provides a good example of how an environmental problem in one country can have detrimental effects on surrounding countries. Radioactive debris from that nuclear power plant drifted over parts of the western Soviet Union, Eastern Europe, Scandinavia, the UK, and the US. People in Ukraine, Belarus, and Russia had to be resettled because of the effects of this radioactive spill.[54] Thus, environmentally detrimental behaviour of one state can affect other states. Domestic decisions protected by the principle of sovereignty become similarly domestic issues for other countries. For obvious reasons, this creates a complex situation for thinking about sovereignty. Environmentalists have suggested that we need to stop thinking of sovereignty as an absolute principle, and instead think in terms of globality—that the only way to combat global problems associated with the environment is through global co-operation.

The growing environmental movement has helped to contribute to this holistic approach. The incredible growth in environmental NGOs (e.g., Greenpeace, the Sierra Club) has created a situation in which states are forced to take these entities seriously because they have demonstrated that they can influence public opinion and agenda-setting in many countries around the globe (see Box 2.2).

Finally, whereas the modernist paradigm views development as industrialization and a positive good, environmental theorists reject this outright, suggesting that development theory must be rethought to take into account the finite nature of the Earth's resources and the detrimental effects of resource exploitation and industrial production. Instead, green thinkers from a liberal perspective promote the idea of sustainable development, and more radical environmentalists propose zero-growth and the idea that humans are simply another species on planet Earth

BOX 2.2

The Bombing of the *Rainbow Warrior*

Just before midnight on 10 July 1985, the *Rainbow Warrior*, a 40-metre vessel, was sunk by explosives in Auckland harbour in New Zealand. The crew of the *Rainbow Warrior* managed to escape the bombing, except for Fernando Pereira, an environmentalist photographer. Pereira drowned in that incident.

The *Rainbow Warrior* was the flagship of Greenpeace, an international environmental NGO founded in Vancouver in 1970. The ship was preparing to take part in a protest, along with several other vessels (a 'peace flotilla'), against French nuclear testing in the South Pacific.

The bombing turned out to be a deliberate act of sabotage, carried out by agents of the French secret service. Despite initial denials by the French government, within a few days after the incident French secret service agents Alain Mafart and Dominique Prieur were arrested by New Zealand police as they tried to return their van to an Auckland rental company. These two agents of Direction Générale de la Sécurité Extérieure (DGSE) eventually pleaded guilty on 4 November 1985 to charges of manslaughter and wilful damage in an Auckland court and were sentenced to 10 years' imprisonment.

The *Rainbow Warrior* bombing has to be classified as nothing less than a sordid act of state-sponsored terrorism.

with no more rights than a koala, polar bear, or plants in the Amazon rainforest. From all environmental perspectives, long-term ecological concerns are expected to take precedence over short-term economic and industrial gains.

Among the most influential and foundational thinkers in regard to short-term actions and long-term needs has been Garrett Hardin. In 1968, Hardin published a report called 'The Tragedy of the Commons',[55] which explained why individuals will forgo long-term interests for short-term profit. In short, the argument is that all producers have an immediate interest in maximizing the yield of the resources from which they make their living. The producers understand that in the long-term the rate of extraction is unsustainable, but they pay only a fraction of the cost of this because the effects are shared among the community, and they know that their competitors will continue to maximize their yield. Besides, they probably will not live to see the full deleterious effects of their environmental exploitation. For Hardin, the situation is analogous to the common pasture or commons of earlier times, where everyone in the village or community could pasture their livestock, yet, if everyone maximized their use of the commons there would be no commons left as a result of overgrazing. To ameliorate this situation, most environmentalists propose strong international agreements that legislate production in sustainable directions.

Constructivism

Among the alternative theories that have emerged since the advent of a more critical turn in IR theorizing, constructivism stands as a particularly important contribution to understanding the complexity of global politics. Like other theoretical perspectives, constructivism comes in many different shades. Some critical constructivists draw from a methodological opposition to the positivist methodologies and epistemologies found in much of neo-realism and neo-liberalism, and challenge the idea of a universal truth, while recognizing 'their own participation in the reproduction, constitution, and fixing of the social entities they observe'.[56] Other, more conventional, constructivists seek to employ mainstream methodologies, arguing that it is possible and at times necessary to specify a 'contingent universalism' while proposing a radically different interpretation of the source and persistence of this universalism across time and space. All, however, 'aim...to empirically discover and reveal how the institutions and practices and identities that people take as natural, given, or matter of fact, are, in fact, the product of human agency, of social construction.'[57]

Borrowing from sociological theory, constructivism adopts a more interpretive approach to global politics that calls attention to the influence of norms and identities on the behaviour of the various actors, including states, that participate in global politics. The intersubjective character of social reality is neatly captured by one of constructivism's more prominent exponents, Alexander Wendt: 'anarchy is what states make of it.'[58] Rejecting the assumed objectivity of global order, constructivists challenge us to accept that the structures we often assume to be permanent features of global politics are, in reality, social facts, constructed by individual agents, a view shared by many postmodernists. Constructivists, however, also acknowledge that such structures, while created by agents, in turn shape how these agents subsequently interact with one another.

Constructivism calls attention to the relationship between socially relevant actors and the world around them, between ideas and material reality, between agents and structures.

> Constructivists hold the view that the building blocks of international reality are ideational as well as material; that ideational factors have normative as well as instrumental dimensions; that they express not only individual but also collective intentionality; and that the meaning and significance of ideational factors are not independent of time and place.[59]

Constructivism also calls attention to the importance of identities as a way of determining the interests and likely behaviours of particular actors, and asserts that these identities are based on intersubjective understandings rather than on objective characteristics. According to Hopf, therefore, they reject the parsimonious view found in neo-realist accounts: that the relevant units share a common identity as self-interested states. 'Constructivism instead assumes that the selves, or identities, of states are a variable; they likely depend on historical, cultural, political, and social context.'[60]

Constructivists, while emphasizing the central significance of ideas, do not dismiss the importance of material factors such as economic and military resources. Instead, they call attention to the need to understand the meaning given to these material factors by the actors involved. For example, John Ruggie has argued that American economic resources carried different meanings in the mid-1940s, when they were deployed in support of an embedded liberal economic order, than they did in the 1990s, when the emphasis was much more on unfettered liberal market practices. He argues that a full understanding of the post-1945 global economic order cannot be acquired by considering material conditions alone. Rather, one must take into account 'the efficacy of the concept of authority in international regimes—as distinct from power. Legitimate authority rests on shared social purposes . . . prescribing the domestic social and economic role of state under embedded, as opposed to *laissez-faire*, liberalism.'[61]

Constructivism takes no clear position on the possibility or direction of change in the global polity. It does, however, allow for change by holding that agents can shape and hence alter the structures that define behaviour. On a more substantive level, however, given the central significant role that agency plays in constructivism, one is unable to forecast the likelihood or direction of change. It is only possible that if change is to occur, then it would require a shift in the behaviour and the shared meanings that relevant actors hold about the behaviour. As Hopf writes: 'Constructivism conceives of the politics of identity as a continual contest for control over the power necessary to produce meaning in a social group. So long as there is difference, there is a potential for change.'[62] Given its contingent view of change and its position that identities are socially constructed, constructivism clearly is unable to provide an overarching theory of global politics. It is, instead, a way of describing the means by which the agents and structures that make up global politics are created, reinforced, and changed. Yet, as Hopf concludes, 'the promise of constructivism is to restore a kind of partial order and predictability to world politics that derives not from imposed homogeneity, but from an appreciation of difference.'[63]

Conclusion

This chapter has outlined a number of alternative ways of viewing the world. Each theoretical perspective discussed here (Marxism, modernization theory, dependency theory, post-dependency theory, world systems perspective, the critical theories of postmodernism, including feminism, environmentalism, and constructivism) challenges the traditional liberal and realist theories examined in the previous chapter. The problem for us as students of global politics is to figure out which of these theoretical perspectives offer a better way of understanding how global politics function. The fact is, no single theory of or approach to global politics can tell us how the world actually is, or why it is in the state that it is in. But by having an array of theoretical tools at our disposal, we might just be able to make sense of the world by using several of them in our analysis.

Key Terms

capitalism

communism

dependency theory

environmentalism

feminism

imperialism

Marxism

modernization theory

monopoly capitalism

post-dependency theory

postmodernism

surplus value

world systems theory

Discussion Questions

1. Why did critical theory develop?
2. In what ways does critical theory present an alternative to mainstream approaches?
3. What are the principal concerns of Marxist theories of global politics?
4. To what concerns did feminist theory respond, and how have feminist theorists expanded our understanding of global politics?
5. What contributions have environmentalists made to our understanding of global politics?

Suggested Readings

Enloe, Cynthia. *Bananas, Beaches, and Bases: Making Feminist Sense of International Politics.* Berkeley: University of California Press, 2000. Enloe provides a good illustration of the insights that feminist analysis can provide in re-envisioning how we view and interpret international relations.

Rengger, Nicholas John, and Tristram Benedict Thirkell-White. *Critical International Relations Theory after 25 Years.* Cambridge: Cambridge University Press,

2007. An edited collection that brings together some of the leading exponents of critical theory to assess its contribution to the discipline.

Smith, Steve, Ken Booth, and Marysia Zalewski. *International Theory: Positivism and Beyond.* New York: Cambridge University Press, 1997. This edited collection brings together both traditional and critical scholars to discuss the state of international relations theory and the respective contributions that various approaches can make to the discipline.

⋅•⋅ Global Links

IR Theory
www.irtheory.com/index.htm
   A wiki-type site with brief descriptions of various international theory concepts and links to some useful international relations programs, institutes, and web resources.

Institute for the Theory and Practice of International Relations
irtheoryandpractice.wm.edu/
   A focus on the relationship between international theory and the practice of foreign policy and international relations.

The State of International Relations Theory
www.sussex.ac.uk/Users/hafa3/stateofIR.htm
   This site features a book chapter by Martin Shaw that examines the state of IR today, including ways of conceptualizing international relations. It offers alternative ways of viewing political economy, historical sociology, and the state in a globalized world, and suggests a synthetic approach to IR that allows us to challenge traditional realism on its own grounds.

⋅•⋅ Debate 2

Be it resolved that theory should provide an emancipatory project for reforming global politics.

Chapter Three

World Civilizations and the Origins of the International System

Introduction

As the two previous chapters demonstrate, theories are created to help us make sense of the world. However, theories are abstractions of reality or guides to help us gain a better understanding of reality. Theories are no substitutes for reality. They are, at best, simplifying devices which can assist us in making sense of the complexities of the real world. Different theories act like lenses that allow us to focus on specific facts or aspects of social reality.[1] No single IR theory can provide us with a completely accurate and comprehensive picture of politics at the global level. However, like the story of the blind men and the elephant, if we employ the right combination of theoretical perspectives we might be able to figure out the shape of the complex beast we call 'global politics'.

Furthermore, to inform our theoretical perspective it is useful to have some knowledge of history. If we take a *longue durée* approach to the study of human organization and society, for example, it soon becomes evident that entities other than states have been important players in governance at particular junctures in history. Some of those players include: tribes, clans, fiefdoms, kingdoms, empires, and city-states.[2] Traditional IR scholarship suggests that the contemporary states system is a by-product of the Westphalian treaties of 1648. To a large degree this is the case. But examining, even cursorily, the historical record of world civilization will uncover the Eurocentric bias in much of IR scholarship and perhaps help us to re-imagine the evolutionary process leading to the establishment of the current inter-state system as not terminal but still unfolding. This technique of historical inquiry allows us to imagine an alternative future that reflects the paradigm shift from international to global politics.

A Brief History: Tribes, Clans, City-States, and Empires

Humans are in essence social beings: 'unus homo, nullus homo'.[3] Due to their gregarious nature, humans have tended to organize in groups. From the earliest accounts of recorded time, there have been interactions between these human groups. Some of these interactions came in the form of commercial exchanges, feasts, dynastic marriages, burial and totemistic rituals, the fellowship of common religion, diplomacy, and war. Ragnar Numelin has stated that, as long as there were sources of subsistence, 'the social radius' of these human groups gradually extended 'from the family to organized joint families, clans, tribes, nations'.[4] As these social groups and networks grew, their interactions and relations became increasingly complex in nature. We consider these early 'intertribal relations' as the precursor to 'international relations'.

Adam Watson, borrowing from Martin Wight's *Systems of States*, traces the origin of our international states system not to 1648 but to a period between 3500 BC and 2000 BC that saw the emergence of Sumerian society[5] in Mesopotamia (in present-day southern Iraq), considered by many anthropologists as the birthplace of the first 'civilization' in world history. Sumer consisted of 12 independent city-states. These city-states engaged in trade and other economic interactions with non-Sumer societies located in the area we call today the Persian Gulf region. The people of Sumer established what is widely regarded as one of the oldest known legal systems.[6] Babylonians modified the Sumerian city-states system and formed a 'hegemonial system' that unified the city-states under the rule of the city of Babylon around the third millennium. Babylon exerted its dominance and influence over several neighbouring societies (e.g., Assyrian society) that eventually assimilated a large part of Babylonian culture. A collection of laws, known as the 'Code of Hammurabi', and institutions governed Babylonia's social structures, modes of economic organization, and its relations with other societies.

The kings of Babylon (see Box 3.1) were believed to be entrusted with the sovereignty of the deities and acted as mediators between the gods and those

© Bettmann/Corbis

An artist's rendition of the Hanging Gardens of Babylon.

BOX 3.1

King Nebuchadnezzar

Nebuchadnezzar, the king of Babylonia from 605 to 562 BC, reconstructed Babylon, restored its temples, defeated Egypt, and destroyed Jerusalem before succumbing to a mental illness. When Nebuchadnezzar died in 562 BC, a power struggle ensued within Babylon that led to its defeat and annexation in 538 BC by Cyrus the Great, the king of Persia. But Babylonian culture left a deep imprint on the entire ancient world and, to a large degree, influenced today's civilizations.[7]

over whom they ruled. Babylonian rulers therefore derived their legitimacy from the myth that they were designated the gods' representatives on earth. A dynastic king or 'king of kings' governed the political institutions of Babylonia's city-states with the help of appointed governors and local administrators.

If Babylonia was a model of relations between city-states, then the Assyrians provide one of the earliest examples of 'empire'.[8] Persia provides another example of **empire**.[9] Some have referred to the Persian Empire under Darius I as an example of 'imperial moderation'—a **benign hegemon**.[10] When Xerxes I ascended to the Persian throne and tried to continue his father's plan of aggrandizement he was defeated in several wars, including the Battle of Salamís (480 BC).[11] This series of defeats led to the decline of the Persian Empire and signalled the rise of Greece as a world power.

Ancient Greece (Hellas) occupied what Watson calls 'a central position in the evolution of modern international society'. Watson asserts that 'the Greco-Persian system exercised great influence on the European system, out of which the present inter-states system developed; and for several centuries, aspects of Greek practice served as models for the European society of states.'[12] In the mid-eighth century BC, a novel form of political organization was created by the Greeks, known as the **polis**. The Greek polis was 'a complex hierarchical society' built around an egalitarian 'notion of Greek citizenship'.[13] Each polis consisted of:

> . . . [a] limited corporation of citizens who were the hereditary armed proprietors of the corporation. A citizen had to be male and to be descended from citizens, almost always on both sides; and he had notionally to own some property . . . in addition to being a co-proprietor of the polis.

Each co-proprietor was expected to defend his city-state by force of arms. Based on a democratic decision, the Greek city-state allowed 'the citizens who would do the fighting to assemble and decide for themselves whether to go to war'. This produced 'a high degree of solidarity among the citizens of a polis in the face of external enemies'.[14] However, Greek citizenship was highly exclusionary and non-Greeks, including the Medes and the Persians, were considered 'barbarians'.[15] The **Hellenic** network of polities signified the first real indication of the development of an international society.[16] It was a society in which each polis was considered independent and there was no allegiance to Hellas as a whole (i.e., exhibiting what might be called anti-hegemonic characteristics).

The international society of Greek city-states discovered ways to institutionalize the increasingly extensive relations between city-state entities: city-states engaged not only in activities in the polis but also in inter-city-state ceremonial practices and dispute settlements.[17] However, what appears to have been missing in Greek society was a clear, agreed-upon body of laws to govern the behaviour of individual city-states. To a large degree, despite the commonality of political culture, language, and religion, each individual city-state maintained its independence and did not become part of any overarching or super-state political association. Yet, Greek city-states adopted a form of diplomacy, treaties, standards of conduct, and principles of war,[18] similar to *jus in bello* (justice in war) constraints. For instance, prisoners of war could not be killed but could be held for ransom. Limits were also placed on the pursuit of defeated and retreating enemies. Agreed-upon principles of war stipulated that battles would be fought only during the regular campaigning season (summer). The wanton destruction of property was not permitted and non-combatants could not be hurt intentionally.[19] These norms, however, did not have universal application but were only applied 'to intra-Greek warfare'.[20]

It is important to note that Hellenic 'international' society was dominated by two major city-states—Athens and Sparta. Other city-states often became entangled in the bipolar rivalry between these 'major' powers.[21] In Thucydides's account of the Peloponnesian War (431–404 BC), he notes that the less powerful city-states were subordinated to the powerful ones.[22] The Athenian city-state was the hegemonic power in this system but its over-extension eventually led to its downfall. With the defeat of Athens by an anti-hegemonic alliance initiated by Corinth, Sparta found itself in a unipolar position in the inter-polis system and, like Athens, began to exhibit hegemonic ambitions. It interfered in the internal affairs of other city-states, launched attacks on the Persians, occupied Asian Hellas, and acted in a generally oppressive manner towards members of the anti-hegemonic alliance. Eventually, it was left to Corinth, which acted as a balancer in the system, to initiate another anti-hegemonic alliance, led by Athens, to keep Sparta in check. This was probably one of the earliest examples of a balance-of-power system—a concept still part of the lexicon of global politics.[23]

Apart from balance-of-power mechanisms, one can find early evidence of attempts by city-states to find diplomatic ways of coexisting peacefully. For instance, there were a number of periodic inter-polis conferences during the Hellenic period, and the Persian Empire used peace congresses on the Greek peninsula to maintain peace within the territories it controlled. King Artaxerxes of Persia proposed what we call today a **collective security** arrangement to come to the defence of any territory under his purview that might find itself under attack. In addition, he used the 'good offices' of the Satrap of Sardis (with Persian finances) to impose a 'King's peace' in Hellas. This general peace is frequently compared to the Peace of Westphalia instituted in 1648.[24]

When Alexander the Great (356–323 BC) came to power in Greece in 336 BC, he proclaimed himself the legal successor of the Persian kings and encouraged his Macedonian and Persian subjects to intermarry. Alexander, a pupil of Aristotle when he was only 13 years old, united Asian Hellas and the Persian Empire into a single imperial Hellenistic structure that combined Greek and Persian governance. Through conquest, he extended his empire to northwest India (modern-day Pakistan), where Persian influence remained present for at least two centuries and where Hellenic ideas competed with Buddhist and Jainist religious and social values. Kautilya, an Indian scholar and Machiavellian-like leader, understood the

Alexander the Great.

concept of benevolent hegemony. Kautilya advised Chandragupta Maurya, an Indian leader, to adopt a policy of **neutrality** as a means for India to maintain a degree of independence within the states system. Kautilya also recommended that Chandragupta accept Persia's 'benevolent imperial rule' (i.e., establishing rule over the conquered by respecting their way of life and values as opposed to using force to assert rule). However, Chandragupta's rule turned oppressive and he quickly became isolated from the rest of the world.

The death of Alexander in 323 BC resulted in his empire being divided up among his generals and the Macedonian/Hellenic system. The empire became a multiple kingship system until roughly 65 BC, when the Romans conquered the area and incorporated it into the Roman Empire.

The Roman Empire ruled most of Europe, the Middle East, and North Africa until the Middle Ages, and the eastern half of this far-reaching empire, the Byzantine Empire centred in present-day Turkey, maintained control over a wide area until 1453. The Roman Empire was ruthless, imperialist, and expansionist. But it also used its dominance to support Hellenistic culture and the arts and to expand commercial relations with surrounding areas. The Roman imperial civilization blended Greek and Persian elements. However, like many great powers, the Roman Empire suffered from over-extension and found it difficult to maintain control over its vast territory. Adam Watson describes the situation this way: 'The Roman Empire had become too large to be governed by a city state, especially one controlled by an **oligarchy** and with a pitifully weak and discontinuous executive.'[25] Rome's weak political centre allowed its military leaders to exercise independent authority in the 'provinces'. These military leaders were soon transformed into unwieldy warlords of the Roman Empire.

One of the better-known Roman military leaders was Julius Caesar, an admirer of the accomplishments of Alexander the Great. Caesar was in essence a *dictator perpetuus* and used his status to restore the city of Rome to its former greatness until he was assassinated on the Ides of March (15 March) in 44 BC by a group of Roman senators, including one of his closest associates, Decimus Brutus.[26] Caesar's death plunged Rome deeper into **civil war** as his adopted son and successor, Octavian, battled for control of the Roman Empire with the help of Marcus Antonius. The triumphant Octavian succeeded in reorganizing the war-weary Roman Empire, in restoring the senatorial republic, and in introducing *Pax Romana*—a period in which Rome's commerce, trade, and industry thrived.[27] It was a period of relative peace that also witnessed the standardization of currency, weights, and measures, the protection of sea lanes, which allowed unimpeded trade, as well as the rise of voluntary associations and religious fraternities that abided by strict codes of conduct.

Codes of conduct were also applied to wars by the Romans. War had to be formally declared before it was fought. Adversaries were given the opportunity to avoid war by offering 'necessary reparations'. However, once war was declared, the Romans could be exceedingly ruthless to their enemies[28]—hence the term *bellum Romanum*, which later became associated with brutal warfare 'in which there were no limits and no restraints'.[29] The general response to Rome's **malign hegemony** was either acquiescence or defiance. By the fourth century AD, Rome suffered major defeats at the hands of Persian Sassanids from the East and many of its allies began to declare themselves independent of the Empire. The Roman Empire's Germanic client states also proved unreliable. In addition, the Empire was forced to compete with the rise of a **Semitic** imperial state that evolved into an Arab **caliphate** around the sixth century AD.[30]

Latin Christendom

The demise of the Roman Empire did not happen overnight. It was a slow process in which the Roman Imperium transformed itself into a theocracy to forestall the inevitable.[31] One part of the Roman Empire adopted Latin Christendom, while the other embraced Greek/Orthodox Christianity (Byzantium). Under Constantine, the centre of the Roman Empire moved from Rome to Byzantium, which was later renamed Constantinople (today's Istanbul, Turkey). But Rome's expansive territory was eventually conquered by the Ottoman Turks as part of an emerging Muslim empire. The western portion of the Roman Imperium was dissolved by AD 476, settled by Germanic peoples, and dominated by Christian churches. The Hellenized eastern area remained nominally part of the Roman Empire, experiencing greater wealth and maintaining a more effective administration than the west. A cultural divide grew between the Latin West and the Greek East.[32]

When the Roman Empire finally fell, three civilizations had emerged from its ashes: (1) an Arabic civilization that stretched from the Middle East and Persia to North Africa and the Iberian Peninsula; (2) the Byzantine civilization in Constantinople that was united under the Christian religion; and, (3) the rest of the European area that was formerly under Rome—a pluralistic population with respect to languages and cultures, yet lacking in any central authority once Rome fell. Western Europe, in particular, consisted of **feudal** principalities controlled by lords and fiefdoms that imposed taxes and exercised legal authority. Lords controlled vassals who worked in exchange for the lords' protection. The feudal apparatus was designed as a political system to provide order within the city-states system amid the prevailing disorder.[33]

This medieval period was dominated by religion, with the Roman Catholic Church predominant. Authority and legitimacy were vested in the Church and the Pope was considered to be 'Sovereign' (i.e., God's representative on Earth). Even kings and princes were technically subordinate to the Pope in Rome.[34] However, by the late eighth century, the papacy's monopoly on authority and power was challenged by Carolus Magnus (Charlemagne).[35] The Pope made Charlemagne the Emperor of the Holy Roman Empire and sanctioned his efforts to unite Western Europe against the advances of the Byzantine civilization to the East. In return, Charlemagne guaranteed protection of the papacy and the Roman Catholic Church. However, during the Middle Ages a move also was afoot to separate religious and secular authority,[36] although this did not materialize until the signing of the Treaties of Westphalia in the towns of Münster and Osnabrück (on 30 January and 24 October 1648). Charlemagne and his successors provided the foundation upon which secular authority could eventually challenge 'divine' authority.

Reformation: The Schism in Christianity

On 31 October 1517 Martin Luther, a German professor/priest, dealt a significant blow to the unity of Christendom when he attacked papal abuses and the sale of indulgences by Church officials. Luther felt that secular and materialist elements of the Renaissance were infiltrating the Church and he tried, with his 95 theses posted on the door of the church at Wittenberg, to bring the Church back to what he considered to be a more spiritual path. His actions and teachings caused a major schism among Christians—separating Catholics from Protestants. At the same time, his challenge to papal infallibility[37] had the effect of enhancing the authority of kings.

The **Reformation** was significant not only because it helped to loosen the hold of the papacy on European peoples, but also because, as Daniel Philpott argues, it coincided with an interest in the creation of a states system in Europe and, in fact, influenced the events leading to the signing of the Westphalian treaties.[38] Philpott asserts: 'had the Reformation not occurred, a system of sovereign states would not have developed, at least not in the same form or in the same era as it did.' He further suggests that were it not for the Reformation:

> persistently medieval features of Europe—the substantive powers of the Holy Roman Empire and its emperor, the formidable temporal powers of the church, religious uniformity, truncations of the sovereign powers of secular rulers, Spain's control of the Netherlands—would not have disappeared when they did, to make way for the system of sovereign states.[39]

Reformation theology called for: the confiscation of large tracts of property the Church owned; the emperor to relinquish his authority to enforce religious uniformity; ecclesiasts to refrain from holding temporal offices; and the elimination of the ecclesiastical powers of the pope and emperor. In effect, Martin Luther demanded separation of

Martin Luther.

© David Lees/Corbis

Church and state—something that became an important requirement of state sovereignty when the Peace of Westphalia was achieved over a century later. Secular rulers latched onto this idea and granted protection to the reformers when they became persecuted as heretics during the Counter-Reformation. The spread of the Reformation was aided by a number of developments: the **Enlightenment**; the advent of the printing press; widespread literacy throughout Europe; the rise of a new urban middle class; the willingness on the part of the reformers to take up arms against the emperor in support of secular leaders; the link between the reformers and emerging capitalism; and the perceived corruption of the Church and its leadership.[40]

Of course, the split in Christendom was a catalyst for the religious wars in Europe. The Treaty at Augsburg, signed between the Holy Roman Emperor Charles V and the forces of the Schmalkaldic League on 25 September 1555, proved to be only a temporary truce. But it allowed some families to relocate to lands where their religion (Catholic or Protestant) was being practised.[41] Soon enough, however, the Holy Roman Empire (i.e., the papacy, its appointed secular emperor, and the emperor's armies) sought to maintain tight control over German Protestant regions, and this warfare ultimately drew much of Europe, from Spain to Sweden, into the Thirty Years' War (1618–48), which only came to an end with the Peace of Westphalia. The overall effect of the Reformation was to weaken Christendom, particularly the hold the papacy had on European society at the time. This came at a time when the Islamic Ottoman Empire was on the ascendancy.

The Advent of Islam

The gradual weakening of the papacy, the increasing ineffectiveness of the secular Holy Roman Empire, and the proliferation of small, decentralized feudal entities ensured that centralized governance in Europe would not take hold. The earlier fall of the Roman Empire and the diminishing influence of the Christian Church coincided with the emergence of a Semitic Arabic civilization and the rise of a Muslim empire. The Ottoman Turks toppled the Byzantine Empire at Constantinople—the gateway between Europe and Asia—in 1453, and the Ottoman Empire vanquished Greece, the Ionian Islands, Bosnia, Albania, Budapest, Vienna, and most of the Balkans prior to expanding into North Africa. By the early 1500s, the Ottoman Empire rivalled Latin Christendom (the Holy Roman Empire).

During the sixteenth century 'the Muslim states...formed the most rapidly expanding forces in world affairs'. The Ottoman Turks expanded westward and the Safavid dynasty resuscitated the Persian Empire. Muslim forces controlled silk routes to China, spread Islamic influence into North Africa, overthrew the Hindu Empire in Java, and established the Mogul Empire in northern India in 1526. Muslims led a proselytizing mission, adding large numbers of people to the Islamic faith in Africa and the Indian subcontinent.[42] The Ottoman Empire stretched from the Crimea (Ukraine) and Aegean Sea (the eastern Mediterranean Sea between Greece and Turkey) to the Levant (the eastern Mediterranean region). The empire captured Damascus in 1516 and invaded Egypt the following year. The Turks captured Bulgaria, Serbia, and Hungary, and then besieged Vienna in 1529 and again in 1683.[43] The Ottoman Turks' formidable navy raided ports in Italy, Spain, and along the North African coast and seized

Cyprus. Muslim zeal explains the rapid expansion of Islamic forces; in some cases the expansion was peaceful, but in many other cases it took the form of violent conquest.

The strength of the Ottoman Empire did not depend entirely on its military might and economic prowess. Its unity was premised on a shared Islamic faith, a shared culture, and a common Arabic language. The territory of the Ottoman Empire in fact grew larger than that of the former Roman Empire. The Islamic world proved vastly superior to Europe in terms of advances in mathematics, cartography, medicine, science, and technology. It controlled large urban areas with well-established universities and libraries, and witnessed a proliferation of exquisite mosques. However, by the seventeenth century, the Ottoman Empire itself began to show signs of fraying due in large part to

Victorious Turks entering Constantinople in 1453.

© North Wind Picture Archives/Alamy

imperial overstretch and its inability to derive economic benefit from some of the territories it had captured. The empire suffered due to a series of incompetent sultans (leaders) and experienced a disastrous religious schism with the separation of Shiites (mostly Persians) from Sunnis. As a result of this split, Shiites were willing to form alliances with European states against Sunnis. The growth of a movement that restricted the freedom of speech and expression, limited imports and foreign trade, and resisted technological improvements and modernization spelled the beginning of the end of the powerful Ottoman Empire, though its final demise would not come until World War I.

Thus, by the 1500s it was not a foregone conclusion that Christian Europe would eventually dominate the rest of the world. As mentioned earlier, Europe was a divided region, lacking in central leadership, and it consisted of 'a hodgepodge of petty kingdoms and principalities, marcher lordships and city-states'.[44] Europe failed to create a united force against Islam. It also faced competition from other significant empires to the East that possessed great wealth and vast armies. Paul Kennedy explains:

> placed alongside these other great centers of cultural and economic activity, Europe's relative weaknesses were more apparent than its strengths. It was, for a start, neither the most fertile nor the most populous area in the world; India and China took pride of place in each respect. Geopolitically, the 'continent' of Europe was an awkward shape, bounded by ice and water to the north and west, being open to frequent landward invasion from the east, and vulnerable to strategic circumvention in the south.[45]

In terms of cultural and technological advances, Europe borrowed knowledge from Islam in the realms of culture, mathematics, engineering, and navigation.

Muslims, in the same way, borrowed from the Chinese via trade, conquest, and settlement. Kennedy reaches the conclusion that, around the fifteenth century, 'each of the great centers of world civilization...was at a roughly similar stage of development, some more advanced in one area, but less so in others.'[46]

Other World Civilizations

It is quite conceivable that under slightly different historical circumstances one of the other great world civilizations, other than the European one, might have produced a model of an inter-states system that would be embraced by the entire globe.

At the time European civilization was evolving, an independent Chinese civilization was thriving and, in fact, was more advanced than most other civilizations. Its culture, as well as agricultural and irrigation systems, was quite advanced. It had the equivalent of Italian city-states, a set of fairly sophisticated territorial political units that operated on the basis of 'power politics' and used war as an instrument of interaction between the units.[47] But for much of Chinese history, the individual territorial units were more or less held together under a unified hierarchical administration.

To understand the Chinese system and its relation to the international system, it is useful to examine the period between 770 and 221 BC. At the beginning of this period, the Zhou (Chou) kingdom[48] had assumed legitimate rule over multiple independencies. Upon conquering the Shang dynasty, the Zhou kingdom claimed that its right to rule (*t'ien-ming*) was conferred by the supreme deity (*t'ien*). Zhou kings were expected to forfeit their 'mandate of heaven' if they behaved impiously or sacrilegiously. It was therefore vital for Zhou kings to act in an appropriate manner if they were to maintain legitimate rule because the right to govern was not absolute but was thought to depend on the possession of moral qualities conferred on the leadership via the 'mandate of heaven'.

The Zhou Kingdom actually controlled only one small core territory under its administration. The rest of China was divided into fiefs.[49] However, in almost all cases, the heads of these fiefdoms were either members of the Zhou royal family or garrison commanders loyal to that family. Thus, the Chinese political system at that time was remarkably similar to the feudal system of rule found in Europe during the Middle Ages, with the head of each fief collecting tribute/taxes to pay to the king. In 770 BC, the Zhou capital was sacked, forcing the kingdom to relocate eastward to Loyang (modern-day Honan province). This move signalled the beginning of the era of the Eastern Zhou dynasty (770–256 BC). Similar to the Roman Empire prior to its demise, the fiefdom rulers across China recognized the nominal primacy of the king but were in fact independent from his sovereign authority. This period of the Zhou Kingdom has been characterized as one of turmoil and civil war.[50]

In 679 BC and again in 546 BC, a series of conferences brought together most of the states within the Chinese states system, which was divided roughly into two main groups: those who supported the status quo and those who challenged the status quo. The first group consisted of states occupying most of the traditional Chinese cultural area. They recognized the authority of the Zhou Kingdom, attempted to conserve Chinese civilization, and labelled peripheral states as 'semi-barbaric'. The second group consisted of peripheral or 'marcher' states (populations of non-Chinese origin or mixed race). These border states were generally contemptuous of the prevailing order and sought opportunities to challenge it. The quest to unseat the traditional centres of Chinese power led peripheral states to introduce important innovations in the art of war, including the use of iron spears, cavalry, and crossbows.[51]

Despite the upheaval and disorder in China, this period produced significant intellectual and philosophical ferment.[52] Four main currents of political thought existed in China during this time. The first was **Taoism** (Daoism), an anarchic pacifism that advocated a natural order based on non-violence. Taoists believed that any form of government interfered with the natural order. The second was **Confucianism**, which considered all people to be essentially good, yet believed that the state was necessary for governance and paternal rule. Confucians suggested that if all people subjected themselves to the authority of a just king with a mandate from heaven, virtuous rule and imperial unity would bring an end to inter-state strife. Confucianism provided the basis for a system of hegemonic rule over a society of states. The third was **Mohist**, which reflected the teachings of Mo-Tsu, a less optimistic and less hegemonic figure than Confucius. Mo-Tsu proposed the notion of 'defensive war as the key to peace among states'. This required states to renounce offensive wars and, instead, develop a defensive program of 'armed neutrality'. According to Mohists, if all states chose this path, peace would prevail.[53] The final current of political thought was termed 'legalist' and rested on the basic assumption that all human beings were essentially evil and debased but could be taught to become good and refined through education and the imposition of state laws.[54] Legalist principles laid the foundation for autocratic, authoritarian, disciplinarian, and anti-democratic leadership within the Chinese system and continued to influence Chinese politics over the centuries. As compared to other streams of political thought, the legalist school appealed most strongly to imperialist Chinese leaders.

Confucius.

INTERFOTO/Alamy

This perspective gained dominance because legalist principles were, in many respects, compatible with certain aspects of Confucianism, particularly the notion of imperial unity for all of China.

However, the wholesale adoption of legalism did not result in tranquility over China. Instead, under legalist leaders, such as Li Ssu (d. 208 BC) and Chao Kao, intense civil wars were fought. The Ch'in dynasty (221–207 BC) gained imperial power over all of China as a result of its victory in those civil wars. It adopted legalism as its political mantra, resulting in uniform totalitarianism. Individuals were conscripted to labour camps for extended periods of time to complete state projects (e.g., the Grand Canal and the Great Wall in northern China). Dissension from the government was considered a capital crime. Alternate ways of thinking were outlawed. Although China was unified under this authoritarian regime, Confucian adherents and other intellectuals developed passive resistance to the regime. China's legalist rulers grew determined to eliminate Confucianism and any other system of thought considered threatening to the regime. The leaders of the Ch'in dynasty burned books, executed scholars, and destroyed a significant portion of China's historical literature.

Subsequent Chinese leaders discredited legalist policies, which led to the eventual downfall of the Ch'in dynasty, but the impact of legalist rule in China was not easily erased. In fact, the Han dynasty (206 BC–AD 220) fused legalism with Confucianism, creating the leading political orthodoxy for China from then on. The synthesis of legalism and Confucianism can be summarized as follows:

1. The universe is controlled and governed by a single principle, the Tao or Great Ultimate.
2. The Tao combines two opposing principles—*yin* and *yang*.
3. All opposites perceived in the universe can be reduced to either *yin* or *yang* forces.
4. *Yin* and *yang* are generally distinguished by their roles in producing 'creation' or 'degeneration'. *Yang* represents creative forces and *yin* represents forces of degeneration.
5. *Yin* and *yang* are further differentiated into five material agents—*wu hsing*—that both produce and overcome one another.
6. All historical change in the universe can be explained by the forces of *yin* and *yang* and by activity of the five material agents as they either produce or overcome one another.[55]

The fall of the Han dynasty in AD 220 divided China into two main regions. The northern portion of China was governed by non-Chinese rulers who did not practise Confucianism but embraced Buddhism, an emerging world religion that originated in India. In the south, Chinese rulers also began to develop an interest in Buddhist thought and practices. Buddhism quickly spread not only to the common population but also to government officials and elites within Chinese society. By the fourth century, a large majority in China had embraced Buddhism and the religion spread as well to Japan, Korea, and other countries in the Asian region.

The Rise of Japan and Russia

As the Chinese empire declined, Japan began showing signs of potential greatness. Contact between these two civilizations goes back to around AD 200. The Japanese borrowed a great deal of their religion, culture, and technologies of government and bureaucracy from the Chinese. Japanese cities like Kana and Kyoto were based on Chinese plans for the development of its own capital cities.

Due to its insularity and separation from mainland China by sea, Japan did not have to be concerned about inland invasions. It traded with Europeans, particularly with the Portuguese and the Dutch, who were expanding eastward. However, Japan did not achieve the greatness of an empire due, in large part, to internal clan feuding, particularly following the death of the warlord Hiseyoshi in 1598. The outcome of these struggles was the consolidation of power by Ieyasu and the shoguns of the Tokugawa clan. The Tokugawa clan restricted overseas expansion, halted foreign relations, forbade Japanese subjects to sail on the high seas, limited trade with the Europeans, and murdered Christians (both foreign and native). 'The entire military system ossified for two centuries, so that when

Commodore Perry's famous "black ships" arrived in 1853, there was little that an overawed Japanese government could do except grant the American request for coaling and other facilities.'[56]

By the sixteenth century, Russia was deeply influenced by Europe and established itself as a major power based on the strength of its musket and cannon technology. While Russia engaged in military expansionism and reached the Asian Pacific coast in 1638, it suffered constant setbacks due to internal struggles and frequent land attacks from such enemies as the Poles, who occupied Moscow from 1608 to 1613. Also, 'Russia remained technologically backwards and economically underdeveloped.'[57] Russia's deteriorating state authority was exacerbated by several factors: (1) lack of control over its vast expanse of land; (2) poor communication between its centre and outlying districts; (3) a static feudal agricultural system; (4) an unpredictable bureaucracy; and (5) **despotic rule**. Despite these obstacles, Russia managed to remain intact and emerged as a great power in the nineteenth and twentieth centuries.

Africa: The Forgotten Continent

Most books about IR tend to ignore the existence on the African continent of great civilizations and empires.[58] The earliest African civilization developed along the Nile—the world's longest river—and its tributaries (through Egypt and Sudan) in eastern Africa. You may have heard the term 'Nubia' used in reference to black art. But what most people in the West may not know is that ancient Nubia (much of which today is flooded by Lake Nasser, created by the dams at Aswan) was the site of highly advanced black African civilizations (evidence of which can be traced to the Fayum and Tibesti plateau as early as 7000–4000 BC) that eventually rivalled ancient Egypt in terms of culture, wealth, and power (see Figure 3.1). In fact, for a period of 100 years Nubian kings ruled over Egypt as pharaohs. Yet, Nubian society and culture have been generally overlooked by most Western historians who tend to focus on the Egyptian civilization—which also was an ancient and rich civilization.

The Nubians were just one of several great African civilizations. Another great African civilization was Egypt, whose pharaohs occupied Nubia between 1970 and 1520 BC. Nubia, however, regained its independence in the eleventh century BC. A new Nubian kingdom, centred at Napata, adopted an Egyptian model of monarchy, including royal brother–sister marriages. This showed how much Egyptian culture had influenced Nubia. Today, several hundred thousand Nubians can be found living in Egypt and Sudan.

From around 900 BC to AD 400 the Kingdom of Kush was dominant in Africa. But evidence indicates other great empires that sprung up in Ethiopia, or that developed along the trading routes in today's Zimbabwe, the Democratic Republic of the Congo (Zaire), and Ghana. The continent also has endured waves of strangers who, in some cases, settled temporarily along the well-trafficked trading routes. For instance, Arab merchants populated northern and sub-Saharan Africa, and their influence on language, culture, and religion is still apparent today.[59] There is evidence of Jewish merchants who interacted with tribes along the trading routes in Ethiopia two millennia ago.[60] Remnants of mixed Jewish/African offspring, called the **Falasha**, were officially recognized by the government of Israel in 1975, following the 1973 decree by Israel's Sephardic Chief Rabbi, Ovadia Yossef (and the 1975 decree by his Ashkenazic counterpart, Rabbi Shlomo

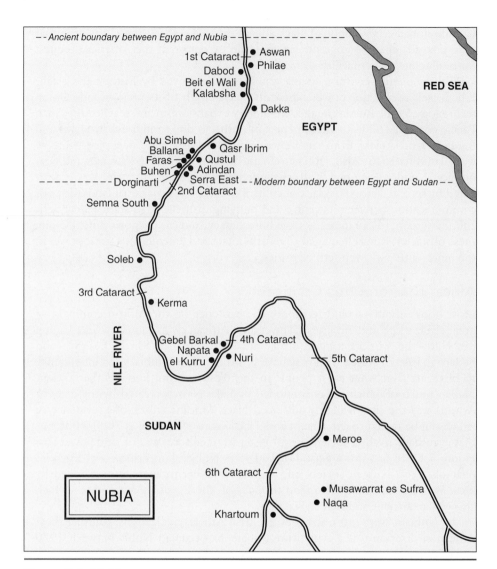

Figure 3.1 Nubia.
Source: Based on <www.crystalinks.com/nubia.html>

Goren) that the Falashas in Ethiopia were in fact descendants of the 'lost' Tribe of Dan and as such should be allowed to emigrate to Israel under the Law of Return (see Box 3.2).[61] A few members of 'Beta Israel' began to migrate to Israel in the 1970s and early 1980s, but the real emigration came in 1985 when Israel airlifted 15,000 Jews, in Operation Moses, out of the midst of an Ethiopian civil war. Three months later, Operation Sheba brought 500 more Falashas to Israel. However, both Ethiopia and Sudan closed their borders, holding almost 15,000 Falasha refugees in camps until 1991, when American diplomats worked out a deal that allowed them to be airlifted to Israel through Operation Solomon.

When the Portuguese first arrived in Africa in 1448, they found a thriving trading system on the continent. The Portuguese were followed by the British and then the Dutch as trade between Europe and Africa expanded to include not just gold, ivory, and copper, but also slaves. Europeans needed a workforce for their sugar plantations

BOX 3.2

A Lost Tribe of Israel in Africa?

Is it possible that one of the Lost Tribes of Israel was actually found in Africa? Or could it be that the lineage of the Africans who call themselves 'Beta Israel' can be traced to an affair between Israel's King Solomon and the Queen of Sheba (Ethiopia). According to this legend, the African Queen of Sheba went to Solomon and shared his bed (a not unlikely scenario, given that the Biblical account of Solomon credits him with having 700 wives and 300 concubines). She then, as the legend has it, returned to Abyssinia carrying his son. When Sheba's son, Menelik, became curious about his father he travelled to Israel where he visited Solomon. Upon leaving, Menelik stole the coveted Ark of the Covenant and brought it back with him to the Abyssinian capital of Axum. Thus, according to the Ethiopian Jews, Axum became the true centre of Zion. Some historians believe that the true ancestor of the 'Beta Israel' is not the legendary son of Solomon and the Queen of Sheba but that they are descendants of Dan, progenitor of one of the Lost Tribes of Israel, who migrated through the Nile Valley to the ancient African kingdom of Kush. Others believe that the 'Falashas' are not genetic descendants of Israel but are Africans who adopted Judaism well over 2,000 years ago as either Yemenite or Egyptian traders flooded the Horn of Africa.

in the Americas and the West Indies. They shipped across the Atlantic approximately 15 million slaves from Africa between 1450 and 1870 to the 'new-found' lands of what is known today as North and South America and the Caribbean.

In most IR texts, discussion about the Americas usually begins with Christopher Columbus's 'discovery' of the New World in 1492, Hernán Cortés's 'discovery' of Mexico in 1519, or Francisco Pizarro's 'discovery' of the Andes in 1533.[62] Such accounts reflect a Western or **Eurocentric bias**. Students of global politics, however, need to recognize that there were also civilizations present in the Americas before the Europeans came. The first such civilizations, the Olmecs and Zapotecs, emerged in Mesoamerica around 1000 BC[63] in present-day southern Mexico. Other pre-Columbian empires in that part of the world include those of the Maya (whose ancestry can be traced to about 1000 BC and whose people occupied present-day Guatemala, Belize, Honduras, El Salvador, and the southern Mexican states of Chiapas, Tabasco, and the Yucatán peninsula), the Aztecs (who dominated southern Mexico between the fourteenth and sixteenth centuries), the Mixtec (who were conquered by the Aztec empire), the inhabitants of Teotihuacán, and the Toltecs (who are known to have dominated the area we call central Mexico from around AD 1000 to AD 1200).

In South America, several distinct ancient civilizations were eventually unified under the Huari and Tiahuanaco empires. Between 900 and 200 BC the Chavín civilization, considered the mother civilization of the Andes, dominated much of the area of modern Peru. Later (from approximately AD 850 to 1470), the kingdom of Chimor ruled along the northern coastal area of Peru. But the most famous of the South American empires was the Inca of Peru (AD 1438 to 1533). The Incas used a combination of peaceful assimilation and military conquest to control most of the western portion of South America.

INTERFOTO/Alamy

Benito Juárez, a Zapotec Indian, served as President of Mexico, 1861–3 and 1867–72. He is the only Aboriginal Mexican to have served as president of that country and is still regarded today as the most beloved of Mexican presidents.

Clearly, in all continents of the globe, civilizations existed and coexisted. Eight hundred to 1,000 years ago, Cahokia, in present-day Illinois, an agricultural and trade centre, had a population of 30,000–40,000 and covered an area greater than that of London, England, at the same period, and, as Dickason writes, except for a written language, 'had all the characteristics of a city-state.'[64] Intertribal relations, which can be considered the precursor to 'international' relations, were not limited to the European continent. Patterns of co-operation and conflict, trade and economic relations, and governance can be found in the history of all civilizations. Many of them showed a predilection for 'empire' as the basic form of socio-political organization. These empires rose and fell, and some of them have legacies that remain with us today. Yet, the legacy of European civilization produced our present-day international system, based on the core concepts of sovereignty and the state.

The Renaissance, Westphalia, and the Evolution of the European States System

The European states system emerged from the city-states of the medieval period as feudal units began to merge into larger territorial units governed by single authoritarian rulers. The territorial states, *stato*, first began to develop during the Italian Renaissance (*Il Rinascimento*) and flourished in the northern part of Italy (Venice, Milan, Florence, and the Papal States) between the fourteenth and sixteenth centuries. The Renaissance was essentially a cultural rebirth that resulted in a period of enlightenment, scientific revolution, and artistic advances.

During the Middle Ages, Muslim scholars had kept alive long forgotten ancient works from the Greek and Roman eras. During the Renaissance this knowledge was rediscovered by the Italians. Also rediscovered were the rules of 'power politics'. Niccolò Machiavelli (1469–1527), a statesman and politician from Florence, wrote about those rules, about what princes had to do to maintain their power in the new states, and about the art of war.[65] Machiavelli was in fact theorizing about 'statecraft' and what we have now come to call 'realism' or **realpolitik**. While the Protestant Reformation planted the seeds of state sovereignty, it was through the Treaties of Westphalia (1648), ending 30 years of religious wars, that sovereignty formally became linked to independent states. To improve the chances of a prolonged peace on the European continent, territorially defined states were established with set rules to govern their interactions. Each state was considered sovereign, which meant that there would be no higher authority than the state within the European states system.

Theoretically, at least four conditions had to be met for an entity to be considered a state. First, it had to have a territory—a geographical expanse of land with delimited borders. Second, it had to have a relatively stable population residing in that territory.

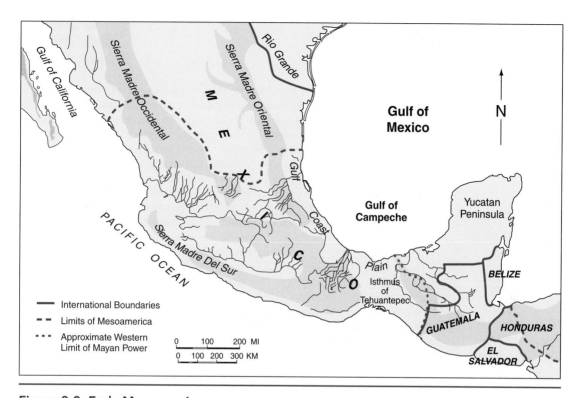

Figure 3.2 Early Mesoamerica.
Source: Based on <weber.ucsd.edu/~anthclub/quetzalcoatl/map1a.jpg>

Third, it had to have some form of government to govern the people, and that government had to have the ability to defend and maintain the territory under its jurisdiction. Fourth, it ought to be recognized by other states through diplomatic and international legal means. The primary characteristic attached to this entity called the state was, however, sovereignty. From 1648 on, no longer would sovereignty reside in the papacy or with an emperor. The state would now be the legal sovereign, which meant that it could not in any way be subject to the commands of another entity.[66]

By establishing and exercising centralized and effective control over its territory, its citizens, and its resources, each state would establish its credentials as sovereign. By mustering its own permanent military, rather than depending on mercenaries and foreign armies, each state would enjoy monopoly of the legitimate use of force within its own borders. By continuing the practice carried out by imperial powers of taxing subjects to pay for its national military and to run its internal affairs, each state would increase its jurisdictional control over its territory and over its subjects. As Seyom Brown put it, 'the jurisdictional integrity of every sovereign state was to be sacrosanct.'[67] This also meant that no state would interfere in the internal affairs of any other state. As long as the above norms were respected, it was imagined that order would be sustained across Europe, and eventually throughout the world.

With the sovereign state at the centre of relations between the main political groupings in Europe, would that bring an end to wars on the continent? Anyone who knows the modern history of Europe would certainly answer in the negative. At the core of the new states system in Europe was a group of powerful states:

BOX 3.3

Decolonization

Decolonization is a process that has occurred since the end of World War II, whereby colonies have been granted independent sovereign statehood. The collapse of imperialism in the twentieth century, due in part to increasing international hostility, led to a transfer of power from the colonial powers, including Britain, France, Belgium, Holland, Portugal, Japan, and Russia, to indigenous peoples. Often, the laws and bureaucracies of colonial powers remained intact.

Decolonization has been premised on the belief that national self-determination should be a guiding principle in international politics. The United Nations Charter and colonialism were increasingly recognized as incompatible in the twentieth century. The process of decolonization was influenced by the attitude and cost analysis of colonial powers, the ideology and strategy of anti-imperialist forces, and the role of external powers.

The legacy of colonization is problematic for several reasons. First, the boundaries carved by colonialists largely did not correspond to ethnic divisions, contributing to ongoing territorial conflicts throughout the world. Second, the end of imperial rule did not always coincide with the full independence of colonized states. This has resulted in neo-colonialism whereby newly sovereign states remain dependent on their former imperial states. Colonial powers and newly emerging sovereign states have had different experiences of the end of imperialism.

Sources: David Weigall, *International Relations: A Concise Companion* (London: Arnold, 2002), 65; John Baylis and Steve Smith, eds, *The Globalization of World Politics: An Introduction to International Relations* (Oxford: Oxford University Press, 1997), 72–3.

Austria-Hungary, England, France, Prussia, Russia, Spain, and the United Provinces (the Netherlands and Belgium). As we shall see in Chapter 5, until the eighteenth century, European politics was dominated by constant rivalries and shifting of alliances between these powerful states. The rivalry was played out not only in Europe but also in the New World as European imperial powers expanded their territorial reach beyond the continent (see Box 3.3). It would take a balance-of-power mechanism and a number of institutional instruments to mitigate the effects of this rivalry.

Conclusion

One can trace the influences that led to the establishment of the international system of states as far back as Sumerian society in Babylon, as well as to the Hellas and Greco-Persian civilizations. As human social organization expanded, patterns of conflict and co-operation emerged.

Forms of governance and leadership developed within and between tribes, clans, empires, and city-states. In ancient civilizations and empires, dynastic kings ruled as divine representatives on earth. In some cases, they appointed governors or local administrators to extract taxes and keep their populations in line. In other societies, leaders and chieftains tended to be 'the oldest men of the group' and were considered the wisest and most influential people within tribes, exerting moral authority and influence in attempts to diffuse conflicts and disputes that arose within or between tribes or clans. In some cases, an inter-tribal council of elders would be formed to address matters of dispute.[68]

But we also can see from this brief historical review that our contemporary international system has inherited several concepts and instruments from previous civilizations. Apart from councils of wise men, various civilizations have used laws, institutions, diplomacy, treaties, codes of conduct and other normative constraints, balance-of-power mechanisms, conferences and congresses, collective security instruments, good offices, and war to address disputes that have arisen between the units of the system—whether tribes, clans, city-states, or empires.

Several different civilizations have coexisted on our planet, sometimes without knowledge of each other's presence. At certain historical junctures, these disparate civilizations have encountered one another (as a result of trade, exploration, and/or conquest). They all left legacies that have influenced our contemporary political systems. Yet, it was the European legacy of the states system that truly became universal, resulting in our international system. Now that the future of the sovereign state is being questioned as a result of globalization forces, it may be a good time for us to consider whether there are alternative forms of governance that might replace the state and the states system. But first it is important to understand the nature of global change and continuity in the historical structure of world order.

Key Terms

benign hegemon
caliphate
civil war
collective security
Confucianism
decolonization
despotic rule
empire
Enlightenment
Eurocentric bias
Falasha
feudal

Hellenic
longue durée
malign hegemony
Mohist
neutrality
oligarchy
Pax Romana
polis
realpolitik
Reformation
Semitic
Taoism

Discussion Questions

1. What is the significance of the Westphalian treaties?
2. What can we learn from studying historical systems of states?
3. What aspects of the Greek city-state system make it important for students of contemporary global politics?
4. What is the relevance of the competing periods of empire and states systems that one finds in history?
5. What role has religion played in shaping global politics in the past?
6. What role has Islam played in the historical evolution of global politics?
7. Is there a useful distinction to be made between civilizations and empires?
8. What is sovereignty and what is its significance for global politics?

Suggested Readings

Aydin, Cemil. *The Politics of Anti-Westernism in Asia: Visions of World Order in Pan-Islamic and Pan-Asian Thought.* New York: Columbia University Press, 2007. The title is self-explanatory as Aydin provides an insightful account of how non-Westerners responded to European efforts to spread their ideas and practices.

Darwin, John. *After Tamerlane: The Global History of Empire since 1405.* New York: Bloomsbury, 2008. An exceptional treatment of the rise and fall of empires from all regions of the globe and of the various factors that shaped both these empires and contemporary global politics.

Wight, Martin. *Systems of States.* Leicester: University of Leicester Press, 1977. Wight provides both a historical description of ancient societies and an analysis of different forms of international systems and societies.

Global Links

World Civilizations

www.wsu.edu/~dee/

An Internet classroom provided by Washington State University with extensive resources.

The War between Athens and Sparta

www.athensinfoguide.com/history/t2–4peloponnesian.htm

This site provides a brief history of the Peloponnesian War.

Alexander the Great

www.historyofmacedonia.org/AncientMacedonia/AlexandertheGreat.html

Biography of the great Macedonian king who conquered Greece, Persia, Egypt, and invaded India.

Martin Luther's 95 Theses

www.iclnet.org/pub/resources/text/wittenberg/luther/web/ninetyfive.html

This site lists the 95 theses published in 1517 by Martin Luther and titled 'Disputation of Doctor Martin Luther on the Power and Efficacy of Indulgences'. Luther's 95 theses became the primary catalyst for the Protestant Reformation.

Internet Global History Sourcebook

www.fordham.edu/halsall/global/globalsbook.html

Fordham University site dedicated to the interaction between world cultures across time and space.

Debate 3

Be it resolved that religion has played a significant role in shaping the evolution of global politics.

PART II

Turbulence and Change in World Order

Chapter Four

Conceptualizing Global Change and Continuity

The trouble with change in human affairs is that it is so hard to pin down. It happens all the time. But while it happens it eludes our grasp, and once we feel able to come to grips with it, it has become past history.[1]

…to treat history as so continuous as to preclude fundamental change—originates in part from a compelling sense that, given a choice, people will opt for long-established ways of doing things and that therefore social and political patterns repeat themselves endlessly.[2]

Introduction

The above quotations, from Ralf Dahrendorf and James Rosenau respectively, provide us with some insight into the dilemma of trying to grapple with change and continuity, particularly as these relate to human societies and polities. To be sure, human affairs never remain static. In the previous chapter we noted that historical changes occur all the time, even though it is difficult for us fully to come to grips with and comprehend the extent of those changes when they occur. For the layperson, it may seem virtually impossible to distinguish important **structural changes** (those that lead to transformation of the global system) from **epiphenomena** (those insignificant surface changes that amount merely to rearranging the deck but on their own do not result in major alterations to the system). And, Rosenau warns, we tend to view episodic crises as leading to significant change when, in fact, a longer-term perspective might reveal these perturbations to be just part of a long-established pattern.[3] Thus, it is important to remind ourselves, as we try to make sense of politics at the global level, that not every crisis or hint of turbulence is necessarily an indication of change.

There has been a predisposition, particularly among realist, neo-realist, and some liberal scholars, to see only the continuities of politics while ignoring the possibility that a number of seemingly insignificant changes might indicate significant cracks in the **historical structure** of global order. Yet, Robert Gilpin, a realist who was influenced by both Marxist-Leninist and liberal economic approaches, is absolutely right to assert that persistence of the problem of war since the days of Thucydides speaks to a certain unalterable aspect of global politics.[4] In his important work, *War and Change in World Politics*, Gilpin concludes that international relations 'continue to be a recurring struggle for wealth and power among independent actors in a state of anarchy.'[5] He is also correct to suggest that the economic system can act as a constraining device on systemic change, thus perpetuating continuity in world affairs.[6] However, we should be careful not to allow the nostalgia of historical continuity to blind us to the possibility of discontinuities in global politics. The fundamental nature of international relations may have remained virtually unchanged for more than a millennium but, as Gilpin readily acknowledges, 'important changes have taken place', and this fact should not be overlooked. For instance, statecraft in the modern era is quite different from statecraft in the pre-modern era.[7] Today we are paying much more heed to environmental issues than we did a century, or even a few decades, ago. Health concerns, in our era of globalization, are no longer limited to specific territories.[8] And the emergence of the human security norm (putting people first when it comes to protection) in our generation is causing serious IR thinkers to reconceptualize the Westphalian notion of state security.[9]

We recognize that a conception of politics at the global level should pay equal attention to changes as well as to continuities. This is why, in writing this book, we have adopted a Coxian historicist approach. **Historicism** is generally contrasted with **positivism** or behaviouralism (that school of thought within the philosophy of science that holds that knowledge about the world in which we live can only be gleaned 'scientifically' through experience, careful observation, and testing). The problem with positivism is that it tends to be **ahistorical**, i.e., 'standing outside of and prior to history', as Robert Cox puts it. In the positivist approach, 'History becomes but a mine of data illustrating the permutations and combinations that are possible within an essentially unchanging human story.'[10] This is not to say that positivism is completely useless. It is useful within defined historical limits.

Robert Cox, drawing on Braudel, Vico, Gramsci, and others, has developed a unique method for studying the social forces that contribute to the development, evolution, and sustenance of global order. His historicist method allows one to combine both the static elements of positivism with the more dynamic aspects of long-range history (i.e., the contradictions and conflicts that result from dialectical social forces operating across time and space). Such an approach also allows one to view the historical terrain of world politics over the *longue durée* and to search out patterns of both continuity and discontinuity. At the same time, in light of what appears to be major turbulence in world affairs at this specific juncture, we agree with Rosenau that there is a need to focus our theoretical attention on anomalies, or what he calls 'breaking points', and disequilibria in contemporary world politics. Moreover, we embrace Cox's critical historical dialectic approach, which recognizes that the antagonisms generated within existing world order can lead to global structural transformation over time. In other words, while accepting that global structures—i.e., those persistent patterns of world order—can constrain and limit change, we do not rule out the possibility that change is still possible and may even be necessary at critical points in history.

As Mohammad Farooq asserts, the history of societies and civilizations cannot be properly understood without some clear conception of the processes of change and continuity. While the absence of continuity in a society or civilization may be a sure sign that it is becoming extinct or is changing so much that something altogether new is being created, the absence of change could also be an indication of stagnation and fossilization of that society or civilization. The failure of certain 'primitive' societies or tribes to adapt to the changing world around them has made them a target of anthropological and archaeological interest. Like Farooq, we make the case that in theorizing global change one should strive for a balance in examining the forces of both change and continuity in human society. In his words, 'it is the balance' in the interaction between forces of change and continuity 'that significantly determines the course of history of a society in particular and human civilization in general.'[11]

In this chapter, we offer a way of conceptualizing global change that takes into account both change and continuity in world politics and order. This conception of global change and continuity is realistic in that it recognizes that while change is always with us, certain structural factors constrain and inhibit it. At the same time, our approach is idealistic in the sense that, in reflectively searching out the discontinuities, it offers hope that structural obstacles to global change can indeed be overcome. Seeking out the nature of the balance between change and continuity in global politics and world order can become the basis upon which a theory of global change and continuity can be built.

Towards a Theory of Global Change and Continuity

How, then, should we go about the task of conceptualizing global change and continuity? The first step is to identify the 'subject' of any analysis on global change. The second step is to pinpoint the 'object' of inquiry with respect to analyses of global change. The third step is to define precisely what is meant by change. The fourth step is to distinguish among epiphenomena, minor changes, and major changes (structural transformation). By definition, an epiphenomenal change cannot itself have effects. That is what makes it 'epiphenomenal'.[12] Minor changes, however, do have their own causal powers, but they do not result in deep changes to the structure of global politics and are therefore not radically transformative. Major (structural) change is transformative in nature. The fifth step is to place the study of change within a *longue durée* historical context so that one can gain a sense of the landscape and trajectory of continuities and changes over a broad expanse of time. Finally, the sixth step is to provide a normative framework to support one's theorization about change and continuity in global politics.

Conceptualizing Discontinuity in Global Politics

Since we are interested in the study of politics at the global level, our concern regarding change is therefore focused on 'world order structures'. The simple reason for this is that those structures either facilitate or constrain the activity of global-wide politics. 'World order' is the term we use to identify established patterns or foundational principles 'by which societies are organized into polities'.[13] These patterns and principles are products of human activity and thought over long historical periods and are embedded in societal institutions. Over time, the collective actions of human beings and the shared ways of thinking about problems and working out solutions to them result in the development of world order structures. It is important, in understanding the 'subject' of global change, to bear in mind at the outset that (1) world order structures are created through human agency, and (2) these structures are historical in nature, i.e., unlike mushrooms, they did not pop up overnight.

To gain a better comprehension of what actually constitutes world order structures we turn to Robert Cox, who, better than any other contemporary thinker, has developed a **heuristic model** for understanding global change. According to Cox, world order structures are frameworks of action or historical structures.[14] Such structures can be viewed as a specific configuration of forces that imposes pressures and constraints on human activity. As human agents we can choose to acquiesce to these pressures and constraints, or we can resist and oppose them. We can also combine forces with other human agents to create and develop alternative historical structures to rival that which is dominant at a particular historical juncture. The antagonistic (dialectical) struggle between two or more rival historical structures will inevitably produce turbulence in the global system, and when a rival historical structure is able to challenge successfully the dominant one, we may begin to see the emergence of a new world order.

Cox explains that three categories of forces interact within a world order (historical structure). These are:

1. *material capabilities* (productive or destructive natural, technological, and organizational capabilities of a society—e.g., the material power that comes from having natural resources, economic wealth, industries, and armaments/military establishments);
2. *ideas/norms* (both the intersubjective meanings shared by a majority of people about the nature of their social relations and the collective images that people hold of social order—the nature and legitimacy of prevailing power relations, meanings of the public good and of justice, etc.). Ideas also can emerge from scientific discoveries and can become embedded in institutions;
3. *institutions* (formal and informal means of organizing society and of embedding the ideas and power relations prevailing within society at the point of origin).[15]

Linked to all three categories is hegemony, both its nature and extent. Here it is important to distinguish between Cox's notion of hegemony (which is drawn from Gramsci) and hegemony as defined by realists. Unlike realists, who equate hegemony with dominance and coercion, Cox defines hegemony as:

> a structure of values and understandings about the nature of order that permeates a whole system of states and non-state entities. In a hegemonic order these values and understandings are relatively stable and unquestioned. They appear to most actors as the natural order. Such a structure of meanings is underpinned by a structure of power, in which most probably one state is dominant but that state's dominance is not sufficient to create hegemony. Hegemony derives from the dominant social strata of the dominant states in so far as these ways of doing and thinking have acquired the acquiescence of the dominant social strata of other states.[16]

Thus, according to Cox, while hegemonic powers are able to maintain their position because of the acquiescence of lesser powers, they tend to have the material power needed to influence the ideas and institutions of a given world order.

Examples of hegemonic influence can be found in the *Pax Romana*, which collapsed about eighteen hundred years ago, the ***Pax Britannica*** of the middle to late nineteenth century, and the *Pax Americana* of the post-World War II period. All three cases reveal that hegemons can be benign.[17] In either case, hegemony cannot be ignored in any conceptualization or discussion of global change. Since hegemons usually have more to gain than other actors in maintaining a global system of order, they can be expected, insofar as possible, to try to preserve the status quo and resist radical changes to a global system that reflects their character and position.[18] Hegemony, therefore, can be considered the glue that holds together a particular historical structure. The strength of its presence in legitimate form, i.e., its political and legal acceptance within the states system, would signify the successful attempt to maintain a particular type of world order. The weakness of its presence (or lack of legitimacy) could be a signal of a deteriorating world order, a collapse in world order, or a major change or transformation in the nature of that order.

It is important for any theory of change to be clear about the 'object' of the analysis (what needs to be analyzed closely) in attempts to verify whether or not change has occurred, or is occurring. Thus, we want to pay close attention particularly to the foundational elements of global politics in a specific world order: the material capabilities of the system/society; the dominant shared ideas/norms within the system/society that are embedded in certain institutions; and the institutions themselves—both formal and informal—created to support these ideas/ norms and particular configurations of power at a given historical moment. If there are significant changes in all three categories, then it is quite possible that a shift in world order and global politics is occurring.

But what do we mean when we speak of global change? Rosenau's description of change in world politics fits with Cox's conceptualization. According to Rosenau, such change refers to 'the attrition of established patterns, the lessening of order, and the faltering of governance, until such time as new patterns can form and get embedded in the routines of world politics.'[19] One can deduce from this that the emergence of disorder and turbulence may be one sign of possible transition in global politics. Both Cox and Rosenau owe their conception of global change to Dahrendorf, who has noted that each society produces within its structure 'the antagonisms that lead to its modification'.[20] If this is so, then in developing a theory of global change we should be searching out and identifying the contradictions within human society that could possibly lead to its transformation, as well as patterns of instability and disorder. Or, to put it in world order terms, there must be conflicting elements within the historical structure that eventually will lead to change and possibly to transformation. If we focus only on patterns of continuity and stability we could be missing important clues that could help us identify crevices or shifts in the structure of world order.

It is important, therefore, to gain an understanding of certain ideational, normative, and empirical aspects of global change. Change may be occurring to world order if the mental constructs that seemed in the past to explain the patterns of established global politics are no longer able to provide an adequate explanation of what is going on in the present. Change may also be occurring if the norms that guided the established global order no longer seem valid or appear to be less robust than formerly was the case. If those established norms are being threatened by emerging or previously suppressed norms, then this could be a sign that the underlying structure of world order is developing fissures. Finally, if the established patterns of world order are actually undergoing changes that can be seen and measured in some form, then one can use this empirical evidence as indicative of global change. There should be measurable and significant changes in institutions, in material conditions, circumstances, and capabilities, and in people's way of thinking about the organization of society if we can honestly say that global change has occurred. Rosenau has this to say about these three elements:

> [O]nce the dynamics of change so strongly challenge the ideational bases of the prevailing order as to result in altered attitudes and orientations, the behavioral and institutional dimensions of that order will surely be weakened and eventually shattered.[21]

Thus, we should take a careful look at the ideas that underpin a particular world order to get an indication of the extent to which they are being challenged.

The next issue of importance in theorizing global change is distinguishing among epiphenomena, minor changes, and major changes (transformation) to the structure of world order. Epiphenomena will result in no change to the overall pattern of global order. Minor changes can cause slight shifts in that pattern, particularly if they are cumulative, even though the overall shape of the pattern may remain relatively unchanged. This type of change is analogous to the rearrangement of furnishings within a classroom. The classroom remains a classroom even though the chairs and desks may be arranged in a different manner to accommodate a particular style of teaching being introduced or to meet a particular pedagogical or functional need of the students. Breaking down a wall separating the classroom from another room in order to expand the seating capacity for students would still not be considered major structural change because the classroom remains functionally 'a classroom', albeit slightly bigger. The third type of change would be analogous to tearing down the classroom altogether and creating in its stead a hospital clinic. Not only would the function of the new room be different from that of the classroom, but the underlying reason for the 'new' room would be significantly changed from a place of learning to a space devoted to caring for the sick. The change would be even more fundamental and radical if the room was transformed into a non-room, e.g., if the building were torn down and a road created in its space.

The distinctions between minor and major/transformative change may not always be that apparent. For instance, in retrospect, we can now recognize the events and episodes that cumulatively resulted in the transformation of the Cold War. Yet, prior to 1989 few scholars and observers of global politics, if any, seemed aware of the momentous nature of the change occurring around them. Indeed, as Ian Clark points out, with the passing of the Cold War there was a mixed reaction to that event.[22] Optimists, usually led by neo-liberal internationalists, tended to view the post-Cold War period as a significant break with the unsavory past and an opportunity for the development of a new and improved world order. President George H.W. Bush was convinced, for instance, that the end of the Cold War ushered in a new world order (NWO) in which the US would play a special role in conjunction with a more assertive United Nations to speed up achievement of the normative goals of peace, stability, justice, and respect for human rights and the rule of law. For him, the end of the Cold War provided a propitious moment, a window of opportunity, for the US to lead in the construction of this NWO and for the UN to operate in the way that institution was intended when it was first created in 1945. The Cold War had stymied the UN's ability to carry out the goals of the UN Charter and it had also

© Bettmann/Corbis

East German workers building the Berlin Wall, 1961.

locked the US into a geopolitical struggle with the Soviet Union. The end of the Cold War meant the termination of that struggle. It also meant that the ideological deadlock within the UN Security Council would come to an end.

Pessimists, on the other hand, argued that the thawing of the Cold War loosened the restraints that had suppressed a number of conflicts, particularly civil conflicts. They predicted that the post-Cold War period would be one of a return, in some cases, to instabilities of the pre-Cold War era. 'There would be a re-emergence of the traditional agenda of international politics that had been concealed by the distracting overlay of the Cold War. The passing of the Cold War was therefore likely to unveil a new age of power politics, untrammelled by the checks and balances of the Cold War.' These individuals feared that instead of a new world order, the post-Cold War period would usher in a new world disorder in which 'vicious national, ethnic, and civilizational conflict' would predominate.[23] Note, however, that despite the differences in position, both optimists and pessimists agreed that the fall of the Berlin Wall (see Box 4.1) and the dismantling of the Soviet Union represented a distinct watershed—a disjuncture in world politics—and that the world would not be the same thereafter.

A very different position was taken by Robert Cox, who emphatically stated in 1996 that the 'Cold War has not ended.'[24] Taking a Braudelian approach, Cox opined that certain structures of Cold War power continue to exist, in the form of intelligence services, abundant supplies of small arms to countries in the developing world from the US, Russia, and other major powers, and a biosphere that remains under constant threat. Cox felt at the time that 'Manichean mental frameworks' preserved the Cold War form while others searched for 'new content' (e.g., Islamic fundamentalism). So, in fact, a certain residue of the Cold War remained even when it was clear that the Cold War was thawing.[25] Cox's take on this subject is that there was a *transformation in* the Cold War, not a *transformation of* the Cold War. Rosenau further explains this nuanced position, maintaining that 'inertia and transaction costs' can 'sustain an order long after the material conditions change and exert pressure for ideational, behavioral, and institutional transformations.'[26] From this point of view, even when change has occurred there can be a lag phase in which patterns of the old order continue to be exhibited at the same time that evidence of a new order abounds. The joyous celebrations at Berlin's Brandenburg Gate when the Berlin Wall was breached in 1989, or the horrific melée when commercial airliners flew into the twin towers of the World Trade Center in 2001, may symbolize change in world order (or disorder), but sea change does not happen overnight.

Another position, taken by Anne-Marie Slaughter, is that the new world order as proclaimed by President Bush was nothing more than a chimera. She also argues that the 'new medieval' proclamation by those who ascribe to the view

BOX 4.1

The Berlin Wall

The Berlin Wall was a barrier and a Cold War symbol that cut Berlin in half—East and West. While the city of Berlin was embedded in the German Democratic Republic (GDR or East Germany), the dividing of spoils among the major powers after World War II originally left Berlin split into four sectors, with the Soviet Union, the United States, the United Kingdom, and France all gaining some control when occupying forces of the Western Allies and the Soviet Union all converged on Berlin at the close of the war. The three Western sectors were soon unified to become West Berlin.

The East German government began constructing the wall on 13 August 1961 to separate West Berlin, a state of the Federal Republic of Germany (West Germany), from East Berlin in the GDR. The wall was built to prevent the flow of East German refugees to the West because the emigration of highly skilled, qualified East German workers threatened to ruin the GDR economy—well over 3 million East Germans had fled to the West before the border was closed. A border, approximately 900 miles long, between East and West Germany was fortified by barbed wire, electrified fences, minefields, tank traps, electronic warning devices, watchtowers, and bunkers. But Berlin itself was seen by the Communist bloc as a porous hole in this border, where refugees from the East could easily cross and either settle in West Berlin, a democratic island in the midst of Communist East Germany, or travel by rail, autobahn, or even waterways across East Germany to West Germany and beyond.

Over the course of the next 15 years, the wall dividing the two Berlins was improved and further fortified until it was a virtually impassable concrete wall, topped with pipe, nails embedded in concrete, and barbed wire, with a 'no man's land' between the wall and West Berlin. After the construction of the wall, the East German government instructed guards to shoot or capture anyone who attempted to cross the barrier and escape East Berlin, and more than 100 people fleeing the East died in such attempts.

The Berlin Wall was a key symbol of the East–West division during the Cold War. The wall became symbolic of imprisonment under communism, the perceived permanence of the divided German state, and Germany's lost hope for reunification. Western powers protested and claimed that East Germany's actions, including the construction of the Berlin Wall, violated agreements following World War II. With the collapse of the Communist regime in East Germany, the East German government announced that their citizens would no longer be prohibited from crossing the border to the West. The subsequent breach and dismantling of the Berlin Wall, on 9 November 1989, symbolized the end of the Cold War and led to Germany's reunification, which formally occurred on 3 October 1990. Before the war, Berlin had been the capital of Germany and East Berlin became the capital of East Germany; today, Berlin is once again the capital city of a unified Germany.

that the end of the Cold War unleashed a new world disorder is equally flawed. On the contrary, however, she claims that a 'new world order is emerging, with less fanfare but more substance than either the liberal internationalist or new medievalist visions.' In Slaughter's view, this new world order is being built, brick by brick, through transgovernmental activity—the creation of an 'effective mode of international governance'. Her conceptualization of the character of the global change taking place does not succumb to the pessimism of neo-realism or to the excessive optimism of Utopianism. It is realist in the sense that it recognizes the constraints of the structure of world order, but it also acknowledges the importance and presence of agents of change on the national and international stages who, through their actions, are remodelling the international architecture, bit by bit, to suit 'an increasingly borderless world'.[27]

In theorizing global change, then, it is important to ask whether the change one is observing 'reflects a decay or a reconstitution of the old order'; whether the transformations 'are so fundamental as to lead to a new order'; or 'whether they are of only limited scope such that some dimensions of the older order remain intact'.[28] We may find, after examining the empirical evidence, that the post-Cold War world order does not really represent as sharp a break from the past as we have been made to believe. As Ian Clark notes, one cannot really 'understand the post-Cold War order without due recognition being accorded to the elements of continuity' as well as those of change. In his view, the post-Cold War order 'is a combination of continuity and discontinuity.'[29] A sophisticated theory of global change should strive to uncover both trends.

Problematizing Global Change and the Persistence of Continuities

Back in 1992, James Rosenau was already taking note of the myriad changes that, in his opinion, were transforming global politics. He speculated at the time that as 'the scope of this transformation widens and its pace intensifies', people will begin to ask urgent questions about the nature of global order and governance.[30] In his *Turbulence in World Politics*, in which he posits a 'theory of change and continuity', Rosenau writes:

> The proposition that the parameters of global politics are undergoing profound and permanent transformation challenges analysts to be open to making corresponding alterations in the conceptual premises with which they organize and interpret the course of events....this can mean that long-standing and comfortable analytic impulses may have to be quelled, even abandoned, if the portents of the observed changes are to be adequately assessed; it can necessitate acknowledgment that what was once given is now problematic; it can even require accepting that what once seemed conceptually impossible may now be emerging as empirical reality.[31]

Another astute observer of politics at the global level, Yoshikazu Sakamoto, also confidently asserted in the early 1990s that 'In light of developments since the late 1980s, it is clear to everyone that a global change is underway.' However, he was quick to add the caution that it is not yet clear as to 'exactly what is changing, how, and into what'.[32] Others, like R.L. Garthoff, considered the end of the Cold War as signifying 'a historic divide'.[33]

More recently, several scholars have pointed out ambivalence about the so-called sea change that accompanied the end of the Cold War. Major questions are being raised about the extent to which the post-Cold War period is actually a break with the past. Like Robert Cox, the noted historian Marc Trachtenberg points out that several enduring features of the Cold War remain present in the post-Cold War period.[34] The fact that NATO persists, and has even been enlarged, is considered an indication of continuity. John Ikenberry argues that the post-Cold War era 'is really a continuation and extension of the Western [liberal] order forged during and after World War II.'[35] Some scholars have pointed out a plethora of cases in which the post-Cold War landscape seems to resemble that of an earlier time—pre-World War II. The Balkans War in the 1990s, for example, is considered by some to be a continuation of a pre-1945 set of events.[36] Others have gone even further to suggest that the instability of the post-Cold War period represents a return to the multi-polar instabilities of the pre-Cold War era.[37] E.J. Hobsbawm presents a similar argument when he suggests that the ethnic violence immediately after the end of the Cold War was, in fact, 'unfinished business' of 1919.[38] Yet others are adamant that the current era is reminiscent of the turbulence and chaos that accompanied the transition from the feudal world order to the early modern period (pre-Westphalian Europe)—a period of 'declining empires, retreating feudal lords and an emerging class of traders and capitalist entrepreneurs'.[39]

What all of these positions seem to imply is that if one takes a long-range view of history one could conclude that the Cold War era was really a disjuncture in world politics, an aberration. 'It is the Cold War period that then takes on the appearance of "exceptionalism".'[40] Indeed, one can make the case that the post-Cold War era is a continuation or resumption of world politics of the pre-1945 era, with the Cold War having been an interregnum.

Whether the above positions have merit can be determined only through meticulous empirical and historical research. But what is clear from the arguments made above is that to understand global change one needs to join, as Eric Wolf puts it, 'theoretically informed history and historically informed theory' in order to map out the trajectory of both change and continuity in world politics.[41]

Conclusion

This chapter has considered some important conceptual and theoretical issues with respect to change and continuity in global politics. It began by identifying the 'subject' of the analyses of global change and the 'object' of inquiries about such change. Clearly, since we want to understand global change, it is necessary for us to examine politics at the global level. What undergirds that politics is the historical structure of world order. That structure, in any historical period, facilitates or constrains the activity of global-wide politics. The structure of governance and relations provides established patterns or foundational principles that guide the global polity. The primary constituents of all world order structures, as Cox has indicated, are ideas, material capabilities, and institutions.

To understand and explain change in world order, we therefore need to examine critically the extent to which the ideas, material configurations of power, and institutions that represent a dominant or prevailing world order are changing or have changed. At the same time, it is necessary to distinguish among epiphenomena, minor changes that can be expected to occur in a system as it adjusts to different circumstances, and major changes that could lead to systemic transformation. Making those distinctions will not always be easy. One way of facilitating the task is to place the study of change within a broad historical context. In so doing, we should be better able to see the overall trajectory of change and, concurrently, establish with a fair amount of certainty patterns of continuity or discontinuity.

To guide our path in the problematizing of global change (i.e., in trying to decipher the balance of change and continuity in world order structures) we need to be aware of the distinction between problem-solving and critical approaches to theorizing as discussed in Chapter 2. An ideological bias—its orientation or commitment to the status quo—underlies **problem-solving theory**. In this sense, neo-realist and neo-liberal paradigms are examples of problem-solving theory.

Critical theory, on the other hand, 'stands apart from the prevailing order of the world and asks how that order came about.' It does not take as given the prevailing ideas, institutions, and material or social power relations. Instead, it calls these into question by focusing on the issue of whether, and to what extent, they might be undergoing change. Unlike ahistorical problem-solving theory, critical theory is a 'theory of history' in that it is concerned with the long view, with historical patterns of change. As such, critical theory has no choice but to 'continually adjust its concepts to the changing object it seeks to understand and explain'. Its ideological and normative bias is explicit. It favours change to the prevailing social and political order of the time and seeks out ways to transform that order. In this sense, critical theory 'contains an element of utopianism'. However, this Utopianism is constrained by the 'comprehension of historical processes'. It rejects improbable alternatives with the same vigour as it rejects the fixity of a particular world order.[42]

Throughout the rest of the book, we embrace both problem-solving and critical theory approaches in an attempt to establish the extent of continuity and change in global politics.

Key Terms

ahistorical

critical theory

epiphenomena

heuristic model

historical structure

historicism

Pax Britannica

positivism

problem-solving theory

structural changes

Discussion Questions

1. What is meant by historicism?
2. What have been some of the more significant breaking points in the history of global politics?
3. What is meant by global order structures?
4. How do different forces—material capabilities, institutions, ideas—shape global order?
5. What is meant by 'hegemony' and what role does it play in global politics?
6. Why is it important to study change?
7. Can we predict change in global politics? Can we explain it?
8. Was the end of the Cold War a significant change in global politics?

9. Were the terrorist attacks of 11 September 2001 reflective of a significant change in global politics, or did political reactions to the attacks indicate change?

Suggested Readings

Bull, Hedley, and Adam Watson, eds. *The Expansion of International Society.* Oxford: Clarendon Press, 1984. This edited collection examines the manner in which the modern state system encountered other regions and cultures undergoing a process of change and adaptation.

Holsti, K.J. *Taming the Sovereigns: Institutional Change in International Politics.* Cambridge: Cambridge University Press, 2004. Holsti assesses the extent to which the fundamental institutions of international politics, such as law, sovereignty, and war, have been transformed over time.

Rosenau, James N., and Ernst-Otto Czempiel, eds. *Governance without Government: Order and Change in World Politics.* New York: Cambridge University Press, 1992. This edited collection examines various aspects of change and transition that have taken place in international relations.

Global Links

Carnegie Endowment for International Peace
www.carnegieendowment.org/
   A good site for reflections on the state of turbulence and change in the world today.

Antonio Gramsci
www.infed.org/thinkers/et-gram.htm
   This site provides a brief biography of Antonio Gramsci, an intellectual, journalist, and major theorist who spent his last 11 years in Mussolini's prisons. While he was imprisoned he wrote 32 notebooks revealing a new Marxist theory that included a reconceptualization of hegemony.

Conversations with History
www.youtube.com/watch?v=O051beio1TE
   A video conversation of 2 May 2008 at the Institute of International Studies, University of California, Berkeley, with host Harry Kreisler and Philip Bobbitt, professor of jurisprudence at Columbia University. Topic: 'Terror and Consent: The Wars for the Twenty-first Century'.

Debate 4

Be it resolved that the Cold War is not over; it has merely been transformed with different antagonists and different issues.

Chapter Five

Conflict, Violence, and War in Global Politics

We're talking about using military force, but we are not talking about war.
—Madeleine Albright, 1998

There's no telling how many wars it will take to secure freedom in the homeland.
—G.W. Bush, 2002

Introduction

'For many generations New York had taken no heed of war, save as a thing that happened far away, that affected prices and supplied the newspapers with exciting headlines and pictures. The New Yorkers felt that war in their own land was an impossible thing.... They saw war as they saw history, through an iridescent mist, deodorized, scented indeed with all its essential cruelties hidden away.' H.G. Wells continued his social commentary *War in the Air* with a description of New York after it was attacked: 'lower Manhattan was soon a furnace of crimson flames, from which there was no escape. Cars, railways, ferries, all had ceased, and never a light lit the way of the distracted fugitives in that dusky confusion.... Dust and black smoke came pouring into the street.' For those who experienced the terrorist attack on New York in September 2001, the description rings eerily familiar, yet Wells wrote this nearly a century ago as a warning of the hell to come if societies did not turn away from war.

The terrorist attacks on 11 September 2001 seemingly marked a new kind of warfare, at least for many observers, and their responses echoed such a refrain. No longer were people in North America insulated from the conflicts that raged in other parts of the world. No longer were innocent civilians an unacceptable target. No longer were the instruments of war limited to tanks and fighter jets. While a few observers acknowledged that little was new in all of this, most popular accounts took a different view. After the Cold War's demise in the early 1990s, many people, especially in Europe and the Americas, were of the opinion that global politics had entered a new era, where war and violence had been replaced by **zones of peace**. For them, the attacks of 9/11 on the United States, which in American government rhetoric suddenly became 'the homeland', marked the beginning of a new era. At the very least, a certain urgency and timeliness were added to discussions of war, and renewed concerns arose about state and individual or human security.

In a more traditional response to this most non-traditional attack, the United States and some of its allies launched counter-attacks, first against Afghanistan and then, amid more controversy, against Iraq. Lost among most of the commentary on these specific attacks, however, was the acknowledgement that this was the third or fourth time in the last decade that member governments of NATO had sent their armed forces to war after more than 40 years of relative peace during the Cold War. In addition to the war in the Persian Gulf against Iraq in 1991 and the air attacks against Serbia over Kosovo in 1999, armed forces from many of these countries also had been deployed to some of the most bitter and violent conflicts of the late twentieth century in Somalia, Bosnia, and elsewhere. Indeed, more Canadian armed forces were on active service in the 1990s than at any time since the Korean War in 1950. While the Canadian experience is not common, it is far from atypical. Moreover, although some world regions did experience a zone of peace, conflicts during the 1990s affected more than three dozen countries and claimed nearly 3 million lives, mostly civilian non-combatants, in addition to generating tens of millions of **refugees**.

At the same time, and despite the end of the Cold War, more than 20,000 nuclear weapons remain in the arsenals of at least eight states—the US, UK, France, Russia, Israel, India, Pakistan, and North Korea. Other states seek to achieve a nuclear weapon capability, and more accessible biological and chemical weapons have become available to a wider array of both state and non-state actors, presenting a considerably deadly arsenal that could threaten the security not only of states and peoples but of the entire human species. All of this reminds us that for a variety of reasons we can no more escape war and violent conflict today than we could in 1914 or in 1939. This makes it all the more imperative for us to consider the nature of modern war, its consequences, and its causes. However much we might wish to be uninterested in war, war continues to be interested in us—or so it seems.

War and Global Politics

Much of what we read and hear about global politics is devoted to violence. War has always been a persistent feature of global politics. Martin Wight describes war as 'the ultimate feature of international relations', just as revolution is the ultimate feature of domestic politics.[1] Yet, while war and political violence seem among the more persistent features of global politics, this area has experienced as much—if not more—change and turbulence as other areas of international relations described in this book. At no time did this change appear more obvious to North American audiences than on the morning of 11 September 2001. Traditional conceptions of war and security seemed to have been turned on their head. The citizens of the world's most powerful country had been directly attacked by a score of individuals acting without state authority, and using non-traditional weapons of destruction. This type of attack was not in any government's military training manual. Most analysts today would dispute the claim that these attacks fundamentally altered the global order, yet the attention given to terrorism and the subsequent wars launched against Afghanistan and Iraq definitely generated a renewed interest in security among observers of global politics. The attacks were also an important reminder that security discussions need to take an expanded view that includes not only states but also groups and individuals. Finally, 9/11 was yet another brutal reminder that the principal victims of modern conflict are civilians. An **expanded security discourse** that requires students of global politics to look beyond states as both the perpetrators and the victims of war and other violent acts had already been initiated in the aftermath of the Cold War,[2] but 9/11 added a degree of urgency and importance for many governments in North America, Europe, and Asia.

The persistence of violent conflict in global politics speaks to the permanence of insecurity in the lives of individuals and governments. It also reminds us of the continuing preference given to military force as a means of resolving conflicts among peoples and states and of trying to gain security in an **anarchic global system**. Attitudes towards war and other forms of political violence have varied over time and have been influenced by one's perspective on human nature and the nature of global politics. In the past, some have viewed war as the highest noble activity in which humans can engage and have considered it an essential part of the development of both human and social character. Sir Francis Bacon, for example, expressed the view that 'a just and honourable war is the true exercise.' War, for others, is seen as inevitable within an anarchic order such as the one that they believe defines global politics. In light of this, preparing for war and prosecuting it effectively become the ultimate, and ultimately, for realists, the most prudent, objective of states. Some of these views were abandoned in the twentieth century and, despite the ongoing presence of war, were replaced by a perspective that war is unnatural and unacceptable for both moral and practical reasons.

Just as the persistence of violence and military force represents the insecurities that confront human society, repeated efforts to ameliorate violent conflict demonstrate the strength and persistence of a desire for peace and non-violent means of conflict resolution in global politics. A desire to limit and prevent war has also been a prominent feature of various proposals for global governance over time. Arguably, the most common perspective today sees war as an aberration, an exception to the normal discourse of global politics with potentially horrific consequences for the entire species. Yet war as an instrument of policy retains considerable support among those who seek to undo the existing order and those who seek to sustain it. Moreover, war continues to attract the attention of analysts and practitioners alike. Indeed, the discipline of international relations can trace its origins to widespread concern about the effects of World War I and the hope to avoid its recurrence. The Scottish-born American industrialist Andrew Carnegie, in establishing one of the first endowments for the study of international relations, proposed that the funds be used to identify the causes of war so that it could be eliminated from the repertoire of global political behaviour.

In this chapter we explore the place of war and violence in global politics. We pay particular attention to the fact that in the contemporary global order war between states has given way to less organized, irregular, and non-state-centric forms of violence. Non-combatants have become (indeed, some would argue, have always been) the primary victims of war. This is especially evident in the contemporary period as armies using high-tech weapons are often far from the actual fields of battle where they do their damage. **'Collateral damage'**—whether of wedding parties, schools, or hospitals—has become part of the lexicon of contemporary warfare. These developments have increased the amount of attention given to the security of individuals in addition to the more traditional concerns over international and state security. Thus, we also address the idea of security as one of the central objectives of global politics. Security crosses the divide between states and society and has received much attention in the discourse of contemporary global politics. Increasingly, this discourse (alongside the practice of some governments, institutions, and civil society organizations) has placed an emphasis on human security amid the rapidly shifting security discourses that have predominated in the post-Cold War world.

Causes of War

The oldest work read by students of global politics is Thucydides's *History of the Peloponnesian War*. In this epic history of the war between Athens and Sparta, Thucydides explores, among other topics, the causes of war. He distinguishes between the immediate and deeper sources of conflict. At the surface level he identifies a series of minor skirmishes, but these, he writes, were incidental to the real cause—Sparta's fears of Athenian power. Thucydides cites the human tendencies towards greed, power, and glory as fundamental sources of conflict among peoples and states—a view that has received repeated attention over the nearly 2,500 years since he made his observations. Both realist and liberal perspectives on war have accepted to some extent these primary causal factors as responsible for much of the violence that has racked international life during centuries past. For realists, the solution has been one of balancing these impulses, usually through displays of force and counter-force. For liberals, the solution lies in developing instruments and institutions that will foster **interdependence** and co-operation among states and thereby make them less inclined to fight over differences, in part by removing the differences. And while realists remain pessimistic about the possibility of bringing an end to war and liberals are more optimistic on that issue, both liberals and realists share a desire to impose constraints on the use of war as an instrument of policy. Utopians share these concerns, but some critical theorists, such as Marxists, take a different position, viewing conflict and struggle as a historical necessity, or, as Isaiah Berlin wrote, 'Genuine progress is constituted not by the triumph of one side and the defeat of the other, but by the duel itself which necessarily involves the destruction of both.'[3]

From the time of Thucydides's efforts to understand the origins of the Peloponnesian War in 431 BC, there have been repeated attempts to identify the causes of war. Many authors have focused on identifying the principal causes of war. Much of their work has been inspired by the objective of understanding war so as to limit its occurrence. Such accounts, whether limited to explaining the sources of specific conflicts or designed to offer more generalized observations, have tended to reflect the theoretical predispositions of the individual authors.[4] One can identify certain patterns in these accounts. For realists, for example, systemic conditions such as the structure and distribution of power among major states are among the most important factors in determining peace and stability. Since many realists have argued that a **balance of power** is the best way to maintain stability, they see a transition in this balance as one of the main sources of war. Power asymmetries and power transitions have been cited as the reason for war since the time of Thucydides. They remain among the most important for contemporary realists such as Mearsheimer and Waltz.[5] Liberals, on the other hand, tend to view war's causes as aberrations or as a result of factors that could be controlled, such as the level of arms expenditures or problems in communications. Many liberals also agreed with their realist counterparts in arguing that a shift in balance of power was responsible for World War I, but unlike the realists, liberals such as US President Woodrow Wilson argued for the construction of an alternative system of international relations to replace power politics.[6]

War during the nineteenth century, particularly in the post-Napoleonic period, while infrequent, nevertheless raised a number of additional factors as potential causes. Many of the systemic uncertainties related to a balance of power had been resolved at the Congress of Vienna in 1815. The Congress laid the foundation for a new European order that relied on conferences and consultative meetings among the dominant powers of Europe to avoid the kinds of disastrous wars fuelled by Napoleon. The resulting Concert of Europe was able to forestall some conflicts from degenerating into violence, but was not always able to avoid war. Wars became more common as time went on and as conditions on the continent began to change. In addition to the more traditional concerns about the balance of power, brought on especially by the unification of Germany, the 1800s were a period of considerable technological change, especially in the latter part of the century, and these changes became the source of considerable uncertainty, not to mention profound social and economic shifts. The nineteenth century also saw the increased significance of domestic factors in shaping a state's international behaviour. By the end of the century the influence and instability of domestic politics, when added to the increased uncertainty brought on by technological, economic, and social change, provided a volatile context for the politicians' efforts to adjust regional and international power balances.

World War I

The Great War, as it was known until the next one came along, has been the object of fairly extensive analysis. Academics and practitioners alike have tried to explain the events that led to a global war that took more than 15 million lives before it ended. The war led to the collapse of the Ottoman and Austro-Hungarian empires, the colossal defeat of Germany, and the transformation of Russia as a result of domestic revolution. Responsibility for the conflict has been attributed to many sources. Political leaders operating from realist assumptions seeking to maintain a balance of power in the face of increased uncertainty and technological change were threatened by Germany's enhanced power position in the early decades of the twentieth century. Flexible **alliances** that had been established to maintain a balance became too rigid for maintaining such a turbulent period. 'What was once a fluid, multipolar alliance system gradually evolved into two alliance blocs, with dangerous consequences for European peace.'[7] Power considerations were of prime importance in this view.

Another systemic factor that has been linked to the war was the level and rate of arms expenditures. While these expenditures pale in comparison to contemporary military spending, many peace advocates argued that military spending was a prime source of conflict and instability in the international system.[8] The relationship between arms expenditures and war has long been of concern to analysts and advocates alike. Arms expenditures became a major issue at the time of World War I, as many observers expressed a concern that an excessive reliance on armaments by the major powers made the decision to go to war more likely and the conflict itself more deadly. Others placed the blame on bureaucratic rigidity, problems of misperception and/or miscommunication among political leaders, or the pressures generated by economic and social change. One can see that such accounts cut across all three levels of analysis—systemic, state, and individual decision-makers.

In response, advocates and policy-makers alike began to press for reforms in a number of arenas. Many looked to **disarmament**, and various conferences were called and agreements signed to limit the development and deployment of weapons. For liberals, it was the failure of the balance of power to maintain stability, order, and ultimately peace that was the underlying cause of the war. For this reason, Woodrow Wilson and other liberals sought to replace balance-of-power politics, with its reliance on military power and alliance politics, with an institutionalized system of law and conflict prevention mechanisms, including collective security provisions outlined in the Covenant of the League of Nations.

The League of Nations was an attempt to create an institutional framework to control war by eliminating or reducing states' concerns about security. The principle of collective security was seen as a remedy for the **security dilemma** that confronted states. A collective security system is based on a number of critical assumptions. It assumes that wars are principally the result of acts of aggression conducted by one state against another. It also assumes that such wars could be deterred if potential aggressors knew that their actions would be met with the combined force of all of the other states in the system, either in the form of harmful sanctions or, ultimately, with armed force. This brings into play still other assumptions, most importantly, the willingness of other states to respond collectively in the face of aggression. Collective security rests on the premise of shared vulnerability among states. As a Haitian delegate stated at the time of Italy's invasion of Ethiopia in 1935, 'Let us never forget that one day we may be somebody's Ethiopia.' Yet, in practice, few states were willing to leave their security in the hands of the collective security instrument devised at the League of Nations. This was especially true for those states—Japan, Italy, and Germany—that were dissatisfied with the prevailing international order. As they sought their own solutions to interwar security issues, other states took notice and felt threatened.

Realists have considered the security dilemma to be one of the more important sources of tension and conflict among states in the global system. As Lord Grey, the British Foreign Secretary, put it on the eve of World War I and in light of German military buildups, 'The distinction between preparations made with the intention of going to war and precautions against attack is a true distinction, clear and definite in the minds of those who build up armaments. But it is a distinction that is not obvious or certain to others.'[9] Dealing with insecurity becomes a matter of assessing both the capability and the intent of potential adversaries. Accurate assessments are not always possible for governments, and so they lean towards worst-case scenarios. Former US Secretary of Defense Donald Rumsfeld has articulated, albeit in a convoluted manner, such a frightening view, in his contemporary rephrasing of the security dilemma. Regarding the threats confronting the United States in the early twenty-first century, he said, 'There are things we know that we know. There are known unknowns. That is to say, there are things that we know we don't know. But there are also unknown unknowns. There are things we don't know we don't know.... Each year, we discover a few more of those unknown unknowns.'[10] To follow along on this Rumsfeldian thinking, defending against such threats requires an indeterminable number of indeterminable measures against an indeterminable number of foes for an indeterminable period of time. It creates a world of persistent threats and thus persistent insecurity that can only be addressed through the maintenance of military forces and their deployment, often in a pre-emptive manner, to address these threats. Yet such a response may simply breed more insecurity.

John Herz defined the security dilemma as 'a structural notion in which the self-help attempts of states to look after their security needs, tend regardless of intention to lead to rising insecurity for others as each interprets its own measures as defensive and the measures of others as potentially threatening.'[11] The security dilemma thus is a reflection of capabilities, mistrust, uncertainty, and fear. It is fostered both by the autonomy of states to decide on their own how best to protect their interests and by the absence of any effective system of overarching rules or authorities that would constrain states from resorting to violence. It has been further affected by advancements in technology, which provide both the incentive and the concomitant fear that through technological improvements one side will be able to acquire a decisive advantage.

World War II

The inability of the League of Nations to overcome the security dilemma by creating an effective structure of conflict resolution has been seen by many as one of the greatest failures of the interwar period, which in turn led to the outbreak of war on the European continent in 1939. Of course, the League was not an entity unto itself; rather, it merely represented the collective will of its member governments. The United States, one of the world's pre-eminent powers, never took up membership, and by the late 1930s most of the disaffected powers—Germany, Japan, Russia—had left the League. Those governments that remained—principally Great Britain and France—were unwilling for a variety of domestic and foreign policy considerations to provide the League with the support it needed to respond to the political and military challenges that developed in the international system during the 1930s. Beginning with Japan's attack on Manchuria, through to Italy's annexation of Abyssinia and on to the German *anschluss* against Czechoslovakia in 1939, the League and its member governments stood by. Yet it would be somewhat misleading to lay the blame for World War II solely on the stoop of the League.

For some, the war that began in 1939 was the continuation of a European-wide war that had not ended in 1919, but merely paused as the combatants regained strength and armour. World War I had failed to resolve the pressing balance-of-power issues that had plagued the continent since the late nineteenth century. States such as Germany and Italy remained dissatisfied with their place in the European power structure. Germany, especially, suffered from the punitive measures imposed as part of the Treaty of Versailles at the end of the Great War. From the Germans' vantage point, there was much ground to recover. Added to these factors, of course, was the emergence of **Fascist regimes** in Germany and Italy led, respectively, by Adolf Hitler and Benito Mussolini. Hitler's ambitious expansionist plans posed a direct and significant challenge to European and international order. In light of these factors, war became more a matter of when, not if.

As was mentioned above, World War I resulted in 15 million casualties. That war is also widely acknowledged as having a significant psychological effect on the soldiers and societies who participated. You can get a sense of the psychological impact of World War I on soldiers by reading poems like 'Suicide in the Trenches' and 'Memory' by Siegfried Sassoon, and 'Dulce et Decorum Est' and 'Mental Cases' by Wilfred Owen. Both of these poets, who were friends and fellow British soldiers, were treated for shell shock. The pernicious use of mustard gas and the miserable life (for as long as it lasted) shared with vermin in the mud of the World War I trenches had a profound impact long before 'shell shock' became medicalized as post-traumatic stress disorder. The dehumanization and cataclysm of the trench warfare of World War I are well documented by Erich Maria Remarque in his acclaimed war protest, *All Quiet on the Western Front* (1929), and by Dalton Trumbo in his anti-war novel, *Johnny Got His Gun* (1939).[12] While the more jaded populations of the 1940s may have been less affected psychologically, the physical costs of World War II were even more horrific. When combined with the holocausts in Germany, Poland, and the Soviet Union, the number of deaths exceeded 50 million.

The end of World War II brought with it the seeds of the next conflict. The destruction of the European order and most of the principal states of Europe created a new order with the United States and the Soviet Union competing for dominance in Central Europe. The **multi-polar** structure that had been in place since the early 1800s was now replaced by a bipolar structure dominated by these two superpowers. The end of the war also brought into play a new era of destructiveness with the unleashing of two atomic weapons on Hiroshima and Nagasaki in August 1945. The overwhelming destructive capacity of these weapons proved to have a sobering effect of sorts on the United States and the Soviet Union, making a direct conflict between them less and less practical, but it did not eliminate conflict. The result was a **Cold War** that persisted for much of the next 40 years. The Cold War was marked by fierce competition between these superpowers as they sought to spread their influence around the globe. Both the US and the USSR worked through formal alliances of their own design, with the North Atlantic Treaty Organization (NATO) and the Warsaw Pact being especially important in organizing the European order. While much of the competition between the two superpowers was fought out in an **arms race** and competition for allies, the two also engaged in numerous **proxy wars**, involving lesser-power allies of the superpowers, fought in contested regions of the globe—Korea, Vietnam, the Middle East, and various parts of Africa (see Box 5.1). Throughout much of the early period of the Cold War, tensions remained high in places such as Berlin and Cuba, but armed conflict was avoided through various forms of diplomacy and brinkmanship.

The Cold War

During the Cold War, the core goal of security policy was primarily the enhancement of stability at the regional and global levels while securing the political survival of the state. The consequences of making a mistake in assessing one's security needs seemed so horrific that radical solutions, such as the abolition of nuclear weapons, were marginalized and a high value was placed on maintaining the status quo. This required a combination of deterrence and reassurance. **Deterrence** was based on a perverse form of security interdependence. The logic of deterrence suggested that if one side attacked the other, the state that had been attacked would retaliate, and given the amount of destruction that would occur in the state that had originated the attack it would be deterred from launching

BOX 5.1

The Vietnam War

Much of the discussion surrounding Western intervention in Afghanistan makes reference to the Vietnam quagmire. The Vietnam War was one of the bloodiest conflicts of the second half of the twentieth century and the most extensive conflict of the Cold War era. It was the longest war the United States has ever been involved in, with American personnel in combat from 1959 to 1975. More than 1 million soldiers from all sides and more than 2 million civilians lost their lives during the conflict. Vietnam, like Korea and Berlin, was divided at the end of World War II, with the French colonial power in control in the South and a Vietnamese nationalist movement led by Communist leader Ho Chi Minh in the North. As the French lost ground and began moving out, leaving the South under increased pressure from the nationalists in the North in the early 1950s, the United States moved in under the influence of the Truman Doctrine, which intended to curb the so-called 'domino effect' of Communist expansion.

The Truman Doctrine first was invoked in 1947 in response to Communist uprisings in Europe. The doctrine essentially committed the US to the defence of free peoples engaged in a struggle against Communist forces wherever they existed. The 'domino theory' held that if one country fell under the influence of communism, neighbouring countries were likely to follow. Operating from this point of view, the Eisenhower government in the US moved in to prop up the government of Ngo Dinh Diem in South Vietnam. Diem refused to hold elections in the South, but the US continued to lend its support to that regime. In the early to mid-1960s a series of events turned an arm's-length relationship between the US and South Vietnam into a full-blown American military intervention that resulted in the deployment of more than half a million American forces, the downfall of an American President (Lyndon B. Johnson), and a political movement that radicalized a generation of young Americans.

The official American sanction of the war, the Gulf of Tonkin Resolution of 7 August 1964, was a ruse by the Johnson administration to secure congressional support for military intervention: the United States supported South Vietnamese attacks on North Vietnam, which led to retaliation that inflicted damage on American vessels in the area. In fact, there had been a minor skirmish a few days earlier in the Gulf of Tonkin, off the coast of North Vietnam. Under this pretense, the US military launched a full-fledged assault on North Vietnam, including an extensive bombing campaign of North Vietnam's capital city, Hanoi. In the midst of growing discontent over the war, the American public withdrew its support of its own government, and President Johnson—in the face of growing anti-war protests, whose shouted slogan had become 'Hey, hey, LBJ! How many kids did you kill today?'—refused to stand for re-election.

After one of the most divisive and violent election campaigns in US history, which included the assassination of Senator Robert Kennedy, the leading Democrat contender for nomination, Richard M. Nixon, a Republican, was elected president in 1968 with a pledge to remove American forces from Vietnam. It would take seven long years, but in 1975, American forces withdrew from Vietnam and forces from North Vietnam quickly assumed control of the entire country, proclaiming Hanoi as the capital of a united Vietnam and renaming Saigon, the former capital of the South, Ho Chi Minh City in honour of the nationalist leader who had led North Vietnam to victory over the most powerful countries in the world. The sight of Americans fleeing onto helicopters on the roof of the American embassy in what was then Saigon is a lasting image of the shame the war had brought to the United States. Except for the Reagan administration's brief forays into Grenada and Panama in the early 1980s, it would be many years before the American government and its military would overcome the Vietnam syndrome and deploy American forces abroad in combat.

●●●●○

such an attack in the first instance. As deterrence evolved, both parties and many analysts came to accept the view that any exchange of nuclear weapons would set off a trail of nuclear escalation leading to universal ruin. This was referred to as **Mutual Assured Destruction (MAD)** or Mutual Assured Deterrence. MAD, it was said, kept the world sane: fear of disaster prevented Washington and Moscow from crossing the line into nuclear war. Deterrence dominated Western strategic policy and thinking for about four decades. Deterrence was also extended to Western Europe through the deployment of the US nuclear capability to that continent beginning in the 1950s and continuing through the 1980s. The proclaimed purpose of these nuclear weapons was to support the **containment** and deterrence of Soviet power.

Containment, proposed by the American diplomat and realist scholar George Kennan in the 1940s, became a cornerstone of American Cold War foreign policy, though not necessarily in the manner Kennan intended. The objective was to limit the spread of Soviet influence throughout the world. Needless to say, the Soviet Union took up the challenge, as exemplified by then Soviet leader Nikita Khrushchev's blunt assertion: 'Whether you like it or not, history is on our side. We will bury you.'[13] This bellicose stance was epitomized by the Cuban Missile Crisis of 1962 (see Box 5.2). Containment policy, in effect, meant an expansion of US involvement in different regions of the world, principally through the use of formal bilateral or multilateral alliances. These alliances also were tangible demonstrations of the US commitment, especially to NATO. The constant reaffirmation of the US nuclear umbrella, so it was imagined, helped to reassure Western Europeans that they would be protected in the event of an armed confrontation with the Soviet Union. Over time, however, the weapons and their threatened use were seen by some as a more significant threat than the adversary and were perceived as undermining the security of peoples and states, as was evidenced by the European opposition to the deployment of a new generation of nuclear weapons in Europe in the late 1970s.[14]

By the late 1970s and into the 1980s, public opinion was uneasy about endorsing a never-ending arms race. The 1982 Report of the

Getty Images

The Big Three, (from left) Joseph Stalin of the Soviet Union, Franklin Delano Roosevelt of the United States, and Winston Churchill of Britain, at the Tehran Conference, 1943.

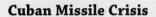

BOX 5.2

Cuban Missile Crisis

On 24 October 1962, then US President John F. Kennedy addressed the American people on national television for 17 minutes. His message was brief, but the implications profound. Surveillance photographs had discovered that installations were being built in Cuba that would house Soviet nuclear-tipped missiles. The effect of this was to bring the threat of a nuclear attack minutes closer to the United States. More significant was the political message that Soviet nuclear forces were advancing into the western hemisphere. For the next 10 days people and governments around the world were on edge as the two antagonists in the Cold War attempted to stare each other down in the most serious confrontation since the crisis over a divided Berlin in 1949.

Many observers report that the Cuban Missile Crisis was the closest the world has come to a nuclear war between these two powers. The US government, in near-constant consultation from the time the missiles were discovered until their removal, drifted between an aggressive response in the form of a military strike against Cuba to a less risky but equally assertive quarantine that would deny Soviet ships access to Cuban ports. In deciding on the quarantine, the Americans left space and time for a Soviet response. For its part, the Soviet leadership responded with a mix of threatening and bellicose messaging and hints of a compromise solution that would see American missiles withdrawn from Turkey in return for their own stand-down in Cuba. As the world teetered on the brink of a potential nuclear war, diplomatic exchanges continued at a frenetic pace. On 27 October a US reconnaissance plane was shot down over Cuba and the pilot killed. Amid the deteriorating climate Soviet Premier Nikita Khrushchev reiterated the missile swap compromise. Despite the opposition of the Turkish government, the compromise position eventually formed the core of the solution, though a further compromise on the part of the Soviet Union meant that it was never formally acknowledged. Complications multiplied and pressures mounted within the US government for an attack on Cuba, but Khrushchev's proposal held. Ten days after his first address, Kennedy returned to the airwaves on 2 November to announce the end of the crisis and the removal of missiles from Cuba.

The Cuban Missile Crisis has been one of the most widely studied confrontations in international relations history. It generated a body of literature on crisis decision-making and brinkmanship. On a more practical level, it also became the catalyst for a series of measures to reduce tensions between the superpowers and thus the likelihood of a recurrence of such a standoff, including such measures as the installation of a telephone link that would connect both leaders in times of crisis (the Red Phone), the development of **confidence-building measures** (CBMs), and later the conceptualization and implementation of more formal **arms control** and arms reduction measures. The Cuban Missile Crisis marked a turning point in the Cold War though it would be a long road back from the brink.

Independent Commission on Disarmament and Security Issues, titled *Common Security: A Blueprint for Survival*, argued for a redefinition of security that would transform the security relationship between the East and the West.[15] This Palme Commission Report, named after its chairman, former Swedish Prime Minister Olaf Palme, was driven by the idea that an arms race was wasteful, harmful to the prospects for development in the Third World, and—above all else—dangerous. The Report noted that:

> nations must strive for objectives more ambitious than stability, the goal of the present system in which security is based on armaments. For stability based on armaments cannot be sustained indefinitely. There is always the danger that the fragile stability of an international system based on armaments will suddenly crumble, and that nuclear confrontation will take its place. A more effective way to ensure security is to create positive processes that can lead to peace and disarmament. It is essential to create an irreversible process, with a momentum such that all nations cooperate for their common survival.[16]

The view proposed by the Palme Report was largely rejected by the political and strategic mainstream, which in the short term continued to emphasize the merits of deterrence. Yet the Commission played a more significant role in reframing the wider debate. First, it supported the concept of **non-offensive defence**. Second, it publicized the usefulness of 'confidence-building measures' (CBMs). Third, it encouraged thinking about the security implications of interdependence. Fourth, it called attention to the growing importance of Third World development issues; poverty in the South was presented as a potential security issue.

One idea fostered at the time was to overcome the security dilemma by shifting the perspective from state security to **common security**. Common security is based on three central themes. The first is interdependence, which leads to the view that states cannot be secure if their policies make others insecure. This view rejects notions of military supremacy and argues instead for a 'non-offensive defence' (whereby armed force would be restructured to emphasize the adoption of defensive measures for defensive purposes) and disarmament. A second theme calls attention to a multi-dimensional view of security, with non-military elements of security given increased recognition. A third theme emphasizes the need to give prominence to individuals rather than states in developing security policies. While such views have gained some acceptance among states, which tend to be more concerned with autonomy than co-operation, they have not completely overtaken the largely self-help-based approach to security.

These reports preceded the major shift in thinking among state leaders that occurred when Mikhail Gorbachev became leader of the Soviet Union in 1985 and emphasized many of the key themes of the common security message. He abandoned the arms race and adopted a new and far more serious approach to arms control. Gorbachev's initiative won support throughout Europe and subsequently in the United States. The two superpowers embarked on a substantive set of arms control measures, the core of which was the elimination of nuclear weapons from Central Europe. In essence, they began to pursue what has been labelled as **co-operative security**—a limited and relatively conservative variant of common security. Proposed initially in the 1970s as an element of the détente then in place between the superpowers, co-operative security acknowledged the mutual interests of the superpowers in avoiding a major war. During the early 1970s, the Americans and the Soviets, under the respective leadership of Richard Nixon and Leonid Brezhnev, had made efforts to reduce the likelihood of armed conflict by pursuing initiatives in a variety of areas. Co-operative security was intended to promote mutual security for both sides in the Cold War through confidence-building measures, arms control, greater transparency, and military exchange visits. Despite its relative conservatism, co-operative security represented a significant shift from more traditional conceptions that stressed the necessity of an arms race, mutual deterrence, and secrecy (see Box 5.3).

The 1980s began with a return to the bellicosity and tensions of the early Cold War period, at least in part the result of the hawkish Margaret Thatcher becoming British Prime Minister in 1979 and the election in 1980 of Ronald Reagan as President of the US. Reagan soon was labelling the Soviet Union as 'the Evil Empire' and pursuing his 'Star Wars' program to weaponize space. But the seeds of change had been planted and a number of developments, led by the

BOX 5.3

Nuclear Proliferation

China and the United States have asserted their right to develop and modernize nuclear weapons, as well as refine the doctrines outlining the deployment and possible use of nuclear weapons. Israel, India, and Pakistan have joined the ranks of nuclear powers. Iran and North Korea have expressed the intention and demonstrated the capacity to acquire nuclear weapons. Libya and Iraq have been suspected in the past of nuclear proliferation activities.

How does the world confront the threat of nuclear weapons in the new millennium? Four choices exist: status quo, proliferation, nuclear rearmament, or abolition.

Restoring the 1995 status quo under the Nuclear Non-Proliferation Treaty (NPT) would require the impossible task of disarming South Asia. In advanced countries, technological flows of materials and expertise in the nuclear power industry can be used to rapidly build a 'virtual' nuclear weapons portfolio. Within the NPT constraints, a non-nuclear industrialized country could build the necessary infrastructure for technological and material advancements in nuclear weapons. Non-ratification, nuclear testing, and/or nuclear weapons proliferation could undermine existing treaties. The abolition of nuclear weapons is unrealistic.

How then does the world deter nuclear weapons capabilities? (1) Nuclear powers must set the example (e.g., the United States needs to adhere to existing international laws on nuclear proliferation). (2) Nuclear weapons must be kept out of the hands of governments and terrorist groups. (3) A drastic reduction should be made in nuclear arsenals and constraints placed on the extra-territorial deployment of nuclear weapons. (4) The Comprehensive Test Ban Treaty must enter into force. (5) Missile test flights and the production of fissile materials should be banned. (6) A pre-emptive ban on the nuclear militarization of outer space is necessary. (7) Nuclear forces, warheads, and missiles should be neutralized.

International security depends on halting the threat of nuclear proliferation.

Source: Adapted from Ramesh Thakur, 'Global Nuclear "Outbreak" Threatens Fragile Status Quo', *Canberra Times*, 6 Aug. 2004. Ramesh Thakur was senior Vice-Rector of the United Nations University (UNU) in Tokyo. He is now Distinguished Fellow at the Centre for International Governance Innovation (CIGI) and Professor of Political Science at the University of Waterloo in Canada.

selection in 1985 of Mikhail Gorbachev to lead the Soviet Union, put in motion a radical transformation of the bipolar security regime. Gorbachev initiated a number of domestic and foreign policy changes and also pursued an aggressive arms reduction campaign with the US, culminating in the historic signing of the Intermediate-Range Nuclear Forces (INF) agreement in 1987, the first treaty in the nuclear era to eliminate a full class of nuclear weapons. As events continued to spiral out of control at home, Gorbachev was forced to confront the demise of his own leadership and of the Soviet Union itself. The bipolar Cold War era passed, fortunately without the bang that so many had feared for so long.

Post-Cold War

At the end of the Cold War, an extensive debate on security and international order was launched. As a result, the concept of security was broadened significantly and traditional views on the security dilemma were challenged. In part because they were seen as too narrow, but also because they justified military force, arms races, and, ultimately, war, even nuclear war, these traditional views were challenged as inherently destabilizing and unsuited to a more integrated and globalizing world community. Such arguments encouraged new approaches to security and altered the discourse surrounding war and the use of force among states. The new debate on security adopted some of the themes of common or co-operative security, comprehensive security, and human security. These themes reflected attempts on the part of different agents in the global community to move beyond traditional approaches to security and to identify alternative approaches that might generate more positive and progressive change. For proponents of co-operative and common security the principal objective was to overcome the divisiveness that the inter-state system had created and to encourage states and other agents to recognize the shared experiences that exist. This more inclusive view of security was designed to recognize the growing interconnections among states, particularly given the increasing significance of economic ties as captured by the concept of globalization.

The Changing Practice of War

Hedley Bull once described war as 'organized violence carried on by political units against each other'.[17] Bull and others, principally in the English school of international relations, have attempted to identify war as a very specific form of inter-state violence. It would be misleading to suggest that this has been a traditional approach to war, yet it does demonstrate an attempt to approach war and security from an inter-state perspective and to limit it to state practice. Others also took a more politicized view of war, considering it to be yet another means for pursuing states' interests in the international realm. Karl von Clausewitz developed a systemic approach to war in his classic work, *On War*.[18] Clausewitz argued that war was diplomacy by other means, or simply another instrument that states would use in pursuing their interests with other states. As an extension of diplomacy, war was thus intended to serve specific political objectives. The use of military force was designed to destroy or weaken an opponent's ability to fight and thus force that enemy into political compromises. Ideally, Clausewitz saw war as a controlled and limited means of serving clearly defined political objectives. He was quick to caution, however, that war was often unpredictable and could not

BOX 5.4

The 'Two Darfurs'

Although genocide continues to plague Sudan, there is an increasing effort by some state leaders to redefine the crisis and present the Darfur region in western Sudan as less urgent and less demanding of international humanitarian intervention. But the grim realities show that the crisis is continuing and deepening throughout the region. If the contrived Darfur governs the response of the international community, the real Darfur will suffer as a result.

United Nations (UN) reports and news releases from the ground evidence increased insecurity and the incapacity of humanitarian operations in Sudan. The African Union (AU) was forced to request that the North Atlantic Treaty Organization (NATO) augment AU deployment in Darfur because the UN denied the AU logistical support.

The 'new Darfur' can be characterized as follows. (1) It is not the site of genocide, despite mounting evidence that all violent actions and killings, as specified in the 1948 UN Convention on the Prevention and Punishment of Genocide, have been committed against non-Arabs and African tribal groups by the military forces of the Khartoum regime and its Janjaweed militia allies. (2) It is the site of genocide by attrition or engineered disease and malnutrition, not violence per se, although violent killings remain the biggest source of overall mortality (approximately 400,000 people have died in the region in the last six years). (3) There is a lack of official human mortality figures and statistical derivations have no context, methodology, data, or explanation. (4) The situation is presented with disingenuous optimism by local, regional, and international media outlets. (5) The alliance between Khartoum and the Janjaweed in sharing responsibility for the genocide is repeatedly denied through elision and indirection, despite human rights reports to the contrary.

The 'real Darfur', on the other hand, is characterized in the following manner. (1) Sudan is experiencing ongoing human suffering, civilian destruction, and massive mortality. (2) There has been a sharp decline in the security of humanitarian staff, operations, and access due to divisive insurgency movements. (3) Agricultural production has stopped and prospects to resume harvesting and yielding crops in the short term are grim. (4) Famine-related mortality is high, including deaths due to related illness (e.g., diarrhea and malnutrition). (5) Humanitarian food relief is inadequate and existing food aid pipelines are hampered by natural disasters, raids by militant groups, and continuing conflict. (6) Almost 2 million people (1.96 million) are categorized as internally displaced, not including 200,000 refugees in Chad and the displaced population in inaccessible rural Darfur. Total displacement exceeds 2.5 million. (7) Khartoum continues with a policy of forced or induced movement and deportations of displaced persons, which increases food insecurity and heightens the risk of rebel attacks.

Critical security tasks need to be met in Darfur: securing refugee camps, protecting humanitarian workers/convoys/operations, providing safe passage of vulnerable civilians in rural areas, allowing civilians to return to their lands, and disarming the Janjaweed. Meanwhile, Khartoum will likely block any efforts to secure Darfur. The international community must address the actual Darfur, not the 'new' Darfur.

Source: Adapted from Eric Reeves, 'The "Two Darfurs": Redefining a Crisis for Political Purposes', 20 May 2005. At: <www.sudanreeves.org>.

always be controlled or kept limited. For these reasons the decision to use military force was among the most important of decisions political leaders ought to take. War was not something to be taken on lightly.

Realists maintain that war has retained its central political role in global politics despite the significant changes in the technology of warfare, the nature of modern states, and the emergence of a new set of issues and actors on the world stage. For example, in response to the terrorist attacks of 9/11, Kenneth Waltz wrote about the continuity in international politics as exemplified by American power, nuclear weapons, and continued international crises.[19] Earlier, John Mearsheimer had argued that while 'nuclear weapons significantly reduced the likelihood of great-power war...war between nuclear-armed great powers is still a serious possibility.'[20] Thus, despite the fact that phenomena such as terrorism, civil war, and unconventional warfare have been as common as inter-state war, if not more so, for many realists armed conflict remains the central prerogative of states in an anarchic global system. It is, they claim, the ultimate means for maintaining stability and order in the anarchic global system and also the principal instrument for change. In the absence of a legitimate authority to enforce international norms, and given the lack of consensus among states on these norms, individual states must rely on their own military forces, or those of other states, to secure their sovereignty, autonomy, and territorial integrity. In relying on military force, realists maintain that states must hold a skeptical view of the intentions of other states and must be prepared to defend themselves with force.

The dictum 'if you want peace, prepare for war' continues to inform many realist debates on security policy. A good illustration of this can be found in the US National Security Policy released in September 2003, which identifies the preponderance of American military power as a necessary prerequisite for international peace and stability. Even smaller states, such as Canada, continue to emphasize the need for a multi-purpose, combat-capable military force to protect their national interests in a potentially hostile global environment. Realists, by and large, also tend to be skeptical of various arguments that suggest a transformation in the nature of global politics, and caution against assuming that states will abandon security concerns as a result of globalization or other considerations.

Mearsheimer, for example, maintains that nothing really has changed and that the global system is still dominated by states locked in power struggles with one another. While the struggle may be complicated by the turn to weapons of mass destruction (WMDs) such as nuclear, chemical, and biological weapons, this does not change fundamentally the overriding importance of balance-of-power considerations. It merely increases the need to equip the states in this new multi-polar balance-of-power system with WMDs. Others, such as Samuel Huntington, have emphasized the growth of non-political sources of identity and argued that clashes across these civilizational divides are likely to be the primary cause of conflict in the future.

Liberal observers have taken a different view, maintaining that changes both within and across various states have led to a transformation of the global political landscape. Where the world was once divided between liberal-democratic and totalitarian regimes, these observers argue that the spread in democratic forms of government and the expansion of liberal ideas and practices have created a more benign international order. Much of this optimism is drawn from analysts led by Bruce Russett and Michael Doyle, who point out that democracies do not fight each other. Since the world is becoming more democratic, then, according to these authors, there will be less conflict.

With the exception of Mearsheimer, all of these attempts to develop new definitions of security in the aftermath of the Cold War reflect a view that the globe has been transformed by the demise of the Cold War and that a new set of security arrangements will likely emerge. Even among realists there is a shared view that new powers will bring a period of instability and turbulence into international security relations. While realists continue to assert that security will remain essentially statist and will be managed primarily through military means, most other analysts reject these assumptions. Rather, they perceive a greater level of uncertainty in a world with considerably less clarity on the nature of the threats to individual, community, and state security. Some have seen the threat in more traditional ways, while others take less orthodox views, but both perspectives understand that the concept of security has changed, with the hope that a strong political/popular consensus can provide a secure foundation for post-Cold War security. Spurred in part by such concerns, human security has emerged as a significant priority among many state and societal actors as well as for many international institutions.

Some realists acknowledge that it is possible to identify patterns in the occurrence and practice of war over the past hundreds of years and that the practice of war has changed over time with important consequences for how we look at war. While realists see war as an inevitable condition among states in an anarchic international order, they are also ready to acknowledge that this does not mean that war will always occur and that war between states declined during the last half of the twentieth century, only to be replaced by new forms of conflict that are not easily accounted for in terms of realist assumptions. In the opinion of Kal Holsti, these 'recent trends and patterns cannot be explained by the standard theoretical devices of international politics, particularly by neo-realist analysis.'[21] Holsti, perhaps as much as any other scholar, has explored patterns in the historical occurrence of war and has identified a number of interesting characteristics. For many generations war was the prerogative of states. It was also principally fought over such issues as territory, commerce, and state survival. Holsti notes that the sources of war have changed significantly through the years, not only in terms of what has been fought over but also in terms of who is doing the fighting. 'War today is not the same phenomenon it was in the eighteenth century, or even in the 1930s. It has different sources and takes on significantly different characteristics.'[22]

Wars today are more often internal affairs and the issues are more likely to involve the acquisition or retention of domestic power and authority, rather than the preservation or expansion of territory. For a long time states—especially more powerful states—had dominated the field of battle. Indeed, much of global history is recounted in the wars among great powers. Yet this, too, has changed. Holsti refers to what he labels 'wars of the third kind' to describe a practice that has become all too common in the contemporary period.

> In wars of the third kind there are no fronts, no campaigns, no bases, no uniforms, no publicly displayed honors, no *points d'appui*, and no respect for the territorial limits of states. There are no set strategies and tactics. Innovation, surprise, and unpredictability are necessities and virtues. The weak must rely on guile, and often crime, to raise funds for the bombings, assassinations, and massacres. People are used as hostages to extract

political gains, terrorist incidents are designed to make publicity, not necessarily to defeat an enemy's armed force. Terror is also used to cow the timid, the 'collaborators,' and the indifferent. The clear distinction between the state, the armed forces, and the society that is the hallmark of institutionalized war dissolves in 'peoples' war.[23]

These 'wars of the third kind' raise many issues surrounding prevention, cessation, and post-conflict peace-building processes in societies that have suffered violent confrontations. Their prevalence in the contemporary period also reflects the degree to which war today differs from past practice. Numerous commentators since 9/11, particularly more recently, have tried to make sense of the special desperation of the state's conduct in the aftermath. David Runciman has gone so far as to argue that what is happening amounts to a genuine mutation of the international state system: Suddenly, the Hobbesian view that states and states alone have the power and security to operate under conditions of lawfulness is threatened by the knowledge that even the most powerful states are vulnerable to assault from unknown and unpredictable sources. It can now be said that in the international arena 'the weakest has the strength to kill the strongest', or they would if only they could get their hands on the necessary equipment:

This, potentially, changes everything ....The common view that 11 September 2001 marked the return to a Hobbesian world is therefore entirely wrong. It marked the beginning of a post-Hobbesian age, in which a new kind of insecurity threatens the familiar structures of modern political life. In one sense, of course, this insecurity is not new, because it carries echoes of the natural uncertainties of individual human beings. But it is new for states, which were meant to be invulnerable to such paranoid anxieties. And since they are not designed to deal with this sort of threat, even the most powerful states don't know what to do about it.[24]

The changing nature of war has been explored by scholars such as Mary Kaldor, who notes how war in the contemporary era is more difficult to keep separate from other activities. She points out the ease with which violent conflict spills across national borders.[25] For example, terrorist attacks can occur far from the sites where grievances are experienced. Civilians cannot

© Ali Ali/EPA/Corbis

Asymmetrical warfare: an Israeli attack on Gaza.

escape the battlefield, as the battlefield shifts to where civilians live. Communities are uprooted, people are displaced, and their vulnerabilities are exacerbated, not just by the level of violence that surrounds them in the conflict but also as a result of the threats to health that come with displacement.[26] Combatants also tend to blur the boundaries between war and crime, so that the two end up reinforcing one another. Finally, ethnic and religious identities begin to consume the conflict and combatants. As Kaldor writes: 'political violence at the start of the twenty-first century is more omnipresent, more directed at civilians, involves a blurring of distinctions between war and crime, and is based on and serves to foment divisive identity politics.'[27] Kaldor goes on to suggest that while much has been done by the international community to contain these new wars, the effort has not turned the tide: 'In most conflict-affected regions, there are still high levels of human rights violations and crime; a variety of armed actors remain at large; high unemployment and a large informal or illegal economy [are the rule]; and very little has been done to confront identity politics.'[28] The end result is the persistence of violence and insecurity for civilian populations.

The link between conflict and crime is only one aspect of the political economy of these new wars. As Mark Duffield, among others, has discussed, armed conflict generates various economic activities that result in conflicts being sustained because they generate economic benefits for some of the parties involved.[29] Similarly, the armaments industry—both lawful and unlawful production and trade—has benefited individuals and economies in some countries and been an engine of economic growth, and also has encouraged acceptance of the inevitability of conflict.[30] Duffield identifies the interconnections among development, foreign assistance, and more nefarious types of economic and criminal activity. Research by David Keen on the conflict in Sierra Leone demonstrates how, in the absence of alternative economic choices, armed conflict becomes the alternative for many in society. 'A key lesson of the war is that Sierra Leone needs a political economy that provides alternative livelihoods to those that have been offered by armed bands.'[31]

Alternatives to War

For as long as states and peoples have gone to war, individuals and groups within society have advocated against war and the use of violence as means of resolving conflict. Indeed, in *Lysistrata*, the well-known comedy by the ancient Greek dramatist Aristophanes, the women of Greece band together to withhold sexual favours from their increasingly priapic men until the men agree to put an end to the interminable Peloponnesian War. Although realists tend to consider war as a necessary if not always desirable factor in global politics, liberals and Utopian/idealists, as well as other more critical scholars, have taken the position that nothing about the persistence of war is inevitable. Rather, it results from imperfections of various sorts in the practice of global politics. If these imperfections were effectively remedied, war and most forms of political violence could be eliminated and a more peaceful global order would persist. At the same time, many liberals have taken the view that war can be justified to serve liberal objectives. This presents what Michael Howard refers to as the 'liberal dilemma'[32]—a dilemma that has become particularly acute in the contemporary era.

Attitudes towards war and the use of force have changed significantly over the course of the past two centuries, yet there have always been voices that have railed against war. In the sixteenth century, for instances, Erasmus made his views on war quite clear: 'There is nothing more wicked, more disastrous, more widely destructive, more deeply tenacious, more loathsome, in a word more unworthy of man, not to say a Christian.'[33] As warfare moved beyond the traditional norms that restricted combat to organized armies and began to involve non-combatants, international norms against the use of force proliferated dramatically. The most concerted effort to debase war and to bring it under the control of an international authority occurred in the twentieth century, continuing through to the present day. Such efforts began as early as the late nineteenth century, with a number of religious and pacifist organizations advocating against war as a policy instrument and seeking its elimination from the practice of global politics, largely through the establishment of international legal regimes. Most types of force are now considered illegal by the international community, save those authorized by legitimate international institutions, best represented by the United Nations.

The UN Charter prohibits the use of force except in the case of self-defence or where the UN, under Chapter VII of the Charter, has authorized such force. Prior to the Charter, attempts were made in the early twentieth century to restrict force by encouraging the establishment of international mechanisms such as the Permanent Court of International Justice (PCIJ) and the League of Nations, which, it was hoped, would resolve inter-state conflicts before they escalated into war. Iraq's invasion of Kuwait in August 1990 and the response of many states to Iraqi aggression suggested for some an attempt to establish a system of collective security. Collective security has long been viewed as a method for preventing war. The UN Charter sets out the pre-eminent state-based approach to security designed to address the insecurities and uncertainties that result from an anarchic international order. As a voluntarist state-based approach, it relies entirely on the willingness of individual state members of the UN system to contribute the necessary financial and personnel support for this approach to be effective, based on the idea that states should band together to enforce international law prohibiting aggression. Collective security was the primary rationale (at least in theory) for the defunct League of Nations, and is a key mission (again in theory) of the United Nations. While these measures have had some limited utility, they have been unable to control national authorities dissatisfied with the existing international order. In brief, although the attempt to prohibit war remains the ultimate objective for many, others have taken a more limited, and less idealistic, view.

A second approach for dealing with war has been to develop a system of rules to be used in making decisions to go to war (*jus ad bellum*) and in governing the use of force within wars (*jus in bello*). The idea of a just war has a long history dating back to Biblical times and has been reasserted through time by various theologians, philosophers, and policy-makers. **'Just war'** doctrine has taken on greater significance especially among the latter group as the legality of war as an instrument of policy was increasingly challenged during the twentieth century. If wars were the exception rather than the rule and were viewed as inherently immoral and procedurally illegal, recourse to war was shrouded in ethical principles and legal justifications that defended the practice, not as an instrument of policy in pursuit of state interests but as a necessary act in support of higher-order, more ethically rooted objectives. There also has been increased pressure to make war consistent with the evolving framework of international law. Many have taken their inspiration from 'just war' doctrine, a set of principles outlined by Thomas Aquinas that was meant to govern a state's decision to go to war. The following constitutes the core of these principles, along with Aquinas's concern that all of this be done in the right frame of mind:

- The decision to go to war must be made by a legitimate authority.
- It must have a just cause.
- Force must be proportionate to the provocation.
- War must be the last resort after other alternatives have been exhausted.
- There must be a reasonable chance of success.

The 'just war' doctrine sought to steer a middle course between a committed pacifist-inspired prohibition against all uses of force and an excessive belligerency on the part of states or other powerful actors. Religious authorities initially advocated 'just war' doctrine, but increasingly some of these authorities have turned away from the doctrine because of the destructiveness of modern weaponry and the sheer difficulty in operationalizing these principles.

Hugo Grotius, who was writing Latin poetry at the age of eight, was one of the first to set out a specific set of rules to govern war. Grotius's *On the Law of War and Peace* was printed in 1625 in the midst of the Thirty Years War.[34] For Grotius, and for many others, that war marked a particularly brutal phase in the history of human relations. As Grotius writes: 'For I saw prevailing throughout the Christian world a license in making war of which even barbarous nations would have been ashamed; recourse being had to arms for slight reasons or no reason, and when arms were once taken up, all reverence for divine and human law was thrown away, just as if men were thenceforth authorized to commit all crimes without restraint.'[35] The solution for Grotius was to impose a set of rules upon a restricted range of actors that would, he hoped, control both the frequency of war's occurrence and the violence accompanying it. In *On the Law of War and Peace*, Grotius accepts that war is a necessary evil, but sketches out a proposal for restricting war to sovereign states and just causes (*jus ad bellum*). He also proposes that states respect a set of rules that would regulate how they conduct their militaries during war (*jus in bello*), for example, by restricting force to proportionate means and protecting non-combatants from physical harm.[36]

A related approach has been the development of rules governing how wars are fought. Throughout time there have been codes of battle to guide the behaviour of soldiers in combat, though more often than not these have been breached rather than respected. Matters such as treatment of non-combatants, prisoners of war, and restrictions on the use of excessively cruel weapons have all been covered at various times. Various humanitarian groups in modern times, most notably the International Committee of the Red Cross, have largely been responsible for these initiatives. Henry Dunant established the Red Cross in response to the horrors he witnessed during the Battle of Solferino in 1859. Through his efforts and the efforts of countless others who shared his concerns, a number of measures have been developed to control the excessive cruelty that accompanies war. Unfortunately, the historical record suggests mixed success. For example, a series of international conventions limit the pain and suffering that can be perpetrated against combatants and non-combatants alike. As well, a wide variety of groups and individuals devote their lives to preventing and/or limiting such acts. Many of these groups, such as the Red Cross, Amnesty International, Médecins Sans Frontières, and the International Campaign to Ban Landmines, have been awarded the Nobel Peace Prize in recognition of their efforts. Despite this commendable body of work, horrific practices continue and civilians seem no better protected from the scourge of war today than they were when Grotius first put pen to paper in the seventeenth century.

Yet another approach to containing war has been to control or prohibit the weapons of war. Activities in each of these areas expanded dramatically during the twentieth century, in part because a very strong opinion developed during World War I that the availability of new and more deadly weapons was primarily responsible for encouraging governments to resort to force.

Some observers at the end of the Cold War spoke of a peace dividend, arguing that states no longer needed to invest in military hardware or armed forces as the likelihood of conflict had been reduced. Data from the 1990s suggest that there was indeed a rather significant reduction in military spending in certain parts of the world, especially Europe, but reductions have been uneven across time and countries and the idea of a peace dividend has been largely illusory. Instead, the proliferation of small arms and light weapons, additional pressures to develop nuclear weapons, and increased concerns over the development and use of WMDs (principally biological and chemical weapons) have tended to increase insecurity at both state and societal levels. Recent data indicate that military spending has returned to Cold War levels, spurred on in part by the wars in Iraq and Afghanistan and accounted for largely by American spending, at 47 per cent of the world's total (see Figures 5.1, 5.2, and 5.3). Indeed, global military spending exceeded Cold War highs of $956 billion in 2003, in 2006 spending reached $1204 billion, and by 2008 it had increased to $1464 billion. The nature of many of the resulting emergent threats and the increased targeting of civilian populations have called attention to the vulnerabilities confronting civilian populations in many parts of the world.[37]

Weapons of violence have always had an influence on the conduct of war. They have also reinforced particular forms of national economic activity and have had

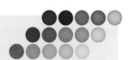

BOX 5.5

Military and UN System Spending

The United Nations and all its agencies and funds spend about $20 billion each year, or about $3 for each of the world's inhabitants. This is a very small sum compared to most government budgets and is just a tiny fraction—about 1.5 per cent—of the world's military spending. Yet for nearly two decades, the UN has faced financial difficulties and has been forced to cut back on important programs in all areas. Many member states do not pay their full dues and have cut their donations to the UN's voluntary funds. As of 31 August 2008, members' arrears to the regular budget topped $919 million, of which the United States alone owed $846 million (92 per cent of the regular budget arrears).

Source: Global Policy Forum, at <www.globalpolicy.org/finance/>.

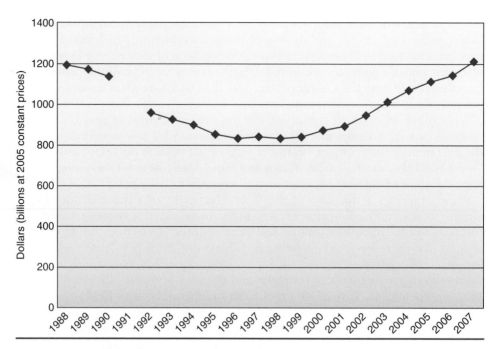

Figure 5.1 World military expenditures, 1988–2007.
Source: www.globalissues.org; Stockholm International Peace Research Institute Yearbook, 2008.

an influence on the organization of national armed forces. Throughout the ages, from the invention of the rifle to the machine gun and other automatic weapons, to the airplane and the tank, to anti-personnel landmines and improvised explosive devices (IEDs), and, most recently, with nuclear, chemical, and biological weapons, as well as intercontinental delivery systems and space-based lasers, the technology of war-fighting has influenced the nature, scope, and consequences of war. The effects of these technological innovations on a state's conduct during times of war are a fascinating story that has been captured by some observers.[38] More recently, some observers have called attention to yet another **revolution in military affairs** (RMA). The RMA refers to the significant developments in military technology and its application to fighting wars.

Technological changes have created weapons that allow states possessing them to fight wars at a considerable distance from their enemy targets.[39] Precision-guided air-launched and sea-launched weapons make it possible to fight a war without directly engaging with the enemy. While some have argued that these high-tech delivery systems potentially allow wars to be fought in such a way as to minimize the killing of non-combatant civilians, the indiscriminate killing of civilians by such high-tech weapons in Iraq, Afghanistan, Gaza, Lebanon, Pakistan, etc. makes such claims ludicrous. The United States has accumulated significant stores of military capabilities, including nuclear-armed intercontinental ballistic missiles, well-stocked carrier fleets circumnavigating the globe, and an air force that could launch attacks throughout the world without even approaching the airspace of target countries. The continued devotion to new technologies for war-fighting and the development of new weapons systems have challenged the considerable efforts that have been expended in the areas of arms control and disarmament. P.W. Singer has discussed in detail the extent to which robotic armaments have appeared on the battlefield.[40] He also raises the profound ethical issues created by the use of robotics to kill people. Equally complicated are the legal restraints that could be employed. The rapid proliferation of such robotics, the disconnect they create between the operators on one side of the world and the victims on the other side, and the fact that they seem to make it easier for states to transgress the borders of other states raise numerous issues that are not only going to change how wars are fought, but also how they are legitimated.

From State to Human Security

War takes its greatest toll on civilian populations. Most civilian victims do not die from direct acts of violence, but

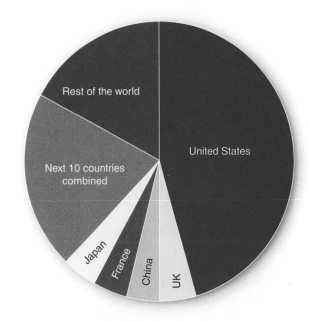

Figure 5.2 Global distribution of military expenditures, 2007.
Source: www.globalissues.org; Stockholm International Peace Research Institute Yearbook, 2008.

from the secondary and tertiary effects of conflict. And often, those many civilians who survive are scarred for life physically and/or psychologically. The human security approach acknowledges that security is a multi-faceted phenomenon that includes not only physical and emotional harm through acts of violence but

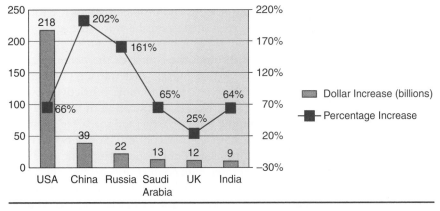

Figure 5.3 Increase in military expenditures, 1998–2007.
Source: www.globalissues.org; SIPRI Military Expenditure Database, Accessed February 2009.

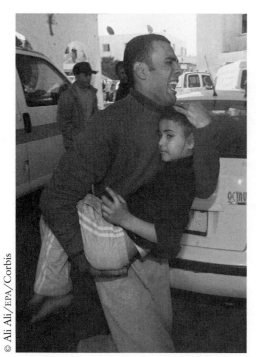

© Ali Ali/EPA/Corbis

A child injured in fighting on the Gaza Strip.

also other forms of harm caused by economic and social vulnerabilities. Human security emerged out of the UN Development Programme and suggested an effort to call attention both to the various insecurities confronting the world's population and to the priority that their alleviation should receive. Human security also developed as a foreign policy paradigm with the potential to serve as a powerful complement to more traditional security concepts in meeting the range of new threats to people and, ultimately, to governments. It took notice of the fact that civilians are the principal victims of the armed conflicts being waged throughout the post-Cold War world. Human security is best seen as a shift in perspective that takes people as the principal point of reference in international affairs.[41]

The human security agenda addresses a range of threats to the safety and security of people. It is fundamentally about putting people first and enhancing our collective ability and capacity to protect human rights and to ensure the essential peace and stability, which is a key prerequisite for sustainable human development. Thus, human security represents one attempt to broaden the security agenda. Indeed, the Commission on Human Security stated in its report that: 'Human security complements state security, furthers human development and enhances human rights. It complements state security by being people-centered and addressing insecurities that have not been considered as state security threats.'[42] In addition, there have been other efforts to broaden the security agenda, for example, by shifting focus from the security of states and nations to the security of the international system as represented in the physical environment and by changing emphasis from military security per se to encompass political, economic, social, environmental, and human security. There also have been debates about shifting the responsibility for security from a state function and from national states up to international governmental organizations (IGOs), down to regional/local organizations, and sideways to non-governmental organizations (NGOs), the market, public opinion, and the media. This more critical security discourse challenges more orthodox views, but also raises many disturbing questions and problems about the sources of insecurity around the globe and the requisite responsibility for managing these insecurities.

Attitudes towards security changed through the course of the twentieth century. The view established in the Concert of Europe that war was a necessary means for ensuring a balance of power began to yield to more restrictive views of war and more encompassing views of security. The culmination of the Cold War conflict between the United States and the Soviet Union (and the latter's demise) brought an end to the overarching threat of a global confrontation between these two nuclear-armed states. Francis Fukuyama was not alone in suggesting that the end of the Cold War meant the end of inter-state conflict. Fukuyama's thesis was that the clash of ideologies had defined global politics during the twentieth century, and now, with liberalism having prevailed over its Fascist and Communist rivals, no further divisions among peoples would lead to conflict.[43] Twenty years later the argument does not sound as reassuring as it did when Fukuyama first proposed it.

As the threat of war between the former Soviet Union and the United States diminished, a number of violent civil conflicts emerged. Prior to 9/11, the most serious in terms of violence were in the former Yugoslavia and in the Great Lakes region of Africa, particularly in Rwanda. These conflicts put to rest any notion that the globe had passed through a period of war into one of a more permanent peace. These conflicts also confirmed that the primary victims of modern warfare, directly or indirectly, are civilian non-combatants. Finally, as Holsti notes, these conflicts demonstrate the new face of war, whereby organized violence against segments of the population are designed as much to terrorize the population as they are to gain control over territory or even resources. Most often, these actions have been used to gain or keep control of political power (e.g., in Sierra Leone, Liberia, Sudan, Somalia).

Many analysts, in the aftermath of the Cold War, have taken the position that the nature of conflict has altered significantly. One view notes that the shift from inter-state to intra-state conflict has become the norm.[44] Others call attention to the apparent prominence of ethnic and state-building factors as sources of conflict in the contemporary system. A shared view among many of these analysts is that the sources, instruments, and manifestations of conflict have become more transnational (less state-centric) and tend to be non-traditional, including such concerns as terrorism, crime, and weapons proliferation.[45] These issues now dominate debate on the nature, scope, and frequency of conflict around the globe. We thus find that contemporary security debates have tended to move away from the more state-centric approaches that dominated most of the discussion of security during the twentieth century and earlier periods. Among the characteristics of this transformation is a conceptual move from securing states to securing human beings, to treating security as a transnational concern rather than as a national matter, and to viewing security in non-military terms.

During the 1990s, human security was adopted as a foreign policy priority by selected institutions, governments, and political leaders. The principle of human security received a vigorous defence from leaders such as the former Czech President Vaclav Havel in a speech to the Canadian Parliament in 1999 and from British Prime Minister Tony Blair in a speech to the Chicago Council on Foreign Relations in 1999. Human security also has become closely associated with regional and international institutions, including the Organization of American States (OAS) and, most especially, the United Nations. Former UN Secretary-General Boutros Boutros-Ghali called for a 'conceptual breakthrough' that would enhance and protect 'the security of people in their homes, jobs and communities'.[46] That breakthrough was championed by his successor, Kofi Annan, who has written that 'individual sovereignty—by which I mean the fundamental freedom of each individual, enshrined in the Charter of the UN and subsequent international treaties—has been enhanced by a renewed and spreading consciousness of individual rights. When we read the Charter today, we are more than ever conscious that its aim is to protect individual human beings, not to protect those who abuse them.'[47] In response to these many concerns, in 2001 the UN launched a commission on human security chaired by Sadako Ogata and Amartya Sen.

Despite the widespread support, defining human security, or determining what governments and advocates of the concept mean when they refer to human security, is a little more problematic. Reviewing the speeches of one of the leading advocates of such a policy, the former Canadian Foreign Minister, Lloyd Axworthy (alongside statements from others, such as Havel and Annan, the Lysøen Declaration, and other documents), reveals a number of key characteristics of the human security agenda. Most importantly, it is a rejection of the primacy that has been given to national/state-based security in the discourse of international politics. It is an attempt to prioritize the individual and to recognize and respond to the multiplicity of threats to the security of individual citizens. Axworthy expands on the idea: 'Human security is much more than the absence of military threat. It includes security against economic privation, an acceptable quality of life, and a guarantee of fundamental human rights.'[48] It entails, then, an explicit challenge to the concept of national security and an implicit charge that some states are not capable of meeting the security needs of their citizens.

Human security initiatives, as applied by most governments and institutions, have tended to focus on security from violence, specifically violence directed at individuals by states or parties to civil conflicts; security from political oppression and violations of political rights; and security from the trade in and effects of illicit drugs. For example, the Canadian–Norwegian Lysøen Declaration of 1998 highlights the following areas of activity: landmines; International Criminal Court; human rights; international humanitarian law; women and children in armed conflict; small arms proliferation; child soldiers; and child labour.[49] As the list demonstrates, less commonly mentioned are references to economic security, the reduction of poverty, and the provision of basic needs, despite the fact that such matters were central to the UN *Human Development Report* of 1994 that emphasized human security. The overwhelming majority of human security initiatives have been reactions to violations of human and political rights and to acts of political violence committed during armed conflicts and/or as a result of criminal activities. Until recently, less attention has been given to what Johan Galtung once described as **structural violence**, the violence against individuals that occurs through economic structures and practices. This, however, may be changing.[50]

Conclusion

Conflict continues to plague global politics in the twenty-first century. Yet, armed conflict in the contemporary period has taken on different forms that some see as a more fundamental change in the way states, and especially civil society actors, conduct their relations with other members of the global community. These changes have been characterized in different ways. Developments during the twentieth century revealed a number of patterns that suggested the declining influence of state-generated laws/norms on the practice of war. Indeed, the very idea of war as it has been traditionally understood in discussions of international relations now seems outdated.

A number of issues have been identified as major security concerns in the contemporary era. In addition to such traditional concerns as shifts in the global balance of power involving the US and China and regional balances of power in the Middle East and South Asia, new concerns have arisen in recent years, including terrorism, weapons of mass destruction, clashes of civilizations, failed and rogue states, and a host of economic conflicts evolving out of globalization and the environmental crisis. During the early months of 2003, as the world watched the American preparations for the armed invasion of Iraq, listened to the increased sabre-rattling emanating from the Korean peninsula over North Korea's development of nuclear weapons, and worried about the next terrorist bombing, the security concern that had the greatest effect on many people was the outbreak of SARS. The threat of SARS emptied airports more quickly and thoroughly than any of these other concerns, demonstrating the extent to which non-military threats to human security had assumed greater prominence. The SARS threat had serious repercussions for airlines and tourism businesses throughout the Pacific Rim. To look at another example, globally, 38 million people are estimated to be living with HIV/AIDS. In 2003, there were approximately 2.9 million deaths as a result of this disease.[51] By 2005 that number rose to 3.1 million deaths per year. In sub-Saharan Africa the HIV/AIDS pandemic has taken more lives and had as much effect on the economies of these countries as the numerous and serious armed conflicts that riddled this world region during the 1990s.[52] The most pressing security issue for many island states is global climate change, in that rising sea levels from the melting of polar ice caps threaten the very existence of some of these entities. Thus, we can frame security issues in many different ways.

It is also important to recognize that states no longer hold a monopoly on the use of force/violence. While it is true that various actors always have been engaged in violence that spills across national borders, states have tended to dominate the battlefields of international history. That has changed in the last few decades, as non-state actors now are increasingly common participants.

As these issues clearly demonstrate, the security concerns of individuals and states have been taken over increasingly by new security threats and new actors using new instruments of violence. These new threats can be distinguished from more traditional ones in a number of ways, which forces us to reconceptualize the nature of security. Threats today are not rooted exclusively in territorially based notions of security or identity. One of the more prominent and problematic threats has been that posed by terrorism, a subject we discuss in more detail in Chapter 13. For many North Americans, terrorism was a minor and ambiguous threat until the attacks on the World Trade Center in New York and on the Pentagon in Arlington, Virginia, brought terrorism to the forefront of North American consciousness. Yet terrorism has been a long-standing concern for many actors in global politics, and prior to 9/11 many North American analysts had identified the increasing threat posed by international terrorism. Just as an increasing number of people believe that the 'War on Terror' is a near-permanent feature of the global landscape, so, too, can we be certain that violence will continue to cause much suffering until effective measures are taken to address the underlying concerns of security and identity that motivate individuals and groups to resort to force in order to resolve their conflicts.

⚬ Key Terms

alliances	common security
anarchic global system	confidence-building measures
anschluss	containment
arms control	co-operative security
arms race	deterrence
balance of power	disarmament
Cold War	expanded security discourse
'collateral damage'	Fascist regimes

interdependence
jus ad bellum
jus in bello
'just war'
multi-polar
Mutual Assured Destruction (MAD)
non-offensive defence

proxy wars
refugees
revolution in military affairs (RMA)
security dilemma
structural violence
zones of peace

Discussion Questions

1. Discuss the different attitudes that have been offered about war and its role in global politics?
2. What is meant by the security dilemma and what is its significance?
3. What is collective security? Is collective security an effective measure for controlling war?
4. What were the principal features of the Cold War?
5. What difference, if any, is there between a bipolar and a multi-polar balance of power?
6. What is deterrence?
7. What is meant by common security; by human security?
8. How has the practice of war changed over time?
9. What are the principal tenets of 'just war' doctrine? Does this doctrine provide an ethical guide for the use of force?
10. Is the effort to control weapons an effective means of limiting war?

Suggested Readings

Clausewitz, Karl von. *On War*. New York: Knopf, 1993. Clausewitz's classic, first published in 1833, remains valuable for its insights on the nature of war, its links with politics, and the conditions under which wars are fought.

Holsti, K.J. *The State, War, and the State of War*. New York: Cambridge University Press, 1996. Holsti provides a broad historical analysis of the causes and consequences of a series of historical conflicts in order to identify changes in the pattern of conflicts and the causes of these conflicts over time.

Kaldor, Mary. *New and Old Wars: Organized Violence in a Global Era*, 2nd edn. Stanford, Calif.: Stanford University Press, 2007. Kaldor examines the state of contemporary conflict, taking note of the shift to non-state combatants fighting with non-traditional methods and forces.

Global Links

Richard Jensen's Web Sources for Military History
tigger.uic.edu/~rjensen/military.html
A very extensive collection of material on different conflicts and different aspects of military history.

Stockholm International Peace Research Institute
web.sipri.org/
   This organization is involved in research and the dissemination of information
   on security, arms control, and disarmament.
International Relations and Security Network
www.isn.ethz.ch/isn
   This international security website based in Switzerland has a strong European
   focus.

⣿ Debate 5

Be it resolved that preparing for war makes war more likely.

Chapter Six

Global Structures: Historical and Contemporary Experiences

Introduction

The structures of global politics both shape and are shaped by ideas, interests, and practices at many levels, including the state, civil society, and regional and international institutions. These structures are not permanent features of the global political scene, though they may be sustained over time. Yet, global structures have a tendency to define how the different levels interact. The structures can be considered the grammar of global politics. In this capacity, they are not immune to change and may experience more turbulence at certain points in time than at others. Often, periods of structural turbulence are coterminous with major wars among the principal powers in the international system. At the very least, they are affected by significant developments in one or more of the following arenas: ideas, material interests, institutions, power distributions, and technological developments.

As we examine the broad landscape of global politics at the present time we encounter many references to a new global order marked by the dominant or hegemonic power of the United States, but also identified by a handful of emerging powers such as Brazil, Russia, India, and China.[1] American imperialism has been widely debated as pundits reflect on the political, economic, and social implications of a situation where the supremacy of American power seems to override all other states. We also see many references to the passing of the Westphalian states system, to a move away from conditions where sovereign states enjoyed relative autonomy and independence.[2] Many observers note the extent to which states have sacrificed their **sovereignty** and have been subjected to various forms of intervention. As we discussed in earlier chapters, realists argue that global politics has always been about power. In this chapter we examine how the sources and distribution of that power influence the character and dimensions of global order. Power, however, is only part of what defines global structures, for we must also consider other factors—ideas, technology, trade patterns, and material and military capability. Examining global structures or world orders is both a theoretical and practical issue. It is also a historical issue as global orders have come and gone and, like in most other areas, history is often our best teacher, in part because it has a tendency of repeating itself.

The historical experience of global structures has been marked by different observers on the basis of what they view as the principal determinants or characteristics of this order. For Adam Watson and other English school theorists, global structures have moved between concentrations of power and more diffuse systems where independence of states has been valued in practice and protected by a diffusion of power.[3] Watson's review of international society, past and present, identifies a spectrum of international arrangements that shift between order and independence: order supports hegemonic and imperial arrangements in the international system; independence supports the more traditional sovereign states system, i.e., the Westphalian states system. For Robert Cox, **modes of production** have played a critical role in defining global structures.[4] James Rosenau emphasizes the prevalence of change over continuity in his assessment of global order. His reading of contemporary patterns of global politics points to a 'historical breakpoint' where 'anomalies are more pervasive than the recurrent patterns and the discontinuities are more prominent than the continuities.'[5] Our task is not to set out a definitive account, but rather to point to the role that different factors have played over time in creating, sustaining, and changing global structures with a view to offering a snapshot of the sources of global order. Michael Mann identifies four sources of power—ideological, economic, technological, and military—that have contributed to global orders.[6] A brief glance into history reveals that what we see as new has been here before.

In 1899 the states, or as they were more commonly (and perhaps accurately) referred to at the time, the 'powers',[7] gathered in The Hague at the invitation of the Russian Czar 'with the object of seeking the most efficacious means for assuring to all peoples the blessing of real and lasting peace, and, above all, in order to put a stop to the progressive development of the present armaments.'[8] The Hague Conference convened as a result of this invitation was, along with the Public International Unions of the late nineteenth century, the foundation on which has been constructed the elaborate network of international organizations that govern so much international activity today. In both the substantive matters under discussion and the activities and interests surrounding the conferences, the Hague meetings that set a path for the states system in the twentieth century seem very familiar to those of us looking at international organizations at the start of the twenty-first century.

For example, Geoffrey Best has written that the meetings at The Hague were 'the first ever occasion on which an intergovernmental, in technical terms a "diplomatic", conference was accompanied by a great show of organized public opinion in its support, not to mention what we now call "media interest".'[9] He quotes the American ambassador's frustration at being badgered by representations from NGOs: 'The queer letters and crankish proposals which come in every day are amazing. . . . It goes without saying that the Quakers are out in full force.... The number of people with plans, schemes, notions, nostrums, whimsies of all sorts, who press upon us and try to take our time, is enormous.'[10] The Hague Conference also had its own parallel summit as 'non-governmental groups organized a parallel salon for diplomats to meet with concerned citizens, [and] various petitions with numerous signatures were submitted to the official conference.'[11] The primary NGO players at the time were representatives of the peace movement, supporters of disarmament, humanitarian organizations such as the International

Committee of the Red Cross, and proponents of women's rights, especially **suf-fragettes**. In addition, there were attempts to devise arbitration mechanisms and international judicial bodies for resolving conflict among states as well as propos-als for limiting weapons and banning those considered to be particularly harmful, specifically the dumdum bullets favoured by the British army in defending the Empire. There was also a great deal of discussion on revising the rules of war.

One of the more perplexing issues surrounded the rights to be accorded to the combatants of a regular army and the non-combatants or ordinary citizens who might be fighting to defend their homeland. The regular soldiers and their leaders looked upon the others as irregulars (or, in an interesting turn of phrase being used by the US government during the 'War on Terror', illegal combatants) and questioned whether they had any rights under the laws of war. It was a conversa-tion that former American cabinet members Colin Powell and Donald Rumsfeld would have recognized. Certainly, the representatives present at The Hague in 1899 would have had something to offer to discussions on American treatment of prisoners captured in Afghanistan and Iraq.

As contemporary observers attempt to comprehend both the nature and impli-cations of globalization, of neo-liberalism, or of American imperialism, some scholars have drawn comparisons between the economic conditions and practices of the late nineteenth and early twentieth centuries and our own time. Accounts of earlier experiences of imperial power, such as Niall Ferguson's *Empire* and John Darwin's *After Tamerlane*, are riddled with events and practices that echo in the contemporary global order. Their research suggests that across various ideational, economic, and political dimensions the world of today is not signifi-cantly different from the way it was during earlier periods. Moreover, anecdotal evidence from earlier periods suggests a great deal of interest and enthusiasm among the civilian population, particularly in Europe, to think and act as global citizens. Much of this activity was accompanied by an expansion of international trade and financial activity, and a great deal of it was facilitated by international organizations.

The unregulated movement of people across national borders during the pass-port-free time of the late nineteenth and early twentieth centuries encouraged globalist views. For example, Craig Murphy quotes John Maynard Keynes, who recalled that a well-off man 'could proceed abroad to foreign quarters, without knowledge of their religion, language or customs, bearing coined wealth upon his person, and would consider himself greatly aggrieved and much surprised at the least interference.'[12] The development of transnational groups was also evident in the growth of international communities of scholars, specialists, and workers, as illustrated in the program of the German Social Democratic Party of 1891 that read: 'With the expansion of world transport and production for the world market, the state of the workers in any one country becomes constantly more dependent upon the state of workers in other countries. The emancipation of the working class is thus a task in which the workers of all civilized countries are concerned in like degree.'[13]

The regular occurrence and popularity of world fairs or exhibitions provide another interesting illustration of the globalist sentiment at the time. It was at the twentieth century's first world fair, in Buffalo, New York, in 1901, that US Presi-dent William McKinley said that 'God and men have linked nations together. No nation can any longer be indifferent to any other.'[14] The next day he was assassi-nated by an **anarchist** (though not for these comments), but his successor shared the same beliefs, if not the same faith. In his first State of the Union address, Theodore Roosevelt declared that 'The increasing interdependence and complexity of international political and economic relations render it incumbent on all civilized and orderly powers to insist on the proper policing of the world.'[15] Global order, or at least internationalism, was not only for civil society; it was also for states, even for the United States, that most isolationist of states in the early part of the last century. These observations serve as an important reminder that events and conditions familiar to our own time and circumstances have occurred before and that there may be lessons in the historical underbrush worth recalling.

Global Order, Globalization, and Globalism

Characterizing the contemporary global order requires a consideration not only of its principal features, but also a comparison of earlier orders and their sources. Two rival versions tend to dominate contemporary discourses of global order. One is globalization, the other hegemony (sometimes labelled 'empire'; see Box 6.1). Global order today is most frequently linked with globalization, a term that has emerged as the most prominent descriptor in discussions on the post-Cold War international system. Though exceedingly popular, the concept and the characterization of globalization are intensely contested and not a little bit confusing as a result.[16]

Jan Aart Scholte, one in a growing list of scholars of globalization, has noted five different usages for the term, each emphasizing different aspects of this

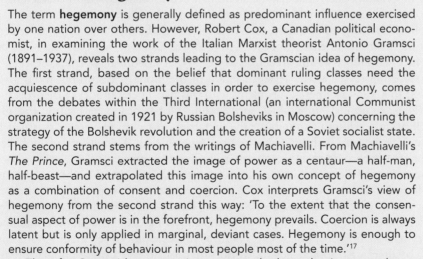

BOX 6.1

Gramsci and Hegemony

The term **hegemony** is generally defined as predominant influence exercised by one nation over others. However, Robert Cox, a Canadian political economist, in examining the work of the Italian Marxist theorist Antonio Gramsci (1891–1937), reveals two strands leading to the Gramscian idea of hegemony. The first strand, based on the belief that dominant ruling classes need the acquiescence of subdominant classes in order to exercise hegemony, comes from the debates within the Third International (an international Communist organization created in 1921 by Russian Bolsheviks in Moscow) concerning the strategy of the Bolshevik revolution and the creation of a Soviet socialist state. The second strand stems from the writings of Machiavelli. From Machiavelli's *The Prince*, Gramsci extracted the image of power as a centaur—a half-man, half-beast—and extrapolated this image into his own concept of hegemony as a combination of consent and coercion. Cox interprets Gramsci's view of hegemony from the second strand this way: 'To the extent that the consensual aspect of power is in the forefront, hegemony prevails. Coercion is always latent but is only applied in marginal, deviant cases. Hegemony is enough to ensure conformity of behaviour in most people most of the time.'[17]

Thus, for Gramsci hegemony is not so much about dominance and control as it is about dominant classes developing an ideological grip over the subdominant classes, not through coercion but through consent and acquiescence. Hegemony, in this sense, is a much more subtle use of power.

phenomenon—internationalization, liberalization, universalization, Westernization, and deterritorialization.[18] Each usage represents a different dimension of the policies and practices that have encouraged analysts and actors to treat global order/globalization as a significant phenomenon.

Global order has been defined in very different ways by academics and other observers. Hedley Bull distinguished between international order and world order. The former he described as 'a pattern of activity that sustains the elementary or primary goals of the society of states'. The latter he referred to as 'those patterns or dispositions of human life that sustain the elementary or primary goals of social life among mankind as a whole'.[19] Indeed, the lack of consensus is quite stark. Some have equated global order with 'globalism'.[20] Ulrich Beck in *What Is Globalization?* defines **globalism** as 'the view that the world market eliminates or supplants political action—that is, the ideology of rule by the world market, the ideology of neoliberalism'.[21] For Beck, globalism is a problem. For others, global order is the path to a more progressive future where **human rights** are protected, greater equality reigns, and peace is guaranteed. Mark Ritchie, for example, draws a distinction between globalization and global order. He defines globalization 'as the process of corporations moving their money, factories and products around the planet at ever more rapid rates of speed in search of cheaper labor and raw materials and governments willing to ignore or abandon consumer, labor and environmental protection laws'—something more akin to Beck's globalism. As an ideology, Ritchie writes, globalization 'is largely unfettered by ethical or moral considerations' whereas global order 'is the belief that we share one fragile planet the survival of which requires mutual respect and careful treatment of the earth and of all its people.'[22] Global order will thus rescue us from the evils of globalization.

For some, global order is neutral in terms of its ideological content and suggests instead a world view that sees the globe as a single unit, more analogous to cosmopolitan beliefs that assume all human beings share common characteristics as consumers or rights holders, as opposed to our different ethnic, religious, or political identities. For others, such as Thomas Friedman, global order describes a world moving ever closer to peace and prosperity, sharing not only Big Macs but democracy and economic freedoms as well. What Friedman applauds, others find threatening or see as the Westernization of the globe, a disturbing trend given what they view as inherent problems with this neo-liberal model of the world.

The definitional ambiguities surrounding global order, globalism, and globalization are found throughout the literature. For example, a report issued by the International Labour Organization reports that 'Definitions of globalization vary according to approach and according to sentiments the word awakes in the definer.'[23] There are no easy exits from these definitional problems, for they reflect normative concerns as much as empirical ones. The problems also reflect the multi-dimensional nature of the issues under study. In considering the presence and effects, not to mention the complexity, of global order in the contemporary scheme of global politics, it is perhaps most helpful to see them as variations of, or alternative approaches to, world order, or, to use a more popular phrase, as alternative forms of global governance. This was how they were presented and debated following World War II when the great powers traded proposals on the framework that would govern the postwar international system. In considering the presence, viability, and desirability of global order and regionalism in the contemporary international system, we must examine these approaches to world order as multi-dimensional phenomena reflecting a plurality of views as to the proper form of global order.

Any particular world order contains a mix of ideas, material interests, political/ institutional relations, and unique distributions of power. While these elements may complement one another, they also may be contradictory or at least move in different directions, especially during periods of transition. The degree of consensus within any one of these elements and the overall convergence or divergence among them tells us a great deal about the viability and stability of any particular global or regional order. It can also tell us about the extent to which an extant world order is undergoing change.

The Ideational Foundation of Global Order

The role of ideas in international relations has received a good deal of attention among contemporary constructivist scholars in the discipline. John Ruggie, among others, has been especially prominent in reinforcing the influence of ideas on international organizations and considerations of global order. Yet even staunch realists such as Henry Kissinger noted the need for ideas or 'vision' to animate American foreign policy in the post-Cold War era. That ideas should and do play such a role is not, however, a new argument, for ideas have always had a prominent place in discussions of world order and international organizations. F.H. Hinsley's excellent survey of European thought and practice around peace and international organizations clearly demonstrates the persistence and influence of ideas in shaping attempts to forge international organizations in the twentieth century.[24] Intellectual histories of the twentieth century also indicate that an ideological convergence, if not exactly a consensus, was instrumental in supporting the efforts to establish the global orders that emerged after both world wars. In both instances this convergence did not embrace all the significant participants, but it was sufficiently robust to support a network of institutions that governed many aspects of international relations. Ideas such as anti-statism, humanitarianism, embedded liberalism, human rights, and anti-militarism have exercised a considerable influence over international organizations in the twentieth century.

One of the issues confronting the contemporary global order is the somewhat shaky ideational foundation for global order. If global order consisted of a single seamless world society it would likely reflect a consensus around certain values, norms, and practices—a common culture. Some maintain that we are already there, or are well on our way, citing shared values/practices such as consumerism, neo-liberalism, human rights, and/or democracy. Others have identified the likely basis for an emergent globalist culture. Authors such as David Held have argued that democratic ideas and practices should serve as the basis for a shift from the modern state to global governance.[25]

Importantly, however, and especially at the elite level, there is not yet any consensus on the main themes/principles/values/practices that should govern the globe. Indeed, a close look at any one of these values and practices reveals that support for them is at best thin, uneven, and unstable. In an essay in which he reviews a number of international reports, Craig Murphy has noted five distinctive views or visions for the contemporary global order. These are: (1) the neo-liberalism of the World Economic Forum (WEF) and the World Trade Organization (WTO) and of Ronald Reagan and Margaret Thatcher and their followers; (2) a 'hard' version of the Third Way liberalism associated with Bill Clinton and Tony Blair, a position shared by the World Bank under James Wolfensohn; (3) a softer version of the Third Way liberalism reflected in the Carnegie Commission on Preventing Deadly Conflict; (4) a global social democratic view exemplified by the reports of the United Nations Development Programme; and (5) an accountable humanitarian view found in the 1999 disasters report of the International Committee of the Red Cross.[26] Murphy argues that each of these views offers a different response to four important questions:

> (1) what are the sources of growing global inequality? (2) to what extent can it be reversed? (3) what connection, if any, does inequality have on the protracted social conflicts that have dominated intergovernmental agendas in recent years and what, if anything, can be done about those conflicts? and (4) to what extent will growing inequality and its consequences thwart the democratic goals that each of these global 'parties' affirm?[27]

These competing views reflect the lack of consensus among elite groups.

A lack of consensus is even more pronounced as one looks towards civil society and considers the numerous challenges to global order/globalization that now proliferate within and constantly surround both global and regional institutional forums.[28] Anti-global order or anti-globalization has been as prominent or even more prominent within the political debate on global order. Many observers have argued that we will not achieve, or should not aspire to, a common global culture. The anti-globalist or anti-globalization movement (discussed in Chapters 10 and 11) reflects a wide array of ideas, some of which are rooted in a desire to protect matters of faith, culture, or national identity. Others express concern about the uneven effects of this process of globalization and argue that whatever has taken place has not touched vast corners of the globe where people still lack the basic necessities of life, not to mention the Internet, cellphones, or access to global financial markets. Many opponents challenge the liberating, democratizing, and equalizing claims of the proponents of globalization. Some fear that it will happen; others fear that it will not and believe that, instead, globalization has done little more than reinforce the positions of those in power, while creating even more inequality and effectively limiting real democracy.

These criticisms cut across the political spectrum, joining linguist and peace activist Noam Chomsky with conservative pundit Pat Buchanan, members of the Taliban with those of the right-wing John Birch Society in the United States, and environmentalists with labour unions, and creating other interesting—though very odd and tenuous—combinations. Such criticisms often reflect strong commitments to nationalism, ethnicity, and religion. They share a common resistance to a unifying global order, a resistance that can manifest (and has manifested) itself in conflict. In many cases this conflict has occurred within cultures, nations, and regions as they seek to determine how they are going to interact with globalist aspirations. In other instances, differing views regarding globalism appear as confrontations between cultures of resistance and the dominant cultures of Western liberal capitalist values, and have a more direct influence on politics at the international level. Thus, in the realm of ideas, global order remains at best an incomplete and highly contested project.

Material Interests and Global Order

Global orders have always been designed to serve economic interests. Murphy's analysis of international organizations, for example, identifies the 'fostering of industry' as one of the primary tasks of international organizations.[29] Many of the most persistent supporters of international organizations have been investors and producers who have grown beyond the territorial borders of the nation-state and sought opportunities to expand their economic practices in the wider regional or global arena. The writings of neo-liberal institutionalists such as Robert Keohane have noted the central significance of material interests in shaping national governments' approaches to co-operation either regionally or globally.[30] Yet, over the long term, the success of international orders, and of the organizations that support them, rests on the ability of industry not only to prosper and thereby sustain a supportive constituency that benefits from these practices, but also to reconcile the dislocations and inequalities that result from the expansion in industrial activity.

Much of the commentary on global order at the present juncture has focused on the apparent fact that the liberal economic practices of the latter half of the twentieth century have created, or at the very least corresponded with, a significant growth in inequality both within and between nations. While some observers argue that the trends have begun to shift and that the income gap has begun to shrink,[31] there is no doubt that the benefits of globalization have been distributed unevenly.[32] For example, most indicators of trade and financial flows demonstrate that the highest concentration of such activity takes place among a relatively small number of national economies in Western Europe, North America, and East Asia. Moreover, the persistence of extreme poverty throughout much of the **global South** presents a potent source of frustration and resentment for those on the margins of the global economy. It also poses a significant challenge for the advocates of a globalized economy.

Patterns of economic globalization reflect a strong regional bias. Flows of trade and investment in the global economy are heavily skewed towards northern states to the neglect of the global South in general and Africa in particular. There are, however, important states that bridge this divide. India, China, and Russia sit on the divide, with expectations that the first two, representing nearly 40 per cent of the world's population, will soon be considered part of the industrialized and post-industrial North. They already account for the overwhelming majority of foreign investment and trade between the North and the South. Such patterns should not cause us to neglect the important differences that exist within the states of both the **global North** and the global South, and in economic developments, including the effects of globalization that have generated new classes of wealth and poverty within states throughout the globe. Significant disruptions in the global financial order since the 1980s also have shaken the material foundations of the neo-liberal economic order. The financial crisis of 2008–9 presents a particularly significant challenge to the principles of unfettered markets and unregulated financial transactions. For some, it suggests the need for a reassertion of the state as the regulator, if not the owner, of major financial institutions and practices. As a consequence of these various factors, the global order project rests on an unsteady foundation because of the shifting patterns of material interests and benefits.

Political/Institutional Dimensions of Global Order

Another element of global order that we need to consider is the political/institutional dimension. In our view, three critical aspects of this dimension need to be considered. One is the issue of global and/or regional institutions and the creation and maintenance of these institutions. A second is the place of the state and, for some analysts, the relevance of the state in this era of globalization. A third issue is the role of civil society in the politics of governance surrounding globalization. A fourth aspect would address the proper relationship among these three. Research suggests a number of identifiable trends along the political/institutional dimension of global order. First is the proliferation of both governmental and, much more significantly, non-governmental organizations (NGOs). The significant growth in the number of intergovernmental organizations (IGOs) has not always been matched by a corresponding growth in the autonomy or influence of these organizations.[33] Some organizations, such as the World Trade Organization (WTO), have laid claim to greater levels of autonomy, while regional organizations, such as the Organization of American States (OAS), remain pretty firmly in the control of their member states. On the other hand, the dramatic proliferation of NGOs or civil society organizations, some have argued, has been accompanied by an increase in their influence and effectiveness.[34] There is no question that the activities of such groups and their participation in the politics of global governance have increased dramatically in recent decades.[35]

Many observers also have noted a significant growth in the relative influence of private regulatory authorities influencing both private- and public-sector activities. As Murphy writes:

> What is really new about global governance in the last decade is neither a shift in power from states to global intergovernmental organizations nor the kind of explosion of international conventions in which a change in quantity (the number of new regimes) has meant a change in quality (the locus or nature of global power). Yet there has been a fundamentally new development: global-level private authorities that regulate both states and much of transnational economic and social life.[36]

The late international relations scholar Susan Strange once referred to this as 'the retreat of the state'.[37] This change, however, may more clearly demonstrate the emergence of multiple centres of power at the national, regional, and international levels.

Regardless of these developments, the state remains a prominent actor. We should not discount the significant expansion that has occurred in the state's involvement in civil society and the economy through taxation, regulation, and the setting of standards. Indeed, one of the more interesting yet understated results of the terrorist attacks on the United States in September 2001 was the dramatic and significant shift to reassert the state's role in everything from border controls to airport security. As one commentator explains:

> Today's world is increasingly populated and enormously affected by non-state and cross-state entities of many kinds, but these changes have not enabled us to escape the necessity of relying upon states, singly and collectively, to manage the process of global governance. In the real world, the function of international organizations is to serve as a vehicle, not a substitute, for collective action by states to promote order and justice.[38]

While states, and especially powerful states, retain considerable freedom of action in the policy realm, many states have had their sovereignty, capacity, and autonomy severely compromised by the regulatory practices of IGOs. 'It is an irony...that the autonomy and capacity of states have come to be doubted just when most of the world's people for the first time live in democracies (generously defined)....If there is a power shift that now disfavours the state, what is the remaining significance of democratic government? Can states any longer govern? Can globalization be democratized?'[39] In addition to falling under the influence of international institutions, some states have also been exposed to more direct forms of intervention. Intervention into the domestic affairs of sovereign states has increased dramatically in both the economic and political realms, and these interventions are supported and implemented increasingly by NGOs and IGOs.

Among the factors shaping global order has been the widely noted shift towards neo-liberal economic practices, or what a century ago was called **laissez-faire**. This shift can be noted within different national economies and in international institutions such as the International Monetary Fund (IMF) and the Bank for International Settlements (BIS). The influence of these neo-liberal ideas within governments and IGOs is also evident in their promulgation by a number of intellectuals: the economic interventionist views of John Maynard Keynes were replaced by the espousal of unfettered markets championed by Milton Friedman and Friedrich Hayek as the ideology of choice by the late 1970s. In some areas, private interests and agents have taken precedence over public ones in areas as diverse as health care, education, development assistance, and security. It also is reflected in the strengthened position of private interests, again within both national and international circles. Neo-liberal economic practices have had a dramatic influence on the role of the state and the perception of the state's role, both in its own national setting and on the world stage. Whether such ideas persist will be an important indicator of the emergence of a different global order.

As mentioned earlier, in the view of observers such as Susan Strange, the contemporary period is defined by the 'retreat of the state' as private interests ranging from corporations to drug dealers move in to fill the void. The era of **embedded liberalism** gave way to a more classical form of liberalism, shifting both discourse and practice. John Ruggie, among others, has noted the importance of these values in shaping social purpose and the longer-term significance of these changes: 'Because social purposes reflect configurations of state–society relations, it suggests that the foremost force for discontinuity at present is not "the new protectionism" in money and trade, which is most feared by observers today. Rather, it is the threat posed to embeddedness by the resurgent ethos of neo laissez-faire.'[40] In addition, these neo-liberal ideas and practices have influenced the process and especially the content of global governance at the regional and international levels. While this is most prevalent within international financial institutions, it has influenced other institutions as well. At the UN, for example, officials are more frequently looking to the private sector to deliver assistance and security to war-torn countries and even to improve the global regime of human rights through better corporate practices.

At the same time that the state was retreating from more direct involvement in managing the domestic and international economies, its legitimacy has been challenged by a second phenomenon, the growing influence of liberal ideas on human rights and human security. International concern and activity in the area of human rights are not a recent phenomenon. Though we have seen a great deal of attention directed to matters of human rights and human security since the 1980s, human rights have animated governments, IGOs, and NGOs for more than a century. The late twentieth century, however, witnessed a return to these liberal themes and a renewed emphasis on individual/human security that continues today, although 9/11 and its aftermath tended for a while to still these concerns. The international status of human rights has been recognized in such documents as the UN's Universal Declaration of Human Rights and the final act of the Commission on Security and Cooperation in Europe (CSCE), the Helsinki Accords of 1975. The status of individual rights and human security also has been asserted by some Western governments, including Canada's, since the end of the Cold War.[41] This, in turn, has led to demands for a more interventionist program of action to protect human rights in foreign societies by international and regional organizations through means such as **military humanitarianism** and the **Responsibility to Protect (R2P)**.[42]

These two themes of neo-liberalism and human security, while supported by different and often oppositional camps, have a significant influence on policy debates and share some common liberal characteristics. A cursory review of the various instruments used to support neo-liberalism, on the one hand, and human security, on the other, reveals a wide and diverse range, including everything from aerial bombardment, economic sanctions, and the creation of norms to the provision of technical, financial, and military assistance. A variety of actors have been involved in the process, including national governments, international and regional organizations, NGOs, and even individuals whose influence and power derive from celebrity and/or wealth, such as Bono, Warren Buffett, George Clooney, Bill Gates, Bob Geldof, Carlos Slim Helú, Angelina Jolie, George Soros, and Ted Turner. The mix of different instruments and actors has created what Emma Rothschild has described as 'problems of psychosocial and political incoherence'.[43] Advocates of neo-liberalism and human security, while at times critical of each other's practices, in different ways have sought to empower NGOs and international institutions as the principal agents for implementing reforms that they favour. States are simply not suited to serve the menu of neo-liberalism. Nor are states always effective in meeting the needs of human security.

These views reflect a persistent pattern within many quarters that challenges the legitimacy and capacity of states. As Ngaire Woods has written:

> Indeed, in the 1980s and in the early 1990s, scholars began a full-fledged assault on state-centered international politics based on sovereignty. Since that time, new rationales for intervention and expanded conditionalities have been opened up, the increased participation of nongovernmental organizations (NGOs) has been encouraged, and concepts of 'global civil society' have been developed. There has been a tendency, in other words, to move away from state-centered views of international relations and toward a more global approach. As regards international organizations, however, the tendency to dismiss sovereignty as anachronistic and illegitimate needs a further rethinking.[44]

At the very least, there are severe limitations on the legitimacy, credibility, and capacity of both non-governmental organizations and international institutions to implement reforms. Among these are the legitimacy, credibility, and accountability of the various agencies that have been empowered to provide human security.

These emerging patterns of global governance suggest the possibility of a more fundamental and long-term change in its processes, institutions, and objectives. One result of these practices has been to transform international and regional institutions into agents of a selective and dominant world view. While this was perhaps less of a leap of faith for the IMF and its Bretton Woods siblings (see Box 6.2), it marked a more significant shift for the UN and its affiliated agencies

BOX 6.2

The Bretton Woods System

After the devastating effects of the global economic crisis of the 1930s, attributed in large measure to the pursuit of nationalistic beggar-thy-neighbour policies, a conference of 45 sovereign states (44 allied nations and Argentina—a neutral nation during World War II) was held in 1944 at the Mount Washington Hotel in Bretton Woods, New Hampshire. This conference created a multilateral system that would regulate and govern the post-World War II economic system and try to prevent a repeat of global economic depression. This was the first time in history that states were able to negotiate a financial and monetary multilateral order to govern the currency relations among sovereign states. The multilateral system created was named after the small resort village in New Hampshire—Bretton Woods.

The Bretton Woods system is in reality an attempt at the institutionalization of international monetary co-operation. In essence, it is a regime (norms, principles, rules, and decision-making procedures around which entities cohere in a specific issue area). This system, or regime, while encouraging co-operation, nevertheless adhered to the principles of state sovereignty. However, unlike some other international organizations, the Bretton Woods system allocated voting rights in relation to quotas, rather than on the basis of one nation, one vote. As a result, wealthier countries in the Bretton Woods system have more voting power than less wealthy countries.

The Bretton Woods agreements signed by the 45 states in New Hampshire in July 1944 resulted in the establishment of the International Monetary Fund (IMF) and the World Bank Group comprised of five organizations: the International Bank for Reconstruction and Development (IBRD), the International Development Association (IDA), the International Finance Corporation (IFC), the Multilateral Investment Guarantee Agency (MIGA), and the International Centre for Settlement of Investment Disputes (ICSID). The IBRD was given the mandate of financing postwar reconstruction, while the IMF was intended to stabilize exchange rates between the currencies of the states and to be a 'lender of last resort' for countries experiencing economic difficulties.

Provision was also made at the New Hampshire conference for the creation of an International Trade Organization (ITO). But when the US Senate refused to ratify the ITO Charter, the Bretton Woods system was left with a General Agreement on Tariffs and Trade (GATT), a temporary multilateral agreement designed to provide a framework of rules and a forum to negotiate trade barrier reductions among nations. This trade regime was built on the Reciprocal Trade Agreements Act, which allowed the US executive branch to negotiate trade agreements with temporary authority from the Congress. By the late 1980s an increasing number of nations felt that the GATT could better facilitate global trade expansion if it became a formal international organization. In 1988 the US Congress passed the Omnibus Trade and Competitiveness Act, which called for more effective dispute settlement mechanisms. This led to the creation of the World Trade Organization (WTO) during the Uruguay Round (1986–93) of GATT negotiations. The WTO has now subsumed the GATT and provides a permanent arena for member governments to address international trade issues.

Under the Bretton Woods system, the US dollar was pegged to gold and all other currencies were pegged to the US dollar. But with the huge amount of money flowing out of the US as a result of the Marshall Plan (a plan designed to rebuild Western European countries devastated by World War II and to repel communism), US defence spending, and the purchase of foreign goods by Americans, the amount of US dollars in circulation quickly exceeded the amount of gold used to back the US dollar. In the 1960s, an ounce of gold could be exchanged in London for about US$40, while that same amount of gold in the US was priced at US$35. Clearly, the US dollar was overvalued and investors picked up on this rather quickly.

A Yale University economist, Robert Triffin, thought he had a solution to the problem. He suggested to the US Congress that the US should reduce the number of dollars in circulation by cutting the deficit and raising interest rates to attract dollars back into the United States. Both strategies, however, pulled the US economy into a recession in the 1960s. By August 1971, US President Richard Nixon declared that the US dollar could no longer be exchanged for gold. This policy prescription was dubbed the 'Nixon shock', and Nixon's unilateral announcement dealt a fatal blow to the Bretton Woods system.

and for regional organizations such as the OAS. It also has led to a very different view of these institutions than that which existed in the immediate post-1945 period. David Kennedy has argued that one of the more significant effects of these changes has been to remove much of the politics from debates about global governance. Formal institutions and legal regulatory regimes replace the discourse and activism associated with political debate and deliberation.

> Internationalists are used to thinking that we have a robust international political order with only the thinnest layer of law. But the reverse is more accurate—we have a robust process of global law and 'governance' without a corresponding strong global political order. Real government is about the political contestation of distribution and justice. Governing an international or global order means making choices among groups.... Development policy means preferring these investors to those, these public officials to those, not the technocratic extension of a neutral 'best practice.' To make these choices we need a world which is open to a politics of identity, to struggles over affiliation and distribution among the conflicting and intersecting patterns of group identity in the newly opened international regime.[45]

Military Dimensions of Global Order

The military dimension of globalization is perhaps less commonly addressed than some of these other dimensions, but as others have noted, the distribution of coercive or military power provides a critically important foundation for whatever form of international order emerges. While major wars between the states of the North now seem to be a thing of the past, the last decade has experienced considerable violence. Moreover, the 9/11 terrorist attacks and the thwarted attempt by a Nigerian youth to blow up Northwest flight 253 near Detroit on Christmas Day 2009 provide a startling reminder of the continuing significance, albeit under changed conditions, of national security. Here, too, there have been some significant changes, two of which help to define global order at the present juncture. One is the changing character of warfare; the second is the hegemonic position of the United States and its increasing use of military force. The effect of these changes was seen in the first days of the Gulf War in 1991.

Fifteen hours before the first attacks on Baghdad on 16 January 1991, seven B-52 bombers left Barksdale Air Force Base in Louisiana. They followed a course over the eastern United States, then across the North Atlantic, over the Mediterranean, and through Egyptian and Saudi Arabian airspace. Without entering into Iraqi airspace they launched nearly three dozen cruise missiles aimed at eight different sites in Iraq. Raid completed, they turned around and flew home—35 hours and 14,000 miles later they landed back at Barksdale Air Force Base having completed the longest air raid in history.

The air raid carries interest at a number of levels, the technical and the military-strategic being among the more noteworthy. However, it is also worth reflecting on the political implications of this act. The United States did not need to send B-52s from the continental US to Iraq. It had forces pre-positioned in Saudi Arabia and aircraft carriers scattered throughout the region. Yet, by launching this air raid the American government demonstrated to itself, and anyone else who was watching, that it had the capacity to project its power at will around the globe. This also marked the beginning of a dramatic shift in how war would be waged, at least for a period of time and at least as it involved the United States.

From the round-trip bombing raid that launched the Gulf War in January 1991 to the air wars during the 1990s against Iraq and Kosovo, and since 2001 in its attacks against Afghanistan and Iraq, there were repeated demonstrations of the American military's ability to project its forces across the globe. At the same time, American practices during this period suggest an uncertain degree of commitment to supporting world order and a strong preference for unilateral approaches over multilateral ones. Krauthammer reflects the spirit of this approach when he writes: 'The essence of unilateralism is that we do not allow others, no matter how well meaning, to deter us from pursuing the fundamental security interests of the United States and the free world.'[46]

When combined with the increased technical sophistication of cruise missiles, these developments now make it possible for the United States (and, by tacit approval, many of its allies) to conduct what Michael Ignatieff has described as a 'virtual war'. Ignatieff and others have raised concerns about the unconventional nature of conventional war in the future. Among the considerations discussed (and considered in greater detail in the previous chapter) are that the source of war is non-territorial; the means of war are technological not personal, and the victims of war are civilian not military. As Ignatieff has discussed, one of the dangers of these developments and the increased use of these technologies that separate the warriors from their counterparts and their victims is that they tend to cloud the warriors and the warriors' fellow citizens from the ends and consequences of their actions. Ignatieff writes:

> Virtual reality is seductive. We see ourselves as noble warriors and our enemies as despicable tyrants. We see war as a surgical scalpel and not a bloodstained sword. In so doing we mis-describe ourselves as we mis-describe the instruments of death. We need to stay away from such fables of self-righteous invulnerability. Only then can we get our hands dirty. Only then can we do what is right.[47]

Related to this has been a certain disconnect between the use of the military for purposes of intervention and the national security interests of intervening states.

As David Kennedy has noted, 'During the Cold War, military interventions and proxy wars were hard wired to the central problem of global security. Now they float more freely into limited police actions, humanitarian gestures, and stabilization at the periphery.'[48] As a result, he argues, such interventions are often seen as options and the result is an inconsistent and uneven response on the part of states to using military force to protect others.[49] We thus find that both the asymmetries of war-fighting capability and the technologies of war-fighting have changed the manner in which states think about using military force as an instrument of policy. The hubris inherent in such war-fighting also only widens the divide between the technologically superior, who fight their antiseptic wars far from their own shores, and those, chiefly civilians, who suffer the consequences in the far-off lands of the global South. During the Iraq War, for example, some of the 'shock and awe' was distributed by a Stealth bomber from a base in Missouri, with the crew back home the next day, after a non-stop round-tripper, in time for family barbecues and Little League games.

Empires Past and Present

Much of the contemporary debate on global order has been focused on the hegemonic position of the United States and its explicit, and repeatedly cited, attempts to secure supremacy among the world's powers. The omnipotence of American power is supported by a number of indicators. The US spends more than all of the other major countries combined on defence, but this represents only 4 per cent of its gross national product (GNP). The US economy is larger than the next three national economies combined. The United States has only 5 per cent of the world's population, but 43 per cent of the world's production, 40 per cent of the world's technology production, and 50 per cent of the world's research and development (R&D). In addition to what Paul Kennedy referred to as an unprecedented concentration of power, the United States under the George W. Bush administration embarked on a plan to use this power to shape the globe in accordance with its interests.[50] For example, in a speech at West Point, President Bush said that the American strategy should be to 'keep military strengths beyond challenge, thereby making the destabilizing arms races of other eras pointless.'[51] Or, to use the words of the often noted Project for a New American Century, 'to accept responsibility for America's unique role in preserving and extending an international order friendly to our security, our prosperity and our principles.'[52]

The accumulation of power was part of a shift to a more unilateralist policy. For example, the turn away from established institutions such as the UN and NATO to what are described as 'coalitions of the willing' suggested that the US no longer sees a need for broad-based material or political (institutional) support for policy initiatives. The willingness to proceed with military action against first Afghanistan and later Iraq, in the absence of a coalition that would provide extensive military resources, demonstrated a preference on the part of the Bush administration for acting alone and a belief that these additional resources are unnecessary for success. These actions implied an abandonment of the hegemonic policies pursued by the US during much of the Cold War, when the United States assumed a comparable leadership role but actively sought the assistance of other states and institutions in support of that role. Current US President Barack Obama appears to be moving the US back to that multilateralist position.

In the aftermath of the criminal attack by a couple dozen terrorists on the symbols of American economic and military power and the tragic death of nearly 3,000 people, commentators rushed to extrapolate from these sad events and proclaimed a total shift in global politics with a variety of phrases—the 'world will never be the same'; 'everything is now changed'; 'we live in a new world'; and 'forget everything that has happened before; we are now in a new era.' The penchant for hyperbole tended to overlook much of the surrounding reality. It represented, in the words of Stanley Hoffmann, 'a misleading interpretation of a horrible event'.[53]

There have been a few noteworthy developments that owe their appearance to the attacks of 11 September 2001, but even more noteworthy have been the persistence and further entrenchment of patterns and practices that were in motion before that day. Thus, despite the common view that the attacks of 9/11 were a defining moment that fundamentally altered the international political and strategic environment, it would seem more accurate to argue that the attacks merely reinforced, confirmed, or rationalized paths that already had been chosen. On balance, it would be difficult to dispute Kenneth Waltz's contention that 'Fighting terrorists provided a cover that has enabled the Bush administration to do what it wanted to do anyway.'[54] Nonetheless, it is important to reflect on possible changes that were instigated or accelerated by this tragic event and we will come back to them later.

In the immediate aftermath of the Cold War, then American President George H.W. Bush displayed an interest in developing multilateral coalitions to support American foreign policy objectives. The coalition of states pulled together at the time of the Gulf War, along with the UN Security Council's sanctioning of military force by this coalition, is reflective of this. In the early months of the Clinton administration there was also much talk among his national security advisers of American support for multilateralism—**assertive multilateralism**. Such comments have re-emerged under the new Obama administration. This modest degree of support for multilateral consultations and institutions has often been superseded by a more unilateralist approach in recent years. While there were indicators of this during the Clinton administration, perhaps most blatantly displayed in Presidential Decision Directive (PDD) 25,[55] in the immediate aftermath of 9/11 there were signals that the American response might serve as an opportunity to restore American commitment to multilateralism, much in the same way President Roosevelt tied American power to multilateral institutions. In the early months of his administration, however, George W. Bush had displayed a blatant and almost contemptuous disregard for various multilateral agreements such as the anti-personnel landmines treaty, the Kyoto Accord, and the International Criminal Court (ICC). In the summer of 2001, Charles Krauthammer described the spirit of the new administration: 'The new unilateralism seeks to strengthen American power and unashamedly deploy it on behalf of self-defined global ends.'[56] When terrorist attacks jolted the post-Cold War complacency of the US and its closest allies, the Bush administration's pattern of rejecting and criticizing international co-operation temporarily yielded to an apparent recognition of the need for multilateral co-operation.[57] The member governments of NATO, for the first time in the history of the alliance, had invoked Article 5, which states that an attack against any member is an attack against all members, and the editor of *Le Monde* declared 'we are all Americans now.' The United States received an outpouring of support from around the globe. Moreover, in response to the 9/11 attacks, governments from all corners of the globe committed themselves to the fight against terrorism. In this atmosphere, it would seem unnecessary for the American President to lay down the threat that 'you

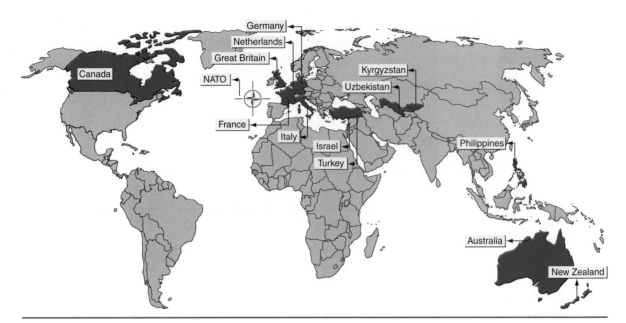

Figure 6.1 The US coalition against Al-Qaeda.

are either with us or against us', when much of the world had already signed the pledge. But the threat was issued and the flirtation with multilateralism began to wane rather quickly—as did the extent to which we were all Americans.

In addition to the American unilateralist approach for addressing international issues, more direct challenges from Washington arose to international institutions, international law, and international agreements. There were, for example, critical rejections of various international agreements on biological weapons investigations, anti-personnel landmines, climate change, the rights of the child, and the ICC, among others. Equally indicative of the general disdain for international agreements and multilateral processes were decisions taken with respect to steel and agricultural products and the administration's decision to proceed with the development (and eventual deployment) of missile defence systems, low-yield nuclear weapons, and a possible return to nuclear testing. How much such practices reflected the temptation of imperial ambitions on the part of a sole superpower and how much were the result of the predilections of a particular president and his coterie of advisers, time will tell. Many of the statements made by members of the Obama administration's foreign policy group, however, indicated a change in direction.

All of this discussion of American practice not only raises the issue of empire, it also points to other considerations in thinking about global order. One is the ongoing need for active American engagement. A second is the importance of institutional arrangements such as international law and organizations. A third is the degree of consensus among states and other agents necessary to support global order. A fourth consideration is how to reconcile empires, like the United States, with the loss of sovereignty that many international agreements involve. There has been an ever-expanding web of international treaties, conventions, and institutions that seek to bind states to norms and practices that are determined through multilateral processes and the compromises that such processes involve.

The preponderance of American power makes multilateral institutions an unnecessary burden on, and/or barrier to, the conduct of American foreign policy. Multilateral commitments and processes constrain unilateral action, and the imperial powers need no longer worry about bringing others under the constraints of international law because they have the necessary will and capabilities to enforce their own view of that law, if and when necessary. Yet, are such imperial practices still possible in our globalized world? This imperial response may stand as an exception to the more general pattern of global politics at the beginning of the twenty-first century. In the ensuing chapters we will examine the manner in which the institutions and practices of global governance have responded to this challenge.

In responding to these developments, international organizations are being challenged in terms of their legitimacy and their effectiveness. This challenge takes two forms. At the global level, state-based institutions are being challenged by non-state actors and domestic lobbies—raising broad issues of global democracy. The democratic governance agenda translates into questions about the very foundations of world order and the place of sovereignty within it. At a more modest level, the legitimacy of international institutions is being contested by states that feel inadequately consulted or represented within these multilateral organizations. The old hierarchy of states within multilateral forums is being challenged and their effectiveness and legitimacy questioned by smaller or weaker states. Here, the good governance agenda can be applied to prescribe greater participation, accountability, and fairness among states within organizations.[58]

For some states, **regionalism** emerges as a response to the fading consensus in support of global governance. In fact, Shepard Forman has asserted that 'the world may be heading toward an interregnum in the trend toward globalism, a period in which regionalism and sub-regionalism will be the organising principle for multilateral action.'[59] Indeed, regionalism may provide places in which viable alternative orders might be created and sustained, as well as offer points of mediation between the global and the local. The uneven degree of integration into the global economy/society may actually help make such regional options more important in the twenty-first century.

In addition, under emerging practices of global governance, international and regional institutions are assuming increased responsibility for the security and welfare of individuals in various parts of the world. This alters the context in which states must operate. It limits or, at the very least, questions their legitimacy, at the same time as states have been encouraged to adopt more democratic forms of domestic government. These practices also are expanding the responsibility of the institutions through which global governance is being conducted. It often appears, however, that the aspirations for these institutions to act are not always in line with the political will and the concomitant resource contributions of member governments. To date, many IGOs and NGOs have demonstrated a lack of capacity to provide welfare and security to people in need. Not only do they not have the necessary resources to make a difference, but they often lack the interest, the political will, the legitimacy, and the long-term commitment. As well, they lack the knowledge and/or the ability to solve many problems, despite the underlying assumptions that all problems are solvable with the proper mixture of international norms, legal mechanisms, institutional arrangements, military force, and political will.

Conclusion

The patterns of activity in each of the dimensions discussed in this chapter suggest a considerable amount of instability in the contemporary global order. Poverty, but perhaps more importantly inequality; the spread in transnational diseases; the pervasiveness of transnational crime; environmental limits to consumption; turmoil in global financial markets; terrorism; and the proliferation of small arms and weapons of mass destruction: all present formidable threats to global order. These threats are not easily countered—the invading armies and aggressive nations of the past could, to some degree, be defended against. Support for global order is also uneven. Among supporters of globalization there is disagreement over the form and content of this global order. Dissenters, of which there are many, also lack a common platform from which they can articulate a unified response to the public and private promoters of continued American **suzerainty** or economic liberalization. The politics of global order more commonly have been in transition than they have been stagnant or stable. It would be premature to attempt to predict the outcome of the debates and conflicts that now dominate the global political economy.

Thus, one of the considerations in the advocacy and activity surrounding new approaches to global governance is the tendency to assume that institutions possess the capacity and will to act. Yet, the capacity of global institutions is, at best, a limited one, influenced by competing interests, shifting material resources and power, and the uneven commitment of supporters. Even the best IGOs and NGOs encounter donor fatigue and a flagging of volunteer spirit. To raise expectations beyond what one is prepared or able to deliver might create a 'false sense of security' and thereby prevent the pursuit or acceptance of a less ambitious alternative. It also might severely undermine the long-term support for specific extant institutions and, more importantly, for the very process of multilateralism itself. As one embarks on a campaign for global governance one must be sensitive to the limits of both ends and means.[60]

Key Terms

anarchist
assertive multilateralism
embedded liberalism
globalism
global North
global South
hegemony
human rights

laissez-faire
military humanitarianism
modes of production
regionalism
Responsibility to Protect (R2P)
sovereignty
suffragettes
suzerainty

Discussion Questions

1. What features define global orders?
2. What are the principal features of the contemporary global order?
3. What significance do you think ideas have had in shaping global order?

4. How have ideas influenced the contemporary global order?
5. Do you think hegemony is necessary for global order? How can global order be established in the absence of hegemony?
6. What are 'historical breakpoints'?
7. What role does military power play in shaping global order?
8. Has the role of military power changed over time? Is it more or less important today?
9. What is an empire?
10. Do you think the United States represents a contemporary empire?

Suggested Readings

Cox, Robert. *Production, Power, and World Order*. New York: Columbia University Press, 1987. Cox provides an analysis that links different modes of production with different forms of world order in a manner that seeks to account for historical change.

Jones, Dorothy. *Code of Peace: Ethics and Security in the World of the Warlord States*. Chicago: University of Chicago Press, 1994. Jones surveys the origins and evolution of the more prominent procedural and substantive norms that have come to define the modern states system.

Mann, Michael. *The Sources of Social Power*. New York: Cambridge University Press, 1986. A sociologist's analysis of the critical role that power plays in shaping both local and global societies.

Global Links

Internet Modern History Sourcebook
www.fordham.edu/halsall/mod/modsbook.html
A comprehensive site from Fordham University that covers many aspects of historical change and transformation, from pop culture to nationalism to military conflicts.

National Intelligence Council
www.dni.gov/nic/NIC_home.html
US government site that engages in over-the-horizon thinking on global issues with reports projecting out to 2020 and 2025.

The Bretton Woods Institutions: Evolution, Reform, and Change
www.reformwatch.net/fitxers/88.pdf
A paper written by Jon-Il You for the fiftieth anniversary of the founding of the Bretton Woods institutions that critically examines the structural changes needed if these institutions are to be relevant to the twenty-first century.

Debate 6

Be it resolved that military power is of declining importance in the contemporary global order.

Chapter Seven

Changes to the Institutions of Global Order since 1945: The UN System

Introduction

As we noted in the previous chapter, the foundational elements of any historical structure of global order are ideas, material capability, and institutions. Observing the shifts and changes within multilateral institutions is of particular importance to understanding how global politics is, or is not, changing. This chapter is concerned with some of the significant changes that have occurred in the UN system, the most universal of international institutions, since the end of World War II and the founding of the United Nations. The post-Cold War period, marked by the intensification of globalization and a new world disorder, has triggered an intense and growing interest not only in the UN system but also in governance at all levels.

While the UN is a clear example of international governance (since it is an organization created to facilitate the interactions of states), its post-Cold War history unveils a characteristic that can be labelled 'embryonic global governance' (in that the UN system has begun to take on challenges of state and non-state actors alike). Indeed, Margaret Karns and Karen Mingst go so far as to suggest that the UN has become 'the centrepiece of global governance'.[1] This should not be too much of a surprise. After all, international institutions are not decisions frozen in time. These bodies can change if the environment within which they operate changes and if they are pressured to adapt by forces operating within them.

Brief History of the Founding of the United Nations

It was amid the smouldering ashes of World War II that the institutional foundation of the postwar global order was laid. In August 1941, just months before the US entered that war, American President Franklin D. Roosevelt joined with British Prime Minister Winston Churchill to establish what became known as the Atlantic Charter. This charter formed the basis for the Declaration of the United Nations, which was signed on 1 January 1942 in San Francisco by some

26 governments who had pledged to continue their fight against the **Axis powers**. In essence, the declaration was an attempt to introduce a permanent system for ensuring general global security once the war was over. The victorious **Allied nations** were envisioned to be at the centre of this new system, which, in effect, constituted the institutionalization of world order at that juncture. In fact, the representatives of China (Taiwan), the Soviet Union, the United Kingdom (UK), and the United States (US) had worked out proposals for the new organization at Dumbarton Oaks, a mansion in the Georgetown section of Washington, DC, between August and October 1944.

However, in San Francisco, on 25 April 1945, two weeks before Roosevelt's death, 50 countries met at the United Nations Conference on International Organization to draft the United Nations Charter. The UN system was initiated with the signing of the Charter (26 June 1945) by those 50 states. Poland, which was not present at the founding, later signed the Charter to become one of the original 51 member states of this organization. The founders promised that this new organization would not be a house of cards, like its ill-fated predecessor, the League of Nations, but rather a stable and authoritative base for global tranquility and a mechanism for preserving international peace and security. The UN was officially ushered into existence on 24 October 1945 when the Charter was ratified by the majority of signatories.[2] This explains why 'UN Day' is celebrated on this date.

The United Nations was a significant improvement on the League. Based on its Charter, the UN promised to be a much more powerful and effective organization than the League of Nations.[3] Its primary mission was 'to save succeeding generations from the scourge of war' (Article 1, UN Charter). Whereas the Covenant of the League made no provision for that organization to be involved in direct military action, the UN Charter envisioned a military staff committee to oversee military enforcement of resolutions passed by its apex body—the Security Council. While the Covenant had contemplated decisions by unanimity, the Charter pictured a majority capable of binding all UN members, and in some cases non-members, to its determinations.

The UN's 51 original members saw this **intergovernmental organization** (IGO) as being at the centre of global multilateral diplomacy in the aftermath of World War II. Its main objectives, according to the UN Charter, included: maintaining international peace and security; developing friendly relations among nations; addressing the economic, social, cultural, and humanitarian problems that the world would face; and promoting respect for human rights. The Charter commits all UN member states to eschew violence and embrace peace.

Unlike the previous experimentations with intergovernmental organization, the UN is truly universal. Its membership has risen from 51 (1945) to 192 (2009)—due in large part to decolonization, **self-determination**, and the post-Cold War breakup of countries like the Soviet Union and Yugoslavia. (Appendix 1 to this chapter lists the UN member states.) In theory, any sovereign state can become a UN member. The UN has a super-bureaucratic structure[4] consisting of six principal organs—the General Assembly, the Security Council, the Economic and Social Council (ECOSOC), the Secretariat, the International Court of Justice (ICJ), and the Trusteeship Council. These sub-organs form an umbrella under which can be found main and sessional committees, standing committees, advisory bodies, offices, subsidiary organs, specialized agencies, functional and regional commissions, expert and ad hoc bodies, **peacekeeping** and peace support operations, and a number of autonomous but related organizations.

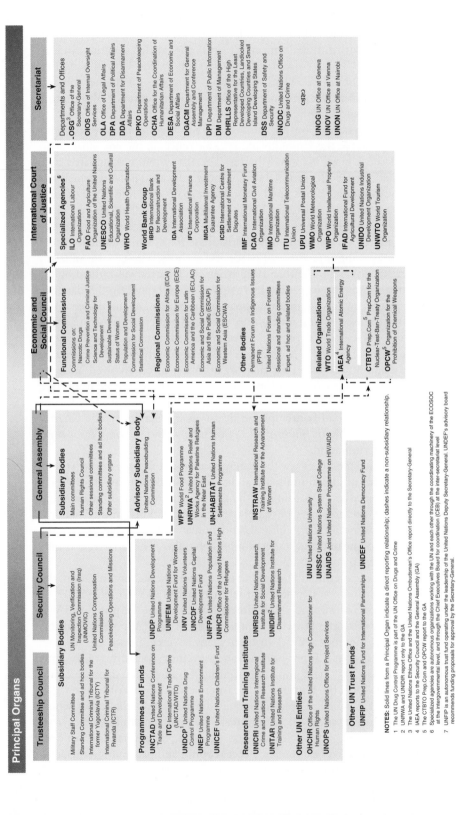

Figure 7.1 The United Nations system.
Source: The United Nations

General Assembly

The General Assembly is the main deliberative organ of the UN and operates like a parliament or congress. This plenary body is composed of representatives of all 192 member states, each of which has one vote. Apart from providing organizational oversight, the General Assembly functions as a forum for all states and lends collective legitimacy to the norms, rules, and actions of the international community. Decisions on important issues, such as peace and security, the election of the Secretary-General, admission of new members, and budgetary matters, require a two-thirds majority in that body. Decisions on other questions and procedural matters are taken by simple majority. Chapter IV of the UN Charter sets out the de jure functions of this principal organ. Those functions are:

- To consider and make recommendations on general principles of co-operation for maintaining international peace and security, including disarmament.
- To discuss questions relating to international peace and security and, except where a dispute or situation is currently being discussed by the Security Council, to make recommendations on them.
- To discuss, with the same exception, and make recommendations on all questions that are within the scope of the Charter or that affect the powers and functions of any UN organ.
- To initiate studies and make recommendations that promote international political co-operation, the development and codification of international law, the realization of human rights and fundamental freedoms, and international collaboration on economic, social, humanitarian, cultural, educational, and health matters.
- To make recommendations for the peaceful settlement of disputes that could impair friendly relations among nations.
- To receive and consider reports from the Security Council and other UN organs.
- To consider and approve the UN budget and establish the financial assessments/contributions of member states.
- To elect the non-permanent members of the Security Council and the members of other UN councils and organs and, on the recommendation of the Security Council, to appoint the Secretary-General.

In November 1950, when there was a stalemate in the Security Council over whether UN action should be taken in the Korean conflict, the General Assembly passed a 'Uniting for Peace' resolution (Resolution 377 [V]) that, from then on, has allowed it to take action in cases threatening the global peace whenever the Security Council fails to act. Because of that resolution, the Assembly is allowed to consider such matters immediately and recommend to its members collective action in order to maintain or restore international peace and security.[5] General Assembly resolutions are considered expressions of general global norms and principles, which often form the basis for 'hard' international law. Those resolutions best approximate, or reflect, the views and wishes of the 'international community'.

At a Summit in 2000, the Assembly passed a landmark 'Millennium Declaration' that commits all member states to reach specific goals, e.g., to attain peace, security, and disarmament along with socio-economic development and the eradication of poverty, the protection of our common environment, meeting the special needs of Africa, instituting good governance and democracy worldwide, and strengthening the UN's organizational capacity. World leaders present at that Summit pledged to meet those Millennium Development Goals by 2015 (Table 7.1). Progress towards meeting the goals is being monitored by a UN Development Group.[6]

Table 7.1 Millennium Development Goals of 2000, To Be Achieved by 2015

HALVE EXTREME POVERTY AND HUNGER

1.2 billion people still live on less than $1 a day. But 43 countries, with more than 60 per cent of the world's people, have already met or are on track to meet the goal of cutting hunger in half by 2015.

ACHIEVE UNIVERSAL PRIMARY EDUCATION

113 million children do not attend school, but this goal is within reach; India, for example, should have 95 per cent of its children in school by 2005.

EMPOWER WOMEN AND PROMOTE EQUALITY BETWEEN WOMEN AND MEN

Two-thirds of the world's illiterates are women, and 80 per cent of its refugees are women and children. Since the 1997 Microcredit Summit, progress has been made in reaching and empowering poor women, nearly 19 million in 2000 alone. These women have benefited from learning how to utilize microfinance.

REDUCE UNDER-FIVE MORTALITY BY TWO-THIRDS

11 million young children die every year, but that number is down from 15 million in 1980.

REDUCE MATERNAL MORTALITY BY THREE-QUARTERS

In the developing world, the risk of dying in childbirth is one in 48. But virtually all countries now have safe motherhood programs and are poised for progress.

REVERSE THE SPREAD OF DISEASES, ESPECIALLY HIV/AIDS AND MALARIA

Killer diseases have erased a generation of development gains. Countries like Brazil, Senegal, Thailand, and Uganda have shown that we can stop HIV in its tracks.

ENSURE ENVIRONMENTAL SUSTAINABILITY

More than one billion people still lack access to safe drinking water; however, during the 1990s, nearly one billion people gained access to safe water and as many achieved better sanitation.

CREATE A GLOBAL PARTNERSHIP FOR DEVELOPMENT, WITH TARGETS FOR AID, TRADE, AND DEBT RELIEF

Too many developing countries are spending more on debt service than on social services. New aid commitments made in the first half of 2002 alone, though, will reach an additional $12 billion per year by 2006.

Sources: UN Department of Public Information, 2002; Susy Cheston and Lisa Khun, 'Empowering Women through Microfinance', at: <www.microcreditsummit.org/papers/empowering_final.doc>.

Under the General Assembly's supervision are subsidiary bodies, which include main committees, the new Human Rights Council, sessional committees, standing committees, and ad hoc bodies. A number of programs, funds, research institutes, and offices also operate under the Assembly's auspices; among other things, these are responsible for refugees, human settlement, development, equality for women, the advancement of women, protection of the environment, emergency food distribution, the global population crisis, trade, children, transnational crime, the HIV/AIDS epidemic, disarmament research, capital development, project services, elections and democratic processes, and education and training. These subsidiary bodies play an important role in addressing specific functional needs of the UN member states and of the international community as a whole.

The Security Council

When the UN founders conceived of the Security Council, they wanted to ensure that this body would be more efficient and effective than the League of Nations' Council. Consequently, they created a limited membership executive body, small in size but relatively representative of the UN membership at the time. Furthermore, to increase the chance of efficiency and effectiveness, the Council's membership is divided into two: five permanent members (the P5), reflective of the global power structure of 1945, and 10 non-permanent members elected on a two-year rotational basis. The P5 members are: the People's Republic of China,[7] France, Russia,[8] the United States, and the United Kingdom. The P5 states have veto power on all substantive resolutions put before the Council. The rationale for this was to ensure that the major powers would always have a say on all major decisions of the Council; this gave them an incentive to stay within the UN organization rather than challenge it from outside.

The 10 non-permanent members are elected by the General Assembly to serve two-year terms, and are not eligible for immediate re-election when the two-year term is over. In electing the non-permanent members, the Assembly is instructed to pay special regard to the contribution of these members to the maintenance of international peace and security and other purposes of the UN, and also to equitable geographical representation. In 1963, the General Assembly passed resolution 1991A (XVIII), which stated that the 10 non-permanent members should be elected according to the following criteria: five from African and Asian states; one from Eastern European states; two from Latin American and Caribbean states; and two from Western European and other states. Each Council member has one vote, and decisions on procedural matters are reached when nine out of 15 members vote in the affirmative. Decisions on substantive matters also require nine affirmative votes, but this must include the concurring votes of all five permanent members. This great power unanimity is referred to as 'the veto'. The presidency of the Council rotates among Council members monthly, based on the English-language alphabetical order of member-countries' names.

The Security Council, although formally equal to other UN principal organs, is in fact the apex body of the organization and bears primary responsibility for maintaining international peace and security.[9] It has evolved into the UN's most powerful forum. It is organized so as to be able to function continuously. To do so, a representative of each of its 15 members must be present at all times at UN headquarters in New York. When the Council hears a complaint concerning a threat to the peace, its first action is to recommend that the conflicting parties

Table 7.2 Non-Permanent Members of the UN Security Council, and Date When Term Expires

Austria (2010)

Bosnia and Herzegovina (2011)

Brazil (2011)

Gabon (2011)

Japan (2010)

Lebanon (2011)

Mexico (2010)

Nigeria (2011)

Turkey (2010)

Uganda (2010)

Source: <www.un.org/sc/members.asp>. (15 Jan. 2010)

try to reach agreement using peaceful means. In some cases, the Council will undertake its own investigation of the matter or offer **mediation** services to the parties involved. In other cases, it may appoint special representatives or request the Secretary-General to do so or to use his **good offices**. In all cases, the Council will suggest principles for peaceful settlement of disputes to dissipate a potential threat to international peace and security.

In the case where a dispute leads to fighting, the Council's first concern is to end the violence as quickly as possible. This may mean issuing **ceasefire** directives, which can prevent widening the hostilities, or establishing a UN peacekeeping force to help reduce tensions in troubled areas, to keep opposing forces apart, and to create conditions of temporary calm so that disputants can be brought to the bargaining table. In certain instances the Council has no choice but to authorize enforcement measures—e.g., **economic sanctions** (such as trade **embargoes**), arms embargoes, or collective military action. A member state against which an enforcement measure is taken may be suspended by the General Assembly from exercising the rights and privileges of its membership. Any member state that persistently violates UN Charter principles may be expelled from the organization by the Assembly, upon the Council's recommendation, although since its inception no state has been suspended or expelled from the UN.

Any UN member that is not a member of the Security Council has the right to participate (without a vote) in Council discussions if that country's interests are in any way affected. Both UN members and non-members, if they are parties to a dispute brought to the Council, may be invited to take part, without a vote, in the Council's deliberations; however, the Council will set conditions for non-member participation.[10]

The Security Council's history can be roughly divided into two periods: (1) the Cold War era, and (2) the **post-Cold War era**.[11] During the Cold War, the Council's work was stymied primarily because of excessive use of the veto. As a result, it became marginalized as a global collective security body. However, innovations allowed the Security Council to become engaged in peacekeeping missions designed to keep warring factions apart long enough for dispute settlement and mediation efforts to take hold. Since the end of the Cold War, the Council's workload has increased exponentially.[12] Beginning with its bold move to offer a settlement plan for the Iran–Iraq War in 1987, and with the thawing of the ideological war between the superpowers by 1989, the Council began to operate as was intended by the UN Charter. Since that time, the veto has been used sparingly. The P5 were actually able to agree on the use of 'collective security' to beat back the aggression of Saddam Hussein when he ordered 100,000 Iraqi soldiers, backed by about 700 tanks, to invade Kuwait in August 1990.[13]

During the immediate post-Cold War period, with the structural and ideological underpinnings of **superpower conflict** dissipating, the major security threat faced by the globe during the Cold War—the Mutual Assured Destruction (MAD) of nuclear war between the Soviets and Americans—was lessened. But the end of the precarious balance of power between the two superpowers created a climate of uncertainty with a rise in the number of civil conflicts and the spread of internecine violence in such places as Afghanistan, the Democratic Republic of the Congo (DRC), Rwanda, Somalia, Sudan, and the former Yugoslavia. In the aftermath of the collapse of the Soviet Union, by 2004 there had been approximately 93 conflicts around the world in which 5.5 million people were killed—75 per cent of whom were civilians.[14] Almost all of these were intra-state conflicts, which in part explains the disproportionate number of civilian casualties. The UN Security Council had to adapt in order to deal with this new reality.

On 31 January 1992, the first summit meeting of the Council was convened at UN headquarters in New York and attended by heads of state and government of 13 of its 15 members, and by the ministers for foreign affairs of the remaining two.[15] That summit confirmed the extent to which the Council had adapted and had begun to influence global politics in ways that it could not during the Cold War era. As David Malone notes, one of the ways in which the UN Security Council affected the nature of global politics was through its decisions, which tended to be 'largely improvised and inconsistent'. Nevertheless, some of those decisions helped to 'erode the foundations of absolute conceptions of state sovereignty' as defined in the UN Charter under Article 2(7). This modification of the concept of state sovereignty, influenced in part by reports like that of the Commission on Global Governance,[16] has altered 'the way in which many see the relationship between state and citizens' today.[17] It also has demonstrated that the UN Security Council has, to some extent, embraced the norms of human rights and human security. For instance, on several occasions since the end of the Cold War the Council has used Chapter VII of the UN Charter to intervene in the internal affairs of states to protect innocent civilians at risk.

The Council's interventions have gone beyond military operations and expanded (second- or third-generation) peacekeeping activity.[18] In some cases, it has assisted countries torn apart by civil conflicts to build peace within their civil societies through the development of liberal democratic governance practices. The UN Security Council has actually been at the centre of this activity in places like Croatia (Eastern Slavonia, Baranja, and Western Sirmium); Western Sahara; Namibia; Angola; El Salvador; Eritrea; Haiti; Mozambique; Nicaragua; South Africa; and Liberia.[19] In certain instances, the Council has experimented with inserting an interim administration when a state's government apparatus is no longer functioning (e.g., Cambodia in 1992). In other cases, the Council has been working hard on a number of important issues:

- to eliminate the practice of child soldier recruitment;[20]
- to authorize humanitarian interventions;[21]
- to implement **smart sanctions** and arms embargoes;[22]
- to deal with the proliferation of small arms and light weapons;[23]
- to increase the level of women's engagement in the political life of countries;[24]
- to shore up failing states and rebuild **failed states**;[25]
- to set up disarmament, demobilization, and rehabilitation processes in post-conflict settings.[26]

The post-Cold War agenda of the Security Council also has been forced to tackle the serious problem of global terrorism on a case-by-case basis. For instance, after the bombing of a Pan American jet over Lockerbie, Scotland, the Council reacted in a punitive manner by imposing sanctions on Libya, using Chapter VII of the UN Charter. These sanctions forced the Libyan government to release the terrorist suspected of carrying out this dastardly deed. Similarly, when Al-Qaeda terrorists bombed the US embassies in Kenya and Tanzania in 1998, the Council responded by condemning the bombings and imposing severe sanctions on the Taliban government in Afghanistan, which had given safe haven to Al-Qaeda and its leader, Osama bin Laden. As we show later in the book, the terrorist attacks on the US on 11 September 2001 resulted in a swift response from the Security Council. Invoking Chapter VII of the Charter, the Council called on all UN member states to take extensive national actions to 'prevent and suppress the financing of terrorist acts' and to prevent terrorists from using their territories to plan and carry out such acts. The Council also created a Counter-Terrorism Committee (CTC) and a Counter Terrorism Executive Directorate (CTED) to work not only with states but also with regional organizations in developing counter-terrorism programs.

From the above it is clear that the UN Security Council's role has been evolving particularly since the end of the Cold War to deal with issues affecting both states and civil society (the state–society complex). It has not been averse to collaborating with the many other agencies of the UN system, regional organizations, and non-governmental bodies to get the job done.

The Economic and Social Council (ECOSOC)

Part of the Dumbarton Oaks proposals of 1944 called for the UN to encourage economic and social co-operation. The UN's role in this area was to be part of the operations of a wider international machinery that included the Bretton Woods system (see Chapter 6).[27] At Dumbarton

Shen Hong/Xinhua/Landov

An ECOSOC meeting at the UN headquarters in New York City.

Oaks the UN founders recognized explicitly the link between peace and security and socio-economic well-being. The proposals crafted there called for the creation of an economic and social council (ECOSOC) that would be a subsidiary body of the General Assembly. ECOSOC emerged as one of the UN's principal organs, with a mandate in two areas: economic and social matters and human rights.[28]

However, ECOSOC has never been at the centre of global economic and social policy-making, as some UN observers had hoped. The weighted voting arrangements in the Bretton Woods institutions made those bodies a more appealing

Table 7.3 Membership in the Economic and Social Council for 2010 and the Expiration Date of Membership

Argentina (2012)	Morocco (2011)
Bahamas (2012)	Mozambique (2010)
Bangladesh (2012)	Namibia (2011)
Belgium (2012)	New Zealand (2010)
Brazil (2010)	Niger (2010)
Cameroon (2010)	Norway (2010)
Canada (2012)	Pakistan (2010)
Chile (2012)	Peru (2011)
China (2010)	Philippines (2012)
Comoros (2012)	Poland (2010)
Congo (2010)	Portugal (2011)
Cote d'Ivoire (2011)	Republic of Korea (2010)
Egypt (2012)	Republic of Moldova (2010)
Estonia (2011)	Russian Federation (2010)
France (2011)	Rwanda (2012)
Germany (2011)	Saint Kitts and Nevis (2011)
Ghana (2012)	Saint Lucia (2010)
Greece (2011)	Saudi Arabia (2011)
Guatemala (2011)	Slovakia (2012)
Guinea-Bissau (2011)	Sweden (2010)
India (2011)	Ukraine (2012)
Iraq (2012)	United Kingdom of Great Britain and
Italy (2012)	North Ireland (2010)
Japan (2011)	United States of America (2012)
Liechtenstein (2011)	Uruguay (2010)
Malaysia (2010)	Venezuela (Bolivarian Republic of) (2011)
Mauritius (2011)	Zambia (2012)
Mongolia (2012)	

Source: <www.un.org/ecosoc/about/members.shtml>. (15 Jan. 2010)

place for the major powers to exert their influence. Instead, ECOSOC plays a co-ordinating and oversight role with respect to a number of autonomous specialized agencies and subsidiary bodies that work under the UN umbrella. They include: the International Atomic Energy Agency (IAEA), the International Labour Organization (ILO), the Food and Agriculture Organization (FAO), the United Nations Educational, Scientific and Cultural Organization (UNESCO), the World Health Organization (WHO), the International Civil Aviation Organization (ICAO), the Universal Postal Union (UPU), the International Telecommunications Union (ITU), the World Meteorological Organization (WMO), the International Maritime Organization (IMO), the World Intellectual Property Organization (WIPO), the International Fund for Agricultural Development (IFAD), and the United Nations Industrial Development Organization (UNIDO). These specialized agencies have a direct reporting relationship to ECOSOC. (Web addresses and other information on these agencies and organizations are listed in Appendix 2 to this chapter.)

Under ECOSOC are also functional commissions responsible for addressing such issues as social development, human rights, narcotic drugs, science and technology for development, sustainable development, status of women, population and development, and demographic and other statistics. The regional Economic Commissions for Africa, Europe, Latin America and the Caribbean, Asia and the Pacific, and Western Asia all report to ECOSOC as well. One should note that ECOSOC has a mandate to involve NGOs in its work (see Article 71 of the UN Charter). As such, it has been instrumental in bridging the gap between the **state-centric world** of international relations and the multi-centric world of global politics.[29]

While the Bretton Woods institutions are generally considered 'sister institutions' of the UN, they operate loosely under the umbrella of the UN system and have an indirect relationship with ECOSOC. Technically, they are considered specialized agencies of the UN. There is no question that both the International Monetary Fund (IMF) and the World Bank Group affect the social and economic planning done within the UN system. They set economic parameters that are followed by UN agencies responsible for development assistance. Yet, the working relationship between the Bretton Woods system and the rest of the UN is loose and tenuous. There is very little co-ordination between those bodies and the UN system as a whole. Indeed, the financing and governance structure of the Bretton Woods organizations ensures their relative autonomy. Unlike the UN, the World Bank and the IMF do not depend solely on their members for financial and operational survival. As noted in Chapter 6, the voting system in the Bretton Woods organizations is also different. Instead of one state, one vote, the IMF and the World Bank have instituted a system of weighted voting. Under that system the US has 17 per cent of the vote in the IMF, whereas India, for instance, with more than three times the population of the US, has 1.9 per cent.

While serious criticisms and demonstrations have been directed at the Bretton Woods institutions, especially from anti-globalization movements (see Chapter 10), for their unaccountable and undemocratic character as well as the strict conditionality attached to the assistance they provide to poor countries, it is important to acknowledge the contribution these organizations are making to post-conflict **peacebuilding** and reconstruction. Recently, in the wake of conflicts in Iraq, Afghanistan, Bosnia-Herzegovina, and the West Bank and Gaza, the IMF and the World Bank have co-ordinated aid delivery, conducted needs assessments, audited aid and assistance efforts, and advised on post-conflict economic policy.[30] This new role is bringing the Bretton Woods institutions into a closer relationship with the UN system.

International Court of Justice (ICJ)

The International Court of Justice, or the World Court, was established as the principal judicial organ of the UN system. Its statute is an integral part of the UN Charter and all UN member states are ipso facto parties to that statute. Learning from the experience of the earlier established Permanent Court of Arbitration (PCA) and the Permanent Court of International Justice (PCIJ), the UN founders decided it was best to make the ICJ an integral part of the UN. The Court has 15 judges, no two of whom are from the same nation-state. The justices of the ICJ are elected by the General Assembly and the Security Council for nine-year terms. The ICJ deals with both contentious and advisory cases brought to it by UN members. But Article 36 of the ICJ statute allows state parties to decide whether or not to give the Court blanket jurisdiction over their disputes. States can accept the rulings of the Court but declare specific reservations. In other words, states usually voluntarily consent to the ICJ's jurisdiction and decisions on a case-by-case basis.

Since the ICJ only hears a few cases each year, some observers consider it an ineffective mechanism of international adjudication and a marginal player when it comes to settling international disputes and preserving international peace and security. However, the ICJ does exert some influence on these matters through its advisory opinions.[31] For instance, in 2003 the UN General Assembly asked the Court to provide an advisory opinion on the legality of the wall being built by Israel in the occupied Palestinian territories. A year later, the Court ruled that construction of this barrier constituted a violation of international law and that it impinged on the human rights of Palestinian people living in the occupied territories. While Israel does not respect this ruling, the advisory opinion helps to give moral and legal weight to the arguments being put forward by those who oppose the construction of this wall.

Trusteeship Council

The Trusteeship Council is, for all intents and purposes, a defunct body. It was created in 1945 to oversee the transition of colonial territories into self-governing states. Chapters XII and XIII of the UN Charter define its mandate. These territories were held under the League of Nations' mandates system (see Box 7.1). The last of the Trust Territories, Palau, gained independence in 1994. Since then, the Trusteeship Council has not been operative. During the 2005 World Summit at the UN, heads of state agreed to wind down the operations of the Trusteeship Council. However, there is now discussion about whether it might not make sense to revive this body under a new mandate, i.e., to assist 'failed states' in getting back on their feet. In such cases, the Trusteeship Council could be responsible for the administrative functioning of those states in which domestic governing mechanisms have collapsed (failed states) until such a time as a local government can be put in place.[32] Thus, the idea of international trusteeship through the UN is still very much afloat, even though the existing Trusteeship Council is nothing more than a defunct body.

The Secretariat

The UN Secretariat can be considered an independent international civil service.[33] The idea for such a service was first floated by Sir Eric Drummond, the first Secretary-General of the League of Nations. Drummond's concept was taken into

BOX 7.1

The League of Nations Mandate System

Once World War I was over, the victorious Allies decided not to appropriate for themselves the colonies of their defeated enemies. Instead, they asked the League of Nations to supervise and administer those territories belonging to imperial Germany and the Ottoman Empire that could not function as independent states. The League created three types of mandates for the administration of these territories by nations acting as 'Mandatories of the League of Nations'. The first type of mandates covered territories considered almost ready to become independent: Iraq, Palestine, and Transjordan, which were to be administered by the UK; and Lebanon and Syria, to be administered by France. The second type of mandates referred to territories for which the granting of independence was considered unlikely in the near term. All of those territories were in Africa: the Cameroons and Togoland, each divided between British and French administration; Tanganyika, placed under British administration; and Ruanda-Urundi, placed under Belgian administration. The third type was reserved for those territories with virtually no prospect of self-government, let alone independence. These included South West Africa, which was to be administered by the Union of South Africa; New Guinea, to be administered by Australia; Western Samoa, to be administered by New Zealand; Nauru, to be administered by Australia under mandate of the British Empire; and a number of Pacific islands that would be administered by Japan.

What the mandates system implied was an acknowledgement by colonial powers that people living under these mandates would at some point be given the right to become independent sovereign states, once they reached a sufficiently advanced stage of development. Yet, no provision in the League Covenant specified what the 'mandatories' would have to do to prepare the administered mandated territories for eventual self-determination.

consideration in the formulation of proposals for the UN Secretariat back in 1944, but the Soviet Union strongly objected to the notion of an independent UN Secretariat. It favoured, instead, an intergovernmental secretariat in which staff members would represent national views. The Soviet position was ultimately rejected by the rest of the UN's membership. Indeed, the UN Charter makes it clear that staff shall not seek or receive instructions from any authority other than the UN. The staff members of the Secretariat are supposed to be recruited based on criteria of efficiency, competence, integrity, and geographical diversity. However, there have been some cases in which those qualities were not strictly followed in the hiring of UN staff.[34]

The Secretary-General, as the chief administrative officer of the UN, heads and oversees the Secretariat. Since its founding, there have been eight UN secretaries-general (see Table 7.4). The Executive Office of the Secretary-General is largely responsible for the day-to-day management of the UN system, including the management of the seemingly perpetual efforts at reforming the institution. To address the issue of 'deadwood' within the Secretariat, the UN has been moving increasingly away from permanent contracts for its staff to short-term contracts (of up to a maximum of six months) and fixed-term contracts (renewable up to a maximum of five years). This move is strongly resisted by the UN staff union,

Table 7.4 UN Secretaries-General: Nationality and Term of Office

Trygve Lie	Norway	1946–52
Dag Hammarskjöld	Sweden	1953–61
U Thant	Burma (Myanmar)	1961–71
Kurt Waldheim	Austria	1972–81
Javier Pérez de Cuéllar	Peru	1982–91
Boutros Boutros-Ghali	Egypt	1992–6
Kofi Annan	Ghana	1997–2006
Ban Ki-Moon	South Korea	2007–

Source: <www.un.org/sg/formersgs.shtml>. (30 July 2007)

concerned that phasing out permanent contracts will simply make it easier to terminate UN employees.

Since 1974 there has been an International Civil Service Commission (ICSC) whose 15 members make recommendations to the UN Secretary-General and the General Assembly regarding salaries and conditions of employment of staff in the professional or higher categories. Secretariat salary scales are determined in accordance with the Noblemaire principles[35] and in comparison with US federal civil service salaries to ensure that well-qualified individuals will be attracted to positions within the worldwide UN system. If a UN staff member wishes to seek remedies for an injustice done, that individual can take the case to the Joint Appeals Board and Panel, the Panel of Counsel, the Administrative Law Unit, the Joint Disciplinary Committees, or the Administrative Tribunal. An Office of the Ombudsman in the Secretariat was created to reduce the resort to the Appeals Board, and the Office of Internal Oversight Services has, from time to time, conducted management reviews of the appeals process.

A position of Deputy Secretary-General was created in 1997 by the General Assembly as part of the UN institutional reform effort. The purpose of this post is to help manage Secretariat operations and ensure coherence of activities and programs. A secondary goal is to elevate the organization's profile and leadership in the economic and social spheres. Canadian-born Louise Fréchette was the first person appointed to that position. She assumed the post on 2 March 1998 and remained until 31 March 2006. Fréchette was followed by Mark Malloch Brown of Britain, and then by Asha-Rose Migiro of Tanzania.

The Multi-faceted Goals of the UN

While the Charter emphasizes the maintenance of international peace and security as the primary goal of the UN, it goes beyond that to list other important goals, such as:

* developing friendly relations among nations based on respect for the principle of equal rights and self-determination of peoples;

- achieving international co-operation in solving global socio-economic, cultural, and humanitarian problems;
- encouraging and promoting respect for human rights and for fundamental freedoms for all;
- becoming the centre for harmonizing the actions of nations in order to attain the above common ends.

Collectively, then, the principal organs of the UN system, along with the specialized agencies, programs, funds, commissions, offices, committees, and peacekeeping and other peace operations, all combine to address almost every conceivable transnational or global issue, and demonstrate the dual task of the world body: to maintain international peace and security while ensuring social and economic development.

Over the years since 1945, the UN has grown in size and mandate. Its Charter goals were extended to include protecting the global commons and encouraging democratization across the globe. As shown earlier, one must add to these the recent goal of countering terrorism reflected in the UN Security Council's resolution 1373, passed on the 28 September 2001 in response to the 11 September 2001 attacks on the US. That resolution also established a Counter-Terrorism Committee (the CTC) made up of all 15 members of the UN Security Council. The CTC monitors the extent to which all states are implementing resolution 1373 and promises to improve the capability of states to fight terrorism. To attain its numerous and multi-faceted goals, the UN system has evolved into a complex bureaucracy.

The UN proper employs 35,000 people in approximately 600 offices worldwide, of whom 14,500 are at the New York headquarters and a further 4,000 work at the UN's European centres in Geneva and Vienna. Together with its various specialized agencies and affiliated bodies, the UN family has just over 64,000 employees. The World Bank is the largest specialized agency with 10,000 employees, followed by the World Health Organization (WHO) with 4,000. Statistically, there is one employee in the UN system for every 100,000 people in the world.

The United Nations had an appropriated regular budget of US$4.19 billion for the biennial period of 2008–9. The budget of the specialized agencies over the same period amounted to US$2.3 billion. Voluntary contributions to aid agencies and related UN organs, as well as the special budgets for financing peacekeeping operations, grew significantly to an estimated US$5.5 billion for the budget year 2007. By comparison, the budget of the European Union (EU) amounted to €116.4 billion for the year 2007, reflecting perhaps a higher degree of regional integration in Europe. According to Article 19 of the UN Charter: 'A Member of the United Nations which is in arrears in the payment of its financial contributions to the Organization shall have no vote in the General Assembly if the amount of its arrears equals or exceeds the amount of the contributions due from it for the preceding two full years.' In July 2007, seven countries fell into this category: Central African Republic; Comoros; Guinea-Bissau; Liberia; São Tomé and Principe; Somalia; and Tajikistan. As noted in Box 5.5, however, at the end of August 2008 total arrears to the UN regular budget were over $900 million, with the United States owing 92 per cent of this total.[36] In June 2009, President Obama signed legislation to erase all US debts to the UN.

The UN Approach to Managing and Suppressing Conflicts

The world body is expected, *inter alia*, to maintain international peace and security, to take effective collective measures for the prevention and removal of threats to the peace, and to suppress acts of aggression or other breaches of the peace. Through its many organs the UN strives to resolve conflicts by peaceful means and in conformity with principles of justice and international law. It has adopted two distinct strategies for dealing with threats to the peace. The first is a reactive strategy. When there is a threat to the peace, certain instruments are available to the organization to manage the conflict by suppressing it (e.g., through collective security arrangements), by separating the warring parties (e.g., through mediation and peacekeeping efforts), or by using peaceful means to bring an end to the conflict (e.g., through diplomacy, **peacemaking**, **arbitration**, etc.). The second is a proactive strategy that searches out the underlying reasons for conflict and attempts to address those before an actual conflict breaks out. The instruments used for the latter include international law, disarmament, deterrence, **preventive diplomacy**, **preventive deployment**, and peace-building.[37]

Prevention

The UN Charter provides for the world body to deal with actual threats to international security in two ways. Article 33 of the Charter states that 'the parties to any dispute, the continuance of which is likely to endanger the maintenance of international peace and security, shall, first of all, seek a solution by negotiation, enquiry, mediation, conciliation, arbitration, judicial settlement, resort to regional agencies or arrangements, or other peaceful means of their own choice.' In other words, peaceful and diplomatic ways ought to be tried first to resolve the problem.[38] The UN experimented with many of these instruments with some success in conflicts in the Suez (1956–67), in Gaza and the West Bank (during the 1950s), in Lebanon and Jordan (1958), and in Laos and the Congo (1961) during the tenure of UN Secretary-General Dag Hammarskjöld. When peaceful measures fail, then the UN can resort to sanctions (both economic and military).

Diplomacy and the Secretary-General's Good Offices

Boudreau has pointed to the importance of the role of the UN Secretary-General in identifying early incipient conflicts and in using the good offices of that position to try and resolve them.[39] This hinges, of course, on the ability of the Secretary-General's office to anticipate, ascertain, and analyze any potential or actual threat to international security. Information-gathering and early warning are central to this preventive diplomatic instrument. The absence of a reliable early warning system in the UN means that the organization continues to react to conflicts after they have erupted rather than anticipate them at the incipient stage. Yet, there have been several successes in UN diplomacy, especially through the office of the Secretary-General.

For instance, the UN played a significant mediation role in the almost decade-long conflict between Iran and Iraq. Secretary-General Javier Pérez de Cuéllar brokered a ceasefire in 1988 between the two warring parties. Similarly, the

Secretary-General's office facilitated the withdrawal of occupying Soviet forces from Afghanistan in the late 1980s. The 1991 Paris agreement that brought relative peace to Cambodia was made possible because of the activist role played by the UN Secretary-General. The result was the end of almost 15 years of conflict in that country. The UN Secretary-General also played a major role in the Central American peace process that led to the Esquipulas II Agreement in 1989. In some cases, the Secretary-General has appointed a Special Representative of his office to oversee mediation efforts. For instance, the general peace agreement that was signed in 1992 in Mozambique by RENAMO (Resistëncia Nacional Moçambicana) and FRELIMO (Frente de Libertação de Moçambique) was implemented with the assistance of the UN Secretary-General's Special Representative, Aldo Ajello.

Clearly, the UN has made important contributions to international security through the Secretary-General's good offices and the mediation efforts of individual secretaries-general and their subordinates. The role of the Secretary-General certainly has evolved through practice, and especially in response to the pressures of globalization and the post-Cold War environment.[40] However, success in this area depends on the qualities and characteristics of the Secretary-General in office at the time and that individual's willingness to use the full weight of the office to end disputes. Some secretaries-general, perhaps most notably Dag Hammarskjöld, have been activist peacemakers (Hammarskjöld died in a plane crash in Africa while brokering the end of conflict in the Congo); others, such as Kurt Waldheim, have acted more as bureaucratic administrators; and still others, of perhaps a more scholarly bent (e.g., Boutros Boutros-Ghali), have produced important documents outlining how peace might be achieved.[41] The absence of a designated and effective early warning system and fact-finding body within the Secretary-General's office has meant that threats to international security are too often allowed to erupt and spread before preventive diplomacy can be used effectively.

Once a conflict erupts, the UN Secretary-General can bring the matter to the UN Security Council's attention. Article 34 of the Charter states that the Security Council can independently investigate any dispute, or any situation that might lead to international friction or give rise to a dispute, to determine whether the continuance of the dispute or situation is likely to endanger the maintenance of international peace and security. But the General Assembly, or a member of the Council, can also bring to the Council matters pertaining to conflicts that threaten global peace.

So, in some respects, the UN Secretary-General is more than an appendage of the UN system and the officeholder can, at times, be quite activist in this role. However, he (and so far only males have been elected to this post) is not an independent actor. The powerful member states can constrain the actions of the Secretary-General, and even coalitions of less powerful states within the organization can pressure the UN leader to go in one direction or another. Yet, this office does have the ability to exercise moral suasion, if the Secretary-General is prepared to use his soapbox skilfully.

Peacemaking and Pacific Settlement

As mentioned earlier, once the Security Council is aware of a threat to the peace, it will first try to recommend peaceful ways of resolving the dispute or suggest terms of settlement. Chapter VI of the UN Charter details the options for peacemaking and pacific settlement. However, if the disputing parties are not favourably disposed to going along with the Council's recommendation, then the Council may be forced to pursue other steps for reducing the threat or suppressing it altogether. Former UN Secretary-General Boutros Boutros-Ghali detailed some of these measures in his *An Agenda for Peace*.[42]

From the very beginning, the UN Charter provided, in Article 7, for the establishment of an International Court of Justice (ICJ) so states could resolve their disputes by recourse to the law. The Court has become an important element in UN peacemaking. However, not all UN member states accept the jurisdiction of this Court. And even those that do can hold out reservations on any of its judgements. This judicial body was created to address disputes between states, not between societal groups or individuals. With the increases in civil conflicts in the post-Cold War era, as noted in the previous chapter, many parties to conflicts are therefore not able to bring their disputes to the ICJ for resolution or arbitration.

The creation in the early 1990s of Ad Hoc International Criminal Tribunals represents a major innovation in how the organization deals with war and other forms of large-scale violence. Unlike the ICJ, the International Criminal Tribunal for the Former Yugoslavia (ICTFY) and the International Criminal Tribunal for Rwanda (ICTR) were established specifically to hold individuals accountable for atrocities committed during hostilities (e.g., **war crimes**, **genocide**, **ethnic cleansing**, and **crimes against humanity**). In many respects, these ad hoc judicial bodies are expected to have the effect of deterrence, i.e., to cause those who might wish to carry out atrocious crimes in conflict theatres to think twice before doing so and perhaps not to act in an inhumane manner. The fact that the ICTFY was able to indict and try high-profile individuals, including former state leaders (e.g., Slobodan Milošević, Milan Milutinovic, Radovan Karadžić, Biljana Plavsic, Ratko Mladić, Dusan Tadic, Goran Borovnica, Dragan Nikolic, Zeljko Raznjatovic), suggests that these instruments can be effective in helping the UN carry out its mission statement.[43] The experience of the ICTR has not been as stellar as that of the ICTFY so far; nevertheless, individuals responsible for war crimes, genocide, ethnic cleansing, and crimes against humanity during the Rwandan genocide are being held to account for their actions.

The UN ad hoc tribunals no doubt provided the needed impetus for the establishment of a permanent International Criminal Court (ICC) in 1998. While this judicial body is separate and distinct from the UN system, it was established by a UN **conference of plenipotentiaries** in Rome. Now that this body is fully functional, it should help to strengthen the UN's ability to address threats to international security and improve international criminal law enforcement. The ICC has already launched a number of investigations into war crimes and crimes against humanity in northern Uganda, the Democratic Republic

United Nations–African Union peacekeeping in Darfur.

© Zohra Bensemra/Reuters/Corbis

of the Congo (DRC), the Central African Republic (CAR), and Darfur in Sudan. So far, the ICC has issued arrests for eight individuals: six are still on the loose, one has since died, and one is now in the custody of the Court. At the time of writing, the ICC had issued an arrest warrant against a sitting head of state for the first time when, on 4 March 2009, it issued a warrant against Sudanese President Omar Hassan al-Bashir charging him with committing crimes against humanity and war crimes in Darfur.[44]

Peacekeeping

One of the more successful innovations within the UN system has been the creation of the unique function of peacekeeping. Peacekeeping, developed during the height of the Cold War, was intended as a halfway-house measure between Chapter VI and Chapter VII of the UN Charter. Lester B. Pearson of Canada, one of the originators of the concept, described it as an intermediary technique between 'merely passing resolutions and actually fighting'.[45] Since the UN does not have military forces of its own, it has to depend on its member states to provide such forces for peacekeeping and other peace support operations. In effect, UN peacekeeping became the employment, under UN auspices, of military, para-military, or non-military personnel or forces in a theatre of political conflict. Its immediate purpose is to separate warring factions long enough to allow negotiations to take place between them. UN peacekeeping was thus conceptually distinguished from the diplomatic enterprises of peacemaking and the coercive activity of **peace enforcement** and, since there is no mention of this mechanism in the Charter, the expression 'a chapter six and a half operation' was first coined by Dag Hammarskjöld to describe it.[46]

Over the course of the Cold War, UN peacekeeping operations fell into two broad categories: (1) military observer missions composed of relatively small numbers of unarmed officers, charged with such tasks as monitoring ceasefires, verifying troop withdrawals, or patrolling borders or demilitarized zones; and (2) peacekeeping forces composed of lightly armed blue-helmeted national contingents of troops, deployed to carry out tasks similar to those of military observers and, often, to act as a buffer between hostile parties. The first UN observer mission was the United Nations Truce Supervision Organization (UNTSO) that operated in Palestine in 1948 and has remained there until the present time. The first actual peacekeeping operation was put to use during the Suez crisis in 1956. A multinational emergency force was established by the UN Security Council to separate combatants in that theatre of conflict, lower tensions, and ultimately facilitate a settlement among the conflicting parties. Table 7.5 lists all of the UN peacekeeping missions from its inception to 2007.

The techniques used and experiences gained by UN peacekeepers during the Cold War era have served as the basis for the evolution of peacekeeping in the post-Cold War period. Today's UN peacekeepers are usually engaged in preventive deployment, temporary administration of governance in countries coming out of conflict, election monitoring and democratization, protecting delivery of humanitarian assistance, and helping create stable and secure environments through disarmament, demobilization, and reintegration processes in ongoing efforts to consolidate peace in the aftermath of conflict. The evolution of UN peacekeeping in response to changing needs has meant that a growing number of peacekeeping missions are now highly complex, comprising a combination of military, civilian

Table 7.5 UN Peacekeeping Operations, 1947–2007

Mission	Date
UN Special Committee on the Balkans (UNSCOB)	1947–52
UN Commission for Indonesia (UNCI)	1947–51
UN Truce Supervision Organization (UNTSO) Egypt, Israel, Jordan, Lebanon, and Syrian Arab Republic)	1948–present
UN Military Observer Group in India/Pakistan (UNMOGIP)	1949–present
UN Emergency Force (UNEF I) (Egypt and Israel)	1956–67
UN Observer Group in Lebanon (UNOGIL)	1958
UN Operations in the Congo (ONUC)	1960–4
UN Security Force in West New Guinea (UNSF)	1962–3
UN Yemen Observation Mission (UNYOM)	1963–4
UN Peacekeeping Force in Cyprus (UNFICYP)	1964–present
Mission of the Representative of the Secretary-General in the Dominican Republic (DOMREP)	1965–6
UN India–Pakistan Observation Mission (UNIPOM)	1965–6
UN Emergency Force (UNEF II) (Egypt and Israel)	1973–9
UN Disengagement Observer Force (UNDOF) (Golan Heights: Israel and Syria)	1974–present
UN Interim Force in Lebanon (UNIFIL)	1978–present
UN Good Offices Mission in Afghanistan and Pakistan (UNGOMAP)	1988–90
UN Iran–Iraq Military Observer Group (UNIIMOG)	1988–91
UN Angola Verification Mission (UNAVEM I)	1989–91
UN Transition Assistance Group (Namibia)	1989–90
UN Observer Mission for Verification of Elections in Nicaragua (ONUVEN)	1989–90
UN Observer Group in Central America (ONUCA)	1989–92
UN Observation Mission for the Verification of Elections in Haiti (ONUVEH)	1990–1
UN Iraq–Kuwait Observation Mission (UNIKOM)	1991–2003
UN Angola Verification Mission (UNAVEM II)	1991–5
UN Observer Mission in El Salvador (ONUSAL)	1991–5
UN Mission for the Referendum in Western Sahara (MINURSO)	1991–present
UN Advance Mission in Cambodia (UNAMIC)	1991–2
UN Protection Force (UNPROFOR) (Croatia and The Former Yugoslav Republic of Macedonia)	1992–5
UN Transitional Authority in Cambodia (UNTAC)	1992–3

(continued)

Table 7.5 (Continued)

UN Operations in Somalia (UNOSOM I)	1992–3
UN Operations in Mozambique (ONUMOZ)	1992–4
UN Observer Mission in Georgia (UNOMIG)	1993–present
UN Observer Mission Uganda–Rwanda (UNOMUR)	1993–4
UN Operation in Somalia (UNOSOM II)	1993–5
UN Assistance Mission for Rwanda (UNAMIR)	1993–6
UN Mission in Haiti (UNMIH)	1993–6
UN Observer Mission in Liberia (UNOMIL)	1993–7
UN Aouzou Strip Observer Group (UNASOG) (northern Chad)	1994
UN Mission of Observers in Tajikistan (UNMOT)	1994–2000
UN Mission in Bosnia–Herzegovina (UNMIBH)	1995–2002
UN Preventive Deployment Force (UNPREDEP) (The Former Yugoslav Republic of Macedonia)	1995–9
UN Confidence Restoration Operation (UNCRO) (Croatia)	1995–6
UN Angola Verification Mission (UNAVEM III)	1995–7
UN Mission of Observers in Prevlaka (UNMOP) (southern Croatia)	1996–2002
UN Transitional Authority for Eastern Slavonia, Baranja, and Western Sirmium (UNTAES) (Croatia)	1996–8
UN Support Mission in Haiti (UNSMIH)	1996–7
UN Transition Mission in Haiti (UNTMIH)	1997
UN Verification Mission in Guatemala (MINUGUA)	1997
UN Civilian Police Mission in Haiti (MIPONUH)	1997–2000
UN Observer Mission in Angola (MONUA)	1997–9
UN Mission in the Central African Republic (MINURCA)	1998–2000
UN Mission in Sierra Leone (UNAMSIL)	1999–2005
UN Organization Mission in the Democratic Republic of the Congo (MONUC)	1999–present
UN Interim Administration Mission in Kosovo (UNMIK)	1999–present
UN Mission in Ethiopia and Eritrea (UNMEE)	2000–present
UN Mission of Support in East Timor (UNMISET)	2002–20 May 2005
UN Mission in Côte d'Ivoire (MINUCI)	2002–present
UN Mission in Liberia (UNMIL)	2003–present
UN Stabilization Mission in Haiti (MINUSTAH)	2003–present
UN Operation in Burundi (ONUB)	2004–present
UN Mission in the Sudan (UNMIS)	2005–present

Source: UN Department of Peacekeeping Operations, 2007.

police, and other civilian personnel. The mandates of these second-generation peacekeeping missions have included: helping to create political institutions and broaden their base; working alongside governments, **non-governmental organizations** (NGOs), and local citizens' groups to provide emergency relief; demobilizing former combatants and reintegrating them into society; clearing landmines; organizing and conducting elections; and promoting sustainable development practices.

Recently, the UN Security Council, relying on its member governments, has been equipping UN peacekeeping operations with credible military capacity. One such example was in 1996 when a 'robust' peacekeeping force, the UN Transitional Administration in Eastern Slavonia, Baranja, and Western Sirmium (UNTAES), was outfitted with some heavy weapons to act as a deterrent. The Council has also authorized UN members to provide close air support or other forceful action in support of some missions. In Sierra Leone, the UN peace operation combined strong political pressure with a strong military posture to dissuade one of the parties from resuming the military option. In July 2000, after UN Mission in Sierra Leone (UNAMSIL) troops were attacked without provocation and after all other options were tried, the UNAMSIL peacekeeping force undertook an offensive 'military' operation to free more than 230 UN peacekeepers trapped for over two months by rebel forces fighting against the government.[47] To facilitate enforcement peacekeeping, the UN Security Council has been incorporating Chapter VII of the UN Charter into some resolutions as a means of securing peace or bringing an end to seemingly intractable conflicts.

Coercion

There are times when neither peacemaking nor even 'robust' peacekeeping will do the job of safeguarding international security. Preserving international peace and security, from time to time, requires further coercive measures.

Comprehensive Sanctions

Sanctions are used by the UN as a means of forcing deviant states or groups to comply with international legal norms or to end threats to international peace and security. Essentially, sanctions are used to persuade the defecting party to reconsider its behaviour and change its delinquent actions and policies. Sanctions are therefore tools of coercion. They are part of what has been called **coercive diplomacy** in that they employ threats or limited force to persuade an opponent to undo an encroachment. To beef up sanctions, Chapter VII of the UN Charter has been used by the Council in about 17 sanctions cases so far: Afghanistan, Angola, Côte d'Ivoire, the DRC, Ethiopia and Eritrea, Haiti, Iraq, Liberia, Libya, Rwanda, Sierra Leone, Somalia, South Africa, Southern Rhodesia, Sudan, the former Yugoslavia, and most recently against Al-Qaeda terrorists.[48]

The range of UN sanctions available to states includes arms embargoes, the imposition of financial and trade restrictions, interruption of relations by sea and air, and diplomatic isolation. When diplomacy fails and the use of military force may be too risky, the UN Security Council may decide to use economic sanctions as a means of dealing with a state that has defected from specific international norms. For example, UN economic sanctions were imposed on South Africa to end apartheid (see Box 7.2) and on Rhodesia to force an end to a racist and illegitimate regime.

BOX 7.2

The End of Apartheid

Under **apartheid** (1948 to 1994), white South Africans engaged in what many considered the racial equivalent of imperialism. Apartheid, the term meaning 'apartness' or 'aparthood' in Afrikaans, the language of the former Dutch colonists in South Africa, was a racial policy of white minority rule. This was the official policy of the ruling Nationalist Party in South Africa. Apartheid involved the territorial separation of non-Europeans from Europeans, who were guaranteed a monopoly of socio-economic and political power.

Apartheid confined black populations to certain townships or tribal homelands and controlled their movement by issuing them internal passports. Apartheid also denied South Africa's black majority political rights and representation in the national parliament.

South Africa's gross violation of human rights under apartheid provoked internal unrest, in addition to international condemnation and sanctions. In the 1980s, the British Commonwealth campaigned to abolish the apartheid system in South Africa. The release from prison in 1990 of Nelson Mandela, the leader of the African National Congress (ANC) who had been unlawfully detained for 27 years, and the lifting of the 30-year ban on the ANC symbolized the end of apartheid. President F.W. de Klerk repealed nearly all apartheid legislation by 1992, including the Population Registration Act.

In December 1991, a Convention for a Democratic South Africa (CODESA) was established. In 1993, CODESA drafted South Africa's new transitional constitution, which was ratified by the national interim government. South Africa's new constitution granted suffrage to all South African adults. In 1994, South Africa held its first multi-racial, democratic elections. The ANC won the majority vote and Nelson Mandela became South Africa's first black president on 10 May 1994. The ANC ratified a new constitution in 1996 that guaranteed equal civil rights to all South Africans regardless of race. In 1995, President Mandela's government formed the Truth and Reconciliation Commission to investigate and provide restitution for crimes committed under apartheid.

Sources: 'Indepth: South Africa', *CBC News Online*, 14 Apr. 2004, at: <www.cbc.ca/news/background/southafrica/>; David Weigall, *International Relations: A Concise Companion* (London: Arnold, 2002), 11–12; John Baylis and Steve Smith, eds, *The Globalization of World Politics: An Introduction to International Relations* (Oxford: Oxford University Press, 1997), 73–4.

Since the end of the Cold War, UN-imposed sanctions have increased exponentially. Former UN Secretary-General Kofi Annan once remarked that the use of sanctions as an instrument of the UN Security Council and of UN member states 'was one of the defining characteristics of the post-Cold War era.' But he warned that 'sanctions remain a blunt instrument, which hurt large numbers of people who are not their primary targets.'[49] Since 1990, economic sanctions have been imposed on the following state and non-state actors: Afghanistan/Taliban, Albania, Algeria, Angola/UNITA, Azerbaijan, Burundi, Cambodia/Khmer Rouge, Cameroon, China, Colombia, Ecuador, El Salvador, Equatorial Guinea, Estonia, France, Guatemala, Haiti, India, Indonesia, Iran, Iraq, Italy, Jordan, Kazakhstan, Kenya, Latvia, Liberia, Libya, Lithuania, Macedonia, Malawi, Nicaragua, Niger, Nigeria, North Korea, Paraguay, Peru, Rwanda, Sierra Leone, Sudan, Swiss banks,

Thailand, The Gambia, Togo, Turkey, Turkmenistan, Ukraine, USSR, Yemen, Yugoslavia, Zaire, and Zambia.

One relatively recent and important test of this peacemaking instrument occurred in August of 1990, when the UN Security Council imposed economic sanctions on Iraq for invading and occupying Kuwait. The result confirms something implied in Kofi Annan's remark: even harsh economic sanctions may not be effective against a dictator who cares little about the plight of his own people. Despite the comprehensiveness of these sanctions, the measures that were taken to enforce them, and the unintended consequences of their use (collateral damage), Iraq initially refused to withdraw its forces. This set in motion the series of events that led to the 1991 Gulf War—a shift from coercive diplomacy to military sanction. Military sanction was also approved by the UN against the Taliban and Al-Qaeda in Afghanistan after the 9/11 terrorist attacks on the US. However, when US President George W. Bush's administration sought similar sanctions against Saddam Hussein to address the dictator's alleged link to global terrorism and the claim that Iraq possessed weapons of mass destruction, the Council was divided on the matter. As a result, in 2003, the Bush administration assembled a 'coalition of the willing' to invade Iraq without UN authorization.[50]

What we have learned from the experiences with the use of UN sanctions is that they can be rather blunt instruments when applied comprehensively upon a target state. They are also punitive in intent, and one recurrent problem with their use has been that of unintended collateral damage to innocent individuals or groups within the target state, to those in neighbouring states, as well as in proximate states locked into an interdependent relationship with the target state. Such unintended consequences forced the UN to develop ways of alleviating the suffering that Iraqi children and much of that country's population had endured as a result of the harsh economic sanctions levied against Iraq. In that case, $46 billion of Iraqi oil export earnings were taken from the Iraqi government over a seven-year period and used to buy food and medical supplies for the Iraqi people.[51] That oil-for-food program was marred by allegations of fraud and corruption on the part of UN personnel and agents, as well as contractors, including entities that entered into contracts with the UN or with Iraq under this program. This scandal led to an independent inquiry set up under the chairmanship of Paul Volcker, a former Chairman of the US Federal Reserve under Presidents Carter and Reagan (and recently appointed chairman of the newly formed Economic Recovery Advisory Board under US President Barack Obama). But the oil-for-food program also had another 'perverse effect'. As Andrew Mack and Asif Khan put it:

> Regime control over much of the food and medical supplies distributed under the oil-for-food program . . . increased the dependence of the [Iraqi] people on the state and further undermined civil society, while providing an additional lever of control and coercion for the [Saddam Hussein] regime.[52]

Smart (Targeted) Sanctions

The problems associated with the implementation of broad sanctions led scholars and practitioners to focus on 'targeted' or 'smart' sanctions—a concept that involves directing sanctions at specific individuals or governing elites responsible for violating international norms while avoiding creating adverse political, social, and economic consequences for the general population of the 'target' state.

The issue of targeted UN sanctions has been the object of intense international diplomatic and academic analyses and processes.

One such effort, labelled the *Interlaken Process*, was initiated by Switzerland and primarily concerned the imposition of financial sanctions.[53] This was followed by another initiative, led by Germany, resulting in the *Bonn–Berlin Process* that focused on other forms of targeted sanctions, notably arms embargoes and aviation and travel sanctions. The above two processes brought together experts, academic researchers, diplomats, practitioners, and NGOs, and produced two volumes that were presented to the UN Security Council in October 2001. Around the same time, Sweden announced the initiation of a third process—the *Stockholm Process*—drawing on a similar combination of expertise. This time, the focus was on the best ways of implementing the suggested measures.[54] The results of this analysis were presented to the UN Secretary-General and the Security Council in early 2003. A parallel, but separate, project on the legal safeguards for individuals placed on target lists also has been undertaken in Sweden.

There are occasions, therefore, when general and comprehensive UN economic sanctions have to be backed up, or supported, by other forms of more specific sanctions, e.g., curtailing financial transactions, freezing bank accounts, limiting travel, and imposing arms embargoes. UN arms embargoes can be considered one of the earliest forms of 'smart sanctions' in that they target instruments of death and the mechanisms used to fuel violent conflicts and threaten the security of the person and the state.[55] As Cortright and Lopez put it, 'By denying aggressors and human rights abusers the implements of war and repression, arms embargoes contribute directly to preventing and reducing the level of armed conflict.'[56]

The UN has used arms embargoes since 1948 to help quell violence in theatres of conflict. Since the end of the Cold War, UN arms embargoes have been imposed on the following states and non-state actors: Iraq, the former Yugoslavia, the Federal Republic of Yugoslavia (including Kosovo), Libyan Arab Jamahiriya, Haiti, Afghanistan under Taliban control, Somalia, Liberia, UNITA in Angola, Rwanda, Sierra Leone and the RUF, and Ethiopia/Eritrea. Several lessons have been learned from this experience with UN arms embargoes.[57] The most important ones are: (1) some states do not have the capacity to enforce embargoes on arms; (2) black market arms dealers and traffickers still find ways to get around arms embargoes; (3) UN resolutions calling for arms embargoes must be as detailed as possible, specifying exactly what types of arms are being prohibited and detailing the nature of the verification mechanism to be put in place for monitoring the embargoes; (4) arms embargoes, like other forms of sanctions, require enforcement capability and measures if they are to be implemented properly.

Military Action

As noted earlier, if UN sanctions and arms embargoes fail to end threats to international security, then the UN Security Council, as a last resort, may invoke Chapter VII of the UN Charter and approve military action against the deviants of international norms and laws. Article 42 of Chapter VII states that the Council 'may take such action by air, sea, or land forces as may be necessary to maintain or restore international peace and security. Such action may include demonstrations, blockade, and other operations by air, sea, or land forces of Members of the United Nations.' With the rise in transnational terrorism, the UN is faced with two choices: (1) to react to every terror incident by condemning it and mobilizing its member states to use force to combat it; or (2) to address the underlying causes of terrorism—a subject that will be discussed in Chapter 13.

Building Sustainable Peace

Part of the UN's counter-terrorism strategy is the notion of addressing the underlying causes of terrorism. This strategy is also linked to sustainable peace-building, which involves addressing the underlying structural causes of conflict. It emphasizes bottom-up approaches and has as its intent the decentring of social and economic structures. In brief, it calls for a radical transformation of society away from structures of coercion and violence to an embedded culture of peace.

Post-Conflict Peace-building

Peace-building became part of the official public discourse in the 1990s when UN Secretary-General Boutros Boutros-Ghali used the term in *An Agenda for Peace*. Initially, the concept was linked specifically with post-conflict societies. Boutros-Ghali defined post-conflict peace-building as 'action to identify and support structures which will tend to strengthen and solidify peace in order to avoid a relapse into conflict'.[58] He saw peace-building as an integral part of the UN's work. Post-conflict peace-building involves disarming warring parties, restoring order, decommissioning and destroying weapons, repatriating refugees, providing advisory and training support for security personnel, monitoring elections, de-mining and other forms of demilitarization, providing technical assistance, advancing efforts to protect human rights, and reforming and strengthening institutions of governance—including assistance in monitoring and supervising electoral processes and promoting formal and informal participation in the political process. It also includes educational exchanges and curriculum reform designed to reduce hostile perceptions of the 'other' and to forestall the renewal of hostilities between factions. Thus, post-conflict peace-building is really about constructing a new environment—political, cultural, economic, social, security.[59]

The UN has an obligation to provide proactive support for the transformation of deficient national structures and capabilities and to work towards strengthening democratic institutions. Most discussions of peace-building thus accept that it is a multi-layered approach, involving participants from many sectors with a view to reconstructing deficient practices and institutions in support of a more **sustainable peace**. The process entails both short- and long-term objectives, for example, short-term humanitarian operations and longer-term developmental, political, economic, and social objectives.[60]

Although Boutros-Ghali's use of peace-building was conceived as a post-conflict activity, UN peace-building can be used conceptually as a mechanism for forestalling the outbreak of violent conflict. This view addresses the underlying economic, social, cultural, and humanitarian problems that might destroy prospects for establishing sustainable peace. Its main aim is to generate and sustain conditions of peace, while managing differences without recourse to violence.

In Cambodia (1993), East Timor (1999), and Kosovo (2000), the UN was given full responsibility for implementing peace-building operations. These operations (and others) were decided on, designed within, and resourced through the UN. The UN also developed specialized instruments in support of peace-building, such as the use of the Secretary-General's Special Representative or the more permanent

UN Office for the High Commissioner for Human Rights. The UN has created, as well, new 'peace-building' roles such as special rapporteurs, district administrators, and representatives for children and displaced persons in societies moving away from violent conflicts. International and regional financial institutions also have become integrally involved in peace-building efforts. The World Bank, for instance, was heavily involved in the peace-building efforts in East Timor. The International Development Association (IDA) of the World Bank was designated the trustee of the reconstruction Trust Fund for East Timor (TFET) and played a major role in community empowerment and local governance there.[61]

Significant concerns have been expressed about the co-ordination of the activities of the many organizations involved in UN peace-building operations. One set of international institutions may be supporting a peace-building process at the same time as another is seeking to enforce policies that directly or indirectly undermine such efforts. Most often cited in this regard are the strict conditionalities imposed by international financial institutions (IFIs) that may impede reconstruction efforts in post-conflict situations. Many other issues, including concerns about the coherence and co-ordination of institutional responses, have also been discussed widely, yet solutions are often difficult to reach or implement.[62]

Peace-building Commission and Fund

At the UN Security Council session on 20 December 2005, the Council made explicit the fact that development, peace and security, and human rights are 'interlinked and mutually reinforcing'. Council members came to the conclusion that there was a need for a co-ordinated, coherent, and integrated approach to post-conflict peace-building and reconciliation if sustainable peace is to be achieved in war-torn countries. The result was the establishment of a **Peacebuilding Commission**—an intergovernmental advisory body to the Council. The makeup of the current Commission is outlined in Table 7.6.

The Peacebuilding Commission is now in full operation. It brings together all relevant actors and marshals resources for the purpose of introducing integrated strategies to deal with post-conflict peace-building, reconstruction, and recovery in countries devastated by violent conflict. It focuses attention on reconstruction, institution-building, and sustainable development in those countries emerging from conflict, and brings together the UN's broad capacities and experience in conflict prevention, mediation, peacekeeping, respect for human rights, the rule of law, humanitarian assistance, reconstruction, and long-term development. Specifically, the Commission is expected to: (1) propose integrated strategies for post-conflict peace-building and recovery; (2) help to ensure predictable financing for early recovery activities and sustained financial investment over the medium to longer term; (3) extend the period of attention by the international community to post-conflict recovery; (4) develop **best practices** on issues that require extensive collaboration among political, military, humanitarian, and development actors.[63]

The Organizational Committee of the Peacebuilding Commission consists of: a chairperson and vice chair; the chairs of country-specific configurations; seven members selected by the Security Council (five of whom must be permanent members of the Council); seven members elected by the ECOSOC; five top providers of assessed contributions to the UN regular budget, and of voluntary contributions to the UN's various funds, programs, and agencies; five top providers of

Table 7.6 Membership of the UN Peacebuilding Commission, 2009

Chairman	Heraldo Muñoz (Chile)
Vice-Chairperson	Park In-kook (Republic of Korea)
Chairs of country-specific configurations	Anders Lidén of Sweden, Chair of the Burundi Configuration; Jan Grauls of Belgium, Chair of the Central African Republic Configuration; Maria Luiza Ribeiro Viotti of Brazil, Chair of the Guinea-Bissau Configuration; Frank Majoor of the Netherlands, Chair of the Sierra Leone Configuration; Carmen María Gallardo Hernández of El Salvador, Chair of the Working Group on Lessons Learned
Members selected by the UN Security Council	Burkina Faso, China, France, Mexico, Russian Federation, United Kingdom of Great Britain and Northern Ireland, United States of America
Members selected by ECOSOC	Algeria, El Salvador, Guinea-Bissau, Luxembourg, Morocco, Poland, Republic of Korea
Five top providers of assessed and voluntary contributions	Canada, Germany, Japan, the Netherlands, Sweden
Five top providers of military personnel	Bangladesh, India, Nepal, Nigeria, Pakistan
Seven members elected by the UN General Assembly	Benin, Chile, Georgia, Jamaica, South Africa, Thailand, Uruguay

Source: United Nations Peacebuilding Commission, 2009.

military personnel and civilian police to UN missions; and seven members elected to the UN General Assembly. On 11 October 2006, a Peacebuilding Fund was launched. This Fund is designed to support interventions considered critical to sustaining peace in war-ravaged countries. It does not seek to address all peacebuilding requirements in a given situation; rather, it aims to have a catalytic effect that will pave the way for the sustained support and engagement of other key stakeholders. The Fund is being managed by the head of the Peacebuilding Support Office, under the authority of the Secretary-General.

Conclusion

Liberal and neo-liberal institutionalists often claim that institutions matter when it comes to understanding and explaining the dynamics of global politics.[64] As Arthur Stein notes: 'Understanding and explaining international politics . . . increasingly requires incorporating the role of international institutions.'[65] This accounts for the fact that scholarship on international institutions continues to grow in the post-Cold War era. Robert Cox suggests that institutions form an important part of the underlying base of world order. According to Cox, international organizations like the UN are by-products of particular historical junctures and specific sets of sociological, political, and economic circumstances. When combined with ideas (particular thought patterns) and material conditions, human institutions reflect world order (or the attempt to achieve world order) at a specific point in time.[66] International organizations represent, in essence, one leg of the tripod of elements that constitute world order at any given moment.[67] This is particularly true of the United Nations, which, in effect, represents an 'ideal', albeit embryonic, form of institutional governance for our contemporary world, particularly because of its universality and penchant for taking on truly 'global' agenda items, i.e., those that transcend national borders.

Both liberal and neo-liberal institutionalists draw on such classical theorists as Immanuel Kant and Jeremy Bentham in arguing that a law-governed international system is indeed possible. They see the UN as embodying the traits of such a system. However, realists and neo-realists are quick, and correct, to point out the inefficiencies and ineffectiveness of this organization. As an example of this criticism, consider a 1984 report of the US Senate, which stated:

> There appears to be a tendency on the part of the [UN] agencies concerned to undertake far more than they can hope to accomplish, and very often without proper regard for the importance of the work undertaken. . . . The result is that funds are spread very thin and very little is accomplished generally. Whenever a particular project appears important at the moment, a new commission or committee is appointed to look into the matter. This ultimately results in a proliferation of bodies, attempting to accomplish a great deal of work, much of which constitutes duplication of effort already being made and some of which overlaps other projects.[68]

Such criticisms have acted as a catalyst for the introduction of reforms to the UN system,[69] although the organization's record in this area has not been stellar.[70]

Since its inception, the UN has been trying to adapt its structure, personnel, and processes in response to global societal pressures.[71] In some instances (e.g., decolonization), change has been foisted on the UN and the organization has adapted in a reflexive manner without too much care as to what the institutional adaptations might mean for the future of the institution. Nonetheless, it is fair to say that UN member states and its Secretariat have generally favoured a reformist impulse, geared towards trying to make the organization more efficient and effective, over a transformative agenda that would result in making the world body more relevant to current global conditions.

The proliferation of UN reform efforts over the years has not made the UN system much more efficient or effective. Indeed, the emphasis on 'reform' has meant that significant institutional transformation gets put on the back burner time and again. However, a historic report, released in December 2004, indicated that UN member governments were finally interested in moving beyond the reformist impulse to engage in a transformative exercise. This report, *A More Secure World: Our Shared Responsibility*,[72] was drafted by a panel of eminent individuals brought together by UN Secretary-General Kofi Annan to assess the post-Cold War threats facing humanity and to suggest far-sighted, but workable, recommendations on how best to refashion the UN system so that it can better address those threats.

Central to the report was the assertion of a need for a new consensus on collective security. The reasoning for this position stemmed from the assumption that

(1) the post-Cold War world is one in which all societies are closely intertwined and interconnected; (2) as a result of global shrinkage, largely a result of globalization, security threats do not respect national boundaries; (3) no state can deal with these transnational threats on its own; and thus, (4) the best way to address global security threats is through multilateral efforts, not through unilateralism.

Despite the effort of this high-level panel to bring about major transformation in the UN system that would make this body more relevant to the twenty-first century, there are major obstacles to significant institutional changes. One of these hurdles is the UN Charter itself, particularly its constricting amendment formula. Article 108 of the Charter indicates the difficulty of making major structural changes to the UN system. It states:

> Amendments to the present Charter shall come into force for all Members of the United Nations when they have been adopted by a vote of two-thirds of the members of the General Assembly and ratified in accordance with their respective constitutional processes by two-thirds of the Members of the United Nations, including all the permanent members of the Security Council.

Indeed, the Charter has been amended only three times since the organization came into being; once in 1963, when Security Council membership was increased from 11 to 15 with an amendment to Article 23 of the Charter, and twice with the enlargement of the Economic and Social Council membership, from 18 to 27 in 1965 and from 27 to 54 in 1973. Other obstacles to bringing about significant changes in the UN stem from lack of political will, the wielding of the veto by the P5 of the Security Council, resistance to major changes coming from the large majority in the UN General Assembly (the developing countries), and bureaucratic inertia.

The United Nations is a universal intergovernmental institution that, by its very nature, can take on tasks that states, acting on their own, have difficulty addressing. The UN's primary mandate is to save us from experiencing another major global war, like World War II. While this world body has not always lived up to the expectations of its founders, not all the blame can be placed on the institution's shoulders. The UN member states must take a large share of this culpability.

Over the years, the UN has expanded its size and operations to accommodate the pressures placed on it, not only by its member states but also by civil society. This expansion is not sustainable indefinitely, given the organization's serious funding constraints, its lack of military and police forces, its constitutional makeup, and the limits of its management capacities. In the twenty-first century, therefore, the UN must make fundamental choices on which combination of its many modes of action most effectively meets the new challenges to international security in a rapidly globalizing world in which both state and non-state actors are making demands on the world body.[73] We will discuss the nature of the globalizing environment within which the UN operates in the next section of the book.

As it decides on how it will operate in the world of this new century, the UN most likely will continue the slow transition it has been making over the past 65 years in response to changing endogenous and exogenous environments. Clearly, change within the UN is linked to ideational shifts. Institutions like the UN are social constructions. As such, they inherently reflect the ideas of their founders, their member states, and their personnel. So it is useful for students of global politics to examine from time to time how new ideas impact the UN system, how those ideas jostle with existing and perhaps outmoded ones for prominence, and what this all means for the governance of the globe.

Because of its universality, the UN will remain a unique forum for the prevention or peaceful resolution of conflicts between states and will field peacemaking, peacekeeping, peace-building, and other peace support operations as required. At the same time, it will be forced to address the agenda and demands of civil societies within and across states, as well as to deal with illicit actors trying to undermine legitimate global governance processes. The UN also will have to act as a linchpin, co-ordinating and partnering with regional organizations, with various state coalitions, and with transnational civil society organizations, if it is to address adequately the state and human security problems that currently confront us. Obviously, the UN cannot handle all of the tasks of global governance on its own. This is why Chapter VIII of the UN Charter, for example, is such an important, although not frequently discussed, constitutional feature. It allows for sharing the burden in international governance between the UN system and regional agencies—something of importance at this particular juncture in world politics.[74] In the present era of **hyperglobalization**, as the Cold War recedes to memory, the UN system has to depend, increasingly, on other intergovernmental organizations, regional bodies, private groups, plurilateral organs, transnational non-governmental organizations, and **grassroots movements** to contribute to accomplishing the task of governing the globe.

The most useful contribution this multi-purpose world body can make specifically to world peace and stability in the long run is to promote conditions within countries (primarily advancing democracy, improving health, eradicating poverty, promoting human rights and equality for women, making available quality education for all, combatting HIV/AIDS, promoting youth employment, improving the quality of life for people with disabilities, combatting illicit drugs, terrorism, and transnational crime, providing access to technology, protecting culture and the environment, and pursuing sustainable development) that will enhance progress and minimize disparity and the prospects of violent conflict. It would seem that conflict prevention (through dealing with root causes of violence and through the development of democracy, equity, and justice), rather than conflict management, ought to be the primary focus for the UN in its quest to preserve international security in an era of accelerating globalization.

❖ Appendix 1:
UN Member States and Dates of Membership

Afghanistan (19 November 1946)
Albania (14 December 1955)
Algeria (8 October 1962)
Andorra (28 July 1993)
Angola (1 December 1976)
Antigua and Barbuda (11 November 1981)
Argentina (24 October 1945)
Armenia (2 March 1992)
Australia (1 November 1945)

Austria (14 December 1955)
Azerbaijan (2 March 1992)
Bahamas (18 September 1973)
Bahrain (21 September 1971)
Bangladesh (17 September 1974)
Barbados (9 December 1966)
Belarus (24 October 1945)[1]
Belgium (27 December 1945)
Belize (25 September 1981)

Benin (20 September 1960)

Bhutan (21 September 1971)

Bolivia (14 November 1945)

Bosnia and Herzegovina (22 May 1992)[2]

Botswana (17 October 1966)

Brazil (24 October 1945)

Brunei Darussalam (21 September 1984)

Bulgaria (14 December 1955)

Burkina Faso (20 September 1960)

Burundi (18 September 1962)

Cambodia (14 December 1955)

Cameroon (20 September 1960)

Canada (9 November 1945)

Cape Verde (16 September 1975)

Central African Republic (20 September 1960)

Chad (20 September 1960)

Chile (24 October 1945)

China (24 October 1945)

Colombia (5 November 1945)

Comoros (12 November 1975)

Costa Rica (2 November 1945)

Côte d'Ivoire (20 September 1960)

Croatia (22 May 1992)[3]

Cuba (24 October 1945)

Cyprus (20 September 1960)

Czech Republic (19 January 1993)[4]

Democratic People's Republic of Korea
    (17 September 1991)

Democratic Republic of the Congo
    (20 September 1960)[5]

Denmark (24 October 1945)

Djibouti (20 September 1977)

Dominica (18 December 1978)

Dominican Republic (24 October 1945)

Ecuador (21 December 1945)

Egypt (24 October 1945)[6]

El Salvador (24 October 1945)

Equatorial Guinea (12 November 1968)

Eritrea (28 May 1993)

Estonia (17 September 1991)

Ethiopia (13 November 1945)

Fiji (13 October 1970)

Finland (14 December 1955)

France (24 October 1945)

Gabon (20 September 1960)

Gambia (21 September 1965)

Georgia (31 July 1992)

Germany (18 September 1973)[7]

Ghana (8 March 1957)

Greece (25 October 1945)

Grenada (17 September 1974)

Guatemala (21 November 1945)

Guinea (12 December 1958)

Guinea-Bissau (17 September 1974)

Guyana (20 September 1966)

Haiti (24 October 1945)

Honduras (17 December 1945)

Hungary (14 December 1955)

Iceland (19 November 1946)

India (30 October 1945)

Indonesia (28 September 1950)[8]

Iran, Islamic Republic of (24 October 1945)

Iraq (21 December 1945)

Ireland (14 December 1955)

Israel (11 May 1949)

Italy (14 December 1955)

Jamaica (18 September 1962)

Japan (18 December 1956)

Jordan (14 December 1955)

Kazakhstan (2 March 1992)

Kenya (16 December 1963)

Kiribati (14 September 1999)

Kuwait (14 May 1963)

Kyrgyzstan (2 March 1992)

Lao People's Democratic Republic
    (14 December 1955)

Latvia (17 September 1991)

Lebanon (24 October 1945)

Lesotho (17 October 1966)

Liberia (2 November 1945)

Libyan Arab Jamahiriya
    (14 December 1955)

Liechtenstein (18 September 1990)

Lithuania (17 September 1991)

Luxembourg (24 October 1945)

Madagascar (20 September 1960)

Malawi (1 December 1964)

Malaysia (17 September 1957)[9]

Maldives (21 September 1965)

Mali (28 September 1960)

Malta (1 December 1964)

Marshall Islands (17 September 1991)

Mauritania (27 October 1961)

Mauritius (24 April 1968)

Mexico (7 November 1945)

Micronesia, Federated States of
    (17 September 1991)

Monaco (28 May 1993)

Mongolia (27 October 1961)

Montenegro (28 June 2006)[10]

Morocco (12 November 1956)

Mozambique (16 September 1975)

Myanmar (Burma) (19 April 1948)[11]

Namibia (23 April 1990)

Nauru (14 September 1999)

Nepal (14 December 1955)

Netherlands (10 December 1945)

New Zealand (24 October 1945)

Nicaragua (24 October 1945)
Niger (20 September 1960)
Nigeria (7 October 1960)
Norway (27 November 1945)
Oman (7 October 1971)
Pakistan (30 September 1947)
Palau (15 December 1994)
Panama (13 November 1945)
Papua New Guinea (10 October 1975)
Paraguay (24 October 1945)
Peru (31 October 1945)
Philippines (24 October 1945)
Poland (24 October 1945)
Portugal (14 December 1955)
Qatar (21 September 1971)
Republic of Korea (17 September 1991)
Republic of Moldova (2 March 1992)
Romania (14 December 1955)
Russian Federation (24 October 1945)[12]
Rwanda (18 September 1962)
Saint Kitts and Nevis (23 September 1983)
Saint Lucia (18 September 1979)
Saint Vincent and the Grenadines
    (16 September 1980)
Samoa (15 December 1976)
San Marino (2 March 1992)
São Tomé and Principe (16 September 1975)
Saudi Arabia (24 October 1945)
Senegal (28 September 1960)
Serbia (1 November 2000)[13]
Seychelles (21 September 1976)
Sierra Leone (27 September 1961)
Singapore (21 September 1965)
Slovakia (19 January 1993)[14]
Slovenia (22 May 1992)[15]
Solomon Islands (19 September 1978)
Somalia (20 September 1960)

South Africa (7 November 1945)
Spain (14 December 1955)
Sri Lanka (14 December 1955)
Sudan (12 November 1956)
Suriname (4 December 1975)
Swaziland (24 September 1968)
Switzerland (10 September 2002)
Sweden (19 November 1946)
Syria (24 October 1945)[16]
Tajikistan (2 March 1992)
Thailand (16 December 1946)
The Former Yugoslav Republic of Macedonia
    (8 April 1993)[17]
Timor-Leste (27 September 2002)
Togo (20 September 1960)
Tonga (14 September 1999)
Trinidad and Tobago (18 September 1962)
Tunisia (12 November 1956)
Turkey (24 October 1945)
Turkmenistan (2 March 1992)
Tuvalu (5 September 2000)
Uganda (25 October 1962)
Ukraine (24 October 1945)
United Arab Emirates (9 December 1971)
United Kingdom of Great Britain and Northern
    Ireland (24 October 1945)
United Republic of Tanzania (14 December 1961)[18]
United States of America (24 October 1945)
Uruguay (18 December 1945)
Uzbekistan (2 March 1992)
Vanuatu (15 September 1981)
Venezuela, Bolivarian Republic of
    (15 November 1945)
Viet Nam (20 September 1977)
Yemen (30 September 1947)[19]
Zambia (1 December 1964)
Zimbabwe (25 August 1980)

Notes:

1. On 19 September 1991, Bylorussia informed the UN that it had changed its name to Belarus.
2. The Socialist Federal Republic of Yugoslavia was an original member of the United Nations, the Charter having been signed on its behalf on 26 June 1945 and ratified 19 October 1945, until its dissolution following the establishment and subsequent admission as new members of Bosnia and Herzegovina, the Republic of Croatia, the Republic of Slovenia, The Former Yugoslav Republic of Macedonia, and the Federal Republic of Yugoslavia. The Republic of Bosnia and

Herzegovina was admitted as a UN member by General Assembly resolution A/RES/46/237 of 22 May 1992.

3. See note 2. The Republic of Croatia was admitted as a UN member by General Assembly resolution A/RES/46/238 of 22 May 1992.

4. Czechoslovakia was an original Member of the United Nations from 24 October 1945. In a letter dated 10 December 1992, its Permanent Representative informed the Secretary-General that the Czech and Slovak Federal Republic would cease to exist on 31

December 1992 and that the Czech Republic and the Slovak Republic, as successor states, would apply for UN membership. Following the receipt of its application, the Security Council, on 8 January 1993, recommended to the General Assembly that the Czech Republic be admitted to UN membership. The Czech Republic was thus admitted on 19 January of that year.

5. Zaire joined the UN on 20 September 1960. On 17 May 1997, its name was changed to the Democratic Republic of the Congo.

6. Egypt and Syria were original UN members from 24 October 1945. Following a plebiscite on 21 February 1958, the United Arab Republic was established by a union of Egypt and Syria and continued as a single member. On 13 October 1961, Syria, having resumed its status as an independent state, resumed its separate membership in the United Nations. On 2 September 1971, the United Arab Republic changed its name to the Arab Republic of Egypt.

7. The Federal Republic of Germany and the German Democratic Republic were admitted to UN membership on 18 September 1973. Through the accession of the German Democratic Republic to the Federal Republic of Germany, effective from 3 October 1990, the two German states have united to form one sovereign state.

8. By letter of 20 January 1965, Indonesia announced its decision to withdraw from the UN 'at this stage and under the present circumstances'. By telegram of 19 September 1966, it announced its decision 'to resume full cooperation with the United Nations and to resume participation in its activities'. On 28 September 1966, the General Assembly took note of this decision and the President invited representatives of Indonesia to take seats in the Assembly.

9. The Federation of Malaya joined the UN on 17 September 1957. On 16 September 1963, its name was changed to Malaysia, following the admission to the new federation of Singapore, Sabah (North Borneo), and Sarawak. Singapore became an independent state on 9 August 1965 and a UN member on 21 September 1965.

10. Montenegro held a 21 May 2006 referendum and declared itself independent from Serbia on 3 June. On 28 June 2006 it was accepted as a UN member state by General Assembly resolution A/RES/60/264.

11. Myanmar joined the United Nations as Burma. When the military junta that rules Burma decided in 1989 to rename the country Myanmar, the renaming of which had and still has

political overtones, the UN was among the first entities to recognize the new name.

12. The Union of Soviet Socialist Republics was an original member of the United Nations from 24 October 1945. In a letter dated 24 December 1991, Boris Yeltsin, the President of the Russian Federation, informed the Secretary-General that the membership of the Soviet Union in the Security Council and all other UN organs was being continued by the Russian Federation with the support of the 11 member countries of the Commonwealth of Independent States.

13. See note 2. The Federal Republic of Yugoslavia was admitted as a UN member by General Assembly resolution A/RES/55/12 of 1 November 2000. On 4 February 2003, following the adoption and promulgation of the Constitutional Charter of Serbia and Montenegro by the Assembly of the Federal Republic of Yugoslavia, the official name of 'Federal Republic of Yugoslavia' was changed to Serbia and Montenegro. In a letter dated 3 June 2006, the President of the Republic of Serbia informed the Secretary-General that the membership of Serbia and Montenegro was being continued by the Republic of Serbia, following Montenegro's declaration of independence.

14. Czechoslovakia was an original UN member from 24 October 1945. In a letter dated 10 December 1992, its Permanent Representative informed the Secretary-General that the Czech and Slovak Federal Republic would cease to exist on 31 December 1992 and that the Czech Republic and the Slovak Republic, as successor states, would apply for UN membership. Following the receipt of its application, the Security Council, on 8 January 1993, recommended to the General Assembly that the Slovak Republic be admitted to UN membership. The Slovak Republic was thus admitted on 19 January of that year.

15. See note 2. The Republic of Slovenia was admitted as a Member of the United Nations by General Assembly resolution A/RES/46/236 of 22 May 1992.

16. Egypt and Syria were original members of the United Nations from 24 October 1945. Following a plebiscite on 21 February 1958, the United Arab Republic was established by a union of Egypt and Syria and continued as a single member. On 13 October 1961, Syria, having resumed its status as an independent state, resumed its separate UN membership.

17. See note 2. By resolution A/RES/47/225 of 8 April 1993, the General Assembly admitted as a UN member the state being provisionally referred to for all purposes within the United Nations as 'The Former Yugoslav Republic of Macedonia' pending settlement of the difference that had arisen over its name.

18. Tanganyika was a UN member from 14 December 1961 and Zanzibar was a member from 16 December 1963. Following the ratification on 26 April 1964 of Articles of Union between Tanganyika and Zanzibar, the United Republic of Tanganyika and Zanzibar continued as a single member, changing its name to the United Republic of Tanzania on 1 November 1964.

19. Yemen was admitted to UN membership on 30 September 1947 and Democratic Yemen on 14 December 1967. On 22 May 1990, the two countries merged and have since been represented as one member with the name 'Yemen'.

❖ Appendix 2:
Specialized Agencies and Related Organizations Maintaining Liaison Offices at United Nations Headquarters

International Labour Organization

ILO Office for the United Nations
220 East 42nd Street, Suite 3101, New York, NY 10017–5806
Telephone: (212) 697–0150
Telefax: (212) 697–5218
E-mail: newyork@ilo.org
Representative to the United Nations and Director: Mr Djankou Ndjonkou

Food and Agriculture Organization of the United Nations

FAO Liaison Office with the United Nations
One United Nations Plaza, Room 1125,
New York, NY 10017
Telephone: (212) 963–6036
Telefax: (212) 963–5425
E-mail: fao-lony@fao.org
Representative to the United Nations and Director: Ms Florence A. Chenoweth

United Nations Educational, Scientific and Cultural Organization

UNESCO Office at the United Nations
Two United Nations Plaza, Room 900, New York, NY 10017
Telephone: (212) 963–5995
Telefax: (212) 963–8014
E-mail: newyork@unesco.org
Representative to the United Nations and Director: Mrs Hélène-Marie Gosselin

World Health Organization

WHO Office at the United Nations
Two United Nations Plaza, Room 970, New York, NY 10017
Telephone: (212) 963–4388
Telefax: (212) 963–8565
Representative of the Director General to the United Nations system and other intergovernmental organizations and Executive Director: Mr Andrey V. Pirogov

World Bank

Office of the Special Representative of the World Bank to the United Nations
One Dag Hammarskjöld Plaza, 885 Second Avenue, 26th Floor, New York, NY 10017
Telephone: (212) 355–5112
Telefax: (212) 355–4523
Special Representative to the United Nations: Mr Oscar A. Avalle

International Monetary Fund

International Monetary Fund Office at the United Nations
885 Second Avenue, 26th Floor, New York, NY 10017
Telephone: (212) 893–1700
Telefax: (212) 893–1715
E-mail: rmunzberg@imf.org, rbrauning@imf.org, lnielsen@imf.org, lhernandez1@imf.org
Representative to the United Nations: Mr Reinhard H. Munzberg

World Meteorological Organization

WMO Office at the United Nations

866 United Nations Plaza, Room A-302,
New York, NY 10017
Telephone: (212) 963–9444, (917) 367–9867
Telefax: (917) 367–9868
E-mail: zbatjargal@wmo.int, batjargal@un.org
Representative and Coordinator to the
United Nations and other intergovernmental
organizations: Mr Zamba Batjargal

World Intellectual Property Organization

WIPO Coordination Office at
the United Nations
Two United Nations Plaza, Room 2525,
New York, NY 10017
Telephone: (212) 963–6813
Telefax: (212) 963–4801
E-mail: wipo@un.org
Representative to the United Nations and Director:
Mr Orobola Fasehun

International Fund for Agricultural Development

IFAD Liaison Office with the United Nations
Two United Nations Plaza, Room 1128/1129,
New York, NY 10017
Telephone: (212) 963–0546
Telefax: (212) 963–2787
E-mail: ifad@un.org
Representative to the United Nations and Director:
Kanayo F. Nwanze

United Nations Industrial Development Organization

UNIDO Office at New York
One United Nations Plaza, Room 1110,
New York, NY 10017
Telephone: (212) 963–6890/6891
Telefax: (212) 963–7904
E-mail: sabriy@un.org
Representative to the United Nations, Assistant
Director-General and Director: Mr Alberto Di Liscia

World Tourism Organization

Office of the Special Representative of the World
Tourism Organization to the United Nations
304 East 45th Street, Room 1513, New York, NY
10017
Telephone: (212) 906–5375
Telefax: (212) 906–6705
Representative to the United Nations:
Mr Rafeeuddin Ahmed

International Atomic Energy Agency

IAEA Office at the United Nations
One United Nations Plaza, Room 1155,
New York, NY 10017
Telephone: (212) 963–6012/6011/6010
Telefax: (917) 367–4046
E-mail: iaeany@un.org
Representative of the Director General to the United
Nations and Director: Mr Gustavo R. Zlauvinen

Source: United Nations Protocol's Blue Book, 'Permanent Missions to the United Nations No. 295', Apr. 2006,
last updated 3 Oct. 2006.

Key Terms

Allied nations
apartheid
arbitration
Axis powers
best practices
ceasefire
coercive diplomacy
conference of plenipotentiaries
crimes against humanity
economic sanctions
embargoes
ethnic cleansing
failed states
genocide
good offices
grassroots movements
hyper-globalization

intergovernmental organization (IGO)
mediation
non-governmental organizations
peace-building
Peacebuilding Commission
peace enforcement
peacekeeping
peacemaking
post-Cold War era
preventive deployment
preventive diplomacy
self-determination
smart sanctions
state-centric world
superpower conflict
sustainable peace
war crimes

Discussion Questions

1. What role have international organizations played in maintaining global order?
2. What are the principal characteristics of the United Nations?
3. What are the main purposes of the UN, according to its Charter?
4. Does the United Nations reinforce the role of states in global politics?
5. Why and how has the UN become involved in non-security issues?
6. How effectively has the UN responded to changes in global politics?
7. Has the UN made a difference in the practice of global politics?
8. How has the UN contributed to management of peace and security?
9. Are sanctions an effective instrument for punishing or influencing states?
10. Should the UN be reformed? If so, how and in order to do what?

Suggested Readings

Claude, Inis L., Jr. *Swords into Plowshares: The Problems and Progress of International Organizations.* New York: Random House, 1971. One of the better and more readable and insightful accounts of the principles surrounding the formation of the UN.

Knight, W. Andy, ed. *Adapting the United Nations to a Postmodern Era: Lessons Learned.* New York: Palgrave Macmillan, 2005. An eclectic and largely critical examination of the UN and its operations at the end of the turbulent 1990s and as it embarks on the next century, with essays focused on such subjects as UN reform and the UN's involvement in and response to a number of security threats.

Murphy, Craig N. *International Organizations and Industrial Change: Global Governance since 1850.* Cambridge: Polity Press, 1994. Murphy provides a sweeping historical overview of the evolution of global governance from the formation of public unions in the nineteenth century to the contemporary era as viewed through the lens of a neo-Gramscian critique.

Weiss, Thomas, and Sam Daws, eds. *The Oxford Handbook on the United Nations.* Oxford: Oxford University Press, 2009. This edited collection will likely stand as one of the most comprehensive accounts of the United Nations system as it brings together more than 40 contributors to reflect on the many varied aspects of the UN, from the office of the Secretary-General to the institution's finances and everything in between, all written by subject matter experts.

Global Links

Academic Council on the United Nations System
www.acuns.org
The ACUNS is devoted to the study and dissemination of information and analysis on the UN and other aspects of global governance.

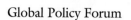

Global Policy Forum
www.globalpolicy.org
>The Global Policy Forum has consultative status at the UN and reports on issues related to that organization.

United Nations
www.un.org
>The official United Nations site.

 Debate 7

> Be it resolved that the UN should be dissolved.

PART III

Globalization

Chapter Eight

Globalization's Impact on the State and the Inter-State System

Introduction

On Monday, 10 September 2001, a group of researchers gathered in the United States to plan a global public opinion survey. The principal concern for these researchers was identifying the most important issue that needed to be addressed in their survey. They asked, 'Could anything supplant globalization as the top international issue in the foreseeable future?'[1] They quickly concluded that nothing else was on the horizon. The events of the next morning surprised them and most others, demonstrating, if nothing else, that forecasting global politics is a risky and often uncertain business. The researchers changed their collective minds and their survey addressed a very different set of priorities.

So what happened to globalization and what effect does it have on global politics? The prominence of globalization as a matter of concern has certainly diminished in the wake of the obsessive focus of some governments on terrorism. Yet the near collapse of the global financial system seven years after 11 September 2001 has returned globalization to the front page. The rapid spread of collapsing banks, credit freeze-up, falling bourses, and sharp stock market declines showed little respect for national borders.[2] In response to this global economic crisis, political leaders are calling for the strengthening of international regulatory regimes and for caution against a return to nationalist and protectionist measures. In early 2009 *The Economist* warned that the integration of the global economy was in retreat.[3]

Indeed, events since 9/11 continue to demonstrate the tension between the traditional forces of state sovereignty in a hostile world defined by the security dilemma and a postmodern global community where sovereignty is more frequently circumscribed by economic, technological, and social forces than reinforced by political or security concerns. Borders have been reinforced and many states have asserted more intrusive domestic measures to keep surveillance on citizens and immigrants alike. But the events of 9/11 were another indication of the impact of globalization. Joe Stiglitz has argued, for instance, that the terrorist attacks on the United States 'brought home a...darker side of globalization... it provided a global arena for terrorists.'[4] It would be a mistake, however, to conclude that globalization—or the institutions, ideas, and practices that have commonly been associated with globalization—is no longer relevant. In fact, modern terrorism itself has been heavily influenced by globalization. Globalization remains a significant feature of contemporary global politics, and the various debates on its meaning and prevalence among scholars and practitioners are important for students of global politics. In this chapter we explore the meanings and practice of globalization with particular reference to the implication for states in the contemporary global order.

The Many Meanings of Globalization

As indicated in previous chapters, 'globalization' is a catch phrase designed to capture the processes and conditions that make up the contemporary global political economy. The term has been widely and variously used by scholars from many disciplines such as economics, sociology, and law, in addition to political scientists. Their definitions tend to reflect the priorities of their respective disciplines and the result has been some degree of confusion over what forms the core of globalization. There is little sense or need in trying to sort out the confusion here. Indeed, if it were not for its common usage, it might be best to avoid the concept entirely. One should, however, be attentive to how different authors have used the term.

Globalization has been used variously to refer to technological change, to political and economic practices of liberalization and privatization, to the politics of interdependence and **internationalization**, and to increased cultural homogenization through transportation and mass media. Primarily, 'globalization' describes global economic practices, but it also refers to politics, culture, and civil society. At times its scope and influence have been widely exaggerated by proponents and opponents alike. Claims can be found in both popular and academic literatures that globalization is now a permanent feature of global politics, that it has erased national borders rendering them and national governments meaningless, and that it is a source of excessive disparities and a threat to local economies, cultures, and communities.

Such views tend to assume that globalization is an unprecedented phenomenon unique to our times, with an internal dynamic that cannot be managed by contrary economic, social, or political forces. One must, however, be attentive to historical experiences, a close reading of which demonstrates that characteristics of globalization have been evident in the past and they have not always survived economic, social, and political challenges. William Rosen's description of practices in the sixth century reads like some contemporary accounts of globalization: 'A bishop in Gaul could anoint a novitiate with oil from the olive orchards of Greece, bless the event with wine from the vineyards of Italy, and celebrate the sacrament with bread baked with the wheat of Africa while wearing a garment made by Syrian weavers from Chinese silk.'[5]

It is difficult to identify a specific starting point for the developments in the global economy or in society at large that fostered contemporary globalization. Some trace the origins to the advent of capitalism, the latest system being its most recent variant. Others emphasize the Bretton Woods system designed at the end of World War II that established a host of international financial institutions, most of which continue to operate today, albeit with different mandates. Yet others point to ideological and policy shifts commencing in the late 1970s that resulted in a shift to a more liberalized international economic order and that came to be widely adopted throughout much of the world, either through consent or coercion.

Much of the considerable activity that took place in the waning months of World War II continues to define the contemporary global political economy. As noted in Chapter 6, the Bretton Woods system that emerged from these war-time negotiations was itself a reaction to the devastating economic conditions that affected much of the world in the inter-war years. These conditions were, in turn, the result of the collapse of the fragile global economic order that was patched together after World War I. Prior to that war, much of Europe and the United Kingdom enjoyed a period of rather considerable economic interaction, not unlike the interactions that characterize our own global economy. The geographical reach of these activities was limited, but as is argued below, they also are limited in the contemporary period. In considering the factors that shape the global economy it is useful to distinguish the respective influences of states, institutions, private actors, and advances in transportation and communication technology, for each has played a role in the global economy.

Despite the fact that globalization is a defining feature of the contemporary environment, there is little consensus on its implications for the state, national economies, and global politics at large. The objective of this chapter is to review conditions in the global environment that will have implications for the role of the state. The implications for society and the state/society complex are examined in Chapter 10. More specifically, the current chapter will examine the nature, extent, and influence of competing tendencies towards globalization and regionalism and their effects on national governments, including the authority, legitimacy, and capacity of the state. It should be kept in mind that while much of the commentary suggests that globalization acts to constrain or diminish the state and its role in the local and global political economy, globalization does not preclude the need for a role for national governance and thus may even serve to enhance state capacity.

The chapter will not attempt to provide a conclusive interpretation of these tendencies, but will instead offer a sketch of their scope and depth and the range of views that exist. It is important to stress, however, that from our perspective globalization is driven both by political forces at the local, national, and transnational levels and by socio-economic forces arising from the practices of corporations, financiers, and the activities of civil society. The significance of this assumption is that globalization does not have a dynamic of its own, but relies on political, economic, and social practices for its past and future existence and evolution. Thus, globalization can be transformed. It has been historically and will be in the future. How it will evolve depends on who influences the policies and practices that will shape globalization in the future.

Characteristics and Drivers of Globalization

There are many different perspectives on the primary sources of globalization in the contemporary era. For some it is an outgrowth of the progressive development of history. For others it is rooted in ideological positions that shape individual and social practices. Still others view globalization as a result of transformations in economic practices as technology and shifting modes of production redefine social and political relations.

Some observers have traced the origins of the recent wave of globalization to significantly reduced costs in transportation and communications. Technological developments have helped people and firms to overcome time and distance and operate in a fashion where the globe becomes as accessible as the office used to be. Technology also has been extremely beneficial for terrorists, drug lords, money launderers, pirates, and other nefarious elements of global society, as we shall see. As a result of globalization, the globe has become the playground of transnational criminals. The cross-border transfer of capital and the growth of international credit stand out as additional features that have helped to promote a growth in cross-border flows. The result has been a significant expansion in the volume and value of international economic transactions. Alongside these factors, and in part in anticipation of and/or in response to these developments in the private sector, many governments adopted liberal policies designed to facilitate or encourage this expansion of trade and financial flows across national borders.

Anxious to keep up with other more prosperous states, some national governments undertook policies that imitated those of these more prosperous states. Governments in the global South often had little choice as they were forced to design policies within the confines of IMF **structural adjustment programs** and the rules of the World Trade Organization (WTO). In addition, regional and global institutions adopted measures to facilitate transborder flows. There also has been an expansion in the reach and influence of individual and group economic, social, political, and cultural practices that are no longer bound by territorial borders, as individuals travel, study, and otherwise become aware of and interact with other cultures. Often, this interaction is more virtual than real for many who interact through Facebook, YouTube, or Twitter. Identities become blurred and are no longer restricted to nationality and local citizenship, being enhanced or replaced by such transnational identities as feminists, environmentalists, artists, **Islamists**, etc. It is difficult in this vast realm of activity to argue that these developments in the global economy, polity, and society have been driven exclusively or even primarily by technology or by economic interests in the private sector alone, or even solely by governments. In looking at each of these areas we gain a fuller perspective on the nature and scope of globalization in the contemporary period. Globalization refers both to the compression of the world and to the growing perception of the world as an organic whole. It also is both a process and a project. Moreover, although many speak of globalization as simply an economic phenomenon, it is multi-disciplinary in its causes and its impacts.

Globalization Indicators

In his book on globalization, Jan Aart Scholte provides an interesting comparison of some indicators of the degree of access to integrative technologies and the size of global activity.[6] Table 8.1, a slightly revised and updated version of that comparison, reveals that these indicators continue to increase over time.

These data suggest that despite the assertion of national borders and business and personal decisions to review international activities after 9/11, very significant growth in cross-border activities continues. Granted, such figures do not provide definitive evidence of the expansion of globalization itself, but they do represent a continued amount of activity that can fuel conditions of globalization.

Table 8.1 Global Growth in Communications and Finance

Fixed telephone lines	150 million in 1965	1.3 billion in 2006
Mobile telephones	0 in 1978	2.7 billion in 2006
Internet users	0 in 1985	1.1 billion in 2006
Radio sets	57 million in 1930s	3.2 billion in 2006
Television receivers	75 million in 1956	1.5 billion in 2006
International air travellers	25 million in 1950	763 million in 2004
Export Processing Zones	0 in 1953	3,000 in 2002
Daily foreign exchange	$100 billion in 1979	$1.9 trillion in 2006
World stock of Foreign Direct Investment	$66 billion in 1960	$9 trillion in 2006
Transborder companies	7,000 in 1960s	70,000 in 2006

Source: Revised and updated from Jan Aart Scholte, *Globalization: A Critical Introduction* (London: Macmillan, 2000).

Technological Changes

Technological changes have certainly played a part in reducing the costs of transportation and communication and making these available to small businesses and individuals. Many observers, such as Thomas Friedman, have noted that these developments have transformed the global political economy. 'The world is flat', argues Friedman, because people across the globe can be on a competitive footing with one another. Friedman identifies ten levellers that have eliminated differences created by size, distance, and national borders, five of which are related to computer technologies (Netscape IPO, work flow software, open-sourcing, informing, wireless), four of which involve business practices that have been facilitated by the relative ease of transportation and communications (**outsourcing**, offshoring, supply-chaining, insourcing), and only one of which—the fall of the Berlin Wall—that is linked directly to political developments.[7] These technological developments have been important in facilitating the movement of capital, goods, services, and peoples across national borders. Technology, for some, has helped to distinguish the current period of globalization from its historical antecedents.

Others have questioned the significance of these developments. Daniel Cohen maintains that nineteenth-century inventions such as the telegraph and refrigeration and the opening of the Suez Canal were even more instrumental in altering global economic and social practices than the computerization and other phenomena of recent times.[8] In the late nineteenth and early twentieth centuries it was in many respects easier for people to negotiate the political barriers that enabled them to travel and function in different countries, even though costs of travel limited opportunities for many. Following advancements in transportation these costs have been reduced to the point that travel is accessible to increasingly large segments of the population, though today the political barriers to migration pose a more significant challenge. Globalization has not provided for labour mobility, and the political barriers to the movement of peoples are in many respects much greater today than they were in the past.

Movement of People

Citizenship laws, passports, and border controls, unheard of in the past, now seek to control the flow of people across national borders. Clearly, migration remains an important feature of contemporary global politics, but it does not distinguish the contemporary era of globalization from its antecedents. Immigrant numbers in 2005 were about 3 per cent of the world's population, well below those recorded in 1913 when about 10 per cent of global population were immigrants. While the absolute number of people migrating in the contemporary system is quite significant, it pales in relation to the number of people prevented from moving or those forced into illegal and increasingly risky paths of migration to Europe and North America. Efforts to restrict mass migration are frequently accompanied by selective immigration policies by wealthy countries of the North that cull the best and the brightest from the global South. The end result is something quite different from the alleged open borders that the advocates of globalization often applaud. The labour mobility of earlier periods has taken on a somewhat different form.[9] 'For the past century or so, the pattern of migration has shifted a good deal, with changes in government policy playing a key role. Until 1914 governments imposed almost no controls. This allowed the enormous nineteenth-century movement of migrants from Europe to North America. The United States allowed the entry of anybody who was not a prostitute, a convict, a "lunatic"—or, after 1882, Chinese. Travel within Europe was largely uncontrolled: no passports, no work permits.'[10] While the EU has returned to these unrestricted days, much of the rest of the world is demarcated by national border controls.

It would be difficult to imagine such freedoms existing today even before the so-called 'threat' posed by terrorists and economic migrants led some governments to seal borders even more tightly. On the other hand, one should not discount the continued importance of migration and the extent to which it has been facilitated by transportation and communication links. It is, however, important to keep in mind the ability of national governments to exercise some constraints on the movement of people across national borders. In contrast, an ongoing proliferation of unofficial or illegal migrants and refugees continues. It is estimated, for example, that 8–20 million unofficial migrants are in the United States and another 5–10 million are in the EU countries, and refugee numbers around the world stand at more than 10 million. In addition, low-cost travel has encouraged a steady growth in global tourism as a record 842 million tourist arrivals were charted around the world in 2006, and the World Tourism Organization forecast a 4 per cent increase for 2007 and a 2 per cent increase in 2008 to reach another record figure of 922 million. By 2020, it is estimated that international tourist arrivals worldwide will reach 1.6 billion.[11]

Reduced Transportation Costs

Lower transportation costs also have played a significant role in facilitating the movement of goods across national borders. Just as railways, steamships, and refrigeration encouraged an expansion in trade in the nineteenth century, more recent developments have provided yet further incentives for moving goods around the world. In addition to reducing costs, developments in containerization and improved refrigeration have perhaps played the major technological contribution to the considerable growth in international trade in recent decades.

The steam engine, then the diesel engine, the railroad, shipping, highway transport, and the airplane all have driven down the price of delivering goods and people. This has occurred to the point that distance hardly matters for much of the world's population.

> Containerisation had huge consequences for world trade. The most obvious was that the cost of shipping fell precipitously, as ships could be loaded by a few dozen longshoremen rather than hundreds, and as pilferage was reduced. The need to build wooden crates to protect individual items was eliminated, making it feasible to ship consumer goods such as toys and stereo systems halfway around the world. International shipping capacity soared, driven by large increases in the volumes of goods shipped.[12]

Containerization plays a major role in international trade. 'As many as 15 million containers are in circulation, criss-crossing the globe by sea and making over 230 million journeys each year. . . . Most international trade—about 80 per cent of the total by volume—is carried by sea. About half the world's trade by value, and 90 per cent of the general cargo, is transported in containers.'[13] Technological developments, of course, were not the only factors that encouraged the tremendous growth in international trade over the past half-century, as will be discussed below; political choices also have been significant.

BOX 8.1

Containerization and Controversy

© Rafael Ramirez Lee/iStockphoto.com

The *Emma Maersk*, said to be the world's largest container vessel, unloaded 45,000 tonnes of Christmas goods from China at Suffolk, England, in 2006.

Hundreds of spectators lined the shore to watch the *Emma Maersk* as it was guided into Felixstowe by three tugs. The ship is a quarter of a mile long, 200 feet high, and as wide as a motorway. Its cargo of toys, books, computers,

Christmas crackers, decorations, and food is bound for Britain and mainland Europe. The vessel's master, Henrik Solmer, expressed pride at being the first person to take charge of it and said he was often hailed by other ships that it passed. Mr Solmer said: 'They say, "Hey, we heard about you and it is nice to see you coming. You are beautiful and it is a nice speed that you are doing."'

The *Emma Maersk*, a PS-class vessel, can carry 11,000 20-foot containers, and the ship's anchor weighs 29 tons. The ship is equipped with over 40,000 metres of pipes and can be operated by a crew of just 13, whose accommodation and the ship's bridge are as high as a 12-storey building.

But campaigners have warned of the environmental damage such giant ships could cause. 'The environmental costs of long-distance trade need to be properly taken into account', said Dr Caroline Lucas, Green Party MEP for South East England. 'We must manage international trade in a way which is socially and environmentally sustainable, working towards global agreement on a raft of measures such as taxation on fuel and import tariffs designed to support home-grown businesses. This will help offset the environmental damage caused by ships like the *Emma Maersk* plying international waters filled with MP3 players and plastic toys.'

Paul Davey, of the Port of Felixstowe, said the size of the load reflected the increase of trade with China. 'This year alone we have seen a 16 per cent increase in the volume of goods coming in from China. The year before that it was 24 per cent, so it is continuing at a considerable pace of increase', he said. The ship's Danish owner, Maersk Line, said the *Emma Maersk* was 'one of the most environmentally friendly' container vessels built. On its website, the company says the ship is the largest container vessel in the world.

The ship is on its maiden voyage and has previously called at Yantian in China, Hong Kong, and Tanjung Pelepas, in Malaysia. A total of 3,000 containers are being unloaded in the Suffolk port. The ship will then move on to mainland Europe to deliver other containers.

Source: Adapted from BBC News, at <news.bbc.co.uk/go/pr/fr/-/2/hi/uk_news/england/suffolk/6117080.stm>. © BBC MMVII.

Communications Technology

Communications technology has had far-reaching effects on cross-border contacts for business and, perhaps even more significantly, for individuals. The dramatic decline in the costs of information-processing and expanding accessibility to computers have increased the potential for individuals in different corners of the world to communicate in real time at insignificant costs. The ramifications of this are significant on a number of levels. Expanded access to and use of communications technology reduces the significance of time and space, allowing for virtual contact between individuals on different sides of the planet. This facilitates the movement of capital around the globe on a continuous basis, the effects of which can be seen in the rapid and near-universal spread of market and currency changes from one part of the world to another. It also makes it easier for firms to house production plants and management offices in different corners of the planet, and allows individuals and civil society associations from different countries to organize and co-ordinate political action, thus empowering them and in the process limiting the effectiveness of government measures to control the flow of information and political activity across national borders.

Capitalism, MNCs, and Transborder Economic Activity

Economic interests, to be sure, have played a major role in fostering globalization. Capitalism has, for some, a dynamic of its own that fosters the development of monopolies operating beyond territorial borders. Many firms have favoured the elimination of border controls and national regulatory measures in the interests of **economies of scale** and larger profits. This has been especially true with lower communication and transportation costs and with a reduction in some of the risks of operating in overseas markets. Multinational corporations (MNCs) have long been plying international waters and crossing borders in search of resources and markets. Some countries, such as Canada, were settled and developed to a considerable extent in response to the practices of such firms, in Canada's case, beginning with the Hudson's Bay Company and its rival, the North West Company and, later, with numerous American companies that jumped the tariff wall to manufacture in Canada for the Canadian (and Commonwealth) market. MNCs continue to proliferate, and while they predominantly originate within the core group of capitalist economies, they also emerge out of non-traditional sources such as Brazil, South Africa, and South Korea. These corporations operate in a manner that often disregards political borders and national governments, and many of them do not exhibit corporate social responsibility. At the same time they seek the support and protection of governments when conditions appear unfavourable or risky. Governments compete with other governments in order to have MNCs locate on their territories by offering these companies incentives such as tax breaks, pledges of governmental assistance or improved infrastructure, or lax enforcement of environmental and labour standards. This process of attracting foreign investment has been characterized by some as a **'race to the bottom'**.[14]

The Political and Policy Context

Having considered the role of technology and business in globalization, we now turn to the political dimension and consider the policy decisions that have played a role in furthering or impeding globalization. Governments, often working through regional and international institutions, have taken an active hand in shaping the contemporary global economy. Some scholars have cited the role of hegemonic powers in shaping the global economy. Global economic practices, like other areas of global politics, have been influenced by dominant powers. In the late nineteenth century, Britain took the lead in promoting a liberal system of free trade. Through a series of bilateral agreements, the British government attempted to encourage other governments to adopt liberal principles in their trade relationship. The effort had some results, and for a period of time liberal practices encouraged a considerable amount of cross-border economic activity.

For many within the geographic reach of Europe, barriers to economic transactions were eliminated. Indeed, by 2007 the United States had not equalled the level of trade dependence (as measured by exports and imports as a percentage of total national output) that Britain had experienced in 1900. Many prosperous individuals in the early 1900s considered themselves part of a global economy where national borders and different languages did not impede them from experiencing the goods of other countries. The experience of the early twentieth century, however, demonstrates the fragility of the global economy. Without institutional support, the **liberal trade policy** was difficult to sustain. The outbreak of war on the European continent confirmed the death of this short-lived but intense period of liberalization.

The **Depression** of the 1930s provided the inspiration for the United States to launch an initiative to create another liberal order.[15] Led in part by Secretary of State Cordell Hull, who saw freer trade and the resulting economic interdependence as a foundation for peaceful relations among these trading nations, the US initially turned to **bilateral treaties** as a means of encouraging the proliferation of liberal practices. Operating under the authority of the Reciprocal Trade Agreement Act of 1934, the US executive, freed from the constraints of direct congressional oversight, began to conclude a series of bilateral agreements designed to promote freer trade. A key principle in these agreements was that of most-favoured nation (MFN), which meant that any state concluding a trade agreement with the US would receive the same tariff rate for a product that the US had granted to its most-favoured trading partner. As a result, other countries were guaranteed that they would not be disadvantaged by any other agreements the US might conclude with other states for the same products. This principle became an important cornerstone of the postwar international trading order that developed around the GATT and subsequently the WTO.

As the world fell into World War II, the US government began to favour a more institutionalized approach and worked to secure political support for its initiative. In the days preceding the US government's entry into the war, it called on other states to commit to a postwar international order that would embed liberal economic practices. This was not only of benefit to the expanding American economy, but also secured a more institutionalized approach to trade liberalization than the one promoted by Britain 50 years earlier. The negotiations at Bretton Woods in 1944 gave substance to this **liberal international economic order** in the form of a series of institutions designed to support and regulate that order. The agreement at Bretton Woods to establish the International Monetary Fund and the International Bank for Reconstruction and Development (IBRD), commonly known as the World Bank, and the other institutions of the World Bank Group, was therefore an attempt to secure through these institutions a more liberalized international economic order. The outcome was a clear reflection of American economic, political, and military power, but it also reflected a commitment on the part of the states involved to co-operate in a collective institutionalized effort to secure a more orderly and open global economy. This postwar international economic order encouraged an expansion in

The IMF and World Bank Group buildings in Washington, DC.

© Matthew Cavanaugh/EPA/Corbis

international trade that was, initially, overwhelmingly reliant on an expanding American economy, but has since been sustained by the institutional arrangements established at Bretton Woods.

The Role of the State in Globalization

Globalization, according to Scholte, can be viewed from different perspectives.[16] One perspective interprets globalization as internationalization. This interpretation sees the expansion of activities that cross international borders as an indication of a significant shift in global activity. Internationalization refers to the type and amount of cross-border activity identified by such markers as the extent of international travel, trade, investment, and cultural and communications flows, all of which indicate an increasingly globalized community. A second perspective describes globalization as liberalization or the removal of regulatory barriers affecting the flow of trade, travel, communications, and financial transfers and, therefore, creating a more global economy. A third perspective identifies globalization as the spread of 'supraterritorial' or 'transborder' relations—transgovernmental and transnational social relations less tied to territorial frameworks. In this view, territorial distance and borders are less significant, suggesting a transformation of human geography where local identities are superseded by identities not confined or defined by territorial boundaries.

The editors of *Foreign Policy* magazine have developed a globalization index that seeks to identify the characteristics of globalization and is then used to measure the extent to which states have globalized.[17] The index incorporates a combination of economic, personal, technological, and political indicators, including such specific items as trade and investment flows, telephone use and travel, Internet use, and participation in international organizations and international treaties. The index, which has been used since 2000 to measure the performance of different countries, reveals that globalization has continued to expand, though much of its growth continues to occur among members of the Organisation for Economic Co-operation and Development (OECD), the wealthiest countries on the planet. The index is based on national statistics, clearly the most accessible form of information, but one that does tend to reinforce the view that this is a practice driven by national policies and practices.

We define globalization as a process that widens the extent and form of cross-border transactions among peoples, goods, and services and that deepens the economic interdependence between and among globalizing entities, which may be private or public institutions or governments. Globalization differs from other forms of intensified interdependence between national economies: true economic globalization involves a qualitative shift towards a system based on a consolidated global marketplace for production, distribution, and consumption rather than on autonomous national economies. Equally important, globalization involves more than economics or economic interconnectedness. It increases risks and opportunities for individuals and communities seeking to transform local traditions and modes of behaviour in reaction to processes of globalization that emphasize mobility, simultaneity, pluralism, and alternate routes to the satisfaction of needs and services.

However one defines globalization and regardless of the indicators used, this phenomenon has not occurred at a comparable level across the globe. A closer reading of most indicators reveals that globalization is much more extensive among OECD countries than within any regional grouping. While countries throughout the global South are certainly affected by globalization, often in dramatic ways, the distribution of benefits has become highly skewed both within and between countries. Cohen maintains that 'The paradox that economists have been late to understand is that reducing the costs of transportation and communication does not promote wealth but instead favors its polarization.'[18]

As suggested above, the pace and pattern of globalization have been very uneven among firms, sectors, and countries. While financial markets are largely globalized, for example, most kinds of labour still remain national and regional. For many throughout the world the cumulative effect of open borders, free trade, and economic globalization is the erosion of economic security, in terms of employment, income, and even the stability of local culture and community. Various economic indicators demonstrate that globalization has been accompanied by an increase in inequality both between and within states.

> Far from financing a convergence of fortunes between rich and poor people, globalization has coincided with a decade of increasing concentration of income, wealth, and control over resources. OECD countries, with 19 per cent of the global population, account for 71 per cent of world trade, 58 per cent of foreign direct investment, and 91 per cent of all Internet users. Such growing disparities, with the social upheavals and discontents they represent, impose real demands on governance—demands that more and more governments are unable to answer in the traditional methods that governments use.[19]

The nature of globalization is nicely captured in Figure 8.1, which represents the distribution of international Internet bandwidth. The concentration of linkages in the global political economy are most extensive between Europe and North America and to a lesser extent Asia. They are extremely modest between these regions and Latin America and virtually non-existent between these regions and Africa. The data would look quite similar along such indicators as direct foreign investment, trade, and other economic and technological measures of globalization.

The effects of globalization are profound and its integrative momentum powerful. Globalization challenges the adaptive capacity of the nation-state, demands new processes of democratization,

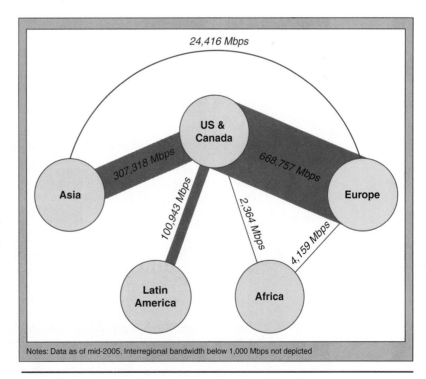

Notes: Data as of mid-2005. Interregional bandwidth below 1,000 Mbps not depicted

Figure 8.1 Interregional Internet bandwidth, 2005.
Source: *The Digital Divide Report: ICT Diffusion Index 2005* (New York: UNCTAD, 2006), 12.

shapes tendencies towards ideological extremism and religious fundamentalism, influences the evolution of North–South relations, and enables NGOs to generate new norms and policies for global governance. In response, several parallel counter-forces, grounded in regionalization, decentralization, and localism, are taking root throughout the globe.

Disenchantment arising from the very uneven rewards and benefits of globalization has led to strong reactions, discussed in greater detail in Chapter 10. These reactions are expressed as **religious extremism**, various forms of terrorism, and efforts to assert the salience of particular ethnicities/cultures and local identities. One response has been the formation of various regional groupings of states that have formed economic coalitions in an effort to enhance their position vis-à-vis larger economic players. Other responses include the establishment of a slow-food movement in Italy (see Box 8.2), the return to Islamic teaching in Central Asia, and the rise in secessionist movements in places like Algeria, the Philippines, Sri Lanka, and Spain.

Finally, globalization may create a need for supranational global governance regimes to maximize welfare globally. Such institutions and regimes may be needed to address cross-border market failures that national governments are unable to surmount or compensate for fully. For example, in response to the crisis in financial markets in 2009, British Prime Minister Gordon Brown, among others, called for a strengthening of global regulatory regimes. The fields of satellite communications, seabed exploration, nuclear proliferation, and protection of the ozone layer, for example, may demand the attention of global institutions to reduce the co-ordination and transaction costs of such activities or to capture the external benefits of intergovernmental networking. These international public and social goods will increasingly require pluralist and multi-level governance structures if they are to produce truly global public value.[20]

BOX 8.2

The International Slow Food Movement

Founded in 1986 by the leftist Italian journalist Carlo Petrini, the International Slow Food Movement is an anti-globalization response to the trend towards the homogenization of food around the world. This movement was spurred on by the opening of Italy's first McDonald's restaurant in Rome. Petrini regarded the introduction of the Golden Arches' fast food to Italy as a cultural affront to the local cuisine. He was determined to save local and regional foods and small producers in various parts of Italy from extinction, to revive and celebrate taste and the senses, and to preserve traditional plant varieties.

Ironically, the movement for slow food has become globalized. It now has 100,000 members in some 132 countries. But its headquarters are located in the Piedmont region of northern Italy, near Turin. There one can find a worldwide collection of small *convivia*, or chapters, that meet informally to share and promote local small producers, to learn about culinary traditions and culture, and to arrange food and wine tastings. These chapters are being replicated in many countries of the globe, including in the US and Canada.

Globalization and the Theory of the State in Global Politics

A common issue in discussions of globalization is its effects on the state. 'One of the chief characteristics of these globalizing dynamics is that they overwhelm the attempts of states to manage globalization alone or control its effects.... Even in the smallest details of domestic legislation and regulation, every state is now constrained by international norms, law, political obligation, and opinions in world markets.'[21] Yet it is also clear that states have not yielded the policy-making field to these economic forces.

In the aftermath of 9/11 it also has become quite clear that states can, with some costs, assert a considerable degree of control over their borders.[22] Conditions will generally determine what those costs are and a state's willingness to absorb them; but the point remains that they can and have been used. It is thus important to recognize that, despite some claims to the contrary, globalization is not an inevitable force clearing everything in its path. Traditional realist views of the state in international politics maintain that a distinction remains between the domestic and the foreign. According to this view the state can still provide a barrier of sorts to protect a domestic community from interference from external forces. While conceived principally in security terms, the view is implicitly extended to other arenas.

The principle of state sovereignty holds that the state, in the form of a national government, can exercise full and final authority over domestic affairs. That view has always been somewhat exaggerated and reflects more of a legal ideal type than a practical reality for most states and peoples. Yet, it has been important to realist theory in that it reaffirms the primacy of the state as an actor in global politics and the potential impermeability of the state—thus dividing and separating, in effect, the 'domestic' from the 'international'. Globalization presents a formidable challenge to this view of the state, and much evidence demonstrates that states cannot provide complete protection for their citizens from economic, environmental, or physical threats. The reality is that borders are neither irrelevant nor impenetrable. It is, however, as important to recognize that the state still functions, and in some cases thrives, amid the myriad cross-border activities that define globalization.

Contemporary political, social, and economic discourse is riddled with phrases such as the **'borderless world'**, the 'demise of the state', and 'end of sovereignty'. Each of these in different ways calls attention to the generic phenomenon referred to as globalization. Globalization has become one of those terms that has achieved a common acceptance though lacking a clear and generally accepted definition. What exactly is globalization? What has created and sustained globalization? To what extent is globalization today different from international linkages of the past? More generally, who promotes globalization and who seeks to arrest its expansion, and to what effects? In what ways has it contributed to the challenges of governance? How has it affected civil societies within various countries around the world? Are there significant differences between its impacts in economically developed societies and in less developed countries? To what extent does globalization lead to cultural consensus and how does it contribute to cultural particularisms, including religious fundamentalisms?

Globalization as the Triumph of Economics

'The nation-state is just about through as an economic unit', wrote Charles Kindle-berger 40 years ago.[23] His was not a lone sentiment, even at that time, as many have speculated that economic practices fuelled by the inevitable dynamic of economic liberalization would soon make national borders irrelevant. The argument about the ability of economic globalization to penetrate national borders, rendering them porous to external influences and incapacitating local authorities, has been prevalent among proponents and opponents alike. Proponents maintain that the state makes little sense in a world organized along the principle of economic efficiency.

Globalization has been cited frequently as a powerful dynamic that will sweep away our traditional notions of territorial states, as these states find it increasingly problematic to establish authoritative and effective national regulative control over key economic factors. As a result, national governments, so the argument goes, will become increasingly dependent on or responsive to developments and decisions taking place at the regional or global level. At times labelled 'hyperglobalizers' because of their claims regarding the strength of the globalizing dynamic, some of those individuals making the above case argue for the need to look differently at global politics and the place of states in global politics. They see a single global market emerging with the decline of states. In the words of Susan Strange: 'the impersonal forces of world markets…are now more powerful than the states to whom ultimate political authority over society and economy is supposed to belong …the declining authority of states is reflected in a growing diffusion of authority to other institutions and associations, and to local and regional bodies.'[24]

Thomas Friedman describes this new world fostered by globalization as 'a global, Web-enabled playing field that allows for multiple forms of collaboration without regard to geography or distance—or soon, even language'.[25] While not everyone accepts the sort of arguments put forward by hyperglobalists such as Friedman,[26] one must admit that Friedman has a way of capturing for the popular imagination the dynamics of change at work in the world today. A columnist for the *New York Times*, Friedman has provided two popular accounts of globaliza-tion in his books *The Lexus and the Olive Tree* (1999) and *The World Is Flat* (2004). Both works look at globalization as a powerful force in global politics driven largely by economic and technological forces that have privileged markets and individuals over the authority of national governments. Friedman notes that globalization confronts the tribal politics that defined the nation-state system, and he maintains that the dynamics driving globalization are largely impervious to political control.[27]

Others have expressed similar views, highlighting different features of this changed socio-economic environment. Jean-Marie Guehenno, for instance, has written that:

> The spatial solidarity of territorial communities is disappearing, to be replaced by tem-porary interest groups. Now, the nation-state …is prisoner to a spatial conception of power…space has ceased to be the pertinent criterion.… If solidarity can no longer be locked into geography, if there is no longer a city, if there is no longer a nation, can there still be politics.[28]

Alongside Friedman's arguments about the levelling effects of globalization, John Naisbitt, in *Global Paradox*, takes the view that, 'the bigger the world economy, the more powerful its smallest players'.[29] He argues that technological revolution is creating a giant global economy in which the nation-state is losing significance as its borders become highly permeable.

Globalization: The State Transformed

The most popular interpretation of the relationship between this phenomenon of globalization and the state is that the process has in some way transformed the state, rendering it rather different from the type of state that existed in the past. Those who hold this position have been described as 'transformationalists', but they cover a wide array of theoretical perspectives and offer different accounts of precisely how the state has been changed by globalization. Linda Weiss, for example, emphasizes 'state adaptivity and its continued advantages rather than diminution of state capacity in an increasingly "global" environment. State capacity, far from becoming irrelevant, has acquired new significance in a changing world economy.'[30] Other arguments tend to focus on different features of state adaptation. For example, according to David Held et al., 'Rather than globalisation bringing about the "end of the state", it has encouraged a spectrum of adjustment strategies and in certain respects, a more activist state.' Thus, 'the power of national governments is not necessarily diminished by globalisation but on the contrary is being reconstituted and restructured in response to the growing complexity of processes of governance in a more interconnected world.'[31]

Ian Clark sees globalization as the result of transformations that take place at the national level. 'Globalisation is not some external process standing apart from sovereignty, but is instead another way of describing changes that sovereignty is undergoing. They are not subject and object, but two alternative formulations of the same set of transitions.'[32] Raimo Väyrynen acknowledges that despite changes that seem to enhance the power, or at least flexibility, of non-state actors, the state retains some capacity to access its authority. He argues that:

> as a result of globalisation, transnational social, political, economic, and cultural spaces have expanded and their autonomy has increased. It is probably misleading to claim that these spaces have acquired an agentive power of their own. However, they have a degree of autonomy in the sense that governments and international organisations are unable to control effectively many of their aspects.[33]

That is, 'the expansion and deepening of transnational spaces need not entail the loss of state sovereignty. States have a surprising capacity to reinvent their tasks and mobilise new resources, many of them immaterial.'[34]

Richard Falk takes a somewhat different approach and argues that while the state remains significant, the state system has become redundant. In his words, 'The state remains a pre-eminent political actor on the global stage; but the aggregation of states, what has been called "a states system", is no longer in control of the global policy process.'[35] A slightly different take on the effect of globalization on the state looks at the issue of territory and national boundaries. Jan Aart Scholte associates globalization with **deterritorialization** or 'supraterritoriality' and avers, 'State sovereignty depends on territorialism…the end of territorialism has, therefore, brought the end of sovereignty.'[36] But he does not necessarily associate it with the end of the state; rather, he describes the state as post-sovereign. In his words, 'The rise of supraterritoriality has encouraged changes in the character of the state undermining the state itself.'[37] In his article, 'Global Capitalism and the State,' Scholte opines, 'The persistence of the state does not imply the immutability of the state, however. For one thing, while the state has retained pivotal significance in globalising capitalism it has lost its former core attribute of sovereignty.'[38]

Stephen Gill, on the other hand, refers to this as the **new constitutionalism**. 'The new constitutionalism can be defined as the political project of attempting to make transnational liberalism, and if possible liberal democratic capitalism, the sole model for future development.'[39] This has significant implications for the state and for the possibility of state autonomy.

> Central…to new constitutionalism is the imposition to discipline on public institutions, partly to prevent national interference with the property rights and entry and exit options of holders of **mobile capital** with regard to particular political jurisdictions. These initiatives are also linked to efforts to define appropriate policy, partly by strengthening surveillance mechanisms of international organizations and private agencies, such as the bond raters.[40]

For Gill, therefore, one of the key features of the emerging global economy has been external agents of surveillance and their efforts to control the actions of states. 'At the heart of the global economy there is an internationalization of authority and governance that not only involves international organizations (such as the BIS, IMF, and World Bank) and transnational firms, but also private consultancies and private bond rating agencies which act, as it were, as arbiters of the supply of capital for public finance and corporate investment, and as "private makers of global public policy."'[41] The net effect of this development has been to reframe the context in which states interact in the international system. That such a change is occurring at the same time when there has been an increase in the number of national governments using democratic mechanisms suggests an interesting relationship between the two levels, but also poses some significant problems that will be discussed later.

David Held and Anthony McGrew write that globalization has created numerous constraints on the state:

> a global system of production and exchange which is beyond the control of any single nation-state; extensive networks of transnational interaction and communication which transcend national societies and evade most forms of national regulation; the power and activities of a vast array of international regimes and organizations, many of which reduce the scope for action of even leading states; and the internationalization of security structures which limit the scope for the independent use of military force by states.

The net result, according to Held and McGrew, places national governments as much in a global setting as in a domestic one and leads to a political process in which decision-making responsibilities, political influence, and salient political constituencies are diffuse and in transition and are no longer organized exclusively along national lines. 'The contemporary global order is defined by multiple systems of transactions and coordination which link people, communities and societies in highly complex ways and which, given the nature of modern communications, virtually annihilate territorial boundaries as barriers to socio-economic activity and relations.'[42]

Globalization: The State Remains

The final group of scholars discussed here question the arguments about the extent to which the state has changed in response to globalization. These skeptics maintain that the state has been largely responsible for the practices and policies that make up globalization. Skeptics emphasize the persistence of states and acknowledge that globalization is not a new phenomenon. Here, too, however, there are profound theoretical differences in the reasons for arguing about the ongoing role of the state. These observers argue that the state continues to define much of what is most relevant about global politics, that globalization has not removed the state from the stage, nor has it transformed the state in significant ways. The argument builds on an assumption that the state, in principle, retains the authority to exercise control over the forces of globalization. The arguments vary, however, in terms of whether the state acts in response to external security threats or because it is being shaped by dominant economic forces that continue to benefit from a territorially based state. Such arguments also include certain caveats, for example, that a state may pay a considerable price in controlling globalization, that not all states may be able to control these forces to the same degree of cost effectiveness, and that the state itself remains in control of the process but may be encouraging globalization through deliberate policy choices.

Thus, one can see that both realists and Marxists might share the view that the state retains a considerable degree of capacity. Stephen Krasner, for example, writes:

> I do not want to claim that globalization has no impact on state control, but these challenges are not new.... There is no evidence that globalization has systematically undermined state control or led to homogenization of policies and structures.... Transnational activities have challenged state control in some areas, but these challenges are not manifestly more problematic than in the past.[43]

Paul Hirst and Grahame Thompson are equally skeptical of the view that the state is making an exit. They suggest that the impact of globalization on the state is highly exaggerated and that states continue to enjoy their place in global governance. According to them, 'nation-states are now simply one class of powers and political agencies in a complex system of power from world to local levels', but states are still important because 'they are the key practitioners of the art of government.'[44] Kenneth Waltz has noted that: 'The international economy, like national economies, operates within a set of rules and institutions. Rules and institutions have to be made and sustained. Britain, to a large extent, provided the service prior to World War I; no one did between the wars, and the United States has done so since. More than any other state, the United States makes the rules and maintains the institutions that shape the international political economy.'[45] Not surprisingly, as a realist, Waltz sees power as the key ingredient in accounting for the shape of the global political economy. In his view dominant powers determine the type of system, and dominant powers are required to sustain the system in the face of challenges.

Among more critical scholars, Eric Helleiner contests the view that economics drives this globalization process. In a detailed analysis of financial reforms undertaken in the post-World War II period, Helleiner concludes that 'today's globalized financial order should be seen as being actively made by state choices and state decisions.'[46] He adds:

> Most governments in the advanced industrialized world are not nearly as shackled by economic globalization as is commonly believed. They retain substantial autonomy in regulating their economies, in designing their social policies, and in maintaining institutions that differ from those of their trading partners.[47]

The view is shared by others, such as Leo Panitch, who says that 'globalisation is a process that is authored by active states; states that are not victims of the process, but active agents of making globalisation happen, and are increasingly responsible...for sustaining it, and even burdened with the increasing responsibility of managing its contradictions and crises.'[48]

Another strong indicator of the continuing relevance of the state is the increased attention given to the state as a necessary agent of economic development. While some observers still discount states, it is also apparent that some form of competent state authority is essential for stable economic activity to take place. The World Bank, since the late 1990s, has emphasized the importance of governance in accounting for the performance of national economies. This follows from an earlier effort to establish international standards that ignored national authorities who were seen as incompetent and hence irrelevant to economic development. This view also rested on neo-liberal ideas that allowed only a minimal role for the state. Yet, discounting the state has proved problematic. 'For the moment, only the state can guarantee political and legal order, without which there is no profitable investment, no sustainable production, no sustained consumption. Companies and markets, therefore, cannot scoff at national regulations, unless there exist supranational entities that take over from states.'[49]

Conclusion

During the twentieth century the number of issues being addressed at the regional or global level expanded greatly. There was a phenomenal growth in the number and range of activities of both intergovernmental and non-governmental organizations. The number of international conferences and congresses grew exponentially and the growth in international agreements was equally impressive. In response, national governments appeared to experience a certain loss of control or, at the very least, an inability to act on their own and within their own sphere. Rather than dismiss the state, the alternative is to recognize that the global stage is now shared with other actors besides the state. As Mark Zacher has written: 'What is occurring in the world is not a serious demise of states as the central actors in the system but rather their acceptance that they have to work together in controlling a variety of interdependencies.'[50] Increasingly, governments turn to international institutions and international agreements as a means of addressing social, economic, and political problems. Such recourse, however, is not limited to government and is not their only option.

Developments in the international economy and especially the growing interconnections between and among national economies have encouraged the process of globalization. Increased trade has been accompanied by the growth and expansion of multinational firms and by international financial transactions, which have proliferated at a phenomenal rate. The responses to the most recent financial crisis will help to illustrate these conflicting pressures and will demonstrate if and how governments are able to assert national measures. Early indications in the response of the US government to the crisis suggested a reversion to nationalist practices through measures such as 'buy American' provisions, but, on balance, the US and other governments have attempted to co-ordinate fiscal and monetary measures in the short term. They also have undertaken negotiations in the G20 towards developing comparable if not fully compatible responses in such areas as regulatory policy.

One of the effects of these interconnections has been an increased reliance by national governments on international regulatory measures to manage trade and financial transactions. Some observers argue that this has altered the nature of states and has direct implications for national-level policy choices. Evidence suggests that these developments have forced states to seek national policy adjustments at the international level, or at the very least in collaboration with one or more other states. The bottom line is that, in some states and for some issues, authority has been transferred from the national level to the regional and/or international level. Twenty years ago, for example, Robert Cox noted that 'Globalization transforms the bases of state authority from within and produces a multilevel **post-Westphalian world order** in which the state remains important but only as one among several levels of authority.'[51] Indeed, few arenas of national life have not been touched by these developments. In addition to their appearance in the economic realm, international regulations also are evident in the areas of environment, communications, transportation, and maritime affairs, among many others. In the end, however, a multi-layered or more networked system of global governance does not eliminate the state or even necessarily diminish its significance. It does, however, force the state into a different policy-making environment where agendas and processes are not easily controlled.

Key Terms

bilateral treaties	liberal trade policy
'borderless world'	mobile capital
depression	new constitutionalism
deterritorialization	outsourcing
economies of scale	post-Westphalian world order
internationalization	'race to the bottom'
Islamists	religious extremism
liberal international economic order	structural adjustment programs

Discussion Questions

1. What is meant by globalization?
2. Does globalization provide a useful descriptor for the contemporary global political economy?
3. What are the most important features of globalization?
4. How has globalization transformed global politics?

5. How has globalization influenced the state and its involvement in global politics?
6. How has the state responded to globalization?
7. How is globalization different from/similar to interdependence?
8. What is 'hyperglobalization'?

Suggested Readings

Friedman, Thomas. *The World Is Flat: A Brief History of the Globalized World in the Twenty-First Century.* London: Allen Lane, 2005. This is Friedman's second book on globalization and argues that various factors are reducing the barriers that used to prevent people in different parts of the world from accessing the benefits resulting from globalization.

Scholte, Jan Aart. *Globalization: A Critical Introduction*, 2nd edn. New York: Palgrave Macmillan, 2005. This is one of the better introductory surveys of a process that has defined many aspects of our contemporary era.

Singer, Peter. *One World*, 2nd edn. New Haven: Yale University Press, 2004. Singer provides an ethical challenge for those confronted by the myriad changes brought on by globalization.

Global Links

BBC Globalization Website
www.bbc.co.uk/worldservice/programmes/globalisation/
  Good overview of issues and practices involved in globalization from a high-quality news service.
The Globalist
www.theglobalist.com/
  Online source of information and short reflections and reviews on a wide variety of globalization issues.
Yale Global Online
yaleglobal.yale.edu/
  A website developed out of Yale University's Center for the Study of Globalization with news and analysis.

Debate 8

Be it resolved that globalization is responsible for global economic downturns.

Chapter Nine

The Globalization of Business and Business in Global Governance

By what right do a self-selected group of druggists, biscuit makers, and computer designers become the architects of the new world?[1]

Introduction

The state shares the global stage with a large number and wide variety of non-state actors. This has always been the case, yet the process of globalization has tended to increase the number, presence, and prominence of these non-state or sovereignty-free actors. In this chapter we examine one such group of non-state actors—multinational corporations (MNCs) and affiliated commercial agents. In the following chapters we examine two other prominent non-state groups—**civil society organizations** and **criminal networks**. These increasingly active and empowered agents have come to play an important role in the politics of **global governance**, though much debate surrounds their ability to override the authority or influence of the state. Many observers have called attention to the increased prominence of these groups, suggesting that they now compete with and in some instances circumvent or supersede the influence and authority of states. To note the increased prominence of these non-state actors it is not necessary to argue that states have lost the prominent position they have held for many years. It is, instead, to recognize that the stage of global politics has become increasingly crowded and that, as a result, the art of governance has increased in its variety and complexity.

Fuelled, in part, by the factors driving globalization—trade, investment, transportation, and information technologies—the cross-border activities of these non-state actors also are supported by increased migratory flows of people across national borders and by pressing economic, social, and environmental issues that cannot be contained by territorial divisions. These non-state actors represent a wide array of concerns: private corporations committed to maximizing their profits wherever they invest; religious groups committed to expanding their adherents and helping those in dire need; anti-globalization activists aiming to close down the World Trade Organization (WTO); illicit bodies seeking to undermine institutions of global governance. These agents have now become a permanent feature, or perpetual concern, of many international meetings and regional and global institutions. As former UN Secretary-General Kofi Annan noted, 'The UN once dealt only with governments. By now we know that peace and prosperity cannot be achieved without partnerships involving governments, international organizations, the business community and civil society. In today's world we depend on each other.'[2]

In examining the role of non-state actors in global politics, it is first necessary to distinguish between these various actors. They play very different roles and have different status within the institutions and processes of global governance. For our purposes, there are three general categories of such actors: corporations, civil society organizations, and criminal organizations. The first and third operate for profit, the middle ones do not. Corporations and civil society organizations usually work within the law and have been accorded at least some degree of legitimacy in most circles, while criminal organizations obviously do not. Given their non-state status, however, they all tend to operate both apart from and, at times, within the established state-based and state-authorized processes and institutions. They all share a concern with and a desire to influence the course of global politics. It is worth spending a little time looking at each in turn to understand the effect of these non-state actors on global governance.

Biersteker and Hall, among others, have noted how the terrain of global governance is now populated by authorities other than the state. They refer to these authorities as 'market authority', 'moral authority', and 'illicit authority', represented respectively by the private sector, civil society, and criminal agents. From their vantage point, private authority has come to rival the authority wielded by states and the international organizations to which they contribute. 'Markets, market actors, transnational movements, mafias, and mercenaries are each recognized socially as possessing authority within certain issue domains. Their authority is legitimate to the extent that they obtain the consent of the governed and exercise certain rights within those domains.'[3] There are two principal sources of authority of private-sector, corporate actors. 'The first regards the capacity to successfully establish manufacturing, productive, regulatory, and reporting standards that become recognized by others and that are subsequently adhered to by others. The second form regards the increasing acceptance by people, particularly in **advanced industrialized countries**, of market based decision-making over politically based decision-making, often both on efficiency and normative grounds.'[4]

Part of the difficulty in unravelling the distribution of power among states, let alone among states and these non-state actors, is the assumption that power is a limited commodity and that if one party has some it must be at the expense of others. This obviously is not the case as power is always relational. Thus, for example, corporations may be able to exercise power with some states, but not with others. Power also is situation-specific, that is, the ability to exercise influence may depend on the issue at hand, the individuals involved, and the particular circumstances at play. Corporations may wield power with some states on some issues at some times but not at other times with the same state and the same issue. It all depends. That is why arguments about whether corporation 'x' is more powerful than state 'y' are usually pointless. One needs to be more specific. Having said that, it is possible to maintain that corporations have gained influence over many areas of global politics and play a very significant role in many of the issues and practices that concern us. It is certainly the case that a review of contemporary global politics is incomplete without a consideration of the role that these corporations play in our world.

Corporations have been both a primary source of and distinctively advantaged by many of the developments, policies, and practices that have supported globalization. For example, the declining relevance of space and distance brought about by improvements in information and communications technologies and substantial reductions in their costs, as well as in the costs of transportation, have made it possible for corporations to set aside geographical considerations in making decisions about the location of manufacturing facilities, suppliers, and markets. National borders also took on less significance as governments adopted policies of **privatization**, **liberalization**, and **deregulation** in the 1980s. Consequently, business firms encountered fewer restrictions as regulations were eased and financial flows increasingly became unfettered. Both small and large investors were able to move their money virtually anywhere in the world with few restrictions, leading eventually to a 24/7 financial web that connects national stock exchanges around the globe. The abdication of regulatory schemes by national governments also has enabled and encouraged the business sector to devise its own regulations, becoming in some instances a private authority for the global market. These developments have led some to suggest that corporations exercise the real pre-eminent power in the global political economy.

As we will see in the next couple of chapters, for some observers of the non-state actor phenomenon, this has become a major concern that must be restrained. For others, it is what globalization is truly about. American consumer activist Ralph Nader describes globalization as 'the global economic and political structure that makes every government increasingly hostage to a global financial and commerce system engineered through an autocratic system of international governance that favors corporate interests.'[5] Not surprisingly, Nader's interpretation is not universally shared. Globalization advocates such as Thomas Friedman believe that such practices act as a 'golden straitjacket' that rightly limits the political power of states so that the market can flourish to the betterment of all. Either way, sorting out the role of corporations in global governance becomes an essential requirement for an understanding of contemporary global politics.

Multinational Corporations Defined

The term 'multinational' was first applied to corporations with overseas operations in the 1960s, despite the fact that commercial enterprises conducting multinational activities can be traced much further back in time. Siemens, a German electrical company, and the US-based Singer sewing machine corporation established foreign operations as early as the 1850s. But even earlier, governments frequently chartered corporations such as the East India Company and Hudson's Bay Company to facilitate the exploitation of raw materials and markets as part of the process of colonization. Geoffrey Jones defines a multinational corporation as 'a firm that controls operations or income-generating assets in more than one country. Multinationals are owned in their home economy and invest in host economies.'[6]

Some organizations and observers, including the UN, use the term 'transnational' to identify such firms. Others also make distinctions among 'firm', 'enterprise', 'business', and 'corporation', but here such terms will be used interchangeably.

One also might distinguish such firms on the basis of the number of countries in which they operate, referring to those with operations in a widely dispersed range of countries as global. Again, for our discussion, such distinctions are unnecessary, though it is worth keeping in mind that the wider the scope and size of operations, the greater the possibility that the multinational corporations may be able to wield more influence. MNCs, however, should be distinguished from corporations that are involved simply in exporting their products, no matter how extensive in both number and scope, for they are not multinational unless they have some part of their operations in a more than one country. While much of the attention and concern about multinational corporations tends to focus on large enterprises such as Cisco Systems, Intel, Lucent Technologies, Microsoft, Nike, Toyota, Wal-Mart, and the like, most multinationals are actually small firms with relatively few employees.

Multinational corporations emerge for different reasons. At the start of the twentieth century, Hobson noted how capitalism tended to create monopolies that would outgrow their domestic market and would need to go abroad in search of raw materials and additional markets.[7] For him, multinationals were an inevitable part of the unrestricted capitalist system. Not all firms, however, become multinationals. The decision for a corporation to move abroad is not a simple matter. The potential liability in operating in 'foreign' territory requires that a firm overcome distance that, in Jones's view, has the potential to increase costs and risks.[8] Distance takes many different forms. In addition to time and space, it also can be conceived in terms of politics and culture as different countries and societies have very different operating practices that firms must adjust to if they are to function effectively. Some observers have distinguished among multinationals operating from resource-scarce home economies and resource-rich home economies. One common form of the latter is described by Wilkins:

> In what I call the 'American model' the firm began at home in the domestic market, developed core competencies, and then, typically, if its product was unique, began to export, locate foreign agents, and soon established foreign sales branches and subsidiaries. If barriers to trade, transportation costs, and such made markets abroad inaccessible or costly to reach, the firm would assemble, pack, bottle, or process near its customers and—at different paces in different markets and in different industries— would move into manufacturing abroad or integrate backward into buying or investing in raw materials at home, abroad, or both.[9]

One commonly used measure of multinational activity is **foreign investment**. Foreign investment takes one of two forms and is used by the United Nations Conference on Trade and Development (UNCTAD) in its annual reports as a rough measure of the growth and distribution of multinational corporate activity. Portfolio investment refers to investments where the investor, either an individual or a corporation, does not acquire control over the management of the foreign enterprise, but loans the capital to local producers. Direct investment refers to those investments where the investor does acquire control. MNCs require at least some foreign direct investment for them to own and control enterprises in foreign countries. Of course, multinationals might also start new enterprises in foreign countries. These are sometimes referred to as greenfield investments. Foreign direct investment (FDI) is sometimes used as a measure of the amount of activity by multinational corporations.

For example, UNCTAD in its reports on multinationals frequently refers to FDI figures as a way of determining the scope and rate of change in multinational activity. Susan Strange, among others, however, has argued that FDI is not necessarily the most accurate indicator of the size and scope of MNC activity. Measures of FDI do not always fully account for such practices as joint ventures or the increasingly common practice of licensing, franchising, or contracting out aspects of a firm's operations. At the same time, FDI may overstate the actual amount of investment to the extent that it includes acquisitions and mergers, which have become a frequent phenomenon as global firms jockey for monopoly status in various sectors. Alternatively, it may understate the potential impact of multinationals where these corporations borrow from local sources of capital to invest in branch plants and other foreign operations. It also tends to ignore the more common practice in recent years where multinationals rely on short-term contractual relationships with suppliers rather than invest directly in foreign plants. Thus, for example, despite its global reach, Nike owns no foreign manufacturing plants.

History of Multinational Corporations

The idea of corporate interests driving the creation and operations of international institutions has caused much consternation among anti-globalization activists. As suggested by the quotation that opens this chapter, many see MNCs as the worst face of globalization, a reflection of selfish corporate interests seeking to create a framework of rules that will serve and protect their own narrow commercial interests at the expense of other social, cultural, and environmental concerns. They also see this as a manifestation of the process of globalization that has been at play since the late twentieth century. The idea, let alone the practice, of commercial interests participating directly in global governance is not unique to this contemporary period of globalization. A historical overview reveals that business elites have long taken an interest in the practice and content of global governance and regularly have been involved in the process for more than a century.

Craig Murphy's examination of global governance since 1850 reveals the very considerable involvement of commercial interests in the creation of public international unions, or business and industry-wide trade organizations (as opposed to the trade unions of workers), in the late nineteenth century that became the foundation for the network of international institutions that exist today. While acknowledging the important role played by British hegemony in supporting a peaceful international order, Murphy finds that 'the political leadership needed to create the Public International Unions came from aristocrats.'[10] These aristocrats received important assistance and support from what Murphy refers to as public system builders—public administrators who sought to apply their expertise and experience in different settings and across national borders. The result was a fairly significant process of institution-building spanning the period from 1864 to 1914. More than half of the institutions created during this first wave of global governance were designed to 'foster industry' and many of these were initiated directly by the commercial interest concerned, by proposing designs, calling international conferences, using events such as World Fairs to gather like-minded individuals together, and supporting experimental unions that would then generate a constituency of supporters based on their success.[11]

These institutions were designed to facilitate order, economic and political efficiency, and, potentially, universality 'in order to create the larger markets in which liberal economic policies would result in the division of labor (from the global level to the factory floor), thus contributing to human progress'.[12] One can see from this the ongoing concern that corporate interests have had with global governance as well as some indication of the methods used to advance their interests in this process.

While the participation of business in global governance is not new, the size and scope of the corporate presence in the global economy has certainly increased during the contemporary period of accelerated globalization. Multinational corporations have been around as long as capitalism, but they became particularly active in the late nineteenth and early twentieth centuries when they proliferated in a number of sectors. Jones identifies two waves of MNC activity over the past century. The first wave actually began in the late nineteenth century and peaked at the time of World War I. This expansion ebbed with the onset of the global Depression in the 1930s. This first wave witnessed a rapid expansion in foreign direct investment as firms began to take advantage of new opportunities provided by the transportation links of the Suez and Panama Canals. Corporations began to use these routes in their search for new markets and additional supplies of raw materials. At its peak, according to estimates by Dunning, FDI reached 9 per cent of total global output during this period, a percentage not reached again until the 1990s.

The second, ongoing wave of MNC expansion began in the 1950s, but really took off in the 1980s and 1990s and, despite a brief relapse in the early 2000s, has continued to expand.[13] It was evident in the 1970s that in spite of concerns about new forms of colonialism and imperialism, most of the investment by MNCs was focused on the larger consumer markets in North America and Europe. This was the case as many countries imposed barriers against MNCs and foreign investment during the 1970s, especially in the natural resource sector. MNCs, however, remained firmly in control of the transportation, processing, and marketing of these resources. Beginning in the 1980s there has been a significant expansion in multinational activity as barriers to foreign investment began to be eliminated throughout the world, particularly in emerging markets. This marked the second wave of multinational activity.

According to Stephen Kobrin, the current period can be distinguished from earlier periods in three respects. It is, first, much broader in the number of national economies affected by multinationals. It also is much deeper in that the 'density of interaction' in areas of trade and investment is much greater than previously was the case. Third, and most importantly in Kobrin's view, the current phase of 'the dominant mode of organization of international economic transactions changed significantly in the late twentieth century from the market (trade and portfolio investment) to hierarchy or the internationalization of production through the multinational enterprise (MNE).'[14]

Today, multinationals have a significant presence in the global economy. The data demonstrate that FDI has become one of the most significant sources of capital transfers across national borders in recent decades. Prior to the 1990s, **official development assistance (ODA)**, funds moving from one government to another, either directly through bilateral means or multilaterally through regional and international agencies such as the World Bank (IBRD), the UN Development Programme (UNDP), or various regional development banks in Latin America, Asia, and Africa, accounted for the majority of funds moving from the rich developed world to poor developing economies. This changed during the 1990s as private

FDI became the principal source of capital moving from the global North to the global South. Unlike public funds, which were primarily designed to support development projects regardless of their commercial potential in many cases, private investment has been directed at profit-making opportunities. The result has been a more narrowly focused distribution of capital with particular attention to commercially viable projects and larger consumer markets.

Despite increases in development assistance (largely attributed to debt forgiveness arrangements) since 2000, FDI remains the major source of capital transfer from the North to the South. Remittances—funds transferred by **diaspora** populations and migrant workers to their home countries—also have become an increasingly significant portion of such transfers. The transfer of remittances has grown so significantly that it has spawned its own network of profit-seekers as money transfer agencies have been established to facilitate (and profit from) the movement of personal capital across national borders. In this, as in other areas, much of the activity has been taking place with little, if any, government involvement on either side of the respective borders.[15] 'Remittances are among the most tangible links between migration and development. Officially recorded flows totaled over US$280 billion worldwide in 2006. Nearly three-quarters were sent to developing countries. In 22 countries, remittances were equal to more than 10 per cent of **gross domestic product** (GDP) in 2006; in six countries they were equal to more than 20 percent of GDP.'[16]

While noting the increased significance of FDI moving from the North to the South, it is important to keep certain factors in mind. First, the overwhelming majority of FDI continues to remain within the global North among OECD members. While much of the attention surrounding MNCs has examined their role in the global South, the US has been both the principal source and recipient of FDI since the end of World War II. Canada and the countries of Western Europe also have been significant sources and recipients, and along with the US accounted for about 70 per cent of the global stock of foreign direct investment by the end of the 1970s. A second factor is that the FDI moving from North to South is highly concentrated in a few select countries of the South. Many of the more impoverished regions of the globe remain untouched by this privately controlled capital and must continue to rely on public sources for whatever assistance they receive. Public assistance programs thus retain some continued significance for what have been described as the **'bottom billion'**. A third factor that looks as if it will be even more important for the future is that an increasing percentage of FDI is now flowing out of emerging markets in the global South both to OECD countries and to other areas of the global South. In other words, emerging markets in the global South, especially China, Brazil, and India, are becoming significant sources of foreign direct investment for the global economy.

The annual reports of UNCTAD on FDI reveal relatively steady growth in FDI globally, with a notable relapse in 2001 and 2002 following the terrorist attacks of 9/11. The reports also reveal a steady increase in the percentage of FDI in the service sector, with relative declines in manufacturing and extractive industries.[17] 'According to estimates by UNCTAD, the universe of TNCs [transnational corporations] now spans some 77,000 parent companies with over 770,000 foreign affiliates. In 2005, these foreign affiliates generated an estimated $4.5 trillion in value added, employed some 62 million workers and exported goods and services valued at more than $4 trillion.'[18] There also has been a shift in the locale of FDI. China hosts more affiliates than any other country and has the highest employment levels related to FDI, though US corporations remain the largest employers. FDI from emerging markets has also increased at a much higher rate than that originating from developed economies.[19] This represents a significant shift that is forecast to reshape the global economy in the years ahead.

Emerging Markets

The largest cement company in the US is Cemex, a Mexico-based MNC. It is also the second largest cement company in England and the third largest in the world. Embraer, based in Brazil, is the world's leading producer of small and mid-sized passenger aircraft. Samsung out of Korea and LG out of China stand near the top of the world's electronics producers. These and many other examples illustrate the need to alter some of the common assumptions about multinationals and about the global economy. There is a tendency in conversations about MNCs to view them as originating exclusively in the countries of the global North. One of the more important developments that will shape the future of global politics can be seen in the growth of MNCs from the emerging markets of the global South. More than 10 per cent of the world's largest corporations as listed in the Fortune 500 can be found in the emerging markets of Brazil, Russia, India, China, among others. Some of these corporations are rivalling the world's largest. In *The Emerging Markets Century*, Antoine van Agtmael notes that emerging markets will be as large as the developed economies by 2030, and that the four largest emerging markets—Brazil, Russia, India, and China (BRIC)—combined will be larger than all currently developed economies by 2050.[20]

One of the reasons for the growth of MNCs in emerging markets is the increased number of consumers in the BRIC area. Many MNCs are able to establish regional markets and use these as a base for additional expansion. Another common assumption is that multinationals are primarily interested in pursuing cheap labour pools. While labour costs may have been one reason for Western MNCs to establish plants in foreign countries with lower wages, it would not appear that cheap labour alone can account for the growing number and size of emerging market corporations. Van Agtmael, in an examination of 25 of the leading emerging market corporations, ranks cheap labour last on his list of the 12 key success factors for these corporations, just behind natural resources. Ranking much higher in importance are such management-driven factors as commitment to export markets, a focus on superior execution and quality, an emphasis on technology and design, and developing a niche overlooked by more established companies.[21]

This transition in the global economy and the emergence of significant national economies in the South underscore the severe legitimacy and credibility issues facing institutional arrangements such as the G8 and the UN Security Council, with their limited membership, and help to account for the increased attention given to more inclusive bodies such as the G20. It also points to the important role that specific emerging markets like China, Brazil, and India will have in the future, given the extent of their expansion and their increasingly influential role in global economic affairs.

Comparisons are frequently made between multinationals and states. Many books and articles make reference to data that suggest that multinationals are larger and, often more by implication than assertion, more powerful than states. Comparisons are often made between the **gross national product** (GNP) of a country and the global sales and/or revenues of firms compared with revenues of national governments. Such comparisons commonly reveal that nearly half of the top 100 entities are corporations. The implications of such comparisons are that these multinationals are hence more powerful than states. However, for a host of reasons, this conclusion does not necessarily follow, not least because it assumes that power is both fungible and based primarily on economic factors. MNCs are narrowly focused on maximizing their revenue. 'Whatever their other differences, this much they have in common: increasingly they think and act globally; the territorial state is not their cardinal organizing principle; nor is serving national interests their primary driver.'[22] Yet this very objective has been the source of much of the controversy surrounding MNCs because their pursuit of profit brings them into conflict with a host of other, state- and civil society-based objectives (political, social, and environmental).

Multinational Corporations: The Controversy

The role of multinational corporations in the global economy has been the source of a considerable amount of controversy through the years. Critics have argued that MNCs have had a deleterious effect on the economies of both home and host countries, have ignored the effects of their practices on the environment, human rights, and labour conditions, and have exerted undue influence on governments. The first round of this debate occurred in the 1970s when MNCs became a significant economic and political force, especially in the global South. Many of the concerns raised about corporations at that time focused on the ability of corporations to wield power over weaker developing countries. In particular was a concern that these corporations had a direct role in supporting governments that protected their interests while interfering in those that did not. A prominent example was the role of the International Telephone and Telegraph (ITT) Corporation in the *coup d'état* that deposed the democratically elected government of Salvador Allende in Chile in 1973. Representatives from ITT proposed an informal economic blockade of Chile to prevent Allende from assuming power. When this failed they actively promoted various economic sanctions designed to undermine the Allende government. On 11 September 1973, the Allende government was overthrown by the Chilean army and ITT's holdings in Chile were secured. The activities of ITT, which at the time controlled more than 70 per cent of Chile's phone services, demonstrated both the power and the nefarious activities of MNCs.

Alongside these concerns, critics in the developed world began to question the practices of MNCs in host countries, especially the economic benefits that such investments allegedly had for host states. A significant wave of criticism developed in Canada through the 1960s and into the 1970s. The extent of the concern over foreign investment led to the establishment of the Foreign Investment Review Agency (FIRA), a federal program designed to regulate foreign investments to increase their benefits to the Canadian economy. Similar regulatory devices were established elsewhere and some governments moved to nationalize the assets of multinational corporations. Critics at the time argued that foreign investment, while providing some capital investment, created a number of side effects that diminished the potential benefits of this investment. Among the issues were limited research and development activities in the host country; removal of material and financial resources from host countries through transfer pricing and other intra-firm practices; restrictions on export activity by branch plants in host countries; limited managerial opportunities for host country citizens; and a tendency to source supplies and services from the home country rather than from the host country.

All of these practices reduced the potential beneficial side effects created by foreign direct investment.[23] The bottom line for MNCs was maximizing revenue and opponents criticized their lack of commitment to the communities in which they had invested. Sufficient concern about the activities of MNCs developed during the 1970s that the United Nations established an agency to monitor these corporations and to assess their impact on host countries.

A second wave of critical commentaries on the activities of MNCs developed in the 1990s amid growing interest in the process and effects of globalization and the considerable expansion in FDI that had taken place since the 1980s. MNCs have played a central role in the globalization process. They also have been among the principal beneficiaries of the various developments that have fuelled globalization. Clearly, corporations have sought unfettered access to resources, labour, and markets in different parts of the world. It is also evident that in their primary concern with the bottom line, MNCs have been the source of some major social, economic, and environmental disasters. On the environmental front, one can note the horrific consequences created by Union Carbide's accident at Bhopal, India, where a noxious gas leak in December 1984 resulted in the immediate death of nearly 4,000 people, with thousands more experiencing various long-term disabilities and premature death. The damage caused by this accident continues to plague the region. Union Carbide offered an initial payout of $7 million, but a year of litigation saw that figure rise to $477 million by way of compensation to victims of the disaster.

In March of 1989, off the west coast of North America, an oil tanker, the *Exxon Valdez*, owned and operated by major oil MNC Exxon, ran aground, spilling more than 10 million US gallons of crude oil into the ecologically sensitive waters of Prince William Sound. The environmental consequences have been severe to marine and bird life and to the aesthetic beauty of the region. In an initial court decision Exxon was asked to pay $5 billion in punitive damages, but on appeal the US Supreme Court in 2008 reduced that amount to $500 million—for a company with an annual profit in 2007 of $40.6 billion that was larger than the GDP of two-thirds of the countries in the world. Meanwhile, some scientists say the damage will persist for decades, a view Exxon disputes.

In the area of labour practices, multinationals frequently have been criticized for the exploitation of labour in their branch-plant operations, including their use of child labour and sweatshop working conditions. The use of branch plants staffed by low-cost labour working under difficult and hazardous conditions has long been used as a symbol for the global reach of multinationals. Repeatedly, attention has been directed to the practices of prominent multinationals and the extent to which their concern with maximizing their profit margins has placed many individuals and communities at considerable risk. In response, the firms defend their practices on the grounds that the wage labour they provide is greater than what would otherwise be there. Pools of cheap labour have been one of the incentives for MNCs' decisions to establish operations in foreign countries, and the violation of labour standards and the effects of MNCs on labour at large have been an ongoing concern. Equally important have been complaints that the pursuit of cheaper labour abroad has led to the creation of unemployment in MNC home countries and the disastrous effects that such plant closures have had on many communities.

A more general critique cites MNCs as both responsible for and representative of the commoditization of more and more aspects of social life, including health, education, and culture. These concerns result from the view that MNCs have been promoting policies of deregulation and privatization and have fostered the view that the market is the most effective means for producing and distributing services.

The Growth of Private Power

Every January, a collection of leading CEOs, past and present policy officials, representatives and leaders of IGOs, and a handful of other celebrities pack up their parkas and skis and fly off to Davos, Switzerland, for a week-long gathering of wealth, power, and ideas to reflect on the fate of the globe. The annual meeting of the World Economic Forum (WEF) since 1971 has brought together the global elite to share ideas, not least about how the present global order can continue to meet their aspirations. For many, the Forum represents the extent to which the growth of private power has overwhelmed all challengers. In Davos, public officials come to impress the private corporate elite as much as the latter seek to influence the policies of the former. It is difficult to compare with any degree of precision the specific policy influence of the annual Davos gathering with entities such as the annual economic summits of the G8 or deliberations of the UN Security Council. This 'invitation only' event has all of the features that suggest money and power, and raises concerns among civil society actors throughout the world in regard to what might result from an exclusive group, overwhelmingly corporate in content, meeting in relative seclusion to discuss matters of public policy.[24] The model of the WEF has been adopted by a number of regions, for example, the establishment of the North American Competitiveness Council.

Another source of private power has been the manner in which international agreements have privileged the position of corporations. Many critics of the North American Free Trade Agreement (NAFTA) cite the agreement's privileging of corporate rights as one of its principal problems. Chapter 11 of NAFTA provides investors, most of whom are corporations, with the right to sue governments for damages. So many corporations have taken advantage of this provision that even those who initially devised the agreement have expressed concern about its repercussions. The idea of protecting investors' rights, however, has become more widely accepted among many states, and there are now literally thousands of bilateral and multilateral investment agreements that provide varying degrees of protection for foreign investors. The expansion of investors' rights speaks to the growing influence of corporate interests on policy-makers at the national, regional, and global levels.

Policies of privatization and deregulation also have had a significant influence on the growth of corporate governance, or what Claire Cutler has referred to as private power. 'In many states, the privatization of government activities, the deregulation of industries and sectors, increased reliance on market mechanisms in general, and the delegation of regulatory authority to private business associations and agencies are expanding the opportunities for the emergence of private and self-regulatory regimes.'[25] National governments, in pursuing such policies, have legitimized private power, providing private sources of authority with greater credibility by sanctioning their existence and empowering them to exercise authority over specified policy sectors. Once devolved, of course, power can be recaptured by the state, but not always easily and never without some costs. As Rodney Bruce Hall notes: 'In the meantime,...private authorities exercise effective and legitimate control over areas that previously were conducted in the public sphere.' He continues:

As a consequence of these processes, Cutler argues that we are witnessing three trans-formations. First, the welfare state is being replaced by the 'competition state' as the globalization of liberalism induces states to adjust to a neo-liberal global environment. Second, the world is moving from national to transnational patterns of capital accumu-lation characterized by a third transformation. This third transformation, in turn, is the emerging dominance of 'flexible accumulation' constituted by a combination of capital mobility and a high degree of flexibility in transnational production arrangements.

Cutler concludes that these transformations are facilitated by the extent to which private transnational interests determine and adjudicate the legal and regulatory regime overseeing their own actions.[26]

When one considers other forms of power, there is also a noticeable extension of private actors into areas that were, could, or, in the view of some, should be in the public sector. Regulatory power, for example, has been an instrument used by governments to restrain the unbridled pursuit of wealth by private capital. Regulatory regimes have been employed to protect health, safety, and the envi-ronment, along with other social concerns. It is not uncommon, however, to find firms actively engaged in various forms of self-regulation operating at a consider-able arm's length from government control and democratic accountability.

In her discussion of the private sector's power in the process of global governance, Doris Fuchs distinguishes among instrumental, structural, and discursive power.[27] The instrumental power of the firm is represented by its efforts to influence in a direct manner the process and outcome of policy-making. Susan Sell's analysis of the manner in which multinational pharmaceutical firms shaped the WTO's agreement on intellectual property rights (TRIPs) provides an illustration of instrumental private power in practice.[28] The **structural power** of corporations is largely exercised by the corporation's ability to transfer its operations elsewhere. The fluidity of transnational capital carries with it an implicit threat to policy officials that allows firms to shape policy outcomes without necessarily intervening in any overt manner in the process. Finally, the discursive power of business derives from its ability to legitimate market practices and the general acceptance of privatization and self-regulation.

The influence of corporate actors and the consensus on the value of unfettered markets may have been shattered by the financial crisis of 2008–9. The financial crisis was the result of the persistent expansion of financial firms into unregulated and ever more complex investment schemes that were increasingly removed from the real productive centres of the global economy. These investments became the source of unprecedented profits for investors. They also were a temptation for unconstrained greed. The practices of these financial institutions began to unravel in 2008 as the banks' practice of supporting sub-prime mortgages, particularly in the US, proved unsustainable and people began to walk away from their debts. So, too, did the banks, and major financial institutions, notably in the US and UK, began to collapse. The economic crisis spread quickly as credit markets froze and stock exchanges went into free fall around the globe. With the collapse of banks and credit markets consumption declined dramatically, economic output declined substantially, and unemployment rose. By the early months of 2009 few parts of the world remained unaffected by these events, a testament to the interrelatedness and globalization of economies. Arguments about the source of the crisis varied greatly, with some observers like Walden Bello suggesting that it resulted from a crisis of overproduction set in motion by corporate practices in response to policies of liberalization and deregulation.[29]

Governments moved quickly to provide financial support to some financial institutions while allowing others to collapse. The bailouts were not without controversy as governments debated the desirability of imposing restrictions on bank practices in such areas as compensation of chief executives. Proposed reforms emphasized the need to restore a more assertive regulatory regime at both the national and the international levels.[30] The crisis may lead to a retrenchment of the expansive corporate activities of the 1990s and has generated widespread discussion on the desirability of more restrictive practices on the part of governments, including nationalization of some corporations. The longer-term effects on global enterprises, however, remain unclear.

Many have challenged the apparently unbridled pursuit of private power by corporate interests over the past two decades and have argued that mechanisms are needed to check and balance the power of MNCs. In the following chapter we look at how civil society has responded to these and other concerns. However, initiatives already have been undertaken in an attempt to hold corporations accountable for their actions. A challenge to the persistent promotion of the invisible hand of the market through much of the 1990s appeared from the UN's Research Institute for Social Development in 2000 in a report titled *Visible Hands*. This report argued that MNCs had accumulated far too much power and that much of this was unchecked. While noting that MNCs are not uniformly exploitive of this situation, this UN institute noted that some are and others could become so.[31] Corporations also have begun to respond, and considerable interest has developed in the idea of **corporate social responsibility**.

Corporate Social Responsibility

Milton Freidman's oft-quoted phrase that 'the social responsibility of business is to increase profits' reflects the view that the firm is primarily responsible to its shareholders. The idea that corporations should even think about being accountable to a wider society/community is anathema to those who hold to this mantra. The idea of corporate social responsibility emerged in the 1970s. At that time Archie B. Carroll identified four responsibilities that corporations shared: the economic responsibility to be profitable; the legal responsibility to abide by the law; the ethical responsibility to engage in just and ethical behaviour; and the social responsibility to contribute to the betterment of society in multiple ways, such as culturally and recreationally. Since that time, much of the discussion of corporate social responsibility has focused on the latter two types, though some voices from the right, more critical of the direction that corporate social responsibility has gone, worry that the first responsibility has been neglected.[32]

Many MNCs have changed their rhetoric, if not always their actual performance, and the idea of social responsibility has become a significant concern. The idea has been pressed upon firms by activists, consumers, and governments and now finds its way into corporate boardrooms around the world. The annual reports of many MNCs now include sections on social responsibility, and many firms have formal divisions devoted to the issue and spend significant amounts responding to concerned publics and promoting their virtues to an often skeptical public. There are many different versions of corporate social responsibility and many different explanations about if, when, and how various MNCs have undertaken commitments to it.

For many corporations, such as Nike and The Gap, an onslaught of bad publicity and sustained public pressure about their corporate practices, primarily questionable labour practices in their overseas manufacturing sites, compelled them to turn their attention to the idea and the practice of corporate social responsibility. Other firms, such as Body Shop, have pursued ethical and socially responsible practices from the beginning, but it is an area of activity that does not come easily to many firms. Much of this debate is a response to the negative effects that multinational corporations' operations have had in many societies around the globe. Concerns and complaints about the extent to which these corporations have interfered with, and impeded, the promotion and protection of labour and civil rights, and with their contribution to economic inequalities, distorted social programs, and deleterious effects on health and the environment, have led some to argue that multinationals bear a special responsibility and obligation to assist in ameliorating some of the harms that they have caused.[33] Some commentators and economists, such as the aforementioned Milton Friedman, have dismissed such concerns out of hand, arguing that corporations have only one responsibility: to maximize the returns on their investments for the benefits of their shareholders. The UN-initiated Global Compact has contributed to a broader debate on the role that corporations, both multinational and others, should play in supporting non-commercial social and humanitarian needs in the communities in which they operate.

The Global Compact

In response to the shifting terrain brought on by globalization, the UN decided to take a more direct approach in dealing with MNCs. In 1997 UN Secretary-General Kofi Annan launched the Global Compact (see Box 9.1). Beginning with 50 participating corporations in 2000, more than 4,300 corporations from 126 countries had signed on to the Compact by 2007, with another 1,300 additional members from UN agencies, labour organizations, and civil society. The principal focus of the Global Compact has been to develop a working relationship between the UN and corporations whereby the corporations make commitments to abide by a set of principles. These principles relate to human rights, labour standards, the environment, and anti-corruption, and are drawn from various UN conventions.[34] As the UN describes it, 'the Global Compact is first and foremost concerned with exhibiting and building the social legitimacy of business and markets.' It is an attempt to respond to the increased criticisms of MNCs and to work with these firms to establish a more acceptable presence in the global economy. It is not designed to regulate the practices of MNCs, restrict their activities, or otherwise enforce measures against them. Rather, it involves a voluntary commitment from the corporations and is intended to enable them to operate more effectively and widely in the global community on the assumption that MNCs make a necessary and important contribution to global prosperity and peace. Increasingly, too, it becomes good business practice for a company to be involved in the Global Compact, which is based on a view that these corporations are well placed to support the UN's efforts in delivering a range of services to the global community, including, for example, the Millennium Development Goals. As John Ruggie explains, 'International organizations cannot adequately compensate for the resulting governance gaps because they simultaneously lack the global reach of markets, firms and civil society actors on one side, while being tightly constrained by territorial states on the other.'[35]

BOX 9.1

The Global Compact

The UN Global Compact is a strategic policy initiative for businesses committed to 'best practice' principles in such areas as human rights, labour, the environment, and anti-corruption. By becoming part of this UN initiative, business, as a primary agent driving globalization, can help ensure that markets, commerce, technology, and finance advance in ways that benefit economies and societies everywhere. The Global Compact today stands as the largest corporate citizenship and sustainability initiative in the world—with over 7,700 corporate participants and stakeholders from over 130 countries.

The Global Compact is a leadership platform, endorsed by chief executive officers, that offers a unique strategic platform for participants to advance their commitments to sustainability and corporate citizenship. Structured as a public–private initiative, the Global Compact is a policy framework for the development, implementation, and disclosure of sustainability principles and practices. Participants have available a wide spectrum of specialized workstreams, management tools and resources, and topical programs and projects—all designed to help advance sustainable business models and markets in order to contribute to the initiative's overarching mission of helping to build a more sustainable and inclusive global economy.

The UN Global Compact has two objectives:

1. Mainstream the 10 principles in business activities around the world.
2. Catalyze actions in support of broader UN goals, including the Millennium Development Goals (MDGs).

With these twin and complementary objectives in mind, the Global Compact has shaped an initiative that provides collaborative solutions to the most fundamental challenges facing both business and society. The Global Compact seeks to combine the best properties of the UN, such as moral authority and convening power, with the private sector's solution-finding strengths, and the expertise and capacities of a range of key stakeholders. The initiative is global and local; private and public; voluntary yet accountable. The Global Compact has a unique constellation of participants and stakeholders—bringing companies together with governments, civil society, labour, the United Nations, and other key interests.

The benefits of engagement include the following:

- Adopting an established and globally recognized policy framework for the development, implementation, and disclosure of environmental, social, and governance policies and practices.
- Sharing best and emerging practices to advance practical solutions and strategies to common challenges.
- Advancing sustainability solutions in partnership with a range of stakeholders, including UN agencies, governments, civil society, labour, and other non-business interests.
- Linking business units and subsidiaries across the value chain with the Global Compact's Local Networks around the world—many of these in developing and emerging markets.
- Accessing the United Nations' extensive knowledge of and experience with sustainability and development issues.

- Utilizing UN Global Compact management tools and resources, and the opportunity to engage in specialized workstreams in the environmental, social, and governance realms.

Finally, the Global Compact incorporates a transparency and accountability policy known as the Communication on Progress (COP). The annual posting of a COP is an important demonstration of a participant's commitment to the UN Global Compact and its principles. Participating companies are required to follow this policy, as a commitment to transparency and disclosure is critical to the success of the initiative. Failure to communicate will result in a change in participant status and possible delisting.

In summary, the Global Compact exists to assist the private sector in the management of increasingly complex risks and opportunities in the environmental, social, and governance realms. By partnering with companies in this way, and leveraging the expertise and capacities of a range of other stakeholders, the Global Compact seeks to embed markets and societies with universal principles and values for the benefit of all.

Source: Abridged and adapted from United Nations Global Compact, 'Overview of the UN Global Compact', at: <www.unglobalcompact.org/AbouttheGC/>. (15 Nov. 2009)

The growing power and independence of MNCs provide them with exceptional opportunities to become directly involved in many host countries' most important economic, political, and social issues. Even if and when these multinational firms attempt to limit their activities to their areas of immediate commercial interest, their sheer size and economic power place them in a position in which their activities could reverberate in other areas of society. And while many efforts have been made to limit or restrict the ability of civil society organizations to operate freely and effectively across national borders, corporations have not encountered any restrictions of this sort.

Ruggie notes a number of limitations with existing practices of corporate social responsibility, including the limited number of corporations that truly embrace this paradigm, the tendency for corporations to undermine social objectives by lobbying for contradictory policies, the recent appearance of many new MNCs from emerging markets where socially responsible practices have yet to be defined, and the lack of effective involvement by public authorities in standardizing and enforcing appropriate social practices. Despite these limitations, Ruggie is of the view that 'CSR initiatives nevertheless have established new sites and new means for social action as well as new political dynamics' that can provide a check on unfettered neo-liberal practices.

Conclusion and Future Directions

The proliferation of multinational corporations has been one of the central features of globalization. These corporations also have been the focus of much of the dissent surrounding globalization and policies of trade liberalization. Yet, at the very point where MNCs seem to overwhelm the capacity of states to control their territorial space for economic objectives, a shift may be occurring where these multinationals return to a more distinctly 'national' basis, conducting business with other 'national' firms through triads, joint ventures, subcontracting, networks, and extensive use of cyberspace. As Kobrin suggests, 'globalization entails a qualitative transformation of the international world economy.' He points to 'three related propositions' to explain this phenomenon and the possibly diminishing role of MNCs in its further development:

> First, dramatic increases in the scale of technology in many industries—in its cost, risk, and complexity—have rendered even the largest national markets too small to be meaningful economic units; they are no longer the 'principal entities' of the world economy. National markets are fused transnationally rather than linked across borders. Second, the recent explosion of transnational strategic alliances is a manifestation of a fundamental change in the mode of organization of international economic transactions from markets and/or hierarchies (i.e., trade and MNEs) to global networks. Last, and related to the second point, the emerging global economy (and many emerging global political actors) is digitally integrated and entails the migration of markets from geographic space to cyberspace.[36]

This transformation represents a new stage in the global economy, where the firm may no longer hold the degree of influence that it once held, yet where the state has as much difficulty as it recently has had in managing and exploiting the economic activity that transpires. To the extent that economic transactions become digitalized, the economic significance of cyberspace increases. To date 'geography and territorial jurisdiction do not map on cyperspace.'[37] Networks have become a common feature of this evolving global economy. These networks have no clear centre of power because they rely on the interdependent relationships among diffuse members. And, importantly, transnational networks render boundaries of whatever kind largely irrelevant. The result may well be an emerging global economy where both the firm and the state are sidelined to the extent that other actors, mainly transnational regulatory regimes, assume greater responsibility for managing the global economy.

Key Terms

advanced industrialized countries
'bottom billion'
civil society organizations
corporate social responsibility
coup d'état
criminal networks
deregulation
diaspora

foreign investment
global governance
gross domestic product (GDP)
gross national product (GNP)
liberalization
official development assistance (ODA)
privatization
structural power

Discussion Questions

1. Who/what are sovereignty-free actors?
2. Why should non-state actors be included in decision-making of global governance institutions?

3. Which non-state actors work to undermine global governance?
4. Which actors provide the following: (a) market authority; (b) moral authority; (c) illicit authority?
5. What does it mean to say that 'power is relational'?
6. What are greenfield investments?
7. Why are MNCs generally considered 'the worst face of globalization'?
8. What explains the exponential increase in the number of MNCs emerging from the global South?
9. What are some examples of the growth of private power?
10. Is corporate social responsibility sufficient to curb the excesses of private firms?

⁂ Suggested Readings

Agtmael, Antoine van. *The Emerging Markets Century*. New York: Free Press, 2007. This book provides an excellent introduction to the corporations and governments that are reshaping the global economy as corporate power begins its move to the global South.

Sagafi-Nejad, Tagi, and John H. Dunning. *The UN and Transnational Corporations: From Code of Conduct to Global Compact*. Bloomington: Indiana University Press, 2008. As part of the UN's intellectual history project, two of the world's leading experts on MNCs chronicle the history of UN efforts to understand, regulate, and eventually work with these influential corporate entities.

Yunus, Muhammad. *Creating a World without Poverty: Social Business and the Future of Capitalism*. New York: Public Affairs, 2007. The Nobel Peace Prize-winning director of the Grameen bank, the 'banker to the poor', explains and provides examples of how corporations can act in a socially responsible fashion.

⁂ Global Links

Global Edge
globaledge.msu.edu
   A Michigan State University site that focuses on international business activities.
Peterson Institute for International Economics
www.iie.com/
   A good collection of papers and other resources on contemporary issues.
Everything International
faculty.philau.edu/russowl/russow.html
   A very comprehensive website managed by Lloyd C. Russow of Philadelphia University with links to most major international business and economic entities.

⁂ Debate 9

Be it resolved that the UN's Global Compact cannot provide a proper check to unfettered capitalism.

Chapter Ten

Anti-Globalization Transnational Movements

> All movements of contestation . . . have an impact on their participants and in this sense the Battle of Seattle was truly a watershed. The anti-globalization movement had made its mark, brought together disparate social movements and created a myth-making event in Seattle.[1]

Introduction

As shown in Chapter 8, globalization is one of the most important macro trends to influence local, national, regional, and global politics over the second half of the twentieth century and into the twenty-first century. In fact, it is safe to posit that globalization has become *the* defining feature of our contemporary world. The intensification of globalization during the past few decades caused some observers to pronounce that this phenomenon is 'new'.[2] But, as noted in the previous section of this book, evidence of what we now call 'globalization' dates back to the fifteenth century with European expansion into the New World. Some historians even argue that this process is traceable to a much earlier time.

So globalization is not new. What differentiates current globalization from earlier forms is its level of intensity, extent, velocity, and pervasiveness. When one takes a long view, evidence can be found of 'distinctive historical forms of globalization which have been associated with quite different kinds of historical world orders'.[3] As well, over time, globalization 'has been marked by advances and retreats, by hope and disappointment.'[4] Clearly, the phenomenon of globalization, while generating much socio-economic and cultural transformation, has had both positive and negative impacts.

While the previous chapter examined the impact of globalization specifically on the state, this chapter asks: What societal challenges does globalization pose? How has globalization affected the relationship between the state and its societal elements? What has been the impact of globalization on the state/society complex?

State/Society Complexes

In trying to understand the phenomenon of globalization it is not sufficient to examine solely its impact on the state. One should also explore globalization's broader effect, which includes its impact on society within the state and across the states system. By treating the state/society complex as a distinct unit of analysis, we are addressing what Robert Cox identified many years ago as a problematic feature of the IR discipline. Cox notes that one of the traditional intellectual conventions that contributed to defining the IR discipline is the practice of making a distinction between 'the state' and 'civil society'. While this distinction may have made sense in the eighteenth and early nineteenth centuries, in our contemporary era of intensified and accelerated globalization it is difficult to maintain such rigid compartmentalization. As Cox puts it:

> There has been little attempt within the bounds of international relations theory to consider the state/society complex as a basic entity of international relations. As a consequence, the prospect that there exists a plurality of forms of state, expressing different configurations of state/society complexes, remains very largely unexplored, at least in connection with the study of international relations.[5]

The state/society complex, as a basic entity of global politics, reflects the relationship between a particular state and the people within it. Taking the state and society together as a unit of analysis forces us to pay more specific attention to the interactive struggles between society and the state apparatus and to consider the 'state' 'not as a single entity with a single interest, but rather as a "naturally" divided entity, made up of particular relationships' that can cut across state boundaries.[6] Those relationships can be broken down into two categories: (1) those in which the state nurtures all groups within the polity and allows them to play meaningful participatory roles so that they can fulfill their dreams and aspirations; and (2) those in which the state plays a role in repressing certain groups within the polity or in allowing a majority group to marginalize, or carry out atrocities against, minority groups within that polity.[7]

Focusing on the state/society complex requires, as well, an examination of what occurs both *within* domestic political 'space' and *across* the domestic–international (or **intermestic**) divide. So when we examine the phenomenon of globalization in the context of the state/society complex it is important to gain an understanding of that phenomenon's impact not only on the society within the state but also on what can be called 'transnational' societal groups (e.g., groups advocating indigenous peoples' rights, women's rights, gay rights, workers' rights, religious rights, human rights, human security, anti-segregation, national liberation, pacifism, environmental protection, child protection, and consumer protection).

Counter-Movements as Safety Valves

One way to conceptualize the counter-movements that have emerged as a response to the globalization phenomenon in recent years, as well as during past centuries, is to consider those movements as necessary 'resistance safety valves'. Social protest, dissent, demonstrations, and **social movements** can be viewed as situated struggles that allow a society to vent its frustration and anger in ways that do not cause the state/society structure to collapse entirely. Social groups will seek to protect themselves from what they perceive as the pent-up pressure of the global extension of the market economy into their lives. The embrace of globalization has meant the acceptance by states and the states system of certain policies, such as privatization, liberalization, and market fundamentalism—all of which produce various counter-reactions, or 'rebuttals', within state/society complexes. This 'action/counter-reaction' can be viewed as a 'double movement'[8]—i.e., states adopt certain policies, which in turn trigger negative reactions in **civil society** within and across state borders. Or one can conceptualize this dynamic in Gramscian terms, as Robert Cox has done, as a counter-hegemonic struggle against the prevailing and dominant neo-liberal orthodoxy and the inequitable forces of global financial markets.[9]

To provide a concrete example, consider the so-called 'Washington Consensus'. The **Washington Consensus** denotes that set of views about 'effective development strategies' that has come to be associated with the policies of Washington-based institutions such as the IMF, the World Bank, and the US Treasury.[10] The Washington Consensus, at least as first articulated by John Williamson, focused on two broad policy elements: (1) the promotion of economic stability through fiscal adjustment, openness to the global market economy, and macroeconomic discipline (or market orthodoxy); (2) a radical reduction in the role of the state in economic and social matters.[11] These two broad policy elements translated into the imposition on the state/society complex of at least 10 specific policy reforms:

- fiscal discipline with the goal of eliminating public deficits;
- a change in the priorities of public spending, e.g., withdrawing government subsidies, decreased spending on health, education, etc.;
- tax reforms—broadening tax bases and reducing tax rates;
- positive real interest rates that are determined by the market;
- exchange rates determined by the market but that must guarantee competitiveness;
- liberalization of trade and opening up the economy;
- no restrictions on foreign direct investment;
- privatization of public enterprises;
- deregulation of economic activity;
- a solid guarantee of property rights.[12]

Naturally, such policy changes have provoked strong reactions within the state/society complex.[13] It would seem that the Washington Consensus, which rose to prominence around 1989, lost its credibility with the Wall Street meltdown in late 2008.[14] In this chapter we examine some bottom-up reactions (i.e., resistances or counter-movements) against the neo-liberal ideology that provides the foundation for economic strategies like those of the Washington Consensus.

One of the visible negative impacts of globalization on the state/society complex has been the subordination of people within global capitalism. The general reaction to this affront (and perhaps a positive outcome) has been the production of local, national, transnational, and global resistance or contestation movements—which we label broadly here as counter-globalization movements.[15] We use the umbrella term of 'counter-globalization movements' because within those movements are at least two streams: (1) those who are in opposition to globalization (members of anti-globalization, anti-capitalist, and anti-corporate movements), and (2) those who present alternative projects to neo-liberal globalization (i.e., they are not necessarily opposed to globalization per se, but want a better, more humane globalization). The latter is described by Louise Amoore this way: 'global resistance takes on a very specific and benign meaning in the form of a potential global civil society that can be usefully invited to "counterbalance" the neoliberal institutions of global governance.'[16] The remainder of the chapter is devoted to examining examples of the two directions taken by counter-movements.

Precursors of Counter-Globalization Movements

At least three waves of global protest have marked the advent of counter-globalization movements. The first wave began in the mid-1970s as a protest movement against the austerity measures of the structural adjustment policies imposed on developing states by the IMF. This wave of global protest was in part activated by the mounting debt crisis in the developing world and materialized in the form of strikes and street demonstrations. According to Walton and Seddon, between 1976 and 1992 there were approximately 146 such incidents in Third World countries as well as in the so-called Second World (socialist countries) during this first wave of global protestation.[17]

The second wave in the early 1990s can be characterized as more co-ordinated and organized than the previous set of protests. These contestations coincided with the end of the Cold War, the collapse of the Soviet bloc, and the embrace of democratization in formerly authoritarian states. Mary Kaldor has described civil society movements that sprung up against authoritarian states and actually brought down some of those regimes.[18] The end of several authoritarian governments—most in Central and Eastern Europe—opened the door for the emergence of a number of social counter-movements. One should note, as well, that this wave coincided with the emergence of a transnational militant Islamic movement and with the coalescing of a number of other social movements (environmentalists, feminists, human rights activists, indigenous peoples, etc.). This combining of concerns among various social movements led directly to a third wave.

The third wave of global protests was triggered by the celebrations in 1994 of the fiftieth anniversary of the Bretton Woods system. A societal campaign was mounted that year, using the slogan 'Fifty Years Is Enough', which targeted the IMF, the World Bank, and the trade regime of the General Agreement of Tariffs and Trade (GATT), which at the end of the Uruguay Round of trade talks morphed into the more formally institutionalized World Trade Organization (WTO) that came into force on 1 January 1995. Here we see the first signs of a growing counter-globalization network that drew on a number of issue-based contestation groups that operated in solidarity with each other across some 65 countries to agitate for changes to the practices, policies, and programs of the Bretton Woods institutions. There were elements of the two streams of the embryonic counter-globalization movement present within the 'Fifty Years Is Enough' campaign (see Box 10.1).

A series of low-level demonstrations in Australia and Canada during 1997 hinted at the growing predilection of ordinary people across the globe to reject the neo-liberal claim that 'there is no alternative' (TINA) to globalization. In Australia, a number of newly formed grassroots movements blockaded the city centres

BOX 10.1

50 Years Is Enough

50 Years Is Enough: US Network for Global Economic Justice is a coalition of over 200 US grassroots, women's, solidarity, faith-based, policy, social- and economic-justice, youth, labor, and development organizations dedicated to the profound transformation of the World Bank and the International Monetary Fund (IMF). The Network works in solidarity with over 185 international partner organizations in more than 65 countries. Through education and action, the Network is committed to transforming the international financial institutions' policies and practices, to ending the outside imposition of neo-liberal economic programs, and to making the development process democratic and accountable. We were founded in 1994, on the occasion of the 50th anniversary of the founding of the World Bank and IMF. We focus on action-oriented economic literacy training, public mobilization, and policy advocacy.

Source: <http://orgs.tigweb.org/4692>.

of Melbourne, Perth, Sydney, and Darwin in protest against globalization.[19] In Canada, student groups protested the Asia–Pacific Economic Cooperation (APEC) summit in Vancouver that year. Three student members of the APEC-Alert group were jailed for several days for protesting against the summit in front of the campus home of Martha Piper, at the time the president of the University of British Columbia. This protest was targeted more at China and Indonesia, two members of APEC with notorious human rights records, although several protestors railed against 'corporatization'.[20]

The three waves of global protests augured what became known as an **anti-globalization movement** that quickly developed from a local to a transnational and, in some cases, a global anti-imperial lobby. The counter-movements came together to protest against the WTO in what became known as the 'Battle of Seattle' in 1999, as well as for protests that soon followed at G8 summits, Organization of American States meetings, and IMF and World Bank conferences.

Counter-Movements

The end of the twentieth century and beginning of the twenty-first century proved to be a defining moment for bottom-up struggles against top-down globalization—what may be called a 'Grotian Moment'.[21] One such counter-movement to globalization took shape at the end of 1999 when the Third Ministerial Meeting of the WTO collapsed due to major street protests in Seattle, Washington. About 50,000 people joined in that protest against one of the symbolic agents of top-down globalization. This societal struggle was indirectly supported by rebellious developing country delegates inside the Seattle Convention Center.

Although it was difficult to pinpoint the position of all of the protestors, what seems to have united them in large part was 'their opposition to the expansion of a system that promoted corporate-led globalization at the expense of social goals like justice, community, national sovereignty, cultural diversity, and ecological sustainability.'[22] There was a general feeling among protestors that the WTO represented 'the darker side of globalization'.[23] This implied that perhaps global-ization had a 'bright side', if only it could be steered in the 'right' direction.

Many considered the Seattle protests as a turning point in the clash between bottom-up and top-down forces in the struggle for how the global economy ought to be governed in the future.[24] But this contest did not erupt out of the blue.

The Battle of Seattle

According to Jackie Smith, many of the activists in the streets of Seattle in 1999 got their feet wet back in the 1980s in the mobilization against 'Third World debt and its relationship to conflict and economic justice in Central America and other developing regions'.[25] And, as Ronaldo Munck notes, the background to Seattle was not only linked to the earlier historical waves of global protests but also had a local, 'context-setting' dimension.

The city of Seattle is known, historically, for its labour militancy. That history goes back to 1919 when workers in that city engaged in a general strike, and to 1934 when longshoremen organized a major strike that paralyzed the harbour. The latter event was considered one of the bitterest labour disputes of the twentieth century. It was a struggle that pitted the International Longshore-men's Association (ILA), later reorganized as the International Longshoremen's and Warehousemen's Union (ILWU), against steamship owners, police, and very hostile public officials. It also embroiled ILA leader Harry Bridges and the head of the Teamsters Union at the time, Dave Beck, in a drawn-out battle for control of the country's waterfronts. Seven people, including Seattle ILA leader Shelvy Daffron, were killed during that violent strike.

Seattle is also well known as the organizational base of the Wobblies (the Indus-trial Workers of the World)—an anarcho-syndicalist and internationalist union that had considerable workplace traction in the early twentieth century—and as one of the first unionized cities in North America. Since the mid-1990s there had been major labour strikes in Seattle against Boeing plants and, buoyed by the suc-cess of the American Federation of Labor–Congress of Industrial Organizations (AFL–CIO) unions, companies like Microsoft and other software companies based in Seattle, which were known to resist unionization, became targets of organized union drives.

So the Battle of Seattle did not just 'simply happen'; it was '*organized* by clearly identifiable social and political organizations', such as the People for Fair Trade (PFT) network comprised of labour, trade, and environmental groups that previ-ously had been engaged in a mobilization effort against the signing of the North America Free Trade Agreement. The PFT also joined forces with the Network Opposed to the WTO (NO! WTO), thus expanding the number of participants in this counter-movement.[26] In addition, in order to garner broad community sup-port for the movement, organized labour spent months before the confrontation in Seattle educating and informing the public about the negative and devastating impacts of the WTO.[27] Adding their weight to the activism of those civil soci-ety groups were student groups, religious-based groups like Jubilee 2000, envi-ronmentalist organizations like the Sierra Club, radical organizations like Direct Action Network (DAN) and Shock Troops, and a cluster of affinity groups that included the Black Bloc, whose members support an anarchist philosophy and wear black clothing and masks to hide their identity and carry makeshift armour to indicate that they are ready for violent battle.[28]

For the most part, the massive street protests outside the Seattle Convention Center were relatively peaceful and festive. The motley coalition of protestors (which included religious groups, labour groups, student groups, and environmental groups from several countries) took up a chant that is well known to the labour movement in Chile—'The people united can never be defeated!' Despite the general peacefulness of the protests, in a few instances protestors became violent—engaging in vandalism and property destruction—and they persisted in acts of civil disobedience, blocking off streets and intersections to hinder confer-

Sponsored by ANSWER Coalition

Members of Black Bloc during an anti-war demonstration, Washington, DC, 12 April 2003.

ence delegates from reaching the convention centre, where the WTO meetings were to take place. The reaction of state authorities exacerbated an already tense situation.

The critical moment for this civil society demonstration came on 30 November, when North American students marched into the city from the north while individuals from developing countries marched in from the south. Those in this permitted march were soon joined by unpermitted marchers who clashed with Seattle riot police. Those police were quickly joined by members of the King County Sheriff's office and together they tried to break up the protestations using pepper spray, tear gas, and rubber bullets. According to Walden Bello, 'The assaults on largely peaceful demonstrators by police in their Darth Vader-like uniforms in full view of television cameras made Seattle's mean streets the grand symbol of the crisis of globalization.'[29] The police actions provoked the demonstrators, and members of the Black Bloc began to smash storefront windows (of companies like Nike, Gap, and Starbucks) while other protestors dragged dumpsters into the middle of streets and lit them on fire. Police vehicles were overturned in the protest and general commercial activity came to a screeching halt.[30]

Eventually, the police were so completely overwhelmed by the tens of thousands of protestors who converged on the city that the opening of the WTO meeting was delayed, President Bill Clinton was prevented from addressing the delegates, and the meeting was eventually cancelled. Over 600 people were arrested over the next few days. The mayor of Seattle imposed a curfew and a 50-block 'no-protest zone' to try to bring the situation under control. Damage to commercial businesses in Seattle during the protests amounted to an estimated $20 million.[31]

What came out of that watershed Battle of Seattle was a sense that some members of civil society were growing wary of the efforts of neo-liberal institutions to marginalize them. The collective mantra was that there would be no globalization without the representation of members of civil society. At the same time, globalization became 'the unifying focus for a whole series of struggles around the environment, indigenous peoples' rights, jobs and people's livelihoods, and a general feeling of cultural alienation.'[32] The Battle of Seattle therefore became a symbol of a Polanyian double movement—an epic struggle between the architects of globalization and a growing transnational counter-globalization movement.

Jubilee 2000 Counter-Movement

Just prior to the Battle of Seattle, a coalition of civil society groups calling itself Jubilee 2000 met in Birmingham, England, to protest the G8 summit. This coalition grew out of alliances between aid agencies such as the Debt Crisis Network, the New Economics Foundation, Christian Aid, Action Aid, Tools for Self-Reliance, Tear Fund, and the World Development Network. Eventually, about 70 secular and religious organizations became part of this transnational movement, along with a number of celebrities (including famous actors, comedians, and musicians) and some members of political parties.

The work of this coalition actually was in part a response to such incidents as the 1982 Mexican debt crisis, which had been precipitated by Mexico's inability to service its outstanding debt to US commercial banks and other creditors. Technically, unlike cases of personal debt, countries are unable to declare bankruptcy when they are saddled with an unpayable debt burden. Poor less developed countries (LDCs) find themselves having to borrow from one creditor to pay off the debt to another creditor, and in so doing they spiral into the abyss of debt.

The Mexican crisis began on 12 August 1982, when the country's finance minister informed the US Federal Reserve chairman, the US Secretary of the Treasury, and the International Monetary Fund managing director that Mexico would be unable to meet its 16 August obligation to service an $80 billion debt (mainly dollar denominated). This situation worsened not only in Mexico but in other heavily indebted countries as well. By October 1983, 27 countries owing $239 billion had either rescheduled their debts to banks or were in the process of doing so. Others soon followed suit. Sixteen of those countries were from Latin America. Four of the largest countries in that region—Argentina, Brazil, Mexico, and Venezuela—owed various commercial banks $176 billion, or roughly 74 per cent of the total outstanding LDC debt.[33] Of that amount, roughly $37 billion was owed to eight of the largest banks in the US, and this amounted to roughly 147 per cent of their capital and reserves at the time.[34] As a result, several of the world's largest banks faced the possibility that several LDCs would default on their loan.

Like the Mexican crisis, the crisis in Southeast Asia during the same period was one of reckless over-lending exacerbated by the lending policies of the Bretton Woods institutions and, particularly, the structural adjustment strategies provided to these poor countries by the IMF. The Jubilee 2000 coalition also was concerned with the effect of the debt burden on African countries. High debt has served to undermine the democratic institutions in several African states, the leaders of which are forced to seek elections on the basis of economic policies that would not be tolerated by the electorate of any of the most developed countries (MDCs). As a result, it is no wonder that some African leaders resort to vote rigging when faced with these economic conditions.[35]

The Jubilee 2000 supporters challenged the acceptance of trade in debt, which tends to remove choice from developing countries' governments and deny their people control over their own destinies. The strategy of this coalition was to focus on advocating debt relief for the bottom 50 countries of the globe. Indeed, this coalition made such an impact on the World Bank and the IMF that in 1996 the international financial institutions proposed a debt relief package for the world's poorest countries, a package known as the heavily indebted poor countries (HIPC) initiative, which was later supplemented by the Multilateral Debt Relief Initiative (MDRI). Essentially, the aim of the first initiative was to ensure that no poor country would face a debt burden that it could not manage. This entailed 'the coordinated action of the international financial community, including multilateral organizations and governments, to reduce to sustainable levels the external debt burdens of the most heavily indebted poor countries'.[36] However, when many of the global creditors put obstacles in the way of this initiative, the Jubilee 2000 coalition decided to bring the issue of debt to the attention of the broader public.

The Jubilee 2000 protest in Birmingham was part of this wider attempt at publicity for the counter-movement. It drew approximately 70,000 people, some coming by foot, others by bike, by coach, by train, by a flotilla of barges, by a coracle, and even by rickshaw. Some of the protestors wanted to fly in by balloon but this idea was nixed by the security forces. While the largest number of people came from northern England and Scotland, a number of protestors arrived from the US, Canada, Germany, Italy, Norway, Sweden, Finland, Spain, Holland, Belgium, Portugal, and Austria. A group also came from the so-called 'Poor 8': Jamaica, Bolivia, Nicaragua, Bangladesh, Tanzania, Malawi, Mozambique, and Ethiopia.

Among the many speakers at this event were Martin Dent and Bill Peters (the individuals in the UK who first proposed the idea of Jubilee 2000 and the need to link this movement to debt relief for the poorest of the developing countries). However, the original concept of Jubilee 2000 can be traced to the 1986 encyclical letter of Pope John Paul II titled *Tertio Millennio Adveniente*.[37] The Pope had drawn on the custom of 'Jubilee' celebrated in the Old Testament, a time dedicated, according to the Law of Moses, to the liberation of slaves and the cancellation of debt.[38]

Thus the Jubilee 2000 coalition pressed the MDC leaders, particularly those in the G8, to 'break the chain of debt' that continued to keep the poorest countries in a state of bondage or slavery.[39] For this coalition, delivering the LDCs from the bondage of debt did not mean 'debt forgiveness' because that would imply that falling into debt was somehow a 'sin'. The creditors, including the G8 countries, are just as responsible for the debt situation as the debtors. Creditors aggressively promote 'credit' to encourage poor countries to purchase goods from the capitalist markets of the MDCs. Some of those goods include small arms and light weapons, as we shall see in the following chapter. The G8 countries are considered by Jubilee 2000, for all intents and purposes, as agents for the international creditors, including the IMF.

The protestors formed a human chain surrounding Birmingham's international conference centre, where the summit was supposed to be held.[40] This human chain symbolized the yoke of debt that kept LDCs in a kind of slavery to international capital.[41] But the organizers also felt that a human chain might be a way of altering the dynamics between large protest groups and the authorities.

Anti-Globalization Movements: From Bangkok to Washington

Over the next few years similar, albeit smaller, anti-globalization protests erupted around the globe. For instance, in February 2000, during the Tenth Assembly of the United Nations Conference on Trade and Development (UNCTAD X) in Bangkok, assembled protestors were critical of the WTO as well as of the entire Bretton Woods system. At this meeting Michael Camdessus, the outgoing managing director of the IMF, received a pie in the face from anti-IMF activist Robert Naiman.

The UNCTAD event received international attention because of the pie-in-the-face incident and, in some ways, helped set the stage for the first major post-Seattle confrontation between pro- and anti-globalization forces at the spring meetings of the IMF and the World Bank in Washington, DC. At those meetings, about 30,000 protestors gathered in the US capital only to find themselves confronted by 10,000 police who cordoned off a significant portion of the northwest part of the city, thus protecting the IMF–World Bank complex. Police made hundreds of arrests as the demonstrators tried, in some cases, to break through the barriers. Although the police declared victory over the protestors, the image portrayed on television was one of siege of the Bretton Woods institutions by a large mob of individuals who decried the fact that these institutions were responsible for inflicting poverty and misery on people in the developing world. In some sense, therefore, the message of the protestors was heard globally, above that of the police.

The next major protest by anti-globalization demonstrators occurred in Chiang Mai, Thailand (in May 2000), where the Asian Development Bank (ADB)—a multilateral body notorious for funding major projects that disrupt communities and destabilize governments—was holding its thirty-third annual meeting. Although the number of protestors was quite small (about 2,000 people) compared to the major demonstrations in Seattle, Birmingham, and Washington, the executive of the ADB set up a task force after the conference to 'deal with civil society'.[42] At the same time, the ADB determined to hold its next meeting at a more secure site in Honolulu. The significance of the Chiang Mai protest was that the majority of demonstrators were local poor Thai farmers, not middle-class youth or organized labour from advanced countries. Key organizers of this local protest saw Chiang Mai as part of the larger global resistance movement against globalization.[43]

In June 2000, some of the same individuals who demonstrated against the globalization of trade at the WTO meeting in Seattle turned up in Windsor, Ontario, Canada, to protest the General Assembly meeting of the Organization of American States (OAS). The 3,000 protestors included free trade, environmental, human rights, and labour activists. The police, who outnumbered the protestors, used pepper spray and unnecessary force to arrest 40 of the demonstrators who tried to infiltrate the barricades set up around six city blocks.

AFP/Getty Images

Protestors in Chiang Mai, Thailand, at the Asian Development Bank meeting, May 2000.

Other major battle lines were drawn at the Asia-Pacific Summit of the World Economic Forum (WEF) held in Melbourne, Australia, in September 2000. The attempt to portray globalization with a 'more liberal face' only cemented in the minds of observers what was wrong with globalization. The meeting held in the Crown Casino on Melbourne's waterfront further magnified the symbolic image of globalization as a 'finance-driven' speculative phenomenon that produces a few big winners and many, many losers. This time, about 5,000 protestors were present, blocking the main entrance to the casino and forcing WEF organizers to bring some of the delegates in by helicopter. The mistreatment by police of the ostensibly peaceful protestors, again in full view of the television cameras, only further served to paint globalization and 'top-down' neo-liberal governance in a negative light before the eyes of the public.

Towards the end of September 2000, the Bretton Woods institutions held their annual meeting in Prague, Czech Republic. About 10,000 people came from all over Europe to protest against globalization and these institutions. This protest was much less peaceful, to the point where the organizers felt it best to end the annual meeting one day early. Czech President Vaclav Havel tried to bring the two sides together on 23 September. However, the gap between the protestors and the representatives of the Bretton Woods institutions only seemed to widen, as the World Bank president, James Wolfensohn, and the managing director of the IMF, Horst Koehler, blew the opportunity of making concrete concessions to civil society.

The assertion that MNCs are in collusion with powerful countries in reaping the benefits of globalization at the expense of the majority of the world's population was only confirmed in the minds of the protestors when US President George W. Bush bent to pressure from US industry to pull the US out of the Kyoto Protocol in March 2001, following the impasse that had occurred at the conference of parties meeting held in The Hague in December 2000. That decision, along with growing attempts by government leaders in the major industrial states to find ways to keep demonstrators away from major summit meetings, only served to anger many within civil society. The overwhelming nature of the show of force at these headline-grabbing demonstrations ratcheted up the violence even more.

Quebec City, the Summit of the Americas, and the FTAA

André Drainville calls the Summit of Americas, held in Quebec City in April 2001, a 'polycentric gathering of would-be hemispheric actors—from globalizing elites intent on creating a "Free Trade Area of the Americas" (FTAA), to sundry "Peoples of the Americas" collected in a parallel summit, to a saturnalia of protests at the periphery of both events'. Drainville goes on to say that this particular event provides us with an understanding of how transnational subjects are constructed.[44]

The Summit of the Americas was the third such meeting to discuss the implementation of an FTAA. The first was held in Miami (1994) and the second in Santiago, Chile (1998). The Quebec Summit was a continuation of the discussion among the leaders of 34 democratic states in the western hemisphere to establish a new trade architecture that would have major implications not only for the sub-regional trade arrangements currently in place throughout the region but also for the global neo-liberal project spearheaded particularly by US capitalism.[45] The impact of such a monumental trade arrangement on the global economy would be difficult to ignore given the fact that the FTAA would create a marketplace of

854 million people from Alaska to Patagonia—a population twice the size of that of the European Union—and would comprise countries with a combined gross domestic product of over US$13 trillion and total exports of more than US$1 trillion annually. As one author put it, in 'an increasingly regionalized world economy, the FTAA would become a very powerful regional grouping.'[46] While the formal plans for an FTAA were launched publicly at the first Summit of the Americas and endorsed openly by the then-US President Bill Clinton, it has been argued that the roots of the idea for such a free trade area can be traced to a much earlier time when organizations controlled largely by the Rockefeller family, such as David Rockefeller's Council for the Americas, developed strategies for building a network through a common market of 'insider allies' in Latin America.[47]

But one can go even further back to find an earlier example of the seed of the idea of an FTAA. According to a right-wing American journalist, William Jasper, this idea originated with a proposal by Fidel Castro in 1959 for a regional common market at a conference in Buenos Aires. Of course, this was before Castro had publicly acknowledged his Communist ties, according to the journalist. Less than two years later, members of US President John Kennedy's administration advanced a similar proposal, 'The Alliance for Progress', which aimed to meld the countries of the region into a common market through free trade and infusions of aid and investment.[48]

In essence, the immediate forerunner of the FTAA was George H.W. Bush's Enterprise for the Americas Initiative (EAI), while the foundation of the proposed FTAA was built on the neo-liberal ideology that underpinned the Washington Consensus. Some scholars and journalistic observers see the FTAA process as a deliberate attempt by the US to consolidate its hegemony in the western hemisphere through peaceful/benign economic integration that would, at the same time, strengthen its position in global trade negotiations taking place at the level of the WTO.[49] It is this view, in part, that stirred up the counter-hegemonic and counter-globalization movements to target the Summit of the Americas.

Due to the extraordinary security measures, the Summit's 9,000 participants were more or less shielded from direct confrontation with the protestors. The meeting was held in the Centre des Congrès on René Lévesque Boulevard near the provincial parliament. The security perimeter consisted of about a 3.5-kilometre-fence, three metres high, and guarded by a large number of municipal, provincial, and federal police officers. The Canadian government, learning the lessons of previous contestations, strategized to find ways of co-opting certain elements of civil society in order to diffuse or reduce the protests. Academics, youth, and representatives of government-created and -sponsored NGOs were brought together with national and global governing bodies just before the Summit began to contribute to the Summit's Declaration and Plan of Action.

Countering this attempt at co-option, those civil society groups opposed to the secret deliberations of the Summit set up a tent, well removed from the security perimeter, at the old harbour in Lower Town (Old Quebec), for the Peoples' Summit of the Americas—organized by the Réseau québécois sur l'intégration continentale and Common Frontiers. The theme for the Peoples' Summit was 'Resisting. Proposing. Together.' In a number of 'teach-ins' and plenary sessions, the Peoples' Summit dealt with such issues as the impact of globalization on women, education, labour, agriculture, communications, human rights, and the environment. A Peoples' Hemispheric Agreement was drafted and then the protestors, about 50,000 to 60,000 strong, marched towards the security perimeter, forming the largest such protest group in Quebec's history. The majority of the people were quite peaceful, but a breakaway group of about 1,000, including some radical Black Bloc members, tried to take direct action against the security perimeter and the police guarding the security fence. A number of 'professional' protestors, who had been well versed in 'civil disobedience', tried to launch a 'sit-in' close to the security fence. In a matter of moments, a surging group broke down a part of the security fence and directly confronted the police, who used tear gas and rubber bullets to disperse the anti-FTAA crowd.[50]

What the Quebec Summit indicates is that there are a number of different approaches within the 'community of resistance'.[51] Some of the protestors were quite content to voice their opinions in opposition to the FTAA negotiations, and globalization in general, in a peaceful manner. Others took a more confrontational approach. Regardless, it was clear that these protestors learned lessons from previous contestations and were prepared for dealing with potential assaults from the police. Drainville put it this way:

> Connecting the dots, we could show that, indeed, the making of protests in Québec City was linked to like happenings elsewhere, by specific people and organizations who shape the aesthetics of anti-summit protests (anti-capitalist carnivals too are made, by such groups as the Ruckus Society or Reclaim the Streets), give them their language, tactics (lock-downs, street parties, property destruction, affinity groups, civil disobedience, etc.) and a measure of political coherence.

The counter-globalization movements that gathered in Quebec City were by and large more conscious of other such movements around the globe and were more reflective and politically deliberate than previous protest gatherings. There was also an element among the protestors that was willing to use more violent and confrontational tactics.

The July 2001 mass demonstrations in Genoa, Italy, produced perhaps one of the worst outcomes of such tactics. One protestor, Carlo Giuliani, was killed—shot twice in the face by the police—and several others were injured as over 200,000 people from all across the globe descended on Genoa the weekend of 19–21 July 2001 to protest against the G8 summit.[52] Among the demonstrators were those who were there to protest against the right-wing Berlusconi government. Thus, this contestation brought together local, national, and international dimensions of a coalition opposed to globalization and to a government that embraced the neo-liberal agenda. Over 16,000 police and 3,000 soldiers were mobilized to keep protestors at bay and insulate the G8 leaders and their entourage from the protest. But violent elements (mostly from Black Bloc members) seeped into the demonstration.

This mounting resistance to globalization was the outcome of a growing awareness around the globe of the illegitimacy of the global governance institutions that use the neo-liberal credo to subordinate ordinary people and to marginalize those who were already hurting from structural adjustment policies and free trade deals. These counter-globalization movements had truly become transnational. Again, this demonstrated a global movement against capitalist globalization.

A major protest, billed as Seattle II, was planned for September 2001 in Washington. This would have brought together a 'perfect storm' of organized labour, anti-globalization activists, anarchists, members of NGOs, anti-capitalists, and members of the Latin American solidarity movement. However, the attacks on

© Reuters/Corbis

Over 200,000 demonstrated in Genoa against the Group of 8 in July 2001.

the twin towers and the Pentagon on 11 September 2001 derailed those plans. Instead, rabid patriotism and jingoism emerged in the US in the aftermath of 9/11, and state responses to the terrorist attacks essentially muted the counter-globalization movements. Many anti-globalization activists feared that they would be labelled as 'pro-terrorists' after 9/11. The focus of attention quickly shifted to the wars in Afghanistan and Iraq, and this brought to the fore the peace movement. The anti-globalization movement seemed to have faded for a while and the transnational peace movement grew with massive rallies in 2003 all across Europe protesting what was considered by many as the illegitimate war in Iraq.

During the WTO negotiations in Cancún in 2003, there was a reconfiguration of the counter-globalization movement. Intergovernmental economic organizations had begun courting and co-opting **international non-governmental organizations** (INGOS) and there seemed to be a deliberate attempt to segregate mainstream INGOS from the more volatile and unpredictable grassroots groups. As well, one should not rule out the 'burn-out' factor and the costs some activists incurred by travelling from city to city to be part of this counter-movement. In addition, severe divisions arose between certain activists groups, as the issue of violence divided the protestors and there was little agreement over exactly what the targets of these protests were (e.g., capitalism, globalization, imperialism, the Bretton Woods system, or MNCs).

Organizations like the World Bank began to open up their consultation processes to intellectuals and women's organization. Terms like 'partnership' and 'networks' began to be used within the sphere of intergovernmental organizations (IGOs) to refer to the new relationships being developed with civil society groups. Of course, consultations and interactions between the IGOs and INGOS were not brand new ideas. In 1945 the first significant success of NGOs in influencing the UN system was to obtain two major amendments to the proposed UN Charter. The end result was Article 71, which provided for consultation arrangements between NGOs and the Economic and Social Council, and a provision for the promotion of human rights, which was incorporated into the UN Charter as one of the purposes of the UN. But NGOs were unable to get governments to agree to involve civil society more directly in the work of the General Assembly or the Security Council. In those days, NGOs were seen as 'non-political'. In practice, however, economic and social questions cannot be separated from 'politics'.

From the end of the Cold War, there has been an exponential increase in the number of NGOs and in the density of interactions between NGOs and international organizations. As the number of NGOs increased, the number of opportunities for interactions between them and IGOs also increased. In addition, improvements in travel and advancements in information and communication technologies (ICTs) allowed thousands of NGOs operating at all levels (local, national, regional, trans-regional, transnational, and global) to increase their contact with representatives of IGOs and with UN agencies, commissions, and committees. Many of these NGOs stepped up their pressure on the field offices and headquarters of IGOs and began attending parallel peoples' conferences whenever IGO conferences were planned. Slowly, IGOs began to involve mainstream NGOs in preparatory meetings, actual IGO conferences, and follow-up meetings. Some were even allowed to help set the agenda for those conferences and meetings.[53] Organizations and agencies like the International Fund for Agricultural Development (IFAD), the United Nations Development Programme (UNDP), the World Health Organization (WHO), and the United Nations High Commissioner for Refugees (UNHCR) all have annual NGO consultative meetings. The World Bank has gone further and now has pluri-annual and regional consultative meetings with NGOs. However, as Peter Uvin points out, just because 'NGOs' voices are heard does not mean they are heeded, especially not those representing the poor and the marginal.' And, generally speaking, consultation between IGOs and grassroots NGOs is 'still weak and unsuccessful'.[54]

In April 2004, state representatives and activists from all over the globe converged on Washington as part of the celebrations of the sixtieth anniversary of the IMF and the World Bank. But while the international bureaucrats were congratulating each other within the walls of these institutions, militants were in the streets protesting against the over half-century of IMF and World Bank structural adjustment programs, undemocratic decision-making, and destructive free trade agreements. The carnival-like atmosphere in the streets of Washington was tempered by the presence, again, of heavily armed police.

Conclusion

Despite the calls for reforms to top-down institutions of global governance, little has been done to make the international financial institutions more democratic and accountable. The lack of confidence in the Bretton Woods institutions today may be an indication that these bodies are losing their legitimacy. The proliferation of counter-globalization and counter-hegemonic protest movements represents the need for bottom-up governance, i.e., governance in which individuals in civil society can have a greater say in decisions that directly affect them. The tensions that emerged on the streets of Seattle, Cancún, Quebec City, Prague, and Washington are indications of the difficulty in getting the state-centric world to accommodate an increasingly multi-centric one. The actual implementation of true bottom-up governance is far from easy. A major problem in implementing bottom-up structures at the global level is the difficulty sometimes in deciphering which among these groups are truly 'representative', not to mention who has the sovereign or supra-sovereign right to do this deciphering and necessary restructuring, and truly to open the doors to non-state actors. But an even bigger problem is finding effective existing institutional structures that can accommodate broadly inclusive representation. Finally, a major critique of the counter-globalization movement is that is it mainly white and largely from the affluent North. The following chapter explores a number of counter-globalization movements from the global South to demonstrate the extent to which these movements are becoming quite transnational and heterogeneous.

Key Terms

anti-globalization movement
civil society
intermestic
international non-governmental
　organizations (INGOs)

social movements
state/society complex
Washington Consensus

Discussion Questions

1. What differentiates globalization today from earlier forms?
2. What is the state/society complex?
3. What is the intermestic divide?
4. Why did the Washington Consensus provoke such a strong negative reaction from civil society?
5. Identify two distinct streams of transnational counter-globalization movements?
6. What were some of the precursors to the current counter-globalization movements?
7. Explain the '50 Years Is Enough' campaign.
8. Why was the Battle of Seattle considered a 'globalization-from-below' movement?
9. What impact has the Jubilee 2000 counter-movement had on inter-state relations?
10. Which neo-liberal institutions have been the most targeted by anti-globalization protestors? Why?

Suggested Readings

Bello, Walden. *Deglobalization: Ideas for a New World Economy*. London: Zed Books, 2005. Bello is the director of one of the more prominent anti-globalization networks, Focus on the Global South, and this book presents a clear critique of globalization from one of its most informed and critical observers.

Cameron, Angus, and Ronen Palan. *The Imagined Economies of Globalization*. London: Sage, 2003. This book includes a review of theoretical arguments related to globalization before examining the influence of globalization on capitalism, the state, culture, and the public sphere.

Serra, Narcis, and Joseph Stiglitz, eds. *The Washington Consensus Reconsidered: Towards a New Global Governance*. Oxford: Oxford University Press, 2008. This collection starts with a concise account of the Washington Consensus and proceeds to a series of critiques and alternatives from some of the world's leading experts in development studies.

Global Links

One World Net

oneworld.net/

This site brings together news and views from more than 1,500 organizations, most of them non-governmental and involved in human rights and development activities.

50 Years Is Enough

orgs.tigweb.org/4692

Website of the organization that has been campaigning for the radical transformation of international financial institutions such as the World Bank and the International Monetary Fund.

Jubilee Debt Campaign

www.jubileedebtcampaign.org.uk/

A non-governmental group organized to promote debt relief for impoverished countries.

Debate 10

Be it resolved that globalization is not new and there is no alternative to it.

Chapter Eleven

Resistance Movements in the Global South

Introduction

While many of the counter-globalization movements have been located in the global North and the majority of the protestors have been white, several counter-movements have their origin in the global South. Not all local resistance movements become transnational or global. But many do. This chapter examines a number of those movements: the Ogoni resistance movement and its actions versus Shell and the Nigerian government; the Chipko Movement in India; the Green Belt Movement in Kenya; the Zapatista uprising in Chiapas, Mexico; and Brazil's landless workers' movement—the Movimento Trabalhadores Rurais Sêm Terra or MST. The chapter concludes with a look at the Porte Alegre World Social Forum (WSF)—an umbrella counter-forum that embraced counter-globalization movements from the global North and global South. The WSF began as an initiative of the MST from Brazil and ATTAC (Association for the Taxation of Financial Transactions to Aid Citizens), an NGO with its origin in France.

The Ogoni Resistance Movement

In the Niger Delta region, a local counter-globalization movement sprang up in the early 1990s to challenge Shell, the Anglo–Dutch global oil giant and an agent of globalization, which produces about half of Nigeria's oil. The Movement for the Survival of the Ogoni People (MOSOP) was born as a direct reaction not only to the fact that the Ogoni, indigenous landowners, were alienated from the produce of their land but also to the fact that Shell BP, the multinational oil giant, was allowed by the Nigerian government to expropriate land belonging to the Ogoni, to exploit that land in drilling for oil, and to pollute the ecosystem of that region of Nigeria without providing for restitution.[1] The MOSOP resistance also targeted the government of Nigeria, which was considered to be in cahoots with Shell. The Ogoni protest was therefore also about the quest for self-determination and control over their lands.

The Nigerian state itself is a product of colonialism. Under the British, it became an interventionist and patrimonial state that tried to integrate forcefully all parts of Nigeria into the global capitalist society. Nigeria became a source of supply for cheap raw materials. At the same time it was a ready market for more expensive finished products from the global centres of industrial capital. As is the case in much of post-colonial Africa, the Nigerian state is a reflection of the colonial past and encompasses people of different nationalities and ethnicities, as well as pre-capitalist modes of production. In so doing, this forcefully contrived state creation has tended to privilege the ethnic majority over minorities. Minority ethnic groups like the Ogoni have used ethnicity to push for self-determination and autonomy over their lands and resources, although they often have lost out to the state and its global capitalist counterparts, during the colonial era and in more recent post-colonial times.

As far back as 1938, Ogoni lands were marked out and given to Shell by the colonial masters of Nigeria. These areas, in the words of Giddens, became 'integrated into **globalized capitalist relations**'.[2] At that time, Shell (later Shell BP) was granted exploration rights to an area of roughly 367,000 square miles (almost the entire mainland of Nigeria). Just before Nigeria gained independence, the area of lands over which Shell had control was reduced to 16,000 square miles, much of this in the oil-rich Niger Delta. Although the Nigerian state began collecting taxes/rent from oil companies beginning in 1959, it wasn't until 1969 that the state gained control, via nationalization, of oil from the oil companies operating within the country. This coincided with the abrogation of the 1914 Petroleum Act. By 1970, oil accounted for over 80 per cent of Nigeria's national revenue and for approximately 95 per cent of its foreign exchange earnings, due largely to joint ventures between the Nigerian government and companies like Shell.[3] Thus, the state's very existence depends on maintaining a relationship with the giant global oil companies, and Nigeria has become essentially a weak partner in that relationship.

Since 1990, Shell's gross annual income was more than the combined GNP of Tanzania, Ethiopia, Nepal, Bangladesh, Zaire, Uganda, Nigeria, Kenya, and Pakistan—countries that represent one-tenth of the world's population.[4] Indeed, Shell has oil production operations in over 100 countries. 'Shell's position in Nigeria's political economy and its role at the cutting edge of the global control of Nigeria's oil offers its "unequal partner"—the state—little autonomy vis-à-vis the imperatives of globalization.'[5] The Nigerian state projects itself as protector of the national interest while repressing any local opposition to Shell. The Ogoni resistance was therefore seen not only as having the potential to obstruct the expansion of global oil capital but also as a subversive enemy of the state.

Ken Saro-Wiwa, the most prominent leader of and spokesperson for the Ogoni people until his execution by the state, called this movement a struggle against 'internal colonization'.[6] But what seemed like a local resistance movement was in fact linked to the global struggle against the globalization project. This type of struggle illustrates the critical nexus between local resistance and the contradictions that stem from the global **social relations of production**. There is obviously a strategic link between the oil giants, like Shell, and the energy needs of the major industrial powers. As Cyril Obi put it, 'control of oil is directly linked to the reproduction and expansion of capital on a global scale.'[7]

The Ogoni live atop some of the richest real estate in Africa and occupy one of the most industrialized areas of Nigeria, yet very few Ogoni benefit from the jobs, development, or amenities coming from the oil industry. Instead, the Ogoni people have been suffering from the oil companies' pollution of their streams and freshwater sources and from the spills and blowouts that degrade their arable land.[8] Julian Saurin explains that:

> the destruction of Ogoni lands in Southern Nigeria by oil companies including alleg-edly Royal Dutch Shell satisfies the covetous and distanced shareholders who derive huge financial benefit from those lands and people. At the same time, the Ogoni pay the permanent costs of ecological degradation and repression, whilst relinquish-ing their control over what happens to their land, to the oil, or the product of their labour.[9]

Shell did not employ Ogoni people. It did not contribute to building basic infra-structure in the region, which was sorely lacking. Furthermore, pollution by Shell plants more or less destroyed the local Ogoni economy—farming, fishing, hunting, and petty trading—and caused illness among the local people, thus threatening their very existence. This reality, combined with the harsh economic conditions brought on by structural adjustment policies and the actions of an insensitive military dictatorship, produced what became the Ogoni counter-globalization movement.[10] As Cyril Obi explains, 'It is this struggle for achiev-ing control of the land, and re-imposing environmentally sustainable local economic practices, that pitched the Ogoni against the further penetration of global capital.'[11]

When MOSOP was formed in 1991, it started out as a relatively peaceful resistance movement. It soon became more militant and radicalized, however, when the Nigerian government failed to meet its five basic demands. According to Ken Saro-Wiwa, those demands were: (1) social justice for minorities; (2) equity in power-sharing; (3) compensation for the devastation done to the environment and funds to restore the environment; (4) release of economic rent payments to the people of the oil-producing areas; and (5) human dignity and self-actualization.[12] The MOSOP resistance gained strength when the struggle became international-ized as the leaders of the movement took their case to the UN system and NGOs known for addressing such issues as human rights, the environment, and demo-cratic representation (e.g., Amnesty International, Greenpeace, the London Rain-forest Action Group, and the Unrepresented Nations and Peoples Organisation). Its campaign was waged in newspaper articles and opinion pieces, documentary films, and lecture tours that highlighted the atrocities being committed by Shell and the Nigerian government against the Ogoni people. The international expo-sure of human rights abuse, environmental degradation, and government repres-sion basically shocked the international community into putting pressure on the oil companies operating in Nigeria as well as on the Nigerian government.

By 1993, MOSOP was transformed from a local resistance movement into a popular social movement with transnational linkages. The more conservative elements within the movement were literally forced out and more youthful and militant elements, such as the National Youth Council for the Survival of Ogoni People (NYCOP) and the Federation of Ogoni Women's Associations (FOWA), took their place with Ken Saro-Wiwa at the helm. The increasingly radicalized movement began blocking access to oil wells, thus forcing Shell to stop operations for long periods of time. 'To the domestic dominant class, the revolutionary activities of MOSOP were a direct threat to its hegemony, as well as the legitimacy of the oil minorities faction aligned to the dominant class.'[13]

Once the Nigerian state began mobilizing armed troops into the Niger Delta region, the MOSOP struggle quickly became militarized. A reign of terror was unleashed by the Nigerian armed forces against MOSOP and any of the Ogoni people who expressed sympathy with the movement. Ogoni villages were occupied by the military, entire villages were ransacked, and people were injured and killed in the crackdown. On 10 November 1995, Ken Saro-Wiwa was hanged by the Nigerian military, along with eight leaders of MOSOP, after being convicted of the trumped-up charge of incitement to murder following the deaths of four Ogoni elders. His death provoked international outrage, and as a result Nigeria's membership in the Commonwealth was suspended. On the day of Saro-Wiwa's death, Thilo Bode, the executive director of Greenpeace International, issued a statement: 'Ken Saro-Wiwa was hanged today for speaking out against the environmental damage to the Niger Delta caused by Shell Oil through its 37 years of drilling in the region. Ken Saro-Wiwa was campaigning for what Greenpeace considers the most basic of human rights: the right for clean air, land and water. His only crime was his success in bringing his cause to international attention.'[14]

Ken Saro-Wiwa, Nigerian writer and activist who was executed for leading the cause of the Ogoni people against exploitation by Shell Oil and the Nigerian government.

© Colin McPherson/Corbis

Ken Saro-Wiwa wrote the following for his closing testimony at the military trial held to convict him:

> I and my colleagues are not the only ones on trial. Shell is here on trial and it is as well that it is represented by counsel said to be holding a watching brief. The Company has, indeed, ducked this particular trial, but its day will surely come and the lessons learnt here may prove useful to it for there is no doubt in my mind that the ecological war that the company has waged in the Delta will be called to question sooner than later and the crimes of that war be duly punished. The crime of the Company's dirty wars against the Ogoni people will also be punished.[15]

The Chipko and Green Belt Movements

Like the MOSOP case, the Chipko and Green Belt movements are concerned with environmentally destructive practices linked indirectly to globalization and global capital. The Chipko Movement emerged in India and the Green Belt Movement began in Kenya.

We all have some understanding of the complex relationship that humans have with forests. The ecosystems of forests are vitally important to human survival. We depend on forests for the clean air that we breathe, for food and watersheds, for shade and shelter, and for economic gain. Early *homo sapiens* were known to worship trees, and even today many Aboriginal peoples still hold forests in awe and some even treat the forest with the kind of respect normally reserved for the divine. As populations grew, some forests have been cleared to make room for agriculture, habitation, roads, and mining. The Food and Agriculture Organization (FAO) has estimated that the rate of natural forest loss in the tropics each year is about 13 million hectares—the equivalent of clear-cutting the area of 36 football fields a minute.[16]

The forests of India are a critical resource for the subsistence of rural peoples throughout that country, but especially in the hilly and mountainous regions, both because of their direct provision of food, fuel, and fodder and because of their role in stabilizing the soil and water resources. As these Indian forests have been increasingly targeted for clear-cutting by commercial and industrial interests, some Indian villagers have been doing their best to protect them and their livelihoods by using the Gandhian method of *satyagraha* or non-violent resistance. During the 1970s and 1980s, resistance to these environmentally destructive practices spread rapidly across India and became known as the Chipko Movement.

This local counter-movement was linked to transnational interests in preserving forests and reducing the effects of global climate change. But it was also a counter to the wasteful, polluting, and resource-intensive consumption patterns of industries representing global capital—hence the link to globalization. Women constitute the vast majority of those involved in the Chipko Movement. The first Chipko action, led by Bali Devi, took place spontaneously in April 1973 in Uttar Pradesh, as villagers, mostly women, interposed their bodies between trees and contractors' axes. They did so by hugging the trees—and this explains why the movement became known in Hindi as 'Chipko', or 'embrace' in English.[17]

Over the next five years or so, the actions of this peaceful movement were imitated in many districts across the Himalayas. Incredibly, the Chipko protests in Uttar Pradesh achieved a major victory in 1980 when the Prime Minister of India, Indira Gandhi, imposed a 15-year ban on green felling in the Himalayan forests. Since that time, the resistance movement has continued to spread—first to Himachal Pradesh in the north, then to Karnataka in the south, to Rajasthan in the west, to Bihar in the east, and to the Vindhyas in central India. Apart from the 15-year ban, the Chipko Movement has managed to stop clear-cutting in the Western Ghats and the Vindhyas and to push for a natural resource policy in India that would be more sensitive to the economic needs and ecological requirements of the average Indian.

Sunderlal Bahuguna, a prominent activist, environmentalist, and philosopher of the Gandhi tradition, supported the many women who made up the Chipko counter-movement. In fact, he was instrumental in bringing their case to Indira Gandhi. As he has said:

© Bagla Pallava/Corbis Sygma

Sunderlal Bahuguna, Indian social activist, environmentalist, and philosopher.

The solution of present-day problems lies in the re-establishment of a harmonious relationship between man and nature. To keep this relationship permanent we will have to digest the definition of real development: development is synonymous with culture. When we sublimate nature in a way that we achieve peace, happiness, prosperity and, ultimately, fulfilment along with satisfying our basic needs, we march towards culture.[18]

According to the United Nations Environment Programme (UNEP), the Chipko Movement has demonstrated how ordinary women, by their actions, can make a difference to their communities.[19] In this case, the Chipko resistance was about wresting control of the forests in the Himalayas from the hands of a distant bureaucracy that was more concerned with cutting down the forest to make urban-oriented products than with ensuring sustainable development for the local people. Since the announcement of the National Forest Policy in 1988, in response to the pressure from the Chipko resistance, considerable progress has been made in forest conservation in India. Indeed, the result of this counter-movement has been reclamation of the Himalayan forests[20]—satellite imagery indicates that net deforestation in India is being arrested. As a Chipko slogan states: 'ecology is permanent economy.'

Like the Chipko Movement, the Green Belt Movement grew out of a local context and was headed by a woman. It also took the view that sustainable development must be linked to preservation of the environment.

The principal promoter of the Green Belt Movement is Professor Wangari Maathai, who was awarded the Nobel Peace Prize in 2004 for her work in empowering local people to make a difference environmentally and politically. Maathai has been active on the National Council of Women in her home country of Kenya for many years. Within this Council the idea of a Green Belt Movement was born. The specific goals of the movement can be summarized as follows:

- Avoid desertification.
- Promote awareness of the need to strike a balance between development and preservation of the environment.
- Provide fuel wood for the energy needs of local people.
- Promote the planting of a variety of trees for human and animal use.
- Encourage soil conservation and land rehabilitation.
- Create jobs in rural areas through tree-planting.
- Create self-employment opportunities for young people in agriculture.
- Give women a positive image.
- Promote sound nutrition based on use of traditional foodstuff.
- Carry out research in rural areas.
- Develop a replicable methodology for rural development.

In the first 10 years of its existence, the Green Belt Movement realized most of these goals.

By World Environment Day (5 June) in 1977, this movement had become a broad-based grassroots reforestation project, and by the mid-1980s it had about 600 tree nurseries, providing earnings for 2,000 to 3,000 women, involving about a half-million schoolchildren, and assisting roughly 15,000 farmers in planting

Wangari Maathai, leader of the Green Belt Movement and Nobel Peace Prize winner.

private green belts. The movement has since grown from its local origins to become regional, transnational, and international. The stated mission of the Green Belt Movement International is 'to empower individuals worldwide to protect the environment and to promote good governance and cultures of peace'.[21]

In 1989, the Kenyan government decided to build a world media centre in collaboration with Robert Maxwell, the British media magnate who recently had bought a large share in the *Kenya Times*, which was to include the construction of the tallest building in Africa and a larger-than-life statue of the Kenyan President, Arap Moi. Maathai and her movement opposed this project because of the negative impact it would have on Nairobi's principal inner-city parks. As international support for the resistance movement grew, the Kenyan government retaliated by vilifying Maathai and placing her under house arrest. Maathai received a tremendous outpouring of support from many quarters, including from the Norwegian government. When the Norwegian ambassador to Kenya protested Maathai's house arrest, he was asked by the Kenyan government to go back to Norway immediately. In November 1990, Maathai was prevented from returning to Kenya during one of her overseas trips to the US.

Looking back over her years with the Green Belt Movement, Wangari Maathai remarked, 'If I have learned one thing, it is that humans are only part of this ecosystem. When we destroy the ecosystem, we destroy ourselves, for in its survival depends our own.'[22] The Green Belt Movement is a good example of how a local resistance movement, under charismatic leadership, can expand to a region and then became a transnational and even international counter-movement.

Zapatista Uprising in Chiapas

When masked Zapatista rebels took over the administrative offices in San Cristóbal de las Casas on 1 January 1994, the entire world's attention was drawn to the Mexican state of Chiapas. Anyone who knows the history of Mexico would remember that San Cristóbal de las Casas was named after Fray Bartolomé de Las Casas, a Catholic priest who accompanied Christopher Columbus on his third voyage to the New World. Las Casas is remembered in Latin America as an ardent defender of 'the native Indians'—the indigenous population of the hemisphere—against mistreatment at the hands of the Spanish colonists. He had seen 'countless indigenous people die of imported infections, mistreatment, and outright slavery'.[23] Despite Las Casas's efforts, which included petitioning Spain's rulers to recognize the 'full humanity' of the Indians, the indigenous people of Mexico remained marginalized in their own country from the mid-1500s to the present.

In fact, today, the divide between the rich European elites in that country and the poor *indígenas* is blatantly evident. The many years of being treated like second-class citizens in their own environment finally got to the indigenous people of Chiapas. To the surprise of those of European heritage living there, a radical movement—the Ejército Zapatista de Liberación Nacional (EZLN)—emerged in the 1980s and early 1990s and took root among the indigenous people of the Tzeltal, Tzotzil, and Chil communities in Chiapas. Widespread militia training and effective democratic control of local communities evolved over the course of the late eighties and early nineties. Just as the rest of the world was turning away from leftist revolutionary tactics with the fall of the Berlin Wall, the demise of other leftist political movements in Latin America, and the growing global embrace of the capitalist imperative, the indigenous people of Chiapas were seeking to develop a new grassroots model of socialist revolution. They were, after all, the poorest of the poor, severely malnourished and without the basics of health care and community hygiene, living in the midst of what is the breadbasket of Mexico. As they perceived it, their homeland was being exploited for capitalist profit beyond their region and outside their country. The Zapatista rebels took their name from Emiliano Zapata, a revolutionary who fought at the beginning of the twentieth century for the land rights of Mexico's extremely poor *campesinos* and was summarily executed in 1919.[24] It was evident that 'Government repression, electoral fraud and failure to deal with a pressing land question created the conditions for rebellion.'[25]

The night before they launched the uprising, the Zapatistas broadcast their manifesto—the Declaración de la Selva Lacandona (or Declaration from the Lacandón Jungle)—on a local radio station in Ocosingo, to the east of San Cristóbal and close to their jungle hideout. The Declaration began with the words: ¡Hoy decimos basta! (Enough is enough!) It went on to list major events in the 500 years of struggle for the indigenous people of Chiapas, including the fight against slavery, the insurgent War of Independence against the Spanish colonial power (1810–21), the expulsion of French colonists from Mexican soil in 1755, the promulgation of the local constitution in 1917, and the Zapata revolution. That long struggle did not bring social equity to the indigenous people of Chiapas. As the Declaration noted:

> We have been denied the most elemental education so that others can use us as cannon fodder and pillage the wealth of our country. They don't care that we have nothing, absolutely nothing, not even a roof over our heads, no land, no work, no health care, no food, and no education. Nor are we able freely and democratically to elect our political representatives, nor is there independence from foreigners, nor is there peace or justice for ourselves and our children.[26]

The Zapatista uprising occurred on the same day that the North American Free Trade Agreement (NAFTA) was signed. This was hardly a coincidence. The guerrilla leader of the EZLN, Subcomandante Marcos, understood the importance of NAFTA to the President of Mexico, Carlos Salinas de Gortari. When President Salinas ignored the demands of the EZLN, it would appear that Marcos and the Zapatistas planned the uprising to begin on the same day that the NAFTA treaty was scheduled to be signed by Mexico. The EZLN, after all, has labelled NAFTA as 'a death sentence' against Mexican Indians.

In any event, the uprising had its desired effect—it provoked the government to act, but that action was deadly—a 12-day war against the rebels in the Chiapas Highlands in which many were killed. But what the Mexican government did not realize was the extent to which the Zapatistas had generated sympathy for

© Reuters/Corbis

Subcomandante Marcos, leader of the Zapatistas.

their cause both inside and outside Mexico. 'Their supporters had access to electronic mail, and their mysterious and mediagenic spokesman, Subcomandante Marcos, issued volley after volley of trenchant communiqués.'[27] The radical **egalitarianism** expressed by the EZLN was deeply appealing to many in Mexico, and transnational groups opposed to neo-liberal globalization saw in the Chiapas struggle another example of globalization's negative impacts and an attempt to bring about social justice. 'What was most remarkable—and most interesting to the theme of globalization and contestation—was the speed at which this solidarity movement spread and consolidated its activities.'[28] One can attribute this to the fact that the Zapatista leader was able to use the computer and the Internet to generate international solidarity for this movement.

The Mexican government therefore found it difficult to suppress the Zapatista uprising, even though it increased its military presence in the area. The Mexican army, seemingly ill-prepared to fight this insurgency, resorted to torture, beatings, and illegal arrests of locals suspected of being sympathetic to the Zapatistas. Suspected guerrillas were detained without due process and, in many cases, tortured or killed.[29] But transnational non-governmental organizations and solidarity networks began to monitor the human rights abuses committed by the Mexican state against the Zapatistas following the Mexican army's invasion of EZLN territory.[30] One of those cases of human rights violations occurred in the small village of Acteal in Chiapas, where 45 people of the Tzotzil pacifist community who were attending a prayer meeting of Roman Catholic indigenous people, including children and pregnant women, were slaughtered in December 1997 by members of a paramilitary group linked to the Mexican army and funded by the Mexican state.[31] As a result of pressure from both Mexican and transnational solidarity groups, the Mexican government, nine years after the Acteal massacre, decided to appoint a special prosecutor to investigate this horrendous crime. Thirty civilians (mostly Mayans who supported the ruling PRI Party in Mexico), 15 civil servants, and 11 state policemen were subsequently sentenced for their roles in this massacre.[32]

Thomas Olesen, in discussing the impact of modern electronic communications on the Zapatista social movement, has noted that 'the interest and attraction generated by the EZLN beyond its national borders is matched by no other movement in the post-Cold War period.'[33] As Ronaldo Munck argues, the impact of this first informational guerrilla movement (to use a term popularized by Castells)[34] 'in creating and providing a beacon of hope' for the transnational anti-globalization movement 'has been considerable'.[35]

Some observers, however, are quick to make a distinction between the 'virtual Chiapas' and the 'real Chiapas'. Judith Hellman, for instance, in critiquing the transnational solidarity network that coalesced around the Zapatista movement, writes: 'Virtual Chiapas holds a seductive attraction for disenchanted and discouraged people on the left that is fundamentally different than the appeal of the struggles underway in the real Chiapas.'[36]

Hellman and other critics are understandably concerned about the romanticized image of the indigenous Chiapas people that gets relayed on the Internet. The situation on the ground may be much more complex than that being portrayed in virtual forums. In fact, these critics suggest that the transnational solidarity of armchair activism could in fact do damage to the real grassroots activism of the various indigenous groups in Mexico.

On the other hand, other observers argue that the struggle by the Zapatistas for dignity and social justice is a universal one, and this explains why so many civil society groups across the world identified with and wanted to support that struggle. Indeed, several activists from various parts of the globe have visited Chiapas to get a first-hand glimpse of the situation facing the indigenous people there. Such visits help them become more informed citizens, and from that point of view 'the Zapatista revolt has an overwhelmingly positive resonance around the world, teaching and energizing a whole generation of young activists that another world is, indeed, possible.' According to Munck, the Zapatista movement 'touched certain chords' and 'served to create common ground for various diverse struggles against globalization.' Zapatistas basically said '*Ya Basta!* (enough) to neoliberal globalization and its failure to create a modernization process characterized by social inclusion and basic human dignity.'[37] In this sense, that local counter-movement has much in common with other transnational counter-globalization movements.

Movimento dos Trabalhadores Rurais Sem Terra

In Brazil, a social revolt against state authoritarianism gave birth to Movimento dos Trabalhadores Rurais Sem Terra (MST). The landless workers in this movement were supported by a radical element in the Roman Catholic Church and had been struggling for years for the right to work the land they were developing in southern Brazil. Bear in mind that Brazil was under military dictatorship from 1964 to 1985.

When he took over as President in 1979, João Figueiredo had promised that he would move quickly to make Brazil a democracy. But during the transition from military to democratic rule, Figueiredo faced significant socio-economic problems. Inflation was soaring, productivity had declined, and Brazil was faced with a mounting foreign debt. In addition, Brazilian capitalism proved unable to alleviate the existing contradictions that blocked economic and social progress, especially in the rural areas of the country. Poor farm workers were expelled from rural areas as agriculture became increasingly mechanized and there was a corresponding mass exodus to the cities by former salaried farm workers, renters, and sharecroppers. Foreign Roman Catholic priests involved in the land reform struggle were expelled from the country. Union leaders (including the future three-time presidential candidate and current President of Brazil, Luís 'Lula' Inácio da Silva) were arrested for violating national security laws. In addition, the downturn in the world economy at the end of the 1970s further contributed to Brazil's weakening economic state.

Partly in response to the economic and social hardship exacerbated by the IMF's imposition on Brazil of a severe austerity program, the landless peasant movement coalesced into the Workers' Party—Partido dos Trabalhadores—and began to challenge the government, making significant electoral gains during the 1980s, especially in Porto Alegre. By 1985, realizing that it would have to appeal to the entire Brazilian population in order to be successful in its struggle, the MST officially organized itself at the national level at the first-ever National Congress of the Landless. It didn't take long for much of the wider Brazilian society to throw their support behind the MST's actions and to pledge solidarity to the landless who occupied large farms (or *fazendas*) and pushed for land redistribution and agrarian reform. The actions of the movement were also instrumental in highlighting the need for the promised democratic national system to replace the authoritarianism of the military. Furthermore, the MST soon realized that its struggle was not just against state elites but also against the neo-liberal economic model that had penetrated the state. This explains why members of the movement began to occupy the headquarters of public and multinational entities and to carry out marches, hunger strikes, and other political actions.

Today, the MST is active in 23 of Brazil's 27 states and involves more than 1.5 million people. As a result of this struggle, approximately 350,000 families have been settled on their own land, and another 80,000 families live in encampments awaiting the government's recognition of their right to own those lands. Again, as a result of this movement, a large number of associations and co-operatives are engaged in commercialization and services, and the processing of fruit, vegetables, dairy products, grains, coffee, meat, and sweets. These MST economic enterprises generate a great deal of employment as well as revenue for farmers, and this has provided an indirect benefit to roughly 700 small towns in Brazil's interior. The MST also has managed to team up with international bodies such as UNESCO to ensure better-quality education for children and for university students. In addition, the MST has developed a literacy program for approximately 19,000 teenagers and adults in the settlements and offers training to students in the management of settlements and co-operatives, so that they have the skills needed for development work in settlements.

With support from the Brazilian Minister of the Environment, the MST developed an environmental education program for leaders, teachers, and technical experts in the settlements. The MST also collaborated with the Cuban government to ensure that some of the MST members would be able to study medicine at the Latin American School of Medicine in Cuba.

But the MST has not forgotten its roots as a resistance movement. In 2002, it participated with labour, environmental, and religious groups in the fight to stop the Free Trade Area of the Americas when the economic ministers of all the countries in this hemisphere (with the exception of Cuba) met in Quito, Ecuador, to advance the negotiations on this US-backed free trade arrangement. The influence of the MST on this particular issue was tremendous, as more than 10 million Brazilians voted in an unofficial referendum to reject the FTAA. Today, the MST continues its fight for agrarian reform, for a free, sovereign, and egalitarian Brazil, and for a continent free from the FTAA. At the same time, it has joined forces with movements from the global North in an effort to counter the ill effects of globalization.

The Porto Alegre World Social Forum

During the 1990s, the **World Economic Forum** (WEF) became, for all intents and purposes, the leading think-tank for leaders of the major industrial states. It was therefore considered one of the main proponents of the globalization process. The end of that decade witnessed an attempt to develop an umbrella counter-movement in Davos, Switzerland, where the WEF has its annual meetings.

This umbrella counter-movement became known as the **World Social Forum** (WSF). This North–South initiative, spearheaded in January 1999 by a French NGO, ATTAC, and the Brazilian landless people's movement, MST, led to the birth of a movement to create a 'parallel summit' to the World Economic Forum—a top-down and hegemonic governance forum for the global elite.

The World Social Forum had its origins in a relatively innocuous article published in *Le Monde Diplomatique* in France. The English title of that article was 'Disarming the Markets'. The article called for action to control the tyranny of the financial markets. In response to that article, an organization called ATTAC was formed in 1998. ATTAC (or the Association for the Taxation of Financial Transactions to Aid Citizens) has, as its mission, the goal of offering alternatives to the profit-driven global financial markets. Indeed, one of its first proposals was to tax financial transactions to create a development fund. Another early proposal was to develop measures for curbing stock market speculation.

At an international meeting in December 1998, ATTAC issued a platform statement that explicitly blamed financial globalization for increasing economic insecurity and social inequities across the globe. The statement noted that globalization tends to bypass and undermine the popular decision-making of democratic institutions, as well as of sovereign states that are supposed to be responsible for protecting the general interests of their citizens. It accused financial globalization of substituting states' democratic institutions with 'a purely speculative logic that expresses nothing more than the interests of multinational corporations and financial markets.'[38]

The signatories of this statement promised to work with the international ATTAC network to create new instruments of governance/control and pursue the following goals:

1. to hamper international speculation;
2. to tax income on capital;
3. to penalize tax havens;
4. to prevent the generalization of pension funds;
5. to promote transparency in investments in developing/dependent countries;
6. to establish a legal framework for banking and financial operations in order not to penalize further consumers and citizens;
7. to support the demand for the general annulment of public debt of dependent countries and use the freed-up resources in behalf of populations and for sustainable development—i.e., paying off the social and ecological debt;
8. to reclaim the sphere of finance lost by democratic governments;
9. to oppose any new abandonment of national sovereignty on the pretext of the 'rights' of investors and merchants;
10. to create a democratic space at the global level.

ATTAC now has semi-autonomous branches in Africa (Burkina-Faso, Côte D'Ivoire, Sénégal, and Togo); in the Americas (Argentina, Chile, Colombia, Costa Rica, Ecuador, Peru, Quebec, Uruguay, and Venezuela); in Asia–Oceania (Australia and Japan); in Europe (Andorra, Austria, Belgium, Denmark, Finland, France, Germany, Greece, Hungary, Ireland, Italy, Jersey, Luxembourg, the Netherlands, Norway, Poland, Portugal, Romania, Spain, Sweden, and Switzerland), and in the Middle East and North Africa (Lebanon, Morocco, and Tunisia).

When the first World Social Forum was being planned, Porto Alegre was chosen by representatives of ATTAC as an ideal site for this meeting, which would bring together coalitions and networks from both the global South and the global North that had been involved in countering globalization.[39] Leaders in the MST met with Bernard Cassen (of *Le Monde Diplomatique*) to organize this umbrella counter-summit. Both the MST and ATTAC agreed that the WSF was in essence a global response to the growing international movement towards neo-liberal globalization and to the negative effects of neo-liberal economic policies on most less developed countries. They realized that while international financial and trade institutions such as the World Bank, the International Monetary Fund, and the World Trade Organization generally make prescriptions that are to be rigorously followed by developing countries, the effects of those policies on the lives of people in those countries are generally poorly understood: not only are the people in developing countries affected negatively by those policies, but the poor and excluded sectors of developed countries also can be hurt by them.

The World Social Forum was therefore conceived for civil society participants to explore how to develop alternatives to globalization. It was also envisioned as a place where proposals could be developed and a free exchange of experiences could be shared and articulated by those civil society organizations and movements opposed to neo-liberal globalization, neo-imperialism, and other forms of capitalist domination of the world. The WSF was conceived as a 'plural and diversified, non-confessional, non-governmental and non-partisan' forum (see Box 11.1).[40]

The first World Social Forum (WSF I) was held in Porto Alegre, Brazil, in January 2001 in explicit opposition to the World Economic Forum, an annual event since 1971 in Davos, Switzerland. The reason why the WSF was billed as a direct opponent of the WEF had to do with the fact that the latter plays a strategic role in formulating the thought of those who promote and defend the neo-liberal policies undergirding the globalization phenomenon. Approximately 20,000 people attended WSF I, representing some 117 countries, Youth Camp, and Indigenous Nation Camp. Eight organizations constituted the executive secretariat that organized the first of these forums: Brazilian Association of Non-Governmental Organizations (ABONG); Association for the Taxation of Financial Transactions for the Aid of Citizens (ATTAC); Brazilian Justice & Peace Commission (CBJP); Brazilian Business Association for Citizenship (CIVES); Central Trade Union Federation (CUT); Brazilian Institute for Social and Economic Studies (IBASE); Centre for Global Justice (CJG); and the Landless Rural Workers Movement (MST).

The event was such a huge success that some commentators even called it 'a revitalization of the left'. While this comment might have been a bit premature, the event did underscore the extent to which a large number of groups within

BOX 11.1

World Social Forum Charter of Principles

The committee of Brazilian organizations that conceived of and organized the first World Social Forum, held in Porto Alegre, January 25th to 30th, 2001, after evaluating the results of that Forum and the expectations it raised, consider it necessary and legitimate to draw up a Charter of Principles to guide the continued pursuit of that initiative. While the principles contained in this Charter—to be respected by all those who wish to take part in the process and to organize new editions of the World Social Forum—are a consolidation of the decisions that presided over the holding of the Porto Alegre Forum and ensured its success, they extend the reach of those decisions and define orientations that flow from their logic.

1. The World Social Forum is an open meeting place for reflective thinking, democratic debate of ideas, formulation of proposals, free exchange of experiences and interlinking for effective action, by groups and movements of civil society that are opposed to neo-liberalism and to domination of the world by capital and any form of imperialism, and are committed to building a planetary society directed towards fruitful relationships among Mankind and between it and the Earth.

2. The World Social Forum at Porto Alegre was an event localized in time and place. From now on, in the certainty proclaimed at Porto Alegre that 'Another World Is Possible', it becomes a permanent process of seeking and building alternatives, which cannot be reduced to the events supporting it.

3. The World Social Forum is a world process. All the meetings that are held as part of this process have an international dimension.

4. The alternatives proposed at the World Social Forum stand in opposition to a process of globalization commanded by the large multinational corporations and by the governments and international institutions at the service of those corporations' interests, with the complicity of national governments. They are designed to ensure that globalization in solidarity will prevail as a new stage in world history. This will respect universal human rights, and those of all citizens—men and women—of all nations and the environment and will rest on democratic international systems and institutions at the service of social justice, equality and the sovereignty of peoples.

5. The World Social Forum brings together and interlinks only organizations and movements of civil society from all the countries in the world, but intends neither to be a body representing world civil society.

6. The meetings of the World Social Forum do not deliberate on behalf of the World Social Forum as a body. No one, therefore, will be authorized, on behalf of any of the editions of the Forum, to express positions claiming to be those of all its participants. The participants in the Forum shall not be called on to take decisions as a body, whether by vote or acclamation, on declarations or proposals for action that would commit all, or the majority, of them and that propose to be taken as establishing positions of the Forum as a body. It thus does not constitute a locus of power to be disputed by the participants in its meetings, nor does it intend to constitute the only option for interrelation and action by the organizations and movements that participate in it.

7. Nonetheless, organizations or groups of organizations that participate in the Forum's meetings must be assured the right, during such meetings, to

deliberate on declarations or actions they may decide on, whether singly or in coordination with other participants. The World Social Forum undertakes to circulate such decisions widely by the means at its disposal, without directing, hierarchizing, censuring or restricting them, but as deliberations of the organizations or groups of organizations that made the decisions.

8. The World Social Forum is a plural, diversified, non-confessional, non-governmental and non-party context that, in a decentralized fashion, inter-relates organizations and movements engaged in concrete action at levels from the local to the international to build another world.

9. The World Social Forum will always be a forum open to pluralism and to the diversity of activities and ways of engaging of the organizations and movements that decide to participate in it, as well as the diversity of genders, ethnicities, cultures, generations and physical capacities, providing they abide by this Charter of Principles. Neither party representations nor military organizations shall participate in the Forum. Government leaders and members of legislatures who accept the commitments of this Charter may be invited to participate in a personal capacity.

10. The World Social Forum is opposed to all totalitarian and reductionist views of economy, development and history and to the use of violence as a means of social control by the State. It upholds respect for Human Rights, the practices of real democracy, participatory democracy, peaceful relations, in equality and solidarity, among people, ethnicities, genders and peoples, and condemns all forms of domination and all subjection of one person by another.

11. As a forum for debate the World Social Forum is a movement of ideas that prompts reflection, and the transparent circulation of the results of that reflection, on the mechanisms and instruments of domination by capital, on means and actions to resist and overcome that domination, and on the alternatives proposed to solve the problems of exclusion and social inequality that the process of capitalist globalization with its racist, sexist and environmentally destructive dimensions is creating internationally and within countries.

12. As a framework for the exchange of experiences, the World Social Forum encourages understanding and mutual recognition amongst its participant organizations and movements, and places special value on the exchange among them, particularly on all that society is building to centre economic activity and political action on meeting the needs of people and respecting nature, in the present and for future generations.

13. As a context for interrelations, the World Social Forum seeks to strengthen and create new national and international links among organizations and movements of society, that, in both public and private life, will increase the capacity for non-violent social resistance to the process of dehumanization the world is undergoing and to the violence used by the State, and reinforce the humanizing measures being taken by the action of these movements and organizations.

14. The World Social Forum is a process that encourages its participant organizations and movements to situate their actions, from the local level to the national level and seeking active participation in international contexts, as issues of planetary citizenship, and to introduce onto the global agenda the change-inducing practices that they are experimenting in building a new world in solidarity.

Source: <wsfindia.org/?q=node/3>. (28 July 2008)

civil society in the global North and the global South were willing to consider alternatives to globalization. In some respects, the WSF was an attempt to move beyond the mass protests, marches, and demonstrations of the anti-globalization movements of the past (dealt with in the previous chapter), and to move towards a new strategy of developing concrete proposals for alternatives to neo-liberal globalization. What united all those involved was a visceral and intellectual opposition to the neo-liberal hegemony of the type of globalization advanced by the participants in the World Economic Forum in Davos.

By allowing for the inclusion of all networks already involved in the struggle against neo-liberal globalization, the WSF promised to be an inclusive process. This inclusiveness, plus its democratic process of decision-making, ensured that the alternatives proposed to neo-liberal globalization would be 'bottom-up' as opposed to the 'top-down' approaches of the WEF. In fact, although political parties and military organizations are not allowed to be members of the WSF, government leaders and members of legislatures who accept the WSF's Charter of Principles may be invited to attend and participate in a personal capacity.

The success of the first WSF led to a number of other social forums. For example, the Genoa counter-summit to the G8 meeting in 2001 was unofficially dubbed a 'social forum', as was the 2001 Durban alternative meeting to the World Conference against Racism. In Latin America a number of meetings were called 'regional social forums'. The second official WSF, again held in Porto Alegre (January 2002), was attended by 15,000 registered delegates along with 55,000 people from 131 countries. The slogan chosen for WSF II was 'Another World Is Possible'. WSF III, also held in Brazil, attracted over 100,000 people, including several state leaders and parliamentarians.

After this forum, the International Council of the WSF, at a meeting in Porto Alegre in January 2003, decided that the next Forum in 2004 would be held outside of Latin America. That meeting, WSF IV, was held in Mumbai, India. 'Mumbai demonstrated the flexibility of the WSF's identity, which enables it to adapt to local social and political contexts without losing its energy.'[41] This meeting, attended by close to 1 million people, was a wake-up call for many participants from the global North who came face to face, some for the first time, with many of the issues they had been fighting for, such as the glaring gaps between rich and poor, and the presence of a large number of marginalized groups (ranging from the **Dalits** or untouchable caste to sex workers). Instead of focusing on a single issue, such as neo-liberal or capitalist globalization, WSF IV embraced a wide range of topics, including race, caste, religious fundamentalism, gender discrimination, and patriarchy. The sense is that the WSF has undertaken to pursue issues that affect people of particular regions—whatever those issues may be.[42]

WSF IV was followed, in January 2005, by the next 'edition' of the Forum in Porto Alegre, Brazil, attended by over 1.2 million delegates. Clearly, the WSF process has continued to grow over the years and has attracted increasingly larger participation from across the globe. However, there is some concern with 'gigantism' and the 'Woodstock' feel that these events are beginning to exhibit.[43] Table 11.1 outlines the growth of the social forum phenomenon, regionally and thematically, from 2002 to 2006.

In 2006, the International Council of the WSF decided to promote the decentralization of the WSF process by proposing 'polycentric WSF events' instead of one global event. These polycentric events were organized in Caracas, Venezuela,

---

Table 11.1 WSF Expansion since 2001: Thematic and Regional Forums

- Thematic Forum: Crisis of the neo-liberal model, Buenos Aires, Argentina (August 2002)
- European Social Forum: Florence, Italy (November 2002)
- Thematic Forum: Negotiated solutions for conflicts, Ramallah, Palestine (December 2002)
- Asian Social Forum: Hyderabad, India (January 2003)
- African Social Forum: Addis Ababa, Ethiopia (January 2003)
- Panamazonic Social Forum: Belém, Brazil (January 2003)
- Thematic Forum: Democracy, human rights, wars, and drug trafficking, Cartagena de Indias, Colombia (June 2003)
- European Social Forum: Paris, France (November 2003)
- Pan-Amazon Social Forum: Ciudad Guayana, Venezuela (February 2004)
- Social Forum of the Americas: Quito, Ecuador (July 2004)
- European Social Forum: London, UK (October 2004)
- Pan-Amazon Social Forum: Manaus, Brazil (January 2005)
- Mediterranean Social Forum: Barcelona, Spain (June 2005)
- European Social Forum: Athens, Greece (May 2006)

Source: wsfindia.org/?q=node/3, accessed on 28 July 2008.

and Bomako, Mali, in January 2006, and in Karachi, Pakistan, in March, 2006. The next 'edition' of the global WSF event was held in Nairobi, Kenya, 20–25 January 2007, and marked another next step in the advance of the global process of the WSF. In 2008, there was a return to the polycentric approach, with the WSF reflecting the shape being taken all over the world for resistance and movements for change. Rather than attempting to gather into one, worldwide mass celebration, it was broken up into what some have called 'unity in diversity'. Indeed, thanks in no small part to the Internet, small local anti-globalization movements are cropping up across the world and connecting through regional, national, and global alliances. At the present rate of growth in the movement, an aggregate increase is anticipated in common awareness of the problems facing humanity as a result of the imposition of the top-down capitalist version of globalization.

Conclusion

Dorval Brunelle reminds us that 'civil society is the quintessential home of politics and the constituent power underpinning the political structure.'[44] By 'political structure' he is referring particularly to the state. But as shown above and in the previous chapter, civil society has begun to organize beyond the national level and has become an important actor on the transnational and global stage.

Today we are witnessing an increase in the number of global social movements. These are non-state (sovereignty-free) actors who organize locally and across national boundaries to protest what many consider to be the negative impacts of globalization and the democratic deficit in governance. Some of these protestors are quite vocal and demonstrative. Others choose to agitate in a more circumspect manner.

Social movements, as forms of resistance, are complex in that they have a variety of goals that may not entirely coalesce. These goals can range from tinkering with the current global practices and institutions, reforming them, reflexively adapting them, transforming them, or rejecting them outright. Some of the counter-movements may express themselves through formal organizational structures (e.g., Greenpeace, Friends of the Earth, Amnesty International). These NGOs operate at national and international levels. Some have chosen a strategy of **benign resistance**, i.e., merely counterbalancing the neo-liberal institutions of global governance that perpetuate the globalization phenomenon in order to lessen dissent, disorder, and conflict. Indeed, many of these types of counter-groups are co-opted by states or state-based institutions (IGOs).[45] They may, for instance, be invited as 'experts' to present their grievances in a sanitized manner within an IGO, such as the United Nations Economic and Social Council (ECOSOC). As such, their particular grievance becomes incorporated into the extant global governance agenda and decisions to address the grievance become 'routinized'. These NGOs may be convinced that, by co-operating with the purveyors of globalization, they can give globalization a 'human face'. In the final analysis, though, this often simply means business as usual, and no structural change or shift in the locus of power has been accomplished.

Former US President Bill Clinton was adept at such co-option. In one of his overtures to the liberal globalization resistance movement, President Clinton said:

> We must do more to make sure that this new economy lifts living standards around the world and that spirited economic competition among nations never becomes a race to the bottom in environmental protections, consumer protections and labor standards. We should level up, not level down. Without such a strategy, we cannot build the necessary public support for the global economy. Working people will only assume the risks of a free international market if they have the confidence that this system will work for them.[46]

In fact, President Clinton appealed to the WTO to create a forum that would allow the dissent from labour, consumer, business, and environmental groups to be heard. In doing so, the WTO, of necessity, would become more open and public and would put a human face on globalization.[47] This is yet to happen.

Some counter-movements may express themselves through **ad hoc collectivities** (i.e., occasional mass rallies and protest movements that bring together various anti-globalization groups for a specific purpose). These groups can get their point across by being loud and confrontational. Other counter-movements find expression for their causes through cyberspace. This particular site of resistance attracts every type of counter-discourse as well as an instantaneous audience, and, more than any other site, facilitates the globalization of counter-movements, including terrorist movements, and their causes and encourages borderless solidarity. It also helps to interconnect the various issues and causes advocated by disparate social movements.

Other counter-movements express themselves through 'submerged networks' that have no clearly defined organizational structure. 'The presence of submerged networks gives new meaning to resistance.' Individuals engaged in this kind of counter-movement may not always be the loudest or they may not choose to mobilize in public protest.[48] They may simply engage in low-level acts that make their point of resistance, e.g., not buying tuna caught using methods that destroy dolphin populations; refusing to purchase consumer products made by companies engaged in environmental degradation; trading in an SUV for a smaller and more efficient vehicle; riding a bike to school instead of taking the family gas guzzler; deciding not to wear designer clothing with logos of companies that employ child labour; wearing a hijab or **chador**; eating at home instead of in a fast-food joint like McDonald's; or choosing not to watch the Olympic Games when they are being hosted by a country that abuses human rights.

Thus, some counter-globalization struggles grab headlines, while others tend to be more circumspect or 'under the radar'.[49] In any event, civil society movements of whatever type can help build defences 'against the predatory attacks of globalization'.[50] The situated struggles of resistance exhibited by social movements are located at local, national, regional, and global sites in reaction to 'economic globalization that slices across geopolitical borders'.[51] The multi-site and interconnected locales within which these counter-movements operate require multi-level governance if global disorder is to be forestalled. This is the subject of the next section of the book. First, however, we need to consider two significant aspects of global disorder: organized crime and terrorism.

Key Terms

ad hoc collectivities
benign resistance
chador
Dalits
egalitarianism

globalized capitalist relations
satyagraha
social relations of production
World Economic Forum
World Social Forum

Discussion Questions

1. How do local resistance movements become transnational?
2. In what way can the Ogoni movement be considered a struggle against internal colonization?
3. What are the similarities and differences between the Chipko Movement and the Green Belt Movement?
4. Why did the Zapatista revolt have such a positive resonance across the globe?
5. What was the link between the MST and the FTAA?
6. How does the World Social Forum counter the World Economic Forum and liberal globalization?

Suggested Readings

Munck, Ronaldo. *Globalization and Contestation: The New Great Counter-Movement.* London: Routledge, 2007. This book addresses the contestation of globalization by the anti- or counter-globalization movement, showing how globalization is 'contestable' in many different ways and how counter-movements are advocates for an alternative to globalization.

Okonta, Ike, Oronto Douglas, and George Monibiot. *Where Vultures Feast: Shell, Human Rights and Oil.* London: Verso, 2003. Okonta, Douglas, and Monibiot present a devastating case against the world's largest oil company, Shell, whose irresponsible practices have degraded agricultural land and left the Ogoni people destitute. But the book also shows how a courageous people in the Niger Delta are determined to resist this multinational corporation and corruption in their central government.

Taylor, Bron Raymond, ed. *Ecological Resistance Movements: The Global Emergence of Radical and Popular Environmentalism.* Albany: State University of New York Press, 1995. This book brings together a team of international scholars to examine the proliferation of ecological resistance movements around the world. Some of these movements are explicitly radical in their ideas and militant in their tactics, while others have emerged from a variety of social movements that have taken up ecological sustainability as a central objective.

Global Links

Movement for the Survival of the Ogoni People (MOSOP)
www.mosop.org/
   The official site of the Ogoni movement.
The Green Belt Movement
www.greenbeltmovement.org
   The official site of the Green Belt Movement.
Movimento dos Trabalhadores Rurais Sem Terra
www.mstbrazil.org/
   The official site of Brazil's landless workers' movement.
Zapatista Index
flag.blackened.net/revolt/zapatista.html
   A collection of English-language material on the Zapatista rebellion.
World Social Forum
www.wsfindia.org/
   A sample of the World Social Forum and its activities, this from the 2006 meeting in India.

Debate 11

Be it resolved that the World Economic Forum is an anachronism and needs to be replaced.

Chapter Twelve

Transnational Organized Crime

Just as a globalized economy provided new opportunities for business, it also provided new opportunities for criminal enterprises.[1]

Introduction

Crime has existed alongside legal commerce for centuries and is an integral component of human societies. Today, the business of crime is soaring because globalization has facilitated the intensification and expansion of crime. Globalization has made crime increasingly 'transnational' and, in the process, it has facilitated the rise of complex global criminal networks—'criminals without borders'. The most successful transnational criminal networks are those that have learned how to take advantage of the globalization phenomenon. These networks understand that globalization has diminished the significance of time and geographic distance, has made state borders more porous, and has provided a globalized financial system that can enable criminal networks to flourish alongside legal global activity, thus blurring the line between licit and illicit. As one author puts it, 'It is in the international finance system that underworlds and upperworlds unite and merge.'[2] When you hear the term 'organized crime', the first thing that might spring to mind is *The Sopranos* or the Italian Mafia, or even the Hell's Angels. Such depictions and organizations are the visible tip of a much deeper and broader iceberg of global crime.

Like the licit civil society movements discussed in the previous two chapters, transnational organized criminal groups can also operate within and across state boundaries. Phil Williams and Gregory Baudin-O'Hayon point out that since the 1980s we have been witnessing a 'criminalization syndrome' that has infected large portions of the globe. By this they are referring to the noticeable increase in drug trafficking, trafficking in women and children, money laundering, illicit/underground markets, corruption, piracy, extortion, and other forms of organized crime.[3] While these criminal activities are most evident in failed and failing states, and in transitional states and developing countries, they can be found in more developed states as well. Also, while it is important to draw a distinction between licit and illicit organizations, it is equally important to recognize that legitimate groups sometimes can be caught up in illegal activity, that some criminal groups may actually claim that their actions are somehow legitimate, and that illicit organizations may use their criminal proceeds to set up legitimate businesses or agencies.

Clearly, one reason for a surge in organized crime is that some states are losing their capability to regulate and govern activity within their boundaries. Criminals have learned how to take advantage of the 'functional holes' in government. As we have learned in earlier chapters, globalization has played a role in creating these 'spaces' in which both licit and illicit non-state actors operate.

There is definitely a relationship between the exponential acceleration of globalization over the past few decades and the proliferation of transnational organized crime. The growth of global crime is intricately intertwined with advances in technology, especially with the revolutionary changes in computer and communications technologies. This growth in cross-border crime also is linked to improvements in transportation and to the pervasiveness of finance vehicles. In the world of finance, it is extremely difficult these days to separate criminal activities from legitimate global transactions. In fact, just as globalization has helped local businesses to be launched onto the global stage and access global markets, so, too, globalization has facilitated the expansion of local organized crime into transnational and global venues.[4]

Some national boundaries have become so porous that criminal gangs and organizations find it easy to penetrate those countries. The more sophisticated **transnational organized crime groups** are able to take advantage of porous national boundaries in order to operate within different states, but then use the Westphalian norm of sovereignty to protect themselves against global counter-crime governance bodies by locating head operations or financial practices in states that afford them the protection of sovereignty. States that are failing or collapsing are more susceptible to being overrun by organized criminals than more established states, but as we know, well-functioning states also can be penetrated by organized crime. No state, acting on its own, can hope to combat transnational organized crime successfully. In fact, states can become havens for transnational organized criminal groups, both wittingly and unwittingly.

Some observers have argued that the forces of cultural globalization contribute to the rise in transnational crime.[5] Cultural globalization can erode traditional value systems and influence people to experiment with non-traditional lifestyles, such as illegal drug use, which have a tendency to attract criminal gangs and organizations. The end of the Cold War also saw an increase in global crime. The disintegration of the Soviet Union contributed to the unleashing of criminal organizations that quickly used the vehicles of globalization to construct transnational criminal networks in the areas of drug trafficking, human trafficking, money laundering, illegal trade in small arms and light weapons, and sexual slavery.[6] Poverty and inequality are also linked to the spread of global crime.[7]

As we will see later, even transnational, regional, and global organizations designed to counter organized crime are usually fraught with deficiencies that make governing in this particular issue area difficult at best. In addition, some states regard certain criminal activity with more seriousness than others. For instance, some governments turn a blind eye to money laundering activity because it brings in incredible amounts of revenue for the national treasury. Also, some cultures tolerate certain criminal activity more so than other cultures. Thus, for example,

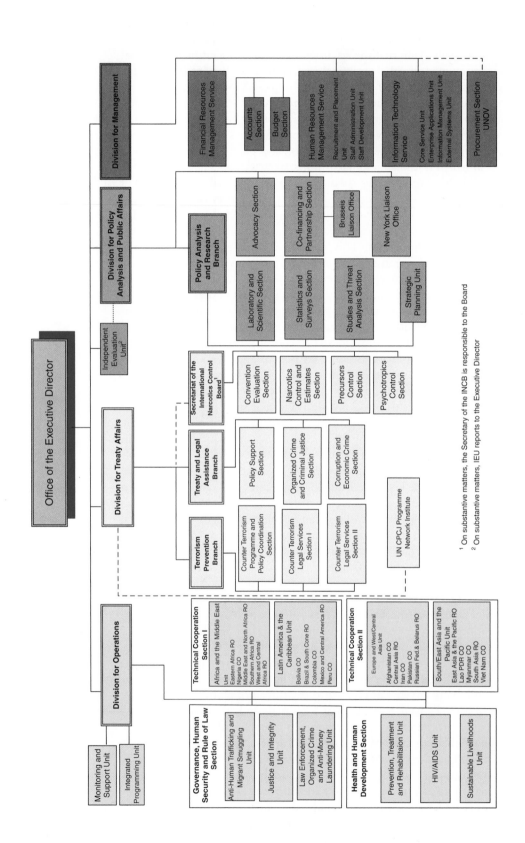

Figure 12.1 United Nations Office on Drugs and Crime (UNODC).

Source: <www.unodc.org/unodc/en/about-unodc/index.html/>

bribery seems to be an acceptable activity in certain cultures, but in other cultures it is frowned upon and dealt with harshly. As Richard Payne writes:

> The multiplicity of values, conflicting interests, inadequate resources, ineffective global cooperation, the cumbersomeness of national sovereignty, rapid economic and political change, ethnic conflicts, and the existence of weak states help fuel the growth of global crime and militate against efforts to reduce it.[8]

This chapter examines the growth of transnational organized crime and its links to globalization. The following global crimes are examined: drug trafficking, smuggling of migrants, sexual slavery and human trafficking, criminal gangs and kidnapping, money laundering, counterfeiting, illicit trade in small arms and light weapons, illicit trade in exotic animals and plants, illicit trade in human organs, **cybercrimes** and theft of intellectual property, piracy on the high seas, stolen art and antiques, and corruption. It is exceedingly difficult to arrest the growth in transnational crime because it is lucrative and because it is facilitated by the same vehicles that are used to expand capital, trade, finance, and production. Criminal financial flows are massive, and, as Payne notes, 'The social, economic, and political costs of global crime are incalculable.'[9]

Who Are Transnational Organized Criminals?

Many transnational organized criminals provide goods and services that are otherwise prohibited. This is why some international relations scholars refer to transnational organized crime as 'the continuation of business by criminal means'.[10] Frank Madsen defines transnational organized crime as 'an informal, loosely structured open system that is reactive to fluctuations in the economic, political, and legal environment', and argues that the symbiosis between transnational organized crime bodies and licit commercial enterprises may, at times, make it 'difficult to discern between the corrupter and the corrupted'.[11] Organized crime is certainly a major threat to the social and economic well-being of the world's population. What makes this problem difficult to solve is the fact that at times there can be a relationship between licit and illicit worlds or what is referred to by Madsen as between the 'upperworld' and the 'underworld'. Recently, we have seen how **white-collar crime** can overlap with corporate crime, organized crime, and state crime, the primary distinction among these being the agent primarily responsible for the crime: an individual, a corporation, organized groups, and finally the state itself. Criminal activities would include but not be limited to insider trading, antitrust violations, defamation, fraud, bribery, corruption, industrial espionage, environmental damage, labour exploitation, violation of health and safety laws, and failure to maintain fiduciary responsibility to shareholders/stockholders. Although the worldwide gross criminal product (GCP) can only be estimated, some observers set the value at between $600 billion and $1.5 trillion, or about 2 to 5 per cent of the world's gross national product. Estimates of the annual take for illegal narcotics range from $300 billion to $500 billion; smuggling of arms, other goods, people, and counterfeiting is valued at between $150 billion and $470 billion; and proceeds from computer crimes alone are valued at $100 billion.[12] Some scholars believe that these figures underestimate the amount of profit in transnational crime, while others claim that such numbers are an overestimation of criminal activity and profit. But there is no question that the GCP is large.

Counterfeiters and Intellectual Piracy

Both counterfeiting and piracy are intellectual property infringements. Counterfeiting is the crime of wilful trademark infringement, while piracy is related to general copyright infringement. Examples of counterfeiting include the production by criminal groups of replica designer jeans, fake Rolex watches, and imitator Adidas running shoes. An example of piracy would be the unauthorized downloading of music from a site on the Internet to your iPod. These two sets of criminal activity are of concern to governments because: (1) they can have a very negative impact on innovation; (2) they can pose serious threats to the welfare of consumers; and (3) they channel substantial resources to criminal networks, organized crime, and terrorist groups that disrupt and corrupt society. These activities are of particular concern to business because of their impact on sales and licensing, brand value and firm reputation, and the ability of firms to benefit from breakthroughs make in developing new products. They are of concern to consumers because they can pose a significant health and safety risk, particularly when the produced products are substandard counterfeit and pirated products.

Counterfeiting has been a major source of income for organized criminals and for terrorist organizations. The WTO has begun a formal investigation into claims that China is providing safe haven for counterfeiters.[13] Also, China is considered the world's biggest source of piracy. But China is not alone as a source of fake and pirated goods. Globalization has made it relatively easy for counterfeiters and pirates to operate in almost any corner of the globe.

Counterfeiters produce almost every type of product available. Some counterfeit items are generally quite substandard and may pose major risks to the public. Examples include automobile brake pads made with sawdust, Chinese-made toothpaste or toys containing high levels of lead, and deadly fake prescription drugs. As Anthony Mangione of the Immigration and Customs Enforcement Agency in the US warns: 'This isn't a victimless crime. The trafficking of counterfeit goods costs US citizens jobs, costs tax revenue and affects the reputations of companies big and small.'[14] Such criminal activity also can cost lives. In December 2006, for example, a 58-year-old Vancouver Island woman died because she took counterfeit pills bought from a bogus on-line pharmacy.[15] The EU has expressed concern that the major increase in counterfeit items coming into Europe is a 'threat to public health and the region's economies'.[16] Organized crime is behind much of the multi-billion dollar counterfeiting industry. In a 2007 OECD report on *The Economic Impact of Counterfeiting*, the value of the global trade in counterfeit goods was estimated at around US$450 billion annually,[17] or approximately 5–7 per cent of the value of global trade. Put differently, the value of trade in counterfeit and pirated items is greater than the GDP of 150 economies.[18] The OECD report also noted that organized crime (particularly in Asia) is heavily involved in this activity.

Illicit Drug Trafficking

The production, trafficking, and use of illicit drugs are a major problem today. As Payne explains, 'No society has managed to escape the consequences of the global drug trade, largely because the global drug problem is so closely intertwined with other areas of globalization.'[19] Indeed, many of the things we associate with globalization—communication, travel, tourism, migration, transportation, financial transactions, and trade—help to 'facilitate the globalization of illegal drugs.'[20] But it should be borne in mind that **drug trafficking** is not a recent phenomenon, just as globalization is not new. Europeans trafficked in Asian opium production during the days of European expansion and colonization. During the eighteenth century, the British East India Company paid Asian farmers to grow opium and then sold the product to wholesalers. The British government forced the Chinese to import opium from India, even though opium was prohibited in China by imperial decree. The illicit traffic in opium was made possible through the connivance of profit-seeking merchants and a corrupt bureaucracy. By 1839, the Qing government decided to adopt drastic laws prohibiting the opium trade. A commissioner, Lin Zexu (1785–1850), was sent by the Emperor to Guangzhou to suppress illicit opium traffic. Lin seized illegal stocks of opium owned by Chinese merchants and then proceeded to detain the entire foreign community and to confiscate and destroy 20,000 chests of illicit British opium. The British retaliation resulted in the first Anglo-Chinese war—the Opium War (1839–42). The Chinese were defeated in this war and that defeat tarnished its image as an imperial power. Subsequently, Britain used its hegemonic power and military might to force China to import opium and to legalize this drug (in 1858). '[T]he Portuguese, French, Spanish, and Dutch also participated in the trade, creating opium addicts in their colonies as well as in Europe.'[21] The Spanish got enslaved Indians and blacks to consume coca leaves so that they would be able to endure the hard labour their masters imposed on them. Towards the end of the nineteenth century there was an increase in the demand for opium in Europe and America.

The most recent phase of globalization has led in many cases to the deregulation, privatization, and outsourcing of governmental functions, which has had the effect of weakening the capacity of some governments to police their borders adequately. Heroin was and is smuggled into Europe and North America from the so-called Golden Triangle countries (Burma/Myanmar, Thailand, and Laos) as well as from the Golden Crescent countries (Afghanistan, Pakistan, and Iran). Cocaine is illegally brought into North America from Mexico, Jamaica, Colombia, and Thailand. To accommodate and profit from this illicit trade, global trafficking networks have developed to produce, distribute, and sell illegal drugs, and global commerce and migration have helped to facilitate the illegal drug trade. For instance, Mexican drug traffickers have taken advantage of the large number of Mexican immigrants living in the US and freer North American trade to turn certain US states (e.g., Georgia, North Carolina, and Tennessee) into major depots for illegal drug distribution. Mexican producers of the illicit drugs have shifted production sites closer to the consumers of those drugs in places like the Central Valley of California, and Mexican traffickers have moved across the Northwest and Midwest of the US, hiding among migrant fruit pickers in Washington, resort workers in Colorado, and construction workers in Minnesota.[22] The estimated value of the global illicit drug market in 2003 was US$13 billion at the production level, US$94 billion at wholesale level, and US$322 billion at the retail level.[23]

As mentioned earlier, weak and failing states are a magnet for transnational criminals. The same holds true for criminal gangs involved in the illicit drug trade. Powerful drug cartels, for instance, often exercise significant control within weak and failing states, largely because weak governments are often entangled with corruption and are unable to control many parts of their countries.

Agents of Corruption

Corruption is pervasive throughout the world. One can find corrupt officials in developed as well as underdeveloped states. Basically, corruption serves to undermine democratic institutions and can retard economic development as well as destabilize governments and their institutions. In fact, corruption attacks the very foundation of democratic institutions. We have seen this occur in Zimbabwe, where President Mugabe and his corrupt party—the ZANU PF—managed to distort the electoral process to remain in power, even after being defeated electorally by the opposition party leader, Morgan Tsvangirai. Corruption also can pervert the rule of law and create bureaucratic quagmires whose only reason for existence is the soliciting of bribes. We are constantly reminded in the media that bribery is a way of life in some Third World countries, especially on the African continent. But even in developed countries, like the US, bribery is present. The *Washington Post* reported in July 2006 an increase in the level of bribery cases among US customs agents patrolling the border between the US and Mexico.[24] Several border guards allegedly had taken bribes from Mexicans to allow illegal immigrants into the US. In fact, in early July 2006, two border patrol supervisory agents pleaded guilty to accepting close to US$200,000 in payoffs to release smugglers and illegal immigrants who were detained. This corruption basically undermines the US government efforts to beef up security at its borders and cut down on the level of illegal immigrants getting into the country. A corrupt US border guard can basically make the equivalent of his/her monthly salary in a couple of nights.

Economic development is also stunted by corruption, in some cases because it can discourage direct investment that comes from outside of the country. Due to corruption, small businesses within the country can often find it next to impossible to overcome the start-up costs required to establish a business, since those costs will include the payment of bribes to officials in various government licensing and regulatory agencies of a bloated bureaucracy.[25]

Money Laundering

The process that involves moving money from illegitimate sources to the legitimate economy is called money laundering. **Money laundering** is a significant transnational crime. According to Louise Shelley, the Director of the Center for Transnational Crime and Corruption at American University in Washington, this crime occurs when an individual or organization knowingly disguises 'the source, origin or ownership of illegal funds'. As she points out, many criminal transactions are generally carried out using cash. The money launderer then converts that 'dirty' cash, in small sums, into a larger, more liquid sum that is difficult to trace and easier to invest.[26] This is the laundering process.

The transnational scale of money laundering has been facilitated by the globalization of the world economy and the internationalization of organized crime. Money earned through criminal activity in one part of the globe can easily be transferred to another part of the globe in a way that prevents it from being traced or eventually recovered by law enforcement officials. The new technologies that facilitate globalization are the same technologies that make it easy for tainted funds, obtained in one part of the globe, to be collected, consolidated, and transferred to another part of the globe. With the rapid improvements in transportation technology, money, goods, and people are moving increasingly and in large numbers across national borders. Both licit and illicit funds are taken daily by all means of transportation into and out of countries in every region of the world. Increasingly, a number of professionals—accountants, bankers, lawyers, and real estate agents—make their services available to individuals involved in the criminal activity of money laundering. These corrupted professionals look the other way because of the usually huge amounts of money provided by their clientele. While not privy to the original criminal activity, many of these professionals are in fact complicit in perpetuating criminal and corrupt acts through their services.[27]

Money launderers benefit especially from the expanded global financial markets. They exploit the differential regulatory regimes and are able to move money quite easily across jurisdictions because the detection and regulatory ability is uneven across many countries. In other words, transnational criminals, such as drug traffickers, traffickers in women and children, individuals involved in sex slavery, and terrorists, know how to take advantage of the discrepancies that currently exist between countries' customs agencies and regulatory systems. These criminals particularly seek out countries with weak regulations related to money laundering, or those that have offshore banks known for their culture of corporate secrecy. The culture of secrecy is the cornerstone of most offshore banking centres, and this culture can abet criminal activity like money laundering.

While offshore banking centres are legal and can facilitate global distribution of finance from the developed world to the underdeveloped world, they can also be used to hide large-scale financial assets that are often illegal and that are diverted from companies controlled by organized crime groups. Thus, offshore banks can contribute to the underground economy by turning a blind eye to shady business practices that bring extraordinarily large sums of money into their coffers. But even major legitimate banks such as Citibank, the Bank of New York, Union Bank of Switzerland (UBS), and their offshore branches have been involved in money-laundering schemes.[28]

BOX 12.1

Offshore Bank Accounts

An offshore bank account is an account at a bank located outside the country of residence of the banking client. These bank accounts are known for having low tax liabilities and are therefore often referred to as **tax havens**. Offshore bank accounts can provide financial and legal benefits, such as (1) lax legal regulation of deposits; (2) little to no taxation; (3) greater secrecy; (4) easy access to funds; (5) higher interest rates; and (6) protection against local financial or political instability.

The most popular and widely known offshore banking centres in the global market are found in the Cayman Islands and Switzerland. But other well-known offshore banking centres are found in Andorra, the Bahamas, Barbados, Belize, Bermuda, the British Virgin Islands, Cyprus, Dominica, Gibraltar, Ghana, Hong Kong, Labuan, Malaysia, Liechtenstein, Luxembourg, Malta, Macau, Mauritius, Monaco, Montserrat, Nauru, Panama, Seychelles, St Vincent, and the Turks and Caicos Islands.

Furthermore, some money-laundering schemes are associated with high-level government corruption. Many of these cases of laundered money attained through government corruption have occurred in the post-Cold War period, but the practice certainly precedes the end of the Cold War. Numerous deposed leaders of Caribbean, Latin American, African, and Asia–Pacific countries, with the millions and billions of dollars they laundered while in power, have enjoyed opulent lifestyles in foreign countries once they have left or been thrown out of office. Some corrupt leaders launder money siphoned out of their national treasury or diverted from foreign assistance. Others launder funds obtained through payoffs from foreign investors or through contractors working on development loans from multilateral organizations. Yet others launder funds gleaned from the proceeds of privatization.

Privatization, particularly since the 1990s, has been a by-product of globalization. It has contributed to the wave of funds being deposited into unregulated offshore accounts. After the disintegration of the Soviet Union, several of the former Soviet states were in a hurry to plug into the global capitalist economy. To speed up the process, these states engaged in wholesale privatization of what had been state-owned enterprises. During the transitional period from governmental ownership to private ownership, when there is limited transparency, many of the insiders have managed to appropriate significant resources of privatizing firms and, through elaborate trust agreements consistent with the laws of the locale, have parked valuable national resources in financial tax havens.[29]

The money laundered through privatization has resulted in high-profile investigations, such as the Raúl Salinas case in Mexico and the Pavlo Lazarenko case in Ukraine. In the Salinas case, money obtained through bribes from drug traffickers was commingled with money obtained through bribes from individuals who benefited from the Mexican government's privatization of key state-owned industries. Raul Salinas de Gortari, the older brother of Mexico's president at the time, Carlos Salinas, used Citibank's private banking services to transfer his ill-gotten funds to secure offshore financial institutions.[30] The Swiss government and court determined that much of Raul Salinas's over $100 million placed in Swiss accounts was protection money paid out by the drug cartels. Salinas invented fictitious persons and used Citibank, whose high-ranking executives helped to engineer some of his financial operations, to set up paper companies with Swiss bank accounts. He was able to deposit large sums of money into accounts in Banque Pictet, Citibank Zurich, Julius Baer Bank, and Banque Edmond de Rothschild.[31]

In the case of Pavlo Lazarenko, privatization of the oil and gas industries allowed the former prime minister of Ukraine to accumulate and launder at least US$114 million through Swiss and American banks. According to the 53-count indictment filed by US prosecutors, Lazarenko used his political clout to establish an international underground network of bank accounts to launder profits made through clandestine schemes (bribery, fraud, and graft) involving natural gas, agribusiness, housing, and other businesses in Ukraine. His criminal activity finally led to his indictment for money laundering in Swiss and American courts.[32] The large sums of money involved in this case reminded observers of similar cases in the 1980s and early 1990s of graft and corruption by President Ferdinand Marcos of the Philippines (who was removed from power in a 'people's revolution') and by President Mobutu Sese Seko of the Democratic Republic of the Congo (who died in exile in Morocco in 1997). Both of these leaders also had access to large portions of their national treasuries and siphoned off an incredible portion through money-laundering schemes.

In the investigations following the end of the General Sani Abacha government in Nigeria in 1998, US$650 million was traced to Switzerland and US$120 million was traced to Liechtenstein.[33] Such large sums illustrate the absence of preventive legislation. Furthermore, many countries in the global South have no laws to facilitate the confiscation of the proceeds of corruption and, thus, have allowed massive transfers of assets to countries in the North.[34] Prosecutors in South Korea who followed the embezzlement of their past president tracked over US$700 million and were able to recover several hundred million of the laundered money. A major question is whether mechanisms will be created to deter such deposits and whether procedures will be established to make such sums more easily recoverable by the source country.[35]

As the corruption issue is no longer taboo for employees of multinational financial institutions, the significant money laundering associated with project and structural adjustment loans has become a permissible topic of discussion. The former international banking practice of turning a blind eye—of 'see no evil, hear no evil, speak no evil'—is no longer quite as acceptable as it was, as the banking culture is slowly being forced to change after so many headline-grabbing accounts of corruption in high places. For example, researchers at the IMF now acknowledge that they could observe the financial flows out of Haiti immediately after international loan funds flowed into the country.[36] An investigator examining the diversion of a World Bank loan to Pakistan traced $30 million to a Swiss bank.[37] Increasingly, the investigators of corruption in these international financial institutions must be trained to find money laundering because both bribe money and actual project loans wind up in the banking centres of Western countries.

Economists at the IMF suggested in 1996 that 2 per cent of global GDP was related to drug crime and that the laundered money associated with corruption and tax evasion represented an even larger percentage.[38] Other experts have said that offshore banks may hold up to 26 per cent of the world's wealth. According to a *World Wealth Report* produced in 2000 by Merrill Lynch and Gemini Consulting, as much as US$6 trillion may be held in offshore banking centres.[39] It is well known that laundered money invested in dollarized accounts and other strong currencies tends to escape significant losses through currency devaluations in origin countries. In offshore regimes where financial capital is untaxed, the growth in laundered funds is much faster than that of money from taxed and regulated regimes. And banks are not the only institutions engaged in money laundering.[40] This criminal activity also occurs through other financial institutions, currency exchange and wire transfer businesses, stock brokerage houses, real estate agencies, gold dealers, luxury hotels, and casinos, as well as insurance and trading companies.[41]

Human Trafficking

How would you answer the question: when did slavery end? If you are American with some knowledge of history, your answer would probably be 1808—the year that the US outlawed the slave trade. However, if you are an African American you would probably contest the previous answer because of your knowledge that, in fact, it was still legal to own slaves in the US right up until the Civil War (1861–5). So your answer, in that case, might be 1863—when US President Abraham Lincoln issued the Emancipation Proclamation[42] to free slaves held within the 'rebellious states' (i.e., those states that had seceded from the

BOX 12.2

The End of Slavery

Throughout the eighteenth and early nineteenth centuries, African slaves were forced to work on plantations in the Caribbean and southern United States. By the nineteenth century, the international dimension of liberalism and its indeterminate universalism emerged as humanitarians pressed for international standard-setting on human rights. In this context, the Great Powers accepted an obligation to end the slave trade at the Congress of Vienna of 1815. The slave trade was finally abolished by the Brussels Convention of 1890. Slavery was formally outlawed by the 1926 Slavery Convention.

Although global laws outlaw slavery and related practices, these laws exist in a context that takes notions of sovereignty and non-intervention for granted. Notions of state sovereignty are only overridden with great reluctance. Although norms of international society condemn gross violations of human rights, they do not support intervention under less extreme circumstances. Therefore, abolishing the slave trade, which involves international transactions, has proven easier than abolishing slavery, which concerns how states treat their citizens. Slavery and slave trafficking still exists today in parts of the world, such as West Africa and Eastern Europe.

Source: John Baylis and Steve Smith, eds, *The Globalization of World Politics: An Introduction to International Relations* (Oxford: Oxford University Press, 1997), 474–5.

Union)—or 1865—the year that the Thirteenth Amendment to the US Constitution was ratified. If you are British with a good knowledge of history, your answer would probably be 1807—the year when the British Parliament heeded the demands of a growing number of abolitionists and made slavery illegal. But if you are from one of the former British colonies, your answer might be 1833—the year the British government finally decided to abolish slavery in its colonies.

The reality, however, is that slavery hasn't ended. Today, slavery still exists, although the modern name for it is **human trafficking**. Human trafficking 'has a devastating impact on individual victims, who often suffer physical and emotional abuse, rape, threats against self and family, and even death.'[43] But the impact of human trafficking goes beyond individual victims; it undermines the health, safety, and security of all nations it touches. In this sense, it can be considered a multi-dimensional threat in that it deprives individuals of their human rights and freedoms, increases global health risks, and fuels the growth of transnational organized crime.[44]

According to the 'Not for Sale' campaign—the campaign to end slavery in our time—27 million people are enslaved today.[45] Forms of slavery include, among others, forced child labour, debt bondage, sex slave exploitation, and chattel slavery. According to The Protection Project, a human rights research institute based in Washington, DC, an estimated two million women and children are treated as commodities and sold into sexual slavery each year. Contemporary slavery in many cases involves the transportation of victims, using false pretenses, from one country or state to another for forced labour or prostitution. Work is demanded and maintained through violence, threats, addictive substances, and other forms of coercion.[46] According to the US Central Intelligence Agency (CIA), approximately 800,000 people around the world are enslaved each year, including about 20,000 in the United States.[47] This global criminal activity is growing in large part because it reaps very high profits, state borders have become more porous because of globalization, and global labour migration is thus difficult to manage. Of course, human trafficking is facilitated by transnational criminal organizations, and low-cost labour in many fields is in increasing demand. For example, tens of thousands of boys from such countries as Pakistan, Bangladesh, and India, as young as four and five years old, have been kid-

Camel racing in Qatar.

© Reuters/Amr Dalsh

napped or sold by beggar parents into slavery, are 'employed' as camel jockeys in Middle Eastern countries. If they are not soon crippled or killed in the work, they remain as malnourished and enslaved jockeys for the camel races of sheiks in such places as the United Arab Emirates. Likewise, many women are trafficked and then used as low-paying domestic workers, or as dancers, strippers, and/or sex workers.[48]

Most of the women who are trafficked come from Southeast Asia (particularly Nepal, Thailand, and the Philippines), Africa (especially Ghana and Nigeria), Latin America (particularly from Colombia, Brazil, and the Dominican Republic), Eastern and Central Europe, and Central Asia, especially after the demise of the Soviet Union. This shows the extent to which this criminal activity has become truly global.

BOX 12.3

From Romania to the UK

Lila, a 19-year-old Romanian girl who had already endured physical and sexual abuse from her alcoholic father, was introduced by an 'acquaintance' to a man who offered her a job as a housekeeper/salesperson in the UK. When she arrived in the UK, the man sold her to a pimp and Lila was forced into prostitution. She was threatened that she would be sent home in pieces if she did not follow every order. After an attempted escape, her papers were confiscated and the beatings became more frequent and brutal. Months later, after being re-trafficked several times, Lila was freed in a police raid. She was eventually repatriated back to Romania where, after two months, she fled from a shelter where she had been staying. Her whereabouts are unknown.

Source: US State Department, *Trafficking in Persons Report*, 4 June 2008, at <www.state.gov/g/tip/rls/tiprpt/2008/105376.htm>. (2 August 2008)

© AFP/Getty Images

Young trafficking victims at a halfway house in Manila, Philippines. Human trafficking—the biggest money spinner for organized crime after drugs and firearms—has been steadily increasing in Canada and around the world.

The main destinations for many of these women include the Netherlands, Germany, Japan, the United Arab Emirates, Israel, Greece, South Korea, Turkey, Austria, Bosnia, Belgium, the United States, and Canada.

Half of the migrants in the world are being smuggled by organized crime. Human smuggling is the fastest-growing criminal activity in the world. 'Human trafficking is a low-risk, high-profit enterprise, and because it looks to the casual observer—and even to cops—like garden variety prostitution, it is tolerated. And worse, it is growing.'[49] Richard Poulin argues convincingly that the global sex industry now occupies a strategic and central place in the development of international capitalism, and for that reason the sex trade is increasingly looking more like an ordinary sector of the global economy. In his view, the industrialization of the sex trade has involved the mass production of sexual goods and services structured around a regional and international division of labour. These 'goods' are human beings who sell sexual services. Prostitution and related sexual industries—bars, dancing clubs, massage parlours, pornography producers, etc.—depend on a massive subterranean economy controlled by pimps connected to organized crime. At the same time, businesses such as international hotel chains, airline companies, and the tourist industry benefit greatly from the sex industry.[50]

The explosive growth in human trafficking is usually associated with the changes that have resulted from globalization. Richard Payne argues that many young women worldwide are seduced by romantic images of the West and as a result become victims of exploiters who promise them the possibility of living that lifestyle.[51] While this is true in some cases, it is definitely not the only motivating factor in human trafficking. In fact, this line of argument places blame on those who are already victimized. A more plausible explanation is that poverty and inequities associated with globalization are likely factors in influencing human trafficking. Another plausible explanation, more specific to Eastern and Central Europe, is that the rapid economic changes accompanying the fall of the Soviet Union and the transition from a centralized economy to a market-based economy actually served to undermine economic security for many women. 'The rapid privatization process, required for Russia to participate in the global economy, contributed to the elimination or reduction of employment opportunities, especially for women. Women became more vulnerable to trafficking as they attempted to find employment in other countries to support their families.'[52]

The revolution in communications and transportation also facilitates the proliferation of matchmaking services, many of which are owned and operated by organized crime.[53] Some women who subscribe to those services may actually end up in brothels. Another factor influencing the increase in human trafficking is the HIV/AIDS epidemic. Individuals in the market for sex may be of the opinion that young girls or boys are less likely to be infected with the HIV/AIDS virus. Therefore, human traffickers are being instructed to find younger and younger victims for those customers.

Criminal Gangs and Covert Groups

Criminal gangs have existed for a long time in many parts of the globe. However, globalization has intensified the activity of criminal gangs and expanded their territory. The same communications and technological revolutions that drive globalization also help to facilitate the growth of criminal gangs. In March 2006 the Communications Fraud Control Association estimated that annual global fraud losses in the telecommunications sector were now between $54 billion and $60 billion, an increase of 52 per cent from 2003. A common scam for fraudsters is to direct calls to their own premium rate services by tricking mobile users to call their premium rate number. The mobile operator ends up paying a commission to the premium rate service owner but is not able to recover the costs. Others involve false identities and are part of the wider trend of identity theft.[54]

The Mafiosos

Several recent studies have maintained that a number of criminal organizations, such as the Sicilian Mafia, the 'Ndrangheta, the Cali Mafia, the Hong Kong Triads, the Russian Mafia, and the Japanese Yakuza, are part of the same species, collectively referred to as 'mafias'.[55]

The Italian Mafia

The term 'Mafia' was used in Italy around 1865 for some powerful Sicilians, or Sicilian families, who were engaged in violent and criminal activity in that country and who, as a result, achieved considerable control of the local economy. In fact, the Mafioso played a critical role in mediating between peasants, landowners, and the state and between the Italian countryside and the outside world. Although the Italian Fascist government tried to dissolve the Mafia between 1925 and 1929 and to re-establish the government's control over violence in that country, those efforts failed when the Fascists later fell. The Mafia became even more firmly planted in Italian society, beginning in 1943 when the Allied occupation unwittingly drew on the Mafia bosses for assistance in governing the country. So, in a sense, the Italian Mafia grew out of certain social and political conditions that allowed it to fill a gap in governance.

While there are four types of Italian Mafia,[56] most people have heard of the Sicilian Mafia because it is the most powerful transnational criminal organization to have come out of Italy. This criminal organization is based in Palermo but now has operations in over 40 countries, including the US and Canada.[57] There are approximately 186 ruling families in the Sicilian Mafia, and its clan-based hierarchical structure, modelled largely on Catholic confraternities and Freemasonry, consists of a board of directors, crime bosses, and soldiers/workers.[58] Individuals who join this criminal organization adhere to a strict code of silence (*Omertà*) and are loyal for life; some would argue that the only way out of this criminal group is through 'death'. The Sicilian Mafia wields a tremendous amount of clout within political and economic circles in Italy but also in many parts of the globe. Its transnational operation generates much of its profits from heroin trafficking.

Since the 1930s, the Sicilian Mafia has operated in the US as La Cosa Nostra. This group, in conjunction with its Italian counterparts, pursues a multi-faceted criminal agenda involving drug trafficking, illegal gambling, arms trafficking, prostitution, extortion, and development of the porn industry.

The 'Ndrangheta

Apart from the Sicilian Mafia, one of the most active Italian-based criminal groups is the 'Ndrangheta (or Honoured Society).[59] This Calabrian-based organization may have already 'surpassed the Sicilian Mafia in the international drug trade'.[60] Formed in the 1860s by Sicilians who were banished from Sicily by the Italian government, the 'Ndrangheta settled in Calabria and operated as a network of small criminal groups. Initially, this group developed as a defence network for impoverished rural peasants against aristocratic landlords. Federico Varese has argued that certain features of the local economy, in particular an economy that is unprotected by the state, generate the demand for criminal protection and groups like 'Ndrangheta fill that gap.[61]

Today, the organization consists of 160 loosely connected clan cells with approximately 6,000 members. Its organizational structure, unlike the Sicilian Mafia's pyramidal and hierarchical structure, is loosely based on blood ties and intermarriage, with Godfathers giving direction to the units. Apart from cocaine and heroin trafficking, this network is heavily involved in gambling, fraud, theft, labour racketeering, loansharking, kidnapping, alien smuggling, prostitution, bombings, arms trafficking, murder, and political corruption. According to Italian anti-organized crime agencies, the 'Ndrangheta earns roughly US$30 billion annually, mostly from illegal drugs, but also from legal businesses such as construction, restaurants, and supermarkets.

Like its Sicilian counterpart, 'Ndrangheta is now transnational, with between 100 and 200 members and associates estimated to be active in locales such as New York and Florida, as well as network contacts in various countries, including Australia, Belgium, Canada, Colombia, France, Germany, Holland, and Turkey. In 2007, in the German town of Duisburg, six Italian men between the ages of 16 and 39 were found dead with bullet wounds to the head. Their slaying was linked directly to the execution style of the 'Ndrangheta.[62] It is also alleged that 'Ndrangheta is 'directly involved with paramilitary groups in Colombia and the ETA terror group in Spain.'[63]

The Cali Mafia

The Cali Mafia was founded in the 1970s by Gilberto Rodriguez-Orejuela and José Santacruz-Londoño. It grew from a small gang of criminals called Los Chemas into a loose association of five independent drug trafficking organizations.[64] Initially, the Cali Mafia confined its operations to counterfeiting and kidnapping. Gradually, however, it expanded its activities to include cocaine smuggling. From its bases in Peru and Bolivia, the Cali Mafia smuggled cocaine into Colombia and other Latin American countries. It now operates as a global network of cocaine production, transportation, wholesale distribution, and money-laundering operations.[65] It smuggles hundreds of tons of cocaine into the United States and launders billions of dollars of the proceeds.[66]

The Cali Mafia is known for its ability to bribe, intimidate, and corrupt political officials. This cartel of narco-traffickers likes to give the appearance of being a legitimate business, so it uses laundered money to set up licit companies worldwide. It also has worked closely with a number of Mexican criminal organizations that facilitate the transportation of drugs into North America. Those Mexican organizations include: the Tijuana organization, the Sonora cartel, the Juarez cartel, and the Gulf Group. Since June 1995, however, the Cali Mafia suffered a severe setback to its global operations when seven of its top leaders surrendered or were arrested. Some of its key operators also have been killed. This transnational criminal organization has nevertheless shown a facility in working between the upperworld and the underworld and across porous national borders.

The Russian Mafia (*Russkaya Mafiya*)

Organized crime has existed in Russia (former Soviet Union) for centuries. Under the Communist regime there was always space for corruption and the 'black market'. Criminals began to thrive especially during the Brezhnev era when the Soviet economy was stagnating. Crooks known as 'thieves in law' (*vory y zakone*) began to fill a gap in the economy, supplying on the black market luxury goods that the state could not provide—including jeans, cigarettes, vodka, chewing gum, and hi-fi equipment—to those who could afford them.[67] The biggest gangs operating in Russia are the Dolgopruadnanskaya and the Solntsevskaya.

During the 1970s and 1980s a wave of Russian émigrés fled to North America. Most of these émigrés were of Jewish descent. However, among them were many Russians with fake Israeli passports, and some of them were criminals. Most of the Russians settled in Brighton Beach in New York, which has the largest Russian population outside of Russia. Organized Russian crime was therefore able to plant its roots in the US and in Israel.

The disintegration of the Soviet Union in 1989 left an economic, moral, and social vacuum that organized crime has been only too happy to fill. Hundreds of ex-KGB men and veterans of the Afghan war, whose incomes were very minimal, in some cases offered their skills to the crime bosses in the Russian Mafia. The Russian Mafia filled a social welfare function left void by the state by providing money and jobs to young men in Moscow, St Petersburg, and Kiev who were struggling to cope following the collapse of the Communist safety net. The acceleration of globalization also facilitated the unleashing of Russian criminal elements into the world. Among other places, the Russian Mafia set up operations in the US, the UK, Israel, France, Spain, Switzerland, and states that were formerly within the Soviet Union. For instance, there are signs that the Russian Mafia has taken over the Israeli underworld and is using that country to launder vast amounts of drug profits as well as to invest in real estate, businesses, and banks.[68] Also, more than 150 business and political leaders and 90 Swiss firms are suspected of having ties to the Russian mob. Billions of dollars obtained through criminal means are laundered by the Russian Mafia in Swiss banks. It is estimated that approximately US$25 billion of dirty Russian money has left the country since the fall of communism—most of which has been laundered by banks in Switzerland, Liechtenstein, and

Cyprus.[69] Russia's former President, Boris Yeltsin, once referred to Russia as 'the biggest mafia state in the world' and as 'the superpower of crime'.[70]

Today the Russian Mafia is considered among the most powerful criminal networks in the world, primarily because of the multi-dimensionality of its criminal activities, which include: fraud, transnational money laundering, extortion, drug trafficking, weapon smuggling, auto theft, white slave trafficking/prostitution, hostage-taking, extortion of immigrant celebrities and sport figures, transportation of stolen property for export, insurance (staged auto accidents) and medical fraud (false medical claims), counterfeiting, credit card forgery, and murder. This transnational criminal organization collaborates with prostitution and gambling rings in Sri Lanka and with drug cartels in Colombia—even to the point of selling to the Colombians an old Soviet submarine for the purpose of smuggling drugs into the US. The Russian Mafia has expanded its operations, especially in the Caribbean, taking advantage of lax tax regulations and offshore incentives to buy property and establishing legitimate businesses to conceal their illicit financial transactions.[71]

Writing at the turn of this century, Robert Friedman reported that Russian gangsters operated in over 50 countries. They 'smuggle heroin from Southeast Asia, traffic in weapons all over the globe, and seem to have a special knack for large-scale extortion.' They also have 'plundered the fabulously rich gold and diamond mines in war-torn Sierra Leone, built dazzling casinos in Costa Rica with John Gotti Jr., and through . . . control of more than 80 per cent of Russia's banks, siphoned billions of dollars of Western government loans and aid.' Even the game of hockey, sacred to most Canadians, has been infiltrated by the Russian Mafia. Well-known Russian hockey players in the National Hockey League, such as Alexander Mogilny, Alexei Zhitnik, Vladimir Malakhov, Sergei Fedorov, and Oleg Tverdovsky, have been subject to extortion, threats, and even beaten by members of the Russian Mafia. Some Russian-born NHL hockey players, such as Pavel Bure, Valeri Kamensky, and Slava Fetisov, have been personally linked to the Russian mob.[72] In the US, the Russian Mafia has infiltrated the financial markets, laundered billions of dollars through American banks, and penetrated the real estate business. But, perhaps the biggest fear of the US government and its intelligence agencies is that the Russian Mafia will one day help terrorist organizations gain access to nuclear materials, fissile weapons, or other weapons of mass destruction (WMDs).[73]

The Albania Mafia

The Albania mafia began as a local criminal organization in the inaccessible regions of northern Albania but has now become transnational. This criminal organization can be traced to 15 families that formed the core group of Albanian criminals during the Communist dictatorship of Enver Hoxha (1945–85) and were heavily involved in the black market. When the Communists were toppled in the late 1980s, these 15 families increased their criminal control of Albania and, during the collapse of the Albanian state into anarchy, they made deals with the Kosovo Liberation Army (KLA) that kept them in control of such criminal activity as gun smuggling.

Back in the 1970s, Albanian immigrants to the US were actively recruited as couriers, transporters, or assassins for the Italian Mafia. Those recruits performed their assignments so efficiently and brutally that by the 1990s the main assassins for the Gambino crime family were Albanians. Fierce loyalty to family clans (*fis*), vendetta killings, and a code of silence are features that are similar in both the Albanian and Sicilian mafias.

Since 1991, this criminal organization has spread its tentacles into the European Union and North America. In fact, according to a CNN report, ethnic Albanian gangs (including immigrants from Kosovo, Macedonia, and Montenegro) are replacing the Italian La Cosa Nostra as the leading organized crime outfit in the US, especially since the success of US law enforcement agencies in cracking down on Italian Mafia outfits. These Albanian criminals are much less sophisticated than those in the Russian Mafia and much more violent and brutal in their approach to crime than either the Russian or the Italian Mafia.[74] Albanian criminals are known to work in tandem with Italian organized criminal groups in such areas as prostitution, trafficking in illegal drugs, small arms, humans, and human body parts, illegal immigration, counterfeiting, sex slavery, abductions, and murders.[75] The FBI is particularly concerned that militant Islamist elements in the Albanian mafia may have ties to terrorist organizations like Al-Qaeda.

The Yakuza

The Yakuza is the Japanese equivalent of the mafia. Like the other mafioso described above, the Yakuza began as a local crime group and became a transnational criminal organization with the acceleration of globalization. 'With a membership that has been put at from 88,000 to as high as 110,000, the Yakuza may be the world's oldest and largest criminal organization.'[76] Yamguchi-gumi constitutes the largest Yakuza group.

Members of this criminal organization are said to be descendants of the seventeenth-century *kabuki-mono* (crazy ones), a group of rather outlandish samurai who revelled in dressing outlandishly, in speaking in elaborate slang, and in carrying unusually long swords in their belts. In the Tokugawa era, a period of extended peace in Japan, the services of the *kabuki-mono* were no longer needed, and as a result they became essentially a band of thieves and community troublemakers. Yakuzas today like to think of themselves as modern-day Robin Hoods, but their actions are more reminiscent of the mafia groups discussed above. Yakuza members are well known for their elaborate, almost full-bodied tattoos. 'The application of these extensive tattoos is painful and can take hundreds of hours, but the process is considered a test of a man's mettle.'[77]

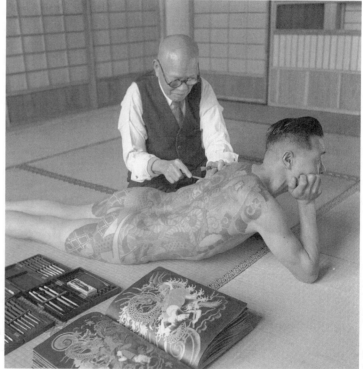

© Horace Bristol/Corbis

A Yakuza gang member in a tattoo parlour in Japan.

The Yakuza has a similar power structure to some Italian criminal organizations, such as La Cosa Nostra, with a patriarch at the top and loyal underlings of various ranks below him. If a Yakuza member disappoints his boss, the punishment is often *yubizume* (the amputation of the last joint of the little finger). A second offence may result in the severing of the second joint of that same little finger, and additional offences might require moving on to the next finger. 'A man knows that he must commit *yubizume* when his immediate superior gives him a knife and a string to staunch the bleeding. Words are not necessary. The origin of this practice dates back to the days of the samurai.' Removing part of the smallest finger weakens the hand's ability to hold the sword. So with a damaged hand, the swordsman became more dependent on his master for protection.[78]

Yakuza gangs can be found operating in South Korea, Australia, Costa Rica, Brazil, Hawaii, and some major cities on the American west coast. They are engaged in smuggling amphetamines and firearms, money laundering, and trafficking of women.[79]

Other Transnational Criminal Gangs

Some transnational criminal organizations operate more like traditional gangs than businesses. Examples include the Sonora, Medellin, and Bogata cartels, the Khun Sa gang, the Jamaican Yardies, the Chinese Triads, the Big Circle Boys, the Nigerian crime syndicates, Vietnamese gangs, outlaw motorcycle gangs, and pirates on the high seas.

The Cartels

A number of cartels, which have expanded as a result of globalization, are involved in transnational criminal activity. The Sonora Carmetel, which began in north-central Mexico and is headed by a trio of brothers (Miguel, Jorge, and Genaro Caro-Quintero),[80] specializes in the trafficking of marijuana, cocaine, and methamphetamine. This polydrug cartel has strong links to the Colombian criminal organizations, particularly the Cali Mafia.

The Medellin cartel is named after the Colombian city of Medellin. Founded by Juan David Ochoa and his brothers, along with Pablo Escobar, this cartel at its height had total revenues in excess of $60 million per month and was estimated to be worth as much as $28 billion. During the 1970s and 1980s it was considered the most powerful drug trafficking organization to have emerged out of Colombia. It had a well-connected and functioning smuggling, marketing, and money-laundering network operating from coast to coast in the United States.[81] In August 1989 the Medellin cartel murdered Colombia's leading presidential candidate, Luis Carlos Galán, and declared 'total and absolute war' against the Colombian government as a means of stopping the extradition of its members to face trial in the US.[82] It carried out several hundred assassinations across Colombia, including of high-profile politicians and police, in an attempt to intimidate anyone who stood up against the cartel. However, this criminal organization lost much of its consolidated power and influence after the death or capture of many of its leading figures, particularly that of Pablo Escobar, which led to its disappearance as a unified entity. Several of its surviving associates and former members continue to be involved in transnational drug trafficking.

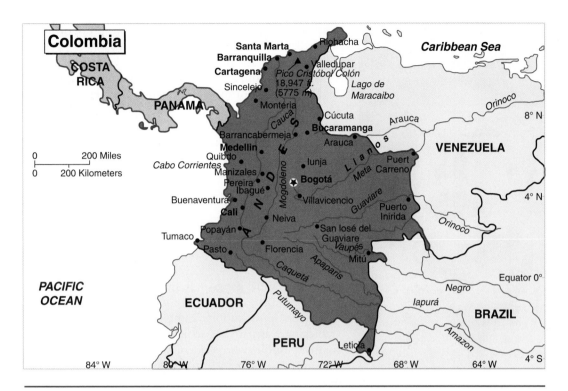

Figure 12.2 Colombia, the cocaine gateway to the world.
Colombia has long been a centre of cocaine trafficking and other criminal activity because of the ready availability of the coca shrub, the leaves of which are used to produce cocaine. Colombia's criminal culture, corrupt politics, and its strategic location as the entry point to Central and North America and to the Caribbean have been important factors in the continuing drug trade.
Source: <cocaine.org/colombia/index.html>

A less well-known but nonetheless very powerful drug trafficking organization is the Bogota cartel (also known as the North Coast cartel). This group engaged initially in contraband smuggling and later gained prominence by associating itself with American criminal organizations in 1980s that were involved in drug trafficking.[83]

The Khun Sa gang is named after Khun Sa, a Burmese warlord of Chinese and Chan background, who earned the nickname of 'Opium King' because of his control of opium trafficking in the Golden Triangle of Burma, Thailand, and Laos. Also known as Chan Shi Fu, Khun Sa was in fact a guerrilla leader in the separatist Shan movement in Burma who used his criminal activities to finance an army of tens of thousands of soldiers. His drug empire traded opium for guns and used those weapons to consolidate control over the rugged, remote, and impoverished Shan region. At the height of his power, in the 1980s, he controlled approximately 70 per cent of the country's heroin business, which enabled him to finance large-scale heroin laboratories. Much of the drugs that passed through his network were shipped to the US during the 1980s and 1990s.

In 1980 the Thai Prime Minister, Prem Tinsulanonda, ordered the air force to bomb his base but failed to dislodge him. In 1982 the Thai army, led by General

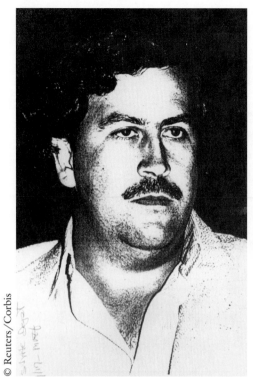

Pablo Escobar, founding member of the Medellin cartel.

Chavalit Yongchaiyut, who later became Prime Minister of Thailand, launched an assault on Khun Sa's compound, killing 130 of his men. Khun Sa retreated into Burma, where he continued to run his heroin business until he and his Shan United Army surrendered to Burmese authorities in 1996. His heroin trafficking group was disabled a year earlier.[84] Khun Sa finally died in 2007 at age 73.[85]

The Jamaican Yardies are criminal groups that originated in the Caribbean island of Jamaica.[86] Yardies tend to be single males, usually between 18 and 35 years old, who are unemployed, often by choice. They come to Britain usually as tourists or to visit their 'relatives'. Or, they may simply assume false identities and use forged credentials when they enter into the country. Most Yardies come to Britain with criminal convictions or are wanted by the Jamaican police.

These criminal gangs have infiltrated most of the major cities in Britain, and they are primarily engaged in drug trafficking, prostitution, gambling, and illegal weapons trafficking.[87] Britain has actually become the staging point for many Yardies who seek entry to the United States using fraudulently obtained British passports. They see the US as a more lucrative market for their illegal activities. However, US immigration authorities are making it difficult for Yardies to enter that country.[88]

Anyone who has seen the 'Rush Hour' movies would recall Jackie Chan and Chris Tucker doing battle with the Chinese Triads. The Chinese Triads originated as secret societies and a resistance movement during the rule of the Ching dynasty (from the early seventeenth century to 1911). Today, the Triads form perhaps the world's largest criminal outfit, with over 100,000 members.[89] The largest of the Triads is Sun Yee On, which is based in Hong Kong and whose membership is somewhere in the range of 47,000 to 60,000.[90] This Triad is extremely powerful, with what is akin to an armed force and its own stockpiles of ammunition.

There are about five or six main Triads and each of them has smaller satellite criminal groups. These groups are involved in various illegal activities, including drug trafficking, money laundering, corruption, computer software piracy, racketeering, credit card forgery and fraud, identity theft, counterfeiting, extortion, contract murder, and human smuggling. Many of the Triads' operations can be found in Hong Kong, Macau, Taiwan, and mainland China. But elements of the Triads also are visible in cities in developed countries throughout the world that have large Chinese populations. These cities are new centres of Triad activity. This shows the extent to which the Triads' criminal activity has become transnational in scope.

The Big Circle Boys (*Dai Huen*) is another transnational criminal syndicate with an original base in China. In fact, it has its origins in the Red Guards, the paramilitary troops of the Chinese Cultural Revolution who terrorized intellectuals and the upper class. After Mao Zedong's death in 1976, many Red Guards were sent to re-education prison camps around the city of Canton—represented on maps by a big circle, hence the name 'Big Circle Boys'. In these camps they

Khun Sa, Burmese warlord and drug kingpin, who died in 2007.

© EPA/Corbis

were tortured and starved. Having been through this degrading treatment and having military training, they developed a fearsome reputation. A number of them escaped to Hong Kong where they obtained falsified documents to enter Canada in the early 1980s. Most of them went to Vancouver and were able to blend into the large Chinese population there. But the members of the Big Circle Boys (BCB) are extremely mobile and now have created a transnational network that covers major cities in both Canada and the US. They are very difficult to detect because they work in small cells, where infiltration is practically impossible. The BCB indulge in several nefarious operations, including drug trafficking, loan-sharking, human smuggling, counterfeiting, credit card forgery and fraud, and the export of stolen vehicles.[91]

Nigerian crime syndicates operate as adaptable, transnational multi-crime organizations engaged in money laundering, car theft, human smuggling, and the trafficking of narcotics and small arms. However, these criminal groups are best known for their focus on Internet-based and letter-based financial frauds. The advance-fee frauds—known as '419 scams', after an article of Nigeria's criminal code—usually target elderly people in the West with the intent of stripping them of large amounts of money, and in some cases their life savings.[92] Members of these criminal organizations first dupe unsuspecting individuals residing in different countries into sending money or sharing their bank account information by promising that a much larger amount of money will follow once certain administrative formalities are completed.[93] The US Secret Service has estimated that Nigerian advance-fee scams cost Americans somewhere in the vicinity of $250 million a year.

Nigerian criminal enterprises are organized and active in about 60 countries across the globe. Their growth is attributed to the globalization of the world economy as well as to the lawlessness that prevails in Nigeria. The presence today of hundreds of convicted Nigerian traffickers in Indian, Pakistani, Thai, Turkish, and other international prisons is indicative of the international reach of the Nigerian crime rings, which 'launder money in Hong Kong, buy cocaine in the Andes, run prostitution and gambling rings in Spain and Italy, and corrupt legitimate business in Great Britain with their financial crimes.'[94] Nigerian drug-trafficking rings are especially notorious and they continue to evolve. Where once they limited their membership to those from ethnic-based clans, they have come to recognize that international law enforcement targets Nigerian nationals. Consequently, they use surrogate couriers, especially young women, to carry out trafficking activity.

Apart from the Nigerian criminal groups, Vietnamese gangs are believed to be 'the fastest growing ethnic criminal groups in America today and could become a major force in the lucrative business of international drug trafficking.'[95] These gangs have a reputation for extreme violence and for engaging in 'illegal activities ranging from property crime, drug trafficking, and cigarette smuggling to high-technology theft, financial fraud, and other white-collar crime. Vietnamese gangs have established [a] presence in Asia, Eastern Europe, Australia, and North America.'[96]

A number of outlaw motorcycle gangs are involved in nefarious criminal activities. Their undertakings include:

- murder for hire
- prostitution
- the operation of massage parlours
- international white slavery
- kidnapping
- burglary
- gun running
- insurance frauds
- loansharking
- motorcycle and automobile theft
- gambling
- truck hijacking
- arson
- forgery of government documents
- extortion
- the fencing of stolen goods
- theft from military bases
- assault
- rape
- the by-now ubiquitous narcotics trafficking.

The Big Four among these motorcycle clubs are the Pagans, the Hell's Angels, the Outlaws MC, and the Bandidos. The Pagans were founded in Maryland in 1959 by Lou Dobkins. By 1968, this outlaw motorcycle gang had more or less dominated the entire US east coast. This group has done major battles with the Hell's Angels over territory and drugs. The Hell's Angels motorcycle club is without doubt the largest and most notorious of the outlaw motorcycle clubs. Formed in 1948 and headquartered in Oakland, California, it truly has a transnational reach,[97] with about 180 chapters around the world—including Canada, a country with more Hell's Angels per capita than any other country in the world. The Canadian headquarters of the Hell's Angels is located in the small town of Lennoxville, Quebec, near Sherbrooke in the Eastern Townships.[98] The Outlaws motorcycle club has been around even longer than the Hell's Angels and is the main rival of that organization. Formed in 1935 in Illinois, this transnational criminal gang now has about 200 chapters in the US, Canada, Australia, New Zealand, Russia, Japan, and Europe, and has a simple motto that says: GFOD—'God Forgives, Outlaws Don't'. The Bandidos motorcycle club was founded in Texas in 1966 by John Chambers (a former US marine who served in Vietnam), and has grown into a major transnational criminal gang with 195 chapters in about 14 countries. Some consider this criminal group to be an outcrop of the Outlaws. Regardless, it is now the fastest-growing outlaw motorcycle club.

A band of Somali pirates.

© Badri Media/EPA/Corbis

Finally, pirates of the high seas have become a significant factor in international crime. 'There are few more enduring romantic myths than those related to pirates and piracy—those handsome bearded swash-buckling renegades, a seafaring equivalent to Robin Hood or William Tell. Such fanciful myths at best overlook and at worst serve to obscure the fact that piracy is not a historic curiosity, rather it is a contemporary and increasingly criminal activity, involving the violent loss of human life.'[99] We normally think of these pirates as remnants of the sixteenth to eighteenth centuries, but with the increase in ocean travel as globalization has intensified we are beginning to see a return of piracy on the high seas.

It is estimated that the losses resulting from piracy—in cargo, ships, and rising insurance costs—amount to $16 billion a year.[100] Not only are incidents of piracy on the rise, but pirate attacks have become increasing violent and the new privateer organizations are linked to sophisticated crime syndicates that use the latest advances in communication technologies and benefit from the illicit trade in small arms. The advantage that merchant vessels once had as a result of their modern size and speed is now offset by technological advances that have significantly improved pirate ships' speed and firepower.

Piracy has now become a serious threat to international commerce, especially in the Southeast Asian archipelago where it has been a nagging problem for many years. Commercial ships in this area are particularly vulnerable to piracy due to the narrow waterways and countless small islands that define the region's geography. The situation is even worse in the Malacca Strait and Singapore Strait because this has become a busy and significant sea lane. The Malacca Strait gave particular cause for concern because it is one of the busiest waterways in the world, connecting the Pacific Ocean and Indian Ocean with the narrowest point of only 1.3 km wide; 200 ships a day on average pass through and 50 per cent of these ships are oil tankers. The Strait, in some stretches, is shallow and narrow and requires precise navigation.

The strategy used by the pirates was to board a steaming ship at night, undetected, and make their way to the ship's bridge. Once there, they would overpower the officer of the navigational watch and either tie him up or handcuff him to the rail while the rest of the gang made for the master's and crew cabins to demand money and valuables. Apart from the danger to the crew of the ship under attack, there is always the horrifying hazard posed by ships carrying dangerous cargoes, steaming at full speed, unattended, in confined waters.

There was a sharp increase in maritime piracy during the late 1990s following the massive unemployment and political instability caused by the Asian economic crisis. Nearly two-thirds of the attacks in 1999 occurred in Asia, with 113 of the 285 reported cases taking place in Indonesia's waters and ports.[101] The risk of attack is increasing, with 90 per cent of the world's goods trade moving via ship and 45 per cent of all shipping moving through the pirate-infested waters of Asia. According to the International Maritime Organization (IMO), in 2004 there were 173 reported cases of pirate attacks in the South China Sea and the Malacca Strait, making up more than half of all pirate incidences around the world. In 2006, there were 61 actual pirate attacks in the waters of Southeast Asia and 22 attempted attacks.[102]

Between 1982 and 1986, West Africa—particularly Nigeria—had the highest reported number of cases of piracy and armed robbery. About 25 cases were reported annually, mainly against ships at anchor awaiting berth. In 2001, 58 incidents of piracy and armed robbery occurred in West Africa. In 2006, there were 41 actual pirate attacks in that region. Many kidnappings and attacks were against foreign oil workers. It appears that the local politics are having a direct impact on the shipping of the area. There has been a marked increase recently in pirate attacks and hijackings off the southern part of Somalia, particularly off Mogadishu.[103] The attacks mainly target vessels with cargo for Somali ports.

Conclusion

Some analysts have proclaimed that no area of international affairs has remained untouched by organized crime. This is because criminal groups have taken advantage of the vehicles of globalization to become transnational in their activities. 'The globalization of organized crime has occurred in tandem with the globalization of the world economy.'[104] Political and economic systems and the social fabric of many countries are deteriorating under the increasing financial power of international organized crime groups. Concomitantly, organized crime finds a place of birth and relatively safe haven in weakened and failed states, such as Somalia, Afghanistan, and Russia and its satellites following the demise of the Soviet Union. There is clearly a need for global governance institutions to respond to the global reach of criminal organizations; otherwise, 'the twenty first century will belong to transnational criminals.'[105] Before we consider, in the final section, the institutions for bringing some order to a disorderly world, we need to examine terrorism, a form of transnational organized crime perpetrated primarily for a cause rather than for financial profit and raw power.

Key Terms

cybercrimes
drug trafficking
human trafficking
money laundering

tax havens
transnational organized crime
   groups
white-collar crime

Discussion Questions

1. How has the globalized financial system allowed criminal networks to flourish?
2. How would you describe and explain 'the criminalization syndrome'?
3. Why did the end of the Cold War contribute to the expansion of global crime?
4. In what ways does transnational organized crime pose a major threat to the social and economic well-being of people across the globe?
5. Explain the symbiosis that exists between the licit and illicit worlds?
6. How is economic and social development stunted by corruption?
7. How has globalization facilitated transnational money laundering?
8. What is the link between human trafficking and sexual slavery, and what accounts for this transnational crime in Central Asia?
9. How did the disintegration of the USSR result in this former superpower becoming 'the superpower of crime'?
10. In your opinion, why has there been a spike in piracy off the coast of Somalia?

Suggested Readings

Bales, Kevin, and Ron Soodalter. *The Slave Next Door: Human Trafficking and Slavery in America Today.* Berkeley: University of California Press, 2009. This is a revealing primer about the re-emergence of practices of human bondage, and is essential reading for those who want to understand and do something about the human rights abuses associated with the transnational crime of human trafficking.

Fichtelberg, Aaron. *Crime without Borders: An Introduction to International Criminal Justice.* Upper Saddle River, NJ: Prentice-Hall, 2007. *Crime without Borders* discusses the nuts and bolts of international crime and international law enforcement as well as the theoretical issues that will help students to think about the best ways to address the transnational problems associated with global crime.

Kindt, Michael T., Jerrold M. Post, and Barry R. Schneider, eds. *The World's Most Threatening Terrorist Networks and Criminal Gangs.* Houndmills, UK: Macmillan/Palgrave, 2009. This important new edited volume examines a diverse group of sub-state and trans-state actors such as Al-Qaeda and its jihadist fellow travellers, as well as Hezbollah and its terrorist state sponsor, Iran. There are also chapters on Hamas, Jemaah Islamiyah, the FARC, the Mexican drug cartels, and the criminal gang, Mara Salvatrucha 13.

Global Links

Terrorism, Transnational Crime and Corruption Center at George Mason University
policy-traccc.gmu.edu/
> A site with a variety of information, research reports, and links on a wide range of transnational criminal practices.

UN Office on Drugs and Crime
www.unodc.org/
> An excellent site on how the international community, through the UN, is trying to fight the trafficking of illicit drugs and the pervasiveness of international crime, including human trafficking, migrant smuggling, money laundering, piracy, corruption, organized crime, and terrorism.

Transparency International
www.transparency.org/
> Transparency International is a global civil society organization that leads the fight against corruption around the world.

Debate 12

Be it resolved that no areas of international affairs have been left untouched by transnational crime.

Chapter Thirteen

Terrorism: Understanding the Causes of Radicalism and Extremism

This form of radicalism exploits Islam to serve a violent, political vision: the establishment, by terrorism and subversion and insurgency, of a totalitarian empire that denies all political and religious freedom. These extremists distort the idea of jihad into a call for terrorist murder against Christians and Jews and Hindus—and also against Muslims from other traditions, who they regard as heretics.

—George W. Bush[1]

Introduction

Many people can recall precisely where they were and what they were doing on the morning of 11 September 2001 when the US sustained its worst terrorist attack. This event was an eye-opener for many in North America who had become accustomed to thinking that the terrorist threat was 'over there'—in the Middle East, in Asia, in Africa, even sometimes in parts of Europe—but certainly not 'here'. With 9/11, academics who had studied **terrorism** and other acts of **extremism** were suddenly plunged into the spotlight. Policy-makers, particularly those in the United States, were desperate to understand the causes of radicalism and extremism. Why would individuals gravitate towards an ideology of hate that would cause them to want to kill innocent people in large numbers and in such a spectacular fashion?

Unfortunately, many of those policy-makers jumped the gun and pursued 'coalition of the willing' counter-terror measures without reflecting critically on those questions or without seeking out well-researched answers to them. The end result has been the fiasco in Iraq, a military and societal quagmire in dusty Afghanistan, and a **War against Terror** that appears unwinnable.

The nineteenth-century Russian novelist Fyodor Dostoevsky once said: 'While nothing is easier than to denounce the evildoer, nothing is more difficult than to understand him.'[2] US government decision-makers were quick to denounce Osama bin Laden and his Al-Qaeda network of extremists, once they realized that there was a connection between the 9/11 attacks and this band of modern-day 'outlaws'. President George W. Bush, as quoted above, expressed that sentiment in a clear and unequivocal manner.

Policy-makers, like those around the US President, tend to act with some sort of 'concept' or 'theory' in mind—even though it sometimes may be unsophisticated and not all that well thought out or articulated. The concept of a **'clash of civilizations'**,[3] for instance, was an implicit theoretical element in the Bush foreign policy and its counter-terrorist strategy.[4] But even ordinary citizens depend on conceptual and theoretical frameworks to help make sense of the world. We use such frameworks to order and systematize the multiple facts and news items that bombard us every day as we watch television, read the newspaper, or examine scholarly journals and books. Without concepts and theories to guide our thinking process, we would become overwhelmed by the abundance and proliferation of facts and data arising from the very complex world in which we live.[5]

This is particularly true today in regard to the plethora of facts and maelstrom of information concerning the causes of radicalism and extremism. We want to understand why individuals employ acts of terror as a means of drawing attention to their causes. We may even ask ourselves: Aren't there less destructive ways that these causes can be presented and possibly resolved? Are the counter-measures being used to combat acts of extremism designed to address the underlying reasons why people choose to embrace radical and extreme positions, ideologies, and actions?

For students living in Canada (a country well known for its tolerance, diversity, multiculturalism, and social cohesion), similar questions must have been raised in June 2006. During that month, the Royal Canadian Mounted Police (RCMP),

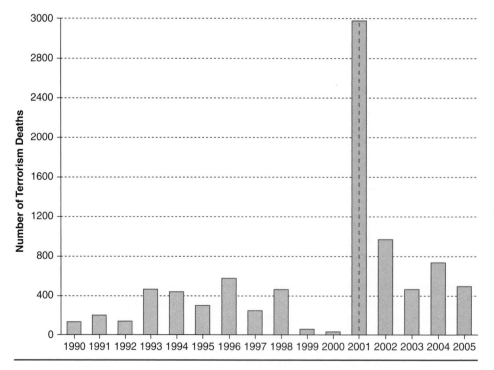

Figure 13.1 Deaths from international terrorism, 1990–2005.

with the assistance of the Canadian Security Intelligence Service (CSIS),[6] foiled an alleged attack by **homegrown terrorists** in Toronto by arresting 18 suspects who appeared to be inspired by the violent ideology of Al-Qaeda. According to official reports, these individuals had obtained three tons of ammonium nitrate—three times the amount of the explosive ingredient used in the Oklahoma City bombing of 1995 that killed 168 people and injured over 800.[7] Five of these suspects were under the age of 18 and the others were between the ages of 19 and 43. They were all Canadian citizens or landed immigrants.

If the accusations against these individuals are true then what would have caused these young Muslim men to want to behead the Prime Minister of Canada, to blow up the Canadian Parliament buildings, or to kill innocent people by targeting the CN tower, one of the world's tallest free-standing structures? It has been suggested that they had bought into the extremist ideology of Osama bin Laden. And we know that the infamous international terrorist named Canada as one of five 'Christian' nations that should be targets of terror and that the other countries—the US, Britain, Spain, and Australia—all have been targeted by terrorists. But was there a direct relationship between bin Laden's wishes and the actions of the Toronto 18? Again, as students of global politics, these are some of the questions that bedevil us. We want explanations that would make sense of what appears to be senseless.

Conceptualizing Radicalism and Extremism

Radical and extreme ideologies and behaviour have complex historical, political, social, and economic roots and therefore evade any simplistic type of cause–effect analysis. It is thus important for students of IR to reflect critically on the diversity of perspectives and the complex multi-dimensional variables that can inform our understanding of the wellsprings from which both extremism and radicalism flow.

Defining these terms is not as simple or straightforward a task as may seem at first. **Radicalism** is conceived by some as '[t]he active pursuit of and support for far-reaching changes in society which may constitute a danger to the democratic legal order through the threat or use of violence or other undemocratic means'.[8] One can read into this definition that radicals may or may not opt to use violence as a means of bringing about the 'far-reaching' societal changes they desire. Clearly, not all radicals are necessarily violent. A recent government report that analyzed violent **jihad** in the Netherlands after the shocking murder of Theo van Gogh (Box 13.1) admits that 'Only a limited number of radicalised individuals make the leap from radicalism to extremism.'[9]

Indeed, some people who hold radical ideas may decide to pursue those ideas through peaceful methods. For instance, Mahatma Gandhi, for all intents and purposes, was a radical in that he espoused revolutionary changes to the way in which Indian society was governed. He envisioned the transformation of Indian society along the path of *satyagraha*.[10] Yet, he chose to pursue a non-violent strategy to guide India's struggle for independence from Britain and to agitate for major societal changes in that country. His non-violent approach did not make him any less radical. As Vinay Lal put it, Gandhi may have been orthodox in his pronouncements, but 'refreshingly radical and experimental in his practices'.[11]

The word 'radical' is linked to 'extreme' when individuals or groups hold positions that are uncompromising and make a conscious decision to use violence to effect political and societal change. Thus, today's spate of terrorists can be

BOX 13.1

The Murder of Theo van Gogh

Theo van Gogh, 47, was the great-grandson of art dealer Theo van Gogh and the great-grandnephew of the famous Dutch painter Vincent van Gogh. He was a prominent, well-respected film director, author, journalist, actor, and producer. But he was also very outspoken and knew how to use the media to convey his controversial views—some of which dealt with ideologies and religion.

Theo van Gogh.

Theo van Gogh was not afraid to be provocative and offensive, but these characteristics ensured that he would not only be constantly in the national spotlight in the Netherlands but also be very unpopular among certain groups in his country. Van Gogh was highly critical of all religions, including Christianity and Judaism. But he reserved his most vitriolic criticisms for the Muslim religion and for Muslims who had immigrated to Holland.

In April 2004, van Gogh combined forces with equally controversial Ayaan Hirsi Ali (a Dutch politician) to produce a short film, *Submission*, that depicted Muslim women in a bad light. In the 10-minute film there were four partially nude women dressed in dark, but transparent, veils. Each of them had words from the Qur'an written in calligraphy on their bare skin. Some of the women had what appeared to be 'whip' marks on their legs and back, insinuating that they were most likely beaten by their husbands for being disobedient.

Once the film was released, Theo van Gogh began to receive death threats. On 2 November 2004, van Gogh was attacked brutally outside a city council building in Amsterdam by an unknown assailant dressed in a traditional Moroccan 'djelleba'. He was stabbed repeatedly in the chest and then shot by his attacker as he stumbled across the street. The attacker, later identified as 26-year-old Mohammed Bouyeri (an Islamic extremist of Moroccan and Dutch citizenship), then slit van Gogh's throat with a large butcher's knife as onlookers stood by gasping in horror.

considered both radical and extreme. Their goals may be just and they might be fighting for worthy causes, but by intentionally targeting and killing people (many of them innocent) in support of their mission these individuals and groups shift from being radicals to being extremists. Louise Richardson has argued that 'the legitimacy . . . of the goals being sought should be irrelevant to whether a group is a terrorist group. Many terrorist groups . . . have been fighting for goals that many share, and that may even be just. But if they deliberately kill civilians to achieve that goal they deserve to be considered terrorists.'[12]

According to this view, then, the movement in **Islam** that pursues the goal of transforming society so that it reflects what that movement considers to be the original objectives of the Qur'an and the **Sunna** is without doubt a 'radical' movement. It is fundamentalist in its desire to return to the roots of Islam. But it does not necessarily have to be an extremist movement. 'Extremist Islamists' are those 'who propagate violence against perceived enemies of Islam in order to effect social and political change which accords with their radical religious (jihadist) ideals.'[13] Muslims are generally peace-loving people who are opposed to the use of violence against the innocent. Those individual Muslims who become extremists are, like other extremists, first radicalized. Radicalization 'is the growing readiness to pursue and/or support—if necessary by undemocratic means—far-reaching changes in society that conflict with, or pose a danger' to the so-called 'established political order'.[14]

Terrorism as Radical Extremism

While there is no internationally established definition of terrorism, it is generally considered as the commission of premeditated violence, or the threat to commit such violence, aimed at destroying human lives and/or inflicting serious material damage that will disrupt social, economic, and political processes and inculcate fear among a general population (i.e., beyond the immediate victims of the violence) with the view of forcing changes in society and/or influencing political decision-making.[15]

For some, there are clearly problems with this definition[16]—perhaps best encapsulated in the well-worn adage that 'one man's terrorist is another's **freedom fighter**.' When the African National Congress (ANC) planted bombs indiscriminately during the 1980s in trash cans in Johannesburg, South Africa, was this organization engaged in terrorism or freedom fighting? One can make the case that the ANC resorted to this kind of extremism only because there was no other avenue within apartheid South Africa for opposition groups to express dissent. Prior to the founding of the ANC, the blacks in South Africa had struggled with the British and Dutch colonizers to regain control over their land and resources. The many wars between the locals and foreigners ended in 1878 with the colonial power's resounding victory over the indigenous people of South Africa. By 1900, the British had broken the backs of the African kingdoms and for the first 50 years of the ANC's existence it was for all intents and purposes a non-violent movement for national liberation.[17] By the 1960s, however, the ANC decided to take up arms against the racist South African government because blacks were being systematically discriminated against, marginalized, and, in some cases, deliberately slaughtered, as happened in the Sharpeville massacre of 21 March 1960, when several thousand black South Africans, peacefully protesting the government's pass laws, were fired on by police, resulting in an official death toll of 69 and many more injured.

In a leaflet issued by the *Umkhonto we Sizwe* (MK)—the military wing of the ANC—in December 1961, one can observe, clearly, the ANC's frustration with the Nationalist government of South Africa. Part of that document reads:

> The time comes in the life of any nation when there remain only two choices: submit or fight. That time has now come to South Africa. We shall not submit and we have

no choice but to hit back by all means within our power in defence of our people, our future and our freedom. The government has interpreted the peacefulness of the movement as weakness; the people's non-violent policies have been taken as a green light for government violence. Refusal to resort to force has been interpreted by the government as an invitation to use armed force against the people without any fear of reprisals. The methods of Umkhonto we Sizwe mark a break with that past.[18]

At this point the radical ANC embraced a form of extremism (asymmetric warfare). In his autobiography, Nelson Mandela explained what he thought were the various violent options available to the ANC at the time:

We considered four types of violent activities: Sabotage, **guerrilla warfare**, terrorism and open revolution. For a small and fledgling army, open revolution was inconceivable. Terrorism inevitably reflected poorly on those who used it, undermining public support it might otherwise garner. Guerrilla warfare was a possibility, but since the ANC had been reluctant to embrace violence at all, it made sense to start with the form of violence that inflicted the least harm against individuals: sabotage.[19]

Despite Mandela's attempt to provide a nuanced explanation for the nature of the ANC's resistance against the immoral South African government, at that time the government labelled him a terrorist, as did the US government and many within academia, and the ANC organization was viewed as a radicalized extremist (terrorist) group. Nelson Mandela spent 27 years in prison for **sabotage** because of his role in the ANC's armed struggle. In retrospect, many in the West now look upon Nelson Mandela as a hero, a freedom fighter, and a cultural icon comparable to Mahatma Gandhi. He even went on, at the age of 75, to become the first President of his country to be elected (1994–9) in a multi-racial, democratic vote, and he won the Nobel Peace Prize in 1993. Today, Nelson Mandela is an elder statesman who denounces terrorism—a far cry from his days as co-founder of a 'terrorist' organization. What this clearly shows is that someone who was considered a radical extremist and terrorist at one point in time can be viewed completely differently the next.

Apart from Mandela, other examples of individuals who made that personal transformation include Menachem Begin, Gerry Adams, Colonel Muammar Abu Minyar al-Qadhafi, and Yasser Arafat. Since radical extremism can be reversed, is it then possible that some of the same people who are labelled as 'terrorists' by the US today will be viewed in the future as national liberators and statespersons?

The late Yasser Arafat is well remembered for his speech at the United Nations in 1974 when, with holster attached to the hip, he effectively renounced terrorism. But his renunciation sounded more like a justification of his brand of extremism than an abandonment of terrorism per se. He felt at the time that Fatah, the militant wing of the Palestinian Liberation Organization (PLO) he headed, was engaged in a just cause—the liberation of the Palestinian people from Zionist Israel. He saw himself as a **revolutionary**, not as a terrorist, and explained the difference this way:

The difference between the revolutionary and the terrorist lies in the reason for which each fights. For whoever stands by a just cause and fights for the freedom and liberation of his land…cannot possibly be called terrorist.[20]

More recently, Osama bin Laden also has tried to justify his brand of radical extremism by declaring that there are good and bad forms of terrorism. He claims that terrorism should be considered 'reprehensible' when it unjustly terrorizes innocent people. He called his brand of terrorism 'commendable' because it terrorizes 'oppressors and criminals and thieves and robbers' and because 'it is directed at the tyrants and the aggressors and the enemies of Allah...the traitors who commit acts of treason against their own countries and their own faith and their own prophet and their own nation.'[21] When asked whether he thought it was fair to target all Americans in his *fatwa*, bin Laden replied:

> Through history, America has not been known to differentiate between the military and the civilians or between men and women or adults and children. Those who threw atomic bombs and used the weapons of mass destruction against Nagasaki and Hiroshima were the Americans. Can the bombs differentiate between military and women and infants and children? America has no religion that can deter her from exterminating whole peoples. Your position against Muslims in Palestine is despicable and disgraceful. America has no shame....We believe that the worst thieves in the world today and the worst terrorists are the Americans. Nothing could stop you except perhaps retaliation in kind. We do not have to differentiate between military or civilian. As far as we are concerned, they are all targets, and this is what the fatwah says ....The fatwah is general (comprehensive) and it includes all those who participate in, or help the Jewish occupiers in killing Muslims.[22]

But for some observers, like Louise Richardson, neither Arafat's nor bin Laden's justification carries much weight. As she puts it, 'A terrorist is a terrorist no matter whether or not you like the goal s/he is trying to achieve, no matter whether or not you like the government s/he is trying to change.'[23] Thus, while there are some real problems with the definition of terrorism, we can probably agree that the activities labelled as 'terrorist' are both radical and extreme. They are radical in the sense that their goals aim at bringing about far-reaching change in society or at forcing a government to make major adjustments to policy. They are extreme in the sense that the methods chosen to achieve those aims focus on premeditated violence that can cause indiscriminate deaths.[24] Terrorists are aware that those methods (whether mortar attacks, ambushes, kidnappings, hijackings, bombings, assassinations, crashing planes into skyscrapers) neutralize the strength of conventional forces, create theatre to bring much media attention to their cause, and strike fear in the hearts of a general population.[25]

Now that we have reflected on the concepts that undergird the object of our analysis, it is necessary to place our subject in historical perspective.

Drawing on History to Understand Extremism

Any cursory historical survey of radicalism and extremism would reveal a plethora of reasons why individuals have resorted to various forms of extremism. Cindy Combs traces individual acts of terrorism to ancient Greek and Roman republics. The assassination of Julius Caesar in 44 BC, for instance, can be considered one of the early individual acts of terrorism.[26] Around AD 66–72, a Jewish resistance movement, the **Zealots** (or Sicarii), was responsible for a wave of extremist activity, including killing Roman soldiers and systematically destroying Roman property.[27] David Rapoport, in his analysis of the historical evolution of terrorism, discerns at least four distinct waves of this form of extremism: anarchist, anti-colonial, New Left, and religious.[28]

In the first phase, terrorism was seen as the only way for certain individuals or groups to redress societal wrongs. The nature of this kind of extremism involved revolutionary upsurges and the assassinations of high-profile political figures. Rapoport designates the 1890s the 'golden age of assassinations' because during that decade a significant number of monarchs, prime ministers, and presidents were struck down by assassins. However, the assassination of Archduke Franz Ferdinand (on 28 June 1914) by Gavrilo Princip, a Serbian terrorist, proved to be counter-productive as it precipitated the advent of World War I. In essence, this extremist act brought to an end the first wave of modern terrorism.

The second wave of modern terrorism took the form of anti-colonial resistance. This wave saw the emergence of nationalists who, emboldened by the principle of self-determination, considered themselves 'freedom fighters' in their quest to be freed from the shackles of colonial bondage. During the anti-colonial struggle, transnational connections became vital, as diasporas not necessarily directly involved in the struggle provided funds, weapons, and other forms of support to the nationalists (including the exertion of moral pressure on colonial powers in support of the anti-colonial struggle). Extremist actions were critical in the establishment of new states such as Ireland, Israel, Cyprus, and Algeria. Terrorist campaigns continued in those territories where special political problems made the withdrawal of colonial power less attractive as an option.

An example is the rise of the Irish Republican Army (IRA) in Ireland, where the majority of the people in Protestant Northern Ireland wanted to remain under British rule. Another example involves the fiasco of partition that has resulted in animosity between Arabs and Jews over Palestine. The Zionist terrorist group, Irgun, led by a Polish Jew—Menachem Begin, who in 1977 would become the first Likud Party Prime Minister of the state of Israel—fought colonial Britain using underground terrorism in an attempt to have the new state of Israel control the whole of Palestine. However, ultimately, this group had to settle for 'partition'.[29] One other example of anti-colonial extremism is the case of Algeria, where resistance by Europeans residing in that country to France's abandonment of its colony led to the establishment of the terrorist organization the Front de Libération Nationale (FLN). With the dissolution of empires, this form of anti-colonial extremism has begun to peter out.

The third wave, left-wing extremism, took hold during the period of the late 1960s and early 1970s and saw the emergence of extremist ethno-nationalist and separatist groups bent on liberating ethnic groups from already established state entities. The Basque **separatists** (Euskadi Ta Askatasuna, or ETA) emerged in reaction to the Spanish government's political and cultural repression of the Basques' language and culture. The ETA, which in 1965 adopted a Marxist-Leninist ideology, staged a series of high-profile attacks on Spanish officials and government buildings. Similar to the Basques, the 25 million or so Kurds have a culture and language of their own, but no territory upon which to establish a national state. The Kurdish Workers' Party (the PKK), another Marxist-Leninist extremist group, was formed in 1978 with the goal of establishing, through violent means if necessary, an independent Kurdish state in southeast Turkey, northern Iraq, and parts of Iran and Syria. It has carried out attacks on Turkish security forces and on government targets both within Turkey and in several Western European countries. Factions within the Palestinian Liberation Organization (PLO) provide an example of a group that has felt it has to use extremist means in order to take back territory—lost to Israel during a series of brief wars.

According to Rapoport, the fourth wave of modern extremism combines right-wing elements with elements of **religious fundamentalism**. The phenomenon of right-wing terrorism is often neglected in the literature or given short shrift, perhaps because 'right-wing violence tends to be poorly organized' and because 'there are only a few readily identifiable right-wing terrorist organizations.'[30] Since the late 1980s there has been evidence of a rise in right-wing extremism in Western Europe, and following the collapse of the Soviet Union in 1990 there was also a spike in the number of right-wing extremist groups across Eastern Europe. Some of these groups include neo-Nazis, neo-Fascists, and skinheads. The objective of many of these **xenophobic** groups was to use violence to bring down democratic governments and replace them with totalitarian ones. At the heart of their grievance was the fact that democratic states were too accepting of diversity and that immigration and refugee laws were too lax.

This cursory historical overview of radical extremism reveals that, in most cases, the driving reason for the embrace of extremist acts has been a longing for freedom: to be rid of an oppressor; to preserve a particular identity; or to preserve a particular way of life. However, it is important to conduct a more in-depth analytical search to see if there are any other causes of radicalized extremism. This can be accomplished by using a **levels of analysis** approach.

Explaining Multiple Causes of Extremism using 'Levels of Analysis'

Kenneth Waltz made a significant contribution to the theory of international relations by advancing three main levels of analysis—the *individual* level, the *state* level, and the *systemic* or international level—that can be used to provide a means of sorting and arranging data for systematic analysis of potential causes of particular phenomena. While these three levels are useful, they are insufficient for discovering some of the reasons for extremism. This phenomenon exhibits a degree of multi-dimensionality that forces one to seek out levels of analysis besides the individual, the state, and the international system. Here we advance three additional levels—group, societal, and state/society—that should help get at some of the potential causes of extremism that cannot be easily deciphered with Waltz's schema. Thus, the remainder of the chapter will demonstrate how we can bring systematic organization to our thinking about extremism by examining this phenomenon at individual, group, societal, state/society complex, state, and transnational/global levels.

Explanations of Extremism from the Individual Level

The individual level of analysis is generally concerned with perceptions, choices, and actions of individual human beings. With respect to extremism, some of the questions that can be asked using this level of analysis are: Why would an individual choose to take up a radical position and then move beyond that to kill or maim others who may have little or nothing to do with her/his plight?

Why would someone choose to go outside of the law to commit hideous crimes against fellow humans for a cause and take the risk of being imprisoned for a very long time or killed? Or, why would anyone decide to kill herself or himself to further an abstract cause?

Many studies have been done by psychologists, behavioural scientists, sociologists, criminologists, and political scientists to find answers to these questions. Policy-makers, too, are interested in this level of analysis because they hope to develop a profile for would-be terrorists in order to identify them before they can carry out their despicable deeds. But there is a lot we still don't know about the 'terrorist mind'. Are there innate characteristics of extremists that would make them prone to carry out acts of terror? What role do brain damage, mental deficiencies, personality defects, narcissism, paranoia, hormonal changes, self-aggrandizement, delusion, arrested psychological development, impulsiveness, irrational behaviour, or other forms of psychological or physiological maladjustment play in the decision of an individual to become an extremist?

Several popular assumptions have been proffered that seem to imply that such individuals must be crazy, that they are unable to reason normally. Former US President Ronald Reagan once characterized 'terrorists' as 'the strangest collection of misfits, looney tunes, and squalid criminals since the advent of the Third Reich'. He also referred to extremists as: 'irrational', 'flaky', and 'zealots' who demonstrated 'fanatical hatred'.[31] While it may be true that some extremists or terrorists might be 'crazed fanatics', the available evidence does not bear this out.[32] Most psychologists suggest that 'terrorists are psychologically normal—that is, not clinically psychotic. They are not depressed, and not severely emotionally disturbed, nor are they crazed fanatics.'[33]

An expert on terrorist psychology for the US Department of Justice, Jerrold Post, had the opportunity of interviewing extremists who were apprehended for carrying out terrorist attacks. In one such interview with Omar Rezaq, a member of the Abu Nidal organization who played a central role in the 1985 hijacking of an Egyptian airplane, Post came to the conclusion that Rezaq was quite sane but full of hatred for Jews from his early childhood. This was a person who had been socialized from birth to become 'a heroic revolutionary' fighting for the freedom of the Palestinian people. Rezaq's mother had passed on stories of how the Israelis forced her family from their home in the West Bank during the 1948 Arab–Israeli war. His mother was only eight years old at the time of the expropriation, but that event nonetheless left an indelible impression on her and most probably left her emotionally scarred. She obviously passed on the animosity she held for Israelis to her son.

But what cemented this hatred of Jews in Omar Rezaq was the Six Day War in June 1967, when he himself was eight years old. Once again, his family was forced to flee, this time from a refugee camp in Jordan. The young boy attended a school where his teachers were members of the PLO. He idolized one of his teachers and became radicalized. Omar was taught that the only way he could become a real man was if he took up the cause of the revolution and helped to take back the lands the Israeli army stole from his parents. In carrying out the hijacking and in shooting the five hostages (two Israeli women and three Americans), Omar Rezaq was taking up his family's cause—'a cause that had been *bred in the bone*'.[34]

Based on a survey of the literature, the causal factors for extremism, using the individual level of analysis, are multiple. They include: ideological indoctrination at an early age; hatred of an oppressor; humiliation and other forms of degradation;

loyalty to a particular people or cause; empathy for the suffering of others; a strong sense of justice; and seeing oneself as a victim who is then justified in taking action (revenge).[35] What complicates this research at the individual level of analysis is that one has to take into account the link that individuals have to groups and to society, including the impact on the individual of transnational/global extremist networks. In many cases, for instance, individual terrorists choose to subordinate their individual identities to the collective identity of a group, organization, or network that supports their particular cause.

Explanations of Extremism at the Group Level

A group level of analysis is probably more helpful than the individual level for determining the reasons for extremism. Certainly there are examples of the 'lone wolf' syndrome, such as Theodore 'Ted' Kaczynski, the infamous Unabomber (see Box 13.2), but more often than not individual terrorists lack the financial

BOX 13.2

The Unabomber

Theodore 'Ted' Kaczynski was a child prodigy, a Harvard graduate, and a Ph.D. in mathematics from the University of Michigan before becoming a brilliant professor of mathematics at the University of California, Berkeley in 1967. However, by 1969 Kaczynski resigned without explanation from his teaching position and chose to live as a recluse in a remote cabin he built in Lincoln, Montana.

He was given the codename 'UNABOM' (UNiversity and Airline BOMber) by the US Federal Bureau of Investigation after he carried out a string of bombings that began in the late 1970s, using mail bombs and other handmade, untraceable explosive devices, killing three people and wounding 23 others.

Ted Kaczynski.

© Ralf-Finn Hestoft/Corbis

His first bombing, at Northwestern University, occurred in 1978 and was unsuccessful. But this was followed by 15 other bombings that targeted engineering/math/science professors, logging company CEOs, airline executives, technological advocacy writers, and other propagandists for industry. Because of these bombing, Kaczynski was declared as one of America's most dangerous domestic terrorists by the FBI.

Kaczynski was finally caught only because his brother turned him in to authorities, after Kaczynski's 35,000 word *Manifesto* was published in major American newspapers in 1995.

resources, technical know-how and information, and support needed to launch a successful terror attack. Such individuals usually rely on an organization or group. The difficulty in gaining answers about the cause of extremism through the group level of analysis is that several different types of radicalized extremist groups emerge out of a variety of different social, economic, and political conditions and circumstances. Thus, while these groups may be fundamentally similar in their techniques and ultimate goal of imparting terror, they differ in several respects (e.g., their structure, ideology, membership, etc.).

The goals of Russian revolutionaries, anarchists, anti-colonialists, ethno-nationalists/separatists, the radical New Left, right-wing reactionaries, state-sponsored terrorists, and religiously motivated extremists have been quite different even if they shared some of the same tactics and strategies. Some extremist groups may be motivated to seize power, others may not. Some of them are motivated by a desire to address grievances or to improve the political, social, or economic conditions of a specific people. Some may simply be fed up with political repression and humiliation faced by the society represented in the membership of the group. Other extremist groups and organizations are driven by a particular ideology, whether Marxist or religious. And many extremist groups have multiple motivations for carrying out indiscriminate violence and other acts of terror. Consequently, it is important, in trying to understand the causes of radicalism using the group level of analysis, to understand the differences between various extremist groups, their motivations, and the socio-political circumstances from which they emerge, rather then simply paint them all with the same brush.

What we do know is that extremist behaviour practised by a group cannot be properly understood without reference to 'group identity' and 'shared ideological commitment'. Being a member of an extremist group can make an individual feel like part of a larger cause. Membership in such a group provides the terrorist with a sense of belonging, purpose, perceived social status, and empowerment that he (or she) would not otherwise enjoy. It also gives the individual terrorist a sense of anonymity that could provide a crucial explanation for the justification of using violence against innocent victims. Then there is the reality of **'group-think'** with respect to the decision-making process in extremist groups or organizations. The essence of group-think is the drive towards uniformity, conformity, and group solidarity. Those qualities become extremely important in maintaining an individual's focus on achieving stated objectives. Dissenting voices are generally silenced quickly within such groups, and this sense of solidarity and comradeship helps to generate a bond among extremists that can lead to lunatic acts of 'bravery'.[36]

Explanations of Extremism from the Societal Level

To expand our knowledge of what causes extremism, we need to look beyond individual and group explanations and see whether societal elements, such as cultural clashes, changing socio-economic conditions, religious and other particularist ideologies may have something to do with facilitating the embrace of radical and extreme thought and action. At this level of analysis, one should also be concerned with trying to understand situations in which certain whole societies collectively engage in protest and provide encouragement and support for those individuals and groups who decide to go beyond radicalism and use violence to address societal grievances.[37] Societal explanations of extremism take into account the impact of the social environment on the behaviour of individuals and groups. That environment may produce social, political, and economic inequalities or racial or religious prejudices, and these, in turn, can spur an individual or a group to engage in violent acts.[38]

Although we all know that one does not have to be poor and oppressed to empathize with the poor and oppressed, or even to take up arms on their behalf, poverty is a societal condition that some believe may spur on radical and extremist thought and action. However, the fact that extremists have emerged from both rich and poor countries, and from both developed and developing regions of the world, calls this supposition into question. Some observers have noted that, at best, the link between poverty and extremism is indirect, complicated, and most likely weak.[39] Certainly, if there was a direct correlation between poverty and terrorism, then the poorest continent (Africa) should have the highest rate of terrorism, but it does not. But it is true that poverty in weak and failing states can create a permissive environment for terrorist and other criminal activity, particularly recruitment in those states, thus making them vulnerable to terrorist networks and drug cartels.[40] A more nuanced perspective on this issue can be found in Johan Galtung's notion of 'structural violence'. According to Galtung, 'structural violence' stems from political and economic inequalities between different groups within society that cause harm to the disadvantaged group. Poverty, hunger, homelessness, oppression, and discrimination are all results of structural violence.[41] Victims are generally those at the margins of society, including women, children, the elderly, ethnic and racial minorities, homosexuals, and those from non-mainstream religious groups. One can expect that those who have been subject to structural violence may lash out at their oppressors. In this sense, structural violence can lead indirectly to extremism.

Another societal factor usually blamed for nurturing extremism is religion.[42] Prior to the eighteenth century, religion was a prime motivating factor for extremist groups like the Jewish Sicarii, the Indian Thugs, the Shia Ismaili assassins, and the Christian crusaders. Between the 1800s and the 1970s, religion took a back seat to nationalism, Marxism, and other ideologies as a driving force

BOX 13.3

How to Keep Your Children from Becoming Terrorists and Extremists

If we want to protect our young children from one day becoming fanatics or terrorists, we need to provide them with a completely new culture that is radically different than the religious, intellectual, and social culture that has dominated us for many decades, and still does. Instead of teaching your children hostility, or letting someone else teach them hostility, towards those of other religions, teach [them] religious tolerance, which will [ensure that while] they differ from others in religion, they will share with them their common humanity.

Source: Quotation from Mamdouh Al-Muhaini, 'In Order to Keep Our Children from Embracing Terrorist Ideology, We Need to Block the Entryways That Lead to It', *Al-Riyadh* (Saudi Arabia), 6 Feb. 2009.

for extremism. However, since the Iranian Islamic revolution in 1979, religious terrorism has come back to the fore.

Clearly, some extremists today are using religion to justify their violent acts. We see this in the case of Christian extremists in the US who are convinced that God prohibits abortions. Some of these extremists target medical doctors who perform those procedures on women and, ironically, are willing to kill to deter future abortionists. We have also seen Muslim extremists use their religion to justify the indiscriminate killing of civilians in New York, Washington, London, Madrid, Bali, and elsewhere. And Jewish settlers in Gaza and the West Bank have used religious arguments to justify their use of terrorist tactics. But are certain violent acts associated with extremists the fault of religious absolutist thinking? Or, to pose Mark Juergensmeyer's very different question: 'has the innocence of religion been abused by wily political activists who twist religion's essential message of peace for their own devious purposes? Is religion the problem or the victim?'[43]

Extremist religious elements do not, in fact, represent the majority of the people who adhere to any particular faith. Those elements are generally unrepresentative of the true normative traditions of mainstream religions. So, for instance, most Buddhists immediately distanced themselves from the Aum Shinrikyo sect, a fanatical Japanese religious cult best known for its terror attack of 20 March 1995, using sarin nerve gas, on the Tokyo subway system during the early morning rush hour. Most Muslims were appalled by the 9/11 terrorist attacks on US soil and cannot believe that any good Muslim would contemplate, far less do, such a thing. Most Christians in the US refused to consider Timothy McVeigh, a US army veteran who was convicted of bombing the Alfred P. Murrah Building in Oklahoma City on 19 April 1995, as a 'Christian terrorist'. Rather, they saw him as anti-Christian and even anti-religious. What makes violence done in the name of a religion particularly savage is that its perpetrators are able to convince themselves that their worldly political battle is an evocation of a much larger or higher 'spiritual confrontation'.[44] Religion is obviously a powerfully motivating force for anyone who thinks he or she is doing God's bidding and who honestly believes that, even if the struggle is a trans-historical one, victory is inevitable. The real danger comes when religious images of 'cosmic war' are used in the service of secular or worldly political struggles. When this happens, religious zealots can kill indiscriminately and without remorse.

Explanations of Extremism from a State/Society Complex Level

Extremists can be by-products of the relationship between specific forms of state and their societies. Several political regimes in the Muslim world are repressive, undemocratic, and illegitimate. Some have tried to modernize and industrialize too rapidly, only to be met with resistance from rebellious sectors within their societies concerned about the erosion of traditional institutions and value systems. In such cases, radicalized Islamist groups have entered the picture offering an alternative to the state. Their fundamentalist religious message generally appeals to those who yearn for a return to the past. When these autocratic governments crack down on dissenters, this has led to a counter-reaction—in most

BOX 13.4

Wahhabism

Wahhabism is a radical constructionist interpretation and practice of Islam based solely on literal puritanical readings of the Qur'an (the holy book of Islam) and the Sunna (Prophet Muhammad's teachings). It is concerned with 'purifying' Islam from innovations (*bid'a*) and rejects interpretations of Islamic thought after the tenth century, when most Islamic judicial rulings on holy texts and schools of jurisprudence were established. Wahhabism requires the performance of communal prayer, stresses monotheism and the oneness of God (*tawhid*), and condemns mystical Islam.

Wahhabism emphasizes Muslims' duty to wage holy war (jihad) against those who do not follow Wahhabi principles. Jihad means 'to strive' and refers to both 'greater' jihad (resisting evil deeds and supporting what is right) and 'lesser' jihad (waging war against enemies and those who attack Muslims). Although lesser jihad is rare, it is still practised by extremist Islamic groups to achieve political change and to make a self-righteous call for a return to the 'pristine' Islam of the past. The view that all non-Wahhabi societies are pagan (*jahiliyya*) has justified Wahhabi **insurgency**.

Wahhabism was founded in the eighteenth century by Mohammed ibn Abd Al-Wahhab (1703–91). Inspired by medieval jurist Ahmad ibn Hanbal (d. 855), the originator of the Hanbali school of Islamic jurisprudence, Wahhabism became a political tool in 1744 when Al-Wahhab, a religious authoritative leader, forged an alliance with the political leader Sa'ud ibn Mohammed and built an empire based on Wahhabi doctrine. The empire threatened nomadic and sedentary populations with jihad if they resisted mental and physical coercion, but promised spiritual rewards if they submitted to assimilation. Al-Wahhab collected a regular financial payment (*zakath*) like the Christian tithe, which was said to be Muslims' religious obligation to pay. By 1803, the empire had conquered much of modern-day Saudi Arabia, which became an official state in 1932.

Saudi Arabia has historical importance to Muslims because it is the birthplace of Islam (AD 610). Saudi Arabia is also the home of Islam's holiest cities—Mecca and Medina—and the direction that most of the world's one billion Muslims turn to pray five times a day (*quibla*). Wahhabis believe Saudi Arabia is the religious and political centre of the Islamic world. Therefore, since the oil boom in the 1970s, a major plank of Saudi Arabian foreign policy has been to export Wahhabism to the rest of the Islamic world. The Saudi government incites jihad by providing financial support and arms to anti-government groups in Wahhabi-dominated areas including the Middle East, Central Asia, the Balkans, and North Africa. Saudi funds are often disguised as charitable contributions that offer free education, food, and shelter to poor youth. In reality, Saudi funds help indoctrinate youth with Wahhabism and train them as militants in Wahhabi religious schools (*madrassas*) all over the world.

The government of Saudi Arabia has never owned or controlled the Wahhabi movement. This became evident in 2001 when Al-Qaeda attacked the United States—a major Saudi trade partner. Osama bin Laden, leader of Al-Qaeda and figurehead of modern-day Wahhabi terrorism, sees the Saudi government as an enemy—a corrupt and abusive regime that maintains power due to the assistance of the US government. Bin Laden recruits Saudis because they witness first-hand how the Saudi government employs the guise of Wahhabi religiosity while developing a collusive relationship with the US government. Bin Laden issued his first declaration of jihad after King Fahd invited US troops into Saudi Arabia during the Iraqi invasion of Kuwait in 1990, and he has sworn to use every instrument to wage war against US 'foreign occupation' of the Middle East.

A rapid proliferation of independent Islamic terrorist groups has occurred in the Middle East and North Africa: Al-Qaeda scattered in various countries, especially Afghanistan, Pakistan, Somalia, and Yemen; Al-Gama'a al-Islamiyya in Egypt; the National Islamic Front in Sudan; Hezbollah in Lebanon; and Hamas within the Palestinian movement. The most high-profile jihad is currently waged against the United States by independent Wahhabi groups. Bin Laden has openly stated his willingness to employ chemical and biological weapons to achieve his aims and has demonstrated that he is not adverse to killing civilians, as in the bombings of US embassies in Kenya and Tanzania in 1995 and 1996. In the 9/11 terrorist attacks, 15 of the 19 hijackers were Saudi Arabian and all professed to follow the Saudi doctrine of Wahhabism. Clearly, the repercussions of Wahhabism, particularly under bin Laden, are likely to be far-reaching and of some duration.

●●●○○○

cases, to a further hardening of the opposition and, in certain instances, to the embrace of radical and extreme thought and actions.[45]

Many Muslims who left their countries of origin and moved to countries in the West often find themselves subject to discriminatory, exclusivist state policies. Some have experienced both state and societal discrimination, racial profiling, cultural alienation, socio-economic marginalization, religious suppression, and political repression. In France, poor disenfranchised Muslims, many born and raised in France, have been subjected to the state's forced secularization and assimilation policies and not so subtle racism, as well as other forms of discrimination from within the mainstream population in regard to housing, education, and employment. The French government and mainstream society have generally tended to treat French Muslims as sojourners rather than full citizens. Instead of respecting difference and diversity, the French have pushed integration as a means of forcing Muslims to conform to their principle of *laïcité*. It is not surprising, therefore, that many within the French Muslim communities, embedded in a strongly secular society, have reacted negatively to policies that force them to separate private and public demonstrations of faith.[46]

Indeed, the hijab policy is a case in point. France's insistence on banning the wearing of the hijab in public places was an affront to adherents of the Islamic faith in that country and contributed to growing resentment within Muslim communities (or, as one writer put it, 'the rebellion of the French underclass'). This policy, combined with religious intolerance, the expulsion of 'radical' imams, the imprisonment of certain Muslim clerics, the ghettoization and socio-economic marginalization of Muslim youth, the dilapidated conditions in the housing projects, and general **Islamophobia** within the French mainstream population, may have pushed some Muslims into the arms of Islamic extremists. In addition, some in the French Muslim communities doubtless harbour long-standing grudges because of French imperialism in their countries of origin. Some of the extremism demonstrated by immigrant communities in France is an outgrowth of that historical resentment.[47]

Explanations of Extremism from the State Level

Several states are involved in both direct and indirect forms of terrorism and other extremism. Both superpowers, for example, engaged in state-sponsored terrorism during the Cold War. Iran has been a leader in state-sponsored terrorism since 1979. It has actively supported radical Islamic organizations in Kuwait, Saudi Arabia, Bahrain, and Lebanon with funds, weapons, safe haven, training, and technical expertise as part of its quest to export its Islamic revolution. It has also supported Hezbollah in southern Lebanon against Israel, as well as Palestinian extremist groups like Hamas, Palestinian Islamic Jihad, and the Popular Front for the Liberation of Palestine-General Command. Iran is suspected of having provided safe haven to some Al-Qaeda operatives or of allowing them transit through its territory.

There is another aspect of state-level explanations of extremism. Some observers have noted that weak and failing, or failed, states provide fertile ground for extremism to flourish. Terrorist organizations can take advantage of vacuums of governance to plant their seed of extremism. The 'permissive environment' created by state failure provides ideal conditions for extremists to operate and expand. Transitioning states (e.g., states making the transition from autocratic to democratic, or from command closed economies to free-market economies) may also attract extremist groups and activity.[48] Finally, there is some debate in the literature about whether particular forms of state are more conducive to breeding extremist elements. Certainly, the apartheid regime of the South African state developed a deliberate and sophisticated strategy of extremism, by supporting terrorist movements in the front-line states (FLS) in an effort to combat the African National Congress. Both Syria and Libya have sponsored terrorism in the past. And, of course, the Afghanistan state, under the Taliban, and the Sudanese government earlier provided safe haven for Osama bin Laden and his Al-Qaeda operation.

© Mohammed Saber/EPA/Corbis

Hamas militants.

BOX 13.5

Palestinian Jihad

Valour in battle, including intentional self-destruction, has always been characteristic of armed conflicts. Since 1984, disheartened by numerous failed peace negotiations between the Israeli government and the Palestinian Liberation Organization, radical groups including Hamas and the Palestinian Islamic Jihad have employed suicide terrorism against hundreds of Israeli civilians in order to achieve Palestinian national aspirations in statehood. In response, Israel has retaliated with collective punishment, which has increased the rate of Palestinian suicide bombings.

Are there explanations for support of Palestinian suicide bombings and the proneness to participate in them? Hilal Khashan argues that the Palestinian suicide bombing phenomenon has a pattern: political Islam, deteriorating social functionality in the context of refugee camps, and youth. Political Islam refers to persons who not only perform standard religious obligations but also believe that the Islamic faith has a central role in the lives of adherents in the Muslim community, feel strongly that there is a need to create an Islamic state, and see jihad as a religious obligation. In addition to the strength of political Islam, grave humanitarian conditions in Palestinian refugee camps in the Gaza Strip and southern Lebanon lead to a feeling of relative deprivation—frustrations resulting from a gap between rising expectations and a deteriorating poverty-stricken reality. For this reason, many Muslim clerics consider suicide attacks by Palestinian refugees legitimate martyrdom missions and acts of self-defence against the enemy. In addition, youth tend to be more willing to carry out suicide operations. Faced with low-income, manual labour jobs in which they are often mistreated, marginalized Palestinian youth are easily recruited by extremist groups. By identifying the causal factors behind Palestinian suicide bombings, there is hope that violence and inter-group conflict in Israel can be resolved.

Source: Hilal Khashan, 'Collective Palestinian Frustration and Suicide Bombings', *Third World Quarterly* 24, 6 (2003): 1049–67.

Some neo-conservative scholars have suggested that the democratic form of state is the ideal form for stemming the tide of extremism.[49] After all, in democracies people, at least in theory, have an outlet for their grievances and frustrations—i.e., the ballot box. Close study, however, reveals that while democracy may be the preferred political system for the US, Britain, France, Spain, Canada, and other states in the West, it is certainly not necessarily a recipe for dampening or extinguishing the spread of extremism. Some observers have demonstrated that acts of terrorism are, in fact, more prevalent in democracies than in any other form of state.[50] Perhaps this is because democracies provide settings within which it is relatively easy for terrorists to plan and commit violent acts. In fact, the presence of terrorist groups could affect the quality of democracy in at least two ways: (1) it could result in bringing physical harm to the population of that form of state; (2) it could result in the weakening of democratic structures as the government revokes civil liberties and institutes extreme security measures as a way of countering terrorists. Many analysts have remarked on this second point in regard to North America post-9/11.

Explanations of Extremism from the Transnational/ Global Level

One of the major reasons why studies of extremism have become so important today is the recognition that this phenomenon is transnational and global in its character and reach. But what is causing the transnational and global spread of extremism? According to Samuel Huntington, the answer lays in the 'clash of civilizations'—a fundamental cultural and ideological incompatibility between Islam and the West.[51] Benjamin Barber presents a slightly more nuanced position when he argues that:

> the struggle of Jihad against McWorld is not a clash of civilizations but a dialectical expression of tensions built into a single global civilization as it emerges against a backdrop of traditional ethnic and religious divisions, many of which are actually created by McWorld and its infotainment industries and technological innovations.[52]

According to Barber, what we are witnessing today is a struggle not between civilizations but within one global civilization, as individuals, groups, societies, and governments try to cope with the phenomenon of globalization. Globalization has obvious benefits to some sections of the globe and to some people. It promotes economic growth and prosperity and can be an instrument for the spread of democratic values. It also enhances the ease with which labour, ideas, capital, production processes, technology, and profits can move across borders. But globalization comes with significant costs to other sections of the globe and to other people, particularly in the developing countries of the world. Those living in the global South are generally suspicious of globalization because it smacks of a neo-colonialist or neo-imperialist strategy that allows the US, as the sole remaining hegemon, to maintain and spread its hold on much of the world. It is the homogenization tendencies of globalization against which Muslims have to guard. But other negative impacts of globalization have provided radicals and extremists with the justification for redress. Economic practices associated with globalization have also fostered greater inequalities within countries. These inequalities exacerbate tensions as the gulf between haves and have-nots has led to a proliferation of gated communities and private security agencies.

Globalization also has resulted in the migration and resettlement of people looking for a better way of life. Diasporas do not always leave behind the conflicts that are brewing in their state of origin. Some of them actually fund the work of extremists who are living and working in the home country, thus contributing to the transnationalization of conflicts and the globalization of extremism. Of course, this globalization of extremism has been aided and abetted by technological advances, including computers, satellite television, the Internet, expansion of air travel, the wide availability of news coverage, etc. Meanwhile, radicalism and extremism are sustained by funds and other resources that are gleaned transnationally or globally and sometimes obtained illegally. Underground arms trade and drug trafficking are two examples of the transnationalization or globalization of instruments that facilitate extremism.

The Response of the United Nations to Terrorism

International terrorism has occupied the UN agenda since the late 1960s. In 1972, the UN General Assembly explicitly addressed this issue as an international security problem. UN Secretary-General Kurt Waldheim brought the issue to the attention of the General Assembly in the wake of several major acts of terror, most notably the attack on Lod Airport in Israel and the 1972 slaughter of Israeli athletes at the Summer Olympics in Munich. Expressing deep concern with acts of international terrorism and the toll it was taking in human life, the General Assembly urged states to search for the 'underlying causes which give rise to such acts of violence'.[53] Yet, at the same time, the Assembly reaffirmed the inalienable right of peoples to self-determination and upheld the violent struggle of national liberation movements as a legitimate form of resistance against colonial and racist regimes. In effect, the early response of the UN to acts of international terrorism was somewhat ambivalent.

In part, the latter response reflected the views of several 'radical' new states that had, during the 1960s and early 1970s, obtained independence from colonial and imperial powers—some through violent struggle—and were now members of the UN system. An ad hoc committee was formed to find ways to end terrorism. The Soviet Union and several of the more radical leftist countries of the Third World pointed to the fact that the US, Israel, and South Africa were involved in what they called 'state terrorism' against leftist/Marxist movements, Palestinians, and anti-apartheid activists respectively. In the mid-1980s, the Reagan administration in the US exhibited this pattern of state terrorism in its fight against leftists in Central America. The end result was disagreement within the UN over the definition of terrorism. Essentially, the dispute has centred on what constitutes a terrorist act and, in particular, how one should classify Palestinian suicide bombings and Israeli military actions in the West Bank and Gaza. Some UN member states have held on to the adage that 'one man's terrorist is another's freedom fighter.'

Consideration of terrorism as an international security problem as well as a human security and human rights problem remained on the UN General Assembly's agenda throughout the 1970s and 1980s, during which time a number of conventions were adopted to deal with various aspects of the problem (see Table 13.1). However, terrorism as an agenda item became the purview of the Sixth Committee, otherwise known as the legal committee of the General Assembly. The end of the Cold War opened up a window of opportunity for the UN membership to reach some consensus on ways of dealing with terrorism. In 1991, the first resolution passed unanimously by the Assembly on 'measures to eliminate international terrorism' shifted the concern from distinguishing between legitimate armed struggle and terrorism to the means employed by terrorists. At this point, too, a link was made between the international security problem of terrorism and the transnational security problem of drug trafficking (narco-terrorism) and the proliferation of 'paramilitary gangs'. This resolution called on states and on UN special agencies and other intergovernmental organizations to do all in their power to combat this growing transnational threat to state and human security.

Despite the normative framework laid down by the Assembly, acts of terrorism continued to threaten individual states, innocent citizens, and the international community at large. Terrorist attacks like those against Pan Am Flight 103 over

Table 13.1 International Conventions to Address the Problem of Terrorism

Convention	Date	Location of Signing/ Adoption
Convention for the Suppression of Unlawful Seizure of Aircraft	16 December 1970	The Hague
Convention for the Suppression of Unlawful Acts against the Safety of Civil Aviation	23 September 1971	Montreal
Convention on the Prevention and Punishment of Crimes against Internationally Protected Persons, including Diplomatic Agents	14 December 1973	New York, adopted by UN General Assembly
International Convention against the Taking of Hostages	17 December 1979	New York, adopted by UN General Assembly
Convention on the Physical Protection of Nuclear Material	3 March 1980	Vienna
Protocol on the Suppression of Unlawful Acts of Violence at Airports Serving International Civil Aviation, supplementary to the Convention for the Suppression of Unlawful Acts against the Safety of Civil Aviation	24 February 1988	Montreal
Convention for the Suppression of Unlawful Acts against the Safety of Maritime Navigation	10 March 1988	Rome
Protocol for the Suppression of Unlawful Acts against the Safety of Fixed Platforms Located on the Continental Shelf	10 March 1988	Rome
International Convention for the Suppression of Terrorist Bombings	15 December 1997	New York, adopted by UN General Assembly

Source: <www.nti.org/e_research/official_docs/inventory/pdfs/intlterr.pdf>

Lockerbie, Scotland (December 1988), and against Union des Transports Aériens (UTA) Flight 772 over Niger (September 1989) prompted some of the permanent members of the UN Security Council (namely France, Britain, and the US) to involve the Council in the fight against this transnational security threat. The subject became a serious issue for the UN Security Council in 1992 when, at the Council's first-ever Meeting of Heads of State and Government, Council members expressed deep concern over acts of international terrorism and stressed the importance of addressing this problem.

By March of that same year, the Council took action against a known terrorist state, Libya, by imposing mandatory sanctions on that country for its involvement in the terrorist bombing of a discotheque in Germany. It determined as well that there was Libyan involvement in the downing of Pan Am Flight 103. In addition, the British had evidence that Libya was providing support to the Irish Republican Army (IRA), whose brand of terrorism had crossed the line between armed resistance against an occupying power to indiscriminate acts of violence that targeted innocent people. The Council resolution declared Libya's actions a 'threat to international peace and security' and invoked Chapter VII of the UN

Charter to counter that threat. Apart from the earlier economic sanctions, an arms embargo was imposed on Libya as well as restrictions on flights coming into and out of that country. UN member states were also asked to freeze specified Libyan government assets. Eventually, Libya caved into the Council demands and handed over two Libyan-born suspects to be tried under Scottish law in a court in the Netherlands. The effect of this result was that the norm criminalizing terrorism was upheld and made more robust by Libya's eventual compliance, albeit reluctantly, with UN Security Council resolutions.[54]

In 1996, the Council again backed up its rhetoric with action, this time imposing economic sanctions against Sudan for serving as a refuge, nexus, and training hub for a number of international terrorist organizations, primarily of Middle Eastern origin. The Sudanese government refused to extradite three individuals who were suspected of carrying out a failed assassination attempt on the life of the Egyptian President, Hosni Mubarak, while he was visiting Addis Ababa, Ethiopia, on 26 June 1995. Sudan failed to comply with the UN Security Council's demand that it cease support to terrorists and turn over the three Egyptian Al-Gama'a al-Islamiyya (IG) fugitives who had been linked to the assassination attempt.

The Sudanese government denied any foreknowledge of the planning behind the Mubarak assassination attempt and claimed that it did not know the whereabouts of the assailants. Only after the passage of three critical UN Security Council resolutions and the bombing of a pharmaceutical plant in Khartoum (suspected of being a dual-use facility for the Al-Qaeda network) did the Sudanese government order Osama bin Laden to uproot his terrorist organization from Sudan. In return for Sudan's co-operation, the Security Council lifted the sanctions placed on that country. One would have to conclude that it was the impact of UN sanctions coupled with the backing of US military might that forced the Sudanese government to comply finally with its international legal obligation.

After leaving Sudan, Osama bin Laden and his Al-Qaeda terrorist organization moved to Afghanistan, receiving the support of the Taliban regime there. Al-Qaeda was linked to several terrorist attacks, including the 1998 bombings of US embassies in Nairobi, Kenya, and Dar es Salaam, Tanzania, that killed at least 301 individuals and injured more than 5,000 others. The UN Security Council condemned the Taliban for allowing Afghanistan to be used as a base for terrorist training and activities and for facilitating the exportation of terrorism. The Council demanded that the Taliban turn over Osama bin Laden, without delay, 'to appropriate authorities in a country where he has been indicted or to appropriate authorities in a country where he will be returned to such a country, or to appropriate authorities in a country where he will be arrested and effectively brought to justice.'[55]

The Council also imposed financial and travel 'smart' sanctions on the Taliban regime. Resolution 1333, adopted on 19 December 2000, tightened the earlier imposed sanctions, and demanded that the Taliban act swiftly to close all terrorist training camps in the territory under its control. These resolutions seemed to have little effect on the Taliban regime or on the Al-Qaeda network, which was now operating as a global terrorist and criminal organization with approximately 4,000 to 5,000 well-trained fighters located in about 50 countries around the world. In December 2000, the Council strengthened the sanctions on the Taliban by imposing an arms embargo. In this case, UN sanctions proved futile against an already illegitimate regime and against non-state criminal actors who were operating covertly outside the confines of international law and norms.

On 11 September 2001, when the US sustained an Al-Qaeda terrorist assault, tackling terrorism with more coercive instruments became a top priority for the UN Security Council. Within hours of the attack, a draft resolution was circulated among Council members strongly condemning the attack on American soil and paving the way for a US-led military response targeting Afghanistan. A few weeks later the Council adopted resolution 1373, which obliged all UN member governments to use domestic legislation and executive action in an effort to combat future terrorist acts. It called for the freezing of terrorists' assets, the prohibition of fundraising for terrorist activities, the denial of safe haven or passage, a ban on providing arms or other material assistance to terrorists, and the sharing of information between states about terrorists operations. UN member states were obligated under this resolution to report to the Counter-Terrorism Committee (CTC) about the legislative and administrative steps they were taking to fulfill the above requirements.

One important element of the UN Security Council's response to the 9/11 attacks was that it lent legitimacy to unilateral military action by states that are subject to terrorist attack and threat. This action, in some respects, helped to weaken the norm prohibiting the use of force that has been a central plank of the UN Charter. It also presents another problem for the international community. Some states have difficulty carrying out the anti-terrorist measures laid out by the Council because many of these measures require institutional and material resources that several developing countries, and even some industrial ones, may not have at their disposal. If a majority of UN member states are unable or unwilling to comply with the Council's demands on this issue, then this could undermine or weaken the authority and legitimacy of not only the Council but also of the entire UN system.

A positive outcome of the Council's response to 9/11 was the creation of the Counter-Terrorism Committee. One task of the CTC is to help states draft legislative and executive measures needed to combat terrorism. All UN member states are expected to provide the CTC with reports indicating the steps they have taken to deal with international terrorism. Only 15 states did not submit their reports by the fall of 2002. From the 176 reports received it is clear that most states are not yet able, legislatively or administratively, to tackle the problem. It would seem that the CTC is not in a position to help bridge the gaps in administrative and legal capacity that most states have. It has a staff of only 12 and no independent budget. Furthermore, UN member states remain at odds over what constitutes terrorism.

Nevertheless, both the General Assembly and the Security Council have determined that terrorism is a global and transnational concern and that it poses a global threat that cannot be dealt with adequately by states acting unilaterally. Terrorism poses a threat to security (both human and state) that calls for a multilateral response. That response is best provided through the United Nations and the norms that criminalize terrorist acts. In addition, the UN also possesses the requisite socio-political and legal framework for addressing the underlying root causes of international terrorism.

However, while the UN already has adopted a number of treaties designed to counter various aspects of terrorism (as noted earlier), it has not yet been able to reach agreement among its member governments on a comprehensive convention on global terrorism—something that is sorely needed at this particular stage in our history. The draft of a 'comprehensive convention on international terrorism' has been stalled in the UN's legal committee since 1996, where negotiations have repeatedly been bogged down over the definition of terrorism. Recent suicide bombings in Afghanistan, Bali, Egypt, Iraq, Spain, and the UK have once again spurred UN member governments to take another stab at developing consensus over the definition of terrorism.

Conclusion

As shown above, reflecting critically on radicalism and extremism can produce a rich set of explanations as to their causes. Understanding the subtle differences in the concepts of 'radicalism' and 'extremism' helps to focus on the significant question: what causes a radical to embrace extremism? That question is important if we want to understand the terrorism we are witnessing today. By first drawing on history and then organizing the vast literature on the subject through the lens of 'levels of analysis', this chapter demonstrates that there are multiple causes of extremism and terrorism. Understanding those causes ought to be a first step in developing any counter-terrorism policy. Thus, careful and critical theoretical reflection on a subject can be of enormous benefit to policy-makers. It can help them understand the complexities and nuances of the subject under examination and, as well, to arrive at the most plausible solution for addressing particular problems.

Key Terms

'clash of civilizations'
extremism
fatwa
freedom fighter
'group-think'
guerrilla warfare
homegrown terrorists
insurgency
Islam
Islamophobia
jihad
laicité
levels of analysis

madrassas
radicalism
religious fundamentalism
revolutionary
sabotage
separatists
Sunna
terrorism
Wahhabism
War against Terror
xenophobic
Zealots

Discussion Questions

1. Why has the War on Terror failed?
2. How can you distinguish between a radical and an extremist?
3. What are levels of analysis and how can this approach be used to explain the causes of extremism?
4. To what extent are poverty-stricken areas a prime source for terrorist recruiting?
5. Can the US be considered a terrorist state? Why? Why not?
6. How is the UN's approach to counter-terrorism different from that of the US?
7. How would you devise a counter-terrorist response to the 9/11 attacks on the US?

Suggested Readings

Katona, Peter, Michael D. Intriligator, and John P. Sullivan, eds., *Countering Terrorism and WMD: Creating a Global Counter-Terrorism Network*. London: Routledge, 2006. This book—essential reading for all serious students of terrorism and political violence, security studies, and defence and policy analysts—identifies the nature of a global counter-terrorism network, shows how such a global network might be created, and provides some guidelines for gauging its future effectiveness.

Merkl, Peter H., and Leonard Weinberg, eds. *Right-wing Extremism in the Twenty-first Century*. London: Frank Cass, 2003. The contributors scrutinize the rise of right-wing extremist groups in a number of states, including Britain, Germany, Austria, Russia, and France.

Rapoport, David, ed. *Inside Terrorist Organizations*. London: Frank Cass, 2001. This excellent collection of essays and case studies sheds light on the internal workings of terrorist organizations since the nineteenth century. Special attention is given to their conflicts, strategies, divisions of labour, rivalries between competing organizations, and strife among terrorists, sponsors, and supporters.

Global Links

Columbia University Library: Terrorism Information Sources
www.columbia.edu/cu/lweb/indiv/lehman/guides/terrorism.html
    A very useful guide to a variety of resources, some in libraries and some found on-line from a major American university library.

Terrorism Research Center
www.terrorism.com/
    The Terrorism Research Center is an independent institute dedicated to the research of terrorism, information warfare and security, critical infrastructure protection, homeland security, and other issues of low-intensity political violence and grey-area phenomena.

The International Centre for the Study of Radicalisation and Political Violence
www.icsr.info/
    This site—a partnership among institutions in the UK, the US, and the Middle East—is a good source for papers on political violence and radical extremism.

Center for Defense Information
www.cdi.org/program/document.cfm?DocumentID=3391
    This page provides a brief explanation of how statistics collected on terrorism can be flawed, or can be the result of political fashion rather than 'hard facts'.

Debate 13

Be it resolved that Hamas extremists are not terrorists but freedom fighters.

PART IV

Multi-Level Governance

Chapter Fourteen

Governing the Global Environment

Introduction

Environmental issues have become front-page news. After all, the environment has a direct and significant influence on the daily lives of people throughout the world. Regardless of where we live, changes in climate patterns, extreme weather events, loss of **biodiversity**, depletion of fish stocks, and rising sea levels affect all of us either directly or indirectly. Likewise, environmental pollution from oil spills and other industrial 'accidents' create significant loss of human life and property. Not surprisingly, given its crucial importance for our daily lives, managing the global environment has emerged as one of the more significant political issues over the past few decades. One of the reasons for this has been the increasing attention given to climatic events, especially a notable warming in the earth's surface temperatures. The more important reason is that human activity is having a profound impact on our natural environment, an impact so profound in the view of some that it calls into question the sustainability of the ecological order that supports life on the planet. As Bo Kjellen describes the current situation, humankind 'has reached a point where the increase in population and economic development has given us the power to influence the global environment in such a way that a prominent group of environmental scientists argue that we have entered an era of *Anthropocene* in which human behavior has a decisive impact on the whole earth system.'[1]

The attention given to environmental issues is a reflection of the connections that exist between environmental conditions and resource management, habitat, and health. Environmental conditions also have been linked to conflict. Responding to environmental concerns has raised profound issues of economic development and intra- and inter-generational justice. In examining the governance of environmental issues and efforts to regulate environmental practices at the national, regional, and global levels, one encounters a wide range of actors, institutions, norms, and practices found in other areas of global governance. Thus, an examination of the governance of environmental issues is not only of intrinsic importance but also illustrates the need for, the process of, and complexity involved in global governance.

Environmental Issues

Many different types of environmental issues enter onto the agenda of global politics. They reflect the fact that the environment is both local and global. The array of environmental issues that crowd onto policy agendas also reflects the diversity and complexity of these issues and the challenges they present to those attempting to design effective mechanisms to protect the environment. James Gustave Speth and Peter Haas identify 10 major global environmental challenges: **acid rain** and regional air pollution; **ozone depletion**; climate disruption; deforestation; land degradation and desertification; freshwater degradation and shortages; marine fisheries decline; toxic pollutants; loss of biological diversity; and excess nitrogen.[2] To these one could add others, such as species loss, reduction of the polar ice caps, waste disposal, and threats to sensitive ecosystems. The multiplicity of environmental threats displays no preference for any particular region of the planet, yet the effects are often most severely felt by those living in marginal conditions. These environmental threats also pose little regard for national borders. They thus force governments and concerned citizens to think beyond local and national policy-making instruments for ameliorating these threats. It is the case, however, that these environmental threats present different types of problems for governance.

One way of approaching the governance of environmental issues is to look at them as types or classes of issues, each involving a slightly different set of characteristics. The first such set of issues and the ones that raise perhaps the most profound difficulties are those described as global commons issues. **Global commons** are those places on or around the planet outside of national jurisdictions, have value for many if not all citizens, and are affected by individual actions. The global commons of most relevance for environmental practices are the oceans, space, and especially the atmosphere and climate. Polar regions also present a potentially important illustration of the global commons. The use of the term 'commons' calls to mind Garrett Hardin's seminal article of more than 40 years ago on 'The Tragedy of the Commons'.[3] In a discussion on the difficulty of controlling population growth, published in the journal *Science*, Hardin borrowed from a pamphlet written in 1833 by William Forster Lloyd. The commons, of rural and village agricultural life of a century and more ago, was the unregulated, common pasture where individuals were free to exercise their own independent choices about how the area was to be used. Because the commons is shared and open to all, however, the individual choices to maximize personal gain have implications for the entire community. Lloyd drew his example from sheep grazers using a common plot of land. Any individual's decision to increase his flock would reduce the available land for others. At the same time, there was no incentive for an individual to resist the temptation to increase his flock size since the land was accessible to all. The net result of these individual decisions would lead to the depletion of the common property resource to the detriment of the entire community, hence the **tragedy of the commons**. At the global level, concern about the commons—oceans, biodiversity, the air we breathe—has become one of the most prominent and problematic classes of environmental issues confronting the global community.

Global commons issues are exceedingly difficult for a number of reasons. Given that these resources are shared but cannot be 'owned' in any strict sense, any damage created by harmful practices has widespread effects. These effects also may be far removed both in time and distance from when and where the harmful practice takes place, and what may appear to be a local or regional issue can have far-flung ecological implications. Fish farming, for example, can have a negative local impact on wild species and water quality, but it also can have a regional impact when exotic species, such as Atlantic salmon farmed on the Pacific coast of Canada, escape and intermingle with local species. At the same time, this aquaculture has a much wider effect because the pellets used to feed the fish are made of ground fish meal from species caught and processed—and hence removed from local food webs—thousands of miles away in the global South. As a result, demonstrating the causal linkages and assigning responsibility are often difficult. It is also difficult to control the incentives that may exist for neglecting to manage the common property resource. How does one tell the South American fisher that he cannot catch fish for the pellet industry because aquaculture is polluting some inlets along the coast of British Columbia, and because the fish he catches are a necessary part of a local food web, when this is his livelihood?

In addition, the proverbial free-rider problem is particularly acute when dealing with common property assets. Among the measures that have been used to govern the global commons and thereby to mitigate potential harmful effects to the environment include such practices as regulatory measures distributing private property rights; or attempting to restrict common property rights. Below we will examine more fully measures to manage the global commons.

A second class of environmental issues exists where natural resources are shared among two or more states, as has been the case with the sharing of Pacific salmon quotas between the US and Canada, with the Great Lakes that form part of the boundary between these two countries, and with various important river systems that flow through several countries. While issues raised by shared natural resources bear some relationship to those of the global commons, the number of states involved is substantially less. In many instances, only two or three states are involved in such issues. Among the specific environmental concerns in this class are migratory species, fisheries, forests, and water. One can also make a distinction between renewable and **non-renewable resources** in this category.

The management of fresh water presents an interesting illustration of the complexities involved in environmental policy-making on transboundary externalities. The complexities are the result of the multi-layered nature of governance surrounding many freshwater issues in which local communities in different states are often in competition for limited water supplies. It also results from the multiple interests—commercial, agricultural, and recreational—involved with freshwater use. A further complication arises out of ongoing debates on the privatization of water in many parts of the world. To cope with these competing and conflicting demands, governments have responded in different ways and with varying degrees of co-operation. Canada and the United States established the International Joint Commission (IJC) in 1909 to assist the two governments in identifying mutually acceptable solutions for the joint management of the numerous freshwater sources that criss-cross the border between these two countries. Even with the IJC, however, the two governments often come into conflict over competing demands on river systems and pollution threats to the numerous lakes along the border. Other approaches have been adopted for rivers like the Danube and the Nile that pass through a number of countries.

A third class of issues involves transboundary externalities. In these situations, practices in one country have adverse environmental effects in neighbouring countries. One of the earliest examples of this that eventually led to litigation in 1928 involved pollution from what was then one of the largest lead and zinc smelters in the British Empire in Trail, British Columbia. The toxic fumes from the smelter dispersed downwind over forests and farms in the state of Washington in the United States. American farmers rose in protest that eventually involved governments on both sides of the border. The end result would not come for nearly 15 years, but an international tribunal eventually awarded compensation from the smelter to the American farmers for damages created by the smelter's emissions. The Trail smelter case was the first instance where an international tribunal adopted the principle of 'polluter pays' in determining that compensation must be paid by the corporation. It also stands as an interesting example of citizens holding corporations socially responsible for their actions. Other more recent examples of transboundary externalities include such occurrences as acid rain and the somewhat more spectacular and tragic nuclear accident at the Chernobyl reactor in Ukraine in 1986. The radioactive fallout that spread across Northern Europe and was recorded around the world resulted in the deaths of thousands and widespread acute and chronic illness.

A fourth class of environmental issues relates to those areas where environmental conditions and practices have repercussions for other areas of social, economic, or political affairs. Among the more prominent are such issues as trade, development, energy security, and even conflict. One area that has received much attention is the linkage between international trade agreements and environmental practices. Attempts to restrict trade on products that harm the environment have generally run afoul of international trade rules that seek to limit discriminatory trade restrictions. Some of the more widely cited instances involve trade in marine products such as tuna and sea turtles. In many of these cases international trade regulations have impeded efforts to address environmental concerns. One such illustration was the Canadian government's attempt to restrict trade in MMT, a gasoline additive manufactured by Ethyl Corporation, an American subsidiary operating in Manitoba. Ethyl successfully sued the Canadian government on the grounds that the ban on trade would reduce the value of Ethyl's assets and thus, under the North American Free Trade Agreement, was 'tantamount to expropriation'. Often, environmental issues are linked with these other issues in a manner that either enhances or detracts from efforts to address the underlying environmental problems.

Thus, depending on the particular environmental issues involved and the number of countries implicated, alternative mechanisms are available to promote, design, and implement sustainable environmental practices. Not all environmental problems require global responses. Some do not even require international measures of a bilateral nature. On the other hand, efforts at the regional and global level to develop multilateral environmental agreements and to create global environmental regimes with attendant norms and procedures serve as an important framework that can instigate and facilitate effective action at the national and local levels.

A Precursor to Global Governance of the Environment

Governance in the interests of sound environmental management originated, for the most part, within national societies. Local efforts to conserve and protect species and land encouraged the initiation of conservation schemes in many countries in the early twentieth century. The early conservationists, such as Ducks Unlimited in North America, became strong proponents of establishing protected areas in order to preserve both species and potentially vulnerable land. In response, some governments established national preserves and parklands to protect special and unique geographic areas from degradation or from industrial and commercial activity. Over time, however, it became clear that local efforts would never effectively mitigate problems that originated outside of a country's border. Moreover, as cross-border activity increased and as industrial activity expanded, the volume and variety of environmental threats increased dramatically. The ineffectiveness of abatement measures in the absence of co-ordinated transborder governance became more and more obvious. As a result, once environmental consciousness increased, so did the demand for more effective measures of global governance of the environment.

A sustained round of discourse and activity to address environmental issues emerged in the 1960s, spurred by Rachel Carson's landmark 1962 book, *Silent Spring*. At this time policy-makers were confronted with a combination of pressing environmental problems, widespread and growing popular concerns about environmental conditions, and some effective entrepreneurial activity that had the effect of jump-starting a round of diplomatic efforts intended to develop a regime of environmental management at the global level. Speth and Haas provide a concise summary of the environmental conditions found in the United States during the late 1960s:

> Threats were highly visible and impossible to ignore: smog, soot, and resultant smarting eyes and cough from air pollution; streams and beaches closed to fishing and swimming because of water contaminants; plastic trash and toxic chemicals that would not go away; birds threatened by DDT; pesticide poisoning; fish kills; power plants and highways in the neighborhood; marshes filled for new tract houses, and streams channelled for navigation and drainage; clear-cutting and strip-mining.[4]

As if this were not enough, perhaps foremost among the pressing environmental problems at the time was the occurrence of oil spills by tankers in the Pacific and North Atlantic; the polluted Cuyahoga River in Cleveland, Ohio, which caught fire as a result of its toxicity, symbolized for many the extent to which industry had been allowed to lay waste to the natural environment. There was also an emerging environmental consciousness raised by individuals such as Ralph Nader and US President Lyndon Johnson's wife, Lady Bird, and her 'Beautify America' campaign, and by environmental NGOs such as the Sierra Club and Greenpeace.

By the early 1970s, conditions were ripe for a political response. Public attention on environmental matters was instigated in part by the work of scientists and advocates who publicized the environmental repercussions of certain industrial, agricultural, and consumer practices.

One such advocate was Rachel Carson, whose pioneering work in the 1950s and 1960s raised public awareness of the harmful effects of pesticides on animal, plant, and human life. Carson was an American scientist interested in marine biology. She had published extensively on the ecology of the seas when her attention shifted to the extensive use of chemicals in the agricultural sector. In 1962 she published her paradigm-shifting *Silent Spring*. In this book, Carson not only challenged the chemical companies and how their products were being used, she also called for a change in perspective and for recognition that humans were intimately connected with their natural environment. The book was a manifesto for a new environmental consciousness. Not surprisingly, Carson was widely attacked by the chemical industry and others, but her research and her ideas have prevailed. *Silent Spring* remains one of the foundational works of the environmental movement. So, too, is Jacques-Yves Cousteau's book, *The Living Sea*.[5] Both books galvanized environmentalists and raised the public's consciousness about the importance of the interactions between humans and the environment.

By the late 1960s, as US astronauts went to the moon and relayed pictures of the earth from outer space, people began to realize the extent to which our planet was, in fact, a single ecosystem. Garrett Hardin's pivotal article essentially helped to set the stage for a concerted effort at the international level to address 'the collective goods dilemmas posed by many environmental issues'[6] and to negotiate practical governance mechanisms to deal with this complex transnational problem.

The Launch of Global Negotiations

One response to these events and the growing popular concern with environmental degradation was the launch of negotiations at the UN. Two sets of negotiations were influenced by environmental concerns. One was a decision to launch a third round of conferences to negotiate a comprehensive law of the sea. The decision to undertake the UN Conference on the Law of the Sea (UNCLOS III) in 1973 was initially motivated by concerns that were primarily environmental. It was soon taken over by other considerations. Indeed, many aspects of sea law had remained unresolved following extensive negotiations in the 1950s and early 1960s. Developments in the exploitation of fisheries and the potential expansion of deep seabed mining, however, raised concerns among a number of observers about the potential environmental implications for the oceans and the potential economic implications for those who rely on the resources of the oceans for their national wealth. At the same time, developing states were concerned that the continued exploitation of the rich resources of the world's oceans would benefit the wealthy countries of the world and leave landlocked and less developed regions wanting.

In response, there was an attempt to establish a new guiding principle that would inform the conference negotiations, that of the 'common heritage of humankind'. The principle was first articulated by Arvid Pardo, the Maltese representative to the UN, in a speech to that institution's General Assembly in 1967. As described by Agius, the characteristics of the principle had a distinctive intergenerational quality:

> These resources are not property, not being owned either by a sovereign state or by humanity itself, but are resources to which all present and future human beings have or will have a right of access. Every generation has obligations to humanity to conserve and transmit this heritage. The heritage should thus be managed internationally on behalf of humanity, and for the shared benefit of humanity (present and future).[7]

The principle did eventually influence negotiations, perhaps most concretely in the establishment of the International Seabed Authority (ISA). The ISA was designed to ensure that any benefits derived from the exploitation of the seabed 'would be equitably shared by all peoples taking into account the specific needs of developing countries and non-self-governing peoples.'[8] In the end, however, the Law of the Sea that was concluded in 1982 confirmed an incredible expansion of coastal state jurisdiction over the waters adjacent to their coastlines. In this case, the management of the global commons was partly resolved by transferring vast portions of the commons to states for their exclusive use.

A second initiative was to undertake another global conference under the auspices of the UN to examine environmental issues and their implications for development. The move reflected a concern among many developing states that the industrialized world's sudden concern for sound environmental practices might serve to undermine their efforts to industrialize and develop their national economies. The developing countries feared that they might be held to a more rigid set of environment protection measures that would increase their costs of production or curtail production altogether.

The Stockholm Conference, or the UN Conference on the Human Environment (UNCHE), was held in 1972 as a follow-on to the first international conference ever held on the biosphere (convened in 1968 by UNESCO). The 1972 conference marked one of the first instances where the UN had turned to a global forum as a means of addressing a collective environmental problem. The conference generated a considerable amount of interest, especially on the part of civil society: 134 non-governmental organizations made the trip to Stockholm to demonstrate their concern and voice their demands for collective action. Out of this conference came the notion of 'Spaceship Earth' and the now familiar slogan: 'Think Globally, Act Locally.' For the non-governmental groups that observed this conference, it represented at least a partial answer to their efforts at the national level to increase awareness about pollution and environmental degradation and the need to develop policies to protect the natural environment. The response on the part of states was considerably less enthusiastic, as only two political leaders (Sweden's Olaf Palme and India's Indira Gandhi) decided to attend.

For her part, Gandhi was there to caution against using the environment as a way to stifle the economic development of countries in the global South. 'Are not poverty and need the greatest polluters? How can we speak to those who live in villages and slums about keeping the oceans, rivers and the air clean when their own lives are contaminated at the source? The environment cannot be improved in conditions of poverty.'[9] As Kjellen relates, 'Gandhi...underlined...that the central problem for developing countries was not environmental deterioration but unacceptable poverty and lack of resources.' The final agreements in Stockholm, with the help of Canadian Maurice Strong, managed to bridge the divergent interests of North and South by forging a link between development and the environment, but 'the reality has haunted environmental negotiations ever since.'[10]

The Stockholm Conference did not reach any major agreements, but it did mark a turning point: the environment had moved onto the agenda of national governments and from there onto the international stage. 'Symbolically important for moving what were often parochial and national environmental concerns onto the international political agenda, the Stockholm Conference was also significant in a very practical sense for setting up the United Nations Environment Programme (UNEP), which was charged with implementing the recommendations that emerged from Stockholm and from subsequent environmental conferences.'[11] UNEP was located in Nairobi, Kenya, in large measure to illustrate to members of the Group of 77 (a collection of countries from the global South formed in the early 1960s as part of the UN Conference on Trade and Development) that environmental governance would not ignore the concerns of development and to win their support for ongoing efforts by the UN to develop an environment portfolio. UNEP has proven to be an important agency for providing and disseminating information, contributing to the development of norms, and fostering the development of a consensus in support of global environmental policies. 'The global environmental agenda thus emerged and moved forward due primarily to a relatively small, international leadership community in science, government, the United Nations, and NGOs.'[12]

The Brundtland Commission

Throughout the 1970s and into the 1980s a number of UN agencies, such as the World Meteorological Organization (WMO), the International Maritime Organization (IMO), and the Food and Agriculture Organization (FAO), developed or assumed responsibility for monitoring environmental practices in their respective fields of jurisdiction. The next major environmental governance initiative came with the UN's decision to convene a **World Commission on Environment and Development** in 1983. The Commission, under the direction of former Norwegian Prime Minister Gro Harlem Brundtland, issued its report, *Our Common Future*, four years later. This report sought to reconcile environmental management with economic growth without having to compromise the ability of future generations to meet their needs. This was the principle of **sustainable development**.[13]

Far from requiring the cessation of economic growth, this principle recognizes that 'the problems of poverty and underdevelopment cannot be solved unless we have a new era of growth in which developing countries play a large role and reap large benefits.'[14] Some have adopted a more expansive view of what 'sustainable development' means, including specific principles on: 'the duty of states to ensure sustainable use of natural resources, equity and the eradication of poverty, on common but differentiated responsibilities, on a precautionary approach to human health, natural resources and ecosystems, on public participation and access to information and justice, on good governance and the principle of integration and interrelationship, in particular in relation to human rights and social, economic and environmental objectives.'[15] For others, however, the link between environmental responsibility and economic development seems irreconcilable. 'The sustainable development model suggested by the Brundtland Report is still framed in the traditional interpretation of the relationship between the environment and economic growth. Thus (it) does not directly challenge industrialism and consumerism, nor does it seriously question their undesirable consequences for the environment.'[16]

One of the more significant contributions of *Our Common Future* has been its recommendation to create a mechanism to assist developing countries in meeting their obligations under international environmental agreements. In response, UNEP, joined by the UNDP and the World Bank, created the Global Environment Facility (GEF). The GEF is a collaborative enterprise that has transferred billions of dollars to developing countries. 'That collaboration between UN agencies that provide technical assistance and environmental management experience; governments who provide funding on a voluntary basis; the World Bank, which is responsible for investment projects and mobilizing private sector resources; and

NGOs that assist in implementing projects, has earned the GEF the reputation as an innovation in global governance.'[17] This extensive collaboration has been responsible for some of the criticisms levelled against the GEF for the unevenness of its operations, but it remains an important agent for supporting developing country involvement and compliance with international environmental governance.

Despite the debate over if and how sustainable development should be applied to environmental management, the Brundtland Report had considerable influence on policy developments. Many governments, especially those in the North, pressed for yet another global conference to address environmental issues. Southern governments, while initially reluctant, eventually agreed and the UN General Assembly recommended a global conference that 'should elaborate strategies and measures to halt and reverse the effects of environmental degradation in the context of increased national and international efforts to promote sustainable and environmentally sound development in all countries.'[18]

The Montreal Protocol

As the UN General Assembly debated another conference, governments and scientists gathered in Montreal in 1986 to address yet another pressing environmental problem—the depletion of the ozone layer in the stratosphere due to the use of chlorofluorocarbons (CFCs). In September 1987, 24 governments signed the **Montreal Protocol** to ban the use of CFCs by all states. The Montreal Protocol, which Kofi Annan referred to as 'perhaps the single most successful international agreement to date', derived its success from a number of factors. One was the clear and unambiguous scientific consensus on the problem, its source, and its effects. A study first published in 1974 was quickly confirmed and, despite claims of denial from the chemical industry, achieved popular and political credibility and legitimacy.[19] Negotiations commenced in 1982 and were facilitated and mediated by UNEP. Equally significant was the fact that leading producer states, initially the US and subsequently the EU, supported the ban. In addition, the ban was applied to all countries and was applied to producers and consumers alike. Finally, the ban on CFCs was permanent, thereby forcing industries and consumers to develop and use alternative, less harmful products. For some, the success of the Montreal Protocol stands as a model that should be replicated in other areas.

The Rio Conference

The 1992 UN Conference on Environment and Development (UNCED) in Rio de Janeiro is frequently cited as a watershed in global governance and a major achievement on the road to effective governance of the global environment. It certainly stands as a significant stage in the ongoing efforts to address **climate change**. UNCED, however, was about more than climate change; it represented an attempt to catalyze both governments and civil society around a broad base of change in how the global community would address the environment. As Speth and Haas report: 'The conference was attended by 178 nations, with 118 heads of state or government, 8,000 official delegates, nearly 1,400 NGOs represented by 3,000 accredited observers, 9,000 journalists, and approximately 15,000 to 20,000 visitors. The scale of the conference—soon dubbed the Earth Summit—was unprecedented.'[20] The conference changed the way many observers looked upon global governance. The process was far more fluid, and power seemed more dispersed than had been the case in the past. The result was a more expansive agenda and a litany of issues and proposals for the governments to tackle.

Bo Kjellen, the chief negotiator for Sweden at UNCED, described his feelings at the end of the negotiations.

> The package of Rio was agreed. Our expectations for the future were high. An agenda for the twenty-first century had been drafted, a blueprint for a sustainable world. The new conventions on Climate Change and on Biological Diversity had been signed. Coming on top of the major political changes after the end of the Cold War it seemed to us that the new millennium had already started and that the road to international co-operation on major survival issues was open.[21]

A longer-term view is considerably less optimistic, but UNCED remains a significant achievement, and its accomplishments were many. Governments agreed on a fairly comprehensive list of 27 principles, including the principle of common but differentiated responsibility and the precautionary principle. The former acknowledges that some states and societies bear a larger responsibility for cleaning the environment based on their past use. The precautionary principle acknowledges that 'Where there are threats of serious or irreversible damage, lack of full scientific certainty should not be used as a reason for postponing cost-effective measures to prevent environmental degradation.'[22] These principles provide the basis for an emerging international environmental law. In addition, the Earth Summit saw agreement on a much broader set of proposals known as Agenda 21, which encompassed social and economic development, conservation, and resource management for development, and strengthened the role of a variety of non-governmental actors and the means for implementation. The Rio conference led to a linkage of trade and environmental issues in the WTO and to the 'greening' of World Bank programs. 'It also led to the recognition that the goal of sustainable development depends not only on governments, businesses, IGOs, and NGOs, but also on ordinary people.'[23]

Finally, the meeting saw agreement on a series of conventions, among them the Conventions on Biodiversity and Desertification and the Framework Convention on Climate Change (UNFCCC). The UNFCCC became the conduit for a global response to the pressing issue of climate change.

Climate Change, Kyoto, and an Uncertain Future

Concerns about the implications of climate change are growing in number and importance. In a report released in 2007, International Alert reported, as had many others, that climate change would have its most serious effects on poorer regions of the planet. The report went on to note that unless climate change and its effects on these regions are reversed it is likely to become a source of conflict and instability.[24] In a somewhat different vein, it has been suggested that the principal security threat to small island republics in the Pacific is climate change. Rising sea levels resulting from global warming will effectively erase large sections of these countries from the planet. Nicholas Stern warned that the failure to respond to global warming and climate change will have substantial adverse consequences for the global economy as well as many national ones.[25] The President of Uganda, Yoweri Museveni, refers to climate change as 'an act of aggression by the rich against the poor'.[26] Clearly, climate change, like many of the other issues referred to here, is not just an environmental issue.

BOX 14.1

What Is Global Warming?

Carbon dioxide and other gases warm the surface of the planet naturally by trapping solar heat in the atmosphere. This is a good thing because it keeps our planet habitable. However, by burning **fossil fuels** such as coal, gas, and oil and by clearing forests we have dramatically increased the amount of carbon dioxide in the earth's atmosphere and temperatures are rising.

The evidence of global warming is overwhelming and undeniable. We're already seeing changes. Glaciers are melting, plants and animals are being forced from their habitat, and the number of severe storms and droughts is increasing.

- The number of Category 4 and 5 hurricanes has almost doubled in the last 30 years.
- Malaria has spread to higher altitudes in places like the Colombian Andes, 7,000 feet above sea level.
- The flow of ice from glaciers in Greenland has more than doubled over the past decade.
- At least 279 species of plants and animals are already responding to global warming, moving closer to the poles.

If the warming continues, we can expect catastrophic consequences.

- Deaths from global warming will double in just 25 years—to 300,000 people a year.
- Global sea levels could rise by more than 20 feet with the loss of shelf ice in Greenland and Antarctica, devastating coastal areas worldwide.
- Heat waves will be more frequent and more intense.
- Droughts and wildfires will occur more often.
- The Arctic Ocean could be ice-free in summer by 2050.
- More than a million species worldwide could be driven to extinction by 2050.

There is no doubt we can solve this problem. In fact, we have a moral obligation to do so. Small changes to your daily routine can add up to big differences in helping to stop global warming. But people need to understand the severity of the situation, which is a full-blown crisis that has already begun to occur. A recent posting in the blog of former US Vice-President Al Gore describes the irrefutable proof that the Antarctic is warming: 'Previously, there was some uncertainty with regard to the rate of warming in areas of Antarctica outside of the Antarctic Peninsula and west Antarctic. In fact, some claimed that East Antarctica—the largest part of the frozen continent—was actually cooling.' Recent reports, however, based on 'evidence from more than 100 manned and unmanned weather stations both inland and along the continent's coasts to determine climate trends for the past 50 years came to a very clear conclusion....all of Antarctica—including East Antarctica—has been warming since 1957. In addition,...the West Antarctic Ice Sheet is warming more extensively and rapidly than we thought.' As Gore concludes, 'it's clear now that all seven continents are manifesting the impact of the global climate crisis. As a result, our sense of urgency must increase yet again as we work to build the political will necessary to solve this rapidly worsening planetary emergency.'

Sources: Adapted from <www.climatecrisis.net/thescience/> and <blog.algore.com/2009/02/the_antarctic_is_warming.html>

Major growth is expected in the global population over this century. The **Inter-governmental Panel on Climate Change (IPCC)** estimated in 2001 that the global population would grow from 5.3 billion in 1990 to between 7 billion and 15 billion in 2100, and also estimated that the global economy would expand from $21 trillion to between $200 trillion and $500 trillion over the same period. Consequently, world energy demand, without a concerted international effort to mitigate climate change, was expected to increase from 351 exajoules a year to somewhere between 515 and 2,740 exajoules per year.[27] If these projections are correct, then carbon emissions could rise as high as 36.8 gigatonnes (Gt) per year by 2100 compared to the 1990 figure of 6.0 Gt per year. 'The resulting global mean temperature increase from the 1990 level would be between 1.4°C and 5.8°C or approximately between 2.5°F and 10.4°F.'[28]

The standard of living enjoyed by many in the developed world is only possible because of the consumption of huge amounts of energy. Vast improvements in technology—such as sea-bottom oil drilling from stationary platforms, extraction of oil from oil sands, more efficient long-distance transport of gas and oil through pipelines, strip-mining for coal that drastically changes topography by flattening mountains, and massive hydroelectric projects that flood many thousands of hectares of land—have made it easier for humans to exploit the scarce natural resources used to generate that energy. Now that the developing world has gained access to these same technologies, the countries in the global South are beginning to follow the lead of those in the developed world and to exploit their resources to meet energy demands.

The issues of climate change and global warming have been on the radar of the scientific community for decades. Their appearance on the policy agendas of national governments has been more recent, but at least since the 1980s the international political community has known that the time to act is now. Concern was triggered by phenomena such as more frequent and intense storms, more widespread and prolonged droughts, and more intense and deadly summer heat waves. Yet, while many took note of these climatic changes, there was little by way of consensus as to their source, scope, or long-term effect. Into this scientific uncertainty stepped the Intergovernmental Panel on Climate Change. The IPCC was created in 1988 by the World Meteorological Organization and UNEP as a means for addressing the scientific uncertainty surrounding climate change. Debates among scientists as to whether the earth's climate was cooling or warming and uncertainty over the source of a transition to more abnormal or aberrant climatic events were difficult to resolve. Given the complexity of the earth's climate and the extensive research being conducted, the IPCC was mandated to make sense of the cacophony of scientific data and report on its significance. In establishing the IPCC as an intergovernmental body, the WMO and UNEP wanted it to provide policy-relevant reports and advice that would easily feed into the governance process. While the broader issue of climate change remains embroiled in some controversy, the IPCC has gone a considerable distance in compiling a scientific consensus around the issue.

The IPCC is a scientific body: the information it provides with its reports is based on scientific evidence and reflects existing viewpoints within the scientific community. The comprehensiveness of the scientific content is achieved through contributions from experts in all regions of the world and all relevant disciplines.... Because of its intergovernmental nature, the IPCC is able to provide scientific technical and socio-economic information in a policy-relevant but policy neutral way to decision makers.[29]

One of the principal activities of the IPCC is to issue periodic reports that provide an assessment of the current state of research on climate change. To date, four such reports have been issued, each of which has highlighted a slightly different theme. The reports have informed ongoing policy debates on how to respond to these themes and the broader issue of climate change, and each report has provided additional currency to the extent and seriousness of the problem created by climate change.

Consequences of Global Warming

The greenhouse gas effect has meant that the surface temperature of the earth over the past 100 years has increased by about 0.6°C (or 1.1°F). The effects of this global warming consist of rising sea levels, bleached coral reefs, the thinning of sea ice, the retreat of glaciers, changes in precipitation patterns, lengthening and shortening of seasons, increases in pest and disease outbreaks, population changes, and changes in the cultivable ranges of certain crops. 'The connection between human energy use and climate change has become extremely difficult to deny.'[30]

Natural systems related to snow, ice, and frozen ground (including permafrost) are affected. The IPCC has observed an enlargement, and increased numbers, of glacial lakes; increases in ground instability in permafrost regions and rock avalanches in mountain regions; changes in some Arctic and Antarctic ecosystems, including those in sea-ice biomes; negative impacts on predators such as polar bears at high end of the food web. As well, increased runoff and earlier spring peak discharge occurs in many streams fed by glaciers and snow-melt, and the lakes and rivers in many regions have warmed measurably, which impacts thermal structure and water quality.

The IPCC has declared that 'warming of the climate system is unequivocal, as is now evident from observations of increases in global average air and ocean temperatures, widespread melting of snow and ice and rising global average sea level.'[31] The rise in sea level threatens the existence of several small island states (e.g., the Maldives in the Indian Ocean) and low-lying alluvial areas (such as the heavily populated delta regions around the Ganges and Brahmaputra rivers in the South Asia region of Bengal (Bangladesh and the state of West Bengal in India), where flooding has killed thousands and left over 30 million people homeless in the last decade or so.[32]

It should be noted that many of the world's largest cities, including many heavily populated ones in the developing world, are built along coastlines or near river valleys. The rise in sea levels, as well as flooding in river basins due to increased precipitation, could actually submerge many of these cities.

While global precipitation is expected to rise due to global warming, there will be significant variations across latitudes. Upper latitudes will most likely receive more rain and snow while areas in and around the tropics could experience erratic weather conditions—with increased tropical storms, cyclones, and hurricanes bringing very heavy precipitation causing severe floods, and dry seasons accompanied by major droughts. The areas expected to suffer greater droughts include the Mediterranean, Mexico, Central America, central Chile, northeastern Brazil,

Mesopotamia, South Africa, and western Australia. Unfortunately, the areas that will suffer most severely from drought due to climate change are peopled by those 'who are already poor and have few resources and little technological or social capacity to deal with such a change'.[33] Reduction in precipitation will certainly reduce the potential for energy derived from hydroelectric and biomass sources. This, in turn, could increase the dependence on fossil fuels, which would most certainly worsen the environmental conditions even further.

One would expect that the changes accompanying global warming might lead to major human migratory flows in the direction of those countries that will benefit from increased precipitation and improved agricultural production. It could also result in stiff competition for scarce resources, including water, and possible outbreaks of violent conflicts.

Global warming and deforestation certainly result in the extinction of species, which means that 'many ecosystems would suffer a devastating loss of biodiversity.'[34] At the same time, as the temperature warms, we are likely to witness an increase in the range of species, such as mosquitoes, that carry infectious diseases, and a significant growth in water-borne micro-organisms that will cause the eutrophication of ponds, lakes, and streams, thereby reducing supplies of potable water and diminishing the numbers of aquatic species that humans depend on as a food source. Added to this is the possible spread of water-borne diseases like cholera—as is occurring already in places like Zimbabwe—which could cause much suffering and death. According to WHO estimates in early 2009, the cholera outbreak in Zimbabwe 'has so far infected more than 60,000 people and killed more than 3,100 since August 2008.'[35]

There is also an indication that the recent trend in global warming is strongly affecting terrestrial biological systems, including an earlier timing of spring events such as the leafing of trees and other plants and bird migration and egg-laying, and poleward and altitudinal shifts in ranges in plant and animal species. In many regions, the trend is towards earlier 'greening' of vegetation in the spring, which is directly linked to longer thermal growing seasons due to global warming. Added to the above are major shifts in ranges and changes in algal, plankton, and fish abundance in high-latitude oceans; increases in algal and zooplankton abundance in high-latitude and high-altitude lakes; and range changes and earlier fish migrations in rivers. Some aspects of human health are affected by this global warming trend. These include: excess heat-related mortality in Europe, changes in infectious disease vectors in parts of Europe, and earlier onset of and increases in seasonal production of allergenic pollen in northern hemisphere high and mid-latitudes. Global warming is also contributing to sea-level rise, as noted earlier, which together with human development has resulted in losses of coastal wetlands and mangroves and increased damage from coastal flooding in many areas.[36]

The economic costs of preventing, mitigating, and adapting to the climate change problem could be astronomical. This is a particular concern in the midst of the current global economic downturn. But the costs of doing nothing will be even greater. 'In the absence of any serious effort to reduce net emissions of...**greenhouse gases**, the effects of climate change on ecological, social, and economic systems during the rest of the century will be dramatic—threatening, among other things, the sustainable development of today's low- and middle-income countries and their elimination of poverty.'[37] The possible negative effects on human health also have to be calculated in any costing of the impact of global warming and climate change.

Nobel Peace Prize award: Al Gore and the IPCC's Rajendra Pachauri pose on the podium in Oslo.

Former US Vice-President Al Gore won a Nobel Peace Prize in 2007 for his passionate advocacy work on global warming and climate change.[38] His popular and Academy Award-winning movie, *An Inconvenient Truth*, paints a gloomy picture of the devastating effects that climate change could have on our world if we do nothing about it today, and this is obviously a problem that governments

BOX 14.2

Definitions of Climate Change

Climate change in IPCC usage refers to a change in the state of the climate that can be identified (e.g., using statistical tests) by changes in the mean and/or the variability of its properties, and that persists for an extended period, typically decades or longer. It refers to any change in climate over time, whether due to natural variability or as a result of human activity. This usage differs from that in the United Nations Framework Convention on Climate Change (UNFCCC), where climate change refers to a change of climate attributed directly or indirectly to human activity that alters the composition of the global atmosphere and that is in addition to natural climate variability observed over comparable time periods.

Source: IPCC, Climate Change 2007 Synthesis Report, at: <www.ipcc.ch/pdf/assessment-report/ar4/syr/ar4_syr.pdf>.

acting unilaterally cannot solve. They have to solicit the assistance of international governmental and non-governmental organizations, as well as the members of their societies, if they are to get this problem under control.

The Response to Climate Change

The UNFCC came into force in March 1994 and by 2008 had 192 signatory nations, reflecting a virtual global consensus on the nature of the problem and the need to undertake measures in response. The Convention includes a number of important principles and while these may not be binding, in signing this agreement, governments are acknowledging a degree of commitment to these principles. In addition to admitting a problem and that humans are part of the problem, other principles include stabilizing emissions, undertaking national programs to slow climate change, acknowledging that greater responsibility for the problem rests with industrialized nations and the particular vulnerabilities of developing countries, and, importantly, reasserting the precautionary principle that encourages mitigation even in the absence of clear scientific evidence. The UNFCC put in motion a series of meetings of the 'supreme body' of the Convention, the Conference of the Parties (COP), which are held annually. The COP began to outline more specific programs that could and should be adopted to contain the progress of climate change.

The first significant step was taken at COP3 in Kyoto, Japan, in 1997, where 37 industrialized countries and the EU agreed to reduce greenhouse gas (GHG) emissions by an average of 5 per cent from 1990 levels by 2012. The measure was designed to bring the non-binding principles of the UNFCC into binding commitments to pursue real reductions. States were given more than a decade to make the necessary policy adjustments to achieve these targets. The protocol came into force in 2005 when over 55 states representing more than 55 per cent of total GHG emissions ratified it. More than 180 parties to the Convention have ratified this **Kyoto Protocol**. The United States and Australia stood out as not having ratified it, though Australia has subsequently changed its position and completed its ratification in 2007. The Australian decision followed a change in government, but the country also has been ravaged by drought and fires.

The Protocol followed the 'common but differentiated responsibilities' principle found in most environmental agreements, which recognizes the far greater impact that GHG emissions from industrialized countries have had and continue to have on the atmosphere. The Protocol thus attempted to address considerations of equity. In this regard, it should be mentioned that the Kyoto agreement had already provided for financial assistance, technology transfer, and special considerations as a way of easing the burden of compliance for developing countries. Equity considerations have become quite significant within negotiations on climate change. The IPCC weighed in on equity issues, noting in its 2001 report that 'The challenge of climate change mitigation from an equity perspective is to ensure that neither the impact of climate change nor that of mitigation policies exacerbates existing inequities both within and across nations.'[39]

Environmental Governance

The existing international framework of environmental governance is very diverse and fragmented. Following the 1992 Earth Summit, with the optimism of the Rio Declaration that recognized the environment as a critical global good and linked to development, the global environmental regime has proliferated. There now are a number of governance mechanisms, including treaties and protocols.

The wide array of agencies associated with various environmental issues and agreements has posed a serious challenge to effective coherence and co-ordination of the international environmental regime. While the United Nations Environment Program exists as the core internationally recognized environmental organization, it has struggled to co-ordinate and influence the diverse set of programs geared at environmental protection. The fragmentation of programs and activities reflects the diversity of issues relating to the environment, which range from curbing carbon dioxide emissions to banning the trade in endangered species. The resulting effect has been a lack of any central authority within the environmental governance regime.

Along with this governance incoherence, the multitude of environmental issues has contributed to what some have called 'negotiation fatigue' with respect to environmental issues. Just five to six years ago, there were something like 700 multilateral and over 1,000 bilateral international environmental agreements aimed at reducing the impact of humans on the environment.[40]

Frank Biermann notes the general frustration that persists regarding the state of international environmental policy. Not only does UNEP appear incapable of dealing with the plethora and complexity of the environmental issues before it, but parallel institutions focused on other issues such as economic growth are extremely powerful when juxtaposed against the meagre resources of UNEP.[41] UNEP basically lacks an effective mandate to launch negotiations on, or to take any self-initiative to address, environmental issues, and both it and its associated ECOSOC Commission on Sustainable Development are among the weakest of multilateral organizations. UNEP lacks a stable base of funding that would ensure its sustainability. Bilateral donors have been quick to develop their own separate agencies relating to environmental issues, and while UNEP's staff barely reaches 300 professionals, this is 'a trifle compared to its national counterparts such as the German Federal Environmental Agency with 1,043 employees and the US Environmental Protection Agency with a staff of 18,807.[42] Many international organizations, such as the Food and Agriculture Organization, have also initiated environmental programs outside of the aegis of UNEP. This organizational fragmentation compounds the difficulty of co-ordinating international environmental governance, along with the incoherence and fragmentation of various agreements that have been implemented without developing a clear linkage to, or understanding the repercussions they will have on, other policy areas. International agreements tend to be negotiated in isolation with neglect of the overall operational context.[43] The proliferation of organizations and issues severely hampers the ability of UNEP to manage environmental governance at the global level.

Departing from the optimism established in Rio, the international environmental governance regime has suffered serious setbacks. While the negotiation of various agreements has represented the importance of dealing with environmental issues at an international level, there has been little real action to curb activities that are exhausting the earth's natural resources and posing serious challenges to development. The current state of the environment paints a rather dismal picture but reflects the intense need for effective global governance mechanisms. In 'A New Green Regime', James Speth succinctly captures the precarious nature of the environment. Deforestation, species extinction, destruction of photosynthetic processes through human activity, declining availability of fresh water, overfishing, desertification, soil degradation, climate change, population growth and consumption, carbon dioxide emissions, and declining fossil fuels represent a snapshot of the challenges posed to the environment.[44] Compounding human-inflicted impacts on the environment are natural disasters, which have revealed the fragility of the environment as well as the vulnerability of concentrations of very poor populations that live in already ecologically fragile environments. Hurricane Mitch in Central America, Hurricane Katrina in the US, Cyclone Nargis in Myanmar, floods in Bangladesh, Fiji, and the Caribbean, Tropical Storm Ketsana in the Philippines, earthquakes in India, Iran, Pakistan, Turkey, Indonesia, and Haiti all have devastated local environments and populations in countries without the capacity to handle such disasters. Such disasters have a spillover effect in that they impact long-term economic and political issues within the affected countries.

Despite these challenges and the awareness of the fragility of the environment, unsustainable consumption continues and is spreading globally due to the conveyor belts of globalization and the capitalist imperative to secure ever-greater profits. Financial aid to address this problem, which was promised at Rio, has decreased and the transfer of environmentally sound technology to the developing world has not taken place. The WTO's TRIPS agreement 'has facilitated intellectual property rights regimes of a higher standard in developing countries, making it more costly to transfer environmentally sound technology'.[45] The TRIPS agreement and financial aid to developing countries typify the fundamental dilemma facing global environmental governance: there are divisions among countries and regions, 'often manifesting themselves as North–South divides in terms of environmental priorities and perceived responsibilities'.[46]

Environmental damage has been further compounded as a result of the globalization trend towards economic liberalization. The macroeconomic policies promoted by the World Bank and the IMF often run counter to the norms of sustainable development, have had adverse effects on the environment, and have destabilized national economies while contributing to social disruption in some cases.[47] Unstable economic and social conditions put pressure on the environment and on available resources, particularly as those who dwell in poverty struggle to make ends meet. Despite the unsustainable and consumptive lifestyles in developed countries, the developmental model being followed in much of the developing world is formulated on the patterns of developed countries. This further promotes activities and decisions in developing countries that run counter to the notion of maintaining a sustainable environment.

The outlook for global environmental governance is not that rosy. The unilateral rejection of the Kyoto Protocol by the United States frustrated international negotiations and optimism towards meeting climate change objectives. This move, along with overall negotiation fatigue, has jeopardized the needed multilateralism to sustain effective environmental governance. There is a clear lack of political will on the part of several governments to make commitments on environmental governance and it appears unlikely that the excessively consumptive lifestyles within developed countries will change any time soon. Curbing global warming requires immediate and drastic action by the world's leaders, yet their current level of commitment does not encourage optimism that such action will be forthcoming. It would appear that the bread-and-butter issues of domestic politics and, in liberal democracies, of re-election will win the day until such time—sooner than many of us might think—as the bread and butter are all gone because of environmental degradation.

Assessing Environmental Governance

What, then, are we to make of this record of global governance in the environmental arena? Hundreds of multilateral environmental agreements and thousands of bilateral ones have been reached. Yet a look around the planet reveals the persistence of global environmental problems.

> In fact, glaciers are shrinking worldwide and the melting of polar ice and large areas of permafrost in Alaska, Canada, and Siberia is accelerating. Carbon dioxide levels in the atmosphere have reached record highs and climate change will continue for possibly hundreds of years, even assuming that atmospheric concentrations stabilize. Scientists are also warning that we are in the midst of a mass extinction of species, that the world's fisheries are depleted, and that water shortages loom worldwide.[48]

There is thus an important distinction to be made between effective governance, on the one hand, and effective environmental management, on the other. While the two may overlap, this is not necessarily or always the case.

Haas has opined on the extent to which global governance in the environmental field may reflect a more general pattern of governance at the global level:

> Without the prospects of hegemonic leadership, and in light of the substantial growth of influence of international institutions and non-state actors, international rule making has become the domain of multiple overlapping actors and regimes, rather than the clear-cut leadership by one state or multilateral conformity with a small and homogeneous set of shared rules backed by enforcement mechanisms.[49]

This admittedly messier approach to global governance has raised concerns about the need for and potential benefits of a more centralized approach to environmental governance, 'an overarching centralized structure in the form of a World Environment Organization'. An institution such as this would 'avoid the current overlap,...ensure greater coherency and create economies of scale in the current system—and...produce an organization similar in stature and power to that of the World Trade Organization.'[50]

Others see certain strengths in the existing dispersal of institutions and clustering of agreements. The proliferation of environmental assessment mechanisms provides alternative mechanisms responsive to some of the pluralisms that exist both in different environmental arenas and in different parts of the world. But it also allows for synergies. As Peter and Celia Bridgewater conclude:

> Without an overarching structure or process to provide guidance, the key to establishing and maintaining coherency within the governance of sustainable development lies in the relationships between regimes, including those for the environment, trade, health, and peace and stability. The development of strong and clear complementarities will help both to create, and reflect, a balance between the economic, social and environmental pillars of sustainable development.[51]

One important aspect of global governance that has been significantly advanced by activities in the environmental arena has been the increased participation of non-governmental or civil society representatives in the process. The growth of

NGOs has been noted elsewhere in this text, as has their diversity. Over the past few decades, they have become an increasingly integral part of the global governance process, attending and participating as observers at international meetings and holding parallel NGO meetings.[52] The practice of parallel conferences has almost become an institution that mirrors the formal state-centric institutions of global governance. While discussions on the influence of these parallel summits continue, they clearly have provided an opportunity for greater levels of popular involvement in global affairs. These NGO summits also have acted as a device for catalyzing alternative viewpoints and for presenting these viewpoints in a manner that they get picked up and distributed, if not by the political leaders themselves then by the media and other civil society groups. While it would be difficult to conclude from this that global governance has been democratized, it has certainly been transformed. Whether this transformation has been constructive remains to be determined.

One issue that confronts all aspects of global governance and is evident in the environmental area is the problem of implementation. Haas argues that 'international conferences seldom have direct causal influences on member states' behavior, but their outputs are part and parcel of this broader process of multilateral governance and may contribute to stronger and more effective environmental governance by states.'[53] Yet, if global environmental governance is to have any real effect on practice, then it is important to consider how agreements can be implemented. A number of factors have been identified as assisting in the implementation of agreements. Among these are effective and timely data gathering, sharing, and monitoring, the more effective involvement of both industry and NGOs, financial support, and, in some circumstances, sanctions.[54]

On the environmental front, the experience to date suggests a number of important issues that will need to be resolved if a comprehensive and effective environmental management regime is to be adopted. Among the issues that will need to be addressed are those dealing with scientific, economic, and social uncertainty, matters of inequity including intra-generational and intergenerational justice, and the role and practices of private actors.

Conclusion

This review of global governance on environmental issues reveals the extent to which the processes and institutions of global governance have evolved. It also demonstrates the continued difficulty in developing instruments of governance that can respond rapidly and effectively to immediate global problems. Pressing environmental issues have repeatedly been forced onto the agenda of states and institutions. In response, efforts have been made to establish processes of global governance and some success has been achieved in articulating principles and in designing mechanisms that could alleviate these problems. Galvanizing relevant actors (both state and non-state) into undertaking such changes remains a significant barrier to the implementation of such measures. It is possible that reforms to procedures and institutions may overcome such obstacles. It also may be necessary to recognize the limits of global governance in the face of public and private actors able and willing to resist the necessary changes in practice to address the problem.[55]

⚽ Key Terms

acid rain	Kyoto Protocol
biodiversity	Montreal Protocol
climate change	non-renewable resources
fossil fuels	ozone depletion
global commons	sustainable development
greenhouse gases	tragedy of the commons
Intergovernmental Panel on Climate Change (IPCC)	World Commission on Environment and Development

⚽ Discussion Questions

1. Why are environmental issues considered 'intergenerational' and what makes them so prominent in today's news?
2. What are the various classes and characteristics of today's environmental issues?
3. How did Rachel Carson contribute to raising awareness of environmental issues?
4. What is the tragedy of the commons?
5. What was Arvid Pardo's contribution to our understanding of the importance of resource management?
6. What influence did the Brundtland Report have on the development of environmental governance?
7. What are the basic consequences of global warming and what can we do about this problem?
8. What has been Al Gore's contribution to the issues of climate change and global warming?
9. How has the international community responded to environmental degradation? Is this response enough?

⚽ Suggested Readings

Delmas, Magali A., and Oran R. Young, eds. *Governance for the Environment: New Perspectives.* Cambridge: Cambridge University Press, 2009. This volume begins from the assumption that confidence in the capacity of governments to meet this demand is waning and, therefore, effective policies for environmental governance have to be developed without relying exclusively on government.

Gore, Al. *Our Choice: A Plan to Solve the Climate Crisis.* New York: Rodale Books, 2009. The former US Vice President and Nobel winner lays out a comprehensive global 'blueprint' for solving the climate crisis and appeals to all of us to answer the call.

Soroos, Marvin S. *The Endangered Atmosphere: Preserving a Global Commons.* Columbia: University of South Carolina Press, 1997. With the atmosphere increasingly being used as a convenient sink for myriad pollutants, humanity faces the daunting problem of conserving a vital resource that, like the oceans, outer space, and Antarctica, defies geographical boundary. This comprehensive book examines how the atmosphere is being altered and degraded by a rapidly growing and industrializing human population and what is being done to preserve it.

Global Links

Intergovernmental Panel on Climate Change
www.ipcc.ch/
>   This site reports on the work of the IPCC, the research of which provides governments with scientifically sound information on climate issues.

International Institute for Sustainable Development
www.iisd.org/
>   A wide collection of commentaries and reports on many environmental issues.

Greenpeace
www.greenpeace.org/international/
>   Site of one of the best-known and most active international environmental NGOs.

Debate 14

Be it resolved that the 'tragedy of the commons' is nothing more than a myth.

Chapter Fifteen

Governing Global Politics in an Era of Globalization

Governance is not about structures but about practice.[1]

Introduction

While wars and conflict dominate our daily news, global politics is about much, much more. The number, variety, and scope of interactions that cross national boundaries are staggering. Moreover, the overwhelming majority of these interactions are not restricted to governments or their representatives. They involve ordinary people—students, tourists, business people, missionaries and pilgrims, immigrants, and some not so ordinary people—refugees, slaves, drug traffickers, money launderers, criminals, and terrorists. The movement of these people and their interactions are to varying degrees facilitated, monitored, and regulated by myriad norms, rules, and practices that constitute the 'institutions' of global governance. In the previous chapter we looked at the need for and the difficulties related to global governance in one issue area—the environment—as well as some of instruments developed in this area. Here, we explore the arrangements that have been devised to manage the multiplicity of cross-border transactions, their sources, and their effects.

The process by which norms, rules, and practices are made and enforced in global politics is both complex and fascinating because of the absence of clearly defined authoritative procedures and institutions. Instead, the procedures are more fluid and the institutional setting more variable than those of governance processes found within states. The process through which these norms, rules, and practices are defined takes place within multi-level governance **networks** that involve states, institutions, groups, and individuals bringing different interests and capacities and using mechanisms that are both traditional and, in many instances, innovative. As Robert Keohane and Joseph Nye Jr write:

> To understand global governance for the twenty-first century, we will have to go well beyond understanding multilateral cooperation among states. We will have to understand how agents in networks—including agents that are organizationally parts of

governments as well as those who are not – interact in the context of rapidly changing norms. Governance is likely to be fragmented and heterogeneous. Whatever else it is, it is unlikely to be based on the domestic analogy.[2]

Global governance involves, but is not limited to, the formal intergovernmental institutions that most of us are familiar with, including the United Nations, the European Union, and some of the more specialized ones such as the World Trade Organization, the International Monetary Fund, and the World Bank. Global governance is a more encompassing process that also involves civil society organizations, transgovernmental networks, multinational business and financial actors, and informal regimes and norms—all of which play a role in that process.[3]

> In addition to the multiplication of countries seeking a voice in international fora, transnational movements of civil society, NGOs, multinational corporations and even wealthy individuals are influencing the ways in which international public policy is made and implemented. Through advocacy, lobbying and direct service provision (and now global terrorism), these non-state actors are changing perceptions and behavior in fields as diverse as international health, environmental management, peace and security, human rights, and trade.[4]

Indeed, the value of thinking in terms of global governance is to recognize that most of the transactions that cross national borders are managed not by formal institutions or **codified international law**, but by informal norms, rules, and practices that manage, with varying degrees of effectiveness, the extraordinary movement of people, goods, and services criss-crossing the world.

The Evolution of Global Governance

As long as there have been borders there have been measures to manage the movement of people and things across them and to regulate the relations among the political communities they inhabit. To gain a clearer understanding of how global governance has changed over time, as well as to recognize the different forms of governance that have been employed throughout time, it is worthwhile to provide a brief historical review of some of the alternative mechanisms of governance. It is also important to note that global governance has been shaped by any number of changing considerations, but especially by considerations of power, ideas, institutional arrangements, and material interests, as detailed in Chapter 6.

Many different arrangements have been developed in an attempt to manage the cross-border relations among states and peoples. Until the nineteenth century there was a limited amount of traffic across national boundaries. At certain periods, however, more intensive interactions within selected collections of political societies have led to different forms of governance structures. At one extreme, and perhaps among one of the oldest methods of regulation, is imperialism—that ideology that underpins a type of governance in which centres of power exercise dominant control over other regions and their populations. Empires, the political entities associated with imperialism, have had a long history and have recurred in many different regions of the globe, including Europe, the Indian subcontinent, East Asia, and parts of what is now Latin America. Imperialism inevitably involves a considerable degree of centralization as the dominant power seeks to define the terms and conditions that other members of the empire must follow. Imperialism is a relationship of political control that rests on **power asymmetries**, **coercion**, and efforts to enforce a degree of **homogeneity**. The effect, however, is to impose rules governing the relations among the members of the empire and especially between them and the imperial power, but also the internal or domestic practices of these members. Imperialism can be traced back to the Greek city-state of Athens and has reappeared at different junctures throughout history.[5] At the same time, the historical record demonstrates a clear pattern of resistance and the subsequent decline of imperial states. Interest in imperialism and its implications for global governance has been revived in light of the preponderant power assumed by the United States since the end of the Cold War.

Following the Peace of Westphalia in 1648 and for many decades during the initial period of the modern states system, one of the principal mechanisms used to maintain international order was the balance of power. A balance of power was at various times actively promoted by the reigning sovereigns of Europe during the seventeenth and eighteenth centuries, albeit with varying degrees of success. The primary objective in a balance-of-power order is self-preservation, at least on the part of those in positions of power. It also seeks to prevent the emergence of a hegemonic or imperial power and thus reflects an implicit commitment to a more **pluralist** global order. Balance-of-power systems do not necessarily lead to the absence of war, as violent conflict can be used to maintain or create the balance. In terms of the process of governance, a balance of power rests heavily on diplomacy conducted by state authorities to manage relations among participating states. The balance-of-power system is largely driven by external/systemic considerations and is most conducive to a system in which independent states have little interaction across their borders. Indeed, a balance of power would necessarily need to be isolated from such influences as public opinion, economic interests, and ideological and religious values. Balance of power is an important feature in many realist accounts of global politics, including in the scholarly work of Kenneth Waltz and John Mearsheimer, and among practitioners such as Henry Kissinger.[6] For these realists, the balance of power is the most valuable means of ensuring order and, most importantly, the sovereignty of powerful states. In their view, a balance of power allows states and the citizens of these states to conduct their internal business with little interference. Such a system, however, carries with it the threat of war as a means of preserving the balance. It is also unsuited for addressing the number and variety of cross-border transactions that began to define international relations in the nineteenth century.

The Concert of Europe, which lasted from the defeat of Napoleon in 1815 to the end of the Crimean War in the mid-1850s, marked an attempt to move away from a balance of power through a series of plurilateral conferences among the great powers of the European continent in the nineteenth century. Rather than seek a tenuous balance through unilateral efforts to maintain a relative distribution of material and political power, these states used the conferences to co-ordinate their behaviour, or at the very least, to provide sufficient information that would reduce uncertainty and alleviate fears that some states might be seeking to gain power at the expense of others. The Concert stopped short of establishing formal institutions, but relied instead on a series of intermittent conferences at which states could relay their interests and concerns and seek commonly accepted remedies to address developing areas of concern. Inis Claude has called attention to the fact that the Concert was the first attempt to consider a more formal organization to govern inter-state relations. This, in turn, was the result of a number of developments that made such attempts desirable, if not necessary. These developments included the existence of independent states with 'a substantial measure of contact', 'an awareness of the problems which arise out of their coexistence', and the recognition of 'the need for (the) creation of institutional devices and systematic methods for regulating their relations with each other'.[7]

While the principal concern of the Concert was to maintain order among the great powers in the aftermath of the Napoleonic Wars, it evolved into a more extensive array of activities. It 'gave Europe for the first time since the rise of national states, something imperfectly resembling an international parliament, which undertook to deal by collective action with current problems ranging from the regulation of international traffic on the great rivers of the Continent to the adjustment of relations between **belligerent** and neutral states, and from the redivision of Balkan territories to the carving up of Africa.'[8] The Concert was something more than a great power directorate, but it was still very much under the control of these great powers and when they began to fall out with one another, so did the governance structures they had devised. The Concert was unable to withstand a number of pressures that developed during the mid-nineteenth century and states began to revert to alternative means to serve their interests. In a concluding comment on the Concert, Inis Claude has written: 'When all is said and done, the political conference system contributed more to awareness of the problems of international collaboration than to their solution and more to opening up the possibilities of multilateral diplomacy than to realizing them.'[9]

Two structural deficiencies of the Concert needed to be remedied as the nineteenth century gave way to the twentieth. The first was its **Eurocentrism** and the second was its **statism**. The Concert made little effort to look beyond the European continent to include the emerging powers of the Americas and Asia, and also provided little opportunity for private commercial interests and civil society organizations to participate in this governance process. The first deficiency was bridged at The Hague conferences in 1899 and 1907, where governance structures and processes took on a more global flavour that they retained through much of the twentieth century. The second deficiency was addressed by civil society interests themselves as they began to promote their own concerns and pursue their own methods in an effort to shape global politics. As Craig Murphy recounts, civil society organizations emerged in the mid- to late nineteenth century and began to establish a presence in the arena of global governance.[10]

Many of these groups emerged out of domestic contexts, but in their efforts to address global issues they moved onto a broader stage. One of the first efforts to meet with some success in this area was the **anti-slavery movement**. Financial and corporate interests were even more successful in their efforts at governance on the global stage. Considerable evidence from the later decades of the nineteenth century indicates an expanded set of associations, norms, regulations, and institutions that emerged to facilitate the cross-border movement of goods and capital. While states played a role in this expansion, they were by no means alone, as private interests in the form of both associations and individuals took an active role in the process. The effect of these arrangements was a rather dramatic increase in the volume and scope of international transactions.

As Murphy notes, the conferences brought into practice by the Concert of Europe encouraged the expansion of international activity on the part of individuals and groups.

> By getting European governments into the habit of meeting together, the conference system contributed to the further institutionalization of world politics. Ironically, it could have this effect because it was so imperfectly institutionalized itself. It was never clear who had the right to call such meetings, what topics could be broached, or which dignitaries and officials from invited states should attend. Yet the trend was always toward increasing the scope of the conference system along each of these three dimensions.[11]

The effect of these arrangements was a rather dramatic increase in the volume and scope of transnational efforts on the part of many different segments of states and societies to shape the development of global order.

During the twentieth century, much of the effort turned to the creation of formal international organizations that have become increasingly active on the world stage. These organizations continue to stand as the manifest representation of the system of governance that regulates interactions around the globe. The efforts began as early as the 1860s with the establishment of the International Public Unions to regulate such areas as telecommunications and postal service. As Murphy relates, more than two dozen organizations were established between the 1860s and the start of World War I in 1914. In response to the **Industrial Revolution**, these organizations addressed transnational issues that had become increasingly vital to national, regional, and global economic activity. While peace may have been the primary motive for many in creating these international organizations, the vast majority of them were created to serve economic and social needs. In his review of international organizations, Murphy identifies their principal tasks as fostering industry and managing social conflicts. He also suggests two secondary tasks for these organizations—strengthening states and the state system and strengthening society.[12] Murphy links the creation of international organizations to changes in the international political economy commencing in the late eighteenth century. These changes helped to create international markets in industrial goods by linking communications and transportation infrastructure, protecting **intellectual property**, and reducing legal and economic barriers to trade.

A more sustained attack on the balance-of-power approach and an initial effort to establish a multi-purpose universal organization developed in the wake of World War I. Led by Woodrow Wilson, the challengers sought to supplant the balance-of-power and concert system with a structure of norms and a body of public international law, supported by institutions, principally the League of Nations. Rather than relying on a balance of power, Wilson's 14th point proposed that 'A general association of nations must be found by treaties, which would mutually guarantee our political independence and territorial integrity of all states.'[13] The League was an attempt to expand upon ideas and practices that had been initiated by the Concert of Europe and reasserted in The Hague conferences of 1899 and 1907.

The establishment of a permanent organization whose primary objective was to preserve the peace marked a significant departure from the more ad hoc arrangements of the past. The League adopted a decidedly legalistic approach to conflict resolution favouring such techniques as inquiry, mediation, and arbitration, including the use of the Permanent Court of International Justice, which came into force in 1921. The League also promoted formal treaty-making through more traditional diplomatic methods. It should be noted that the League never abandoned the state system or sought to replace it with an alternative. The League's 'founders approved the basic principles of the traditional multistate system; they accepted the independent sovereign state as the basic entity, the great powers as the predominant participants, and Europe as the central core of the world political system.'[14] The League was designed to assist states in restraining themselves from reverting to armed conflict without considering other alternatives. It also provided an institutional framework in which states were able to pursue other interests and objectives such as disarmament, economic expansion, and more specialized activities in such areas as health and refugees.

A commission under the direction of former Australian Prime Minister Stanley Bruce recommended that the League play a co-ordinating role in various areas of economic activity, a recommendation that foreshadowed the UN's Economic and Social Council. This recommendation also recognized the potential in fostering transgovernmental networks of government officials responsible for specialized areas of activity. Some of these efforts were absolute failures, but others met with greater degrees of success. As with all League activities, they tended to be dominated by states' representatives, but as the Bruce Report suggests, there was a value in disaggregating the state and enabling international agencies to pursue co-operation in functional areas.

One of the foremost problems that confronted the League was the deterioration in global politics created by World War I. In the midst of economic problems, resurgent nationalism, and ongoing political conflicts, states fell back on their own national interests rather than considering the interests of any wider global community. Such unilateral actions in economic and security affairs undermined the principles on which supporters of the League had placed their hope. As the South African statesman Jan Christiaan Smuts, one of the most ardent supporters of the League, wrote at the time:

> It is not sufficient for the League merely to be a sort of *deus ex machina*, called in very grave emergencies when the spectre of war appears; if it is to last, it must be much more. It must become part and parcel of the common international life of states, it must be an ever visible living, working organ of the polity of civilization. It must function so strongly in the ordinary intercourse of States that it becomes irresistible in their disputes, its peace activity must be the foundation and guarantee of its war power.[15]

The League of Nations never obtained these ideal conditions and fell into disuse as states opted for more unilateral measures. The League did, however, foster a number of institutional efforts that not only survived, but prospered as the years went by. It also encouraged a more global outlook for many non-governmental organizations that were looking beyond their national governments to gain recognition and support for their causes.[16]

The most extensive period of global institutionalization occurred during and immediately after World War II. Led in large measure by the United Kingdom and the United States, with the tacit approval of the Soviet Union and with significant support from other governments such as Canada and Australia, substantial additions were made to the institutional framework of an embryonic global governance, principally in the form of the United Nations, its specialized agencies, and the Bretton Woods institutions of the IBRD, the IMF, and the GATT. These were subsequently complemented by important regional institutions such as the EU, the Organization of American States (OAS), and the Organization of African Unity (OAU) and a considerably expanded set of codified international laws.

The vast range of activities that have engaged international organizations is illustrated in the UN and its network of specialized agencies. As we saw in Chapter 7, the UN is a **multi-purpose organization** involved in a number of areas such as economic development (UN Development Programme), health (World Health Organization), communications (International Telecommunications Union), social concerns such as refugees (UN High Commissioner for Refugees), women (UN Development Fund for Women), environment (UN Environment Programme), drugs and crime (UN Office on Drugs and Crime), and children (UN Children's Fund). The UN retains its support for state sovereignty as exemplified in its membership and its resistance (until recently) to intervention. It has been the principal forum in which newly independent states seek recognition and confirmation of their independence and sovereignty. At the same time, it has been pursued by human rights advocates as the organization through which the rights of individuals against the state are to be advanced and ultimately protected and by civil society organizations to gain their own recognition and opportunities for participation in the process of global governance. The structure of the UN recognizes the asymmetrical distribution of power among states through its Security Council, but also pays lip service to democracy in allowing each state equal standing in the General Assembly.

The UN also recognizes the importance of **regional arrangements** and agencies. Chapter VIII of the Charter states that these can be used to address issues related to peace and security, as long as the arrangements and/or agencies and activities are consistent with the purposes and principles of the UN. At a time when the UN system seems overburdened and overstretched, this part of the Charter is becoming increasingly noticed. Furthermore, there seems to be a trend towards using existing regional mechanisms (or creating new ones, such as the Trans-Pacific Partnership or TPP) to deal with some of the transnational issues facing the global community (see Box 15.1). In fact, some scholars believe that regional arrangements may be one way in which states try to respond to the onslaught of globalization.[17] Viewed from this vantage point, regionalism might be not only a reaction against globalization but a force for enhancing global governance over the long run.[18]

The most established set of regional organizations can be found in Europe. Most students will be familiar with the European Union and its institutions (the European Commission, the European Parliament, the Council of Ministers, the European Council, the European Court of Justice, the European Central Bank, and the Court of Auditors). The European regional bodies are the by-products of a long history of attempts at regional integration on a continent known in the past for some of the most brutal wars in human history. European regionalism, especially since 1945, has resulted in gradual integration, with the establishment of a European Parliament in 1979, the formal founding of the EU in 1993, and the creation of a European currency (the euro) in 2002. The EU began with six members (Belgium, France, West Germany, Italy, Luxembourg, and the Netherlands),

BOX 15.1

The Trans-Pacific Partnership

The Trans-Pacific Economic Partnership (TPP) was known as the P4 agreement, until November 2009 when the United States decided to join in this strategic economic partnership. TPP is a multilateral free trade agreement that was initially between four countries—Brunei, Chile, New Zealand, and Singapore. It was signed on 3 June 2005 and came into force on 28 May 2006. The US began negotiations with the four countries in September 2008 with the intention of entering into this partnership. But there were concerns among the group of countries that with the election of President Barack Obama, the US might turn its back on the TPP, since members of the Democratic Party were generally considered to be less friendly towards free trade arrangements than their Republican counterparts. Although the scheduled negotiations were delayed after Obama became President, on 14 November 2009 the President announced at an APEC Summit that the US will join the TPP. With the US joining, it is expected that Vietnam, Australia, and Peru also will join, thus turning this arrangement into an eight-country partnership. This bodes well for trans-regional economic co-operation among APEC countries.

as the European Coal and Steel Community (ECSC), with the signing of the Treaty of Paris in 1951. But the organization grew over the years, and with the signing of the Maastricht Treaty in 1992 it became a truly supranational institution. The EU has now expanded to 27 members and has become an important political and economic actor that sometimes rivals the United States with its unified foreign and security policy. Unlike the UN General Assembly, whose member states are appointed national representatives, the EU Parliament consists of individuals. The EU itself is a system of multi-level governance, for within it is a plurality of actors from the supranational, to the national, to the sub-state levels.

Regional organizations also operate in the Americas. Examples include the OAS, NAFTA, the Central American Integration System (SICA), the Central American Common Market (CACM), the Caribbean Community (CARICOM), the Andean Community (CAN), the Common Market of the South (MERCOSUR), the South American Community of Nations (SACN), and the Latin American Integration Association (LAIA). Much of this regionalism has been in response to the presence of the United States—the hegemon in the region as well as the global hegemon. The Americans were the ones to push for the first Pan-American conference in 1889–90, which resulted in the establishment of the Pan-American Union that later, in 1948, became the OAS. During the Cold War, the OAS was largely viewed as an instrument of US foreign policy, and this did not sit well with many of the states in Latin America and the Caribbean. After extensive negotiations that first involved only the US and Mexico, since the US and Canada had earlier signed a free trade agreement that came into effect in 1989, NAFTA was signed in 1992 by US President George H.W. Bush, Canadian Prime Minister Brian Mulroney, and Mexican President Carlos Salinas de Gortari, and came into effect in 1994. The 1990s saw a wave of regionalism in the western hemisphere. Part of this related to an idea to create an omnibus free trade arrangement.

The Free Trade Area of the Americas (FTAA), if it became a reality, would have extended NAFTA to 31 other nations in the hemisphere.[19] The proposed arrangement would have been the most far-reaching trade agreement the world has ever seen. However, disagreements between Brazil and the United States and some concerns expressed by labour groups in many of the 34 countries have meant that the FTAA has been put on the back burner for the time being.

On the continent of Africa, most students will be familiar with the African Union (AU)—formerly the Organization of African Unity (OAU). But a plethora of other sub-regional organizations operate on that continent, including the Arab Maghreb Union (UMA), the Community of Sahel-Saharan States (CEN-SAD), the Economic Community of West African States (ECOWAS), the West African Economic and Monetary Union (WAEMU), the Central African Monetary and Economic Community (CEMAC), the Economic Community of the Great Lakes Countries (ECPGL), the Economic Community of Central African States (ECCAS), the East Africa Community (EAC), the Common Market for Eastern and Southern Africa (COMESA), the Intergovernmental Authority for Development (IGAD), the Southern African Customs Union (SACU), and the Southern African Development Community (SADC). Many of these organizations, although strapped for cash and resources, are trying to respond to problems of insecurity, poverty, undemocratic practices, and corruption across the African continent. Some have been more successful than others. But it is clear that African regionalism provides a potential governance framework for addressing African problems, as opposed to having actors from outside the region insert themselves as they have done since the colonial era.

Regionalism in Asia began with the formation of a US-backed collective defence organization, the South East Asian Treaty Organization (SEATO), which was established in 1954. It was essentially a trans-regional product of the Cold War—an attempt by the US to block further Communist expansion in Southeast Asia. Thus, its members included France, the United States, the United Kingdom, Australia, New Zealand, Thailand, the Philippines, and Pakistan. But when SEATO failed to live up to American expectations, it dissolved in 1977 not long after the Vietnam War ended. The Association of South East Asian Nations (ASEAN) was established in 1967 in Bangkok. The original five members were Indonesia, Malaysia, the Philippines, Singapore, and Thailand. Brunei Darussalam joined in 1984, Vietnam in 1995, Lao PDR and Myanmar in 1997, and Cambodia in 1999. This organization has two important goals: (1) to accelerate economic growth, social progress, and cultural development in the region; and (2) to promote regional peace and stability through abiding respect for justice and the rule of law in the relationship among countries in the region and adherence to the principles of the United Nations Charter. In 2003, the ASEAN members decided to create an ASEAN Security Community, an ASEAN Economic Community, and an ASEAN Socio-Cultural Community by 2020. In this sense, ASEAN is moving in the supranational direction of the EU.

A competing institution in this region is APEC—Asia-Pacific Economic Co-operation. APEC is really a trans-regional arrangement that consists of 21 member states with a geographic presence on the Pacific Rim: Australia; Brunei Darussalam; Canada; Chile; People's Republic of China; Hong Kong, China; Indonesia; Japan; Republic of Korea; Malaysia; Mexico; New Zealand; Papua New Guinea; Peru; the Philippines; the Russian Federation; Singapore; Chinese Taipei; Thailand; the US; and Vietnam. The primary purpose of this body is to further enhance economic growth and prosperity for the region and to strengthen the Asia-Pacific community. But it is clear that a not so hidden reason for establishing APEC was to ensure that the countries involved would adhere to open market principles.[20]

In Eurasia, we have witnessed attempts at regionalization among the former states of the Soviet Union. The most important regional body in this area is the Commonwealth of Independent States (CIS), created in 1991 at the end of the Cold War. This body included all members of the former USSR with the exception of the three Baltic states. Georgia initially joined the CIS but withdrew. In 1995 a CIS customs union was formed among Russia, Belarus, and Kazakhstan. This was followed by the establishment of a Collective Security Treaty in 1992, which by 2002 was transformed into the Collective Security Treaty Organization (CSTO). The members of that latter body are Russia, Belarus, Armenia, Kazakhstan, and Tajikistan. In 2006, Uzbekistan was enticed to join this security **treaty** organization. Some former members of the CIS, like Georgia, have complained that Russia is trying to create a new 'Cold War' with the establishment of CSTO. With the dismantling of the Warsaw Pact at the end of the Cold War, Russia has been trying to find a way to re-establish the equivalent to that security pact in order to counter the enlargement of NATO. CSTO has even adopted a logo that looks very similar to that of NATO. In addition, it has a clause in its charter that resembles Article 5 of the NATO Charter, which states that aggression against one signatory would be perceived as an aggression against all.

From the above, it is clear that the UN has not always been able to address the concerns of its member states. In fact, the founders of the UN understood that the burden of governance at the global level could become too great for the organization. With its large and expanding mandate, the UN system could use the assistance of other institutions that are willing to abide by the UN Charter and its principles. In fact, the explosion of regionalism and the creation of regional bodies could be a blessing to the universal global governance institution. In addition to various regional organizations, there have been attempts to construct alternative institutional frameworks to meet diverse sets of interests, such as **coalitions of the willing** and smaller more exclusive groupings of states around specific issues such as the G20 finance ministers, established in 1999 and, more recently, the G2 consisting of China and the United States. In some cases these could be seen as alternatives of a complementary sort, but they also could be seen as alternatives that would challenge the legitimacy and credibility of the UN.

If the contemporary global agenda seems crowded by the number and scope of activities that occur in so many different sectors, the response in governance terms is equally staggering. While the total number of governance mechanisms is seemingly countless, the variety is clearly evident. At the inter-state level alone, there are numerous formal groupings: G2, G3, G8, G20, G21, G25, G77, G90. In addition are the seemingly ubiquitous 'coalitions of the willing'. Andrew Cooper has made an important distinction between the various forms of coalitions that have emerged in the governance arena, distinguishing those that grow from the bottom up and those that are led from the top down.[21] In either case, multilateralism has become a necessity in a globalizing world (Box 15.2).

This brief history demonstrates the evolution of governance mechanisms at the international level and suggests some of the alternative patterns that have defined this governance process over time. Not only does it suggest considerable variety, but it also reinforces the idea that global politics is not a fixed phenomenon but is subject to considerable change and variation across time and space. The particular form of governance reflects a number of considerations.

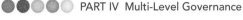

BOX 15.2

Multilateralism

Multilateralism has begun to receive much attention in the literature on international politics and foreign policy. Multilateralism calls attention to the foreign policy activity of states. As compared with unilateral or bilateral strategies, **multilateralism** refers both to the practice of multilateral diplomacy and to policies supporting the establishment and maintenance of institutions and associations that facilitate and support the practice of multilateral diplomacy. Multilateral diplomacy involves working with coalitions of states, primarily but not exclusively within formal associations or institutions, to achieve foreign policy objectives. It also implies a willingness to maintain solidarity with these coalitions and to maintain support for these institutions. In practice, it often involves greater attention to the process by which decisions are made than to the more substantive elements of those decisions. Support for multilateral diplomacy also necessitates encouraging others to follow the same procedures.

John Ruggie has written that multilateralism should be viewed as having some substantial content as well as being merely a process. A commitment to multilateralism involves more than a procedural strategy for conducting one's foreign policy. It suggests a subjective approach and a conscious commitment to the process and substance of the associations—more specifically, a conscious interest in the substantive content of the international order that is supported by multilateral activity along with a commitment to abide by the rules set by these multilateral associations. Multilateralism, in this sense, shares certain characteristics with how international regimes have been described in the literature. Support for regimes, analysts note, derives from their ability to reduce the costs and risks to governments from co-operation. International regimes also provide a greater degree of predictability for governments because they make it easier to anticipate the response of other governments involved in the same regime. These views of multilateralism emphasize the role of states in the process of co-operation and tend to perceive international co-operation primarily as a top-down process, one organized and implemented by states in service to interests that have been defined by the states involved.

In contrast to this, some analysts have argued that for both empirical and normative reasons, multilateralism needs to be examined from the bottom up. This argument stems from the increased prevalence and participation of non-governmental organizations (NGOs) in global politics. This 'new multilateralism', as it has been described, takes a different view from that of realist, liberal, or constructivist views of multilateralism. In these more traditional approaches, the state plays a central role. In contrast, the bottom-up element embodies the reconstitution of civil society, and is most manifest in the rise of new social movements and other civil society actors who seek to participate more directly in international institutions and other forms of multilateral governance.

Source: Adapted from Tom Keating, *Canada and World Order: The Multilateralist Tradition in Canadian Foreign Policy* (Toronto: Oxford University Press, 2002), 4–6.

Craig Murphy and John Ruggie, among others, have noted the importance of power and material interests in addition to ideas, social purpose, and normative considerations in understanding the origins and operations of the institutions of global governance.[22] Formal international institutions, such as the UN, have generally recognized, legitimized, and to a degree empowered the state and national governments as significant actors in the work of global governance. In turn, these institutional structures reflect a commitment on the part of governments to a more regulated international order designed through a governance process of multilateral diplomacy. Many institutions, and especially the UN, were also designed to recognize the existence of competing substantive views of world order and sought to accommodate or tolerate these competing views within this governance framework.

Finally, there appears to have been a fairly clear recognition of the limitations of these institutions, and of the necessity for active state involvement in this process. Clearly, many of these institutions were established under a set of ideas that enshrined state sovereignty while recognizing the material benefits that would be derived from co-operation in selected arenas. Ultimate authority has remained with member governments, which are in a position to determine the overall effectiveness of the institutions themselves. It would be a gross misunderstanding, however, to conclude that global governance has been driven exclusively by states and their formal **agents**. Moreover, the normative framework in which these institutions were established has been altered in recent years, as has the state's ability to control fully the material benefits that can be derived from global activity. As a result, global governance now encompasses a much wider variety of non-state actors operating in many different forums than has been the case in the past.

One of the most noteworthy features of the late twentieth and early twenty-first centuries has been the proliferation of NGOs in the structures and processes of global governance. As we have noted earlier, these organizations have played some role in global governance for well over a century, especially since the late nineteenth century. NGOs could be identified in the establishment of the international public unions (IPUs) during the late nineteenth century and in the corridors at The Hague conferences at the turn of the century. Such groups were instrumental in pushing for the Geneva Conventions in the 1860s as well as for various labour conventions during the early twentieth century. Though granted no formal role in the League of Nations, NGOs were actively involved on the sidelines. They sought and received a more permanent role in the activities of the UN, and under Article 71 of the UN Charter were granted consultative status with ECOSOC. The involvement of NGOs in global governance was, of course, hardly limited to the UN system and other formal institutions, as they have regularly formed transnational coalitions and worked with, through, and around national governments. There are numerous instances in which these groups have forged transnational coalitions to promote particular interests or to prevent other interests from gaining support. Yet, despite all of this activity, only in the last few decades have NGOs really come into prominence.

The proliferation and expanding influence of NGOs can be attributed to many factors. One widely noted factor has been the technological developments in transportation and communications that facilitate the growth of transnational contacts among NGOs and their participation in meetings around the globe. Jessica Matthews has noted the influence of these changes in communications technology:

> The most powerful engine of change in the relative decline of states and the rise of non-state actors is the computer and telecommunications revolution, whose deep political and social consequences have been almost completely ignored. Widely accessible and affordable technology has broken governments' monopoly on the collection

and management of large amounts of information and deprived governments of the deference they enjoyed because of it. In every sphere of activity, instantaneous access to information and the ability to put it to use multiplies the number of players who matter and reduces the number who command great authority.[23]

Another related factor has been the process of globalization itself, which has done much to change the agenda of global politics by adding issues that impact more directly on the daily lives of individuals. Globalization has led to the distribution not only of goods and services and financial capital, but also to the dissemination of values, ideas, and practices. As a result, NGOs can emulate and learn from activities taking place in far corners of the globe.

The end of the Cold War and the spread of democratic ideas and practices also have opened considerable space for NGOs to participate at the national, regional, and global levels. Many governments and organizations have become increasingly receptive to the participation of NGOs in deliberations on policy issues. The UN probably deserves special mention here since, through a series of global conferences during the 1990s, '[r]epresentatives of NGOs and the business world were invited to attend and make inputs to UN Conferences, such as the 1992 Earth Summit in Rio, the 1995 World Summit on Social Development, and the WSSD in Johannesburg in 2002.'[24] NGOs were afforded repeated opportunities to gain experience and recognition. In part, as a result of this increased exposure, NGOs have become an important constituency for national governments and for many international organizations, including the UN. Finally, as Rosenau has pointed out, we must recognize the increased competencies of individuals and groups who increasingly have the knowledge, skills, and access to take on an active role in the process of global governance.[25]

The Expanding Agenda of Global Governance

As we have witnessed historically and continue to experience today, governance at the global level is most often a response to pressures emanating from the cross-border activities that proliferate around the globe. Not surprisingly, as activities have increased in support of and in response to globalization, so, too, has global governance.

> International organizations are still coming to terms with unprecedented growth in the volume of international problem-solving. Between 1972 and 1992 the number of environmental treaties rocketed from a few dozen to more than 900. While collaboration in other fields is not growing at quite that rate, treaties, regimes, and intergovernmental institutions dealing with human rights, trade, narcotics, corruption, crime, refugees, antiterrorism measures, arms control, and democracy are multiplying. '**Soft law**' in the form of guidelines, recommended practices, nonbinding resolutions, and the like is also rapidly expanding. Behind each new agreement are scientists and lawyers who worked on it, diplomats who negotiated it, and NGOs that back it, most of them committed for the long haul. The new constituency also includes a burgeoning, influential class of international civil servants responsible for implementing, monitoring, and enforcing this enormous new body of law.[26]

These civil servants have themselves become important players in the process of global governance.[27]

In addition, we should not forget the emergence of celebrities who have become important players on the global political stage. Individuals like the popular musicians Bob Geldof, Bono, and Sting, the super-rich entrepreneur Bill Gates, the actress Angelina Jolie, and the former Brazilian soccer star Pelé all are involved in specific global causes either on their own or on behalf of international institutions. These celebrities are changing the way in which diplomacy has traditionally been done, and they are calling attention to such transnational issues as the spread of HIV/AIDS, the enduring problems of poverty and malnutrition in Africa, abandoned children, and child soldiers.[28] These are issues that states are having problems addressing on their own.

The ever-expanding agenda of global governance has generated a number of important concerns about the legitimacy, capacity, and efficacy of the governance process and of individual institutions involved in this process. Besides the sheer volume of global activity, regulatory efforts undertaken by global actors to override or supplant the authority of national governments have increased in order to bring governments into compliance with accepted or emerging global norms. Beginning in the 1990s, the UN, along with a number of regional organizations including the EU, the OAS, the African Union, the Organization for Security and Co-operation in Europe (OSCE), and NATO, set aside considerations of sovereignty and non-interference and intervened directly in the domestic affairs of a number of states involved in domestic conflicts or serious violations of human rights. These interventions represent a change in practice, if not in principle, for many of these institutions. The change has been fostered by a number of factors, including:

- the increased prevalence and significance of intra-state conflicts;
- pressing demands from victims and observers alike for some measure of relief for the civilians who have been caught up in these conflicts;
- a changed normative environment surrounding these organizations that places greater emphasis on the rights and protection of individuals than on sovereign states;
- some institutionally driven pressures as these institutions have sought to make themselves more relevant in an evolving international security framework.

A good example of this can be found in the report of the UN Secretary-General's High Level Panel (HLP) on threats, challenges, and change, *A More Secure World: Our Shared Responsibility*, released in December 2004. This report envisions an empowered UN assuming greater responsibilities for protecting individuals who are in harm's way. The Panel draws from the International Commission on Intervention and State Sovereignty (ICISS), established by the Canadian government in 2000, and its December 2001 report, *Responsibility to Protect*. The High Level Panel recommends a recasting of sovereignty and of the role of the UN in ensuring that states meet their responsibilities to protect and serve their citizens. The HLP report goes on to state that 'Governments have the primary responsibility to protect their own citizens from such catastrophes, [but] when they are unable or unwilling to do so that responsibility should be taken up by the wider international community—with it spanning a continuum involving prevention, response to violence, if necessary, and rebuilding shattered societies.'[29] In advocating for greater and more assertive involvement on the part of the international community, the HLP report acknowledges both the increased demands placed on international organizations in recent years and their limited capacity to respond effectively to these demands. It also speaks to the multiplicity and complexity of the tasks confronting the organizations that assume this responsibility.

It should be noted that the leaders and representatives of 191 countries voted unanimously to adopt a version of the ICISS proposal for the Responsibility to Protect (R2P) norm as part of an omnibus package in an 'Outcome Document' of the World Summit at the UN in 2005 (Box 15.3). Unfortunately, since that time, there has been 'buyers' remorse', especially from some members of the Non-Aligned Movement (NAM) and among some major countries such as China and Russia. This backsliding prompted Michael Ignatieff, one of the members of the ICISS, to lament that while the 'demand for humanitarian intervention is high,...the supply has dried up.'[30]

The expanded mandates, discussed above, impose a considerable responsibility on institutions to provide for the well-being of local citizens, with all that this entails. As Philippe Sands reports, these more intrusive rules also caught the attention of many individuals and groups outside of government: 'At some point in the 1990s these arcane rules moved out of the corridors of foreign ministries and into the boardrooms of businesses, the lobbying newsletters of non-governmental organizations, and the front pages of our newspapers. International law went public. The monopoly which states held over the rules began to crumble.'[31] The recent history of peace-building activities undertaken by the UN and other agencies provides a good illustration of the complexity of the tasks undertaken by these organizations. It also reflects how intimately involved these institutions have become with local populations.[32] Most importantly, when one considers how such actions have been undertaken, it demonstrates how dramatically global governance has changed.

BOX 15.3

The 2005 World Summit

From 14 to 16 September 2005, the Heads of State and Government of the countries that make up the United Nations came together for a High Level Plenary meeting of the UN General Assembly in New York. The significance of this meeting is that it fell on the sixtieth anniversary of the UN. Then UN Secretary-General Kofi Annan considered this World Summit to be a 'once-in-a-generation opportunity' for UN member governments to assemble and take action on some of the 'grave global threats that require bold global solutions'. He also felt that this meeting offered the chance for the UN to undergo an important and necessary revitalization. Out of the World Summit came some significant proposals and resolutions. Most important among them was the Outcome Document adopted by the UN General Assembly as resolution 60/1 on 24 October 2005, which included, among other things, the acceptance by the world body of the Responsibility to Protect (R2P) norm.

Source: For further details, see <daccess-dds-ny.un.org/doc/UNDOC/GEN/N05/487/60/PDF/N0548760.pdf?OpenElement>. (15 Nov. 2009)

For example, the UN has consulted with various humanitarian NGOs to determine the nature of crises and to receive expert information on the type of responses required. In the field, operations are no longer simply government affairs, as NGOs have taken on increased responsibility for the delivery of (broadly conceived) security. Many NGOs in the humanitarian field have budgets in excess of those of some national governments. The UN itself has sought to work in strategic external partnership with both NGOs and private interests (including transnational corporations), most notably through Kofi Annan's Global Compact, to respond in a 'multi-stakeholder' manner to some of the negative consequences of global capitalism.[33]

The mandates of international economic organizations are even more noteworthy for their contributions to global governance, for the extent to which they intervene in the domestic affairs of sovereign states, and for their direct impact on people's lives. For many years the activities of the institutions of the Bretton Woods System—the GATT, the IMF, and the World Bank—held little interest for citizens of most countries. Today that is clearly not the case. As was evident in Seattle in 1999, and noted in Chapter 10, a WTO meeting can bring hundreds of thousands of demonstrators onto the streets. The WTO, along with the World Bank and the IMF, plays a major role in the daily lives of countless citizens throughout the world. Increasingly, the Bretton Woods institutions have redefined their mandates to address matters of social policy and governance issues. These areas traditionally fell within the exclusive purview of national authorities, but no longer is this true. The sanctions of international agencies often trump domestic policy choices and render citizens much more responsive to the international institution than to the local authority. The WTO, for its part, has been involved in ruling certain domestic legislation illegal on the grounds that it interferes with free trade, thus challenging national sovereignty while raising the ire of environmentalists, economic nationalists, and other concerned citizen groups.

As one looks to other policy areas, similar instances can be found: more international institutions undertaking more intrusive activity that brings them into direct contact with local citizens. From human rights monitoring to the World Health Organization's authority to verify disease outbreaks, national authorities must increasingly share the policy turf with international institutions. For some observers, this continues a growing tendency within many quarters to challenge the legitimacy and capacity of states.

> Indeed, in the 1980s and in the early 1990s, scholars began a full-fledged assault on state-centered international politics based on sovereignty. Since that time, new rationales for intervention and expanded conditionalities have been opened up, the increased participation of nongovernmental organizations (NGOs) has been encouraged, and concepts of '**global civil society**' have been developed. There has been a tendency, in other words, to move away from state-centered views of international relations and toward a more global approach.[34]

This more global approach is marked by a wider variety of actors operating across different levels. The international landscape is now littered with a multiplicity of actors pursuing their policy interests in decision-making processes that have no clearly defined centre, but instead, at different times, incorporate global networks of states, regional and international organizations, private and public non-state agents, coalitions of the willing, and other formal or loose associations. As Keohane and Nye write:

> The world system of the twenty-first century is not merely a system of unitary states interacting with one another through diplomacy, public international law, and international organizations. In that model, states as agents interact, constituting an international system. But this model's focus on the reified unitary state fails sufficiently to emphasize two other essential elements of the contemporary world system: networks among agents, and norms—standards of expected behavior—that are widely accepted among agents. . . . It is therefore a helpful simplified model with which we can begin to ask about global governance, although it by no means provides us with the basis for a comprehensive account.[35]

It is to this more comprehensive account that we now turn our attention.

These emerging patterns of global governance suggest the possibility of a more fundamental and long-term change in its processes, institutions, and results.[36] Perhaps foremost among these is the underlying assumption that a proper formula exists for dealing with various problems and that one only needs to empower international institutions with this formula and set them to work. One effect of this, as David Kennedy has noted, has been to remove much of the politics from debates over global governance by assuming that there is a consensus where in fact one may not exist. Kennedy explains that 'long-term economic security cannot be "managed" without attention to distribution, any more than long-term humanitarianism can be enforced without political choices. . . . Both aspire to clean hands—but governance is a messy business, globally as [well as] locally.'[37]

Part of this messiness is driven by the issues involved—a subject to be tackled in the Conclusion—and their increased salience. Part of it is driven by the lack of clear lines of authority and the absence of definitive processes for making decisions and resolving disputes. And part of it is driven by the numbers of players involved in global governance and how they criss-cross in their governing activity and networks. Global governance also has been influenced by concerns of legitimacy, capacity, and efficacy.

Anne-Marie Slaughter has called attention to the proliferation and significance of global networks in the process of global governance. In her discussion, these networks include transgovernmental networks of bureaucratic officials interacting with their counterparts in other jurisdictions, sometimes with considerable autonomy from their national governments.[38] These networks have expanded in part in response to the demands for more effective governance to address concerns emanating from globalization and from the related disaggregation of the state discussed in Chapter 8. Many observers have noted that power centres have shifted so dramatically in the global arena that it makes little sense to try to identify a locus of power or a locus of decision-making at the international level. Instead, a diffusion of power has created space for these new governance networks to emerge and, in instances such as in international finance, to flourish.[39] At the same time, the diffusion of power has opened up space also for criminal organizations and terrorist groups to thrive, as discussed in Chapters 12 and 13.

This is not to suggest that states have completely lost their capacity to act or that their formal authority has been completely eroded or withdrawn. But states are no longer able to operate free of the external restraints erected by institutions and practices of global governance. Thus, even while states, and especially powerful states, retain considerable freedom of movement, many of them have had their sovereignty, capacity, and autonomy severely compromised by the regulatory practices of international institutions. Intervention in the internal affairs of states has increased dramatically in both economic and political realms. In areas as diverse as security, trade, and environmental management, international institutions have assumed an increasingly greater responsibility for an ever-expanding array of international and domestic activity. International politics has been dominated by the meetings and activities of these organizations, and the organizations have become a principal source of attention for supporters and detractors alike. The expanding number of institutions and, more importantly, the expanded mandate that these institutions have acquired are integral to global governance and must be examined. The emergent situation suggests a move to a more institutionalized approach to global politics and towards a more intrusive international regulatory regime in which the establishment and enforcement of a rules-based order would be carried out by, or through, international institutions.

Assessing Global Governance

It has become evident that if international institutions are to acquire the authority and capacity to regulate international relations effectively, they will need to gain greater legitimacy and transparency.[40] As Michael Zurn has argued: 'The more intrusive these international institutions become, the more justified and intense the demands will be for their democratization.[41] Without an improvement of the legitimacy of decision-making processes, i.e., the incorporation of affected societal actors into the decision-making process, there is a danger that the effectiveness of international institutions will weaken.'[42] The net effect has been a significant expansion in the number, scope, and efficacy of NGOs and other non-state (or sovereignty-free) actors now interacting on a regular basis with these organizations—interactions that bring NGOs onto one of the principal stages of global governance.[43] By itself, however, this will not necessarily resolve the concerns about legitimacy.

The emerging structure of global authority brings with it concerns about the legitimacy of international institutions. International institutions traditionally have derived their legitimacy from their member governments. In undertaking action, international institutions were reflecting what Inis Claude referred to as collective legitimation, meaning quite simply that the decisions of these institutions reflected the collective will of the member governments involved. Yet, as these institutions have expanded and sought to regulate domestic societies, so their need has grown for a wider form of legitimacy to reflect their increasingly politicized role. Ian Hurd explains that '[l]egitimacy refers to the normative belief by an actor that a rule or institution ought to be obeyed. It is a subjective quality, relational between actor and institution, and defined by the actor's perception of the institution. The actor's perception may come from the substance of the rule or from the procedure or source by which it was constituted.'[44] Keohane writes that legitimacy 'must facilitate persuasion rather than coercion or reliance on sanctions as a means of influence....Voluntary cooperation based on honest communication and rational persuasion provides the strongest guarantee of a legitimate process.'[45] The legitimacy of global governance becomes critically important in light of the fact that compliance in the international system is generally voluntary. At the same time that the legitimacy of international institutions as the main framework for conducting global governance has become more important, it has also become more difficult to attain. To achieve such legitimacy, international institutions must appeal not only to their member governments, but also to individual citizens and the civil society organizations that claim to speak on behalf of these citizens.[46]

As witnessed in recent years, the UN has had a difficult time in establishing its role as the legitimate authority on the right to use force. One of the most significant problems faced by the international community has been achieving widespread acceptance of the right of humanitarian intervention.[47] As former UN Secretary-General Kofi Annan noted, the Kosovo issue is illustrative of this problem. NATO's actions in Kosovo raised an important issue involving the legitimacy of international action in support of human security. According to Annan:

> It has cast in stark relief the dilemma of so-called 'humanitarian intervention'. On the one hand, is it legitimate for a regional organization to use force without a UN mandate? On the other, is it permissible to let gross and systematic violations of human rights, with grave humanitarian consequences, continue unchecked? The inability of the international community to reconcile these two compelling interests in the case of Kosovo can be viewed only as a tragedy. Nothing in the UN charter precludes the recognition that there are rights beyond borders. What the charter does say is that 'armed force shall not be used, save in the common interest.' But what is that common interest? Who shall define it? Who shall defend it? Under whose authority? And with what means of intervention?[48]

The appropriation by NATO of responsibility for defining and defending the common interest might be commendable if the **alliance** had more legitimacy in the international system. The dilemma became even more acute in the months preceding the American-led invasion of Iraq during the winter of 2003. Once again, the UN's role as the legitimate authority for using force was questioned and then summarily dismissed by the US government, with the support of Britain, Spain, and others. Problems of legitimacy and relevance remain, however, for the institution and for its Charter-mandated role of maintaining global peace and stability.[49]

Determining legitimacy in the international community is an admittedly complicated and uncertain task. Yet, if a global order is to be successful in moving states and civil society actors towards more humane and just practices, it needs an authority that is legitimate, credible, and accountable to ensure the habit of compliance with international norms. The activities of international institutions have met with considerable resistance as these institutions 'invade' domestic societies and seek to implement societal change. In view of their more direct contact with civil society, 'international organizations can no longer afford to bypass the concerns of transnational actors who have successfully mobilized around many global issues and have strengthened their bargaining position with significant moral, financial and knowledge resources.'[50] This resistance comes from left and right alike as both sides of the political spectrum rail against the intrusiveness of these institutional mandates. On the right, conservatives—largely, but not exclusively, in the United States—have taken exception to many efforts to push forward a more intrusive role for international institutions. Some populist factions such as the John Birch Society and the Heritage Foundation in the US have voiced opposition to the UN and other multilateral associations for decades. The resistance has manifested itself in reactions against, for example, UNESCO, the IMF, the Anti-Ballistic Missile (ABM) Treaty, the Biological and Toxin Weapons

Shuttle diplomacy: Barack Obama and UN Secretary-General Ban Ki-moon on a flight from Washington, DC, to New York, 2 February 2007. Obama had yet to become President but was already developing a good relationship with the UN Secretary-General. Since the 2008 US presidential election, President Obama and the UN Secretary-General have pledged to have the US and the UN work more closely together on a number of major global issues. This is certainly in contrast to the relationship that existed between former US President George W. Bush and the UN organization.

Convention (BWC), the Kyoto Protocol, the Convention to Ban Anti-Personnel Landmines, and the establishment of the International Criminal Court (ICC), among other global institutional initiatives.[51]

Opponents of international economic institutions, mostly on the left, have waged an even more active campaign against such institutional intrusions. These voices, mostly from the street, have shadowed meetings of international economic agencies as they have moved around the world (see Chapters 10 and 11). In demonstration after demonstration when they are not castigating the whole process of globalization, they are calling upon global institutions to democratize their decision-making processes and to become more accountable to a wider variety of people and interests.[52] The lack of consensus among these critics of global institutional intrusion is, however, quite pronounced. The anti-globalization movement reflects a wide array of ideas, some of which are rooted in a desire to protect matters of faith, culture, or national identity. Others express concerns about the uneven effects of the process of globalization and argue that it has yet to touch people in vast corners of the globe who still lack the basic necessities of life, not to mention the Internet, cellphones, or access to global financial markets. 'Resisters' from across the ideological spectrum also reflect the persistently strong commitments to nationalism, ethnicity, and religion being demonstrated in many parts of the globe. They share a common resistance to many aspects of global governance as currently conducted. Yet their diversity and absence of collective strategy make them a difficult, though no less essential, constituency to cultivate.

> The controversies surrounding accountability and legitimacy are critical to the political future of the [international economic institutions]. Suspicion of supranational governance and embrace of market alternatives on the right have been matched by left-wing hostility towards globalization and its promotion by [these economic institutions]. The domestic base of support for these institutions has eroded. Addressing the issue of accountability is essential for rebuilding that support.[53]

In response to the above challenges to their legitimacy, international institutions have begun to make some efforts at becoming more inclusive. As Zurn notes, 'in the light of growing societal resistance, the [World Bank, IMF, and WTO] have taken measures to 1) increase control over the decision-makers through various evaluation procedures, 2) improve the ability to scrutinize the decision-making processes and 3) increase the share of power of transnational society.'[54] Both the World Bank and the IMF have instituted consultative mechanisms, for instance. The consultative process of the World Bank is more elaborate and incorporates representatives from various NGOs into policy review and policy planning. The IMF's contact with NGOs is slightly more circumspect, but it has facilitated some consultations. The WTO is looking at establishing something similar, but nothing has been done thus far.

> The capacity to deliver effective policies is a basic requirement of the legitimacy of any political system, but usually it is not sufficient. This is because the conception of political legitimacy prevalent in most countries today is hostile to the idea of any form of power that is unaccountable to those over whom it is exercised and especially to those who are most affected by it. The legitimacy crisis of international institutions such as the International Monetary Fund (IMF), the World Trade Organization (WTO) and the UN Security Council shows that the question of the public accountability of global governance is unavoidable and cannot be answered simply by pointing at the control exercised by national governments over them.[55]

The response on the part of some observers has been at the same time more elaborate and less substantial. There have been various proposals for a people's assembly and numerous studies have focused on making the global decision-making process more representative of the range of member governments. To date, however, very little substantial reform has been undertaken beyond informal consultation. There seems to be a clear difficulty in reconciling a formal international order built around sovereign states with the more diffuse, multi-centred processes involving both states and NGOs, alongside organizations and numerous private-sector interests,[56] not to mention transgovernmental networks of officials. No amount of tinkering with the structure of institutions such as the UN will fully come to grips with this new reality.

Conclusion

Amid the calls for democratization, transparency, and accountability, existing structures face a number of difficult choices. As Miles Kahler notes: 'Few clear guidelines exist at the global level for enfranchising those who are not member governments. Issues of representation and internal accountability are profound and divisive among governments and nongovernmental organizations.'[57] Yet the need to confront these issues is equally profound if international institutions are to maintain a constructive and effective role in global governance. International institutions have assumed a central role in many areas of contemporary international relations. They have made a contribution to a more stable order and facilitated the move away from a strictly state-based international system. As the range and substance of their activities have expanded, however, so, too, has the resistance to these activities and, by association, to the institutions themselves, not only by non-state actors but by some member states as well. Zurn describes the dilemma:

> The more intrusive these international institutions become, the more justified and intense the demands will be for their democratization. Without an improvement of the legitimacy of decision-making processes, i.e., the incorporation of affected societal actors into the decision-making process, there is a danger that the effectiveness of international institutions will weaken. In order to avoid an acceptance crisis, and consequently an effectiveness crisis, it therefore appears that some kind of societally backed multilateralism with full multimedia coverage is necessary to save multilateralism by putting an end to executive exclusiveness.[58]

International institutions have the potential to be significant contributors to a stable, peaceful, and progressive global order. If they are to play such a role, however, they must undergo reform to secure the support of both governments and civil society. Their greatest potential ostensibly rests on their ability to be accepted as legitimate and accountable sources of global governance.

According to Keohane and Nye: 'Rulemaking and rule interpretation in global governance have become pluralized. Rules are no longer a matter simply for states or intergovernmental organizations. . . . As a result any emerging pattern of governance will have to be networked rather than hierarchical and must have minimal rather than highly ambitious objectives.'[59] In the Conclusion we examine in more detail the evolution of these multi-level governance structures and their contributions to politics at the global level.

❖ Key Terms

agents	Industrial Revolution
alliance	intellectual property
anti-slavery movement	multilateralism
belligerent	multi-purpose organization
coalitions of the willing	networks
codified international law	pluralist
coercion	power asymmetries
deus ex machina	regional arrangements
Eurocentrism	'soft law'
global civil society	statism
homogeneity	treaty

Discussion Questions

1. In what way is global politics about more than war and conflict?
2. What is global governance and how has it evolved?
3. What is the difference between international governance and global governance?
4. What are the limits of global governance?
5. How has the proliferation of NGOs put pressure on the UN system to democratize and to become more transparent?
6. Why does the emerging structure of global authority bring with it concerns about the legitimacy of extant international organizations?
7. How would you explain 'multi-level' governance, and where does the UN fit in this schema?

Suggested Readings

Cooper, Andrew F. *Celebrity Diplomacy.* Boulder, Colo.: Paradigm, 2007. This is the first book-length study of celebrity diplomacy as a serious global project with important implications, both positive and negative. Even if their lofty goals remain elusive, when celebrities speak, other actors in the global system listen. Celebrities bring optimism and 'buzz' to issues that seem deep and gloomy. Cooper considers the diplomacy of popular culture celebrities from Angelina Jolie to Bono and global political and economic figures, including Nelson Mandela, George Soros, and Bill Gates.

Schulz, Michael, Joachim Öjendal, and Fredrik Söderbaum, eds. *Regionalization in a Globalizing World: A Comparative Perspective on Forms, Actors and Processes.* London: Zed Books, 2001. This volume explores the emerging role of regional systems of relations. The contributors focus on key questions: What constitutes a region? How is the historical process of region formation developing? What are the roles of main state and non-state actors involved? What are the future prospects? Eleven different regions are examined and the general conclusion is that regionalization is an uneven, heterogeneous, and multidimensional phenomenon.

Whitman, Jim, ed. *Palgrave Advances in Global Governance.* London: Palgrave Macmillan, 2009. This authoritative edited collection is devoted to clarifying established understandings of global governance as a distinct form of political activity. Whitman, a well-respected scholar in the field, pulls together some of the leading global politics researchers to examine the actors, arenas, means, and purposes of global governance and in the process bring some order and clarity to governance in the twenty-first century.

Global Links

Europa
europa.eu/
   This is the site of the European Union and includes more than you will ever need to know about the EU.

Centre for the Study of Globalisation and Regionalisation
www2.warwick.ac.uk/fac/soc/csgr/
> The University of Warwick in the UK has the largest academic centre in Europe dealing globalization and regionalization.

New Zealand Ministry of Foreign Affairs and Trade
www.mfat.govt.nz/Trade-and-Economic-Relations/Trade-Agreements/Trans-Pacific/index.php
> Among other items of interest, this site includes the terms of the agreement of the Trans-Pacific Strategic Economic Partnership Agreement.

 Debate 15

Be it resolved that the UN has lost its relevance and should be replaced by a world government.

Conclusion

It is hard to overestimate the fluidity of the early twenty-first century.[1]

Introduction

As students of global politics, we try to make sense of the world around us. This involves trying to identify the important events and practices shaping our world amid the cacophony of activities that occur every day. It also requires that we distinguish between those common practices that suggest continuity or a common heritage with the past and practices that appear without historical lineage, that are new and have significance for global politics.[2] As we suggest in this book, it is important that we discern patterns of change from those of continuity. Making sense of the political world requires that we try to understand the underlying sources of continuity and change so that we can identify opportunities for reform, transformation, and progress. Two events help to demarcate the terrain of contemporary global politics.

On 26 November 2008, India's largest and most cosmopolitan city, Mumbai (formerly known as Bombay), experienced a well-planned and co-ordinated terrorist attack that reminded many of the 9/11 attacks on the US World Trade Center and the Pentagon. Heavily armed gunmen, taking advantage of the Indian government's security lapses and intelligence failures, infiltrated this busy financial capital of India, via the sea routes into Mumbai from Karachi, Pakistan. They targeted two famous five-star luxury hotels, the Taj Mahal and Hotel Oberoi, as well as upscale restaurants like Café Leopold, the crowded Chhatrapati Shivaji Terminus railway station (an estimated 6 million people ride the commuter trains through Mumbai each day), and a Jewish community hall. Over 170 people were killed in those attacks, including Mumbai's anti-terror chief, Hemant Karkare, and hundreds more were injured.

Terrorist attacks, like these, remind us that we live in an exceedingly dangerous world, in a new world disorder. Max Weber once noted that the state ought to be the source of legitimacy for any use of violence.[3] States, in fact, used to boast about having the monopoly of force. Maybe they did, but certainly this

The Taj Mahal Hotel before the Mumbai attacks of 26 November 2008.

© Larry Lee Photography/Corbis

The Taj Mahal Hotel during the Mumbai attacks, 26 November 2008.

Arko Datta/Reuters/Landov

is no longer universally true. As we have seen in the Mumbai attacks, non-state actors like the Pakistan-based militant group Lashkar-e-Taiba (LeT) are quite capable of engaging in what has come to be known as **asymmetric warfare**. These sovereignty-free actors not only have access to high-powered automatic weapons, bombs, grenades, and various types of explosives, but they are also quite capable of using many of the tools of globalization (e.g., ATM machines, computers, cell-phones) to facilitate their assault on states. It has been reported, for example, that the gunmen who carried out the terror attacks on Mumbai used cellphones that were enabled with Voice over Internet Protocol (VoIP) services. VoIP uses a complicated digital codes system that makes it very difficult to trace and tap messages using traditional listening technology.

The LeT terrorists were therefore apparently able to get around US and Indian intelligence surveillance. What is even more terrifying to contemplate is that these non-state actors may have had help from a rogue element within the Pakistani Inter-Services Intelligence (ISI) agency. As we all know, Pakistan is a nuclear power, and this raises the horrifying prospect that a non-state actor might some-day get its hands on a weapon of mass destruction (WMD).[4] In fact, a December 2008 US congressional report by the bipartisan Commission on the Prevention of Weapons of Mass Destruction warned that 'unless the world community acts decisively and with great urgency, it is more likely than not that a weapon of mass destruction will be used in a terrorist attack somewhere in the world by the end of 2013.'[5] The combination of sovereignty-free actors bent on destruction with access to technologically sophisticated means of launching devastating attacks creates a new set of circumstances not readily constrained by such **state-centric measures** as the balance of power or deterrence.

In the waning months of 2008, another devastating series of events played out in boardrooms and was reported across the business pages of the world's papers as the international financial system collapsed. What began as a sub-prime mortgage crisis in the United States quickly degenerated in a loss of confidence in the US markets.[6] Walden Bello relates the description of a New York City bus driver, who informed his passengers: 'New York is still here, ladies and gentlemen, but Wall Street has disappeared, like the Twin Towers.'[7] The analogy was not entirely mis-placed as the financial collapse wiped out more than 30 per cent of many persons' and corporations' assets and created a series of corporate casualties, including some of the leading lights of global capitalism. Some non-financial corporations went under, while other prominent firms, such as General Motors, tottered on the brink. The global financial system had expanded rapidly in the preceding decades on the basis of a series of regulatory policy changes and the practices of private and institutional investors who increasingly disregarded national borders and began exchanging **financial commodities** across territories and time zones. They also became involved in more complex financial contracts such as **deriva-tives**, which American investment billionaire Warren Buffett once referred to as 'financial weapons of mass destruction'.[8]

The factors that have defined globalization—such as developments and advances in information and communication technologies—facilitated and encouraged these cross-border financial flows to the point where more than a trillion US dollars were being moved through **bourses** around the world every day. The non-stop 24/7 world of **global capital flows** fuelled an economic expansion the likes of which the world had not experienced. The expansion was without roots, however, as there was 'an increasing disconnect between the real and the financial economies. ... The real economy has grown ... but nothing like that of the finan-cial economy ... until it imploded.'[9] The collapse was swift and widespread. It began with the collapse of major banks in the UK (Northern Rock, Bear Stearns) and mortgage firms in the US (Fannie Mae, Freddie Mac), followed quickly by other financial institutions (Lehman Brothers, Merrill Lynch) that had invested heavily in what proved to be a paper economy built more on the sandy foundation of wishes and hopes, propped up by a healthy dose of greed, than on production of 'real' goods and services.

The construction of the **global financial order** and its collapse represent many of the practices and patterns that we have examined throughout this book. For one, they demonstrate the importance of history in understanding contemporary practices—something we highlighted in Chapters 3 and 6. Comparisons with the **'crash of 1929'** have been common among observers. History also reveals the continuing influence of states in the global political economy, for states play the significant role in creating the conditions under which financial (and other) markets operate. During the early days of the post-World War II period national governments remained deeply involved in national economies even as they fostered a pattern of more liberal exchanges on the international side.

Subsequently, as Eric Helleiner has discussed, beginning in the 1970s, states led by Margaret Thatcher's Conservatives in the UK and Ronald Reagan's Republicans in the US undertook a series of policies aimed at deregulating national financial systems, thereby opening opportunities for a variety of financial institutions to engage

Figure C.1 The crash of 1929.

Source: <www.marketoracle.co.uk/images/1929-stock-market-crash-dow-chart-image005.png>.

© Wally McNamee/Corbis

US President Ronald Reagan and UK Prime Minister Margaret Thatcher in their prime.

in speculative investments at home and abroad.[10] The policies of national governments were complemented by the financial practices of international institutions, specifically the IMF, that supported the liberalization of transnational capital flows. Completing the picture were individuals and corporations that engaged in an unprecedented volume of transborder financial activity.

Banks led the drive to move capital abroad following the OPEC-generated oil price increases in the 1970s. This, in turn, exacerbated the financial costs and debt burden that many developing countries experienced during the recession of the 1980s, the so-called 'lost decade' for many developing economies. Individuals got into the act in ever greater numbers in the 1990s such that, by the early 2000s, transnational financial practices were being marketed in commercials across North America, using a digitally enhanced wise-cracking baby sitting in front of a computer making financial investments on-line. It would not be possible to understand the dynamics that propelled the global financial system to the disastrous collapse of 2008 without taking into account this diverse range of actors and institutions at the local, national, and transnational levels. Solutions to this economic downturn will not come quickly or easily and lie well beyond the capacity of any one state or collection of corporate interests. Instead, those solutions will require a combination of transnational public/private networks and multi-level governance structures.[11] The beginning of this change in governance strategy was, in part, reflected in the gathering of **G20** finance ministers in November 2008 in Washington, as a first step in trying to put 'Humpty Dumpty' together again.

Among many other events that we could recount, these incidents leave little doubt that our contemporary world is in flux. The vertiginous speed of the transformation brought on by the current phase of globalization has not yet been matched by an equally speedy transformation in our governance at the global level. Yet, as we have shown earlier, global governance is undergoing some important changes in order to address old, new, and emerging global problems. States are working in different ways and with different combinations of actors. Civil society organizations are, at times, assuming greater prominence in advocating and directing changing practices. Private actors of all stripes—corporations, prominent individuals, military contractors, humanitarian workers, NGOs, and criminal entities—are shaping global economic, security, and political relations in ways that we never thought possible. We have observed within current practices some indication that the various actors involved are conscious of the need for change. Not surprisingly, however, others are more resistant to change and question the need for new approaches.

Identifying the Terrain of Global Politics

As was discussed in Chapter 6, many observers believe that the terrorist attacks on the United States in September 2001 signalled a significant shift in the pattern of global politics. For others, the tragic event brought little by way of significant change to the practice of global politics. Carolyn Kennedy-Pipe and Nicholas Rengger argue that the widespread assumption that somehow 9/11 represents a radical break in world politics is incorrect. They make a convincing case that global politics since 9/11 displays many more continuities than disjunctions. In their view, the belief that 9/11 marked a radical change is problematic, not just for the way we conceive of global politics but also for the way policy-makers respond at the global level.[12] Much of global politics is still defined by states, and the distribution of power among states continues to have a significant influence on who gets what, when, and how. Military power, in the form of both conventional and nuclear weapons, remains critically important in determining the outcome of many conflicts. Civil society organizations still lack secure access to the corridors of global governance. Most international institutions still restrict formal membership to sovereign states. **International law** remains limited in its reach and efficacy.

In contrast to this reading, others see change as an endemic feature of global politics. As Donald Kirkpatrick argued 25 years ago, albeit during a time when the global situation seemed less ominous and when global governance appeared less onerous:

> Change is inevitable; it is a natural process and can be seen in the incessant flux of aging and evolution in all living systems. It need not, however, be seen as so troublesome, stressful, and indeed, catastrophic as some regard it. Change must rightfully be regarded as the vital, creative, exciting, and energizing force that it really is.[13]

For good or ill, globalization itself has been a powerful force for change. Developments in such areas as technology, transportation, and communications and in practices such as trade, finance, travel and tourism, and migration have furthered the experience in and awareness of the global community. Experiences, problems, and solutions increasingly transcend national borders, and while there are and will continue to be efforts to shore up borders in response to such practices, there remains to a very significant degree a community of actors and practices that are not restricted to traditional conceptions of the nation-state. The nature of warfare also has changed. At the beginning of the twenty-first century, there are now fewer wars between states than at any time during the last century. Yet violence remains a prominent feature of the contemporary global landscape. Despite the end of the Cold War, we have not seen the expected **peace dividend**. Instead, we have been witnessing a rise in civil wars, terrorism and other forms of extremism, human rights abuses, and a return to piracy at sea. We are also witnessing what amounts to a geopolitical reshaping, as new powers (China, India, and Brazil, among others) are clambering up the hierarchical ladder and emerging powers and markets are sitting in the wings itching to jump into the spotlight.[14] New forms of totalitarianism in the guise of 'fundamentalist religions' are popping up in various locales. A related but distinguishable development has been the increase in nationalistic and ethnicity/identity conflicts. US power, although still predominant, seems to be waning, as it struggles with a major war in Afghanistan that seems to offer little hope of ultimate success and the fallout from a war in Iraq that never could be won, as well as an economic crisis that has spread to the rest of the world.[15] Denigrations of multilateralism and the increasing acceptance of plurilateralism and coalitions of the willing are also signs of new forms of 'institutional' co-operation among a limited number of states.

Rosenau's vivid picture of multi-centric and state-centric worlds coexisting may be apt for the contemporary period. And so, too, is his concept of **'fragmegration'**—the simultaneous processes of fragmentation and integration. The boundaries between domestic and international politics have continued to erode because the principles and practices of sovereignty are, in some cases, no longer barriers to external intervention into situations rife with humanitarian crises brought on by famine, tsunamis, hurricanes, typhoons, earthquakes, civil wars, and gross violations of human rights. Individual citizens and subjects today have relatively better analytical skills and emotional competence than people in past international systems and can therefore significantly affect (even as they are affected by) the aggregated dynamics that give shape and direction to global life.[16]

BOX C.1

Fragmegration

Rosenau coined the word 'fragmegration' to describe the complex dynamism of world politics. The word is a combination of 'fragmentation' and 'integration', and signifies a theoretical outlook that attempts to examine the world in two different ways simultaneously. Like combining Newtonian and quantum physics, Rosenau's fragmegration lens views the world of politics as both macro and micro phenomena. By examining the world at micro and macro levels simultaneously, Rosenau hopes to avoid neglecting the findings of either view and to develop a more comprehensive picture. For example, at the micro level, technologies such as television, the Internet, and cellphones 'enable like-minded individuals to be in touch with one another.' At the macro level, on the other hand, those technologies 'render collectivities more open and connected and empower them to mobilize support.' Uniting micro and macro perspectives, the fragmegration lens illustrates how such technologies 'constrain governments by enabling opposition groups to mobilize more effectively' while 'accelerating diplomatic processes and facilitating surveillance and intelligence work'. Though tangential to the finer points of global trade and investment, Rosenau's discussion of fragmegration highlights the conceptual challenge globalization poses and the necessity for new theoretical frameworks able to capture the complex processes of global phenomena.

Source: Adapted from: <gstudynet.org/governance/panels/global_trade.php>.

Using Theory as a Guide

Our review of global politics has revealed a world marked by both change and continuity. It is a world that remains infected by violent competition for political power more within than between states; a world in which hundreds of millions of people remain caught in conditions of abject poverty in substandard housing and lacking the basic necessities of life; a world experiencing significant environmental changes especially in climate patterns not seen in many generations, if ever; a world that faces new health crises, such as SARS and the H1N1 virus pantemic, as it continues to grapple with long-standing ones such as malaria.

Yet, it is also a world where the incidence of inter-state conflict has declined significantly; where hundreds of millions of people have moved out of poverty; where the size of the middle class has expanded in many parts of the global South; where there has been considerable success in identifying, monitoring, and controlling the spread of infectious diseases with a concomitant increase in the lifespan of many people around the globe; where inter-state co-operation through international agreements and institutions continues to proliferate. The images of contemporary global politics represent a mix of despair and hope, pessimism and optimism, constraint and opportunity. They also reflect a myriad of actors, many with no formal affiliation to the state, engaged in global politics. How, then, is one to approach the subject?

Realist scholars often caution against allowing our wishes and hopes for a better world to cloud our knowledge of existing conditions. Any clear understanding of global politics needs to start from the practices taking place. As we saw in Chapters 1 and 2, however, different theories direct our attention to different phenomena, even when we are looking at the same subject matter—at states in the case of realists; at the vulnerable populations of the world in the case of feminists; at the ideas and rationales that motivate the participants in global politics in the case of the constructivists. Each theory not only calls our attention to a different aspect of global politics, it also presents a different set of normative concerns. For realists it is how to act prudently in a dangerous world; for feminists and post-colonialists, how to uncover the sources of power and oppression so that vulnerable populations can emancipate themselves; for Marxists and neo-Marxists, how economic structures and practices shape the political and social behaviours of actors in this globalized capitalist economy. In selecting among these competing approaches one must be aware of their limitations and potential alongside their ability to help us understand what is going on around us. A more balanced approach could be adopted—one that does not succumb to the pessimism so common among certain realists but at the same time recognizes the importance of keeping one's feet firmly planted on the ground.

Above all, central forces in contemporary global politics include dynamic technologies, shrinking social and geographical distances, and a proliferation of actors. The latter includes a series of transnational, large-scale, and powerful social movements, as discussed in Chapters 10 and 11, addressing the issues of women's rights, peace, environmental pollution and climate change, HIV/AIDS, refugees and internally displaced persons, trafficking in women and children, drugs, and currency crises in the context of interdependence and the centralizing dynamics that compel co-operation on a transnational scale.[17] Individual states are unable to deal with these issues acting on their own—hence the need for multilateral or global governance. The emerging multi-centric system is relatively more dynamic

Refugee camp inhabitants.

than the state-centric one. One should also stress that the state-centric system that operates according to sovereign borders is being challenged by a world capitalist system, acting across and above national borders, that is largely out of the control of the states or of any specific non-state actor.[18]

Idealists, in contrast, would propose that we need to transcend power and create conditions and institutions that can mitigate conflicts and support a more just and equitable order. We need to rethink the goals and instruments of institutions such as the United Nations so that they can deal effectively with the increasing challenges to the state-centric system and with the complexities of a turbulent world largely out of control. We assume that multilateralism is, and will continue to be, an evolving phenomenon whose concrete manifestations—multilateral institutions and regimes—must of necessity periodically undergo change to be relevant in responding to the needs, wants, and demands of all members of global society. At the same time, we recognize that multilateral institutions are limited and constrained by global structures of security, production, finance, and knowledge. The multi-centric world is less an arena of power struggles than a shifting sea of locales in which coalitions and networks are formed and reformed through subtle influence processes, leading to what some have called a hybridity of global governance. Unlike states, organizations in the multi-centric world do not rely on coercive power bases 'to affect each other directly as they do on the indirect routes through which they have access to attentive publics, markets, bureaucracies, and other arenas where authority is diffuse and informal.'[19] The turbulence model suggests that the integrating and fragmenting forces are in a rough balance where certain problems are being resolved while others persist. We agree with James Rosenau that 'much depends, in the end, on the kinds of leaders that come to power in the state-centric and multi-centric worlds and the quality of the demands that ever more skillful publics make upon them.'[20] We certainly agree that networked global governance, based on the principle of **subsidiarity**, may prove valuable for our current and future world.[21]

While we share much in common in our views on the state of global politics and its trajectory to this point, we part company on the guiding wisdom that alternative theories can provide for the future. One of us advocates **neo-idealism** or a critical *idealpolitik* for both leaders and publics, whereas the other one advocates a normatively informed, critically engaged realism or *realpolitik*. The normative position of neo-idealism—cosmopolitan and democratic,

© David Turnley/Corbis

humane global leadership and governance in the pursuit of world interests—is based on the assumption that it is possible to go beyond the essential dilemmas presented by the tradition of **Machiavellian realism**. In a post-realist, neo-ide-alist perspective, it is crucially important to debate what ought to be the priority world interests according to an expanded concept of security. Moreover, since the process of positing and ranking of world interests, like national interests, involves values, it necessarily encompasses a combination of empirical and normative theo-rizing and controversies. In general, Seyom Brown has made an excellent start in denying the realist claim that any putative world interest would have to be derived from national interests. On the contrary, 'the securing of world interests ... is the necessary condition for maintaining any of the national and special interests that continue to be highly valued.' Brown continues:

> whatever the scope of the polity—city, province, country, the entire planet—the fun-damental human interests that deserve to be accommodated and reliably secured include not only physical safety and minimal public order, but also economic subsis-tence and basic health of the population [that implies a sustainable ecological envi-ronment], individual civic and property rights, and opportunities for cultural and religious communities to develop their own ways of life.[22]

Brown attributes this idea of world interests to **'higher realism'**—a realism that shares many of its premises with other schools of realism but transcends the rather narrow nationalistic definitions of self-interest and recognizes the interconnect-edness of national and global interests.[23]

Complementing higher realism, critical *idealpolitik* affirms human, not national, survival in dignity as the overriding world interest. Human beings possess dignity, rights, and responsibilities and are not merely means but ends in themselves and part of a universal and transcendent common good. This transcendental good and the ideals that embody it should be given, at least, a balanced priority with the demands of the constraining structures of global 'reality', and whenever pos-sible clear pre-eminence. The application of these principles has to be balanced with the demands of necessity—scarcity of global natural resources, the unin-tended effects of human technologies, the finite limits to human life, knowledge, and power, and the historically well-attested tendencies of human beings to com-pete for power and prestige, and often to behave selfishly as individuals and in groups.

Realists are generally inclined to confine causal power to states and therefore, in the process, largely ignore or minimize the importance of non-state actors. Many realists present a cogent model of unitary state actors interacting according to calculations of relative instrumental power and seeking the overall goal of national interests defined primarily in terms of hard economic, technological, and mili-tary power. As a result, realist theories, at first glance, seem to have lost much of their ability to explain certain contemporary events. Yet theorists such as Hans Morgenthau also have seen in realism the need to respond to changing conditions:

> When the times tend to depreciate the elements of power, [political science] must stress its importance. When the times incline towards a monistic conception of power in the general scheme of things, it must show its limitations. When the times conceive of power primarily in military terms, it must call attention to the variety of factors which go into the power equation and, more particularly, to the subtle psychological

relation of which the web of power is fashioned. When the reality of power is being lost sight of over its moral and legal limitations, it must point to that reality. When law and morality are judged as nothing, it must assign them their rightful place.[24]

Morgenthau, among others, presents a more nuanced view of realism that acknowledges and applauds its normative component while recognizing the need to be attentive to change. The realist repeatedly emphasizes the need to look at things as they are, not as we wish for them to be. Yet realism for Morgenthau 'is supposed to *explain* international relations, but it is also, fundamentally, a normative and *critical* project which questions the existing *status quo*.'[25] At the same time, he retains the commitment to identify the sources and forms of power that are shaping global politics, even as these change.

Realpolitik 'may be defined as a theory revolving around core assumptions, but it is much more than this. In fact, realism is best conceived as an intellectual attitude towards the world one lives in, which accepts its constraints, does not negate its ambiguities, constantly highlights its complexities, and does uphold a profound normative commitment to some fundamental values.'[26] A critical *realpolitik* for the future must recognize both diversity and imperfection while reinforcing what Robert Jackson has described as 'serviceable international norms' in support of a global political ethics.[27] The threat of nuclear war encouraged Morgenthau to look at fusing both Utopian and realist views. He explicitly states that, 'threatened by the unsolved political problems of the day, we have come to think more and more in terms of a **supranational community** and a **world government**, a political organization and structure that transcend the nation state.'[28]

A normatively informed and critically engaged realism is not the antithesis of idealist thinking, for it remains rooted in a fundamental concern for human beings. As Murielle Cozette writes:

> While realism maintains the centrality of the state as an actor in international politics, it never thought of the state as the impassable horizon of political and moral life. To pretend so signals a fundamental misunderstanding of the realist project which is, ultimately, to speak truth to power so that the humanity of man is permanently upheld. Going beyond the state-centric system when the situation demands it is therefore regarded as a moral duty from a realist perspective.[29]

As students considering the future of global politics we are struck by the variety of interests involved and the need to approach policy options from different perspectives and levels. The mix of actors and interests does not lend itself to any simple and straightforward approach to global governance.[30] Clearly, global governance in our contemporary world will be messy.[31] There seems little reason to discount the continued significance of states and nationally focused policy choices as self-interested governments try to retain an advantage in the global political economy. There is also little doubt about the ineffectiveness of national and unilateral measures and the pressing need for these same governments to embed their approaches in a wider network of regional and global institutions, either for essential support or to legitimate their actions and thus allow for a greater level of success. Above all else, it would seem essential that one must never lose sight of the crucial importance of adopting a self-consciously normative approach to one's study of global politics. For these reasons, a perspective that blends the need to understand the world as it is with a view to the need and opportunities for emancipation, reform, and transformation provides an approach for mediating between the contemporary global disorder and a future defined more by peace, justice, and the full security of individuals around the world.

Key Terms

asymmetric warfare
bourses
'crash of 1929'
derivatives
financial commodities
'fragmegration'
G20
global capital flows
global financial order
'higher realism'

idealpolitik
international law
Machiavellian realism
neo-idealism
peace dividend
state-centric measures
subsidiarity
supranational
world government

Discussion Questions

1. Do you make sense of the world around you by drawing on history or by examining current events?
2. What do the global financial collapse and the global epidemic of terrorism tell us about the need for global governance?
3. How will the emergence of new economic powers, such as Brazil, China, and India, change the way politics is conducted at the global level?
4. Are the forces of fragmentation and integration an indication of a new world disorder or a new world order?
5. What theoretical approach best explains the current trends in global politics?
6. How can a critical *realpolitik* and a critical *idealpolitik* be reconciled?

Suggested Readings

Archibugi, Daniele. 'Models of International Organization in Perpetual Peace Projects', *Review of International Studies* 18 (1992): 295–317. This article demonstrates that contemporary international organizations are by-products of the ideas of so-called Utopian thinkers of the past. This intellectual tradition of perpetual peace projects, according to the author, has continuing relevance for the debate about the transformation of international organization and global governance.

Booth, Ken. 'Security in Anarchy: Utopian Realism in Theory and Practice', *International Affairs* 67, 3 (1991): 527–45. Realism—the view that war is inescapable in a system where sovereign states compete for power and advantage to one another's detriment—still dominates IR thinking. But Booth argues that a world view in which war is seen as a rational policy choice is unacceptable.

He proposes a Utopian realism based on the assumption that states are becoming less important as power becomes decentralized and the world moves closer towards a global community of communities.

Schmitt, Gary J., ed. *The Rise of China: Essays on the Future Competition*. New York: Encounter Books, 2009. China's economy and military are expanding to the point where it is positioning itself to challenge the United States as the greatest international power. *The Rise of China* is a collection of essays about the nature of that challenge and what the US and its allies might do in the areas of foreign and defence policy to meet it.

Global Links

South Asia Terrorism Portal
www.satp.org/satporgtp/countries/india/states/jandk/terrorist_outfits/lashkar_e_toiba.htm

Detailed information about Lashkar-e-Toiba ('Army of the Pure')—its objectives, ideology, leadership and command structure, area of operation, training and operational strategies, weapons, and links to Al-Qaeda and the Taliban.

Council on Foreign Relations
www.cfr.org/publication/11644/

This webpage examines the accusations made against Pakistan's Inter-Services Intelligence regarding its involvement in regional terrorist activity and its support for global extremism. It also details the paucity of civilian control over this Pakistani intelligence organization.

Centre for International Governance Innovation
www.cigionline.org/publications/2009/7/picking-your-club-g8-or-g20-brics-or-bricsam

This webpage of CIGI, a research institute at the University of Waterloo, collates a series of opinion articles that examine the evolution of global governance institutions—both plurilateral and multilateral—and the emerging new architecture of global governance.

Debate Conclusion

Be it resolved that we are living in a new world disorder that cannot be explained using traditional theories of IR.

Glossary

acid rain The combination of precipitation with nitrogen oxide and sulphur dioxide, from emissions of industrial plants, power plants, and automobiles, which harms forests, lakes, and human-made structures.

ad hoc collectivities Occasional mass rallies and protest movements that bring together various groups for a specific purpose.

advanced industrialized countries Countries with a very high level of economic development, high income per capita, high gross national product (GNP) per capita, and advanced technology and manufacturing sectors.

agent An individual who operates on behalf of or represents a larger group of individuals or organization.

ahistorical Standing outside of and prior to history.

alliance An agreement between individuals, organizations, or states usually formalized in a pact or treaty; a collection of states formally organized around particular military/ strategic goals.

Allied nations The alliance opposed to the Axis powers in World War II. The prominent or 'big three' members were the United Kingdom, the United States, and the Soviet Union. These nations were joined by the French before their defeat in 1940, British Commonwealth countries such as Canada, India, Australia, and New Zealand, as well as several other minor powers.

anarchic global system A system in which there is no central authority.

anarchist Someone who believes that societies can function effectively without any formal authority structures.

anschluss The forced removal of populations from Czechoslovakia by Germany prior to World War II.

anti-globalization movement A variety of social movements and groups generally opposed to globalized capitalism; while the various groups target numerous grievances, many share opposition to large MNCs, free trade, market deregulation, and the deregulation of various standards such as labour and environmental standards.

anti-slavery movement Typically associated with abolition, a movement of anti-slavery activists who grew in power during the nineteenth century. At the time, the movement sought the emancipation of slaves in Europe, the United States, and colonial countries.

apartheid 'Separateness' or, in Afrikaans, 'apart-hood', a governmental policy of codified social, economic, and political discrimination based on 'racial' characteristics; the policies formally pursued by the white South African government between 1948 and 1994.

arbitration A process through which two or more parties use an arbitrator or arbiter to resolve a dispute.

arms control A practice of limiting the expansion of military spending and arms deployment.

arms race The practice of trying to maintain comparable and increasing levels of military spending with rival states.

assertive multilateralism The use of multilateral associations to exercise military force in response to threats to international peace and security.

asymmetric warfare A type of warfare in which there is a wide power differential between opposing forces, which usually leads to the adoption of non-conventional tactics, such as guerrilla warfare and terrorist actions, or indiscriminate bombing, by one or both sides.

Axis powers The defeated World War II alliance whose central members were Germany, Italy, and Japan. The Axis powers also included several minor powers, including Hungary, Romania, and Bulgaria.

balance of power The condition where the dominant powers in the international system or a particular region are roughly equivalent in their capacity to wield power.

belligerent As employed in IR, an individual, state, or group involved in hostilities.

benign hegemon A dominant power that acts in a benevolent manner to lesser powers in the system.

benign resistance The act of merely counterbalancing neoliberal institutions of global governance that perpetuate the globalization phenomenon in order to lessen dissent, disorder, and conflict.

best practices Benchmark techniques when pursuing a particular aim, which are defined by past experience and the demonstration of success with particular techniques.

bilateral treaties Formalized agreements between two entities.

biodiversity A variety of fauna and flora in a habitat.

bipolar world The world as it was after World War II until around 1989, which was dominated by two superpowers—the United States and the Soviet Union.

bond rating agencies Agencies, such as Standard and Poor's, that rate corporate and government bonds based on risk calculations.

'borderless world' A normative concept of a global environment in which state boundaries no longer have meaning.

Those who advocate for such a world may have various motivations, for example, global free trade or open migration.

'bottom billion' The close to billion people who reside in about 60 impoverished countries whose economies seem irredeemably stuck at the bottom of the global economy.

bourses Exchanges that deal in a particular good, for instance, coins or stamps; derived from the French word for purse and also the name of the French stock exchange.

caliphate The form of government inspired by Islam that represents the political unity of Muslims.

capitalism Economic system based on liberal free-market principles where wealth and the means of production are privately owned. Goods, services, and labour are traded in markets, so it is a market-driven system of economics with emphasis on the generation of profits by individuals and corporations.

ceasefire A temporary stoppage of war agreed upon by the warring parties.

chador A full-length semicircle of fabric open down the front, which is thrown over the head and held closed in front by the hands or by wrapping the ends around the waist. The chador is one way for Muslim woman to follow the Islamic dress code that women must cover their heads and not reveal bare arms or legs.

civil society Individuals and groups who operate outside of formal government organizations to pursue political goals.

civil society organizations Voluntary civic and social organizations and institutions that include NGOs, trade unions, faith-based organizations, indigenous peoples' movements, foundations, and the like. These organizations play a significant role in global politics today.

civil war An intra-state conflict among opposing forces who seek to establish control over a state or, alternatively, achieve independence from a state.

'clash of civilizations' The notion, advanced by Samuel Huntington, that in the post-Cold War world there will be inevitable clashes of cultural and religious identities and that these will be the primary source of conflict.

climate change Any change in climate over time, whether due to natural variability or as a result of human activity.

coalitions of the willing A euphemism for a de facto alliance undertaking a military intervention that is unsanctioned or only partially sanction by an IGO. The term gained prominence when it was used to describe the military alliance led by the United States that invaded Iraq in 2003.

codified international law Laws enacted by an international legislative body.

coercion The act of compelling someone to do something through some form of threat or physical force. Coercion can therefore be violent or non-violent.

coercive diplomacy A diplomatic method used by a country in which the use of force, military action, or economic sanction is threatened or hinted at to force another country to give in to a certain demand or not take a particular action.

Cold War The period of hostility between the two nuclear-armed superpowers, the US and the USSR, that lasted from roughly 1947 to 1990.

collateral damage A euphemism for violent, inadvertent harm inflicted on civilian populations or damage to civilian infrastructure during the course of military action.

collective security An organizing principle designed to prevent or limit conflict among states whereby all states agree to come to the defence of any state that is a victim of aggression.

common security A view that the security of a state rests on the common security of all of the states in a region or the globe at large.

communism Economic system based on principles of central state control over means of production.

conference of plenipotentiaries A conference invested with diplomatic authority to represent a government or international organization. The United Nations has held a series of such conferences on issues ranging from the status of refugees to the establishment of the International Criminal Court.

confidence-building measures Practices designed to reassure adversaries that other parties are respecting treaties, truces, and other such measures.

Confucianism Chinese belief and philosophical system based on such principles as filial piety and love for one's fellows that has ramifications for social, economic, and political affairs; with Taoism, one of two principal Chinese ethical systems.

containment A policy to limit the expansion of another state to keep it from having control or influence in different parts of the world.

co-operative security A view that the security of a state can only be achieved through direct co-operation with another state or states.

corporate social responsibility The initiation and practice of ethical and moral standards by corporations. Such standards may apply to human rights, environmental concerns, and labour regulations.

cosmopolitanism The notion that a person can have citizenship in a world state.

coup d'état The sudden unconstitutional overthrow of a government, usually by a segment of that government's military, to replace the deposed government with another.

'crash of 1929' The most severe stock market crash in the history of the United States, which initiated the Great Depression. Following the speculative frenzy witnessed in the economically prosperous 1920s, the stock market had become highly overbought, often by investors buying on margin (loans). The result was a massive market correction that lasted for several years.

crimes against humanity As defined in the Rome Statute of the International Criminal Court, particularly odious offences that constitute a serious attack on human dignity or a grave humiliation or degradation of one or more human beings.

criminal networks An interconnected system of individuals, groups, and gangs who engage in such criminal activity as illicit drug trafficking, money laundering, trafficking in people, trafficking in illegal arms, prostitution, corruption, fraud, etc.

critical theory According to Robert Cox, this theoretical approach allows one to stand apart from the prevailing order of the world and ask how that order came about. Critical theory does not take as given the prevailing ideas, institutions, and material or social power relations but calls these into question by focusing on the issue of whether, and to what extent, they might be undergoing change.

cybercrimes The use of computers and the Internet to pursue illegal activities.

Dalits A self-designated group of people traditionally regarded as low caste or untouchables (outcastes) in India. Dalits are a mixed population of numerous caste groups all over South Asia, and speak various languages.

decolonization A process that has occurred since the end of World War II in which the colonies of European colonial powers gained independent sovereign statehood.

dependency theory Theory that seeks to account for persistent underdevelopment of certain countries in the global economy, arguing that unequal relationships of economic exchange prevent poorer countries from escaping from poverty.

depression The most severe form of economic recession, as during the Great Depression of the 1930s, characterized by high levels of unemployment, bankruptcies, restricted credit, deflation, and other negative economic indicators; some economists contend that a 10 per cent reduction in a state's real GDP constitutes a depression.

deregulation The removal or simplification of government rules and regulations that constrain the operation of market forces so that businesses and markets are allowed to a greater extent to self-regulate, leading to a freer market.

derivatives A form of market contract, the value of which is based on another form of security or underlying asset. Often derivatives are used as a hedge, a type of insurance, that protects against the change of value of an underlying asset. A common form of derivative is a futures contract where one party agrees to sell an asset at a later date at an agreed price.

despotic rule Rule by a single individual or small group exercising absolute authority.

deterrence The practice of discouraging another party from taking action by threatening punishment if that action is taken.

deterritorialization A process whereby the importance of state boundaries is reduced. Such a process may be formal, in the voluntary reduction of sovereignty by states that participate in regional or international organizations, or organic, for example, by the spread of information, people, and ideas through globalization.

deus ex machina Literally, 'God out of the machinery', which refers to an unexpected event that acts to resolve a plot line in a play or novel, or in real life, the providential appearance of an actor or the occurrence of an event to resolve a difficult or seemingly impossible situation.

diaspora Initially, the dispersion of Jews outside of Israel from the sixth century BC when they were exiled to Babylonia; also, the dispersion of any people from their original homeland.

disarmament The removal and destruction of weapons from the arsenals of states and other parties.

drug trafficking The buying and selling of narcotics, including the production and distribution of illegal drugs.

economic sanctions Trade restrictions or penalties placed on one state or group by another state or group, including tariffs, trade barriers, import duties, export quotas, etc.

economies of scale An economic principle whereby businesses gain a cost advantage through production increases so that per-unit cost of manufacture is reduced.

egalitarianism A belief in equal political, economic, social, and civil rights for all people.

embargoes Partial or complete prohibitions of trade or commercial activity with a particular country that has violated international law or some international norm. The goal is usually to isolate a deviant state.

embedded liberalism The practices that dominated much of the early period after World War II where the state continued to intervene to protect domestic labour from liberal policies designed to promote free trade.

empire A collection of states or region dominated by a single power.

Enlightenment The historical period centred in the eighteenth century during which there was a commitment to the notion of reason and its central role in philosophy and culture.

environmentalism Theory that views the ecosystem as the principal driver of economic, social, and political relations, arguing that neglect of this underlying principle will mean that unless favourable environmental conditions are sustained these relations will not prosper.

epiphenomena Insignificant or surface changes that amount merely to rearranging the deck but on their own do not result in major alterations to the global system.

ethnic cleansing The mass expulsion and/or killing of one ethnic or religious group in an area by another ethnic or religious group in that area.

Eurocentric bias A view that ideas and practices developed out of the European experience are of greatest value and should take precedence in organizing international relations.

Eurocentrism A perspective that views knowledge through a European cultural and political perspective. The term also usually implies a belief in the pre-eminence of European cultures and has been used by neo-colonial scholars to criticize European perspectives on the developing world.

expanded security discourse The inclusion of non-military issues such as the environment, health, and poverty in discussions on global security.

explosive sub-groupism Term used by James Rosenau to refer to global protest movements that emerge from the grassroots to challenge state leaders and state-based political institutions at the local, national, regional, and international levels.

extremism A disposition to go to extremes in ideology, politics, or religion. Extremists tend to use violence as a means to an end.

failed states States lacking the ability to exercise their sovereign control over their territory, population, decision-making, and resources.

Falasha Remnants of a mixed Jewish/African people living in Ethiopia who were officially recognized by the government of Israel in 1975 when they immigrated to Israel.

Fascists Extreme right-wing groups who follow an ideology of strong states and an exclusivist approach to domestic society, as practised by Nazi Germany and Italy under Mussolini.

fatwah A legal opinion, ruling, decree, or pronouncement made by an ulema, i.e., an Islamic scholar or body of Islamic scholars.

feminism Theory that identifies gender as the key principle influencing economic, social, and political relations. Variations within feminism—liberal, socialist, postmodernist—offer some qualifications to this underlying principle.

feudal The practice where land is divided among a few select individuals who then exercise control over the land and people who reside on the land.

financial commodities Any good, or article of commerce, that has underlying value and may be bought and sold; sometimes used to refer to bulk products such as minerals, agricultural goods, and petroleum products.

foreign investment Either portfolio investment, i.e., loans of capital to local producers that do not involve control over the management of the foreign enterprise, or direct investment, where the investor acquires control over enterprise in a foreign country.

fossil fuels Fuels formed by natural resources such as anaerobic decomposition of buried dead organisms (e.g., coal, natural gas, petroleum).

'fragmegration' A term coined by James Rosenau to describe the complexity of the international system as it undergoes both fragmentation and integration processes.

freedom fighters Those engaged in a struggle to achieve political freedom for themselves or to obtain freedom for others.

genocide The systematic killing of a racial or cultural group.

global capital flows The international transmission of currency around the world, often related to foreign direct investment and foreign currency trading.

global civil society A catch-all phrase with multiple interpretations, but generally referring to a broad base of individuals and groups that operate internationally outside of government, such as NGOs, social movements, and other actors concerned with global policy issues.

global commons Those elements of the earth and atmosphere owned by no nation-state or individual and deemed to be the property of all humankind.

Global Compact A UN initiative that encourages businesses worldwide to adopt sustainable and socially responsible policies and to report on their implementation.

global financial order The economic structure of the world. Thus, the global financial order today is generally defined by the legacy of the Bretton Woods agreement, the influence of international organizations such as the World Bank, the IMF, and the WTO, and the economic predominance of certain states.

global governance The political interaction of transnational actors (both state and non-state) aimed at solving global problems affecting more than one state or region, such as environmental degradation and nuclear proliferation.

globalism An ideology that views the entire world as the basis for organizing economy, society, and politics.

globalization A process that involves the transformation of the scale of human relations (economic, social, technological) such that time and space become less relevant and the globe appears to be shrinking.

globalized capitalist relations The relations and interactions that occur in a global economic and social system in which capital is privately controlled and in which labour, goods, and capital are traded in markets; profits then are distributed to owners/stakeholders or invested in technologies and industries.

global North Those countries, practically all of which are located in the northern hemisphere, that experience relatively lower levels of poverty and higher levels of economic development.

global South Those countries, many of which are located in the southern hemisphere, that experience higher levels of poverty and lower levels of economic development.

good offices The use of the prestige and ethical power of an office, such as that of the UN Secretary-General as representative of the world community, for political traction and moral suasion in negotiating and seeking to resolve otherwise intractable issues.

grassroots movements Issue-based movements that originate with the general population rather than from an elite.

greenhouse gases Any of the atmospheric gases that contribute to the greenhouse effect by absorbing infrared radiation produced by the solar warming of the earth's surface. These include carbon dioxide (CO_2), methane (CH_4), nitrous oxide (N_2O), and water vapour.

gross domestic product (GDP) The total market value of all final goods and services produced in a country in a given year, equal to total consumer, investment, and government spending, plus the value of exports, minus the value of imports.

gross national product (GNP) The value of all the goods and services produced in an economy, plus the value of the goods and services imported, less the goods and services exported.

'group-think' When a group of people develop a common perspective on an issue and make a collective decision without considering opposing views.

G20 The Group of Twenty, an international forum established in 1999 consisting of the finance ministers and central bank governors representing the most economically developed states in the world. The group was formed to address financial instability and increase the international representation of emerging economic powers; the G20 meets annually, with deputies' meetings and workshops held more frequently; most recently, heads of state also have attended these meetings.

guerrilla warfare Irregular combat and mobile military tactics (such as ambushes and raids) by a small group of combatants against a larger, less mobile, and more formally structured army.

hegemony Concentration of power in the hands of a dominant actor.

Hellenic Greek language, culture, and ethnicity.

heuristic model General strategies and methods for addressing and resolving problems.

'higher realism' An emerging approach to IR that departs from traditionally conceived forms of realism by recognizing the existence of multiple international actors apart from states, the importance of common interests among these various actors, and the possibilities for co-operation based on these interests.

historical structure Patterns of interaction among principal political units that have been influenced by the experiences of the past.

historicism View that theories must account for local and historical factors rather than rely on fundamental principles.

homegrown terrorists Acts of terror, planned or accomplished, by individuals within their home country, sometimes with influence from extremist individuals and groups outside of the country.

homogeneity The quality of being uniformly similar in composition.

human rights Those basic freedoms seen to be the entitlement of all individuals as human beings.

human security Securing people, rather than simply the state, from physical danger and harm.

human trafficking The coercive transport or recruiting of individuals by others for economic and/or sexual purposes.

hyper-globalization An extension of globalization that involves expanded interconnectedness and essential co-operation among international actors. This may involve greater co-ordination on areas such as the environment, food scarcity, and the diffusion of technology.

idealpolitik A normative approach to state behaviour in which states seek to establish peaceful co-existence.

imperialism The theory and practice whereby dominant powers exercise direct and effective control over other countries and regions of the globe.

Industrial Revolution A historical period in the eighteenth and nineteenth centuries originating in the United Kingdom. During this transformational period agrarian societies became industrialized.

insurgency A subversive organized movement aimed at overthrowing a constituted government through armed violence.

intellectual property Any product of the intellect, usually protected through copyrights and patents.

interdependence Conditions in which different states have so many overlapping interests that changes in one will have direct and significant implications for the others.

intergovernmental organization An organization made up of state governments and established by an agreement to pursue common goals.

Intergovernmental Panel on Climate Change An international body that draws on the expertise of over 3,000 leading scientists, created by the World Meteorological Organization and the UN Environment Program in 1988 to monitor and report on climatological change of human origin.

intermestic The growing interconnectedness of, or blurred line between, domestic and international issues.

internationalization The act of bringing an entity formerly organized under a state orientation to international control.

international law Laws governing the relations among states and other actors active in the international system. International law can be said to originate from norms, rules, customs, and formalized legal principles derived from international organizations/conventions.

international non-governmental organizations NGOs that operate outside of the border and authority of a single state and across several states. For example, the Red Cross and Amnesty International are INGOs.

international relations The relations undertaken between separate national states pursuing separate national interests; also, the study of these relations, abbreviated as IR.

Islam The religion articulated by the Koran, a book considered by its adherents to be the verbatim word of the single incomparable God (Allah) as dictated to and written in Arabic by the prophet Muhammad. It is the second-largest and fastest-growing religion in the world.

Islamists Adherents to the belief system of political Islam, also known as Islamism. Islamists may hold a variety of different beliefs, and in some cases advocate violence.

Islamophobia An irrational fear of, or outright prejudice against, Muslims—the followers of Islam.

jihad Literally, 'to strive', but today generally understood as holy war to defend the Muslim faith. 'Greater' jihad involves resisting evil deeds and supporting what is right; 'lesser' jihad is the waging of war against enemies and those who attack Muslims. Although lesser jihad is rare, it is still practised by extremist Islamic groups to achieve political change and to make a self-righteous call for a return to the 'pristine' Islam of the past.

jus ad bellum A body of legal principles that seek to control if and when a state can go to war.

jus gentium An element of just war principles, i.e., a set of laws that govern how states ought to behave during wartime.

jus in bello Justice in war; a body of law developed over time to constrain the behaviour of combatants during armed conflict.

'just war' A set of principles that establishes specific conditions under which the undertaking of war is permissible. Associated with medieval philosophy and the theories of St Thomas Aquinas, just war is a doctrine based on certain ethical and moral justifications for war.

Kyoto Protocol International agreement signed in 1997 in Kyoto, Japan, in regard to national commitments to reduce greenhouse gas emissions; a number of countries, notably Canada, have failed to meet their targets.

laïcité French term connoting secularity in a society in which religion and the state are separate.

laissez-faire The practice of limited government intervention in the economy.

legitimacy The quality of being valid or legal. In IR, legitimacy has normative, moral, and ethical connotations usually conferred through some form of consensus.

levels of analysis A framework for scholars to analyze political phenomena by examining them at different levels, from the particular to the general: individual, group, state, state–society, regional, international, and/or global.

liberal international economic order The actors, actions, and policies of global deregulation and free trade. The Washington Consensus, a set of economic reform recommendations that originated in the United States, is said to be at the heart of the liberal international economic order.

liberalism The belief that individual citizens are all equal in a juridical sense and should have equal rights to education as well as to the practice of religion and free speech.

liberalization The relaxing of social and economic government regulation. Liberalization also can be characterized as allowing a more market-driven economic system to operate in a state and/or internationally.

liberal trade policy Policy based on non-interference and free-market economics that seeks to limit restrictive policies such as tariffs and import and export quotas.

longue durée Approach of the French Annales school that emphasizes the need to study the long-term historical forces that have shaped society and the economy.

Machiavellian realism Realism that rests on a negative view of human nature and the natural existence of state conflict in the international system. Niccolò Machiavelli's obsession with political power and effective rulership has led some to call him the father of modern *realpolitik*.

madrassas Arabic: any type of educational institution; literally, a place where learning is done.

malign hegemony The situation where a dominant power acts in a malevolent manner to lesser powers in the system.

market fundamentalism Exaggerated faith in the ability of unfettered laissez-faire or free-market economic views or policies to solve economic and social problems across the globe.

Marxism Theory that sees ownership of the modes of production as the key principle accounting for economic, social, and political relations.

mediation An act involving a third party who works with disputing parties to resolve the conflict between them.

military humanitarianism The practice of attempting to provide humanitarian relief as part of or through military intervention.

mobile capital The open and relatively free movement of money across international borders as the result of the reduction or elimination of state regulatory principles such as fixed exchange rates.

modernization theory Theory that identifies key factors as being necessary for the economic advancement of societies.

modes of production The manner in which economic activity (including labour, technology, and relations of production) is organized.

Mohist Chinese philosophy that for a short period rivalled Confucianism and promoted the principles of universal care and armed neutrality.

money laundering The act of processing money gained through illicit activities into proceeds that are disguised or concealed as legal.

monopoly capitalism A stage of capitalism where increasingly fewer entities control more of the means of production.

Montreal Protocol An international agreement, initially signed in 1987, to ban the use of chlorofluorocarbons (CFCs) by all states.

moral relativism A philosophical notion that moral or ethical propositions do not reflect universal moral truths but are relative to certain social, cultural, and historical circumstances.

multi-centric world A multi-centric world may be differentiated from a state-centric world in that inter-state organizations and non-state actors play an important role in international relations.

multilateralism The practice of diplomacy among several or many states on an issue or issues, as well as adherence to policies supporting the establishment and maintenance of institutions and associations that facilitate and support this practice in international relations.

multi-level governance The exercise of authority across multiple levels of government, for instance, across federal, state, and municipal levels.

multinational corporations Businesses that operate in many nations.

multi-polar The presence of more than two major powers in the global balance of power.

multi-purpose organization An organization that pursues multiple agendas.

Mutual Assured Destruction (MAD) A condition that existed throughout much of the Cold War in which the two superpowers, the US and the USSR, could destroy each other and the rest of the world with nuclear weapons if either one started a nuclear conflict.

national interests The interests of a state, usually as defined by its government.

neo-idealism A belief that the reduction of international conflict may come from the growth and increasing prominence of international regimes.

networks Interconnected groups of individuals.

neutrality Practice of not taking sides or providing support to either party in a conflict. As employed in IR it refers to a party that does not support another party involved in some form of dispute.

new constitutionalism A framework of governance reform that seeks to include non-state actors, such as NGOs and corporations, in reshaping global social and economic policies.

non-governmental organizations Organizations, commonly labelled as NGOs, that operate apart from any attachment to government, that generally are supported by individual and/or corporate donations, and that exist for the purpose of maintaining, changing, or improving the societal status quo in a particular narrow or broad issue area.

non-offensive defence A practice of developing defensive systems that afford protection but do not pose a threat to other parties.

non-renewable resources Natural resources that, once exploited, cannot be regrown or regenerated, such as fossil fuels and minerals.

non-state actor An individual or group that acts outside of the parameters of a state.

official development assistance Flows of official aid aimed at improving welfare conditions in developing countries.

oligarchy Rule by a small elite group.

outsourcing A business practice that entails garnering goods or services from an external source. Outsourcing has gained prominence as a business practice in the developed world as companies seek to limit costs by gaining cheaper goods and services from the developing world.

ozone depletion (1) The slow depletion of the total volume of ozone in the earth's stratosphere (ozone layer) that has been noticed since the late 1970s, and (2) a much larger, but seasonal, decrease in stratospheric ozone over the polar regions during the same period.

paradigm A theoretical and philosophical framework sometimes assigned to a particular period of time. A paradigm can affect the questions we pose, how we ask those questions, and what are considered acceptable forms of inquiry in a discipline.

Pax Britannica The period of the late nineteenth and early twentieth centuries when Great Britain ruled large areas of the globe through its empire.

Pax Romana The name given to the empire led by Rome that ruled much of Europe during the first and second centuries.

peace-building A strategy that may have security, economic, and governance development components aimed at preventing the outbreak of violent conflict and/or preventing the reoccurrence of prior hostilities.

Peacebuilding Commission Commission established by the General Assembly of the United Nations in 2005 to aid countries in the rebuilding process in post-conflict environments.

peace dividend A term originally used in the 1990s to describe the benefit of reducing national defence spending. The 'dividend' from such a reduction was to be used for public spending in non-defence areas.

peace enforcement The use of armed force, or the threat of such use, to compel combatants to cease their fighting.

peacekeeping The deployment of UN interpositional forces in an area of conflict, with the consent of all parties to the conflict.

peacemaking An act of reconciling former enemies.

Peace of Westphalia Peace that resulted from the signing of two treaties—the peace treaties of Osnabrück (15 May 1648) and Münster (24 October 1648)—that brought an end to the Thirty Years War (1618–48).

pluralist An individual who promotes diversity among, for instance, cultural, ethnic, and religious groups. Pluralists can be seen as holding normative beliefs on the desirability of peaceful coexistence among peoples with differing identities.

politics A process of contestation and resolution of social and economic issues among a citizenry, carried out through political parties, interest groups, businesses, etc. Put simply, in Harold Lasswell's definition, it is about who gets what, when, how.

politics of meaning The clash of different conceptions and theories about the nature and objective of politics at the global level and over methods of studying, observing, understanding, and explaining global politics.

polis Greek term often equated with the city-state or the citizens thereof.

positivism A philosophy of science that relies on the scientific method and observation for generating theories.

post-Cold War era The period following the end of the Cold War (i.e., after 1989) that saw the dismantling of the Soviet Union and rise of other states and issues to the top of an agenda of Western concern.

post-dependency theory A variation of dependency theory that seeks to account for the increased prevalence of corporate actors and the structural conditions brought on by globalization.

postmodernism Critical theory that is generally distrustful of grand theories and that rejects absolute truths for relativism and contingency, and thus that challenges many of the assumptions underpinning more traditional theories.

post-Westphalian world order A global order in which non-state actors play an increasingly important role, as opposed to the state-driven Westphalian order.

power The ability, through coercion or influence, of an actor (state, political leader, etc.) to get others to do what they might otherwise not want to do or prevent them from doing something they might otherwise do.

power asymmetries The power differential between two forces in which one force has greater power than another.

preventive deployment A proactive deterrent measure designed to facilitate a political solution by avoiding or limiting violent conflict.

preventive diplomacy Diplomatic action aimed at preventing disputes from escalating into full-blown conflicts.

privatization The transfer of government services and/or assets to private individuals and firms; the opposite of nationalization.

problem-solving theory Cox's term for traditional theories that do not reflect on their own assumptions, but proceed to explain phenomena on the basis of these assumptions.

proxy wars Occurrences during the Cold War when the US and the Soviet Union supplied and encouraged other parties to engage in conflict, putatively for either the containment or spread of state socialism (or capitalism).

'race to the bottom' The deregulation of state economies as countries seek to attract businesses with lower taxes and regulatory standards. The race to the bottom has been highlighted by critics who point to the negative side of globalization.

radicalism The political orientation of those who favour change in government and society but who may be willing to accept gradual change. Radicals may or may not use violence as a means to an end.

raison d'état The practical application of the doctrine of realism.

realism A theoretical approach that treats all international relations as relations between states engaged in the pursuit of power and self-interest. It does not accommodate non-state actors in its analysis.

realpolitik A view that holds that power is the central feature of international relations.

Reformation Sixteenth-century European religious movement that challenged the central authority of the Roman Catholic Church and, hence, European unity.

refugees Individuals who have fled their country or local territory of origin for fear of persecution; refugees who seek safer haven within their own country are commonly called 'internally displaced persons'.

regional arrangements Agreements between one or more states in a region.

regionalism Shared identity, interests, and goals among states in a particular region that often translates into the formation of regional political, economic, and/or cultural institutions aimed at pursuing shared interests.

religious extremism A religious interpretation or belief that stands apart from the mainstream of a religion. Such beliefs may be marked by literal or rigid interpretation of religious texts, exclusivity, and the promotion of coercive, even violent, action towards non-believers.

religious fundamentalism Strict adherence to a set of basic or fundamental principles and beliefs as set out in the sacred writings of a religion.

responsibility to protect (R2P) A principle whereby states are considered to be responsible for the well-being of their citizens and if they fail to exercise that responsibility, then it falls to the international community.

revolutionary A person who advocates and works actively towards sudden, drastic, and fundamental changes in society.

revolution in military affairs The set of practices, related to technological advancements, broadened definitions of such concepts as security, and new theatres of military conflict, that have changed the manner in which wars are fought.

sabotage Deliberate damage to property, especially to infrastructure such as power lines, bridges, roads, and rail lines, undertaken to weaken a political state or regime.

satyagraha Non-violent resistance as practised by Mahatma Gandhi as a means of pressing for political reform in South Africa and India.

scientific behaviouralism A method of analysis that focuses on the objective measurement of behaviour (or measured responses to stimuli). It excludes the subjectivity of emotion and inner mental experience.

security dilemma The situation where one state, by increasing its armaments for purposes of defence, presents a threat to another state, which in turn increases its armaments, thus posing a new threat, and so on; in brief, a spiralling deterioration of security between two or more states that may not desire conflict.

self-determination A principle espoused in 1918 by US President Woodrow Wilson that argued that each 'people' should be allowed to govern themselves rather than be governed by colonial powers. The right of self-determination has been codified in international law within the Charter of the United Nations.

self-help When states look out for themselves, i.e., find the means (usually military, economic, and diplomatic-legal) to protect their sovereignty from intruders.

Semitic The linguistic, cultural, and ethnic groups located in what is now the Middle East, i.e., Jews and Arabs, believed to be descended from Shem, the son of Noah.

separatists Those who advocate cultural, ethnic, tribal, religious, racial, governmental, or gender separation from the larger group, often with demands for greater political autonomy and even for full political secession and the formation of a new state.

smart sanctions A form of sanction aimed at affecting a specific group within a state (such as an executive body, specific company, or organization). Smart sanctions are designed to limit their detrimental affect on those parties outside the targeted group or entity.

social movements Groups of people who are united under a common ideology and who seek common goals.

social relations of production The objective material relations that exist in any society independently of human consciousness, formed between all people in the process of social production, exchange, and distribution of material wealth.

society of states A concept originating with the English school of IR that contends that international relations take place within a society of states. This society is based around certain ideas that influence the structural composition of the international system.

'soft law' Quasi-legal instruments without legally binding force, or whose binding force is somewhat 'weaker' than the binding force associated with traditional law. Soft law is often contrasted with 'hard law'—the more binding legal instruments.

sovereignty The principle that a state has absolute authority not subject to any other state's control or approval.

sovereignty-bound Controlled by the rules and constraints of the sovereign state.

sovereignty-free Individuals and groups not beholden to the state that operate outside the bounds of the recognized legitimacy of states; related to the emergence of non-state entities that play an important role in international relations.

state A political entity with a contained territory, permanent population, and government apparatus that has monopoly over the legitimate use of force. To be legally considered a state the entity must be recognized by other states as sovereign.

state-centric The focus on sovereign states as the sole actors of importance in international relations.

state-centric measures International policy initiatives initiated and/or pursued primarily by states.

state-centric world A world in which the focus is on state-to-state relations; thus, the state is deemed to be central to foreign policy-making.

state/society complex A basic unit of analysis in IR that reflects the relationship between a particular state and the people within it, considered by some scholars as a more appropriate unit of analysis than the state-as-actor model because the state does not act in isolation of its relationship with society.

statism The theory or practice of concentrating economic and political power in the state, resulting in a weak position for the individual or community with respect to government and governance.

structural adjustment programs Policies developed by the IMF and World Bank aimed at helping states repay debt that require participating states to initiate free-market reforms such as trade liberalization, privatization, and deregulation.

structural changes Those changes that lead to a major transformation of the global system.

structural power Power embedded in the economic, cultural, political, and ideational characteristics of the international system.

structural violence Harm and injury that result from the structural conditions in which people live, such as poverty, societal discrimination, and unjust legal and penal systems.

sub-national actors Actors operating below the level of the state and within its national boundaries.

subsidiarity A principle of governing that holds that a majority of power should rest with smaller levels of government, such as the local level, rather than at the higher or national level.

suffragettes Women who campaigned for the right to vote.

Sunna The Islamic collection of the sayings and practices of the Prophet Muhammad.

superpower conflict Hostilities between the US and the USSR during the Cold War period.

supranational The transcendence of state borders—at a level above state governance.

surplus value Wealth or profit gained by the capitalist owners of the means of production created by the labour of workers in the production process.

sustainable development Economic development that seeks to ensure that future generations will not be deprived of resources or a healthy environment by economic activity in the present. It requires that the current generation not exceed the regenerative capacity of nature.

sustainable peace A condition in which people can live together in sustained harmony. To achieve such a peace one would have to address the underlying sources of potential conflicts.

suzerainty Conditions under which lesser powers or peoples are controlled by a major power but retain considerable autonomy.

Taoism An anarchic pacifism that advocated a natural order based on non-violence; one of two principal philosophical traditions in Chinese life and thought.

tax havens Countries or territories where certain taxes are levied at a low rate or not at all.

terrorism The systematic use of terror, especially as a means of coercion for political and/or religious ends.

tragedy of the commons Exploitation of the commons, i.e., that which is not or cannot be individually owned, such as oceans, the air we breathe, wildlife, or lands held in common for the public good, by individuals and corporations for short-term profit without recognition of longer-term loss for everyone.

transnational movements Movements that unite peoples across state borders to pursue common purposes and goals.

transnational organized criminal groups Centralized groups involved in organized criminal activity that operate in multiple states.

treaty A recognized formal agreement between two or more nations, relating to peace, alliance, trade, etc.

Utopianism The ideology that holds that there is a perfect future that people can hope to achieve.

Wahhabism A radical interpretation and practice of Islam based solely on literal interpretations of the Koran (the holy book of Islam) and the Sunna (Prophet Muhammad's teachings). It is concerned with 'purifying' Islam from innovations (*bid'a*) and rejects interpretations of Islamic thought after the tenth century, when most Islamic judicial rulings on holy texts and schools of jurisprudence were established.

War against Terror A term introduced by the George W. Bush administration in the US to refer to military, political, and legal actions taken by the US against Islamist-inspired terrorism.

war crimes Clear violations of the laws or customs of war, including but not limited to mass murder, the ill treatment or deportation of civilian residents of an occupied territory to slave labour camps, the murder or ill treatment of prisoners of war, the killing of hostages, and rape.

Washington Consensus A set of free-market and deregulatory principles that originated in the United States. Originally, the term was used by John Williamson to summarize proposed economic reforms for Latin American states in the 1990s. More recently it has become a contentious term that is synonymous with American-led globalization and neo-liberalism.

white-collar crime Any of a variety of non-violent frauds, schemes, and commercial offences committed by business persons and public officials that have cheating as their central element (e.g., stock manipulation, consumer fraud, bribery).

World Commission on Environment and Development UN Commission formed in 1983 and headed by Norwegian Prime Minister Gro Harlem Brundtland, whose 1987 report, *Our Common Future*, has been widely influential in seeking to reconcile environmental management with economic growth.

World Economic Forum Annual meeting held in Davos, Switzerland, established by a Geneva-based non-profit foundation, which brings together top business leaders, international political leaders, selected intellectuals, and journalists to discuss the most pressing issues facing the world, especially involving or as they relate to the economy.

world government The notion of a single common political authority for all of humanity. Inherent to the concept of a world government is the idea that nations would be required to pool or surrender (depending on one's point of view) sovereignty over some areas of their decision-making for the benefit of all humanity.

world order An arrangement that involves more than just states but also individuals and other non-state actors. Ideally, this 'order' would advance security, development, human rights, basic needs, and justice for all of humanity.

World Social Forum Annual meeting, organized by NGOs and activists of the anti-globalization movement, held in different parts of the globe in direct response to the World Economic Forum. This forum is plural, diverse, non-governmental, and non-partisan, and its objective is to develop alternatives to neo-liberalism and the worse elements of globalization.

world systems theory An approach that examines international relations as derived from different historical economic and social systems.

xenophobic An irrational feeling of fear of, or contempt for, people who are strangers or foreigners.

zealots Fanatical individuals who are adherents to a particular (usually religious) way of life, from a first-century AD Jewish sect (the Zealots) that fought against Roman rule in Palestine.

zones of peace Areas of the globe where military conflict among the states in the region is considered to be extremely unlikely.

Notes

Introduction

1. Note that the new political framework that emerged out of the Westphalian Treaty paved the way for a clash between two conceptions of sovereignty: the notion of 'state' sovereignty (or delegated sovereignty) and the idea that sovereignty could reside directly in the hands of the people living within a demarcated territory. The theory of state or 'delegated' sovereignty dominated and developed in parallel with the evolution of the modern state. It described a particular state/society relationship that was shaped by the social, cultural, and economic environment of sixteenth- and seventeenth-century Europe. On this point, see Joseph Camilleri, 'Rethinking Sovereignty in a Shrinking, Fragmented World', in R.B.J. Walker and Saul Mendlovitz, eds, *Contending Sovereignties: Redefining Political Community* (Boulder, Colo., 1990), 13–14.
2. See Evan Luard, *The Globalization of Politics: The Changed Focus of Political Action in the Modern World* (London, 1990), vi.
3. Steve Smith and John Baylis, 'Introduction', in Baylis and Smith, eds, *The Globalization of World Politics: An Introduction to International Relations*, 2nd edn (Oxford, 2001), 2.
4. Harold D. Lasswell, *Politics: Who Gets What, When, How* (New York, 1936).
5. See James H. Mittleman, 'How Does Globalization Really Work?', in Mittleman, ed., *Globalization: Critical Reflections* (Boulder, Colo., 1996), 229.
6. See <www.hm-treasury.gov.uk/d/leitch_finalreport 051206.pdf>. (27 Nov. 2008)
7. On this point, see W. Andy Knight, 'Pluralizing Global Governance: Bottom-up Multilateralism and the Construction of Space for Civil Society', in Claire Turenne Sjolander and Jean Francois Thibault, eds, *Of Global Governance: Culture, Economics and Politics* (Ottawa, 2002).
8. James Rosenau, *Distant Proximities: Dynamics beyond Globalization* (Princeton, NJ, 2003), 8–11.
9. James N. Rosenau and Mary Durfee, *Thinking Theory Thoroughly: Coherent Approaches to an Incoherent World* (Boulder, Colo., 2000), 40.
10. John Burton, *World Society* (Cambridge, 1972).
11. James N. Rosenau, *Turbulence in World Politics: A Theory of Change and Continuity* (Princeton, NJ, 1990), 5.
12. John Mearsheimer, *The Tragedy of Great Power Politics* (New York, 2001).
13. Adam Watson, *The Evolution of International Society* (New York, 1992).
14. Friedrich Meinecke, *Machiavellism: The Doctrine of Raison d'État and Its Place in Modern History*, trans. Douglas Scott (London, 1957), 2–3.
15. Michael Ignatieff, *Virtual War, Kosovo and Beyond* (Harmondsworth, UK, 2001).

Chapter 1

1. Glenn Hastedt and Kay Knickrehm, 'Studying World Politics', in Hastedt and Knickrehm, eds, *Toward the Twenty-First Century: A Reader in World Politics* (Englewood Cliffs, NJ, 1994), 6.
2. See Charles W. Kegley Jr, ed., *Controversies in International Relations Theory: Realism and the Neoliberal Challenge* (New York, 1995), 3.
3. Stephen M. Walt, 'International Relations: One World, Many Theories', in Karen Mingst and Jack Snyder, eds, *Essential Readings in World Politics* (New York, 2001), 27.
4. E.H. Carr, *The Twenty Years Crisis, 1919–1939* (New York, 1964), 4.
5. James E. Dougherty and Robert L. Pfaltzgraff, *Contending Theories of International Relations: A Comprehensive Survey*, 3rd edn (New York, 1997), 541.
6. Robert Cox, 'Towards a Post-hegemonic Conceptualization of World Order: Reflections on the Relevancy of Ibn Khaldun', in Cox with Timothy J. Sinclair, *Approaches to World Order* (Cambridge, 1996), 145.
7. Ibid.
8. Lewis Mumford, *The Story of Utopias* (New York, 1962), 1.
9. Maurice Meisner, *Marxism, Maoism and Utopianism* (Madison, Wisc., 1982), 3.
10. Ibid., 14.
11. See Max Weber, *The Sociology of Religion* (Boston, 1963), 144; Hans Gerth and C. Wright Mills, eds, *From Max Weber: Essays in Sociology* (New York, 1958), 128.
12. Karl Mannheim, *Ideology and Utopia* (New York, 1952), 236.
13. See Dante Alighieri, *De Monarchia*, trans. Herbert W. Schneider, 2nd edn (New York, 1957).
14. Dougherty and Pfaltzgraff, *Contending Theories*, 7.
15. Dubois's thinking in *De Recuperatione Terrae Sanctae* can be found in Frank Russell, *Theories of International Relations* (New York, 1936), 105–10.
16. Hedley Bull, 'The Theory of International Politics 1919–1969', in Brian Porter, ed., *The Aberystwyth Papers: International Politics 1919–1969* (Oxford, 1972), 34.

17. See Steve Smith, 'Paradigm Dominance in International Relations: The Development of International Relations as a Social Science', *Millennium: Journal of International Studies* 16, 2 (1987): 191.

18. Ibid., 192.

19. See David Weigall, *International Relations: A Concise Companion* (London, 2002), 117.

20. Smith, 'Paradigm Dominance', 191.

21. Trevor Taylor, 'Utopianism', in Steve Smith, ed., *International Relations: British and American Perspectives* (Oxford, 1985), 92.

22. Peter Wilson, 'Introduction: The Twenty Years' Crisis and the Category of Idealism in International Relations', in David Long and Peter Wilson, eds, *Thinkers of the Twenty Years' Crisis: Inter-war Idealism Reassessed* (Oxford, 1995), 4.

23. Hans Morgenthau, 'A Realist Theory of International Politics', in Hastedt and Knickrehm, eds, *Toward the Twenty-First Century*, 8.

24. John H. Herz, 'Idealist Internationalism and the Security Dilemma', in Andrew Linklater, ed., *International Relations: Critical Concepts in Political Science* (London and New York, 2000), 261.

25. See Smith, 'Paradigm Dominance', 194.

26. Robert Rothchild, 'On the Costs of Realism', *Political Science Quarterly* 87, 3 (1972): 348.

27. Morgenthau, 'A Realist Theory', 9

28. Ibid.

29. Ibid., 38.

30. Ibid., 11.

31. Ibid., 13.

32. See Hans J. Morgenthau, 'The Evil of Politics and the Ethics of Evil', *Ethics* 56, 1 (1945): 1–18.

33. See Mingst and Snyder, eds, *Essential Readings in World Politics*, 68.

34. Kenneth Waltz, 'Realist Thought and Neo-Realist Theory', *Journal of International Affairs* 44 (1990): 23.

35. Ibid., 26.

36. Ibid., 29.

37. Ibid., 29–30.

38. On this, see Walt, 'International Relations', 28–9.

39. See Duncan Bell, 'Anarchy, Power and Death: Contemporary Political Realism as Ideology', *Journal of Political Ideologies* 7, 2 (2002): 221–39.

40. Kenneth N. Waltz, 'Political Structures', in Mingst and Snyder, eds, *Essential Readings in World Politics*, 82–6; also see N.J. Rengger, *International Relations, Political Theory and the Problem of Order: Beyond International Relations Theory* (London, 2000), 37–49.

41. John Mearsheimer, *The Tragedy of Great Power Politics* (New York, 2001).

42. Bell, 'Anarchy, Power and Death', 229–30.

43. Fred Halliday, *Rethinking International Relations* (Vancouver, 1994), 11.

44. See Stanley Hoffmann, 'An American Social Science: International Relations', *Daedalus* 106, 3 (1977): 48.

45. Smith, 'Paradigm Dominance', 195.

46. Martin Wight, *International Theory, The Three Traditions* (Leicester, UK, 1991).

47. Hedley Bull, *The Anarchical Society: A Study of Order in World Politics* (London, 1977).

48. Ibid., 13.

49. Ibid., 22.

50. Andrew Hurrell, *On Global Order* (Oxford, 2007), 2.

51. Bull, *The Anarchical Society*, 22.

52. On the history, see, e.g., Martin Wight, *Systems of States* (Leicester, UK, 1977); on the evolution, see Adam Watson, *The Evolution of International Society* (London, 1992), and Hedley Bull and Adam Watson, eds, *The Expansion of International Society* (Oxford, 1985).

53. Bull and Watson, eds, *The Expansion of International Society*, 9.

54. Nicholas J. Wheeler, *Saving Strangers: Humanitarian Intervention in International Society* (Oxford, 2002), 11.

55. Alex J. Bellamy, ed., *International Society and Its Critics* (Oxford, 2004), 12.

56. Mark W. Zacher and Richard A. Matthew, 'Liberal International Theory: Common Threads, Divergent Strands', in Kegley, ed., *Controversies in International Relations Theory*, 108.

57. Freedom in this case means the absence of obstruction in the pursuit of given ends. It allows for individualism. See Boris DeWiel, *Democracy: A History of Ideas* (Vancouver, 2000), 72.

58. Michael Doyle, 'Liberalism and World Politics', in Kegley, ed., *Controversies in International Relations Theory*, 83.

59. Joseph Schumpeter, *Capitalism, Socialism, and Democracy* (New York, 1950).

60. Michael Haas, *International Conflict* (New York, 1974), 464–5.

61. See Niccolò Machiavelli, *The Prince and the Discourses*, ed. Max Lerner (New York, 1950).

62. See Liu Feng and Zhang Ruizhuang, 'The Typologies of Realism', *Chinese Journal of International Politics* 1, 1 (2006): 109–34.

63. Herz, 'Idealist Internationalism', 271.

64. Ibid., 272.

65. Although, to be fair, some liberals espouse a kind of Utopian idealism when they propose a neutralist pluralism that tolerates a multitude of competing ideologies, religions, and cultures. A good example of this is found in the work of Robert Nozick, *Anarchy, State, and Utopia* (New York, 1974).

66. Ole R. Holsti, 'Theories of International Relations and Foreign Policy: Realism and Its Challengers', in Kegley, ed., *Controversies in International Relations Theory*. Some scholars have pointed out the many similarities that exist between neo-realism and neo-liberalism. See David A. Baldwin, ed., *Neorealism and Neoliberalism: The Contemporary Debate* (New York, 1993), 4–12.

67. Charles W. Kegley Jr, 'The Foundations of International Relations Theory and the Resurrection of the Realist–Liberal

Debate', in Kegley, ed., *Controversies in International Relations Theory*, 26.

68. Robert O. Keohane, *After Hegemony: Cooperation and Discord in the World Political Economy* (Princeton, NJ, 1984).

69. Robert O. Keohane and Joseph S. Nye, *Power and Interdependence: World Politics in Transition* (Boston, 1977).

70. See, e.g., Ernst B. Haas, *Beyond the Nation State: Functionalism and International Organizations* (Stanford, Calif., 1964).

71. David Mitrany, *A Working Peace System: An Argument for the Functional Development of International Organisation* (London, 1943), 6.

72. Ibid., 27.

73. Karl Deutsch, *Political Community and the North Atlantic Area: International Organization in the Light of Historical Experience* (New York, 1957); Ernst Haas, *The Uniting of Europe: Political, Social, and Economic Forces, 1950–1957* (Stanford, Calif., 1968).

74. Michael Mandelbaum, *The Ideas That Conquered the World* (New York, 2002).

75. Zacher and Matthew, 'Liberal International Theory', 140.

76. Horton argues that the renaissance of liberalism may have created as many problems as it has resolved. John Horton, *Liberalism, Multiculturalism and Toleration* (New York, 1993), 1.

77. See Dougherty and Pfaltzgraff, *Contending Theories*, 24.

78. Ibid., 25.

79. Smith, 'Paradigm Dominance', 189.

80. See Charles Reynolds, *Theory and Explanation in International Relations in Great Britain* (Oxford, 1973).

81. See Richard Little, 'The Evolution of International Relations as a Social Science', in Randolph Kent and Gunnar Neilsson, eds, *The Study and Teaching of International Relations* (London, 1980), 9.

82. Smith, 'Paradigm Dominance', 194.

83. See Dougherty and Pfaltzgraff, *Contending Theories*, 33.

84. Linklater, ed., *International Relations*, 255.

85. Ibid., 258.

86. Ibid.

87. Herz, 'Idealist Internationalism', 276.

Chapter 2

1. Steven L. Lamy, 'Contemporary Mainstream Approaches: Neo-Realism and Neo-Liberalism,' in John Baylis and Steve Smith, eds, *The Globalization of World Politics: An Introduction to International Relations*, 3rd edn (Oxford, 2005), 221.

2. See John Godfrey Saxe, 'The Blind Men and the Elephant', at: <rack1.ul.cs.cmu.edu/is/saxe/doc.scn?fr = 0&rp = http%3A%2F%2Frack1.ul.cs.cmu.edu%2Fis%2Fsaxe%2F&pg = 4>; Don Fabun, *Communications: The Transfer of Meaning* (New York, 1968), 13.

3. See Karl Marx, *Capital*, student edn, ed. C.J. Arthur (London, 1967 [1867]).

4. Vladimir Ilyich Lenin, *Imperialism, the Highest Stage of Capitalism: A Popular Outline*, 13th edn (Moscow, 1966 [1917]).

5. W.W. Rostow, *The Stages of Economic Growth: A Non-Communist Manifesto* (London, 1960).

6. 'Newton' is used here as a symbol for that watershed in history when people widely believed that the external world was subject to a few knowable laws and was systematically capable of productive manipulation.

7. See John Ernest Goldthorpe, *The Sociology of the Third World: Disparity and Involvement* (Cambridge, 1975), 147–8.

8. Paul A. Baran, *The Political Economy of Growth* (New York, 1957).

9. See Raúl Prebisch, *The Economic Development of Latin America and Its Principal Problems* (New York, 1950).

10. André Gunder Frank, *Capitalism and Underdevelopment in Latin America* (New York, 1967).

11. See Fernando Henrique Cardoso and Enzo Faletto, *Dependency and Development in Latin America*, trans. Marjory Mattingly Urquidi (Berkeley, Calif., 1979). For a more comprehensive overview of these and other dependency thinkers, see John Martinussen, *Society, State and Market* (Halifax, 1997); Robert A. Packenham, *The Dependency Movement: Scholarship and Politics in Dependency Studies* (Cambridge, Mass., 1992).

12. Martinussen, *Society, State and Market*, 95.

13. Wallerstein believed that there are three potential world systems: (1) world empire; (2) the global economic system; and (3) socialist world government.

14. For Wallerstein, a world system is a social system with boundaries, structures, member groups, rules of legitimation, and coherence. It is characterized by the existence of conflicting forces that hold it together by the tensions between those forces but that at the same time can tear it apart as each group seeks continually to remould the system to its advantage. Wallerstein compared the world system to an organism, in that it has a lifespan and throughout that lifespan certain elements of its characteristics can change while others may remain stable. Therefore, at some points in its history it may be described as 'strong', while at other times it may be characterized as 'weak' with regard to the internal logic of its functioning.

15. Immanuel Wallerstein, *The Modern World-System*, vol.1: *Capitalist Agriculture and the Origins of the European World Economy in the Sixteenth Century* (San Diego, 1976), 229–33.

16. See Immanuel Wallerstein, *The Capitalist World-Economy* (Cambridge, 1979), 66.

17. Christopher Chase-Dunn, 'World Systems Theorizing', in Jonathan Turner, ed., *Handbook of Sociological Theory* (New York, 2001). Also see Christopher Chase-Dunn, *Global Formation: Structures of the World-Economy*, 2nd edn (Lanham, Md, 1998).

18. Robert Cox, 'Social Forces, States and World Orders: Beyond International Relations Theory', in Robert

Cox with Timothy Sinclair, *Approaches to World Order* (Cambridge, 1996).

19. While the eighteenth century is considered the advent of the 'Enlightenment' era, its roots can be traced to the Aristotelian logic of Thomas Aquinas in the thirteenth century.

20. Two of the primary proponents were Richard Ashley and R.B.J Walker. For a sampling of their work, see Richard Ashley, 'The Geopolitics of Geopolitical Space: Toward a Critical Social Theory of International Politics', *Alternatives* 12, 4 (1987): 403–34, and Richard Ashley and R.B.J. Walker, 'Reading Dissidence/Writing the Discipline: Crisis and the Question of Sovereignty in International Studies', *International Studies Quarterly* 34 (1990): 367–416.

21. See Pauline Marie Rosenau, *Post-Modernism and the Social Sciences: Insights, Inroads, and Intrusions* (Princeton, NJ, 1992).

22. Jean-François Lyotard, *The Post-modern Condition: A Report on Knowledge* (Manchester, 1984), xxiv.

23. See Richard Ashley, 'The Poverty of Neo-Realism', *International Organisation* 38, 2 (1984): 225–86.

24. Steve Smith and Patricia Owens, 'Alternative Approaches to International Theory', in John Baylis and Steve Smith, eds, *The Globalization of World Politics: An Introduction to International Relations*, 3rd edn (Oxford, 2005), 285–7.

25. See Michel Foucault, *Power* (New York, 1994); Foucault, *Politics, Philosophy, Culture: Interviews and Other Writings, 1977–1984* (New York, 1988).

26. On this point, see Smith and Owens, 'Alternative Approaches', 285.

27. Ashley, 'Geopolitics of Geopolitical Space'.

28. For further elaboration, see D. Campbell, *Writing Security: United States Foreign Policy and the Politics of Identity* (Manchester, 1992), 9.

29. Joshua S. Goldstein and Sandra Whitworth, *International Relations*, Canadian edn (Toronto, 2005), 118.

30. See especially Jacques Derrida, *Of Grammatology* (Baltimore, 1976).

31. Smith and Owens, 'Alternative Approaches', 287.

32. Richard Ashley, 'Untying the Sovereign State: A Double Reading of the Anarchy Problematique', *Millennium* 17, 2 (1988): 227–62.

33. See Steve Smith, 'Positivism and Beyond', in Steve Smith, Ken Booth, and Marysia Zalewski, eds, *International Theory: Positivism and Beyond* (Cambridge, 1996), 11–46.

34. See Nicholas Rengger and Ben Thirkell-White, eds, *Critical International Relations Theory after 25 Years* (Cambridge, 2007).

35. Jill Steans and Lloyd Pettiford, with Thomas Diez, *Introduction to International Relations: Perspectives and Themes*, 2nd edn (Essex, 2005), 131.

36. Ibid., 140.

37. Rosenau, *Post-Modernism and the Social Sciences*. Also see D.S.L. Jarvis, *International Relations and the Challenge of Postmodernism: Defending the Discipline* (Columbia, SC, 2000).

38. Robert Jackson and Georg Sorensen, *Introduction to International Relations: Theories and Approaches*, 2nd edn (Oxford, 2003), 252.

39. Among these scholars are: Isobel Coleman, Cynthia Enloe, Charlotte Hooper, Nükel Kardam, Marianne Marchand, Philomena Okeke, Jane Parpart, V. Spike Peterson, Elizabeth Ridell-Dixon, Fiona Robinson, Lydia Sargent, Claire Turenne Sjolander, Heather Smith, Deborah Stienstra, Christine Sylvester, J. Ann Tickner, Sandra Whitworth, Gillian Youngs, and Marysia Zalewski.

40. The UN Development Program has developed a measure of the extent of gender inequality globally. The instrument is called the Gender Empowerment Measure (GEM) and is based on estimates of women's relative income and their access to professional and parliamentary positions. It shows that gender inequality is still a major problem in most countries.

41. Steans and Pettiford, with Diez, *Introduction to International Relations*, 155.

42. Smith and Owens, 'Alternative Approaches', 280–4.

43. The least egalitarian country is Saudi Arabia, where women still are not permitted to vote, to travel unaccompanied by male relatives, or to drive.

44. See the following books by Cynthia Enloe: *Bananas, Beaches and Bases: Making Feminist Sense of International Politics* (London, 1989); *The Morning After: Sexual Politics at the End of the Cold War* (Berkeley, Calif., 1993); *Maneuvers: The International Politics of Militarizing Women's Lives* (Berkeley, Calif., 2000).

45. Enloe, *Maneuvers*, 51.

46. L. Sargent, *Women and Revolution: A Discussion of the Unhappy Marriage of Marxism and Feminism* (Boston, 1981).

47. Marysia Zalewski, 'Feminist Standpoint Theory Meets International Relations Theory: A Feminist Version of David and Goliath', *Fletcher Forum of World Affairs* 17, 2 (1993): 15.

48. Ibid.

49. See, e.g., the critique of Morgenthau's realist postulates in J. Ann Tickner, 'Hans Morgenthau's Principles of Political Realism: A Feminist Reformulation', *Millennium* 17, 3 (1988): 429–40.

50. H. Kinsella, 'For a Careful Reading: The Conservatism of Gender Constructivism', *International Studies Review* 5 (2003): 296.

51. V. Spike Peterson, *A Critical Rewriting of Global Political Economy: Reproductive, Productive, and Virtual Economies* (London and New York, 2003).

52. Judith Butler, *Gender Trouble: Feminism and the Subversion of Identity* (London, 1990).

53. See Gayatri Spivak, 'Can the Subaltern Speak?', in C. Nelson and L. Grossberg, eds, *Marxism and the Interpretation of Culture* (Basingstoke, UK, 1988).

54. For more details on the health effects of this radioactive spill, see David R. Marples, 'A Correlation between Radiation and Health Problems in Belarus?', *Post-Soviet Geography* 35, 5 (1993): 281–92.

55. Garrett Hardin, 'The Tragedy of the Commons', *Science* 162 (1968): 1243–8.

56. Ted Hopf, 'The Promise of Constructivism in International Relations Theory', *International Security* 23, 1 (Summer 1998): 184.

57. Ibid., 182.

58. Alexander Wendt, 'Anarchy Is What States Make of It', *International Organization* 46, 2 (Spring 1992): 391–425.

59. John Ruggie, 'What Makes the World Hang Together? Neo-utilitarianism and the Social Constructivist Challenge', in Ruggie, *Constructing the World Polity: Essays on International Institutionalization* (London and New York, 1989), 33.

60. Hopf, 'The Promise of Constructivism', 175.

61. John Ruggie, 'Embedded Liberalism and the Postwar Economic Regimes', in Ruggie, *Constructing the World Polity*, 84

62. Hopf, 'The Promise of Constructivism', 180.

63. Ibid., 200.

Chapter 3

1. On this point, see John Baylis and Steve Smith, eds, *The Globalization of World Politics: An Introduction to International Relations*, 3rd edn (Oxford, 2005), 3.

2. For an expansion of this history, see Charles Jones, Cristine de Clercy, and W. Andy Knight, *Introduction to Politics: Concepts, Methods, Issues* (Toronto, forthcoming).

3. Ragnar Numelin, *The Beginnings of Diplomacy: A Sociological Study of Intertribal and International Relations* (London, 1950), 18.

4. Ibid., 20.

5. See Adam Watson, *The Evolution of International Society* (New York, 1992), 21–3.

6. For further information on Sumerian society, see Samuel Noah Kramer, *The Sumerians: Their History, Culture and Character* (Chicago, 1971); Kramer, *History Begins at Sumer: Thirty-Nine Firsts in Recorded History* (Philadelphia, 1981).

7. See <ragz-international.com/babylonia.htm>. (11 Aug. 2004)

8. For a map of the Assyrian empire, see <www.angelfire.com/nt/Gilgamesh/images/assyria.gif>. (11 Aug. 2004)

9. For a map of ancient Persia, see <www.livius.org/a/1/maps/persia_map.gif>. (11 Aug. 2004)

10. See Watson, *Evolution of International Society*, 40–6.

11. <encarta.msn.com/encyclopedia_761564512/Persia.html>. (12 Aug. 2004)

12. Watson, *Evolution of International Society*, 47.

13. Ian Morris, 'The Early Polis as City and State', in John Rich and Andrew Wallace-Hadrill, eds, *City and Country in the Ancient World* (London, 1991), 26.

14. Watson, *Evolution of International Society*, 48–50. Descent from citizens on both sides would mean that both one's father and one's mother's father were citizens.

15. Martin Wight, *Systems of States* (Leicester, UK, 1977), 46–7.

16. This Hellenic international society was located on the lower Balkan Peninsula and embraced several islands in the surrounding Aegean, Adriatic, and Mediterranean Sea.

17. The Oracle at Delphi acted as one authority for dealing with disputes between city-states. The Greek concept of *dike* also was used to settle disputes. *Dike* involved a third party to help disputing parties reach a settlement. Nicholson notes the terminology that emerged from Greek conflict resolution practices. Terms such as reconciliation, truce, alliance, coalition, arbitration, peace, and neutrality were used on a regular basis as the interactions, exchanges, and relations between Greek city-states increased. See H. Nicolson, *The Evolution of Diplomatic Method* (London, 1954), 3–14. Nicolson notes that the concept of neutrality was expressed in a Greek word that means 'to stay quiet'.

18. Robert H. Jackson, 'The Evolution of International Society', in John Baylis and Steve Smith, eds, *The Globalization of World Politics: An Introduction to International Relations*, 2nd edn (Oxford, 2001), 38–9.

19. Josiah Ober, 'Classical Greek Times', in Michael Howard, George J. Andreopoulos, and Mark R. Shulman, eds, *The Laws of War: Constraints on Warfare in the Western World* (New Haven, 1994), 13.

20. Guy Van Damme, 'Jus in Bello', in Bruno Coppieters and Nick Fotion, eds, *Moral Constraints on War: Principles and Cases* (New York, 2002), 123.

21. This bipolar structure was known as a 'diarchy'. See Watson, *Evolution of International Society*, 59.

22. Thucydides, *History of the Peloponnesian War*, trans. R. Warner (London, 1954).

23. The term 'balance of power' is used to refer to the general concept of one or more states's power being used to balance that of another state or group of states. Such counterbalancing systems have been used throughout history to prevent one state from conquering a state or group of states and to maintain equilibrium/stability within the international system.

24. See Watson, *Evolution of International Society*, 60–4.

25. Ibid., 98.

26. For more information on Caesar, see <heraklia.fws1.com/>. (26 Aug. 2004)

27. During this period, Octavian suspended expansion of the Roman Empire and introduced a hereditary monarchy, which lasted for five generations. For more on Octavian, see <www.vroma.org/~bmcmanus/antony.html>. (26 Aug. 2004)

28. See Michael Walzer, *Just and Unjust Wars: A Moral Argument with Historical Illustrations*, 2nd edn (New York, 1992), 267.

29. Van Damme, 'Jus in Bello', 124.

30. Watson, *Evolution of International Society*, 101–2.

31. The government of the Roman Empire provides an example of a 'state' becoming coterminous with an organized religion.

32. King Charles of the Frankish Empire was crowned Holy Roman Emperor on Christmas Day, AD 800, which marked the beginning of Latin Christendom.

33. Karen Mingst, *Essentials of International Relations* (New York, 1999), 24.

34. See John T. Rourke, *International Politics on the World Stage*, 6th edn (New York, 2006), 203.

35. Charlemagne (742–814) was leader of the Franks (in present-day France).

36. For example, see Dante, 'De Monarchia', in *The Portable Dante*, ed. Paolo Milano (New York, 1977).

37. See J. Burckhardt, *The Civilization of the Renaissance in Italy*, vol. 1 (New York, 1958), 120–40.

38. For a cogent elaboration of this argument, see Daniel Philpott, 'The Religious Roots of Modern International Relations', *World Politics*, 52 (Jan. 2000): 206–45.

39. Ibid., 214.

40. See Andrew Pettegree, *The Early Reformation in Europe* (Cambridge, 1991).

41. Except that certain Protestants, like the Calvinists and the Anabaptists, were not included in this truce.

42. Paul Kennedy, *The Rise and Fall of the Great Powers: Economic Change and Military Conflict from 1500 to 2000* (New York, 1987), 9.

43. For a more extensive account of the expansionism of the Ottoman Empire, see Paul Wittek, *The Rise of the Ottoman Empire* (London, 1938); M.A. Cook, ed., *A History of the Ottoman Empire to 1730* (Cambridge, 1976).

44. Kennedy, *Rise and Fall of the Great Powers*, 4.

45. Ibid., 3.

46. Ibid., 4. The major power centres at that time included: the Aztec Empire, the Inca Empire, the Ottoman Empire, Western Europe, the Persian Empire, the Mogul Empire, the Ming Empire, Japan, and Muscovy.

47. Sun Tzu described in detail the art of warfare developed by the dynastic powers in these 'state' units that occupied early China. Sun Tzu, *The Art of War*, trans. Samuel B. Griffith (New York, 1963).

48. The Zhou Kingdom was the longest-lasting dynasty in Chinese history.

49. Initially, there were approximately 70 fiefdoms, which expanded to 1,770 by 770 BC.

50. Watson compares the Zhou Kingdom to the Holy Roman Empire of the European Middle Ages.

51. Watson, *Evolution of International Society*, 87.

52. This period is known for its many Chinese classics as well as for the philosophical works of Confucianism, Taoism, and Legalism.

53. Watson, *Evolution of International Society*, 89–92.

54. For further elaboration, see <www.wsu.edu:8080/~dee/chphil/legalism.htm>. (1 Sept. 2004)

55. See <www.wsu.edu:8080/~dee/chphil/hansynth.htm>. (1 Sept. 2004)

56. Kennedy, *Rise and Fall of the Great Powers*, 15.

57. Ibid., 16.

58. Indeed, most of today's civilizations and societies likely had their roots in African civilizations.

59. See Heather Deegan, *Contemporary Islamic Influences in Sub-Saharan Africa: An Alternative Development Agenda*, at <www.islamfortoday.com/subsahara.htm>. (25 Dec. 2005)

60. In 1000 BC it is recorded that the Queen of Sheba (Ethiopia) visited King Solomon (Israel). The story can be found in the Ethiopian 'Book of the Glory of Kings', the *Kebra Nagast* (which is based on several passages from the Jewish Torah), and the Bible, 1 Kings 10:1–13 and 2 Chronicles 9:1–12.

61. Israeli immigration statute guarantees citizenship to anyone who is 'verifiable' Jewish.

62. For example, see Karen A. Mingst, *Essentials of International Relations*, 3rd edn (New York, 2004), 24.

63. For a historical overview, see Michael D. Coe, *The Maya* (New York, 1993); Michael D. Coe, *Mexico: From the Olmecs to the Aztecs*, 4th edn (London, 1994).

64. Olive Patricia Dickason with David T. McNab, *Canada's First Nations: A History of Founding Peoples from Earliest Times*, 4th edn (Toronto, 2009), 27.

65. Niccolò Machiavelli, *The Prince*, ed. Q. Skinner (Cambridge, 1988); Niccolò Machiavelli, *The Art of War*, ed. N. Wood (New York, 1965).

66. Jens Bartelson, *The Genealogy of Sovereignty* (New York, 1995). Also see Jean Bodin, *Six Books on the Commonwealth* (Oxford, 1967), 25–8.

67. Seyom Brown, *New Forces, Old Forces and the Future of World Politics* (Boston, 1988), 14.

68. Numelin, *Beginnings of Diplomacy*, 22–3.

Chapter 4

1. Ralf Dahrendorf, 'The Europeanization of Europe', in Andrew J. Pierre, ed., *A Widening Atlantic? Domestic Change and Foreign Policy* (New York, 1986), 5.

2. James N. Rosenau, *Turbulence in World Politics: A Theory of Change and Continuity* (Princeton, NJ, 1990), 73.

3. Ibid., 72–3.

4. See Robert Gilpin, *War and Change in World Politics* (New York, 1981), 213.

5. Ibid., 7.

6. Ibid., 69.

7. Ibid., 7.

8. Obi Aginam, 'Of Savages and Mass Killing: HIV/AIDS, Africa and the Crisis of Global Health Governance', in Toyin Falola and Matthew M. Heaton, eds, *HIV/AIDS, Illness, and African Wellbeing* (Rochester, NY, 2007).

9. Mary Kaldor, *Human Security: Reflections on Globalization and Intervention* (Oxford, 2007); Sandra Jean Maclean, David R. Black, and Timothy M. Shaw, eds, *A Decade of Human Security: Global Governance and New Multilateralisms (Global Security in a Changing World)* (Surrey, UK, 2006).

10. Robert Cox, 'Postscript 1985', in Robert Cox, 'Social Forces, States, and World Orders: Beyond International Relations Theory', in Robert O. Keohane, ed., *Neorealism and Its Critics* (New York, 1986), 243.

11. Mohammad Omar Farooq, 'Change and Continuity: The Dynamics of Institutional Behavior in Islam', paper presented to the twentieth annual conference of the Association of Muslim Social Scientists, Detroit, 25–7 Oct. 1991.

12. The authors are thankful to Charles Jones for pointing out this distinction.

13. See Robert W. Cox on this point in 'On Thinking about Future World Order', in Cox, *Approaches to World Order* (Cambridge, 1996), 78.

14. Ibid., 97–101.

15. Robert W. Cox, 'Social Forces, States, and World Orders: Beyond International Relations Theory', in Robert W. Cox with Timothy J. Sinclair, *Approaches to World Order* (Cambridge, 1996), 98–9.

16. Robert Cox, cited in Stephen Gill, ed., *Gramsci, Historical Materialism and International Relations* (Cambridge, 1993), 42.

17. For a discussion of hegemony, see Antonio Gramsci, *Selections from the Prison Notebooks*, ed. and trans. Quintin Hoare and Geoffrey Nowell Smith (New York, 1971), 169–70. Instead of coercive hegemony, like that of Japan prior to World War II, benign hegemony seeks to share economic and security benefits, and often will include consultations with other states. For example, following World War II, the US was seen by many as a benign hegemon 'because of its geopolitical strategy of liberal internationalism and its security umbrella in Europe and Asia' that benefited both allies and former foes, as well as because of its tradition of democratic governance. See Tom Berry, 'The Terms of Power', 2 Nov. 2002, at: <www.fpif.org/commentary/2002/0211power_body.html>.

18. On hegemonic stability, see Robert O. Keohane, 'The Theory of Hegemonic Stability and Changes in International Economic Regimes, 1967–77', in Ole Holsti, Randolphe Siverson, and Alexander George, eds, *Change in the International System* (Boulder, Colo., 1981), 131–62.

19. James N. Rosenau, 'Governance, Order, and Change in World Politics', in James N. Rosenau and Ernst-Otto Czempiel, eds, *Governance without Government: Order and Change in World Politics* (Cambridge, 1992), 1.

20. Ralf Dahrendorf, *Class and Class Conflict in Industrial Society* (Stanford, Calif., 1959), 125.

21. Rosenau, 'Governance, Order, and Change in World Politics', 16–17.

22. Ian Clark, *The Post-Cold War Order: The Spoils of Peace* (Oxford, 2001), 19.

23. Ibid.

24. Robert W. Cox, 'Influences and Commitments', in Cox with Sinclair, *Approaches to World Order*, 34.

25. Ibid., 34–5.

26. Rosenau, "Governance, Order and Change in World Politics', 16.

27. See Anne-Marie Slaughter, 'The Real New World Order', in Gregory M. Scott, Randall J. Jones Jr, and Louis S. Furmanski, eds, *21 Debated Issues in World Politics*, 2nd edn (Englewood Cliffs, NJ, 2004), 22–34.

28. Rosenau, 'Governance, Order and Change in World Politics', 19.

29. Clark, *The Post-Cold War Order*, 22.

30. Rosenau, 'Governance, Order, and Change in World Politics', 1.

31. Rosenau, *Turbulence in World Politics*, 37

32. Yoshikazu Sakamoto, 'A Perspective on the Changing World Order: A Conceptual Prelude', in Sakamoto, ed., *Global Transformation: Challenges to the State System* (Tokyo, 1994), 15.

33. R.L. Garthoff, *The Great Transition: American–Soviet Relations and the End of the Cold War* (Washington, DC, 1994), 1.

34. Marc Trachtenberg, *A Constructed Peace: The Making of the European Settlement, 1945–1963* (Princeton, NJ, 1999), 402.

35. John G. Ikenberry, 'The Myth of Post-Cold War Chaos', *Foreign Affairs* 75, 3 (1996): 90.

36. E.J. Hobsbawn, *The New Century* (London, 2000), 7.

37. For an example of this line of reasoning, see John Mearsheimer, 'Back to the Future: Instability in Europe after the Cold War', *International Security* 15, 1 (1990): 5–56.

38. E.J. Hobsbawm, *Nations and Nationalism Since 1870: Programme, Myth, Reality* (Lanham, Md, 1990), 165.

39. Kimon Valaskakis, 'Long-term Trends in Global Governance: From "Westphalia" to "Seattle"', in *Governance in the 21st Centrury* (Paris, 2001), 48.

40. Clark, *The Post-Cold War Order*, 25.

41. Eric R. Wolf, *Europe and the People without History* (Los Angeles, 1982), 21.

42. Robert W. Cox, 'Social Forces, States, and World Orders', 89–90.

Chapter 5

1. Martin Wight, *Power Politics* (London, 1995), 207.

2. See, e.g., Keith Krause and Michael Williams, *Critical Security Studies* (London, 2003).

3. Isaiah Berlin, *Karl Marx* (London, 1948), 116.

4. See, e.g., the discussion in Kalvei J. Holsti, *The State, War, and the State of War* (Cambridge, 1996), especially 1–18; Joseph S. Nye Jr, *Understanding International Conflicts*, 3rd edn (New York, 2000).

5. See, e.g., John Mearsheimer, *The Tragedy of Great Power Politics* (New York, 2001); Kenneth Waltz, *Man, the State, and War* (New York, 2001).

6. Woodrow Wilson, *The Papers of Woodrow Wilson*, vol. 40 (Princeton, NJ, 1984), 536 passim.

7. Nye, *Understanding International Conflicts*, 64; also see George Kennan, *The Fateful Alliance* (New York, 1984).

8. Norman Angell, *The Great Illusion* (New York and London, 1913).

9. Cited in Robert Jervis, *Perception and Misperception in International Politics* (Princeton, NJ, 1976), 69; also Roland Axtmann and Robert Grant, 'Living in a Global World', in Trevor C. Salmon, ed., *Issues in International Relations* (London and New York, 2000), 3.

10. Donald Rumsfeld, cited in John Ikenberry, 'America's Imperial Ambition', *Foreign Affairs* 81, 5 (Sept.–Oct. 2002): 50.

11. John Herz, *Political Realism and Political Idealism* (Chicago, 1951).

12. Also see, for example, Paul Fussell, *The Great War and Modern Memory* (Oxford, 1975). Trumbo, a noted screenwriter, was one of the 'Hollywood Ten' who were blacklisted and spent time in prison after refusing to co-operate with the House Un-American Activities Committee in the late 1940s, which was seeking to ferret out Communist influences in the American film industry. He later won an Academy Award writing under a pseudonym.

13. Quoted in Suzy Platt, ed., *Respectfully Quoted* (Washington, 1992), 372.

14. See Michael Howard, 'Reassurance and Deterrence', *Foreign Affairs* 61, 2 (Winter 1982–3): 309–24.

15. Independent Commission on Disarmament and Security Issues, *Common Security: A Blueprint for Survival* (Palme Report) (New York, 1982).

16. Ibid.

17. Hedley Bull, *The Anarchical Society* (New York, 1977), 84.

18. Carl von Clausewitz, *On War* (London, 1982).

19. Kenneth Waltz, 'The Continuity of International Politics', in Ken Booth and Steve Smith, eds, *World in Collision: Terror and the Future of Global Order* (London, 2002).

20. Mearsheimer, *The Tragedy of Great Power Politics*, 366.

21. Holsti, *The State, War, and the State of War*, 25.

22. Ibid., xi.

23. Ibid., 36–7.

24. David Runciman, 'A Bear Armed with a Gun', *London Review of Books*, 3 Apr. 2003, 5.

25. Mary Kaldor, *New and Old Wars: Organized Violence in a Global Era*, 2nd edn (Cambridge, 2006).

26. For a good summary of the health-related effects arising from conflict, see Michael J. Toole, Ronald J. Waldman, and Anthony Zwi, 'Complex Emergencies', in Michael H. Merson, Robert E. Black, and Anne J. Mills, eds, *International Public Health: Diseases, Programs, Systems, and Policies*, 2nd edn (Boston, 2006), 445–511.

27. Kaldor, *New and Old Wars*, ix.

28. Ibid., x.

29. Mark Duffield, *Global Governance and the New Wars* (London, 2001).

30. A half-century ago, just days before leaving office, US President Dwight Eisenhower warned against the potential for the rise in misplaced power that could result from the US having a permanent military-industrial complex. Today, President Obama is faced with tremendous pressure, mostly exerted by that military-industrial complex, to increase US military forces in Afghanistan even though he wants to curb the excesses of weapons manufacturers and reduce the influence of their lobbyists.

31. David Keen, 'Liberalization and Conflict', *International Political Science Review* 26, 1: 85.

32. Michael Howard, *War and the Liberal Conscience* (New Brunswick, NJ, 1986), 4.

33. Cited ibid., 15.

34. For the full text on-line, see <www.geocities.com/Athens/Thebes/8098/>. (1 Nov. 2008)

35. Hugo Grotius, *The Rights of War and Peace*, An Abridged Translation by William Whewell (Trinity Lodge, Cambridge, 1853), xxxi.

36. Ibid.

37. Note that global military spending surged during 2003, reaching US$956 billion, with nearly half of it by the United States as it paid for missions in Iraq, Afghanistan, and the War on Terror. See Matt Moore, 'Global Military Spending Soars: Peace Group', *CNews World*, at: <cnews. canoe.ca/CNEWS/World/2004/06/09/492268-ap. html>.

38. See, e.g., John Keegan, *The Mask of Command* (New York, 1987); Max Boot, *War Made New* (New York, 2006).

39. See Trevor Nevitt Dupuy, *The Evolution of Weapons and Warfare* (Cambridge, Mass., 1990).

40. P.W. Singer, *Wired for War: The Robotics Revolution and Conflict in the 21st Century* (New York, 2009).

41. See Lloyd Axworthy, 'Putting People First', *Global Governance* 7, 1 (Jan.–Mar. 2001): 19–23; Barry Buzan, *People, States and Fear*, 2nd edn (Boulder, Colo., 1991); United Nations Development Program, *Human Development Report, 1994* (New York, 1994).

42. Commission on Human Security, 'Outline of the Report of the Commission on Human Security', at: <www.human security-chs.org/finalreport/Outlines/outline.pdf>.

43. Francis Fukuyama, 'The End of History?', *The National Interest* no. 15 (Summer 1989).

44. See Holsti, *The State, War, and the State of War*, 123–4.

45. See, e.g., Nye, *Understanding International Conflicts*, 207–25.

46. Emma Rothschild, 'What Is Security?', *Daedalus* 124, 3 (Summer 1995): 56.

47. Kofi Annan, 'Two Concepts of Sovereignty', *The Economist*, 18 Sept. 1999, 49.

48. Lloyd Axworthy, 'Canada and Humane Security: The Need for Leadership', *International Journal* 52 (1997): 184.

49. Canada and Norwegian partnership for action, the Lysøen Declaration, Backgrounder to 'Canada and Norway form new partnership on human security', press release No. 117, Department of Foreign Affairs and International Trade, 11 May 1998.

50. See Commission on Human Security, *Human Security Now*, Final Report (New York, May 2003).

51. <www.unaids.org/en/resources/epidemiology.asp#>. (1 Nov. 2008)

52. See <www.unaids.org/en/default.asp>. (1 Nov. 2008)

Chapter 6

1. See, e.g., Anne-Marie Slaughter, *A New World Order* (Princeton, NJ, 2004).

2. See Gene M. Lyons and Michael Mastanduno, eds, *Beyond Westphalia: State Sovereignty and International Intervention* (Baltimore, 1995).

3. Adam Watson, *The Evolution of International Society* (New York, 1992).

4. Robert Cox, *Production, Power, and World Order: Social Forces in the Making of History* (New York, 1987).

5. James N. Rosenau, *Turbulence in World Politics: A Theory of Change and Continuity* (Princeton, NJ, 1990), 5.

6. Michael Mann, *The Sources of Social Power* (New York, 1986).

7. As Geoffrey Best has written: 'there was no point in any state's participation if it wasn't some sort of a "power", with the proper attributes of such: sovereignty within its own territory, armed force to defend its borders and its national interests, respect for what was known as the "standard of civilization", and ability to shoulder the responsibilities resting on members of the society of states.' Geoffrey Best, 'Peace Conferences and the Century of Total War', *International Affairs* 75 (July 1999): 619.

8. Ibid., 621.

9. Ibid., 620.

10. Cited ibid., 623.

11. Steve Charnovitz, 'Two Centuries of Participation: NGOs and International Governance', *Michigan Journal of International Law* 18 (Winter 1997): 196–7.

12. John Maynard Keynes, cited in Craig Murphy, *International Organization and Industrial Change* (Cambridge, 1994), 88.

13. Cited ibid., 75.

14. For a full text of McKinley's speech of 5 Sept. 1901, see <www.schillerinstitute.org/educ/hist/mckinley0901jba.html>.

15. Quoted in John Gerard Ruggie, *Constructing the World Polity: Essays on International Institutionalization* (London, 1998), 204.

16. See Randall Germain, *Globalization and Its Critics: Perspectives from Political Economy* (London, 2000).

17. Robert Cox, 'Gramsci, Hegemony and International Relations: An Essay in Method', in Louise Amoore, ed., *The Global Resistance Reader* (London: 2005), 37.

18. Jan Aart Scholte, 'The Globalization of World Politics', in John Baylis and Steve Smith, eds, *The Globalization of World Politics: An Introduction to International Relations*, 3rd edn (Oxford, 2005), 14.

19. Hedley Bull, *The Anarchical Society: A Study of Order in World Politics* (London, 1977), 8, 20.

20. Note that globalism is usually equated with a process that has resulted in the 'shrinkage' of the globe.

21. Ulrich Beck, *What Is Globalization?* (Cambridge, 1999), 9. For other definitions of 'globalism', see Robin Hambleton, Hank V. Savitch, and Murray Stuart, eds, *Globalism and Local Democracy: Challenges and Change in Europe and North America* (New York, 2002); B. Hettne, A. Inotai, and O. Sunkel, eds, *Globalism and the New Regionalism* (London, 1999); Stephen Ambrose, *Rise to Globalism: American Foreign Policy, 1938–1976*, rev. edn (New York, 1976); Peter Waterman, Review Article, 'Beyond Globalism and Developmentalism: Other Voices in World Politics', *Development and Change* 27 (1996): 167–82.

22. Mark Ritchie, 'Globalization vs. Globalism: Giving Internationalism a Bad Name', Jan. 1996, at <www.hartford-hwp.com/archives/25a/069.html>. (10 Dec., 2008)

23. International Labour Organization, Bureau for Workers Activities, at: <actrav.itcilo.org/actrav-english/telearn/global/ilo/globe/new_page.htm#Definition>. (10 Dec. 2008)

24. F.H. Hinsley, *Power and the Pursuit of Peace* (Cambridge, 1963).

25. See David Held and Anthony McGrew, 'Globalization and the Liberal Democratic State', in Yoshikazu Sakamoto, ed., *Global Transformation: Challenges to the State System* (Tokyo, 1994), 57–84.

26. Craig N. Murphy, 'Inequality, Turmoil and Democracy: Global Political-Economic Visions at the End of the Century', *New Political Economy* 4, 2 (July 1999): 289–305.

27. Ibid.

28. On this point, see Robert W. Cox with Michael G. Schechter, *The Political Economy of a Plural World: Critical Reflections on Power, Morals and Civilization* (London, 2002), 96–117.

29. Murphy, *International Organization and Industrial Change*.

30. Robert Keohane, *After Hegemony: Cooperation and Discord in the World Political Economy* (Princeton, NJ, 1984).

31. David Dollar and Aart Kraay, 'Spreading the Wealth', *Foreign Affairs* 81, 1 (Jan.–Feb. 2002): 120–33.

32. See Paul Collier, *The Bottom Billion: Why the Poorest Countries Are Failing and What Can Be Done about It* (Oxford, 2007).

33. Bob Reinada and Bertjan Verbeek, *Autonomous Policymaking by International Organizations* (New York, 1998).

34. See, e.g., Mary Kaldor, *Global Civil Society: An Answer to War* (Cambridge, 2003); Peter Willetts, ed., *The Conscience of the World: The Influence of Non-Governmental Organisations in the U.N. System* (Washington, 1996); Thomas G. Weiss and Leon Gordenker, eds, *NGOs, the UN, and Global Governance* (Boulder, Colo., 1996).

35. For a sample of this activity, see Margaret Keck and Kathryn Sikkink, *Activists beyond Borders* (Ithaca, NY, 1998); Jan Aart Scholte and Marc Williams, *Contesting Global Governance* (Cambridge, 2000).

36. Craig Murphy, 'Global Governance: Poorly Done and Poorly Understood', *International Affairs* 76, 4 (2000): 794.

37. Susan Strange, *The Retreat of the State: The Diffusion of Power in the World Economy* (Cambridge, 1996).

38. Inis Claude Jr, 'The Evolution of Concepts of Global Governance and the State in the Twentieth Century', paper delivered at the annual conference of the Academic Council on the United Nations System (ACUNS), Oslo, 16–18 June 2000.

39. Gordon Smith and Moises Naim, *Altered States: Globalization, Sovereignty, and Governance* (Ottawa: International Development Research Centre, 2000).

40. John Ruggie, *Constructing the World Polity* (New York, 1998), 84.

41. See Lloyd Axworthy, *Navigating a New World: Canada's Global Future* (Toronto, 2003).

42. International Commission on Intervention and State Sovereignty, *The Responsibility to Protect: Report of the International Commission on Intervention and State Sovereignty*, at: <www.dfait-maeci.gc.ca/iciss-ciise/report-en.asp>. (27 Apr. 2004)

43. Emma Rothschild, 'What Is Security?', *Daedalus* 124, 3 (Summer 1995): 53–98.

44. Ngaire Woods, 'Good Governance in International Organizations', *Global Governance* 5, 1 (Jan.–Mar. 1999): 39–62.

45. David Kennedy, 'The Forgotten Politics of International Governance', *European Human Rights Law Review* 2 (2001): 123.

46. Charles Krauthammer, 'Unilateralism Is the Key to Our Success', *Manchester Guardian Weekly*, 20–6 Dec. 2001, 22.

47. Michael Ignatieff, *Virtual War, Kosovo and Beyond* (Harmondsworth, UK, 2001).

48. Kennedy, 'The Forgotten Politics of International Governance'.

49. Ibid.

50. Paul Kennedy, 'The Eagle Has Landed', *Financial Times* (London), 2 Feb. 2002.

51. George W. Bush, Graduation Speech at United States Military Academy, West Point, NY, 1 June 2002, at: <www.whitehouse.gov/news/releases/2002/06/20020601-3.html>. (14 Mar. 2009)

52. Project for a New American Century, Statement of Principles, June 1997, at: <www.newamericancentury.org/statementofprinciples.htm>. (14 Mar. 2009)

53. Stanley Hoffmann, 'On the War', *New York Review of Books*, 1 Nov. 2001, at: <www.nybooks.com/articles/14660>. (14 Mar. 2009)

54. Kenneth Waltz, 'The Continuity of International Politics', in Ken Booth and Tim Dunne, eds, *World in Collision: Terror and the Future of Global Order* (New York, 2002), 349.

55. PDD-25, issued on 3 May 1994, was effectively a way for the US to avoid UN peacekeeping responsibilities under UN command and to maintain its hegemonic freedom to act unilaterally. The Directive stated that American military personnel would be deployed for UN peacekeeping only if the operation was deemed in the vital national interests of the US, if US military officers were to be in command of US troops, and if there was broad domestic support for the operation. At the same time, the Directive reduced the American financial commitment to UN peacekeeping.

56. Charles Krauthammer, 'The New Unilateralism', *Washington Post*, 8 June 2001.

57. For a good discussion of this process, see Edward C. Luck, 'The U.S., Counterterrorism, and the Prospects for a Multilateral Alternative', in Jane Boulden and Thomas G. Weiss, eds, *Terrorism and the UN: Before and after September 11* (Bloomington, Ind., 2004), 74–101.

58. See Eşref Aksu and Joseph A. Camilleri, eds, *Democratizing Global Governance* (Houndmills, UK, 2002).

59. Shepard Forman, 'A Manageable World: Taking Hold of the International Public Sector', Centre for International Cooperation. 6 Aug. 2001, at: <www.cic.nyu.edu/peacebuilding/oldpdfs/A_Manageable_World.pdf>. (14 Mar. 2009). Also see Shepard Forman, 'An Interregnum for Globalism', a talk given at a colloquium on Managing Global Issues, Carnegie Endowment for International Peace, 2000, at: <www.cic.nyu.edu>. (14 Mar. 2009)

60. See Jim Whitman, ed., *Advances in Global Governance* (New York, 2009).

Chapter 7

1. Margaret P. Karns and Karen A. Mingst, *International Organizations: The Politics and Processes of Global Governance* (Boulder, Colo., 2004), ch. 4.

2. For an excellent history of the founding of the UN system, see Inis L. Claude Jr, *Swords into Plowshares: The Problems and Progress of International Organization*, 4th edn (New York, 1984).

3. W. Andy Knight, *A Changing United Nations: Multilateral Evolution and the Quest for Global Governance* (Houndmills, UK, 2000).

4. David Pitt, 'Power in the UN Superbureaucracy: A Modern Byzantium?', in David Pitt and Thomas G. Weiss, eds, *The Nature of United Nations Bureaucracies* (New York, 1986), 23–38.

5. 'Uniting for Peace Resolution', *Encyclopedia Britannica* (2009). Encyclopedia Britannica Online, at: <www.britannica.com/EBchecked/topic/617964/Uniting-for-Peace-Resolution>. (12 Dec. 2008)

6. For up-to-date progress reports on the Millennium Development Goals, see <www.undp.org/mdg/>. (8 Mar. 2009)

7. Initially, this seat was held by the Republic of China (Taiwan), but in 1971 UN General Assembly resolution 2758 replaced the Republic of China with the People's Republic of China (mainland China) without going through the required amendment procedure of Article 23 of the UN Charter. Since that time, Taiwan has been refused membership in the UN organization.

8. When the Soviet Union was dismantled in 1991, its seat on the Security Council was given to the Russian Federation without any amendment to the UN Charter, as required in Article 23 of the UN Charter.

9. A number of subsidiary bodies are responsible to the Council, including: the Military Staff Committee (MSC); two ad hoc tribunals—the International Criminal Tribunal for the Former Yugoslavia (ICTFY) and the International Criminal Tribunal for Rwanda (ICTR); the UN Monitoring, Verification and Inspection Commission (UNMOVIC) for Iraq, which replaced the UN Special Commission (UNSCOM) in

1999; the UN Compensation Commission; a number of standing committees and ad hoc bodies; and UN peacekeeping operations and missions. Note that the International Atomic Energy Agency reports to both the UN Security Council and the UN General Assembly.

10. For more on this, see Ian Hurd, 'Legitimacy, Power, and the Symbolic Life of the UN Security Council', *Global Governance* 8, 1 (Jan.–Mar. 2002): 35–51. In several instances the Council has held open meetings with non-Council members who contribute troops to UN peacekeeping. This is allowed under Articles 31 and 32 of the UN Charter. Recently, the Council has been relatively liberal in allowing non-Council members to participate in its deliberations. An example of this is the open Council meeting on AIDS in Africa held on 10 January 2000.

11. David Malone, 'Security Council', in Thomas G. Weiss and Sam Daws, eds, *The Oxford Handbook on the United Nations* (Oxford, 2007), 117.

12. Cameron R. Hume, 'The Security Council in the Twenty-First Century', in David M. Malone, ed., *The UN Security Council: From the Cold War to the Twenty-First Century* (Boulder, Colo., 2004), 607–16.

13. For an excellent survey of the power politics played out in the UN Security Council over Iraq, see David M. Malone, *The International Struggle over Iraq: Politics in the UN Security Council, 1980–2005* (Oxford, 2007).

14. Thomas Keating and W. Andy Knight, eds, *Building Sustainable Peace* (Edmonton and Tokyo, 2004), 1–4.

15. Note that the Council may meet elsewhere other than at UN headquarters in New York City; for example, in 1972 it held a session in Addis Ababa, Ethiopia, and the following year it met in Panama City, Panama.

16. See Commission on Global Governance, *Our Global Neighbourhood: The Report of the Commission on Global Governance* (Oxford, 1995).

17. Malone, *The International Struggle over Iraq*, 117.

18. First-generation peacekeeping activity is the traditional form of peacekeeping of the Cold War era in which the UN Security Council used peacekeepers to monitor ceasefires and act as an interposition force between warring states or groups. First-generation peacekeepers were either unarmed or lightly armed and could use force only in self-defence. Second- and third-generation peacekeeping emerged out of the need to deal with the upsurge of intra-state conflicts at the end of the Cold War. The main aim of UN second-generation peacekeeping operations was to work with conflicting parties to police domestic conflicts that had been at least temporarily settled, whereas the objective of third-generation peacekeeping forces was to protect civilians while trying to terminate persistent civil conflicts. These post-Cold War peace maintenance and peacebuilding operations are known as 'complex peacekeeping' operations because their mandates involve both military and civilian/humanitarian activities coupled with multi-dimensional tasks (such as human rights education and monitoring, landmines removal, organizing and supervising elections, repatriating and resettling refugees and internally displaced persons (IDPs), setting up interim civil administrations, rebuilding infrastructure, re-establishing police and judicial functions, and setting up criminal courts to try individuals involved in war crimes, ethnic cleansing, and other crimes against humanity. Peacekeepers in these second- and third-generation missions tend to be more heavily armed than their predecessors. See Jarat Chopra, ed., *The Politics of Peace Maintenance* (Boulder, Colo., 1998), 1–18.

19. See W. Andy Knight, 'Democracy and Good Governance', in Weiss and Daws, eds, *Oxford Handbook on the United Nations*, 620–32.

20. See Office of the Special Representative of the UN Secretary-General for Children and Armed Conflict, at: <www.un.org/children/conflict/english/index.html>. (8 Mar. 2009)

21. Jennifer M. Welsh, 'Authorizing Humanitarian Intervention', in Richard M. Price and Mark Zacher, eds, *The United Nations and Global Security* (Houndmills, UK, 2004), 177–92.

22. W. Andy Knight, 'Improving the Effectiveness of UN Arms Embargoes', in Price and Zacher, eds, *The United Nations and Global Security*, 39–55.

23. Keith Krause, 'Multilateral Diplomacy, Norm Building and UN Conferences: The Case of Small Arms and Light Weapons', *Global Governance* 8 (2002): 247–63.

24. Louise Olson, 'Mainstreaming Gender in Multidimensional Peacekeeping: A Field Perspective', *International Peacekeeping* 7, 3 (Autumn 2000): 1–16.

25. Ashraf Ghani and Claire Lockhart, *Fixing Failed States: A Framework for Rebuilding a Fractured World* (Oxford, 2008).

26. W. Andy Knight, 'Disarmament, Demobilization, and Reintegration and Post-Conflict Peacebuilding in Africa: An Overview', *African Security* 1 (2008): 24–52.

27. Ngaire Woods, 'Bretton Woods Institutions', in Weiss and Daws, eds, *Oxford Handbook on the United Nations*, 233–54.

28. See Gert Rosenthal, 'Economic and Social Council', in Weiss and Daws, eds, *Oxford Handbook on the United Nations*, 136–48.

29. See the Report of the Panel of Eminent Persons on United Nations–Civil Society Relations, *We the People: Civil Society, the United Nations and Global Governance*, UN Document A/58/817 (11 June 2004).

30. For an example, see the World Bank's operations in the West Bank and Gaza, at: <web.worldbank.org/WBSITE/EXTERNAL/COUNTRIES/MENAEXT/WESTBANKGAZAEXTN/0,,menuPK:294370~pagePK:141159~piPK:141110~theSitePK:294365,00.html>. (8 Mar. 2009)

31. Constanze Schulte, *Compliance with Decisions of the International Court of Justice* (Oxford, 2004).

32. High-level Panel on Threats, Challenges and Change, *A More Secure World: Our Shared Responsibility*, UN Document A/59/565 (2 Dec. 2004).

33. Charles Winchmore, 'The Secretariat: Retrospect and Prospect', *International Organization* 19, 3 (1965): 629.

34. See James O.C. Jonah, 'Secretariat: Independence and Reform', in Weiss and Daws, eds, *Oxford Handbook on the United Nations*, 166–7.

35. The Noblemaire principles are named after G. Noblemaire, a rapporteur for the Fourth Committee of the League of Nations in 1921 who recommended that the level of salaries for international civil servants should be determined by following three basic principles: (1) that remuneration of international civil servants be such as to attract and retain the most competent and efficient citizens of member states of the League; (2) that the expatriation factor be taken into account; and (3) that the level of international civil servants' salaries should be subject to the ebb and flow of public criticism. See Alexander S. Efimov and Nasser Kaddour, *Staff Costs and Some Aspects of Utilization of Human and Financial Resources in the United Nations Secretariat* (Geneva, 1984), JIU/REP/84/12, pp. 4–18. UN Document A/4776 and UN General Assembly Resolution 1797 (XVII) of 11 Dec. 1962, and the Second Report of the Ad Hoc Committee of Experts to examine the finances of the UN and the Specialized Agencies. UN Document A/6343. For further explanations of the Noblemaire principles, see <users.ictp.it/~staff/psalaries.html>. (11 Mar. 2009)

36. Global Policy Forum, 'UN Finance', at: <www.globalpolicy.org/finance/index.htm>. (11 Mar. 2009)

37. See W. Andy Knight, ed., *Adapting the United Nations to a Postmodern World: Lessons Learned*, 2nd edn (Houndmills, UK, 2005).

38. Michael G. Schechter, 'Possibilities for Preventive Diplomacy, Early Warning and Global Monitoring in the Post-Cold War Era; or, the Limits to Global Structural Change', in Knight, ed., *Adapting the United Nations to a Postmodern World*.

39. Thomas Boudreau, *Sheathing the Sword: The UN Secretary General and the Prevention of International Conflict* (Santa Barbara, Calif: Greenwood Press, 1984), 1–4.

40. Edward Newman, 'Secretary-General', in Weiss and Daws, eds, *Oxford Handbook on the United Nations*, 179.

41. Joseph Masciulli and W. Andy Knight, 'Conceptions of Global Leadership for Contextually-Intelligent, Innovatively Adaptive Leaders', in Masciulli, Mikhail A. Molchanov, and Knight, eds, *The Ashgate Research Companion to Political Leadership* (Surrey, UK, 2009), 89–122.

42. Boutros Boutros-Ghali, *An Agenda for Peace* (New York, 1992).

43. However, despite indictments by the ICTFY, Radovan Karadzic and Ratko Mladic, both accused of leading the slaughter of thousands of Bosnian Muslims and Croats between 1992 and 1995, are still on the loose. For the full list of all indicted by the ICTFY so far, see <www.un.org/icty/ind-e.htm>. (11 Mar. 2009)

44. W. Andy Knight, 'Bashir's Day of Reckoning for the Slaughter in Darfur', *Edmonton Journal*, 7 Mar. 2009.

45. Lester B. Pearson, 'Force for UN', *Foreign Affairs* 35, 3 (1957): 401.

46. <www.un.org/Depts/dpko/dpko/intro/1.htm>. (11 Mar. 2009)

47. UN, DPKO, 2003.

48. W. Andy Knight, 'Repensando las sanciones economicas', in Maria Cristina Rosas, ed., *La economia politica de la seguridad internacional: Sanctiones, zanahorias y garrotes* (Mexico City: National Autonomous University of Mexico, 2003), 31–48.

49. United Nations, 'Secretary-General Reviews Lessons Learned during "Sanctions Decade" in Remarks to International Peace Academy Seminar', press release, SG/SM/7360, 17 Apr. 2000.

50. The initial members of this coalition were: Afghanistan, Albania, Angola, Australia, Azerbaijan, Bulgaria, Colombia, Costa Rica, Czech Republic, Denmark, Dominican Republic, El Salvador, Eritrea, Estonia, Ethiopia, Georgia, Honduras, Hungary, Iceland, Italy, Japan, Kuwait, Latvia, Lithuania, Macedonia, Marshall Islands, Micronesia, Mongolia, Netherlands, Nicaragua, Palau, Panama, Philippines, Poland, Portugal, Romania, Rwanda, Singapore, Slovakia, Solomon Islands, South Korea, Spain, Turkey, Uganda, Ukraine, United Kingdom, United States, Uzbekistan.

51. For details, see <www.un.org/Depts/oip/>. (30 July 2007)

52. Andrew Mack and Asif Khan, 'UN Sanctions: A Glass Half Full?', in Price and Zacher, eds, *The United Nations and Global Security*, 112.

53. For a summary of this process, see <www.watsoninstitute.org/tfs/CD/ISD_Summary_of_Interlaken_Process.pdf>. (11 Mar. 2009)

54. See <www.smartsanctions.se/>. (11 Mar. 2009)

55. Knight, 'Improving the Effectiveness of UN Arms Embargoes', 39–55.

56. David Cortright and George A. Lopez, *The Sanctions Decade: Assessing UN Strategies in the 1990s* (Boulder, Colo., 2000).

57. For these lessons, see W. Andy Knight, *The United Nations and Arms Embargoes Verification* (New York, 1998); SIPRI, *United Nations Arms Embargoes: Their Impact on Arms Flows and Target Behaviour*, A report by Stockholm International Peace Research Institute (SIPRI) and the Department of Peace and Conflict Research (Uppsala, Sweden, 2007).

58. Boutros-Ghali, *An Agenda for Peace*, 11.

59. W. Andy Knight, 'Evaluating Recent Trends in Peacebuilding Research', *International Relations of the Asia-Pacific* 3 (2003): 241–64.

60. Keating and Knight, eds, *Building Sustainable Peace*.

61. See Jarat Chopra and Tanja Hohe, 'Participatory Peacebuilding', in Keating and Knight, eds, *Building Sustainable Peace*.

62. Cedric H. de Coning, *Coherence and Coordination in United Nations Peacebuilding and Integrated Missions* (Oslo, 2007).

63. United Nations Peacebuilding Commission, at <www.un.org/peace/peacebuilding/>. (11 Mar. 2009)

64. See Robert O. Keohane and Lisa L. Martin, 'The Promise of Institutionalist Theory', *International Security* 20, 1 (1995): 39–51.

65. Arthur A. Stein, 'Neoliberal Institutionalism', in Christian Reus-Smit and Duncan Snidal, eds, *The Oxford Handbook of International Relations* (Oxford, 2008), 217.

66. Robert Cox, 'Social Forces, States, and World Orders: Beyond International Relations Theory', in Robert Cox with Timothy Sinclair, *Approaches to World Order* (Cambridge, 1996), 97–101.

67. Knight, *A Changing United Nations*, 184.

68. As quoted in Edward C. Luck, 'Reforming the United Nations: Lessons from a History in Progress', in Jean E. Krasno, ed., *The United Nations: Confronting the Challenges of a Global Society* (Boulder, Colo., 2004), 359–97.

69. Kofi Annan, *Renewing the United Nations: A Programme for Reform*, Report of the Secretary-General, A/51/950, 9 Dec. 1997.

70. J. Martin Rochester, *Between Peril and Promise: The Politics of International Law* (Washington, 2006); J. Martin Rochester, *Waiting for the Millennium: The United Nations and the Future of World Order* (Columbia, SC, 1993); Joachim Müller, *Reform of the United Nations*, vol. 1 (New York, 1992).

71. See Knight, ed., *Adapting the United Nations to a Post-modern World*, 2nd edn.

72. High-level Panel, *A More Secure World*.

73. See Peter Willets, ed., *The Conscience of the World: The Influence of Non-Governmental Organizations in the U.N. System* (Washington, 1996).

74. W. Andy Knight, 'Towards a Subsidiarity Model for Peacemaking and Preventive Diplomacy: Making Chapter VIII of the UN Charter Operational', *Third World Quarterly* 17, 1 (Mar. 1996): 31–52.

Chapter 8

1. Andrew Kohut and Bruce Stokes, *America against the World* (New York, 2006), xvii.

2. Tony Porter, 'Why International Institutions Matter in the Global Credit Crisis', *Global Governance* 15, 1 (Jan.–Mar. 2009): 3.

3. 'The Integration of the World Economy Is in Retreat on Almost Every Front', *The Economist*, 19 Feb. 2009.

4. Joe Stiglitz, 'Globalism's Discontents', in Mark Kesselman, *The Politics of Globalization: A Reader* (Boston, 2006), 94.

5. William Rosen, *Justinian's Flea: Plague, Empire, and the Birth of Europe* (London, 2007), 10.

6. Jan Aart Scholte, *Globalization: A Critical Introduction* (New York, 2000).

7. Thomas L. Friedman, *The World Is Flat: A Brief History of the Twenty-First Century* (New York, 2007).

8. Daniel Cohen, *Globalization and Its Enemies* (Cambridge, Mass, 2006), 23–5.

9. Ibid., 27.

10. 'Workers of the World', *The Economist*, 1 Nov. 1997, 81.

11. Chris Wright, 'Global Tourism Soars, China Set to Surpass Spain', at: <nomadx.org/content/view/1287/51/> (16 Mar. 2009); World Tourism Organization, at: <www.unwto.org/index.php>.

12. 'Delivering the Goods', *The Economist*, 15 Nov. 1997, 86

13. Michael Richardson, 'Fighting Marine Terrorism', *Glocom Platform*, 11 June 2004, at: <www.glocom.org/debates/20040611_richardson_fighting/index.html>.

14. William Greider, *One World, Ready or Not: The Manic Logic of Global Capitalism* (New York, 1997).

15. One is left to wonder whether a new order will be created out of the current financial crisis, which is considered the worst since the Great Depression. See Eric Helleiner, 'Introduction—Special Forum: Crisis and the Future of Global Financial Governance', *Global Governance* 15 (2009): 1.

16. Scholte, *Globalization*.

17. A.T. Kearney Inc. and Carnegie Endowment for International Peace, 'The Globalization Index', *Foreign Policy* (Nov.–Dec. 2007): 68–76.

18. Cohen, *Globalization and Its Enemies*, 4.

19. Gordon Smith and Moises Naim, *Altered States* (Ottawa, 2000), at: <www.idrc.ca/en/ev-9412-201-1-DO_TOPIC.html>. (15 Mar. 2009)

20. See Inge Kaul, Isabelle Grunberg, and Marc A. Stern, eds, *Global Public Goods: International Cooperation in the 21st Century* (New York, 1999).

21. Smith and Naim, *Altered States*.

22. See, e.g., James Laxer, *The Border* (Toronto, 2004), which discusses the Canada–US border after 2001.

23. Charles Kindleberger, *American Business Abroad* (New Haven, 1969), 207.

24. Susan Strange, *The Retreat of the State: The Diffusion of Power in the World Economy* (Cambridge, 1996), 4.

25. Thomas Friedman, cited at: <www.wired.com/wired/archive/13.05/friedman.html>. (8 July 2005)

26. See, e.g., the critique at: <www.nypress.com/18/16/news&columns/taibbi.cfm>. (29 Aug. 2007)

27. See Thomas Friedman, *Lexus and the Olive Tree* (New York, 2000); Friedman, *The World Is Flat*.

28. J.-M. Guehenno, *The End of Nation-State* (Minneapolis, 1995), 16–17.

29. John Naisbitt, *Global Paradox* (New York, 1994), 12.

30. L. Weiss, *The Myth of the Powerless State: Governing the Economy in a Global Era* (Cambridge, 1998), 13.

31. David Held et al., *Global Transformation* (Stanford, Calif., 1999), 9.

32. Ian Clark, *Globalisation and International Relations Theory* (Oxford, 1999), 85.

33. Raimo Väyrynen, 'Sovereignty, Globalisation and Transnational Social Movements', *International Relations of Asia-Pacific* 1, 2 (2001): 243.

34. Ibid.

35. Richard Falk, 'State of Siege: Will Globalisation Win Out', *International Affairs* 73, 1 (1997): 124–5.

36. Scholte, *Globalization*, 136.

37. Ibid.

38. Ibid.

39. Stephen Gill, 'Globalisation, Market Civilisation, and Disciplinary Neoliberalism', in *Critical Concepts in Political Science III* (New York, 2004), 1234.

40. Ibid.

41. Ibid., 1238.

42. David Held and Anthony McGrew, 'The End of the Old Order? Globalization and the Prospects for World Order', *Review of International Studies* 24, 4 (Dec. 1998): 283.

43. Stephen Krasner, *Sovereignty: Organized Hypocrisy* (Princeton, NJ, 1999), 223.

44. Paul Hirst and Grahame Thompson, *Globalisation in Question: The International Economy and Possibilities of Governance* (London, 1996).

45. Kenneth Waltz, 'Globalization and Governance', in Robert J. Art and Robert Jervis, eds, *International Politics: Enduring Concepts and Contemporary Issues* (New York, 2007), 344.

46. Eric Helleiner, 'Great Transformations: A Polanyian Perspective on the Contemporary Global Financial Order', *Studies in Political Economy* no. 48 (1995): 150.

47. Dani Rodrik, 'Sense and Nonsense in the Globalization Debate', *Foreign Policy* no. 107 (Summer 1997): 22.

48. Leo Panitch, in Peter Gowan, Leo Panitch, and Martin Shaw, 'The State, Globalization and the New Imperialism: A Roundtable Discussion', *Historical Materialism: Research in Critical Marxist Theory* 9, 1 (Autumn 2001), at: <www.Theglobalsite.ac.uk/press/201gowan.htm>.

49. Pierre de Senarclens, cited in Julien Bauer and Philippe Le Prestre, 'Ménage à trois: The State between Civil Society and the International System,' in Gordon Smith and Daniel Wolfish, eds, *Who Is Afraid of the State?* (Toronto, 2001), 58.

50. Mark Zacher, 'The Decaying Pillars of the Westphalian Temple', in James Rosenau and Ernst-Otto Czempiel, eds, *Governance without Government* (Cambridge, 1992), 67.

51. Robert Cox, 'Globalization, Multilateralism and Social Change', work in progress published by United Nations University, 13 July 1990, p. 2, cited ibid., 81.

Chapter 9

1. Richard Barnet and Ronald Muller, *Global Reach* (New York, 1974), 13, 25, cited in Stephen J. Kobrin, 'MNCs, the Protest Movement, and the Future of Global Governance', in Alfred D. Chandler Jr and Bruce Mazlish, eds, *Leviathans: Multinational Corporations and the New Global History* (New York, 2005), 224–5.

2. <www.rdfs.net/themes/partnership_en.htm>. (15 Mar. 2009)

3. Rodney Bruce Hall and Thomas J. Biersteker, eds, *Emergence of Private Authority in Global Governance* (Cambridge, 2002), 205.

4. Rodney Bruce Hall, 'Private Authority, Non-State Actors and Global Governance', *Harvard International Review* (2005), at: <www.harvardir.org/articles/1390/>.

5. Ralph Nader, cited in Kobrin, 'MNCs', 221.

6. Geoffrey Jones, *Multinationals and Global Capitalism* (Oxford, 2005), 5.

7. J.A. Hobson, *Imperialism: A Study* (London, 1905).

8. Jones, *Multinationals*, 5.

9. Mina Wilkins in Chandler and Mazlish, eds, *Leviathans*, 52.

10. Craig Murphy, *International Organization and Industrial Change* (Cambridge, 1994), 48.

11. Ibid., 71.

12. Ibid., 67.

13. Jones, *Multinationals*, 21; also see J.H. Dunning, 'Changes in the Level and Structure of International Production: The Last One Hundred Years', in M. Casson, ed., *The Growth of International Business* (London, 1983).

14. Stephen J. Kobrin, 'Economic Governance in an Electronically Networked Global Economy', in Hall and Biersteker, eds, *Emergence of Private Authority*, 44.

15. See, e.g., Ester Hernandez and Susan Bibler Coutin, 'Remitting Subjects: Migrants, Money and States', *Economy and Society* 35, 2 (May 2006): 185–208.

16. The Global Remittances Guide, at <www.migrationinformation.org/datahub/remittances.cfm>. (15 Mar. 2009)

17. UNCTAD, *World Investment Report 2007, Transnational Corporations* 16, 3 (Dec. 2007): 108–9.

18. Data from UNCTAD, *World Investment Report 2006, Overview*, 5.

19. Ibid.

20. Antoine van Agtmael, *The Emerging Markets Century* (New York, 2007), 11.

21. Ibid., 46.

22. John Ruggie, 'Global Markets and Global Governance', in Steven Bernstein and Louis W. Pauly, eds, *Global Liberalism and Political Order: Toward a Grand Compromise* (Albany, NY, 2007), 33.

23. For a sample of these criticisms, see Kari Levitt, *Silent Surrender* (Montreal and Kingston, 1970); Glen Williams, *Not for Export*, 3rd edn (Toronto, 1994).

24. Geoffrey Allen Pigman, *The World Economic Forum* (London, 2007).

25. Claire Cutler, 'Private International Regimes and Inter-firm Cooperation', in Hall and Biersteker, eds, *Emergence of Private Authority*, 23.

26. Hall, 'Private Authority, Non-State Actors and Global Governance'.

27. Doris Fuchs, *Business Power in Global Governance* (Boulder, Colo., 2007).

28. Susan K. Sell, 'Big Business, the WTO, and Development: Uruguay and Beyond', in Richard Stubbs and Geoffrey R.D. Underhill, eds, *Political Economy and the Changing Global Order*, 3rd edn (Toronto, 2006), 183–96.

29. Walden Bello, 'A Primer on the Wall Street Meltdown', Inquirer.net, 1 Oct. 2008, at: <opinion.inquirer.net/viewpoints/columns/view/20081001-163889/A-primer-on-the-Wall-Street-meltdown>.

30. Robert E. Litan and Martin N. Baily, *Fixing Finance: A Road Map for Reform* (Washington, 2009), at: <www.

brookings.edu/papers/2009/~/media/Files/rc/papers/2009/0217_finance_baily_litan/0217_finance_baily_litan.pdf> (15 Mar. 2009); also see Stephanie Flanders, 'Will the G20 expand the role of IMF', BBC, 3 Mar. 2009, at: <news.bbc.co.uk/2/hi/business/7922089.stm>.

31. United Nations Research Institute for Social Development, *Visible Hands: Taking Responsibility for Social Development* (Geneva: UNRISD, 2000), at: <www.unrisd.org/unrisd/website/document.nsf/0/FE9C9439D82B525480256B670065EFA1?OpenDocument>.

32. See Mark S. Schwartz and Archie B. Carroll, 'Corporate Social Responsibility: A Three Domain Approach', *Business Ethics Quarterly* 13, 4 (2003): 503–30.

33. Thomas W. Pogge, *World Poverty and Human Rights: Cosmopolitan Responsibilities and Reforms* (Cambridge, 2002). See also Vincent Di Norcia, *Hard Like Water: Ethics in Business* (Toronto, 1998).

34. United Nations Global Compact, at: <www.unglobalcompact.org/AboutTheGC/TheTenPrinciples/index.html>.

35. Ruggie, 'Global Markets and Global Governance', 25.

36. Kobrin, 'Economic Governance in an Electronically Networked Global Economy', 46.

37. Ibid., 52.

Chapter 10

1. Ronaldo Munck, *Globalization and Contestation: The New Great Counter-Movement* (London, 2007), 61.

2. Anthony Giddens, *Runaway World: How Globalisation Is Reshaping Our Lives* (London, 2002), 10.

3. David Held and Anthony McGrew, 'The End of the Old Order? Globalization and the Prospects for World Order', *Review of International Studies* 24, 4 (Dec. 1998): 220.

4. Richard J. Payne, *Global Issues: Politics, Economics, Culture* (New York, 2007), 14.

5. Robert W. Cox, 'Social Forces, States, and World Orders: Beyond International Relations Theory', in Robert W. Cox with Timothy J. Sinclair, *Approaches to World Order* (Cambridge, 1996), 86.

6. See Douglas Chalmers, 'Corporatism and Comparative Politics', in Howard Wiards, ed., *New Directions in Comparative Politics*, rev. edn (Boulder, Colo., 1991), 69–70.

7. For further elaboration on the state/society complex, see Keith Krause and W. Andy Knight, eds, *State, Society, and the UN System: Changing Perspectives on Multilateralism* (Tokyo, 1995), especially the introductory chapter.

8. The idea of the 'double movement' is taken from Karl Polanyi, *The Great Transformation: The Political and Economic Origins of Our Time* (Boston, 1957).

9. On Gramsci's conceptualization, see Antonio Gramsci, *Selections from the Prison Notebooks* (London, 1971). See Robert Cox, 'Civil Society at the Turn of the Millennium: Prospects for an Alternate World Order', *Review of International Studies* 25, 1 (1999): 3–28. Also see George Soros, *The Crisis of Global Capitalism: Open Society Endangered* (New York, 1998).

10. Narcis Serra and Joseph Stiglitz, eds, *The Washington Consensus Reconsidered: Towards a New Global Governance* (Oxford, 2008), 3.

11. This was a marked deviation from the development strategy adopted particularly in Latin America and the Caribbean of 'import substitution'.

12. J. Williamson, 'What Washington Means by Policy Reform', in J. Williamson, ed., *Latin American Adjustment: How Much Has Happened?* (Washington, 1990).

13. See David Held, 'At the Global Crossroads: The End of the Washington Consensus and the Rise of Global Social Democracy?', *Globalizations* 2, 1 (May 2005): 95–113.

14. Michael Hudson and Jeffrey Sommers, 'The End of the Washington Consensus', *Counterpunch*, 12–14 Dec. 2008, at: <www.counterpunch.org/hudson12122008.html>. (12 May 2009)

15. See M. Rupert, *Ideologies of Globalization: Contending Visions of a New World Order* (London, 2000).

16. Louise Amoore 'Introduction: Global Resistance—Global Politics', in Louise Amoore, ed., *The Global Resistance Reader* (London, 2005), 3.

17. J. Walton and M. Seddon, *Free Markets and Food Riots: The Politics of Global Adjustment* (Oxford, 1994), 42.

18. Mary Kaldor, *Global Civil Society: An Answer to War* (Cambridge, 2003).

19. Rhoderick Gates, 'Seattle Explosion: 2 Years Too Late', *Our Time*, 31 Nov. 1999.

20. <www.peak.sfu.ca/the-peak/97-3/issue11/arrest.html>. (15 July 2008)

21. A 'Grotian moment', after the seventeenth-century Dutch diplomat and jurist, Hugo Grotius (Huig de Groot), is a significant development that can result in a reinterpretation of treaty-based law. Richard Falk writes about mobilizing 'the forces of globalization-from-below' to counter the forces of 'globalization-from-above'. However, we are not convinced that the oppositional responses to which Falk is referring will necessarily reflect any of the features of 'globalization'. See Richard Falk, 'Global Civil Society: Perspectives, Initiatives, Movements', *Oxford Development Studies* 26, 1 (1998): 99–110.

22. Waldon Bello, '2000: The Year of Global Protest against Globalization', *Focus on Trade* no. 58 (Jan. 2001), at: <www.nadir.org/nadir/initiativ/agp/free/bello/2000global_protest.htm>. (16 Sept. 2007)

23. See Allen Sens and Peter Stoett, *Global Politics: Origins, Currents, Directions*, 3rd edn (Toronto, 2005), 311.

24. Bello, '2000: The Year of Global Protest', 24.

25. J. Smith, 'Globalizing Resistance: The Battle of Seattle and the Future of Social Movements', in J. Smith and H. Johnson, eds, *Globalization and Resistance: Transnational Dimensions of Social Movements* (Lanham, Md, 2002), 210.

26. Munck, *Globalization and Contestation*, 59.

27. G. Murphy, 'The Seattle WTO Protests: Building a Global Movement', in R. Taylor, ed., *Creating a Better World: Interpreting Global Civil Society* (Bloomfield, Conn., 2004), 32–3.

28. See Alexander Cockburn, Jeffrey St. Clair, and Allan Sekula, *Five Days That Shook the World: The Battle for Seattle and Beyond* (London, 2001).

29. Bello, '2000: The Year of Global Protest'.

30. Janet Thomas, *The Battle in Seattle: The Story Behind and Beyond the WTO Demonstrations* (Golden, Colo., 2000).

31. CBC News, at: <www.cbc.ca/world/story/2000/01/ 06/ wto000106.html>.

32. Munck, *Globalization and Contestation*, 61.

33. Philip A. Wellons, *Passing the Buck: Banks, Government and Third World Debt* (Boston, 1987), 225.

34. Federal Financial Institutions Examination Council, *Country Exposure Report* (Dec. 1982), 2.

35. Ann Pettifor, 'The Economic Bondage of Debt—and the Birth of a New Movement', in Amoore, ed., *The Global Resistance Reader*, 316.

36. International Monetary Fund, at: <www.imf.org/external/np/exr/facts/hipc.htm>. (20 July 2008)

37. <www.vatican.va/holy_father/john_paul_ii/apost_letters/documents/hf_jp-ii_apl_10111994_tertio-millennio-adveniente_en.html>. (20 July 2008)

38. References to the Jubilee Year in the Old Testament can be found in the books of Exodus (23:10–11), Leviticus (25:1–28), and Deuteronomy (15:1–6).

39. Before the Summit, the leaders of the G8 did not have debt on the agenda, but the pressure generated by Jubilee 2000 forced the British hosts of the G8 meeting to add this item to the agenda. See Pettifor, 'The Economic Bondage of Debt', 311.

40. The G8 hosts at the last minute decided to change the site of the summit to Weston Park—well outside the city and beyond the reach of the protests.

41. To put this in perspective, for every US dollar of aid sent from G8 countries to LDCs in the form of aid, $11 is generally returned to service or repay debt.

42. The protestors represented 38 NGOs and student organizations.

43. For more on these protests, see Bello, '2000: The Year of Global Protest'.

44. André Drainville, 'Québec City 2001 and the Making of Transnational Subjects', *Socialist Register 2002*, reprinted in Amoore, ed., *The Global Resistance Reader*, 15–42.

45. See Mario E. Carranza, 'Mercosur and the End Game of the FTAA Negotiations: Challenges and Prospects after the Argentine Crisis', *Third World Quarterly* 25, 2 (2004): 319–37.

46. Ibid., 319.

47. Other organizations credited with conceiving and nurturing the idea include the Americas Society (David Rockefeller, chairman), the Forum of the Americas (David Rockefeller, founder), the US Council of the Mexico–US Business Committee (Rodman C. Rockefeller, chairman), the Council on Foreign Relations (David Rockefeller, former chairman), the Trilateral Commission (David Rockefeller, founder and honorary chairman), the Chase Manhattan Bank (David Rockefeller, former chairman), and the Institute for International Economics (David Rockefeller, financial backer and board member).

48. William F. Jasper, 'Welcome Mat for Terrorists', *The New America*, 29 Dec. 2003, at: <www.stoptheftaa.org/artman/publish/article_89.shtml>. (16 Oct. 2005)

49. See, e.g., the argument made by Peter J. Katzenstein, *A World of Regions: Asia and Europe in the American Imperium* (Ithaca, NY, 2005), 233.

50. Drainville, 'Québec City 2001', 16–20.

51. This is a term used by Michel Foucault in 'Le sujet et le pouvoir', in Michel Foucault, ed., *Dits et écrit—1954–1988* (Paris, 1994), 227–43.

52. The G8 countries are: Canada, France, Germany, Japan, Great Britain, Italy, the United States, and Russia.

53. See Peter Uvin, 'From Local Organizations to Global Governance: The Role of NGOs in International Relations', in Kendall Stiles, ed., *Global Institutions and Local Empowerment: Competing Theoretical Perspectives* (New York, 2000), 19.

54. Ibid., 20.

Chapter 11

1. Ken Saro-Wiwa, *Genocide in Nigeria: The Ogoni Tragedy* (Port Harcourt, 1992).

2. Anthony Giddens, *The Consequences of Modernity* (Cambridge, 1990), 18.

3. Kayode Soremekun and Cyril I. Obi, 'Oil and the National Question', *Proceedings of the Nigerian Economic Society 1993 Annual Conference*, Nigerian Economic Society (1993), 209.

4. Marian Miller, *Third World in Global Environmental Politics* (Boulder, Colo., 1995), 35.

5. Cyril I. Obi, 'Globalization and Local Resistance: The Case of Shell versus the Ogoni', in Louise Amoore, ed., *The Global Resistance Reader* (London, 2005), 322.

6. See Ben Naanen, 'Oil-producing Minorities and the Restructuring of Nigerian Federalism: The Case of the Ogoni People', *Journal of Commonwealth and Comparative Studies* 32, 1 (1995): 46–78.

7. Obi, 'Globalization and Local Resistance', 319.

8. Claude Welch, 'The Ogoni and Self-determination: Increasing Violence in Nigeria', *Journal of Modern African Studies* 33, 4 (1995): 636.

9. Julian Saurin, 'International Relations, Social Ecology and the Globalization of Environmental Change', in John Volger and Mark F. Imbler, eds, *The Environment and International Relations* (London, 1996), 88.

10. Adebayo Olukoshi, ed., *The Politics of Structural Adjustment in Nigeria* (London, 1993).

11. Obi, 'Globalization and Local Resistance', 319.

12. Ken Saro-Wiwa, 'Oil and the Basic Issue at Stake', *Guardian*, 1 Apr. 1994, 17.

13. Obi, 'Globalization and Local Resistance', 324.

14. Thilo Bode, executive director, Greenpeace International, at <archive.greenpeace.org/comms/ken/murder.html>. (18 Nov. 2009)

15. <www.remembersarowiwa.com/lifeksw.htm>. (24 July 2008)

16. <www.panda.org/about_wwf/what_we_do/forests/problems/index.cfm>. (25 July 2005)

17. See Paul Ekins, *A New World Order: Grassroots Movements for Global Change* (London, 1992), 139–65.

18. <www.iisd.org/50comm/commdb/desc/d07.htm>. (25 July 2008)

19. Vandana Shiva and Jayanta Bandyopadhyay, 'The Evolution, Structure and Impact of the Chipko Movement', *Mountain Research and Development* (UNEP) 6, 2 (May 1986): 133–42. Also see <www.unep.org/geo2000/pacha/forests/forests3.htm>. (11 March 2009)

20. Vandana Shiva and Jayanta Bandyopadhyay, 'Chipko: Rekindling India's Forest Culture', *The Ecologist* 17, 1 (Jan.–Feb. 1987): 26–34.

21. <www.greenbeltmovement.org/w.php?id = 21>. (24 July 2008)

22. Ibid.

23. Paul Farmer, *Pathologies of Power: Health, Human Rights, and the New War on the Poor* (Los Angeles, 2005), 92.

24. See J. Womack Jr, *Zapata and the Mexican Revolution* (New York, 1968).

25. Ronaldo Munck, *Globalization and Contestation: The New Great Counter-Movement* (London, 2007), 63.

26. Translated from the Spanish by Farmer, *Pathologies of Power*, 93.

27. Ibid.

28. Munck, *Globalization and Contestation*, 63.

29. Tim Golden, 'Mexican Army Is Said to Abuse Rebel Suspects', *New York Times*, 24 Jan. 1994, at <query.nytimes.com/gst/fullpage.html?res = 9A00E2D81030F937A1575 2C0A962958260&sec = &spon = &pagewanted = 2>. (26 July 2008)

30. See Thomas Olesen, *International Zapatismo: The Construction of Solidarity in the Age of Globalization* (London, 2005), 3.

31. <www.libertadlatina.org/Crisis_Mexico_Chiapas_Acteal_Massacre.htm>. (27 July 2008)

32. *CIMAC Noticias News for Women* (Mexico City), 27 Dec. 2006.

33. Olesen, *International Zapatismo*, 2.

34. Manuel Castells, *The Information Age*, vol. 2: *The Power of Identity*, 2nd edn (Oxford, 2004), 82.

35. Munck, *Globalization and Contestation*, 64.

36. Judith Hellman, 'Real and Virtual Chiapas: Magical Realism and the Left', in Leo Panitch and C. Keys, eds, *Socialist Register 2000* (London, 1999), 175.

37. Munck, *Globalization and Contestation*, 65.

38. See <www.attac.org/spip.php?article2>. (24 July 2008)

39. Porto Alegre is the capital of a state in Brazil that was already well-known globally for its democratic experiences and its opposition to neo-liberalism. See <www.tni.org/detail_page.phtml?page = socforum-docs_origins>. (28 July 2008) A Brazilian, Oded Grajew, is generally credited with the idea of the World Social Forum and for suggesting that it be held in Porto Alegre.

40. <www.wsfindia.org/?q = node/2>. (28 July 2008)

41. Giuseppe Caruso, *Report on the World Social Forum in Mumbai 2004*, at: <www.signofourtimes.org/UK/WSF/html>, p. 205. (28 July 2008)

42. Marwaan Macan-Markar, 'India as Venue Provides a Tough Reality Check', *TerraViva*, 22 Jan. 2004.

43. See Caruso, *Report on the World Social Forum*.

44. Dorval Brunelle, *From World Order to Global Disorder: States, Markets, and Dissent* (Vancouver, 2007), 146.

45. Some NGOs are heavily dependent on governments or IGOs for funding in order to survive, and some basically mirror state bureaucracies.

46. W.J. Clinton, 'Address to the World Trade Organization', Geneva, 1998.

47. Mark Rupert, 'Passive Revolution or Transformative Process', in Amoore, ed., *The Global Resistance Reader*, 200.

48. See James H. Mittelman and Christine B.N. Chin, 'Conceptualizing Resistance to Globalization', in Amoore, ed., *The Global Resistance Reader*, 21.

49. James Scott, 'The Infrapolitics of Subordinate Groups', in Amoore, ed., *The Global Resistance Reader*, 65–73.

50. Brunelle, *From World Order to Global Disorder*, 148.

51. Mittelman and Chin, 'Conceptualizing Resistance to Globalization', 25.

Chapter 12

1. Phil Williams and Gregory Baudin-O'Hayon, 'Global Governance, Transnational Organized Crime and Money Laundering', in David Held and Anthony McGrew, eds, *Governing Globalization: Power, Authority and Global Governance* (Cambridge, 2002), 131.

2. Paul E. Lunde, *Organized Crime: An Inside Guide to the World's Most Successful Industry* (London, 2004), 11.

3. See Williams and Baudin-O'Hayon, 'Global Governance', 128.

4. See Richard J. Payne, *Global Issues: Politics, Economics, Culture* (New York, 2007), 322.

5. K.S. Nair and Gabriel Britto, 'Introduction: Culture and Drugs', in United Nations Education, Scientific and Cultural Organization and United Nations Office for Drug Control and Crime Prevention, *Globalisation, Drugs and Criminalisation*, Final Research Report on Brazil, China, India, and Mexico, part 3 (UNESCO/MOST Secretariat 2002), at: <www.unesco.org/most/globalisation/drugs_vol3.pdf>. (12 Mar. 2009)

6. Joseph Serio, *Investigating the Russian Mafia* (Durham, NC, 2008).

7. Ravi Kanbur, *Poverty and Conflict: The Inequality Link: Coping with Crisis*, Working Paper Series (New York, June 2007).

8. Payne, *Global Issues*, 322.

9. Ibid.

10. Phil Williams, 'Combating Transnational Organized Crime', in Carolyn W. Pumphrey, ed., *Transnational Threats: Blending Law Enforcement and Military Strategies* (Carlisle, Penn., 2000), 185–6.

11. Frank G. Madsen, 'Organized Crime', in Thomas G. Weiss and Sam Daws, eds, *The Oxford Handbook on the United Nations* (Oxford, 2007), 612–13.

12. See Loretta Napoleoni, *Modern Jihad: Tracing the Dollars behind the Terror Networks* (New York, 2005).

13. 'US Prompts WTO Probe into Chinese Counterfeits', *Boston Globe*, 26 Sept. 2007, at: <www.boston.com/business/markets/articles/2007/09/26/us_prompts_wto_probe_into_chinese_counterfeits/>. (12 Mar. 2009)

14. 'U.S. Attorney: Counterfeit Flea Market Items Could Pose Danger', *NBC6.Net*, 1 Aug. 2008, at: <www.nbc6.net/news/5715583/detail.html>. (1 Aug. 2008)

15. Brodie Fenlon, 'Groups Warn of Counterfeit Dangers', *Globe and Mail*, 25 Oct. 2007, at: <www.theglobeandmail.com/servlet/story/RTGAM.20071025.wcounterfeit1025/BNStory/National/home>. (1 Aug. 2008)

16. 'Increase in Counterfeit Imports Poses Risks to EU', at: <www.manufacturing.net/News-Increase-In-Counterfeit-Imports-Poses-Risks-To-EU.aspx?menuid=282>. (1 Aug. 2008)

17. See full report at: <www.oecd.org/dataoecd/13/12/38707619.pdf>. (1 Aug. 2008)

18. This is based on World Bank data for 2005.

19. Payne, *Global Issues*, 324.

20. See ibid.

21. Ibid., 325.

22. See Tim Golden, 'Mexican Drug Dealers Turning US Towns into Major Depots', *New York Times*, 16 Nov. 2002, A1.

23. Madsen, 'Organized Crime'.

24. John Pomfret, 'Bribery at Border Worried Officials', *Washington Post*, 15 July 2006, A01, at: <www.washingtonpost.com/wp-dyn/content/article/2006/07/14/AR2006071401525.html>. (30 June 2008)

25. To get a sense of the pervasiveness of corruption practices, see the report of Kenya's former anti-corruption chief, John Githongo: Africa Focus, 'Kenya: Githongo Report', in *Africa Focus Bulletin*, 26 Feb. 2006, at: <www.africafocus.org/docs06/git0602.php>. (14 Mar. 2009)

26. See <www.respondanet.com/english/anti_corruption/publications/documents/dellasoppa.01.doc>. (2 July 2008)

27. See United Nations International Drug Control Programme, *World Drug Report* (Oxford, 1997), 141; Margaret Beare, 'Money Laundering: A Preferred Law Enforcement Target for the 1990s', in Jay Albanese, ed., *Contemporary Issues in Organized Crime* (New York, 1995), 171–88.

28. US Congress, Senate Committee on Governmental Affairs, Permanent Subcommittee on Investigations, *Suspicious Banking Activities, Possible Money Laundering by U.S. Corporations Formed for Russian Entities* (GAO Publication No. GAO–01–120) (Washington, 2000).

29. For analyses, see Martin Potoucek, *Not Only the Market the Role of the Market: Government and the Civic Sector in the Development of Post Communist Societies* (Budapest, 1999), 80–7, 102–11; Maria Los and Andrzej Zybertowicz, *Privatizing the Police-State: The Case of Poland* (New York, 2000).

30. US Congress, Senate Committee on Governmental Affairs, Permanent Subcommittee on Investigations, *Private Banking: Raul Salinas, Citibank and Alleged Money Laundering* (GAO Publication No. GAO OSI–99–1) (Washington, 1998).

31. See Lucy Komisar, 'Citigroup: A Culture and History of Tax Evasion', Tax Justice Network, The Public Eye on Davos, at: <www.taxjustice.net/cms/upload/pdf/Citigroup_-_a_culture_and_history_of_tax_evasion.pdf>. (14 Mar. 2009)

32. Charles Clover, 'Swiss Investigate the Profits from Unaccountable Ukrainian Gas', *Financial Times*, 9 Dec. 1998, 2.

33. US Department of State, *Money Laundering and Financial Crimes* (2000), at: <www.state.gov/g/inl/rls/nrcrpt/2000/index.cfm?docid=959>. (2 Aug. 2008)

34. T.O. Olaleye-Oruene, 'Nigeria: Confiscation of the Proceeds of Corruption', *Journal of Financial Crime* 8, 2 (2000): 171–7.

35. Jack A. Blum, Michael Levi, R. Thomas Naylor, and Phil Williams, 'Financial Havens, Banking Secrecy and Money Laundering', *United Nations Bulletin of Crime Prevention and Criminal Law* 34 and 35 (Sections 4 and 5) (1998).

36. Vito Tanzi, *The International Anti-Corruption Forum: Corruption's Impact on Economic Performance* (Washington, 19 Jan. 2000).

37. According to an investigator at the Anti-Corruption seminar sponsored by Casals Associates, Washington, DC, 6 Dec. 2000.

38. Vito Tanzi, *Money Laundering and the International Financial System*, IMF Working Paper No. 96, 55 (Washington, 1996).

39. <www.capgemini.com/m/en/doc/WWR00.pdf>. (3 July 2008)

40. Artur Victoria, 'Money Laundering', *Ezine @rticles*, at: <ezinearticles.com/?Money-Laundering&id=1816180>. (14 Mar. 2009)

41. See Howard Abadinsky, *Organized Crime*, 6th edn (Belmont, Calif., 1999), 345–6.

42. A transcript of the Emancipation Proclamation can be found at: <www.archives.gov/exhibits/featured_documents/emancipation_proclamation/transcript.html>. (2 Aug. 2008)

43. US Department of State, 'Facts about Human Trafficking', Fact Sheet, Office to Monitor and Combat Trafficking in Persons, Washington, 7 Dec. 2005, at: <www.state.gov/g/tip/rls/fs/2005/60840.htm>. (14 Mar. 2009)

44. <www.state.gov/g/tip/rls/tiprpt/2008/105376.htm>. (14 Mar. 2009)

45. <www.notforsalecampaign.org/Default.aspx>. (2 Aug. 2008)

46. State of Washington, Department of Community, Trade and Economic Development, Office of Crime Victims Advocacy, *Human Trafficking: Present Day Slavery*, Report of the Washington State Task Force Against Trafficking of Persons (June 2004), at: <www.wcsap.org/advocacy/PDF/trafficking%20taskforce.pdf>. (2 Aug. 2008)

47. See Joel Brinkley, 'A Modern-Day Abolitionist Battles Slavery Worldwide', *New York Times*, 4 Feb. 2006, A4.

48. See, e.g., <www.gluckman.com/camelracing.html>; Elena Tiuriukanova, 'Female Labour Migration Trends and Human Trafficking', in Sally Stoecker and Louise Shelley, eds, *Human Traffic and Transnational Crime* (Lanham, Md, 2005), 98.

49. CBS News, 12 Sept. 2007, at: <www.cbsnews.com/stories/2007/09/11/earlyshow/main3250963.shtml>. (2 Aug. 2008)

50. Richard Poulin, 'Globalization and the Sex Trade: Trafficking and the Commodification of Women and Children', *Sisyphe*, 12 Feb. 2004, at: <sisyphe.org/article.php3?id_article=965>. (2 Aug. 2008)

51. Payne, *Global Issues*, 332.

52. Ibid.

53. See <www.taiwanact.net/article.php3?id_article=82>. (2 Aug. 2008)

54. <www.detica.com/indexed/NewsItem_criminalgangs.htm>. (2 Aug. 2008)

55. See Peter Hill, 'The Changing Face of the Yakuza', *Global Crime* 6 (2004): 97–116; Federico Varese, *The Russian Mafia: Private Protection in a New Market Economy* (Oxford, 2001); Yiu Kong Chu, *The Triads as Business* (London and New York, 2000); Diego Gambetta, *The Sicilian Mafia* (Cambridge, Mass., 1993).

56. The Sicilian Mafia, or Cosa Nostra, the 'Ndrangheta or Calabrian Mafia, the Camorra, and the Sacra Corona Unita.

57. In the US the Sicilian Mafia is now known as La Cosa Nostra.

58. Donald R. Liddock Jr, *The Global Underworld: Transnational Crime and the United States* (London, 2004), 34.

59. See Antonio Nicasso and Lee Lamothe, *Angels, Mobsters and Narco-terrorists: The Rising Menace of Global Criminal Empires* (Toronto, 2005), 33.

60. Ibid., 27.

61. Federico Varese, 'How Mafias Migrate: The Case of the 'Ndrangheta in Northern Italy', *Law and Society Review* 40, 2 (2006): 411–44.

62. CNN, 'Who Are the 'Ndrangheta?', at: <www.cnn.com/2007/WORLD/europe/08/15/germany.ndrangheta.reut/index.html>. (3 Aug. 2008)

63. Nicasso and Lamothe, *Angels, Mobsters and Narco-terrorists*, 29.

64. The heads of the member organizations were: the Rodriguez-Orejuela brothers; José Santacruz-Londoño (deceased); Helmer Herrera-Buitrago; the Urdinola-Grajales brothers; and Raul Grajales-Lemos and Luis Grajales-Posso.

65. See Nicasso and Lamothe, *Angels, Mobsters and Narco-terrorists*, 5–8.

66. <www.druglibrary.org/schaffer/dea/pubs/briefing/2_8.htm>. (4 Aug. 2008)

67. BBC News Special Report, 'The Rise and Rise of the Russian Mafia', at: <news.bbc.co.uk/2/hi/special_report/1998/03/98/russian_mafia/70095.stm>. (4 Aug. 2008)

68. Kevin Connolly, BBC News Special Report, 'How Russia's Mafia Is Taking Over Israeli Underworld', 21 Nov. 1998, at: <news.bbc.co.uk/2/hi/special_report/1998/03/98/russian_mafia/69521.stm>. (4 Aug. 2008)

69. <news.bbc.co.uk/2/hi/special_report/1998/03/98/russian_mafia/70095.stm>. (4 Aug. 2008)

70. See Howard Abadinsky, *Organized Crime*, 7th edn (Belmont, Calif., 2003), 191–205.

71. Lunde, *Organized Crime*, 85

72. See *Frontline*, 'Russian Organized Crime', Centre for Strategic and International Studies (CSIS) Task Force Report (1997), at: <www.pbs.org/wgbh/pages/frontline/shows/hockey/mafia/csis.html>. (14 Mar. 2009)

73. See Robert I. Friedman, *Red Mafiya: How the Russian Mob Has Invaded America* (Boston, 2000), xvii–xix, 173–201.

74. Terry Frieden, 'FBI: Albanian Mobsters "New Mafia"', 19 Aug., 2004, at: <edition.cnn.com/2004/LAW/08/18/albanians.mob/>. (5 Aug. 2008)

75. See Lunde, *Organized Crime*, 87.

76. Ron Chepesiuk, *The War on Drugs: An International Encyclopedia* (Santa Barbara, Calif., 1999), 267.

77. For more information on the Yakuza, see <www.trutv.com/library/crime/gangsters_outlaws/gang/yakuza/1.html>. (5 Aug. 2008)

78. <www.trutv.com/library/crime/gangsters_outlaws/gang/yakuza/2.html>. (5 Aug. 2008)

79. See Lunde, *Organized Crime*, 95–103.

80. Rafael Caro-Quintero was arrested in 1985 in connection with the torture and death of DEA special agent Enrique Camarena. Miguel Caro-Quintero was arrested in 1989, although it is believed that he still maintains control over the organization from behind bars.

81. Chepesiuk, *War on Drugs*, 133.

82. Kevin Noblet, 'Drug Lords Start "War" in Colombia', *Philadelphia Inquirer*, 25 Aug. 1989, A01.

83. Chepesiuk, *War on Drugs*, 15.

84. Michael D. Lyman and Gary W. Potter, *Organized Crime*, 3rd edn (Englewood Cliffs, NJ, 2003), 237.

85. Thomas Fuller, 'Khun Sa, Golden Triangle Drug King, Dies at 73', *New York Times*, 31 Oct. 2007.

86. 'Yardie' is a moniker used by Jamaicans to describe a Jamaican who has just arrived in Britain from 'the back yard' (or back home).

87. Lunde, *Organized Crime*, 83.

88. For more on the Yardies, see Roy A.C. Ramm, 'The Yardies: England's Emerging Crime Problem', Jan. 1988, at: <www.matarese.com/matarese-files/2677/yardies-england-emerging-crime-problem-ramm/index.html>. (6 Aug. 2008)

89. Liddock Jr, *Global Underworld*, 28.

90. See Transnational Criminal Activity: A Global Context, *Perspectives: A Canadian Security Intelligence Service Publication*, Report #2000/07, 3. Note that some observers have traced links between Sun Yee On and the Communist regime in Beijing.

91. See ibid.; Neal Hall, 'Big Circle Boys Born of Red Guards: Drugs, Loansharking among Asian Gang's Specialties', *Vancouver Sun*, 10 June 2005.

92. See BBC News, 'Fraud Ring Uncovered in Nigeria', 6 Sept. 2007, at: <news.bbc.co.uk/1/hi/world/africa/6982375.stm> (6 Aug. 2008); also see John C. Brugger, US Postal Inspection Service, Law Enforcement Report, 'Law Enforcement Weighs in against Nigerian Criminal Gangs' (Spring 1997), at: <www.usps.com/websites/depart/inspect/nigcgang.pdf>. (6 Aug. 2008)

93. *Perspectives*, Report #2000/07, 2–3.

94. Jonathan Winer, Deputy Assistant Secretary for International Narcotics and Law Enforcement Affairs, Statement before the Subcommittee on Africa of the House International Relations Committee, Washington, DC, 11 Sept. 1996, at: <www.fas.org/irp/congress/1996_hr/h960911w.htm>. (6 Aug. 2008)

95. Chepesiuk, *War on Drugs*, 258.

96. *Perspectives*, Report #2000/07, 3.

97. Ibid., 5.

98. Note that members of the Hell's Angels adhere to a strict code of secrecy. They are careful not to use their full names, even with one another. Instead, they use a first name or, more often than not, a nickname. See the official Hell's Angels website at: <www.hells-angels.com/MEMORIAL.html>. (6 Aug. 2008)

99. This comment was made by James McConville, in *Maritime Policy and Management* 31, 2 (2004): 173, about the book *Piracy at Sea: Bibliography*, ed. Rivka Romi-Levin (Haifa, July 2003).

100. 'The Return of Piracy', at <www.marginalrevolution.com/marginalrevolution/2003/12/the_return_of_p.html>. (29 Sept. 2006)

101. Dana Robert Dillon, 'Piracy in Asia: A Growing Barrier to Maritime Trade', The Heritage Foundation (2006), at: <www.heritage.org/Research/AsiaandthePacific/BG1379.cfm?renderforprint=1>. (28 Oct. 2006)

102. International Maritime Bureau (IMB) 'Piracy and Armed Robbery against Ships Annual Report 2006', International Chamber of Commerce, Kuala Lumpur, Malaysia, 2007, at: <www.icc-ccs.org/index.php?option=com_content&view=article&id=27&Itemid=16>.

103. IMB, 'Increase in Hijacking and Piracy off Somalia', 4 Apr. 2007, at <www.mast-yacht.co.uk/news.asp?sectionid=4&newsid=49>. (8 May 2007)

104. Steven L. Spiegel, Elizabeth G. Matthews, Jennifer M. Tow, and Kirsten P. Williams, *World Politics in a New Era*, 4th edn (New York, 2009), 323.

105. See Jeffrey Robinson, *The Merger: How Organized Crime Is Taking Over Canada and the World* (Toronto, 1999).

Chapter 13

1. United States, Office of the Press Secretary, 'President Discusses War on Terror at National Endowment for Democracy', Ronald Reagan Building and International Trade Center, Washington, DC, 6 Oct. 2005.

2. Quoted in Rex A. Hudson, *The Sociology and Psychology of Terrorism: Who Becomes a Terrorist and Why?* Federal Research Division, Library of Congress, 20540–4840 (Washington, Sept. 1999).

3. See Samuel P. Huntington, *The Clash of Civilizations and the Remaking of World Order* (New York, 1996).

4. See Ronald Inglehart and Pippa Norris, 'The True Clash of Civilizations', *Foreign Policy* 135 (Mar.–Apr. 2003): 63–70.

5. Stephen M. Walt, 'International Relations: One World, Many Theories', in Karen Mingst and Jack Snyder, *Essential Readings in World Politics* (New York, 2001), 27.

6. The police raids on these suspects were carried out by the Integrated National Security Enforcement Team.

7. 'Canada Nabs 17 Terror Suspects in Toronto', *USA Today*, at: <www.usatoday.com/news/world/2006–06–03-toronto-terror-suspects_x.htm>. (1 Jan. 2007).

8. This is adapted from a definition provided by the Dutch Ministry of Interior and Kingdom Relations Report 'From Dawa to Jihad: The Various Threats from Radical Islam to the Democratic Legal Order' (2005), 13, in Canadian Centre for Intelligence and Security Studies, The Norman Paterson School of International Affairs, Carleton University, 'Militant Jihadism: Radicalization, Conversion, Recruitment', at: <www.csis.gc.ca/en/itac/itacdocs/2006–4.asp#1>. (14 Jan. 2007).

9. The Netherlands, Ministry of the Interior and Kingdom Relations, General Intelligence and Security Service, *Violent Jihad in the Netherlands: Current Trends in the Islamist Terrorist Threat* (The Hague, Mar. 2006), 11. Van Gogh was murdered in broad daylight by Mohammed Bouyeri, 26, a Dutch-born dual Moroccan-Dutch citizen, who left a five-page note in both Arabic and Dutch attached to Van Gogh''s body with a knife. In the note he threatened jihad against the West in general ('I surely know that you, Oh Europe, will be destroyed'), and specifically against five prominent Dutch political figures. See Daniel Pipes, '[Theo van Gogh and] "Education by Murder" in Holland', *New York Sun*, 16 Nov. 2004.

10. *Satyagraha* is a way of life that guides the modes of political activism undertaken by the followers of its principle (or *satyagrahis*). Following the *satyagraha* path developed by Gandhi involves committing oneself to truth, chastity, non-attachment, and hard work. It also involves using non-violent means for resolving conflicts. A *satyagrahi* should try to convert opponents rather than coerce them. Modes of resistance that can be used by a *satyagrahi* include picketing, refusal to co-operate, peaceful marches and meetings, and a peaceful disobedience of the laws of the land. 'Reverence to the opposition was one of the unique features of the satyagraha preached by Gandhi'. See <www.mapsofindia.com/personalities/gandhi/satyagarh.html>. (15 Mar. 2009)

11. Vinay Lal, 'The Mother in the "Father of the Nation"', *Manushi: A Journal of Women and Society* no. 91 (Nov.–Dec. 1995): 27–30.

12. Louise Richardson, *What Terrorists Want: Understanding the Terrorist Threat* (London, 2006), 24.

13. The Netherlands, Ministry of the Interior and Kingdom Relations, *Violent Jihad*, 11.

14. The Netherlands, Ministry of the Interior and Kingdom Relations, General Intelligence and Security Service, *From Dawa to Jihad: The Various Threats from Radical Islam to the Democratic Legal Order* (The Hague, Dec. 2004), 13.

15. For this definition, we have drawn on a number of sources. Four crucial elements of the terrorism definition can be found in Cindy C. Combs, *Terrorism in the Twenty-First Century*, 3rd edn (Englewood Cliffs, NJ, 2003), 17. This is a clear and analytical conception of terrorism, although her suggestion that the targets of terrorism are always innocent people is not acceptable. Also, some might argue that this definition of terrorism is not much different from a definition of 'acts of war'.

16. For instance, see Charles Townshend, *Terrorism: A Very Short Introduction* (Oxford, 2002), 2–6.

17. The ANC was formed in 1912.

18. Manifesto of Umkhonto we Sizwe, at: <www.anc.org.za/ancdocs/history/manifesto-mk.html>. (1 Feb. 2007)

19. Nelson Mandela, *Long Walk to Freedom* (Boston, 1994), 240.

20. See Yasir Arafat's speech to the UN General Assembly, 13 Nov. 1974, trans. from Arabic, at: <www.mideastweb.org/arafat_at_un.htm>. (20 Feb. 2007)

21. Interview with Osama bin Laden by John Miller, ABC News, *Frontline*, May 1998, two months before the Al-Qaeda bombing of the US embassies in Kenya and Tanzania, at: <www.pbs.org/wgbh/pages/frontline/shows/binladen/who/interview.html>. (20 Feb. 2007)

22. Ibid.

23. Richardson, *What Terrorists Want*, 28.

24. Assaf Moghadam, *The Roots of Terrorism* (New York, 2006), 5.

25. Department of Defence, United States Army, *A Military Guide to Terrorism in the Twenty-First Century*, 15 Aug. 2005, 8.

26. Combs, *Terrorism in the Twenty-First Century*, 20.

27. Franklin L. Ford, *Political Murder: From Tyrannicide to Terrorism* (Cambridge, 1985), 90–1.

28. David C. Rapoport, *Terrorism: Critical Concepts in Political Science* (New York, 2005).

29. The Jewish Irgun and its more radical Stern Gang used terror tactics as a means of trying to force out the British occupying power. See Menachem Begin, *The Revolt: Story of the Irgun* (Jerusalem, 1997).

30. Moghadam, *Roots of Terrorism*, 57.

31. Ronald Reagan, Address to 'American Bar Association', *Weekly Compilation of Presidential Documents*, 8 July 1985, 881; Reagan, 'President's News Conference', 7 Jan. 1986, *Weekly Compilation of Presidential Documents*, 7 Jan. 1986, 26.

32. Louise Richardson, 'The Roots of Terrorism: An Overview', in Richardson, ed., *The Roots of Terrorism* (London, 2006), 3.

33. Jerrold M. Post, 'The Psychological Dynamics of Terrorism', in Richardson, ed., *Roots of Terrorism*, 18.

34. Ibid., 19–21.

35. See W. Andy Knight, 'Research Project on Radicalization and Extremism', unpublished report for the Department of Public Safety, Government of Canada (Mar. 2007).

36. A. Merari, 'The Readiness to Kill and Die: Suicidal Terrorism in the Middle East', in W. Reich, ed., *Origins of Terrorism* (Washington, 1998), 297.

37. See Anne Marie Oliver and Paul Steinberg, *The Road to Martyrs' Square: A Journey into the World of the Suicide Bomber* (Oxford, 2005).

38. Moghadam, *Roots of Terrorism*, 87–8.

39. See Alan Krueger and Jitka Maleckova, 'Does Poverty Cause Terrorism?', *New Republic*, 24 June 2004.

40. Ted Robert Gurr, 'Economic Factors', in Richardson, ed., *Roots of Terrorism*, 87.

41. Johan Galtung, 'Violence, Peace and Peace Research', *Journal of Peace Research* 6, 3 (1969): 167–91.

42. Hector Avalos, *Fighting Words: The Origins of Religious Violence* (New York, 2005).

43. Mark Juergensmeyer, 'Religion as a Cause of Terrorism', in Richardson, ed., *Roots of Terrorism*, 133.

44. Ibid., 141.

45. Anneli Botha, 'Terrorism in the Maghreb: The Transnationalisation of Domestic Terrorism', Institute for Security Studies, Monograph no. 144 (June 2008), at: <www.iss.co.za/index.php?link_id=32&slink_id=6500&link_type=12&slink_type=12&tmpl_id=3>. (15 Mar. 2009)

46. Liz Fekete 'Anti-Muslim Racism and the European Security State', *Race & Class* 46, 1 (2004): 26.

47. Chris Bickerton, 'France's History Wars', *Le Monde Diplomatique*, at: <mondediplo,com/2006/04/01france?var_recherche=+riots>. (19 July 2006)

48. See Edward D. Mansfield and Jack Snyder, 'Democratic Transitions and War', in Chester Crocker et al., eds, *Turbulent Peace: The Challenges of Managing International Conflict* (Washington, 2001), 113–26.

49. See, e.g., George Parker, ed., *The Fight Is for Democracy: Winning the War of Ideas in America and the World* (New York, 2003); Ronald D. Asmus et al., 'Progressive Internationalism. A Democratic National Security Strategy', Oct. 2003, at: <www.ppionline.org/documents/Progressive_Internationalism_1003.pdf>. (15 March 2009)

50. See, e.g., William Lee Eubank and Leonard Weinberg, 'Does Democracy Encourage Terrorism?', *Terrorism and Political Violence* 6, 4 (Winter 1994): 417–35.

51. Huntington, *Clash of Civilizations*.

52. Benjamin R. Barber, 'Terrorism, Interdependence, and Democracy', in James J.F. Forest, ed., *The Making of a Terrorist: Recruitment, Training, and Root Causes*, vol. 3 (London, 2006), 213.

53. UN General Assembly, 1972.

54. One of the convicted Libyan terrorists, Abdelbeset Ali Mohmed al Megrahi, 57, who was suffering with advanced prostate cancer, was released in August 2009 by Scottish authorities on compassionate grounds and sent home to Libya to die. This action caused a major international furor,

made worse when al Megrahi received a hero's welcome in the streets of Tripoli.

55. See UN Security Council, 1999.

Chapter 14

1. Bo Kjellen, 'Diplomacy and Governance for Sustainability in a Partially Globalized World', in Jouni Paavola and Ian Lowe, eds, *Environmental Values in a Globalizing World* (London and New York, 2005), 186.

2. James Gustave Speth and Peter M. Haas, *Global Environmental Governance* (Washington, 2006), especially ch. 2.

3. Garrett Hardin, 'The Tragedy of the Commons', *Science* 162 (1968): 1243–8.

4. Speth and Haas, *Global Environmental Governance*, 57.

5. Jacques Yves Cousteau with James Dugan, *The Living Sea* (New York, 1963).

6. Margaret P. Karns and Karen A. Mingst, *International Organizations: The Politics and Processes of Global Governance* (Boulder, Colo., 2004), 464.

7. E. Agius, cited in Robin Attfield, 'Environmental Values, Nationalism, Global Citizenship and the Common Heritage of Humanity', in Paavola and Lowe, eds, *Environmental Values in a Globalizing World*, 44.

8. Marvin S. Soroos, 'The Evolution of the Global Commons', in Ho-Won Jeong, ed., *Global Environmental Policies* (Houndmills, Basingstoke, UK, 2001), 47.

9. Indira Gandhi, cited in Speth and Haas, *Global Environmental Governance*, 58.

10. Kjellen, 'Diplomacy and Governance', 190.

11. N. Brian Winchester, 'Emerging Global Environmental Governance', *Indiana Journal of Global Legal Studies* 16 (Winter 2009): 10.

12. Speth and Haas, *Global Environmental Governance*, 65.

13. See World Commission on Environment and Development, *Our Common Future* (Oxford, 1987), 8.

14. Ibid., 50.

15. New Delhi Declaration of Principles of International Law Relating to Sustainable Development, cited in Joyeeta Gupta, 'The Climate Change Regime', in Paavola and Lowe, eds, *Environmental Values in a Globalizing World*, 160.

16. Ho-Won Jeong, 'Politics for Global Environmental Governance', in Jeong, ed., *Global Environmental Policies*, 10–11.

17. Winchester, 'Emerging Global Environmental Governance', 21.

18. United Nations General Assembly Resolution 44/228, 22 Dec. 1989, cited in Pamela Chasek, 'The Story of the UNCED Process', in Bertram I. Spector, Gunnar Sjostedt, and I. William Zartman, eds, *Negotiating International Regimes: Lessons Learned from the United Nations Conference on Environment and Development* (London/Dordrecht, 1994), 46.

19. The original study is Mario J. Molina and F.S. Rowland, 'Stratospheric Sink for Chlorofluoromethanes: Chlorine Atom-catalysed Destruction of Ozone', *Nature* 249 (1974): 810–12.

20. Speth and Haas, *Global Environmental Governance*, 69.

21. Kjellen, 'Diplomacy and Governance', 179.

22. Principle 15, Principles of the Rio Declaration, United Nations Environment Program, reprinted in Speth and Haas, *Global Environmental Governance*, 70.

23. Karns and Mingst, *International Organizations*, 467.

24. Dan Smith and Janani Vivekananda, 'A Climate of Conflict: The Links between Climate Change, Peace, and War', *International Alert* (Nov. 2007), at: <www.international-alert.org/pdf/A_Climate_Of_Conflict.pdf>. (19 Mar. 2009)

25. Nicholas Stern, *Stern Review Report on the Economics of Climate Change* (London, 2006), at: <www.hm-treasury.gov.uk/sternreview_index.htm>. (19 Mar. 2009)

26. Cited in Winchester, 'Emerging Global Environmental Governance', 15.

27. An exajoule is 1 quintillion joules.

28. Ian Noble and Robert T. Watson, 'Confronting Climate Change', in Vinay Bhargava, ed., *Global Issues for Global Citizens: An Introduction to Key Development Challenges* (Washington, 2006), 222–3.

29. Intergovernmental Panel on Climate Change, 'Why the IPCC Was Created', at: <www.ipcc.ch/about/index.htm>. (20 Mar. 2009)

30. Noble and Watson, 'Confronting Climate Change', 222.

31. See Intergovernmental Panel on Climate Change, *Climate Change 2007 Synthesis Report*, at: <www.ipcc.ch/pdf/assessment-report/ar4/syr/ar4_syr.pdf>. (18 Mar. 2009)

32. For more on this topic, see Network for Information, Response and Preparedness Activities on Disaster, at: <www.nirapad.org/>. (18 Mar. 2009)

33. Noble and Watson, 'Confronting Climate Change', 225.

34. Ibid., 226.

35. World Health Organization, 'Global, National Efforts Must Be Urgently Intensified to Control Zimbabwe Cholera Outbreak', at: <www.who.int/mediacentre/news/releases/2009/cholera_zim_20090130/en/index.html>. (18 Mar. 2009)

36. IPCC, *Climate Change 2007 Synthesis Report*. Angela Cropper, the UNEP deputy executive director, recently described the seriousness of the current situation: 'Natural disasters caused by climate extremes—including devastating floods, severe droughts, snow storms, heat waves and cold waves—are leaving trails of unprecedented destruction and loss of life.' She pointed to the example of Cyclone Nargis, which devastated Myanmar (Burma) and claimed the lives of about 78,000 people. United Nations Environmental Program, 'Speech by Angela Cropper, UNEP Deputy Executive Director, at the SIDA Climate Game Change Seminar, Bangkok, Thailand', 22 Jan 2009, at: <www.unep.org/Documents.Multilingual/Default.asp?DocumentID=560&ArticleID=6048&l=en>. (18 Mar. 2009)

37. Noble and Watson, 'Confronting Climate Change', 219.

38. It is worth reading Al Gore's Nobel lecture, at: <nobelprize.org/nobel_prizes/peace/laureates/2007/gore-lecture_en.html>. (18 Mar. 2009)

39. T. Banuri and J. Weyant, 'Setting the Stage: Climate Change and Sustainable Development', in B. Metz, O. Davidson, R. Swart, and J. Pan, eds, *Climate Change 2001: Mitigation* (Cambridge, 2001).

40. Ronald B. Mitchell, 'International Environmental Agreements: A Survey of their Features, Formation and Effects', *Annual Review of Energy and Environment 2003* 28 (2003): 429–61.

41. Frank Biermann, 'Green Global Governance: The Case for a World Environment Organisation', *New Economy* 9, 2 (June 2002): 82.

42. Ibid.

43. James Gustave Speth, 'A New Green Regime', *Environment* 44, 7 (Sept. 2002): 20.

44. Ibid.

45. Chee Yoke Ling and Martin Khor, 'International Environmental Governance: Some Issues from a Developing Country Perspective', Working Paper by Third World Network, Sept. 2001, at: <www.twnside.org.sg/title/ieg.htm>. (18 Mar. 2009)

46. World Resources Institute, *2002–2004: Decisions for the Earth: Balance, Voice and Power*, at: <www.wri.org/publication/world-resources-2002–2004-decisions-earth-balance-voice-and-power>. (18 Mar. 2009)

47. Ling and Khor, 'International Environmental Governance'.

48. Winchester, 'Emerging Global Environmental Governance', 11.

49. Peter M. Haas, 'UN Conferences and Constructivist Governance of the Environment', *Global Governance* 8 (2002): 73.

50. Peter Bridgewater and Celia Bridgewater, 'International Environmental Governance', in Paavola and Lowe, eds, *Environmental Values in a Globalizing World*, 205.

51. Ibid., 209.

52. Haas, 'UN Conferences and Constructivist Governance', 86.

53. Ibid., 74.

54. See Jacob Park, 'Global Governance, Institutions, and the Tragedy of the Commons', *Ethics, Place and Environment* 2, 2 (1999): 292–3.

55. See Jim Whitman, *The Limits of Global Governance* (London, 2005).

Chapter 15

1. Vincent Della Sala, 'Constitutionalising Governance: Democratic Dead-end or Dead-on Democracy?' *Constitutionalism Web-Papers*, No. 6–2001, at: <www.qub.ac.uk/ies/onlinepapers/const.html>. (15 Nov. 2009)

2. Robert Keohane and Joeseph Nye Jr, 'Introduction', in Joseph Nye Jr and John D. Donahue, eds, *Governance in a Globalizing World* (Washington, 2000), 26.

3. For a sample of the literature on the topic, see Alice D. Ba and Matthew J. Hoffmann, eds, *Contending Perspectives on Global Governance: Coherence, Contestation and World Order* (London and New York, 2005); David Held and Anthony McGrew, *Governing Globalization* (Cambridge, 2002); William Tabb, *Economic Governance in the Age of Globalization* (New York, 2004).

4. Shepard Forman and Derek Segaar, 'New Coalitions for Global Governance: The Changing Dynamics of Multilateralism', *Global Governance* 12, 2 (Apr. 2006): 205.

5. For a good review, see Michael W. Doyle, *Empires* (Ithaca, NY, 1986). Also see Niall Ferguson, *Empire* (London, 2002).

6. See, e.g., Kenneth Waltz, *A Theory of International Politics* (New York, 1979); John Mearsheimer, *The Tragedy of Great Power Politics* (New York, 2001). Also see Henry Kissinger, *The White House Years* (Boston, 1979).

7. Inis Claude Jr, *Swords into Plowshares*, 4th edn (New York, 1984), 21.

8. Ibid., 27.

9. Ibid., 28.

10. Craig Murphy, *International Organization and Industrial Change* (Cambridge, 1994), 32–7.

11. Ibid., 56.

12. Ibid., 32–7.

13. Woodrow Wilson, Address to the United States Congress, 8 Jan. 1918, at: <www.firstworldwar.com/source/fourteenpoints.htm>. (15 Mar. 2009)

14. Claude, *Swords into Plowshares*, 54.

15. Cited ibid., 44.

16. A good illustration of this can be seen in the women in Latin America who used the League to seek support for their human rights campaign. See, e.g., the discussion in Dorothy Jones, *Code of Peace* (Chicago, 1991).

17. Ramesh Thakur and Luk Van Langenhove, 'Enhancing Global Governance through Regional Integration', *Global Governance* 12 (2006): 233.

18. Bjorn Hettne and Fredrik Soderbaum, 'The UN and Regional Organizations in Global Security: Competing or Complementary Logics?', *Global Governance* 12 (2006): 227–32.

19. Those 34 countries are: Antigua and Barbuda, Argentina, the Bahamas, Barbados, Belize, Bolivia, Brazil, Canada, Chile, Colombia, Costa Rica, Dominica, Dominican Republic, Ecuador, El Salvador, Grenada, Guatemala, Guyana, Haiti, Honduras, Jamaica, Mexico, Nicaragua, Panama, Paraguay, Peru, St Kitts and Nevis, St Lucia, St Vincent and the Grenadines, Suriname, Trinidad and Tobago, the US, Uruguay, and Venezuela.

20. See Richard Higgott, 'Economic Cooperation in the Asia-Pacific: A Theoretical Comparison with the European Union', *Journal of European Public Policy* 2, 3 (1995): 376–7.

21. Andrew Cooper, 'Stretching the Model of Coalitions of the Willing', Oct. 2005, at: <ssrn.com/abstract=857444>. (15 Mar. 2009)

22. Murphy, *International Organization*; also see John Ruggie, *Constructing the World Polity* (New York, 1998).

23. Jessica Matthews, 'Power Shift', *Foreign Affairs* 76, 1 (Jan.–Feb. 1997), at: <www.foreignaffairs.com/articles/52644/jessica-t-mathews/power-shift>.

24. Forman and Segaar, 'New Coalitions for Global Governance'. Forman and Segaar note that Steve Charnovitz, 'Two Centuries of Participation: NGOs and International Governance', *Michigan Journal of International Law* (Winter 1997), claims that the Permanent Court of International Justice and the Economic Consultative Committee of the League of Nations were more open to NGO participation than, respectively, the International Court of Justice or ECOSOC.

25. James Rosenau, *Turbulence in World Politics: A Theory of Change and Continuity* (Princeton, NJ, 1990).

26. Forman and Segaar, 'New Coalitions for Global Governance'.

27. For an interesting account of the role of GATT civil servants during the Uruguay Round negotiations, see Xu Yi-chong and Patrick Weller, *The Governance of World Trade* (Cheltenham, UK, 2004).

28. For more on this, see Andrew F. Cooper, *Celebrity Diplomacy* (Boulder, Colo., 2007).

29. United Nations General Assembly, *A More Secure World: Our Shared Responsibility*, Report of the High Level Panel on Threats, Challenges and Change, Dec. 2004, UNGA Document A/59/565, 64.

30. Michael Ignatieff, 'Whatever Happened to "Responsibility to Protect"?', *National Post*, 10 Dec. 2008.

31. Philippe Sands, *Lawless World* (London, 2005).

32. See, e.g., some of the discussions of peace-building activities undertaken by international institutions in Roland Paris, *At War's End, Building Peace after Civil Conflict* (Cambridge, 2004); Tom Keating and W. Andy Knight, eds, *Building Sustainable Peace* (Edmonton, 2004).

33. See Tagi Sagafi-Nejad with John H. Dunning, *The UN and Transnational Corporations: From Code of Conduct to Global Compact* (Bloomington, Ind., 2008), 215.

34. Ngaire Woods, 'Good Governance in International Institutions', *Global Governance* 5, 1 (1999): 39.

35. Keohane and Nye, 'Introduction', 19.

36. See Jim Whitman, *The Limits of Global Governance* (London, 2005).

37. David Kennedy, 'The Forgotten Politics of International Governance', *European Human Rights Law Review* 2 (2001): 123.

38. Anne-Marie Slaughter, *A New World Order* (Princeton, NJ, 2004).

39. Jan Martin, Wolfgang H. Reinicke, and Thorsten Benner, 'Beyond Multilateralism: Global Policy Networks', *International Politics and Society* 2 (2000).

40. See Andrew F. Cooper, *Tests of Global Governance: Canadian Diplomacy and United Nations World Conferences* (Tokyo, 2004), 1.

41. Eşref Aksu and Joseph A. Camilleri, eds, *Democratizing Global Governance* (Houndmills, UK, 2002).

42. Michael Zurn, 'Global Governance and Legitimacy Problems', *Government and Opposition* 39, 2 (2004): 286.

43. W. Andy Knight, 'Multilateralisme ascendant ou descendant: deux voies dans la quete d'une gouverne globale', *Etudes Internationale* (numero special) 26, 4 (Dec. 1995): 685–710.

44. Ian Hurd, 'Legitimacy and Authority in International Politics', *International Organization* 53, 2 (1999): 381.

45. Robert Keohane, 'Governance in a Partially Globalized World: Presidential Address', American Political Science Association 2000, *American Political Science Review* 95, 1 (2001): 9.

46. Charlotte Ku, 'Global Governance and the Changing Face of International Law', *ACUNS Reports & Papers*, No. 2 (New Haven, 2001).

47. See W. Andy Knight, 'The Development of the Responsibility to Protect: From Evolving Norm to Practice', *Global R2P Journal* (forthcoming 2010).

48. Kofi Annan, 'Two Concepts of Sovereignty', *The Economist*, 18 Sept. 1999.

49. W. Andy Knight, 'Crisis of Relevance Threatens the UN', *Edmonton Journal*, 3 Mar. 2003, A14.

50. Thorsten Benner, Wolfgang H. Reinicke, and Jan Martin Witte, 'Multisectoral Networks in Global Governance: Towards a Pluralistic System of Accountability', *Government and Opposition* 39, 2 (2004): 195.

51. W. Andy Knight, 'The US, the UN and the Global Rule of Law', *Journal of Constitutional Studies* 10, 1 and 2 (2005): 22.

52. See David Cameron and Janice Gross Stein, *Street Protests and Fantasy Parks: Globalization, Culture, and the State* (Vancouver, 2002).

53. Benner, Reinicke, and Witte, 'Multisectoral Networks in Global Governance'.

54. Zurn, 'Global Governance and Legitimacy Problems', 281.

55. David Held and Mathias Koenig-Archibugi, 'Introduction', *Government and Opposition* 39, 2 (2004): 125.

56. Rodney Bruce Hall and Thomas J. Biersteker, eds, *The Emergence of Private Authority in Global Governance* (Cambridge, 2002).

57. Miles Kahler, 'Defining Accountability Up: The Global Economic Multilaterals', *Government and Opposition* 39, 2 (2004): 156.

58. Zurn, 'Global Governance and Legitimacy Problems', 286.

59. Keohane and Nye, 'Introduction', 37.

Conclusion

1. Parag Khanna, *The Second World* (New York, 2008), 320.

2. James Lee Ray and Juliet Kaarbo, *Global Politics* (New York, 2008), 3.

3. Max Weber, *The Theory of Social and Economic Organization* (New York, 1964).

4. See James A. Russell, 'Peering into the Abyss: Non-State Actors and the 2016 Nuclear Proliferation Environment', *Non-Proliferation Review* 13, 3 (Nov. 2006): 645–57.

5. See Ewen MacAskill, 'Terrorist Could Mount Nuclear or Biological Attack within 5 Years, Warns Congress Inquiry', *Guardian*, 4 Dec. 2008, at: <www.guardian.co.uk/world/2008/dec/04/terrorism-nuclear-attack-congress-report>. (10 Dec. 2008)

6. <www.homebuyinginstitute.com/homebuyingtips/2007/12/subprime-mortgage-crisis-explained.html>. (15 Dec. 2008)

7. Walden Bello, 'A Primer on the Wall Street Meltdown', *Focus on the Global South*, 17 Oct. 2008, at: <focusweb.org/afterthoughts-a-primer-on-the-wall-street-meltdown.html?Itemid=1>. (14 Dec. 2008)

8. Ibid.

9. Unnamed financial executive cited ibid.

10. Eric Helleiner, *States and the Reemergence of Global Finance: From Bretton Woods to the 1990s* (Ithaca, NY, 1994).

11. Liesbet Hooghe and Gary Marks, 'Unraveling the Central State, but How? Types of Multi-Level Governance', *American Political Science Review* 97, 2 (May 2003): 233–43.

12. Carolyn Kennedy-Pipe and Nicholas Rengger, 'Apocalypse Now? Continuities or Disjunctions in World Politics after 9/11', *International Affairs* 82, 3 (May 2006): 539–52.

13. Donald Kirkpatrick, *How to Manage Change Effectively* (London, 1985), 31–2.

14. See, e.g., Khanna, *The Second World*; Alexander T.J. Lennon and Amanda Kozlowski, eds, *Global Powers in the 21st Century: Strategies and Relations* (Cambridge, Mass., 2008).

15. Fareed Zakaria, 'The Future of American Power: How America Can Survive the Rise of the Rest', *Foreign Affairs* (May–June 2008): 18–43.

16. James Rosenau, 'The Dynamism of a Turbulent World', in Michael Klare and Chandrani Yogesh, eds, *World Security: Challenges for a New Century*, 3rd edn (New York, 1998).

17. For these and other transnational issues, see Vinay Bhargava, ed., *Global Issues for Global Citizens: An Introduction to Key Development Challenges* (Washington, 2006).

18. Stanley Hoffmann, *World Disorders: Troubled Peace in the Post-Cold War Era* (Lanham, Md, 2000).

19. James Rosenau and Mary Durfee, *Thinking Theory Thoroughly: Coherent Approaches to an Incoherent World* (Boulder, Colo., 2000), 62.

20. Rosenau, 'Dynamism of a Turbulent World', 34.

21. On subsidiarity, see W. Andy Knight and Randolph B. Persaud, 'Subsidiarity, Regional Governance and Caribbean Security', *Latin American Politics and Society* 43, 1 (Spring 2001): 29–56; W. Andy Knight, 'Towards a Subsidiarity Model for Peacemaking and Preventive Diplomacy: Making Chapter VIII of the UN Charter Operational', *Third World Quarterly* 17, 1 (Mar. 1996): 31–52.

22. Seyom Brown, 'World Interests and the Changing Demands of Security', in Klare and Chandrani, eds, *World Security*, 3rd edn, 16.

23. Seyom Brown, *Higher Realism: A New Foreign Policy for the United States* (Boulder, Colo., 2008).

24. Hans Morgenthau, 'The Purpose of Political Science', cited ibid., 12.

25. Murielle Cozette, 'Reclaiming the Critical Dimension of Realism: Hans J. Morgenthau on the Ethics of Scholarship', *Review of International Studies* 34 (2008): 6.

26. Ibid., 27.

27. Robert Jackson, *The Global Covenant* (Oxford, 2000), 401 passim.

28. Hans Morgenthau, cited in Cozette, 'Reclaiming the Critical Dimension', 20.

29. Ibid., 21

30. Jim Whitman, *The Limits of Global Governance* (London, 2005).

31. See Robert Johnstone, 'Global Governance: Creating Rules for Running the World', *Literary Review of Canada* (May 2002): 10–11.

References

Abadinsky, Howard. *Organized Crime*, 6th, 7th edns. Belmont, Calif.: Wadsworth, 1999, 2003.

Africa Focus. 'Kenya: Githongo Report', *Africa Focus Bulletin*, 26 Feb. 2006. At: <www.africafocus.org/docs06/git0602.php>. (14 Mar. 2009)

Aginam, Obijiofor. 'Of Savages and Mass Killing: HIV/AIDS, Africa and the Crisis of Global Health Governance', in Toyin Falola and Matthew M. Heaton, eds, *HIV/AIDS, Illness, and African Wellbeing*. Rochester, NY: University of Rochester Press, 2007.

Aksu, Eşref, and Joseph A. Camilleri, eds. *Democratizing Global Governance*. Houndmills, UK: Palgrave Macmillan, 2002.

Ambrose, Stephen. *Rise to Globalism: American Foreign Policy, 1938–1976*, rev. edn. New York: Penguin, 1976.

Amoore, Louise. 'Introduction: Global Resistance—Global Politics', in Amoore (2005).

Amoore, Louise, ed. *The Global Resistance Reader*. London: Routledge, 2005.

Angell, Norman. *The Great Illusion*. New York and London: G.P. Putnam's Sons, 1913.

Annan, Kofi. *Renewing the United Nations: A Programme for Reform*, Report of the Secretary-General A/51/950. New York: UN, 9 Dec. 1997.

———. 'Two Concepts of Sovereignty', *The Economist*, 18 Sept. 1999.

Ashley, Richard. 'The Poverty of Neo-Realism', *International Organisation* 38, 2 (1984).

———. 'The Geopolitics of Geopolitical Space: Toward a Critical Social Theory of International Politics', *Alternatives* 12, 4 (1987).

———. 'Untying the Sovereign State: A Double Reading of the Anarchy Problematique', *Millennium* 17, 2 (1988).

——— and R.B.J. Walker. 'Reading Dissidence/Writing the Discipline: Crisis and the Question of Sovereignty in International Studies', *International Studies Quarterly* 34, 3 (1990).

Asmus, Ronald D., et al., 'Progressive Internationalism. A Democratic National Security Strategy', Oct. 2003. At: <www.ppi-online.org/documents/Progressive_Internationalism_1003.pdf>. (15 Mar. 2009)

A.T. Kearney Inc. & Carnegie Endowment for International Peace. 'The Globalization Index', *Foreign Policy* (Nov.–Dec. 2007).

Attfield, Robin. 'Environmental Values, Nationalism, Global Citizenship and the Common Heritage of Humanity', in Jouni Paavola and Ian Lowe, eds, *Environmental Values in a Globalizing World*. London and New York: Routledge, 2005.

Avalos, Hector. *Fighting Words: The Origins of Religious Violence*. New York: Prometheus Books, 2005.

Axworthy, Lloyd, 'Canada and Humane Security: The Need for Leadership', *International Journal* 52 (1997).

———. 'Putting People First', *Global Governance* 7, 1 (Jan.–Mar. 2001).

———. *Navigating a New World: Canada's Global Future*. Toronto: Alfred A. Knopf Canada, 2003.

Ba, Alice D., and Matthew J. Hoffmann, eds. *Contending Perspectives on Global Governance: Coherence, Contestation and World Order*. London and New York: Routledge, 2005.

Baldwin, David A., ed. *Neorealism and Neoliberalism: The Contemporary Debate*. New York: Columbia university Press, 1993.

Banuri, T., and J. Weyant. 'Setting the Stage: Climate Change and Sustainable Development', in B. Metz, O. Davidson, R. Swart, and J. Pan, eds, *Climate Change 2001: Mitigation*. Cambridge: Cambridge University Press, 2001.

Baran, Paul A. *The Political Economy of Growth*. New York: Monthly Review Press, 1957.

Barber, Benjamin R. 'Terrorism, Interdependence, and Democracy', in James J.F. Forest, ed., *The Making of a Terrorist: Recruitment, Training, and Root Causes*, vol. 3. London: Praeger Security International, 2006.

Barnet, Richard, and Ronald Muller. *Global Reach*. New York: Simon & Schuster, 1974.

Bartelson, Jens. *The Genealogy of Sovereignty*. New York: Cambridge University Press, 1995.

Bauer, Julien, and Philippe Le Prestre. 'Ménage à trois: The State between Civil Society and the International System', in Gordon Smith and Daniel Wolfish, eds, *Who Is Afraid of the State?* Toronto: University of Toronto Press, 2001.

Baylis, John, and Steve Smith, eds. *The Globalization of World Politics: An Introduction to International Relations*, 3rd edn. Oxford: Oxford University Press, 2005.

BBC News. 'Fraud Ring Uncovered in Nigeria', 6 Sept. 2007. At: <news.bbc.co.uk/1/hi/world/africa/6982375.stm>. (6 Aug. 2008)

Beare, Margaret. 'Money Laundering: A Preferred Law Enforcement Target for the 1990s', in Jay Albanese, ed., *Contemporary Issues in Organized Crime*. New York: Criminal Justice Press, 1995.

Beck, Ulrich. *What Is Globalization?* Cambridge: Polity Press, 1999.

Begin, Menachem. *The Revolt: Story of the Irgun*. Jerusalem: Steinmatsky's Agency, 1997.

Bell, Duncan. 'Anarchy, Power and Death: Contemporary Political Realism as Ideology', *Journal of Political Ideologies* 7, 2 (2002).

Bellamy, Alex J., ed. *International Society and Its Critics*. Oxford: Oxford University Press, 2004.

Bello, Walden. '2000: The Year of Global Protest against Globalization', *Focus on Trade* no. 58 (Jan. 2001). At: <www.nadir.

org/nadir/initiativ/agp/free/bello/2000global_protest. htm>. Reprinted in *Canadian Dimension* 35, 2 (2001).

———. 'A Primer on the Wall Street Meltdown', *Focus on the Global South*, 17 Oct. 2008. At: <focusweb.org/afterthoughts-a-primer-on-the-wall-street-meltdown. html?Itemid=1>. (14 Dec. 2008)

Benner, Thorsten, Wolfgang H. Reinicke, and Jan Martin Witte. 'Multisectoral Networks in Global Governance: Towards a Pluralistic System of Accountability', *Government and Opposition* 39, 2 (2004).

Berlin, Isaiah. *Karl Marx*. London: Oxford University Press, 1948.

Berry, Tom. 'The Terms of Power', 2 Nov. 2002. At: <www. fpif.org/commentary/2002/0211power_body.html>. (18 Nov. 2009)

Best, Geoffrey. 'Peace Conferences and the Century of Total War', *International Affairs* 75 (July 1999).

Bhargava, Vinay, ed. *Global Issues for Global Citizens: An Introduction to Key Development Challenges*. Washington: World Bank, 2006.

Bickerton, Chris. 'France's History Wars', *Le Monde Diplomatique*. At: <mondediplo,com/2006/04/01france?va r_recherche=+riots>. (19 July 2006)

Biermann, Frank. 'Green Global Governance: The Case for a World Environment Organisation', *New Economy* 9, 2 (June 2002).

Blum, Jack A., Michael Levi, R. Thomas Naylor, and Phil Williams. 'Financial Havens, Banking Secrecy and Money Laundering', *United Nations Bulletin of Crime Prevention and Criminal Law* 34 and 35, Sections 4 and 5 (1998).

Bodin, Jean. *Six Books on the Commonwealth*. Oxford: Blackwell, 1967.

Boot, Max. *War Made New*. New York: Gotham Books, 2006.

Botha, Anneli. 'Terrorism in the Maghreb: The Transnationalisation of Domestic Terrorism', Institute for Security Studies, Monograph no. 144 (June 2008). At: <www.iss.co.za/index. php?link_id=32&slink_id=6500&link_type=12&slink_ type=12&tmpl_id=3>. (15 Mar. 2009)

Boudreau, Thomas. *Sheathing the Sword: The UN Secretary-General and the Prevention of International Conflict*. Westport, Conn.: Greenwood Press, 1984.

Boutros-Ghali, Boutros. *An Agenda for Peace*. New York: UN, 1992.

Bridgewater, Peter, and Celia Bridgewater. 'International Environmental Governance', in Jouni Paavola and Ian Lowe, eds, *Environmental Values in a Globalizing World*. London and New York: Routledge, 2005.

Brinkley, Joel. 'A Modern-Day Abolitionist Battles Slavery Worldwide', *New York Times*, 4 Feb. 2006.

Brown, Seyom. *New Forces, Old Forces and the Future of World Politics*. Boston: Scott, Foresman and Company, 1988.

———. 'World Interests and the Changing Demands of Security', in Michael T. Klare and Yogesh Chandrani, eds, *World Security*, 3rd edn. New York: St Martin's Press, 1998.

———. *Higher Realism: A New Foreign Policy for the United States*. Boulder, Colo.: Paradigm, 2008.

Brugger, John C. 'United States Postal Inspection Service, Law Enforcement Report: Law Enforcement Weighs In against Nigerian Criminal Gangs' (Spring 1997). At: <www.usps.com/ websites/depart/inspect/nigcgang.pdf>. (6 Aug. 2008)

Brunelle, Dorval. *From World Order to Global Disorder: States, Markets, and Dissent*. Vancouver: University of British Columbia Press, 2007.

Bull, Hedley. 'The Theory of International Politics 1919–1969', in Brian Porter, ed., *The Aberystwyth Papers: International Politics 1919–1969*. Oxford: Oxford University Press, 1972.

———. *The Anarchical Society: A Study of Order in World Politics*. London: Macmillan, 1977.

——— and Adam Watson, eds. *The Expansion of International Society*. Oxford: Clarendon Press, 1985.

Burckhardt, Jacob. *The Civilization of the Renaissance in Italy*, vol. 1. New York: Harper, 1958.

Burton, John. *World Society*. Cambridge: Cambridge University Press, 1972.

Bush, George W. 'Graduation Speech at United States Military Academy', West Point, NY, 1 June 2002. At: <www. whitehouse.gov/news/releases/2002/06/20020601–3. html>. (14 Mar. 2009)

Butler, Judith. *Gender Trouble: Feminism and the Subversion of Identity*. London: Routledge, 1990.

Buzan, Barry. *People, States and Fear: An Agenda for International Security Studies in the Post-Cold War Era*, 2nd edn. Boulder, Colo.: Lynne Rienner, 1991.

Cameron, David, and Janice Gross Stein. *Street Protests and Fantasy Parks: Globalization, Culture, and the State*. Vancouver: University of British Columbia Press, 2002.

Camilleri, Joseph. 'Rethinking Sovereignty in a Shrinking, Fragmented World', in R.B.J. Walker and Saul Mendlovitz, eds, *Contending Sovereignties: Redefining Political Community*. Boulder, Colo.: Lynne Rienner, 1990.

Campbell, D. *Writing Security: United States Foreign Policy and the Politics of Identity*. Manchester: Manchester University Press, 1992.

Canada and Norwegian Partnership for Action. The Lysøen Declaration, Backgrounder to 'Canada and Norway form new partnership on human security', press release No. 117, Department of Foreign Affairs and International Trade, 11 May 1998.

Canadian Centre for Intelligence and Security Studies, Norman Paterson School of International Affairs, Carleton University for Integrated Threat Assessment Centre (ITAC) of the Canadian Security Intelligence Service (CSIS). 'Militant Jihadism: Radicalization, Conversion, Recruitment', vol. 2006–4, Trends in Terrorism Series. At: <www.csis.gc.ca/en/itac/itacdocs/2006–4.asp#1>. (14 Jan. 2008)

Cardoso, Fernando Henrique, and Enzo Faletto. *Dependency and Development in Latin America*, trans. Marjory Mattingly Urquidi. Berkeley: University of California Press, 1979.

Carr, E.H. *The Twenty Years Crisis, 1919–1939*. New York: Harper & Row Torchbooks, 1964.

Carranza, Mario E. 'Mercosur and the End Game of the FTAA Negotiations: Challenges and Prospects after the Argentine Crisis', *Third World Quarterly* 25, 2 (2004).

Caruso, Giuseppe. 'Report on the World Social Forum in Mumbai 2004'. At: <www.signofourtimes.org/UK/WSF/html>. (28 July 2008)

Castells, Manuel. *The Information Age, vol. 2, The Power of Identity*, 2nd edn. Oxford: Blackwell, 2004.

Chalmers, Douglas. 'Corporatism and Comparative Politics', in Howard Wiards, ed., *New Directions in Comparative Politics*, rev. edn. Boulder, Colo.: Westview Press, 1991.

Chandler, Alfred D., Jr, and Bruce Mazlish, eds. *Leviathans: Multinational Corporations and the New Global History*. New York: Cambridge University Press, 2005.

Charnovitz, Steve. 'Two Centuries of Participation: NGOs and International Governance', *Michigan Journal of International Law* 18 (Winter 1997).

Chase-Dunn, Christopher. *Global Formation: Structures of the World-Economy*, 2nd edn. Lanham, Md: Rowman & Littlefield, 1998.

———. 'World Systems Theorizing', in Jonathan Turner, ed., *Handbook of Sociological Theory*. New York: Plenum, 2001.

Chasek, Pamela. 'The Story of the UNCED Process', in Bertram I. Spector, Gunnar Sjostedt, and I. William Zartman, eds, *Negotiating International Regimes: Lessons Learned from the United Nations Conference on Environment and Development*. London/Dordrecht: Graham & Trotman/Martinus Nijhoff, 1994.

Chepesiuk, Ron. *The War on Drugs: An International Encyclopaedia*. Santa Barbara, Calif.: ABC-CLIO, 1999.

Cheston, Susy, and Lisa Khun. 'Empowering Women through Microfinance'. At: <www.microcreditsummit.org/papers/empowering_final.doc>. (11 Nov. 2009)

Chopra, Jarat, ed. *The Politics of Peace Maintenance*. Boulder, Colo.: Lynne Rienner, 1998.

——— and Tanja Hohe. 'Participatory Peacebuilding', in Tom Keating and W. Andy Knight, *Building Sustainable Peace*. Edmonton and Tokyo: University of Alberta Press and United Nations University Press, 2004.

Chu, Yiu Kong. *The Triads as Business*. London and New York: Routledge, 2000.

CIMAC. *Noticias News for Women* (Mexico City), 27 Dec. 2006.

Clark, Ian. *Globalisation and International Relations Theory*. Oxford: Oxford University Press, 1999.

———. *The Post-Cold War Order: The Spoils of Peace*. Oxford: Oxford University Press, 2001.

Claude, Inis L., Jr. *Swords into Plowshares*. New York: Random House, 1971.

———. *Swords into Plowshares: The Problems and Progress of International Organization*, 4th edn. New York: Random House, 1984.

———. 'The Evolution of Concepts of Global Governance and the State in the Twentieth Century', paper presented at Academic Council on the United Nations System (ACUNS) annual conference, Oslo, 16–18 June 2000.

Clausewitz, Carl von. *On War*. London: Penguin, 1982.

Clements, Kevin P. 'Opportunity for a New Kind of Global Order', some draft talking points on terror and terrorism for CODEP meeting at ODI, 29 Sept. 2001.

Clinton, W.J. 'Address to the World Trade Organization', Geneva, 1998.

Clover, Charles. 'Swiss Investigate the Profits from Unaccountable Ukrainian Gas', *Financial Times*, 9 Dec. 1998.

CNN, 'Who Are the 'Ndrangheta?', in Alexander Cockburn, Jeffrey St Clair, and Allan Sekula, *Five Days that Shook the World: The Battle for Seattle and Beyond*. London: Verso Books, 2001.

Coe, Michael D. *The Maya*. New York: Thames & Hudson, 1993.

———. *Mexico: From the Olmecs to the Aztecs*, 4th edn. London: Thames & Hudson, 1994.

Cohen, Daniel. *Globalization and Its Enemies*. Cambridge, Mass.: MIT Press, 2006.

Collier, Paul. *The Bottom Billion: Why the Poorest Countries Are Failing and What Can Be Done about It*. Oxford: Oxford University Press, 2007.

Combs, Cindy C. *Terrorism in the Twenty-First Century*, 3rd edn. Englewood Cliffs, NJ: Prentice-Hall, 2003.

Commission on Global Governance. *Our Global Neighbourhood: The Report of the Commission on Global Governance*. Oxford: Oxford University Press, 1995.

Commission on Human Security. *Human Security Now*, Final Report. New York: UN, May 2003.

Connolly, Kevin. 'How Russia's Mafia Is Taking over Israeli Underworld', BBC News Special Report, 21 Nov. 1998. At: <news.bbc.co.uk/2/hi/special_report/1998/03/98/russian_mafia/69521.stm>. (4 Aug. 2008)

Cook, M.A., ed. *A History of the Ottoman Empire to 1730*. Cambridge: Cambridge University Press, 1976.

Cooper, Andrew F. *Tests of Global Governance: Canadian Diplomacy and United Nations World Conferences*. Tokyo: United Nations University Press, 2004.

———. 'Stretching the Model of Coalitions of the Willing', Oct. 2005. At: <ssrn.com/abstract=857444>. (15 Mar. 2009)

———. *Celebrity Diplomacy*. Boulder, Colo.: Paradigm, 2007.

Cortright, David, and George A. Lopez. *The Sanctions Decade: Assessing UN Strategies in the 1990s*. Boulder, Colo.: Lynne Rienner, 2000.

Cousteau, Jacques Yves, with James Dugan. *The Living Sea*. New York: Harper & Row, 1963.

Cox, Robert. 'Postscript 1985', in Cox, 'Social Forces, States, and World Orders: Beyond International Relations Theory', in Robert O. Keohane, ed., *Neorealism and Its Critics*. New York: Columbia University Press, 1986.

———. 'Globalization, Multilateralism and Social Change', Work in Progress published by United Nations University, vol. 13, no. 1 (July 1990).

———. 'Influences and Commitments', in Cox with Sinclair (1996).

———. 'On Thinking about Future World Order', in Cox with Sinclair (1996).

———. 'Social Forces, States, and World Orders: Beyond International Relations Theory', in Cox with Sinclair (1996).

———. 'Towards a Posthegemonic Conceptualization of World Order: Reflections on the Relevancy of Ibn Khaldun', in Cox with Sinclair (1996).

———. 'Civil Society at the Turn of the Millennium: Prospects for an Alternate World Order', *Review of International Studies* 25, 1 (1999).

———. 'Gramsci, Hegemony and International Relations: An Essay in Method', in Amoore (2005).

——— with Michael G. Schechter. *The Political Economy of a Plural World: Critical Reflections on Power, Morals and Civilization*. London: Routledge, 2002.

——— with Timothy Sinclair. *Approaches to World Order*. Cambridge: Cambridge University Press, 1996.

Cozette, Murielle. 'Reclaiming the Critical Dimension of Realism: Hans J. Morgenthau on the Ethics of Scholarship', *Review of International Studies* 34 (2008).

Cutler, Claire. 'Private International Regimes and Interfirm Cooperation', in Rodney Bruce Hall, ed., *Emergence of Private Authority in Global Governance*. West Nyack, NY: Cambridge University Press, 2002.

Dahrendorf, Ralf. *Class and Class Conflict in Industrial Society*. Stanford, Calif.: Stanford University Press, 1959.

———. 'The Europeanization of Europe', in Andrew J. Pierre, ed., *A Widening Atlantic? Domestic Change and Foreign Policy*. New York: Council on Foreign Relations, 1986.

Dante Alighieri. *De Monarchia*, 2nd edn, trans. Herbert W. Schneider. New York: Liberal Arts Press, 1957.

———. 'De Monarchia', in *The Portable Dante*, ed. Paolo Milano. New York: Penguin, 1977.

de Coning, Cedric H. *Coherence and Coordination in United Nations Peacebuilding and Integrated Missions*. Oslo: Norwegian Institute of International Affairs, 2007.

Deegan, Heather. *Contemporary Islamic Influences in Sub-Saharan Africa: An Alternative Development Agenda*. At: <www.islamfortoday.com/subsahara.htm>. (25 Dec. 2005)

Della Sala, Vincent. 'Constitutionalising Governance: Democratic Dead-end or Dead-on Democracy?' *Constitutionalism Web-Papers*, ConWEB No.6–2001. At: <www.qub.ac.uk/ies/onlinepapers/const.html>. (15 Nov. 2009)

Department of Defence, United States Army. *A Military Guide to Terrorism in the Twenty-First Century* (15 Aug. 2005).

Department of Foreign Affairs and International Trade. Lysøen Declaration, Backgrounder to 'Canada and Norway form new partnership on human security', press release No. 117, 11 May 1998.

Derrida, Jacques. *Of Grammatology*. Baltimore: Johns Hopkins University Press, 1976.

Deutsch, Karl. *Political Community and the North Atlantic Area: International Organization in the Light of Historical Experience*. New York: Greenwood Press, 1957.

DeWiel, Boris. *Democracy: A History of Ideas*. Vancouver: University of British Columbia Press, 2000.

Dickason, Olive Patricia, with David T. McNab. *Canada's First Nations: A History of Founding Peoples from Earliest Times*, 4th edn. Toronto: Oxford University Press, 2009.

Dillon, Dana Robert. 'Piracy in Asia: A Growing Barrier to Maritime Trade', Heritage Foundation, 2006. At: <www.heritage.org/Research/AsiaandthePacific/BG1379.cfm?renderforprint=1>. (28 Oct. 2006)

Di Norcia, Vincent. *Hard Like Water: Ethics in Business*. Toronto: Oxford University Press, 1998.

Dollar, David, and Aart Kraay. 'Spreading the Wealth', *Foreign Affairs* (Jan.–Feb. 2002).

Dougherty, James E., and Robert L. Pfaltzgraff. *Contending Theories of International Relations: A Comprehensive Survey*, 3rd & 5th edns. New York: Longman, 1997, 2000.

Doyle, Michael W. *Empires*. Ithaca, NY: Cornell University Press, 1986.

———. 'Liberalism and World Politics Revisited', in Charles W. Kegley Jr, *Controversies in International Relations Theory: Realism and the Neoliberal Challenge*. New York: St Martin's Press, 1995.

Drainville, André. 'Québec City 2001 and the Making of Transnational Subjects', *Social Register 2002*, in Amoore (2005).

Duffield, Mark. *Global Governance and the New Wars*. London: Zed Books, 2001.

Dunning, J.H. 'Changes in the Level and Structure of International Production: The Last One Hundred Years', in M. Casson, ed., *The Growth of International Business*. London: Allen & Unwin, 1983.

Dupuy, Trevor Nevitt. *The Evolution of Weapons and Warfare*. Cambridge, Mass.: Da Capo Press, 1990.

Economist, The. 'Workers of the World', 1 Nov. 1997.

———. 'Delivering the Goods', 15 Nov. 1997.

———. 1–7 June 2002.

———. 'The Integration of the World Economy Is in Retreat on Almost Every Front', 19 Feb. 2009.

Efimov, Alexander S., and Nasser Kaddour. *Staff Costs and Some Aspects of Utilization of Human and Financial Resources in the United Nations Secretariat*, JIU/REP/84/12. Geneva: Joint Inspection Unit, 1984.

Ekins, Paul. *A New World Order: Grassroots Movements for Global Change*. London: Routledge, 1992.

Enloe, Cynthia. *Bananas, Beaches and Bases: Making Feminist Sense of International Politics*. London: Pandora Books, 1989.

———. *The Morning After: Sexual Politics at the End of the Cold War*. Berkeley: University of California Press, 1993.

———. *Maneuvers: The International Politics of Militarizing Women's Lives*. Berkeley: University of California Press, 2000.

Eubank, William Lee, and Leonard Weinberg. 'Does Democracy Encourage Terrorism?', *Terrorism and Political Violence* 6, 4 (Winter 1994).

Fabun, Don. *Communications: The Transfer of Meaning*. New York: Macmillan, 1968.

Falk, Richard. 'State of Siege: Will Globalisation Win Out', *International Affairs* 73, 1 (Jan. 1997).

———. 'Global Civil Society: Perspectives, Initiatives, Movements', *Oxford Development Studies* 26, 1 (1998).

Farmer, Paul. *Pathologies of Power: Health, Human Rights, and the New War on the Poor*. Los Angeles: University of California Press, 2005.

Farooq, Mohammad Omar. 'Change and Continuity: The Dynamics of Institutional Behavior in Islam', paper presented to the twentieth annual conference of the Association of Muslim Social Scientists, Detroit, 25–7 Oct. 1991.

Federal Financial Institutions Examination Council (FFIEC). *Country Exposure Report* (Dec. 1982).

Fekete, Liz. 'Anti-Muslim Racism and the European Security State', *Race & Class* 46, 1 (2004).

Feng, Liu, and Zhang Ruizhuang. 'The Typologies of Realism', *Chinese Journal of International Politics* 1, 1 (2006).

Fenlon, Brodie. 'Groups Warn of Counterfeit Dangers', *Globe and Mail*, 25 Oct. 2007. At: <www.theglobeandmail.com/servlet/story/RTGAM.20071025.wcounterfeit1025/BNStory/National/home>. (1 Aug. 2008)

Ferguson, Niall. *Empire*. London: Basic Books, 2002.

Flanders, Stephanie. 'Will the G20 Expand the Role of IMF', BBC News, 3 Mar. 2009. At: <news.bbc.co.uk/2/hi/business/7922089.stm>. (15 Mar. 2009)

Ford, Franklin L. *Political Murder: From Tyrannicide to Terrorism*. Cambridge: Cambridge University Press, 1985.

Forman, Shepard. 'An Interregnum for Globalism', talk given at a colloquium on Managing Global Issues, Carnegie Endowment for International Peace, 2000, Center on International Cooperation, New York University. At: <www.cic.nyu.edu>. (14 Mar. 2009)

———. 'A Manageable World: Taking Hold of the International Public Sector', Center for International Cooperation, New York University, 6 Aug. 2001. At: <www.cic.nyu.edu/peacebuilding/oldpdfs/A_Manageable_World.pdf>. (14 Mar. 2009)

——— and Derek Segaar. 'New Coalitions for Global Governance: The Changing Dynamics of Multilateralism', *Global Governance* 12, 2 (Apr. 2006).

Foucault, Michel. *Politics, Philosophy, Culture: Interviews and Other Writings, 1977–1984*. New York: Routledge, 1988.

———. 'Le sujet et le pouvoir', in Foucault, *Dits et écrit—1954–1988*. Paris: Gallimard, 1994.

———. *Power*. New York: New Press, 1994.

Frank, André Gunder. *Capitalism and Underdevelopment in Latin America*. New York: Monthly Review Press, 1967.

Frieden, Terry. 'FBI: Albanian Mobsters "New Mafia"', 19 Aug. 2004. At: <edition.cnn.com/2004/LAW/08/18/albanians.mob/>. (5 Aug. 2008)

Friedman, Robert I. *Red Mafiya: How the Russian Mob Has Invaded America*. Boston: Little, Brown, 2000.

Friedman, Thomas L. *Lexus and the Olive Tree: Understanding Globalization*. New York: Anchor Books, 2000.

———. *The World Is Flat: A Brief History of the Twenty-First Century*. New York: Picador, 2007.

Frontline. Centre for Strategic and International Studies (CSIS) Task Force Report, 'Russian Organized Crime', 1997. At: <www.pbs.org/wgbh/pages/frontline/shows/hockey/mafia/csis.html>. (14 Mar. 2009)

Fuchs, Doris. *Business Power in Global Governance*. Boulder, Colo.: Lynne Rienner, 2007.

Fukuyama, Francis. 'The End of History?', *The National Interest* (Summer 1989).

———. *The End of History and the Last Man*. Glencoe, Ill.: Free Press, 2006.

Fuller, Thomas. 'Khun Sa, Golden Triangle Drug King, Dies at 73', *New York Times*, 31 Oct. 2007.

Fussell, Paul. *The Great War and Modern Memory*. Oxford: Oxford University Press, 1975.

Galtung, Johan. 'Violence, Peace and Peace Research', *Journal of Peace Research* 6, 3 (1969).

Gambetta, Diego. *The Sicilian Mafia*. Cambridge, Mass.: Harvard University Press, 1993.

Garthoff, R.L. *The Great Transition: American–Soviet Relations and the End of the Cold War*. Washington: Brookings Institution, 1994.

Gates, Rhoderick. 'Seattle Explosion: 2 Years Too Late', *Our Time*, 30 Nov. 1999.

Germain, Randall. *Globalization and Its Critics: Perspectives from Political Economy*. London: Macmillan, 2000.

Gerth, Hans, and C. Wright Mills, eds. *From Max Weber: Essays in Sociology*. New York: Oxford University Press, 1958.

Ghani, Ashraf, and Claire Lockhart. *Fixing Failed States: A Framework for Rebuilding a Fractured World*. Oxford: Oxford University Press, 2008.

Giddens, Anthony. *The Consequences of Modernity*. Cambridge: Cambridge University Press, 1990.

———. *Runaway World: How Globalisation Is Reshaping Our Lives*. London: Profile Books, 2002.

Gill, Stephen, ed. *Gramsci, Historical Materialism and International Relations*. Cambridge: Cambridge University Press, 1993.

———. 'Globalisation, Market Civilisation, and Disciplinary Neoliberalism', *Millennium: Journal of International Studies* 24, 3 (1995).

Gilpin, Robert. *War and Change in World Politics*. New York: Cambridge University Press, 1981.

Global Policy Forum. 'UN Finance'. At: <www.globalpolicy.org/finance/index.htm>. (11 Mar. 2009)

Global Remittances Guide. At: <www.migrationinformation.org/datahub/remittances.cfm>. (15 Mar. 2009)

Golden, Tim. 'Mexican Army Is Said to Abuse Rebel Suspects', *New York Times*, 24 Jan. 1994. At: <query.nytimes.com/gst/fullpage.html?res=9A00E2D81030F937A15752C0A962958260&sec=&spon=&pagewanted=2>. (26 July 2008)

———. 'Mexican Drug Dealers Turning US Towns into Major Depots', *New York Times*, 16 Nov. 2002, A1.

Goldstein, Joshua S., and Sandra Whitworth. *International Relations*, Canadian edn. Toronto: Pearson/Longman, 2005.

Goldthorpe, John Ernest. *The Sociology of the Third World: Disparity and Involvement*. Cambridge: Cambridge University Press, 1975.

Gore, Al. Nobel lecture. At: <nobelprize.org/nobel_prizes/peace/laureates/2007/gore-lecture_en.html>. (18 Mar. 2009)

Gowan, Peter, Leo Panitch, and Martin Shaw. 'The State, Globalization and the New Imperialism: A Roundtable Discussion', *Historical Materialism: Research in Critical Marxist Theory* No. 9 (Autumn 2001). At: <www.Theglobalsite.ac.uk/press/201gowan.htm>. (1 Dec. 2008)

Gramsci, Antonio. *Selections from the Prison Notebooks*. London: Laurence & Wishart, 1971.

———. *Selections from the Prison Notebooks*, ed. and trans. Quintin Hoare and Geoffrey Nowell Smith. New York: International Publishers, 1971.

Greider, William. *One World, Ready or Not: The Manic Logic of Global Capitalism*. New York: Simon & Schuster, 1997.

Grotius, Hugo. 'Preliminary Remarks', *The Rights of War and Peace*, An Abridged Translation by William Whewell. Cambridge University, Trinity Lodge, 1853.

Guehenno, J.-M. *The End of Nation-State*. Minneapolis: University of Minnesota Press, 1995.

Gupta, Joyeeta. 'The Climate Change Regime', in Jouni Paavola and Ian Lowe, eds, *Environmental Values in a Globalizing World*. London and New York: Routledge, 2005.

Gurr, Ted Robert. 'Economic Factors', in Louise Richardson, ed., *The Roots of Terrorism*. London: Routledge, 2006.

Haas, Ernst B. *Beyond the Nation State: Functionalism and International Organizations*. Stanford, Calif.: Stanford University Press, 1964.

———. *The Uniting of Europe: Political, Social, and Economic Forces, 1950–1957*. Stanford, Calif.: Stanford University Press, 1968.

Haas, Michael. *International Conflict*. New York: Bobbs-Merrill, 1974.

Haas, Peter M. 'UN Conferences and Constructivist Governance of the Environment', *Global Governance* 8 (2002).

Haas, Richard. 'Defining U.S. Foreign Policy in a Post-Post-Cold War World', 2002 Arthur Ross Lecture, Remarks to Foreign Policy Association, New York, 22 Apr. 2002. At: <www.state.gov/s/p/rem/9632.htm>. (1 Dec. 2008)

Halliday, Fred. *Rethinking International Relations.* Houndmills, UK: Macmillan, 1994.

Hall, Neal. 'Big Circle Boys Born of Red Guards: Drugs, Loan-sharking among Asian Gang's Specialties', *Vancouver Sun*, 10 June 2005.

Hall, Rodney Bruce. 'Private Authority, Non-State Actors and Global Governance', *Harvard International Review* (2005). At: <www.harvardir.org/articles/1390/>. (1 Dec. 2008)

—— and Thomas J. Biersteker, eds. *The Emergence of Private Authority in Global Governance.* Cambridge: Cambridge University Press, 2002.

Halliday, Fred. *Rethinking International Relations.* Vancouver: University of British Columbia Press, 1994.

Hambleton, Robin, Hank V. Savitch, and Murray Stuart, eds. *Globalism and Local Democracy: Challenges and Change in Europe and North America.* New York: Palgrave Macmillan, 2002.

Hardin, Garrett. 'The Tragedy of the Commons', *Science* 162 (1968).

Hastedt, Glenn, and Kay Knickrehm. 'Studying World Politics', in Hastedt and Knickrehm, eds, *Toward the Twenty-First Century: A Reader in World Politics.* Englewood Cliffs, NJ: Prentice-Hall, 1994.

Held, David. 'At the Global Crossroads: The End of the Washington Consensus and the Rise of Global Social Democracy?', *Globalizations 2*, 1 (May 2005).

—— and Mathias Koenig-Archibugi. 'Introduction', *Government and Opposition* 39, 2 (2004).

—— and Anthony McGrew. 'Globalization and the Liberal Democratic State', in Sakamoto (1994).

—— and ——. 'The End of the Old Order? Globalization and the Prospects for World Order', *Review of International Studies* 24, 4 (Dec. 1998).

—— and ——. *Governing Globalization.* Cambridge: Polity Press, 2002.

—— et al. *Global Transformations: Politics, Economics and Culture.* Stanford, Calif.: Stanford University Press, 1999.

Helleiner, Eric. *States and the Reemergence of Global Finance: From Bretton Woods to the 1990s.* Ithaca, NY: Cornell University Press, 1994.

——. 'Great Transformations: A Polanyian Perspective on the Contemporary Global Financial Order', *Studies in Political Economy* no. 48 (1995).

——. 'Introduction—Special Forum: Crisis and the Future of Global Financial Governance', *Global Governance* 15 (2009).

Hellman, Judith. 'Real and Virtual Chiapas: Magical Realism and the Left', in Leo Panitch and C. Keys, eds, *Socialist Register 2000.* London: Merlin Press, 1999.

Hernandez, Ester, and Susan Bibler Coutin. 'Remitting Subjects: Migrants, Money and States', *Economy and Society* 35, 2 (May 2006).

Herz, John. 'Idealist Internationalism and the Security Dilemma', *World Politics* 2, 12 (1950). Reprinted in Andrew Linklater, ed., *International Relations: Critical Concepts in Political Science.* New York: Routledge, 2000.

——. *Political Realism and Political Idealism.* Chicago: University of Chicago Press, 1951.

Hettne, Bjorn, A. Inotai, and O. Sunkel, eds. *Globalism and the New Regionalism.* London: Macmillan, 1999.

—— and Fredrik Soderbaum. 'The UN and Regional Organizations in Global Security: Competing or Complementary Logics?', *Global Governance* 12 (2006).

Higgott, Richard. 'Economic Cooperation in the Asia-Pacific: A Theoretical Comparison with the European Union', *Journal of European Public Policy* 2, 3 (1995).

High-level Panel on Threats, Challenges and Change. *A More Secure World: Our Shared Responsibility.* New York: UN Document A/59/565, 2 Dec. 2004.

Hill, Peter. 'The Changing Face of the Yakuza', *Global Crime* 6 (2004).

Hinsley, F.H. *Power and the Pursuit of Peace.* Cambridge: Cambridge University Press, 1963.

Hirst, Paul, and Grahame Thompson. *Globalisation in Question: The International Economy and Possibilities of Governance.* London: Polity Press, 1996.

Hobsbawm, E.J. *Nations and Nationalism since 1870: Programme, Myth, Reality.* Cambridge: Cambridge University Press, 1990.

——, Antonio Polito, and Allan Cameron. *On the Edge of the New Century.* London: New Press, 2000.

Hobson, J.A., *Imperialism: A Study.* London: Archibald Constable & Co., 1905.

Hoffmann, Stanley. 'An American Social Science: International Relations', *Daedalus* 106, 3 (1977).

——. *World Disorders: Troubled Peace in the Post-Cold War Era.* Lanham, Md: Rowman & Littlefield, 2000.

——. 'On the War', *New York Review of Books*, 1 Nov. 2001. At: <www.nybooks.com/articles/14660>. (14 Mar. 2009)

Holsti, Kalevi J. *The State, War and the State of War.* Cambridge: Cambridge University Press, 1996.

Holsti, Ole R. 'Theories of International Relations and Foreign Policy: Realism and its Challengers', in Charles W. Kegley Jr, ed., *Controversies in International Relations Theory: Realism and the Neoliberal Challenge.* Florence, Ky: Wadsworth, 1994.

Hooghe, Liesbet, and Gary Marks. 'Unraveling the Central State, but How? Types of Multi-Level Governance', *American Political Science Review* 97, 2 (May 2003).

Hopf, Ted. 'The Promise of Constructivism in International Relations Theory', *International Security* 23, 1 (Summer 1998).

Horton, John. *Liberalism, Multiculturalism and Toleration.* New York: St Martin's Press, 1993.

Howard, Michael. 'Reassurance and Deterrence', *Foreign Affairs* 61, 2 (1982).

——. *War and the Liberal Conscience.* New Brunswick, NJ: Rutgers University Press, 1986.

Hudson, Michael, and Jeffrey Sommers. 'The End of the Washington Consensus', *Counterpunch*, 12–14 Dec. 2008. At: <www.counterpunch.org/hudson12122008.html>. (12 May 2009)

Hudson, Rex A. *The Sociology and Psychology of Terrorism: Who Becomes a Terrorist and Why?* Washington: Federal Research Division, Library of Congress, 20540–4840, Sept. 1999.

Hume, Cameron R. 'The Security Council in the Twenty-First Century', in David M. Malone, ed., *The UN Security Council: From the Cold War to the Twenty-First Century*. Boulder, Colo.: Lynne Rienner, 2004.

Huntington, Samuel P. *The Clash of Civilizations and the Remaking of World Order*. New York: Simon & Schuster, 1996.

Hurd, Ian. 'Legitimacy and Authority in International Politics', *International Organization* 53, 2 (1999).

———. 'Legitimacy, Power, and the Symbolic Life of the UN Security Council', *Global Governance* 8, 1 (2002).

Hurrell, Andrew. *On Global Order*. Oxford: Oxford University Press, 2007.

Ignatieff, Michael. *Virtual War, Kosovo and Beyond*. Harmondsworth, UK: Penguin, 2001.

———. 'Whatever Happened to "Responsibility to Protect"?', *National Post*, 10 Dec. 2008.

Ikenberry, John G. 'The Myth of Post-Cold War Chaos', *Foreign Affairs* 75, 3 (1996).

———. 'America's Imperial Ambition', *Foreign Affairs* 81, 5 (2002).

'Increase in Counterfeit Imports Poses Risks to EU'. At: <www.manufacturing.net/News-Increase-In-Counterfeit-Imports-Poses-Risks-To-EU.aspx?menuid=282>. (1 Aug. 2008)

Independent Commission on Disarmament and Security Issues. *Common Security: A Blueprint for Survival* (Palme Report). New York: Simon & Schuster, 1982.

Inglehart, Ronald, and Pippa Norris. 'The True Clash of Civilizations', *Foreign Policy* (Mar.–Apr. 2003).

International Commission on Intervention and State Sovereignty. *The Responsibility to Protect: Report of the International Commission on Intervention and State Sovereignty*. At: <www.dfait-maeci.gc.ca/iciss-ciise/report-en.asp>. (27 Apr. 2004)

Intergovernmental Panel on Climate Change (IPCC). *Climate Change 2007 Synthesis Report*. At: <www.ipcc.ch/pdf/assessment-report/ar4/syr/ar4_syr.pdf>. (18 Mar. 2009)

———. 'Why the IPCC Was Created'. At: <www.ipcc.ch/about/index.htm>. (20 Mar. 2009)

International Labour Organization, Bureau for Workers' Activities. At: <actrav.itcilo.org/actrav-english/telearn/global/ilo/globe/new_page.htm#Definition>. (10 Dec. 2008)

International Maritime Bureau. 'Increase in Hijacking and Piracy off Somalia', 4 Apr. 2007. At: <www.mast-yacht.co. uk/news.asp?sectionid=4&newsid=49>. (8 May 2007)

International Tribunal for the Former Yugoslavia. At: <www. un.org/icty/ind-e.htm>. (29 July 2005)

Jackson, Robert. *The Global Covenant*. Oxford: Oxford University Press, 2000.

———. 'The Evolution of International Society', in John Baylis and Steve Smith, eds, *The Globalization of World Politics: An Introduction to International Relations*, 2nd edn. Oxford: Oxford University Press, 2001.

——— and Georg Sorensen. *Introduction to International Relations: Theories and Approaches*, 2nd edn. Oxford: Oxford University Press, 2003.

Jarvis, D.S.L. *International Relations and the Challenge of Postmodernism: Defending the Discipline*. Columbia: University of South Carolina Press, 2000.

Jasper, William F. 'Welcome Mat for Terrorists', *The New America*, 29 Dec. 2003. At: <www.stoptheftaa.org/artman/publish/article_89.shtml>. (16 Oct. 2005)

Jeong, Ho-Won. 'Politics for Global Environmental Governance', in Jeong, ed., *Global Environmental Policies*. Houndmills, UK: Palgrave, 2001.

Jervis, Robert. *Perception and Misperception in International Politics*. Princeton, NJ: Princeton University Press, 1976.

Johnstone, Robert. 'Global Governance: Creating Rules for Running the World', *Literary Review of Canada* (May 2002).

Jonah, James O.C. 'Secretariat: Independence and Reform', in Weiss and Daws (2007).

Jones, Charles, Cristine de Clercy, and W. Andy Knight. *Introduction to Politics: Concepts, Methods, Issues*. Toronto: Oxford University Press, forthcoming.

Jones, Dorothy. *Code of Peace*. Chicago: University of Chicago Press, 1991.

Jones, Geoffrey. *Multinationals and Global Capitalism*. Oxford: Oxford University Press, 2005.

Juergensmeyer, Mark. 'Religion as a Cause of Terrorism', in Louise Richardson, ed., *The Roots of Terrorism*. New York: Routledge, 2006.

Kahler, Miles. 'Defining Accountability Up: The Global Economic Multilaterals', *Government and Opposition* 39, 2 (2004).

Kaldor, Mary. *Global Civil Society: An Answer to War*. Cambridge: Polity Press, 2003.

———. *New and Old Wars: Organized Violence in a Global Era*, 2nd edn. Cambridge: Polity Press, 2006.

———. *Human Security: Reflections on Globalization and Intervention*. Oxford: Polity Press, 2007.

Kanbur, Ravi. *Poverty and Conflict: The Inequality Link: Coping with Crisis*. New York: International Peace Academy Working Paper Series, June 2007.

Karns, Margaret P., and Karen A. Mingst. *International Organizations: The Politics and Processes of Global Governance*. Boulder, Colo.: Lynne Rienner, 2004.

Katzenstein, Peter J. *A World of Regions: Asia and Europe in the American Imperium*. Ithaca, NY: Cornell University Press, 2005.

Keating, Tom. *Canada and World Order: The Multilateralist Tradition in Canadian Foreign Policy*. Toronto: Oxford University Press, 2002.

——— and W. Andy Knight, eds. *Building Sustainable Peace*. Edmonton and Tokyo: University of Alberta Press and United Nations University Press, 2004.

Keck, Margaret, and Kathryn Sikkink. *Activists beyond Borders*. Ithaca, NY: Cornell University Press, 1998.

Keegan, John. *The Mask of Command*. New York: Viking, 1987.

Keen, David. 'Liberalization and Conflict', *International Political Science Review* 26, 1 (2005).

Kegley, Charles W., Jr. 'The Foundations of International Relations Theory and the Resurrection of the Realist–Liberal Debate', in Kegley (1995).

———. *Controversies in International Relations Theory: Realism and the Neoliberal Challenge*. New York: St Martin's Press, 1995.

Kennan, George. *The Fateful Alliance*. New York: Pantheon, 1984.

Kennedy, David. 'Background Noise? The Underlying Politics of Global Governance', *Harvard International Review* 21, 3 (1999).

Kennedy, Paul. *The Rise and Fall of the Great Powers: Economic Change and Military Conflict from 1500 to 2000*. New York: Random House, 1987.

———. 'The Eagle Has Landed', *Financial Times* (London), 2 Feb. 2002.

Kennedy-Pipe, Carolyn, and Nicholas Rengger. 'Apocalypse Now? Continuities or Disjunctions in World Politics after 9/11', *International Affairs* 82, 3 (May 2006).

Keohane, Robert O. 'The Theory of Hegemonic Stability and Changes in International Economic Regimes, 1967–77', in Ole Holsti, Randolphe Siverson, and Alexander George, eds, *Change in the International System*. Boulder, Colo.: Westview Press, 1981.

———. *After Hegemony: Cooperation and Discord in the World Political Economy*. Princeton, NJ: Princeton University Press, 1984.

———. 'Governance in a Partially Globalized World: Presidential Address', American Political Science Association 2000, *American Political Science Review* 95, 1 (2001).

——— and Lisa L. Martin. 'The Promise of Institutionalist Theory', *International Security* 20, 1 (1995).

——— and Joseph S. Nye Jr. *Power and Interdependence: World Politics in Transition*. Boston: Little, Brown, 1977.

——— and ———. 'Introduction', in Nye and John D. Donahue, eds, *Governance in a Globalizing World*. Washington: Brookings Institution, 2000.

Khanna, Parag. *The Second World*. New York: Random House, 2008.

Kindleberger, Charles. *American Business Abroad*. New Haven: Yale University Press, 1969.

Kinsella, H. 'For a Careful Reading: The Conservatism of Gender Constructivism', *International Studies Review* 5 (2003).

Kirpatrick, Donald. *How to Manage Change Effectively*. London: Jossey-Bass, 1985.

Kissinger, Henry. *The White House Years*. Boston: Little, Brown, 1979.

Kjellen, Bo. 'Diplomacy and Governance for Sustainability in a Partially Globalised World', in Jouni Paavola and Ian Lowe, eds, *Environmental Values in a Globalizing World*. London and New York: Routledge, 2005.

Knight, W. Andy. 'Multilatéralisme ascendant ou descendant: deux voies dans la quête d'une gouverne globale', *Etudes Internationale* numéro spécial, 26, 4 (Déc. 1995).

———. 'Towards a Subsidiarity Model for Peacemaking and Preventive Diplomacy: Making Chapter VIII of the UN Charter Operational', *Third World Quarterly* 17, 1 (Mar. 1996).

———. *The United Nations and Arms Embargoes Verification*. New York: The Edwin Mellen Press, 1998.

———. *A Changing United Nations: Multilateral Evolution and the Quest for Global Governance*. Houndmills, UK: Palgrave/Macmillan and St Martin's Press, 2000.

———. 'Pluralizing Global Governance: Bottom-up Multilateralism and the Construction of Space for Civil Society', in Claire Turenne Sjolander and Jean-François Thibault, eds, *Of Global Governance: Culture, Economics and Politics*. Ottawa: University of Ottawa Press, 2002.

———. 'Crisis of Relevance Threatens the UN', *Edmonton Journal*, 3 Mar. 2003.

———. 'Evaluating Recent Trends in Peacebuilding Research', *International Relations of the Asia-Pacific* 3 (2003).

———. 'Repensando las sanciones economicas', in Maria Cristina Rosas, ed., *La economia politica de la seguridad internacional: Sanctiones, zanahorias y garrotes*. Mexico City: National Autonomous University of Mexico, 2003.

———. 'Improving the Effectiveness of UN Arms Embargoes', in Richard Price and Mark Zacher, eds, *The United Nations and Global Security*. New York: Palgrave/Macmillan, 2004.

———. 'The US, the UN and the Global Rule of Law', *Journal of Constitutional Studies* 10, 1 and 2 (2005).

———. *Adapting the United Nations to a Post Modern World: Lessons Learned*. 2nd edn. Houndmills, UK: Palgrave/Macmillan and St Martin's Press, 2005.

———. 'Research Project on Radicalization and Extremism', unpublished report for the Department of Public Safety, Government of Canada, Mar. 2007.

———. 'Democracy and Good Governance', in Weiss and Daws (2007).

———. 'Disarmament, Demobilization, and Reintegration and Post-Conflict Peacebuilding in Africa: An Overview', *African Security* 1 (2008).

———. 'Bashir's Day of Reckoning for the Slaughter in Darfur', *Edmonton Journal*, 7 Mar. 2009.

———. 'The Development of the Responsibility to Protect: From Evolving Norm to Practice', *Global R2P Journal* (forthcoming 2010).

——— and Randolph B. Persaud. 'Subsidiarity, Regional Governance and Caribbean Security', *Latin American Politics and Society* 43, 1 (Spring 2001).

Kobrin, Stephen J. 'Economic Governance in an Electronically Networked Global Economy', in Hall and Biersteker (2002).

———. 'MNCs, the Protest Movement, and the Future of Global Governance', in Alfred D. Chandler Jr and Bruce Mazlish, eds, *Leviathans: Multinational Corporations and the New Global History*. New York: Cambridge University Press, 2005.

Kohut, Andrew, and Bruce Stokes. *America against the World*. New York: Times Books, 2006.

Komisar, Lucy. 'Citigroup: A Culture and History of Tax Evasion', Tax Justice Network, The Public Eye on Davos. At: <www.taxjustice.net/cms/upload/pdf/Citigroup_-_a_culture_and_history_of_tax_evasion.pdf>. (14 Mar. 2009)

Kozlowski, Amanda, ed. *Global Powers in the 21st Century: Strategies and Relations*. Cambridge, Mass.: MIT Press, 2008.

Kramer, Samuel Noah. *The Sumerians: Their History, Culture and Character*. Chicago: University of Chicago Press, 1971.

———. *History Begins at Sumer: Thirty-Nine Firsts in Recorded History*. Philadelphia: University of Pennsylvania Press, 1981.

Krasner, Stephen. *Sovereignty: Organised Hypocrisy*. Princeton, NJ: Princeton University Press, 1999.

Krasno, Jean E., ed. *The United Nations: Confronting the Challenges of a Global Society*. Boulder, Colo.: Lynne Rienner, 2004.

Krause, Keith. 'Multilateral Diplomacy, Norm Building and UN Conferences: The Case of Small Arms and Light Weapons', *Global Governance* 8 (2002).

———— and W. Andy Knight, eds. *State, Society, and the UN System: Changing Perspectives on Multilateralism*. Tokyo: United Nations University Press, 1995.

———— and Michael Williams. *Critical Security Studies*. London: Routledge, 2003.

Krauthammer, Charles. 'The New Unilateralism', *Washington Post*, 8 June 2001.

————. 'Unilateralism Is the Key to Our Success', *Manchester Guardian Weekly*, 20–6 Dec. 2001.

Krueger, Alan, and Jitka Maleckova. 'Does Poverty Cause Terrorism?', *New Republic*, 24 June 2004.

Ku, Charlotte. 'Global Governance and the Changing Face of International Law', *ACUNS Reports & Papers*, No. 2. New Haven: Academic Council of the United Nations System, 2001.

Küng, Hans. 'Global Politics and Global Ethics: Status Quo and Perspectives', *Seton Hall Journal of Diplomacy and International Relations* (Winter–Spring 2002).

Lal, Vinay. 'The Mother in the "Father of the Nation"', *Manushi: A Journal of Women and Society* no. 91 (Nov.–Dec. 1995).

Lamy, Steven L. 'Contemporary Mainstream Approaches: Neo-Realism and Neo-liberalism', in Baylis and Smith (2005).

Lasswell, Harold D. *Politics: Who Gets What, When, How*. New York: McGraw-Hill, 1936.

Laxer, James. *The Border*. Toronto: Doubleday Canada, 2004.

Lenin, Vladimir Ilyich. *Imperialism, The Highest Stage of Capitalism: A Popular Outline*, 13th edn. Moscow: Progress Publishers, 1966 [1917].

Levitt, Kari. *Silent Surrender*. Montreal and Kingston: McGill-Queen's University Press, 1970.

Liddock, Donald R., Jr. *The Global Underworld: Transnational Crime and the United States*. London: Praeger, 2004.

Ling, Chee Yoke, and Martin Khor. 'International Environmental Governance: Some Issues from a Developing Country Perspective', Working Paper by Third World Network, Sept. 2001. At: <www.twnside.org.sg/title/ieg.htm>. (18 Mar. 2009)

Linklater, Andrew, ed. *International Relations: Critical Concepts in Political Science*. London and New York: Routledge, 2000.

Litan, Robert E., and Martin N. Baily. *Fixing Finance: A Road Map for Reform*. Washington: Brookings Institution, 2009. At: <www.brookings.edu/papers/2009/~/media/Files/rc/papers/2009/0217_finance_baily_litan/0217_finance_baily_litan.pdf>. (15 Mar. 2009)

Little, Richard. 'The Evolution of International Relations as a Social Science', in Randolph Kent and Gunnar Neilsson, eds, *The Study and Teaching of International Relations*. London: Francis Pinter, 1980.

————. 'The English School's Contribution to the Study of International Relations', *European Journal of International Relations* 6, 3 (2000).

Los, Maria, and Andrzej Zybertowicz. *Privatizing the Police-State: The Case of Poland*. New York: St Martin's Press, 2000.

Luard, Evan. *The Globalization of Politics: The Changed Focus of Political Action in the Modern World*. London: Macmillan, 1990.

Luck, Edward C. 'Reforming the United Nations: Lessons from a History in Progress,' in Krasno (2004).

————. 'The U.S., Counterterrorism, and the Prospects for a Multilateral Alternative', in Jane Boulden and Thomas G. Weiss, eds, *Terrorism and the UN: Before and After September 11*. Bloomington: Indiana University Press, 2004.

Lunde, Paul E. *Organized Crime: An Inside Guide to the World's Most Successful Industry*. London: Dorling Kindersley, 2004.

Lyman, Michael D., and Gary W. Potter. *Organized Crime*, 3rd edn. Englewood Cliffs, NJ: Prentice-Hall, 2003.

Lyons, Gene M., and Michael Mastanduno, eds. *Beyond Westphalia: State Sovereignty and International Intervention*. Baltimore: Johns Hopkins University Press, 1995.

Lyotard, Jean-Francois. *The Post-modern Condition: A Report on Knowledge*. Manchester: Manchester University Press, 1984.

Macan-Markar, Marwaan. 'India as Venue Provides a Tough Reality Check', *TerraViva*, 22 Jan. 2004.

MacAskill, Ewen. 'Terrorist Could Mount Nuclear or Biological Attack within 5 Years, Warns Congress Inquiry', *The Guardian*, 4 Dec. 2008.

Machiavelli, Niccolò. *The Prince and the Discourses*, ed. Max Lerner. New York: Modern Library, 1950.

————. *The Art of War*, ed. N. Wood. New York: Da Capo Press, 1965.

————. *The Prince*, ed. Q. Skinner. Cambridge: Cambridge University Press, 1988.

Mack, Andrew, and Asif Khan. 'UN Sanctions: A Glass Half Full?', in Richard M. Price and Mark Zacher, eds, *The United Nations and Global Security*. Houndmills, UK: Palgrave/Macmillan, 2004.

Maclean, Sandra Jean, David R. Black, and Timothy M. Shaw, eds. *A Decade of Human Security: Global Governance and New Multilateralisms (Global Security in a Changing World)*. Surrey, UK: Ashgate, 2006.

Madsen, Frank G. 'Organized Crime', in Weiss and Daws (2007).

Malone, David M. *The International Struggle over Iraq: Politics in the UN Security Council, 1980–2005*. Oxford: Oxford University Press, 2007.

————. 'Security Council', in Weiss and Daws (2007).

Mandela, Nelson. *Long Walk to Freedom*. Boston: Little, Brown, 1994.

Mandelbaum, Michael. *The Ideas That Conquered the World*. New York: Public Affairs, 2002.

Mann, Michael. *The Sources of Social Power*. New York: Cambridge University Press, 1986.

————. 'Nation-States in Europe and Other Continents Diversifying, Developing, Not Dying', *Daedalus* 122 (Summer 1993).

Mannheim, Karl. *Ideology and Utopia*. New York: Harcourt Brace, 1952.

Mansfield, Edward D., and Jack Snyder. 'Democratic Transitions and War', in Chester Crocker et al., eds, *Turbulent Peace: The Challenges of Managing International Conflict*. Washington: United States Institute of Peace, 2001.

Marples, David R. 'A Correlation between Radiation and Health Problems in Belarus?', *Post-Soviet Geography* 35, 5 (May 1993).

Martin, Jan, Wolfgang H. Reinicke, and Thorsten Benner. 'Beyond Multilateralism: Global Policy Networks', *International Politics and Society* 2 (2000).

Martinussen, John. *Society, State and Market.* Halifax: Fernwood, 1997.

Marx, Karl. *Capital,* student edn, ed. C.J. Arthur. London: Lawrence & Wishart, 1967.

Masciulli, Joseph, and W. Andy Knight. 'Conceptions of Global Leadership for Contextually-Intelligent, Innovatively Adaptive Leaders', in Masciulli, Mikhail A. Molchanov, and Knight, eds, *The Ashgate Research Companion to Political Leadership.* Surrey, UK: Ashgate, 2009.

Matthews, Jessica. 'Power Shift', *Foreign Affairs* 76, 1 (Jan.–Feb. 1997).

Mearsheimer, John. 'Back to the Future: Instability in Europe after the Cold War', *International Security* 15, 1 (1990).

———. *The Tragedy of Great Power Politics.* New York: Norton, 2001.

Meinecke, Friedrich. *Machiavellism: The Doctrine of Raison d'État and Its Place in Modern History,* trans. Douglas Scott. New Haven: Yale University Press, 1957.

Meisner, Maurice. *Marxism, Maoism and Utopianism.* Madison: University of Wisconsin Press, 1982.

Merari, A. 'The Readiness to Kill and Die: Suicidal Terrorism in the Middle East', in W. Reich, ed., *Origins of Terrorism.* Washington: Woodrow Wilson Center Press, 1998.

Miller, Marian. *Third World in Global Environmental Politics.* Boulder, Colo.: Lynne Rienner, 1995.

Mingst, Karen. *Essentials of International Relations.* New York: Norton, 1999.

——— and Jack Snyder, eds. *Essential Readings in World Politics.* New York: Norton, 2001.

Mitchell, Ronald B. 'International Environmental Agreements: A Survey of Their Features, Formation and Effects', *Annual Review of Energy and Environment 2003* 28 (2003).

Mitrany, David. *A Working Peace System: An Argument for the Functional Development of International Organisation.* London: Royal Institute for International Affairs, 1943.

Mittleman, James H. 'How Does Globalization Really Work?', in Mittleman, ed., *Globalization: Critical Reflections.* Boulder, Colo.: Lynne Rienner, 1996.

——— and Christine B.N. Chin. 'Conceptualizing Resistance to Globalization', in Amoore (2005).

Moghadam, Assaf. *The Roots of Terrorism.* New York: Chelsea House, 2006.

Molina, Mario J., and F.S. Rowland. 'Stratospheric Sink for Chlorofluoromethanes: Chlorine Atom-catalysed Destruction of Ozone', *Nature* 249 (1974).

Moore, Matt. 'Global Military Spending Soars: Peace Group', *CNews World.* At: <cnews.canoe.ca/CNEWS/World/2004/06/09/492268-ap.html>. (19 Mar. 2009)

Morgenthau, Hans J. 'The Evil of Politics and the Ethics of Evil', *Ethics* 56, 1 (1945).

———. 'The Purpose of Political Science', in James C. Charlesworth, ed., *A Design for Political Science: Scope, Objectives and Methods.* Philadelphia: American Academy of Political and Social Science, 1966.

———. 'A Realist Theory of International Politics', in Glenn Hastedt and Kay Knickrehm, eds, *Toward the Twenty-First Century: A Reader in World Politics.* Englewood Cliffs, NJ: Prentice-Hall, 1994.

Morris, Ian. 'The Early Polis as City and State', in John Rich and Andrew Wallace-Hadrill, eds, *City and Country in the Ancient World.* London: Routledge, 1991.

Müller, Joachim. *Reform of the United Nations,* vol. 1. New York: Oceana, 1992.

Mumford, Lewis. *The Story of Utopias.* New York: Viking Press, 1962.

Munck, Ronaldo. *Globalization and Contestation: The New Great Counter-Movement.* London: Routledge, 2007.

Munson, C. 'Five Years after WTO Protests', *Counterpunch.* At: <www.counter-punch.org/>. (15 July 2008)

Murphy, Craig. *International Organization and Industrial Change.* Cambridge: Polity Press, 1994.

———. 'Inequality, Turmoil and Democracy: Global Political-economic Visions at the End of the Century', *New Political Economy* 4, 2 (July 1999).

———. 'Global Governance: Poorly Done and Poorly Understood', *International Affairs* 76, 4 (2000).

Murphy, G. 'The Seattle WTO Protests: Building a Global Movement', in R. Taylor, ed., *Creating a Better World: Interpreting Global Civil Society.* Bloomfield, Conn.: Kumarian Press, 2004.

Naanen, Ben. 'Oil-producing Minorities and the Restructuring of Nigerian Federalism: The Case of the Ogoni People', *Journal of Commonwealth and Comparative Studies* 32, 1 (1995).

Nair, K.S., and Gabriel Britto. 'Introduction: Culture and Drugs', in UNESCO and UN Office for Drug Control and Crime Prevention, *Globalisation, Drugs and Criminalisation,* Final Research Report on Brazil, China, India, and Mexico—part 3 (UNESCO/MOST Secretariat 2002). At: <www.unesco.org/most/globalisation/drugs_vol3.pdf>. (12 Mar. 2009)

Naisbitt, John. *Global Paradox.* New York: William Marrow, 1994.

Napoleoni, Loretta. *Modern Jihad: Tracing the Dollars behind the Terror Networks.* New York: Seven Stories Press, 2005.

Netherlands, the, Ministry of the Interior and Kingdom Relations. *From Dawa to Jihad: The Various Threats from Radical Islam to the Democratic Legal Order.* The Hague: General Intelligence and Security Service, Dec. 2004.

———. *Violent Jihad in the Netherlands: Current Trends in the Islamist Terrorist Threat.* The Hague: General Intelligence and Security Service, Mar. 2006.

Network for Information, Response and Preparedness Activities on Disaster. At: <www.nirapad.org/>. (18 Mar. 2009)

Newman, Edward. 'Secretary-General', in Weiss and Daws (2007).

Nicasso, Antonio, and Lee Lamothe. *Angels, Mobsters and Narco-terrorists: The Rising Menace of Global Criminal Empires.* Toronto: John Wiley and Sons, 2005.

Nicolson, H. *The Evolution of Diplomatic Method.* London: Constable, 1954.

Noble, Ian, and Robert T. Watson. 'Confronting Climate Change', in Vinay Bhargava, ed., *Global Issues for Global Citizens: An Introduction to Key Development Challenges.* Washington: World Bank, 2006.

Noblet, Kevin. 'Drug Lords Start "War" in Colombia', *Philadelphia Inquirer,* 25 Aug. 1989.

Nozick, Robert. *Anarchy, State, and Utopia.* New York: Basic Books, 1974.

Numelin, Ragnar. *The Beginnings of Diplomacy: A Sociological Study of Intertribal and International Relations.* London: Oxford University Press, 1950.

Nye, Joseph S., Jr. *Understanding International Conflicts*, 3rd edn. New York: Longman, 2000.

Ober, Josiah. 'Classical Greek Times', in Michael Howard, George J. Andreopoulos, and Mark R. Shulman, eds, *The Laws of War: Constraints on Warfare in the Western World*. New Haven: Yale University Press, 1994.

Obi, Cyril I. 'Globalization and Local Resistance: The Case of Shell versus the Ogoni', in Amoore (2005).

Office of the Special Representative of the UN Secretary-General for Children and Armed Conflict. At: <www.un.org/children/conflict/english/index.html>. (8 Mar. 2009)

Olaleye-Oruene, T.O. 'Nigeria: Confiscation of the Proceeds of Corruption', *Journal of Financial Crime* 8, 2 (2000).

Olesen, Thomas. *International Zapatismo: The Construction of Solidarity in the Age of Globalization*. London: Zed Books, 2005.

Oliver, Anne Marie, and Paul Steinberg. *The Road to Martyrs' Square: A Journey into the World of the Suicide Bomber*. Oxford: Oxford University Press, 2005.

Olson, Louise. 'Mainstreaming Gender in Multidimensional Peacekeeping: A Field Perspective', *International Peacekeeping* 7, 3 (Autumn 2000).

Olukoshi, Adebayo, ed. *The Politics of Structural Adjustment in Nigeria*. London: James Currey, 1993.

Packenham, Robert A. *The Dependency Movement: Scholarship and Politics in Dependency Studies*. Cambridge, Mass.: Harvard University Press, 1992.

Palme Commission. *Common Security: A Blueprint for Survival* (Palme Report). Independent Commission on Disarmament and Security Issues. New York: Simon & Schuster, 1982.

Paris, Roland. *At War's End: Building Peace after Civil Conflict*. Cambridge: Cambridge University Press, 2004.

Park, Jacob. 'Global Governance, Institutions, and the Tragedy of the Commons', *Ethics, Place and Environment* 2, 2 (1999).

Parker, George, ed. *The Fight Is for Democracy: Winning the War of Ideas in America and the World*. New York: HarperCollins, 2003.

Payne, Richard J. *Global Issues: Politics, Economics, Culture*. New York: Pearson/Longman, 2007.

Pearson, Lester B. 'Force for UN', *Foreign Affairs* 35, 3 (1957).

Peterson, V. Spike. *A Critical Rewriting of Global Political Economy: Reproductive, Productive, and Virtual Economies*. London and New York: Routledge, 2003.

Pettegree, Andrew. *The Early Reformation in Europe*. Cambridge: Cambridge University Press, 1991.

Pettifor, Ann. 'The Economic Bondage of Debt—and the Birth of a New Movement', in Amoore (2005).

Philpott, Daniel. 'The Religious Roots of Modern International Relations', *World Politics* 52 (Jan. 2000).

Pigman, Geoffrey Allen. *The World Economic Forum*. London: Routledge, 2007.

Pipes, Daniel. '[Theo van Gogh and] "Education by Murder" in Holland', *New York Sun*, 16 Nov. 2004.

Pitt, David. 'Power in the UN Superbureaucracy: A Modern Byzantium?', in David Pitt and Thomas G. Weiss, eds, *The Nature of United Nations Bureaucracies*. New York: Taylor & Francis, 1986.

Platt, Suzy, ed. *Respectfully Quoted*. Washington: Congressional Quarterly Press, 1992.

Pogge, Thomas W. *World Poverty and Human Rights: Cosmopolitan Responsibilities and Reforms*. Cambridge: Polity Press, 2002.

Polanyi, Karl. *The Great Transformation: The Political and Economic Origins of Our Time*. Boston: Beacon Press, 1957.

Pomfret, John. 'Bribery at Border Worried Officials', *Washington Post*, 15 July 2006. At: <www.washingtonpost.com/wp-dyn/content/article/2006/07/14/AR2006071401525.html>. (30 June 2008)

Porter, Tony. 'Why International Institutions Matter in the Global Credit Crisis', *Global Governance* 15, 1 (Jan.–Mar. 2009).

Post, Jerrold M. 'The Psychological Dynamics of Terrorism', in Louise Richardson, *The Roots of Terrorism*. New York: Routledge, 2006.

Potoucek, Martin. *Not Only the Market the Role of the Market: Government and the Civic Sector in the Development of Post Communist Societies*. Budapest: Central European University Press, 1999.

Poulin, Richard. 'Globalization and the Sex Trade: Trafficking and the Commodification of Women and Children', *Sisyphe*, 12 Feb. 2004. At: <sisyphe.org/article.php3?id_article=965>. (2 Aug. 2008)

Prebisch, Raúl. *The Economic Development of Latin America and Its Principal Problems*. New York: UN, 1950.

Project for a New American Century. Statement of Principles, June 1997. At: <www.newamericancentury.org/statementofprinciples.htm>. (14 Mar. 2009)

Ramm, Roy A.C. 'The Yardies: England's Emerging Crime Problem', Jan. 1988. At: <www.matarese.com/matarese-files/2677/yardies-england-emerging-crime-problem-ramm/index.html>. (6 Aug. 2008)

Rapoport, David C. *Terrorism: Critical Concepts in Political Science*. New York: Routledge, 2005.

Ray, James Lee, and Juliet Kaarbo. *Global Politics*. New York: Houghton Mifflin, 2008.

Reagan, Ronald. 'American Bar Association', *Weekly Compilation of Presidential Documents*, 8 July 1985.

———. 'President's News Conference', *Weekly Compilation of Presidential Documents*, 7 Jan. 1986.

Reinada, Bob, and Bertjan Verbeek. *Autonomous Policy-making by International Organizations*. New York: Routledge, 1998.

Rengger, N.J. *International Relations, Political Theory and the Problem of Order: Beyond International Relations Theory*. London: Routledge, 2000.

——— and Ben Thirkell-White, eds. *Critical International Relations Theory after 25 Years*. Cambridge: Cambridge University Press, 2007.

Report of the Panel of Eminent Persons on United Nations–Civil Society Relations. *We the People: Civil Society, the United Nations and Global Governance*. New York: UN Document A/58/817, 11 June 2004.

Reynolds, Charles. *Theory and Explanation in International Relations in Great Britain*. Oxford: Martin Robertson, 1973.

Richardson, Louise. 'The Roots of Terrorism: An Overview', in Louise Richardson, ed., *The Roots of Terrorism*. London: Routledge, 2006.

———. *What Terrorists Want: Understanding the Terrorist Threat*. London: John Murray, 2006.

Richardson, Michael. 'Fighting Marine Terrorism', *Glocom Platform*, 11 June 2004. At: <www.glocom.org/debates/20040611_richardson_fighting/index.html>. (1 Dec. 2008)

Ritchie, Mark. 'Globalization vs. Globalism: Giving Internationalism a Bad Name', Jan. 1996. At: <www.hartford-hwp.com/archives/25a/069.html>. (10 Dec. 2008)

Robinson, Jeffrey. *The Merger: How Organized Crime Is Taking Over Canada and the World*. Toronto: McClelland & Stewart, 1999.

Rochester, J. Martin. *Waiting for the Millennium: The United Nations and the Future of World Order*. Columbia: University of South Carolina Press, 1993.

———. *Between Peril and Promise: The Politics of International Law*. Washington: Congressional Quarterly Press, 2006.

Rodrik, Dani. 'Sense and Nonsense in the Globalization Debate', *Foreign Policy* no. 107 (Summer 1997).

Rosen, William. *Justinian's Flea: Plague, Empire, and the Birth of Europe*. London: Viking, 2007.

Rosenau, James N. *Turbulence in World Politics: A Theory of Change and Continuity*. Princeton, NJ: Princeton University Press, 1990.

———. 'Governance, Order, and Change in World Politics', in Rosenau and Ernst-Otto Czempiel, eds, *Governance without Government: Order and Change in World Politics*. Cambridge: Cambridge University Press, 1992.

———. 'The Dynamism of a Turbulent World', in Michael Klare and Chandrani Yogesh, eds, *World Security: Challenges for a New Century*. New York: St Martin's Press, 1998.

———. *Distant Proximities: Dynamics beyond Globalization*. Princeton, NJ: Princeton University Press, 2003.

——— and Mary Durfee. *Thinking Theory Thoroughly: Coherent Approaches to an Incoherent World*. Boulder, Colo.: Westview Press, 2000.

Rosenau, Pauline Marie. *Post-Modernism and the Social Sciences: Insights, Inroads, and Intrusions*. Princeton, NJ: Princeton University Press, 1992.

Rosenthal, Gert. 'Economic and Social Council', in Weiss and Daws (2007).

Rostow, W.W. *The Stages of Economic Growth: A Non-Communist Manifesto*. London: Cambridge University Press, 1960.

Rothchild, Robert. 'On the Costs of Realism', *Political Science Quarterly* 87, 3 (1972).

Rothschild, Emma. 'What Is Security?', *Daedalus* 124, 3 (Summer 1995).

Rourke, John T. *International Politics on the World Stage*, 6th edn. New York: McGraw-Hill, 2006.

Ruggie, John Gerard. 'Embedded Liberalism and the Postwar Economic Regimes', in Ruggie (1989).

———. 'What Makes the World Hang Together? Neo-utilitarianism and the Social Constructivist Challenge', in Ruggie (1989).

———. *Constructing the World Polity: Essays on International Institutionalization*. New York: Routledge, 1989, 1998.

———. 'Global Markets and Global Governance', in Steven Bernstein and Louis W. Pauly, eds, *Global Liberalism and Political Order: Toward a Grand Compromise*. Albany: State University of New York Press, 2007.

Runciman, David. 'A Bear Armed with a Gun', *London Review of Books*, 3 Apr. 2003.

Rupert, Mark. *Ideologies of Globalization: Contending Visions of a New World Order*. London: Routledge, 2000.

———. 'Passive Revolution or Transformative Process', in Amoore (2005).

Russell, Frank. *Theories of International Relations*. New York: Appleton, 1936.

Russell, James A. 'Peering into the Abyss: Non-State Actors and the 2016 Nuclear Proliferation Environment', *Non-Proliferation Review* 13, 3 (Nov. 2006).

Sagafi-Nejad, Tagi, with John H. Dunning. *The UN and Transnational Corporations: From Code of Conduct to Global Compact*. Bloomington: Indiana University Press, 2008.

Sakamoto, Yoshikazu. 'A Perspective on the Changing World Order: A Conceptual Prelude', in Sakamoto (1994).

———, ed. *Global Transformation: Challenges to the State System*. Tokyo: United Nations University Press, 1994.

Sands, Philippe. *Lawless World*. London: Penguin/Allen Lane, 2005.

Sargent, L. *Women and Revolution: A Discussion of the Unhappy Marriage of Marxism and Feminism*. Boston: South End Press, 1981.

Saro-Wiwa, Ken. *Genocide in Nigeria: The Ogoni Tragedy*. Port Harcourt, Nigeria: Saros, 1992.

———. 'Oil and the Basic Issue at Stake', *The Guardian*, 1 Apr. 1994.

'Saudi Women Barred from Voting', BBC News, 11 Oct. 2004.

Saurin, Julian. 'International Relations, Social Ecology and the Globalization of Environmental Change', in John Volger and Mark F. Imbler, eds, *The Environment and International Relations*. London: Routledge, 1996.

Saxe, John Godfrey. 'The Blind Men and the Elephant'. At: <rack1.ul.cs.cmu.edu/is/saxe/doc.scn?fr=0&rp=http%3A%2F%2Frack1.ul.cs.cmu.edu%2Fis%2Fsaxe%2F&pg=4>.

Schechter, Michael G. 'Possibilities for Preventive Diplomacy, Early Warning and Global Monitoring in the Post-Cold War Era; or, the Limits to Global Structural Change', in Knight (2005).

Scholte, Jan Aart. 'The Globalization of World Politics', in John Baylis and Steve Smith, eds, *The Globalization of World Politics*. Oxford: Oxford University Press, 1999.

——— *Globalisation: A Critical Introduction*. London: Macmillan, 2000.

——— and Marc Williams. *Contesting Global Governance*. Cambridge: Cambridge University Press, 2000.

Schulte, Constanze. *Compliance with Decisions of the International Court of Justice*. Oxford: Oxford University Press, 2004.

Schumpeter, Joseph. *Capitalism, Socialism, and Democracy*. New York: Harper Torchbooks, 1950.

Schwartz, Mark S., and Archie B. Carroll. 'Corporate Social Responsibility: A Three Domain Approach', *Business Ethics Quarterly* 13, 4 (2003).

Scott, James. 'The Infrapolitics of Subordinate Groups', in Amoore (2005).

Sell, Susan K. 'Big Business, the WTO, and Development: Uruguay and Beyond', in Richard Stubbs and Geoffrey R.D. Underhill, eds, *Political Economy and the Changing Global Order*, 3rd edn. Toronto: Oxford University Press, 2006.

Sens, Allen, and Peter Stoett. *Global Politics: Origins, Currents, Directions*, 3rd edn. Toronto: Thomson/Nelson, 2005.

Serio, Joseph. *Investigating the Russian Mafia*. Durham, NC: Carolina Academic Press, 2008.

Serra, Narcis, and Joseph Stiglitz, eds. *The Washington Consensus Reconsidered: Towards a New Global Governance*. Oxford: Oxford University Press, 2008.

Shiva, Vandana, and Jayanta Bandyopadhyay. 'The Evolution, Structure and Impact of the Chipko Movement', *Mountain Research and Development* (UNEP) 6, 2 (May 1986).

——— and ———. 'Chipko: Rekindling India's Forest Culture', *The Ecologist* 17, 1 (Jan.–Feb. 1987).

Singer, P.W. *Wired for War: The Robotics Revolution and Conflict in the 21st Century*. New York: Penguin, 2009.

Stockholm International Peace Research Institute (SIPRI) and the Department of Peace and Conflict Research, Uppsala University. *United Nations Arms Embargoes: Their Impact on Arms Flows and Target Behaviour*. Stockholm and Uppsala, Sweden, 2007.

Slaughter, Anne-Marie. 'The Real New World Order', in Gregory M. Scott, Randall J. Jones Jr, and Louis S. Furmanski, eds, *21 Debated Issues in World Politics*, 2nd edn. Englewood Cliffs, NJ: Pearson/Prentice-Hall, 2004.

———. *A New World Order*. Princeton, NJ: Princeton University Press, 2004.

Smith, Dan, and Janani Vivekananda. 'A Climate of Conflict: The Links between Climate Change, Peace, and War', *International Alert* (Nov. 2007). At: <www.international-alert.org/pdf/A_Climate_Of_Conflict.pdf>. (19 Mar. 2009)

Smith, Gordon, and Moises Naim. *Altered States: Globalization, Sovereignty, and Governance*. Ottawa: International Development Research Centre, 2000.

Smith, J. 'Globalizing Resistance: The Battle of Seattle and the Future of Social Movements', in Smith and H. Johnson, eds, *Globalization and Resistance: Transnational Dimensions of Social Movements*. Lanham, Md: Rowman & Littlefield, 2002.

Smith, Steve. 'Paradigm Dominance in International Relations: The Development of International Relations as a Social Science', *Millennium: Journal of International Studies* 16, 2 (1987).

———. 'Positivism and Beyond', in Smith, Ken Booth, and Marysia Zalewski, eds, *International Theory: Positivism and Beyond*. Cambridge: Cambridge University Press, 1996.

——— and John Baylis. 'Introduction', in Baylis and Smith, eds, *The Globalization of World Politics: An Introduction to International Relations*, 2nd edn. Oxford: Oxford University Press, 2001.

——— and Patricia Owens. 'Alternative Approaches to International Theory', in Baylis and Smith (2005).

Soremekun, Kayode, and Cyril I. Obi. 'Oil and the National Question', *Proceedings of the Nigerian Economic Society 1993 Annual Conference*. Nigerian Economic Society, 1993.

Soros, George. *The Crisis of Global Capitalism: Open Society Endangered*. New York: Public Affairs, 1998.

Soroos, Marvin S. 'The Evolution of the Global Commons', in Ho-Won Jeong, ed., *Global Environmental Policies*. Houndmills, UK: Palgrave, 2001.

Speth, James Gustave. 'A New Green Regime', *Environment* 44, 7 (Sept. 2002).

——— and Peter M. Haas. *Global Environmental Governance*. Washington: Island Press, 2006.

Spiegel, Steven L., Elizabeth G. Matthews, Jennifer M. Tow, and Kirsten P. Williams. *World Politics in a New Era*, 4th edn. New York: Oxford University Press, 2009.

Spivak, Gayatri. 'Can the Subaltern Speak?', in C. Nelson and L. Grossberg, eds, *Marxism and the Interpretation of Culture*. Basingstoke, UK: Macmillan, 1988.

State of Washington, Department of Community, Trade and Economic Development, Office of Crime Victims Advocacy. *Human Trafficking: Present Day Slavery*. Report of the Washington State Task Force Against Trafficking of Persons, June 2004. At: <www.wcsap.org/advocacy/PDF/trafficking%20taskforce.pdf>. (2 Aug. 2008)

Steans, Jill, and Lloyd Pettiford, with Thomas Diez. *Introduction to International Relations: Perspectives and Themes*, 2nd edn. Essex: Pearson Education/Prentice-Hall, 2005.

Stein, Arthur A. 'Neoliberal Institutionalism', in Christian Reus-Smit and Duncan Snidal, eds, *The Oxford Handbook of International Relations*. Oxford: Oxford University Press, 2008.

Stern, Nicholas. *Stern Review Report on the Economics of Climate Change*. London: HM Treasury, 2006. At: <www.hm-treasury.gov.uk/sternreview_index.htm>. (19 Mar. 2009)

Stiglitz, Joe. 'Globalism's Discontents', in Mark Kesselman, *The Politics of Globalization: A Reader*. Boston: Houghton Mifflin, 2006.

Strange, Susan. *The Retreat of the State: The Diffusion of Power in the World Economy*. Cambridge: Cambridge University Press, 1996.

Sun Tzu. *The Art of War*, trans. Samuel B. Griffith. New York: Oxford University Press, 1963.

Tabb, William. *Economic Governance in the Age of Globalization*. New York: Columbia University Press, 2004.

Tanzi, Vito. *Money Laundering and the International Financial System*, IMF Working Paper No. 96, 55. Washington: IMF, 1996.

———. *The International Anti-Corruption Forum: Corruption's Impact on Economic Performance*. Washington: Brookings Institution, 19 Jan. 2000.

Taylor, Trevor. 'Utopianism', in Steve Smith, ed., *International Relations: British and American Perspectives*. Oxford: Blackwell, 1985.

Thakur, Ramesh, and Luk Van Langenhove. 'Enhancing Global Governance through Regional Integration', *Global Governance* 12 (2006).

Thomas, Janet. *The Battle in Seattle: The Story Behind and Beyond the WTO Demonstrations*. Golden, Colo.: Fulcrum, 2000.

Thucydides. *History of the Peloponnesian War*, trans. R. Warner. London: Penguin, 1954.

Tickner, J. Ann. 'Hans Morgenthau's Principles of Political Realism: A Feminist Reformulation', *Millennium* 17, 3 (1988).

Tiuriukanova, Elena. 'Female Labour Migration Trends and Human Trafficking', in Sally Stoecker and Louise Shelley, eds, *Human Traffic and Transnational Crime*. Lanham, Md: Rowman & Littlefield, 2005.

Townshend, Charles. *Terrorism: A Very Short Introduction*. Oxford: Oxford University Press, 2002.

Trachtenberg, M. *A Constructed Peace: The Making of the European Settlement, 1945–1963*. Princeton, NJ: Princeton University Press, 1999.

Transnational Criminal Activity: A Global Context. Perspectives: A Canadian Security Intelligence Service Publication, Report # 2000/07.

UNCTAD. *World Investment Report 2007, Transnational Corporations* 16, 3 (Dec. 2007).

United Nations (UN). 'Secretary-General Reviews Lessons Learned During "Sanctions Decade" in Remarks to International Peace Academy Seminar', press release, SG/SM/7360 (17 Apr. 2000).

———. *A More Secure World: Our Shared Responsibility*. Report of the Secretary-General's High-level Panel on Threats, Challenges and Change, UNGA Document A/59/565. New York: UN, 2004.

———. At: <www.un.org/Depts/oip/>. (30 July 2007)

United Nations Development Programme (UNDP). *Human Development Report, 1994*. New York: UNDP, 1994.

———. At: <www.undp.org/mdg/>. (8 Mar. 2009)

United Nations Environmental Programme. 'Speech by Angela Cropper, UNEP Deputy Executive Director, at the SIDA Climate Game Change Seminar, Bangkok, Thailand', 22 Jan. 2009. At: <www.unep.org/Documents.Multilingual/Default.asp?DocumentID = 560&ArticleID = 6048&l = en>. (18 Mar. 2009)

United Nations Global Compact. At: <www.unglobalcompact.org/AboutTheGC/TheTenPrinciples/index.html>. (1 Dec. 2008)

United Nations International Drug Control Programme. *World Drug Report*. Oxford: Oxford University Press, 1997.

United Nations Research Institute for Social Development. *Visible Hands: Taking Responsibility for Social Development*. Geneva: UNRISD, 2000. At: <www.unrisd.org/unrisd/website/document.nsf/0/FE9C9439D82B525480256B670065EFA1?OpenDocument>. (15 Mar. 2009)

United States Congress, Senate Committee on Governmental Affairs, Permanent Subcommittee on Investigations, 5th Congress. *Private Banking: Raul Salinas, Citibank and Alleged Money Laundering*. Washington: GAO Publication No. GAO OSI-99–1, 1998.

———, 6th Congress. *Suspicious Banking Activities Possible Money Laundering by U.S. Corporations Formed for Russian Entities*. Washington: GAO Publication No. GAO-01–120, 2000.

United States Department of State. *Money Laundering and Financial Crimes*. Washington, 2000. At: <www.state.gov/g/inl/rls/nrcrpt/2000/index.cfm?docid = 959>. (2 Aug. 2008)

———. 'Facts about Human Trafficking', Fact Sheet, Office to Monitor and Combat Trafficking in Persons, Washington, 7 Dec. 2005. At: <www.state.gov/g/tip/rls/fs/2005/60840.htm>. (14 Mar. 2009)

United States, Office of the Press Secretary. 'President Discusses War on Terror at National Endowment for Democracy', Ronald Reagan Building and International Trade Center, Washington, 6 Oct. 2005.

'Uniting for Peace Resolution', *Encyclopædia Britannica Online*. At: <www.britannica.com/EBchecked/topic/617964/Uniting-for-Peace-Resolution>. (12 Dec. 2008)

USA Today. 'Canada Nabs 17 Terror Suspects in Toronto'. At: <www.usatoday.com/news/world/2006–06–03-toronto-terror-suspects_x.htm>. (1 Jan. 2007)

'U.S. Attorney: Counterfeit Flea Market Items Could Pose Danger', *NBC6.Net*, 1 Aug. 2008. At: <www.nbc6.net/news/5715583/detail.html>. (1 Aug. 2008)

'US Prompts WTO Probe into Chinese Counterfeits', *Boston Globe*, 26 Sept. 2007. At: <www.boston.com/business/markets/articles/2007/09/26/us_prompts_wto_probe_into_chinese_counterfeits/>. (12 Mar. 2009)

Uvin, Peter. 'From Local Organizations to Global Governance: The Role of NGOs in International Relations', in Kendall Stiles, ed., *Global Institutions and Local Empowerment: Competing Theoretical Perspectives*. New York: St Martin's Press, 2000.

Valaskakis, Kimon. 'Long-term Trends in Global Governance: From "Westphalia" to "Seattle"', in *Governance in the 21st Century*. Paris: OECD, 2001.

van Agtmael, Antoine. *The Emerging Markets Century*. New York: Free Press, 2007.

Van Damme, Guy. 'Jus in Bello', in Bruno Coppieters and Nick Fotion, eds, *Moral Constraints on War: Principles and Cases*. New York: Lexington Books, 2002.

Varese, Federico. *The Russian Mafia: Private Protection in a New Market Economy*. Oxford: Oxford University Press, 2001.

———. 'How Mafias Migrate: The Case of the 'Ndrangheta in Northern Italy', *Law & Society Review* 40, 2 (2006).

Väyrynen, Raimo. 'Sovereignty, Globalisation and Transnational Social Movements', *International Relations of Asia-Pacific* 1, 2 (2001).

Victoria, Artur. 'Money Laundering', *Ezine @rticles*. At: <ezinearticles.com/?Money-Laundering&id = 1816180>. (14 Mar. 2009)

Vogel, Steven K. *Freer Markets, More Rules, Regulatory Reform in Advanced Industrial Countries*. Ithaca, NY: Cornell University Press, 1996.

Wallerstein, Immanuel. *The Modern World-System, vol. 1, Capitalist Agriculture and the Origins of the European World Economy in the Sixteenth Century*. San Diego: Academic Press, 1976.

———. *The Capitalist World-Economy*. Cambridge: Cambridge University Press, 1979.

Walt, Stephen M. 'International Relations: One World, Many Theories', in Mingst and Snyder (2001).

Walton, J., and M. Seddon. *Free Markets and Food Riots: The Politics of Global Adjustment*. Oxford: Blackwell, 1994.

Waltz, Kenneth N. *Man, the State, and War*. New York: Columbia University Press, 1959.

———. *A Theory of International Politics*. New York: McGraw-Hill, 1979.

———. 'Realist Thought and Neo-Realist Theory', *Journal of International Affairs* 44 (1990).

———. 'The Continuity of International Politics', in Ken Booth and Tim Dunne, eds, *World in Collision: Terror and the Future of Global Order*. New York: Palgrave Macmillan, 2002.

———. 'Globalization and Governance', in Robert J. Art and Robert Jervis, eds, *International Politics: Enduring Concepts and Contemporary Issues*. New York: Pearson, 2007.

———. 'Political Structures', in Karen Mingst and Jack Snyder, eds, *Essential Readings in World Politics*, 3rd edn. New York: Norton, 2008.

Walzer, Michael. *Just and Unjust Wars: A Moral Argument with Historical Illustrations*, 2nd edn. New York: Basic Books, 1992.

Waterman, Peter. 'Beyond Globalism and Developmentalism: Other Voices in World Politics', *Development and Change 27* (1996).

Watson, Adam. *The Evolution of International Society*. New York: Routledge, 1992.

Weber, Max. *The Sociology of Religion*. Boston: Beacon Press, 1963.

———. *The Theory of Social and Economic Organization*. New York: Free Press, 1964.

Weigall, David. *International Relations: A Concise Companion*. London: Arnold, 2002.

Weiss, L. *The Myth of the Powerless State: Governing the Economy in a Global Era*. Cambridge: Polity Press, 1998.

Weiss, Thomas G., and Sam Daws, eds. *The Oxford Handbook on the United Nations*. Oxford: Oxford University Press, 2007.

——— and Leon Gordenker, eds. *NGOs, the UN, and Global Governance*. Boulder, Colo.: Lynne Rienner, 1996.

Welch, Claude. 'The Ogoni and Self-determination: Increasing Violence in Nigeria', *Journal of Modern African Studies 33*, 4 (1995).

Welsh, Jennifer M. 'Authorizing Humanitarian Intervention', in Richard M. Price and Mark Zacher, eds, *The United Nations and Global Security*. Houndmills, UK: Palgrave/Macmillan, 2004.

Wellons, Philip A. *Passing the Buck: Banks, Government and Third World Debt*. Boston: Harvard Business School Press, 1987.

Wendt, Alexander. 'Anarchy Is What States Make of It', *International Organization 46*, 2 (Spring 1992).

Wheeler, Nicholas J. *Saving Strangers: Humanitarian Intervention in International Society*. Oxford: Oxford University Press, 2002.

Whitman, Jim. *The Limits of Global Governance*. London: Routledge, 2005.

———, ed. *Advances in Global Governance*. New York: Palgrave/Macmillan, 2009.

Wight, Martin. *Systems of States*. Leicester: Leicester University Press, 1977.

———. *International Theory: The Three Traditions*. Leicester: Leicester University Press for the Royal Institute of International Affairs, London, 1991.

———. *Power Politics*. London: Leicester University Press, 1995.

Willetts, Peter, ed. *The Conscience of the World: The Influence of Non-Governmental Organizations in the U.N. System*. Washington: Brookings Institution, 1996.

Williams, Glen. *Not for Export*, 3rd edn. Toronto: McClelland & Stewart, 1994.

Williams, Phil. 'Combating Transnational Organized Crime', in Carolyn W. Pumphrey, ed., *Transnational Threats: Blending Law Enforcement and Military Strategies*. Car-lisle, Penn.: US Army War College, 2000.

——— and Gregory Baudin-O'Hayon. 'Global Governance, Transnational Organized Crime and Money Laundering', in Held and McGrew (2002).

Williamson, J. 'What Washington Means by Policy Reform', in Williamson, ed., *Latin American Adjustment: How Much Has Happened?* Washington: Institute for International Economics, 1990.

Wilson, Peter. 'Introduction: The Twenty Years' Crisis and the Category of Idealism in International Relations', in David Long and Wilson, eds, *Thinkers of the Twenty Years' Crisis: Inter-war Idealism Reassessed*. Oxford: Clarendon Press, 1995.

Wilson, Woodrow. Address to the United States Congress, 8 Jan. 1918. At: <www.firstworldwar.com/source/fourteenpoints. htm>. (15 Mar. 2009)

———. *The Papers of Woodrow Wilson*. Princeton, NJ: Princeton University Press, 1984.

Winchester, N. Brian. 'Emerging Global Environmental Governance', *Indiana Journal of Global Legal Studies 16* (Winter 2009).

Winchmore, Charles. 'The Secretariat: Retrospect and Prospect', *International Organization 19*, 3 (1965).

Winer, Jonathan, Deputy Assistant Secretary for International Narcotics and Law Enforcement Affairs. Statement before the Subcommittee on Africa of the House International Relations Committee, Washington, 11 Sept. 1996. At: <www. fas.org/irp/congress/1996_hr/h960911w.htm>. (6 Aug. 2008)

Wittek, Paul. *The Rise of the Ottoman Empire*. London: Royal Asiatic Society Monographs 23, 1938.

Wolf, Eric R. *Europe and the People without History*. Los Angeles: University of California Press, 1982.

Womack, J., Jr. *Zapata and the Mexican Revolution*. New York: Vintage Books, 1968.

Woods, Ngaire. 'Good Governance in International Organizations', *Global Governance 5*, 1 (1999).

———. 'Bretton Woods Institutions', in Weiss and Daws (2007).

World Bank. 'World Bank's Operations in the West Bank and Gaza. At: <web.worldbank.org/WBSITE/EXTERNAL/ COUNTRIES/MENAEXT/WESTBANKGAZAEXTN/0,, menuPK:294370~pagePK:141159~piPK:141110~theSiteP K:294365,00.html>. (8 Mar. 2009)

World Commission on Environment and Development. *Our Common Future*. Oxford: Oxford University Press, 1987.

World Health Organization. 'Global, National Efforts Must Be Urgently Intensified to Control Zimbabwe Cholera Outbreak'. At: <www.who.int/mediacentre/news/ releases/2009/cholera_zim_20090130/en/index.html>. (18 Mar. 2009)

World Resources Institute (WRI), UNDP, and UNEP. *2002–2004: Decisions for the Earth: Balance, Voice and Power* (2003). At: <www.wri.org/publication/world-resources-2002–2004- decisions-earth-balance-voice-and-power>. (18 Mar. 2009)

Wright, Chris. 'Global Tourism Soars, China Set to Surpass Spain'. At: <nomadx.org/content/view/1287/51/>. (16 Mar. 2009)

Yi-chong, Xu, and Patrick Weller. *The Governance of World Trade*. Cheltenham, UK: Edward Elgar, 2004.

Zacher, Mark. 'The Decaying Pillars of the Westphalian Temple', in James Rosenau and Ernst-Otto Czempiel, eds, *Governance without Government*. Cambridge: Cambridge University Press, 1992.

―――― and Richard A. Matthew. 'Liberal International Theory: Common Threads, Divergent Strands', in Kegley (1995).

Zakaria, Fareed. 'The Future of American Power: How America Can Survive the Rise of the Rest', *Foreign Affairs* 87, 3 (2008).

Zalewski, Marysia. 'Feminist Standpoint Theory Meets International Relations Theory: A Feminist Version of David and Goliath', *Fletcher Forum of World Affairs* 17, 2 (1993).

Zurn, Michael. 'Global Governance and Legitimacy Problems', *Government and Opposition* 39, 2 (2004).

Index

Note: Page numbers in italics refer to illustrations and diagrams.

50 Years Is Enough: US Network for Global Economic Justice, 240, 241

9/11, terrorist attacks of, 3–5, *5*, 133, 135, 146, 148, 150, 181, 301–2, 374; al-Qaeda and, 3, 301, 323; democracy and, 318–19; global change/continuity and, 102, 123, 379; globalization and, 3–5, 198–9, 201–2; global politics and, 3–5, 379; Muslim condemnation of, 314; as muting counter-globalization movements, 249–50; as new kind of war, 108–10, 125; state and, 4, 146, 198–9, 201–2, 211; UN resolution on, 166, 172, 323; US unilateralism and, 153–4, 323; victims of, by country, *4*; Wahhabism and, 316; 'War on Terror' and, 135, 140, 153–4, 302; *see also* terrorism

Abacha, Sani, 283
Abu Nidal, organization of, 310
acid rain, 329
Adams, Gerry, 306
Adorno, Theodor, 56
Afghanistan, 130, 140, 165, 168; al-Qaeda in, 316, 322; Soviet occupation of, 174, 289; Taliban government of, 144, 166, 181, 182, 317, 322; US military action in, 109, 110, 116, 129, 152, 250, 301, 323, 380
Africa: ancient civilizations of, 85–7, *87*; corruption in, 280, 282–3; debt burdens in, 6, 244; Falasha of, 85–6, *87*; HIV/AIDS in, 135; League of Nations mandates in, 170; as part of Global South, 145; proxy wars in, 115; regional organizations in, 358; slave trade and, 86–7, 283–4
African National Congress (ANC), 180, 305–6, 317
African Union (AU), 358, 363; in Darfur, 122, *175*; as OAU, 356, 358
An Agenda for Peace (Boutros-Ghali), 175, 183
Agenda 21 (Earth Summit proposals), 337
Ahmad ibn Hanbal, 315

Ajello, Aldo, 174
Albanian Mafia, 290–1
al-Bashir, Omar Hassan, 176
Alexander the Great, 76–7, *77*
Al-Gama'a al-Islamiyya, 316, 322
Algeria, 308
Allende, Salvador, 227
alliances, global, 112, 115, 159
Allied nations, of World War II, 159
All Quiet on the Western Front (Remarque), 115
al-Qaeda, 166, 179, 181, 301–2, 303, 316; attacks of 9/11 by, 3, 301, 323; embassy bombings and, 322; safe haven for, 317, 322; US-led coalition against, 153–4, *154*, 323; Wahhabism and, 315–16
American Federation of Labour–Congress of Industrial Organizations (AFL–CIO), 242
Americas: indigenous civilizations of, 87–8, *88*, *89*; regional organizations in, 357–8
Amnesty International, 129, 256, 271
anarchist extremism, 308
anarchy, of inter-state relations, 2, 23, 28, 29, 30–1, 38, 39; state self-help and, 2, 30; war and security amidst, 110, 123, 124, 127
Andean Community (CAN), 357
Angola, 165, 182
Annan, Kofi, 171, 220, 336; Global Compact of, 232–4, 365; high level panel of, 186–7, 363–4; on human security, 133, 134, 368; on sanctions, 180, 181
Antarctica, 338, 340
Anti-Ballistic Missile (ABM) Treaty, 368
anti-colonial extremism, 308
anti-globalization movement. *See* counter-globalization movements
anti-slavery movement, 353
apartheid, 179, 180, 305, 317, 320
Aquino, Corazón, 61, 62
Arab Maghreb Union (UMA), 358
Arafat, Yasser, 306, 307
Argentina, 149, 244; women as leaders of, 61, *61*

Aristophanes, 126
Aristotle, 40, 76
arms control and reduction, 121, 129
arms embargoes, 166, 182; *see also* sanctions, UN-imposed
arms expenditures and availability, 112–13, 129
arms race, postwar, 115, 117–21
arms races, 22
Aron, Raymond, 28–29, 30
Artaxerxes II of Persia, 76
Asia, 56, 298; regional organizations in, 358–9
Asian Development Bank (ADB), 246
Asia–Pacific Economic Cooperation (APEC), 358–9; protests against, 241
assassinations, 307, 308
Association of South East Asian Nations (ASEAN), 358
Association for the Taxation of Financial Transactions to Aid Citizens (ATTAC), 265–6
Assyrians, 74, 75
asymmetric warfare, *125*, 152, 306, 375–6
Athens (city-state), 76, 352
Atlantic Charter, 159
Augsburg, Treaty of, 80
Aung San Suu Kyi, 61, 63, 64
Australia, 170, 240–1, 341, 355
Austro-Hungarian Empire, 36, 90, 112
Axis powers, of World War II, 159
Axworthy, Lloyd, 134
Aztec (indigenous civilization), 87

Babylon, *74*, 74–5, 90
Bacon, Sir Francis, 110
Bahuguna, Sunderlal, *258*, 258–9
balance of power, 123, 134, 376; in ancient Greece, 76; asymmetry of, 356; in Cold War era, 30–1, 132; realist advocacy of, 28, 30–1, 111–12, 138, 352; as Utopian concept, 22; in World War I era, 112, 113, 132
Bali, terrorist bombings in, 314
Balkans, 36, 105, 175, 353
Bandaranaike, Sirimavo, 61, 62

Bandidos (motorcycle gang), 296, 297
Bangladesh, 285
Bank for International Settlements (BIS), 147, 214
Ban Ki-Moon, 171, *369*
Baran, Paul, 52, 53
al-Bashir, Omar Hassan, 176
Battle of Seattle, 241–4, 246, 365
Beauvoir, Simone de, 67
Beck, Dave, 242
Begin, Menachem, 306, 308
behaviouralism/positivism, 97
Belgium, 36, 90, 170, 356
Bello, Walden, 230, 243, 376
Bentham, Jeremy, 1, 35, 186
Berlin, Isaiah, 111
Berlin Wall, *102*, 103, 202, 261
Berlusconi, Silvio, 249
Bhopal, India, environmental disaster in, 228
Bhutto, Benazir, *62*, 62, 64
Bhutto, Zulfikar Ali, 62
Big Circle Boys (BCB), 294–5
bilateral trade treaties and agreements, 206, 207
bin Laden, Osama, 8, 166, 301, 303; safe haven for, 317, 322; on terrorism, 307; Wahhabism and, 315–16
biodiversity: loss of, 328, 329; convention on, 337
Biological and Toxin Weapons Convention (BTWC), 368–9
bipolar political systems: of ancient Greece, 76; of Cold War, 7, 115, 117–21
Black Bloc, 242–3, *243*, 249
Blair, Tony, 133, 143
"The Blind Men and the Elephant" (Saxe), 44–5
Bogota Cartel (Colombia), 293
Bolsheviks, 141
bond rating agencies, 6
Bonn–Berlin Process (UN targeted sanctions), 182
Bono, 148, 363
border controls, 203
Bosnia-Herzegovina, 109, 168
Boutros-Ghali, Boutros, 133, 171, 174; peace agenda of, 175, 183
Bouyeri, Mohammed, 304
Braudel, Fernand, 97, 102
Brazil, 56, 206, 244; as emerging power/market, 138, 225, 226, 379; FTAA and, 358; global warming and, 340; IMF and, 264; landless workers' movement in, 263–4; World Social Forum in, 265–70
Bretton Woods System, and institutions of, 148, 149–50, 356, 365; criticisms/denunciations of, 168, 246,

251; environmental issues and, 345; globalization and, 199–200, 201, 207–8; gold standard and, 149–50; lending policies of, 244; protests against, 240, 241, 247, 250; state sovereignty and, 149; UN and, *160*, 166, 167–8; voting at, 149, 167–8; *see also* International Monetary Fund; World Bank
Brezhnev, Leonid, 119
BRIC countries, 226. *See also* Brazil; China; India; Russia; *see also* emerging powers/markets
Bridges, Harry, 242
Britain: liberal trade policy of, 206–7; opium trade and, 279; slavery in, 284; *see also* United Kingdom
Brown, Gordon, 210
Bruce, Stanley, and report of, 355
Brundtland, Gro Harlem, 62; environmental commission of, 62, 67, 335–6
Brussels Convention, 284
Buchanan, Pat, 144
Buddhism, 76, 84
Buffett, Warren, 148, 376
Bull, Hedley, 23, 32–3, 40; on global order, 142; on war, 121
Burma (Myanmar), 191, 293–4; leadership of, 61, 63, 64
Bush, George H.W., 101, 102, 153, 248, 357
Bush, George W., 181; on al-Qaeda, 301, 302; counter-terrorist strategy of, 302; Kyoto Protocol pullout by, 153, 247; UN and, 369; unilateralist policy of, 152–4
business, globalization of. *See* multinational corporations
Byzantine Empire, 77, 78–9, 80

Cahokia (ancient city), 88
Cali Mafia, 288–9, 292
caliphate, Islamic, 78
Cambodia, 166, 174, 183
Camdessus, Michael, 246
camel racing, 285, *285*
Canada: APEC protests in, 241; foreign investment regulation in, 227; global governance and, 355; Hell's Angels in, 297; 'homegrown terrorism' in, 302–3; military activities of, 109, 123
Canadian Security Intelligence Service (CSIS), 303
capitalism: colonization and, 49–50, 55–6; core and periphery/semi-periphery of, 50, 51, 52–3, 54, 55–6; globalization and, 6, 206; hyper-liberal, 6; imperialism and, 49–50; Marx's critique of, 46–9;

modernization and dependency theories of, 50–4; modes of production and, 47–9, 57, 65–6; US as centre of, 53; world systems theory on, 54–6
Cardoso, Fernando Henrique, *53*, 53, 54
Caribbean Community (CARICOM), 357
Carnegie, Andrew, 110
Carnegie Commission on Preventing Deadly Conflict, 144
Caro-Quintero brothers, 292
Carr, E.H., 19, 24
Carson, Rachel, 332–3
cartels, drug-trafficking, 292–3, *293*; Bogota, 293; Cali Mafia, 288–9, 292; Medellin, 292–3, *294*; Sonora, 289, 292; *see also* gangs, transnational
Carter, Jimmy, 181
Cassen, Bernard, 266
Castro, Fidel, 248
celebrity diplomacy, 148, 363
Central African Monetary and Economic Community (CEMAC), 358
Central African Republic (CAR), 176
Central America, 174; US interventions in, 66, 117, 320
Central American Common Market (CACM), 357
Central American Integration System (SICA), 357
Central Intelligence Agency (CIA), 285
Chamberlain, Neville, 25
Chambers, John, 297
Chandragupta Maurya, 77
Chao Kao, 83
Charlemagne, 79
Charles V (Holy Roman Emperor), 80
Chase-Dunn, Christopher, 55–6
Chavín (indigenous civilization), 87
Chernobyl nuclear disaster, 68, 331
Chiapas, Mexico, 260–3
Chile, 243, 357; *coup d'état* in, 227
Chimor, ancient kingdom of, 87
China, early, 82–4; Buddhism in, 84; Ch'in dynasty of, 83–4; Confucianism in, *83*, 83, 84; Great Wall of, 83; Han dynasty of, 84; legalism in, 83, 84; Mohism in, 83; states system in, 82–3; Taoism in, 83; Zhou kingdom of, 82
China, People's Republic of, 56, 61, 163, 241, 359; containerized trade with, *204*, 204–5; counterfeiting/intellectual piracy and, 278; as emerging power/market, 138, 145, 225–6, 379; as nuclear power, 120; opium trade in, 279; R2P norm and, 364; Red Guards of, 294–5; traditional society of, 52; Triads in, 294

China, Republic of (Taiwan), 159
Chipko Movement (India), 257–9
chlorofluorocarbons (CFCs), 336
cholera, 341
Chomsky, Noam, 144
Christianity, 78–80, 314
Churchill, Sir Winston, *117*, 158
city-states, ancient, 74–6, 78, 352
civilian casualties of war. *See*
non-combatants
civil society: counter-globalization
movements and, 240, 242–5, 248,
265–72; global governance and, 8,
220, 346, 351, 353–4, 360, 361–7;
greater prominence of, 378–9; UN and,
250–1; *see also* counter-globalization
movements; non-governmental
organizations
Civil War, US, 283
'clash of civilizations', 302, 319
Claude, Inis L., Jr., 353, 367
Clausewitz, Karl von, 121, 123
climate change, 336, 337; definitions of,
342; global warming and, 337–43;
intergovernmental panel on, 339–40,
342, *342*, 343; responses to, 343;
as security issue, 135; *see also* global
warming
Clinton, Bill, 143, 153, 243, 248, 271
'coalitions of the willing', 359, 366, 380;
against al-Qaeda, 153–4, *154*, 323
Cobden, Richard, 34, 35
cocaine, 279, 288–9
Code of Hammurabi, 74
codified international law, 351, 356
coercive measures, by UN, 176, 179–83;
comprehensive sanctions, 164,
179–81; military action, 181, 182–3;
smart (targeted) sanctions, 166,
181–2, 322
Cold War, 115–21; as aberration of
history, 105; alliances of, 115; arms
race of, 115, 117–21; balance of
power during, 30–1, 132; Berlin Wall
and, *102*, 102, 103; bipolar nature of,
7, 115, 117–21; confidence-building
measures of, 118, 119; Cox on, 102,
104; Cuban Missile Crisis and, 117,
118; deterrence and containment
in, 115, 117; end of, 101–5; global
change/continuity and, 101–5, 123;
Palme Report and, 118, 119; proxy
wars of, 115; realism and, 25, 30–2,
41, 117; scientific behaviouralism
and, 40–1; SEATO and, 358;
state-sponsored terrorism during,
317; superpower conflict of, 165;
UN peacekeeping during, 176; UN
Security Council and, 102, 164–6; US

multilateralism during, 152; *see also*
post-Cold War era
'collateral damage' of war, 110–11
collective security, 22, 76, 127
Collective Security Treaty Organization
(CSTO), 359
Colombia, 288, 290, *293*; drug
trafficking in, 292–3, *294*
colonialism, 21, 90, 353; capitalism and,
49–50, 55–6; decolonization and,
90, 159; drug trafficking and, 279;
exploitation of people/resources and,
50, 55, 254–7; foreign investment
and, 224
Columbus, Christopher, 87
Commission on Security and
Cooperation in Europe (CSCE), 148
Common Frontiers, 248
Common Market for Eastern and
Southern Africa (COMESA), 358
Common Market of the South
(MERCOSUR), 357
common security, 117–19, 121;
confidence-building measures and,
118, 119; individuals and, 119;
interdependence and, 111, 115, 119;
'non-offensive defence' and, 119; as
precursor of arms control initiatives,
119–21
commons, global, 329–30; tragedy of,
69, 329
Commonwealth, British, 180
Commonwealth of Independent States
(CIS), 359
Communications Fraud Control
Association, 287
communications technology, 201, 205–6,
209, *209*
communism (ideology), 46
Community of Sahel-Saharan States
(CEN-SAD), 358
complex interdependence (Keohane/
Nye), 39
comprehensive sanctions, by UN, 164,
179–81
comprehensive security, 120, 121
Comprehensive Test Ban Treaty, 120
Comte, Auguste, 34
Concert of Europe, 112, 132, 352–4
confidence-building measures,
118, 119
Confucianism, *83*, 83, 84
Congo, Democratic Republic of (DRC),
165, 175–6, 191
Congo, Republic of the (later DRC),
173, 174
Congress of Vienna, 112, 284
conservation movement, 331–2
Constantine, 78

constructivism, 69–70
containerization, *204*, 204–5
containment, 117
Convention for a Democratic South
Africa (CODESA), 180
co-operative security, 119–20, 121
Corinth (city-state), 76
corruption, 274, 277, 279, 288,
289, 294; agents of, 280; money
laundering and, 275, 282–3
Cortés, Hernán, 87
Cosa Nostra, 288, 292
Council for the Americas, 248
counterfeiting and intellectual piracy,
278
counter-globalization movements,
144, 168, 219, 237–52, 270–2,
369; as ad hoc collectivities, 271–2;
around the world, 6, 245–51; Battle
of Seattle and, 241–4, 246, 365;
civil society and, 240, 242–5, 248,
265–72; as counter-hegemonic, 239,
319; effect of 9/11 on, 249–50;
as 'explosive sub-groupism', 6;
in Global South, 254–72; by
grassroots movements, 240–1, 250,
251, 254–64; IGOs and, 271; by
individuals, 272; Internet use by,
262–3, 270, 271–2; Jubilee 2000
and, 244–5; local/global nexus of,
255–7; NGOs and, 244–5, 248, 249,
250–1, 254, 265–6, 269, 270–2;
police-protester clashes and, 243,
246–7, 249; precursors of, 240–1,
242; reconfiguration of, 250–1;
representativeness of, 252; as safety
valves, 238–40; two forms of,
239–40; women in, 258–60
counter-globalization movements,
in Global South, 254–72; Chipko
Movement (India), 257–9; Green
Belt Movement (Kenya), 257,
259–60; Movimento Trabalhadores
Rurais Sêm Terra (Brazil), 263–4;
Ogoni resistance movement (Nigeria),
254–7; World Social Forum and,
265–70; Zapatista uprising (Mexico),
260–3
counter-globalization protests and
demonstrations, *11*; ADB meeting
(Chiang Mai, Thailand), 246, *246*;
Battle of Seattle, 241–4, 246, 365;
Bretton Woods meeting (Prague),
247; G8 protest (Genoa), 249,
250; IMF-World Bank meetings
(Washington), 246; OAS meeting
(Windsor, Ont.), 246; Summit of
the Americas (Quebec City), 247–9;
UNCTAD X (Bangkok), 245–6; WEF

Asia-Pacific Summit (Melbourne), 247

Counter-Terrorism Committee (CTC), UN, 166, 172, 323

Cousteau, Jacques-Yves, 333

Cox, Robert, 19–20; on Cold War, 102, 104; on critical theory, 56; on global change/continuity, 97, 99, 100, 102, 104, 105; on globalization, 217; on global structures, 139; Gramsci and, 56, 99, 141, 239; on hegemony, 99, 141; historicist/ heuristic approach of, 97, 99; on IGOs, 185–6; on modes of production, 139; on problem-solving theories, 56; on state/society complex, 238, 239

crime, organized. *See* organized crime, transnational

Crimean War, 352

crimes against humanity, 175–6

critical realist theory, 11–12, 14, 382–5

critical theory, 56, 106; *see also* environmentalism; feminism; postmodernism

Croatia, *30*, 165, 179

Crucé, Emeric, 21

Cuba, 264

Cuban Missile Crisis, 117, 118

Cuyahoga River (Cleveland, Ohio), 332

cybercrimes, 277; Internet frauds, 295

Cyprus, 308

Cyrus the Great, 75

Czechoslovakia, former, 114, 190–1, 191

Daffron, Shelvy, 242

Dalits ('untouchable' caste in India), 269

Dante Alighieri, 21

Darfur, 122, *175*, 175–6. *See also* Sudan

Darius I of Persia, 75

debt crises, in less developed countries, 6, 240, 244–5

Declaration of the United Nations, 158–9

decolonization, 90, 159

deductive vs. inductive approach, to international relations, 39–41

defensive realism, 30–1

deforestation, 329, 341; in India, 257–9

De Klerk, F.W., 180

democracy: in Central and Eastern Europe, 240; extremism and, 318–19; war and, 123–4

Dent, Martin, 245

dependency theory, 50, 52–3; post-dependency theory and, 53–4

Depression, Great, 207, 224

deregulation, 221, 228–9, 230; of financial institutions, 377–8

derivatives, 376

Derrida, Jacques, 58–9

deterrence, 115, 117, 376

deterritorialization, 213–14

Deutscher, Isaac, *26*

developing countries: debt crises in, 6, 240, 244–5; HIPC program and, 6, 245; modernization and dependency theories of, 50–4

Devi, Bali, 258, *258*

Direct Action Network (DAN), 242

Dobkins, Lou, 296

Dostoevsky, Fyodor, 301

Doyle, Michael, 34, 123

drug trafficking, 278–9; cartels/gangs involved in, 288–9, 292–6; colonial history of, 279; extremism/terrorism and, 319, 320; regions involved in, 279, 292–3, *293*

Drummond, Sir Eric, 169

Dubois, Pierre, 21

Ducks Unlimited, 332

Dumbarton Oaks, UN meeting at, 159, 166–7

Dunant, Henry, 128

Earth Summit (Rio Conference), 67, 336–7, 343–4, 345, 362

East Africa Community (EAC), 358

East Germany/East Berlin, 103

East India Company, 221

East Timor, peace-building in, 183, 184

Economic and Social Council (ECOSOC), UN, 159, *160*, *166*, 166–8, 184, 271, 344, 355; agencies reporting to, 168, 192–3; Bretton Woods institutions and, 167–8; membership of, 167, 187; NGOs and, 168, 250–1, 361

Economic Community of Central African States (ECCAS), 358

Economic Community of the Great Lakes Countries (ECPGL), 358

Economic Community of West African States (ECOWAS), 358

Economic Recovery Advisory Board (US), 181

economic sanctions, by UN, 164, 179–81, 182

economies of scale, 206

Egypt, 191, 323; ancient, 85; Al-Gama'a al-Islamiyya and, 316, 322

Ejército Zapatista de Liberación Nacional (EZLN), 261–3; Declaration of, 261; egalitarianism of, 262; government atrocities against, 261–2; international sympathy for, 262–3; leader of, 261, 262, *262*; 'virtual Chiapas' created by, 262–3; *see also* Zapatista uprising

El Salvador, 165

Emancipation Proclamation, US, 283

embargoes: arms, 166, 182; trade, 164, 182; *see also* sanctions, UN-imposed

emerging powers/markets, 138, 145, 225, 226–9, 379–80

Emma Maersk (container ship), *204*, 204–5

empires, ancient, 75–8; hegemony and, 74, 75, 76–7, 78, 83

Engels, Friedrich, 48–9

Enlightenment, 57, 80

Enterprise for the Americas Initiative (EAI), 248

environment, 328–47; climate change/global warming and, 336, 337–43; early advocates of, 331–3; as global capital, 254–9; global politics and, 67–9; governance of, 343–7; issues affecting, 329–31; Kyoto Protocol on, 67, 153, 154, 247, 343, 345, 369; MNC-caused disasters of, 228, 254–7; as multilateral issue, 342–3; NGOs and, 68, 271, 332, 335, 346–7; state sovereignty and, 67–8; trade and, 331; transboundary issues of, 67–8, 330–1; UN conferences/ commissions on, 333–7, 362

environment, issues affecting: climate change/global warming, 336, 337–43; containerization, 205; diverse/fragmented governance, 343–7; global commons, 329–30; as having repercussions in other areas, 331; implementation of agreements, 347; MNC activities, 228, 254–7; natural disasters, 345; shared natural resources, 330; sustainable development, 335, 345; 'tragedy of the commons', 69, 329; transboundary externalities, 67–8, 330–1; unsustainable consumption, 345; World Bank and, 335, 337, 345

environmentalism, 45, 67–9; early advocates of, 331–3; NGOs and, 68, 271, 332, 335, 346–7; as social movement, 240; *see also* Greenpeace

Erasmus, 127

Eritrea, 165, 182

Escobar, Pablo, 292, *294*

Esquipulas II peace agreement, 174

ETA (Basque separatist group), 288, 308

Ethiopia, 113, 114, 182; Falasha of, 85–6, 87

ethnic cleansing, 175

ethno-nationalist/separatist groups, 308–9

Ethyl Corporation, 331
Eurocentrism, 57, 73, 87, 353
    European civilization: after fall of
    Roman Empire, 78, 81; feudalism
    and, 78, 82, 88, 105; inter-state
    system and, 73–82, 88–90; other
    world civilizations and, 82–8; *see also*
    inter-state system; world civilizations
European Coal and Steel Community
    (ECSC), 356–7
European Parliament, 356, 357
European Union (EU), 8, 38, 248, 351,
    356–7, 363; budget of, 172; CFC
    ban by, 336; counterfeiting and, 278;
    history of, 356–7; uncontrolled travel
    within, 203
Euskadi Ta Askatasuna (ETA), 288, 308
extremism, 301; Christian, 314;
    conceptualizing, 303–5; democracy
    and, 318–19; failed/failing states
    and, 317; four phases of, 308–9;
    globalization and, 319; historical
    examples of, 307–9; Islamic, 305–7,
    310, 314–16; levels of analysis
    approach to, 309–19; psychology
    of, 309–11; radicalism and, 301–2,
    303–7, 312–13, 319, 324; religion
    and, 210, 309, 313–14; societal
    marginalization and, 316; of state,
    317–19; structural violence and, 313;
    terrorism as, 303–9; understanding,
    301–2, 307–9; *see also* terrorism
extremism, levels of analysis approach to,
    309–19; group, 311–12; individual,
    309–11; societal, 312–14; state,
    317–19; state/society complex,
    314–16; transnational/global, 319
Exxon Valdez, 228
EZLN. *See* Ejército Zapatista de
    Liberación Nacional

failed/failing states, 166, 169; extremism
    and, 317; organized crime and,
    275, 279
Falasha (Ethiopian Jews), 85–6; possible
    origins of, 87
Faletto, Enzo, 53
Falklands War, 66–7
Fascism and Nazism, 114
Fatah (militant wing of PLO), 306
fatwa (Islamic ruling/decree), 307
Federal Reserve, US, 181, 244
feminism, 45, 60–7; global politics
    and, 381; international relations and,
    60–1, 64–7; liberal, 64–5; post-
    colonial, 67; postmodernist, 64, 66–7;
    realism and, 60–1; sex and gender
    issues of, 66–7; socialist/Marxist,
    65–6; standpoint, 66
feudalism, 78, 82, 88, 105

Figueiredo, João, 263
fish and fish stocks, 328, 329, 330, 332,
    333, 341, 345, 346
Food and Agriculture Organization
    (FAO), *160*, 168, 192, 258, 335, 344
foreign investment: barriers to, 224;
    direct (FDI), 222–3, 224–6, 228;
    portfolio, 222; regulation of, 227
Foreign Investment Review Agency
    (FIRA), 227
Foreign Policy magazine globalization
    index, 208
fossil fuels, 338
Foucault, Michel, 58
'fragmegration' (Rosenau), 380, 382
France, 36, 103, 109, 170, 318, 356;
    Algeria and, 308; Greenpeace
    ship bombing by, 68; Muslim
    marginalization in, 316; as Security
    Council member, 163, 321; Vietnam
    and, 116
Frank, André Gunder, 53, 54
Franz Ferdinand, Archduke, 308
Fréchette, Louise, 171
freedom fighting, vs. terrorism, 305–7
free trade, 21, 34, 35; Wilson on,
    35, 37
'Free Trade Area of the Americas' (FTAA),
    proposed, 247–9, 264, 358
Friedman, Milton, 147, 231, 232
Friedman, Thomas, 142, 202, 212, 221
Friends of the Earth, 271
Front de Libération Nationale (FLN), 308
Fukuyama, Francis, 132–3
functionalism, 38

G2 (US and China), 359
G8 (Group of 8), 226, 229; protests
    against, *11*, 241, 244, 249, *250*
G20 (Group of 20), 217, 226, 378
Galán, Luis Carlos, 292
Galtung, Johan, 134, 313
Al-Gama'a al-Islamiyya, 316, 322
Gandhi, Indira, 61, 64, 334; forest policy
    of, 258, 259
Gandhi, Mohandas (Mahatma), 67, 258,
    303, 306
gangs, motorcycle, 296–7
gangs, transnational, 292–6; Big
    Circle Boys, 294–5; cartels, 288–9,
    292–3, *293, 294*; Chinese Triads, 294;
    Jamaican Yardies, 294; Khun Sa gang,
    293–4, *295*; motorcycle gangs, 296–7;
    Nigerian crime syndicates, 295–6;
    pirates, *297*, 297–8
Gates, Bill, 8, 148, 363
Gaza, 168, 173, 314; Israeli attacks on,
    125, 320; non-combatants in, 130,
    132; refugee camps in, 318
Geldof, Bob, 148, 363

gender and feminist theories. *See*
    feminism
General Agreement on Tariffs and Trade
    (GATT), 149, 207, 240, 356, 365
General Assembly, UN, 159, *160*,
    161–3, 169, 185, 187, 356, 357;
    environmental issues and, 336;
    Human Rights Council of, 163;
    Millennium Development Goals
    of, 161–2, 232; NGOs and, 251;
    Security Council and, 161, 174; Sixth
    Committee of, 320; terrorism and,
    320, 321, 323
Geneva Conventions, 361
Genoa, G8 meeting in, 249, *250*, 269
Georgia, 359
Germany, 62, 64, 103; Nazi regime in,
    24, 25; World War I and, 112,
    113, 114
genocide, 175; in Darfur, 122
Giddens, Anthony, 255
Giuliani, Carlo, 249
global change, 96–106, 379–80;
    attacks of 9/11 and, 102, 123, 379;
    conceptualizing, 98; vs. continuity,
    96, 97–8, 100, 104, 105–6, 123;
    as epiphenomenal, 96, 98, 101;
    hegemony and, 99–100; historicist/
    heuristic approach to, 97, 99, 100–1,
    102, 104, 105, 139; idealist/Utopian
    view of, 98, 104, 106; over *longue
    durée*, 97, 98; neo-liberal view of,
    101–2; positivist view of, 97; post-
    Cold War era and, 101–5, 123;
    problem-solving and critical theory
    approaches to, 106; realist view of,
    96–7, 98, 104, 106; as structural, 96,
    97, 98, 101
Global Compact, 232–4, 365
global economic crisis (2008–9), 6,
    145, 198, 210, 216–17, 230–1, 239,
    376–7, 380
Global Environment Facility (GEF),
    335–6
global financial order, 377–9; 'crash
    of 1929' and, 377, *377*; financial
    deregulation and, 377–8; Great
    Depression and, 207, 224;
    individual investors and, 378; in
    neo-liberal era, 377–8; in postwar
    era, 377; recent economic crisis
    and, 376–7; *see also* global economic
    crisis (2008–9)
global governance. *See* governance,
    global
globalism, 142
globalization, 5–7, 141–2, 198–217,
    237; attacks of 9/11 and, 3–5, 198–9,
    201–2; as benefiting only wealthy
    nations, 6, 208–10, 369; 'borderless

world' of, 211; Bretton Woods System and, 199–200, 201, 207–8; of business, 219–35; characteristics and drivers of, 200–6; colonialism and, 254–7; communications/ finance growth and, 202; cultural, 275; Global South resistance to, 254–72; history of, 199–200, 202, 203, 206–8; indicators of, 201–2; Internet bandwidth distribution and, 209, *209*, 369; meanings/ interpretations of, 199–200, 201, 208; MNCs and, 219–35; movements against, 144, 168, 219, 237–52, 270–2, 369; political/policy context of, 206–10; as 'race to the bottom', 206; regionalism, as response to, 210, 356; state and, 3–5, 198–217; state/society complexes and, 238, 239–40; terrorism and, 198–9, 210, 319; transnational organized crime and, 201, 219, 220, 274–98, 319; as triumph of economics, 212–13; UN and, 187–8; US hegemony and, 319; *see also* state, in era of globalization

globalization, characteristics and drivers of, 200–6; capitalism, 6, 206; communications technology, 201, 205–6, 209, *209*; mass migration, 5, 203, 319; MNCs, 206; reduced transportation costs/ containerization, 201, 203–5; technological changes, 202

globalization, opposition to: by civil society, 240, 242–5, 248, 265–72; counter-movements as, 237–52; in global South, 254–72; by grassroots organizations, 254–64; by individuals, 272; NGOs and, 244–5, 248, 249, 250–1, 254, 265–6, 269, 270–2, 362; protests/demonstrations as, 241–50; religious extremism/activism as, 210; slow food movement as, 210; violence of, 243, 246–7, 249; *see also* counter-globalization movements, *and entries following*

'globalized capitalist relations', 255

global North, 145, 225

global order, 141–52; anti-globalization movement and, 144; competing views/visions of, 142, 143–4; global inequality and, 144, 145; globalism/ globalization and, 141–3; human rights/human security and, 143, 147–8; ideational foundation of, 143–4; IGOs/ NGOs and, 146, 147, 155, 156; vs. international order, 33, 142; material interests and, 144–5; military dimensions of, 150–2; neo-liberalism and, 143, 145, 147;

in North and South, 145; political/ institutional dimensions of, 145–50; power and, 138–41; regionalism and, 155; state sovereignty/relevance and, 138, 139, 146–7; unilateralism vs. multilateralism and, 152–5; US hegemony and, 138, 140, 150–5

global politics: alternative conceptions of, 45–71; attacks of 9/11 and, 3–5, 379; critical realist theory and, 11–12, 14; critical theories of, 56–70; 'fragmegration' and, 380, 382; globalization and, 5–7; vs. international relations, 1–5, 7–8, 12, 168; *longue durée* view of, 97, 98; Marxism and, 46–50, 381; as multi-centric, 6–7; multi-level governance and, 7–12; Mumbai terrorist attacks and, 374–6; 'national interest' and, 8; non-state actors and, 3, 6–7, 8, 9, 219–21; as ongoing process, 7–8, 104–5; power and, 9; security and, 9–10; state and, 3–5, 8–9; theory as guide to, 381–5; *see also* governance, global, *and entries following*; *see also* governance, multi-level

global politics, alternative conceptions of, 45–71; constructivism, 69–70; dependency theory, 50, 52–3; environmentalism, 45, 67–9; gender and feminist theories, 45, 60–7; Marxism, 45–56; modernization theory, 50–2; post-dependency theory, 53–4; postmodernism, 57–60, 69; world systems theory, 54–6

global South: 'bottom billion' of, 225; as constrained by IMF/ WTO policies, 201; counter-globalization movements in, 254–72; dependency theories of, 52–4; development assistance to, 224–5; diaspora remittances to, 225; emerging powers/markets of, 138, 145, 226; foreign investment and, 225–6; Group of 77 and, 334–5; MNCs and, 226–9; as not benefiting from globalization, 208–10; poverty in, as security issue, 119; women in, 67; World Social Forum in, 265–70; *see also* counter-globalization movements, in Global South

global structures, 138–56; Bretton Woods institutions as, 148, 149–50; global order and, 141–52; Hague Conference (1899) and, 139–40; historical experience of, 138–41; international/transnational activities and, 140–1; power and, 138–41; US hegemony and, 138, 140, 150–5

global warming: consequences of, 340–3; definition of, 338; drought and, 340–1; evidence of, 338; rising sea level and, 340; *see also* climate change

Gogh, Theo van, 303, 304, *304*

gold standard, 149–50

'good offices', of political intercessors, 76, 164, 173–4

Gorbachev, Mikhail, 119, 121

Gore, Al, 338, 342, *342*

governance, global, 7–12, 350–71; assessing, 367–70; civil society/ NGOs and, 8, 220, 346, 351, 353–4, 360, 361–7; critical realist theory and, 11–12, 14; evolution of, 351–62; expanding agenda of, 362–7; financial/corporate interests and, 353, 360; IMF and, 351, 356, 365; imperialism and, 351–2; institutions/networks of, 10–11, 350–1; interwar initiatives on, 113, 114, 354–5; legitimacy/ efficacy of, 363, 366–70; MNCs and, 230; multi-centric vs. state-centric, 380, 381–2; as multi-level, 7–12; in post-Cold War era, 7; regionalism and, 155, 356–9; 'soft law' of, 362; state sovereignty and, 5–7, 356, 360–1, 363–7; subsidiarity and, 382; UN and, 356, 359; US and, 355–6; World War I and, 112, 113, 132, 354, 355; World War II and, 142; WTO and, 351, 365

governance, global, institutions/ networks of, 10–11, 350–1; celebrities' role in, 148, 363; civil society/ NGOs, 8, 220, 346, 351, 353–4, 360, 361–7; direct interventions by, 363–7, 368; human security and, 363–4, 368; legitimacy/ efficacy of, 363, 366–70; limitations of, 361; opposition to, 368–71; reform of, 371; regulatory, 354; state sovereignty and, 5–7, 356, 360–1, 363–7; varying goals/interests of, 359–61

governance, global, institutions/ networks of (specific): Bretton Woods institutions, 148, 149–50, 356, 365; Concert of Europe, 112, 132, 352–4; European Union, 351, 356–7; League of Nations, 23–4, 113, 114, 354–5; UN, 158–88, 351, 356; *see also specific institutions/networks*

governance, multi-level, 7–12; critical realist theory and, 11–12, 14; networks of, 10–11, 350–1; politics and, 8; in post-Cold War era, 7; power and, 9; security and, 9–10; state and, 8–9

Gramsci, Antonio, 56, 97, 99, 141, 239
grassroots movements, 188, 240–1, 250, 251, 254–64
Greece, ancient, 90; city-states of, 75–6; influence of, 77, 78; polis of, 75
Green Belt Movement (Kenya), 257, 259–60
greenhouse gases, 341, 343
Greenpeace, 8, *8*, 68, 256, 257, 271, 332
Grenada, US intervention in, 66, 117
Grey, Edward (Viscount Grey of Fallodon), 113
gross domestic product (GDP), 225, 228
gross national product (GNP), 226–7
Grotius, Hugo, 128, 129
group extremism, 311–12
Gulf War (1991), 109, 127, 151, 153, 181

Habermas, Jürgen, 56
Hague Peace Conferences, 139–40, 353, 361
Haiti, 113, 165, 182, 283
Hamas, 316, 317, *317*, 318
Hammarskjöld, Dag, 171, 173, 174, 176
Han dynasty, of China, 84
Hanoi (Vietnam), 116
Hardin, Garrett, 69, 329, 333
Havel, Vaclav, 133, 134, 247
Hayek, Friedrich, 147
heavily indebted poor countries (HIPCs), 6, 245
Hegel, Georg, 47, 57
hegemony, ancient, 74, 75, 76–7, 78, 83; as benign, 75, 77; as malign, 76, 78
hegemony, modern: British, 223, 279; counter-globalization movements and, 239, 319; global change/continuity and, 99–100; Gramsci and Cox on, 99, 141, 239; liberalism and, 38; power and, 9, 141; realist view of, 99; US, 138, 140, 150–5, 248, 319, 352, 357
Hellas, 90; city-states of, 75–6; influence of, 77, 78; polis of, 75
Helleiner, Eric, 215–16, 377
Hell's Angels, 274, 296–7
Helsinki Accords, 148
Heritage Foundation, 368
heroin, 279
Herz, John H., 25, 34, 42, 114
heuristic model, of global change, 99. *See also* global change
Hezbollah, 316, 317
hijab, French policy against, 316
Himalayas, spread of Chipko Movement in, 258, 259
Hirsi Ali, Ayaan, 304
historicism, 97
History of the Peloponnesian War (Thucydides), 76, 111

Hitler, Adolf, 25, 114
HIV/ AIDS, 135, 163, 188, 287, 363
Hobbes, Thomas, 57, 125
Hobsbawm, E.J., 105
Ho Chi Minh, 116
hockey, professional, as infiltrated by Russian Mafia, 290
Holy Roman Empire, 79–80
'homegrown terrorism', 302–3
Hong Kong, 56, 294, 295
Horkheim, Max, 56
Hoxha, Enver, 290
Huari (indigenous civilization), 87
Hudson's Bay Company, 206, 221
Hull, Cordell, 207
human rights: renewed emphasis on, 143, 147–8; UN and, 163, 184, 251
Human Rights, UN High Commissioner for, 184
Human Rights Council, UN, 163
human security, 10, 97, 121, 134–5, 147–8; structural violence and, 134; war and, 10, 110–11, 119, 124, 131–4, 363–4, 368
human trafficking, 283–7; extent of, 284, 285; forms of, 284–5, *285*; of girls and women, 284–7, *286*; HIV/ AIDS and, 287; matchmaking services and, 287; organized crime and, 286; in post-Cold War era, 285, 286; slavery and, 283–4
Huntington, Samuel, 123, 319
Hussein, Saddam, 165, 181
hyperglobalization, 188, 212
hyper-liberal capitalism, 6

idealism, 23–4; cosmopolitanism and, 19; discrediting of, 24, 25, 41–2; 'higher realism' and, 383; *idealpolitik* and, 14, 382–5; liberalism and, 33, 35, 37–8; Morgenthau on, 24–5; neo-idealism and, 382–3; vs. realism, 24–5, 41–2; subsidiarity and, 382; world interests and, 383; *see also* Utopianism
idealpolitik, 14, 382–5
Ignatieff, Michael, 10, 151, 364
imperialism, 21; capitalism as, 49–50; foreign investment and, 224; global governance and, 351–2; liberal, 34; US hegemony as, 138, 140, 150–5, 248, 319, 352, 357
Imperialism, The Highest Stage of Capitalism (Lenin), 49
Inca (indigenous civilization), 87
An Inconvenient Truth (film), 342
Independent Commission on Disarmament and Security Issues, report of, 117–19
India, 56, 168, 269, 285; ancient civilization in, 76–7; Bhopal disaster

in, 228; Chipko Movement in, 257–9; as emerging power/market, 138, 145, 225, 226, 379; Gandhi as leader of, 61, 64; global warming and, 340; independence struggle of, 303; Mumbai attacks and, 374–6, *375*; non-violent radicalism in, 303; as nuclear power, 109, 120; Thugs of, 313; traditional/agricultural society of, *51*, 52
indigenous peoples, of the Americas, 87–8, *88*, *89*, 260–1
individual extremism, 309–11
Indonesia, 191, 241
Industrial Revolution, 354
Industrial Workers of the World ('Wobblies'), 242
intellectual piracy, 278
intellectual property, 354; TRIPS agreement of (WTO), 230, 345
interdependence, and security, 111, 115, 119
Intergovernmental Authority for Development (IGAD), 358
intergovernmental organizations (IGOs), 146, 147–50, 154, 156, 159, 185–6, 351; of Bretton Woods System, 148, 149–50; counter-globalization movements and, 271; global order and, 146, 147, 155, 156; human security and, 132; NGOs and, 39, 250–1; OAS as, 146, 150; regional, 155, 356–9; UN as, 148, 159, 186
Intergovernmental Panel on Climate Change (IPCC), 339–40, 342, *342*, 343
Interlaken Process (UN targeted sanctions), 182
Intermediate-Range Nuclear Forces (INF) agreement, 121
'international' (term), 1
International Atomic Energy Agency (IAEA), *160*, 168, 193
International Bank for Reconstruction and Development (IBRD), 149, 207, 356. See *also* World Bank
International Campaign to Ban Landmines, 129. See *also* landmines
International Centre for Settlement of Investment Disputes (ICSID), 149
International Civil Aviation Organization (ICAO), *160*, 168
International Civil Service Commission (ICSC), 171
International Commission on Intervention and State Sovereignty (ICISS), 363–4
International Court of Justice (ICJ), UN, 21, *22*, 159, *160*, 169, 175
International Criminal Court (ICC), 153, 154, 175–6, 369

International Criminal Tribunals (ICTs), UN, 175
International Development Association (IDA), 149, 184
International Finance Corporation (IFC), 149
international financial institutions (IFIs), 184
International Fund for Agricultural Development (IFAD), *160*, 168, 193, 251
internationalization, 199, 208
International Joint Commission (IJC), 330
International Labour Organization (ILO), 142, *160*, 168, 192
international law, codified, 351, 356, 379
International Longshoremen's Association (ILA), 242
International Maritime Organization (IMO), *160*, 168, 298, 335
International Monetary Fund (IMF), 8, 147, 149, 207, 214, 368; consultative strategies by, 370; debt crises and, 6, 240, 244–5; environmental issues and, 345; global governance and, 351, 356, 365; HIPCs and, 6, 245; money laundering investigations by, 283; protests against, 240, 241, 246, 247; structural adjustment policies of, 201, 240, 244, 251, 264; in UN system, *160*, 168, 192; Washington Consensus and, 239; WSF on, 266
international non-governmental organizations (INGOs), 250
international political economy (IPE): Cox's work in, 19–20; modernization and dependency theories of, 50–3; post-dependency theory of, 53–4; world systems theory of, 54–6
international public unions, 354, 361
international/regional institutions. *See* intergovernmental organizations; regionalism
international relations (IR), 18–42; attacks of 9/11 and, 3–5; complex interdependence theory of, 39; deductive vs. inductive study of, 39–41; development theory of, 50–3; Eurocentric bias of, 57, 73, 87; feminism and, 60–1, 64–7; vs. global politics, 1–5, 7–8, 12, 168; *longue durée* view of, 73; Marxism and, 45–6; modernism and, 57, 68; positivism and empiricism in, 59; power and, 26–8; scientific behaviouralism and, 40–1; as state-centric, 1–3, 57, 376; traditional methodology and, 40–1; World War I and, 23–4, 110
international relations, approaches to: idealism/Utopianism, 20–4;

international society, 32–3; liberalism, 33–9; neo-realism, 29–31; realism, 24–32
International Seabed Authority (ISA), 333–4
International Slow Food Movement, 210
international society, 32–3
International Telecommunications Union (ITU), *160*, 168, 356
International Telephone and Telegraph (ITT) Corporation, 227
International Trade Organization (ITO), proposed, 149
Internet: bandwidth distribution of, 209, *209*, 369; counter-globalization movements and, 262–3, 270, 271–2; organized crime and, 277, 295; VoIP technology of, 376
Inter-Services Intelligence (ISI) agency (Pakistan), 376
inter-state relations: as anarchic, 2, 23, 28, 29, 30–1, 38, 39; debate over study of, 40–1; early approaches to, 19–20; as unsettled, 7–8; *see also* international relations
inter-state system, 73–82; ancient city-states and, 74–6; ancient empires and, 76–8; Christianity/Holy Roman Empire and, 78–80; colonization/decolonization and, 90; feudalism and, 78, 82, 88, 105; Islam/Ottoman Empire and, 78, 80–2; Peace of Westphalia and, 1, 7, 57, 73, 88–90; Reformation and, 79–80, 88; Renaissance and, 88; Roman Empire and, 77–8; *see also* world civilizations
intra-state conflicts, rise of, 102, 133, 165, 175, 363
Iran, 308, 314, 317; war with Iraq, 165, 173
Iraq, 168, 140, 170, 308, 323; ancient civilization in, 74; in Gulf War (1991), 109, 127, 151, 153, 181; invasion of Kuwait by, 127, 165, 181, 316; oil-for-food program and, 181; sanctions against, 181, 182; US bombings of, 130, 151, 152; US invasion of (2003), 109, 110, 129, 134, 152, 153, 181, 250, 301, 368, 380; war with Iran, 165, 173
Ireland, women leaders of, 62, 63
Irgun (Zionist group), 308
Irish Republican Army (IRA), 308, 321
Islamic civilization, rise of, 78, 80–2
Islamic fundamentalism, 102, 240, 305; extremism and, 305–7, 310, 314–16; individual expressions of, 272; in Iran, 314; societal marginalization and, 316, 318
Islamicism, 201, 210
Islamophobia, in France, 316

Ismaili assassins, of Shia Islam, 313
Israel, 61, 169, 308; attacks on Gaza by, *125*, 320; as nuclear power, 109, 120; PLO's struggle against, 306, 309, 310, 318; recognition/rescue of Falasha by, 85–6; state-sponsored terrorism and, 320
Italian Mafia, 274, 287–8, 290. *See also* mafias
Italy, 356; invasion of Ethiopia by, 113, 114; Renaissance-era states of, 88

Jainism, 76
Jamaican Yardies, 294
Janjaweed militia, 122
Japan, 113, 114, 170; early history of, 84–5; Yakuza of, *291*, 291–2
jihad, 303, 315; Palestinian, 317, 318
John Birch Society, 144, 368
Johnny Got His Gun (Trumbo), 115
John Paul II, 245
Johnson, Lady Bird, 332
Johnson, Lyndon B., 116, 332
Johnson-Sirleaf, Ellen, 62, 64
Jolie, Angelina, 148, 363
Jordan, 170, 173
Juárez, Benito, *88*
Jubilee 2000, 242, 244–5
Julius Caesar, 77–8, 307
jus ad bellum, 127, 128
jus gentium, 21
jus in bello, 76, 127, 128
'just war', 21, 126–8

Kaczynski, Theodore 'Ted', 311, *311*
Kaldor, Mary, 125–6, 240
Kant, Immanuel, 22, 34, 35, 57, 186
Karadžić, Radovan, 175
Karkare, Hemant, 374
Kautilya, 76–7
Kellogg-Briand Pact, 23
Kennan, George, 117
Kennedy, David, 150, 152, 366
Kennedy, John F., 118, 248
Kennedy, Robert F., 116
Kenya: embassy bombing in, 166, 316, 322; Green Belt Movement in, 257, 259–60
Keohane, Robert O., 145, 367; Joseph S. Nye and, 39, 350–1, 366, 371
Keynes, John Maynard, 140, 147
Khrushchev, Nikita, 117, 118
Khun Sa gang, 293–4, *295*
Kirchner, Cristina Elisabet Fernández de, *61*, 61, 64
Kissinger, Henry, 143, 352
Kjellen, Bo, 328, 334, 337
Koehler, Horst, 247
Korean War, 109, 115, 161

Kosovo, 109, 182, 183, 368
Kosovo Liberation Army (KLA), 290
Kumaratunga, Chandrika Bandaranaike, 61, 63
Kurdish Workers' Party (PKK), 308
Kush (ancient African kingdom), 85, 87
Kuwait, 317; Iraq's invasion of, 127, 165, 181, 316
Kyoto Protocol, 67, 153, 154, 247, 343, 345, 369

laissez-faire economics, 34, 147; *see also* neo-liberalism
landless workers' movement, in Brazil, 263–4
landmines: campaign to ban, 129; treaty to ban, 153, 154, 369
Laos, 173
Las Casas, Bartolomé de, 260
Lashkar-e-Taiba (LeT), 374–6
Lasswell, Harold, 4, 8
Latin American Integration Association (LAIA), 357
Latin Christendom, 78–9, 80
law, international: as codified, 351, 356; League of Nations and, 354–5
Law of the Sea, UN conference on (UNCLOS III), 333–4
Lazarenko, Pavlo, 282
League of Nations, 159, 169; collective security and, 127; Council of, 163; as idealist concept, 23–4; international law and, 354–5; interwar era and, 23–4, 113, 114, 354–5; mandate system of, 169, 170; NGOs and, 361; promotion of treaties by, 355; state sovereignty and, 355; World War II and, 25
Lebanon, 130, 170, 173, 318; Hezbollah in, 316, 317
left-wing extremism, 308–9
legalism, in early China, 83, 84
Lenin, Vladimir Ilyich, *49*, 49–50, 52, 53
less developed countries (LDCs), debt crises in, 6, 240, 244–5
levels of analysis approach, to examining extremism, 309–19; group, 311–12; individual, 309–11; societal, 312–14; state, 317–19; state/society complex, 314–16; transnational/global, 319
liberal imperialism, 34
liberal international economic order: beginnings of, 206–7; Bretton Woods System and, 199–200, 201, 207–8; in globalization era, 199–201, 208–10; *see also* globalization *and entries following; see also* state, in era of globalization

liberal internationalism, 34, 35–7
liberalism, 33–9; assumptions of, 38; embedded, 143, 147; feminism and, 64–5; free trade and, 34, 35; functionalism and, 38; global change/ continuity and, 101–2; idealism/ Utopianism and, 33, 35, 37–8; imperialism and, 34; internationalism and, 34, 35–7; of Kant, 34, 35; neo-liberalism and, 33–4; pacifism and, 34; vs. realism, 35, 37–8; 'realist', 42; resurgence of, 33–4, 38–9; Third Way, 143–4; on war, 35, 37, 111–12, 113, 123–4, 126, 132–3; on Westphalian state system, 57; of Wilson, 35–7
liberalization, 221
liberal pacifism, 34
liberal trade policies, history of, 206–8
Liberia, 62, 133, 165, 182
Libya, 182; Pan American bombing and, 166, 321, 322; sanctions against, 321–2; state-sponsored terrorism and, 317
Lie, Trygve, 171
Lincoln, Abraham, 283
Lin Zexu, 279
Li Ssu, 83
The Living Sea (Cousteau), 333
Lloyd, William Forster, 329
Locke, John, 35, 57
Lod Airport massacre, 320
London Rainforest Action Group, 256
longue durée, 97, 98
Lula, 263
Luther, Martin, *79*, 79–80
Luxembourg, 356
Lyotard, Jean-François, 57
Lysistrata (Aristophanes), 126
Lysøen Declaration, 134

Maastricht Treaty, 357
Maathai, Wangari, 259, 260, *260*
McAleese, Mary, 62, 63
Machiavelli, Niccolò, *34*, 57, 141; realism of, 34, 88, 383
McDonald's, 210
McKinley, William, 140
McVeigh, Timothy, 314
madrassas (religious schools), 315
Madrid, train bombings in, 314
mafias, 287–92; Albanian, 290–1; Cali, 288–9, 292; 'Ndrangheta, 288; Russian, 289–90; Sicilian, 287–8, 291; Yakuza, *291*, 291–2
Malacca Strait, piracy in, 297–8
Malaysia, 56
Maldive Islands, 341
Malloch Brown, Mark, 171

mandate system (League of Nations), 169, 170
Mandela, Nelson, 180, 306
Mannheim, Karl, 21
Mao Zedong, 294
Marcos, Ferdinand, 61, 282
Marcos, Subcomandante (EZLN leader), 261, 262, *262*
Marshall Plan, 149
Marx, Karl, *46*, 52, 53, 56, 57; on capitalism, 46–9; on communism, 46, 47, 49; Engels' eulogy for, 48–9; on global politics, 46–9; on surplus value, 48, 53
Marxism, 45–56; on capitalism, 46–9; dependency theory and, 50, 52–3; feminism and, 65–6; global politics and, 46–50, 381; on imperialism, 49–50; international relations and, 45–6; post-dependency theory and, 53–4; postmodernism and, 58
Marxist-Leninist extremist groups, 308
Maya (indigenous civilization), 87
Mearsheimer, John, 9; on balance of power, 31, 112, 352; on war, 112, 123, 124
Medellin Cartel (Colombia), 292–3, *294*
Médecins Sans Frontières, 129
mediation, 164
Meir, Golda, 61, 62
Merkel, Angela, 62, 64
Mesoamerica, 89; indigenous civilizations of, 87–8, *88*
Mesopotamia, Sumerian civilization in, 74
Mexico, 56, 340; border bribery and, 280; debt crisis of, 244; drug trafficking and, 279, 289, 292; indigenous civilizations of, 87–8, *88*, *89*; treatment of indigenous peoples in, 260–1; Zapatista uprising in, 260–3
Migiro, Asha-Rose, 171
migration, global, 203, 319
military action and sanctions, by UN, 181, 182–3
military expenditures, world, 112–13, 129–30, *130*, *131*
military humanitarianism, 148
Mill, John Stuart, 35, 57
Millennium Development Goals, 161–2, 232
Milošević, Slobodan, 175
Mitrany, David, 38
Mixtec (indigenous civilization), 87
Mladić, Ratko, 175
MMT (gasoline additive), 331
Mobutu Sese Seko, 282
modernism, 57, 68
modernization theory, 50–2